FIRST
WORLD
WAR

BOOKS BY MARTIN GILBERT

THE CHURCHILL BIOGRAPHY

Volume III *The Challenge of War, 1914–1916*
Volume III (documents in two parts)
Volume IV *The Stricken World, 1917–1922*
Volume IV (documents; in three parts)
Volume V *The Prophet of Truth, 1922–1939*
Volume V *The Exchequer Years 1923–1929* (documents)
Volume V *The Wilderness Years 1929–1935* (documents)
Volume V *The Coming of War 1936–1939* (documents)
Volume VI *Finest Hour, 1939–1941*
Volume VII *Road to Victory, 1942–1945*
Volume VIII *'Never Despair', 1945–1965*

OTHER BOOKS

The Appeasers (with Richard Gott)
The European Powers, 1900–1945
The Roots of Appeasement
Britain and Germany Between the Wars (documents)
Plough My Own Furrow: the Life of Lord Allen of Hurtwood (documents)
Servant of India: Diaries of the Viceroy's Private Secretary (documents)
Sir Horace Rumbold: Portrait of a Diplomat
Churchill: a Photographic Portrait
Churchill's Political Philosophy
Auschwitz and the Allies
Exile and Return: the Struggle for Jewish Statehood
The Jews of Hope: the Plight of Soviet Jewry Today
Shcharansky: Hero of our Time
Jerusalem: Rebirth of a City, 1838–1898
Final Journey: the Fate of the Jews in Nazi Europe
The Holocaust: the Jewish Tragedy
Second World War
Churchill, A Life
In Search of Churchill

ATLASES

Recent History Atlas, 1860–1960
British History Atlas
American History Atlas
Jewish History Atlas
First World War Atlas
Russian History Atlas
The Arab-Israeli Conflict: Its History in Maps
The Jews of Russia: Their History in Maps and Photographs
Jerusalem Illustrated History Atlas
Children's Illustrated Bible Atlas
The Jews of Arab Lands: Their History in Maps and Photographs
Atlas of the Holocaust

FIRST WORLD WAR

Martin Gilbert

WEIDENFELD AND NICOLSON
LONDON

First published in Great Britain in 1994 by
Weidenfeld & Nicolson
The Orion Publishing Group Ltd
Orion House
5 Upper Saint Martin's Lane
London WC2H 9EA

Second impression October 1994
Third impression November 1994
Fourth impression January 1995
Fifth impression February 1995

A catalogue record for this book
is available from the British Library

ISBN 0-297-81312-9

Filmset by
Selwood Systems
Midsomer Norton
Printed by Butler & Tanner Ltd,
Frome and London

The race is not to the swift, nor the battle to the strong. . .
but time and chance happeneth to them all.

ECCLESIASTES ix, 11

Contents

CONTENTS

Maps

MAPS

Illustrations

Introduction

More than nine million soldiers, sailors and airmen were killed in the First World War. A further five million civilians are estimated to have perished under occupation, bombardment, hunger and disease. The mass murder of Armenians in 1915, and the influenza epidemic that began while the war was still being fought, were two of its destructive by-products. The flight of Serbs from Serbia at the end of 1915 was another cruel episode in which civilians perished in large numbers; so too was the Allied naval blockade of Germany, as a result of which more than three-quarters of a million German civilians died.

Two very different wars were fought between 1914 and 1918. The first was a war of soldiers, sailors and airmen, of merchant seamen and civilian populations under occupation, where individual suffering and distress were on a massive scale, particularly in the front-line trenches. The second was a war of War Cabinets and sovereigns, of propagandists and idealists, replete with political and territorial ambitions and ideals, determining the future of Empires, nations and peoples as sharply as the battlefield. There were times, particularly in 1917 and 1918, when the war of armies and the war of ideologies combined, leading to revolution and capitulation, and to the emergence of new national and political forces. The war changed the map and destiny of Europe as much as it seared its skin and scarred its soul.

As a schoolboy in the immediate aftermath of the Second World War, I was very conscious of the First World War, although it had ended twenty-seven years earlier. The school porter, 'Janitor Johnson', a former Royal Marine, was a veteran of the naval attack on Zeebrugge in 1918, and was said to have been recommended for an award for valour there. The headmaster, Geoffrey Bell, had won the Military Cross on the Western Front, but had pacifist instincts which he made known to the boys. One of my first history masters, A.P. White, had also fought in the trenches: he would march up and down the classroom with a broom over his shoulder, singing military songs. When I began work on this book his letters from the trenches were published, revealing great suffering and sensitivity. My father's elder brother, my uncle Irving, had fought on the Somme: his experiences had scarred him, and we boys in the family were warned not to question him. He died as I was writing this book, at the age of ninety-three.

During my National Service in 1954 and 1955, the First World War was an ever-present memory. The infantry regiment with which I trained, the Wiltshires, had lost a battalion at Reutel, in the Ypres Salient, when 1,000 men were all but wiped out, and the few survivors were taken prisoner in October 1914. Another battalion had been all but wiped out, in a few minutes, on the slopes of Chunuk Bair, on the Gallipoli Peninsula, in 1915. A third battalion had been trapped by German naval gunfire on the Salonica Front in 1917. During my academic researches, whatever subject I was working on, whether the British Empire in India at the turn of the century or the establishment of Soviet rule in the Ukraine in the 1920s, the First World War continued to impinge on my researches. My supervisor on Indian history, C.C. Davies, had been wounded on the Western Front and was still troubled by his wound. My work on historical geography in the early 1960s took me to Arnold Toynbee's flat in London. On his mantelpiece were photographs of half a dozen young men in uniform. I asked him who they were. He told me they were his closest friends at university before 1914: all had been killed in the trenches.

Over several decades my travels took me to many of the war zones and places associated with the war. In 1953, encouraged by one of my history masters, Alan Palmer, I travelled through several of the regions whose war memorials introduced me to the differing perspectives on the war: and also to Vienna, where the Hofburg and the Ballhausplatz recalled both the ageing Emperor and his Foreign Ministers; to Ljubljana, which as Laibach had been one of the cities whose Slav population sought independence from Austria and whose soldiers chafed at their role in maintaining the Hapsburg Empire; and to Venice, threatened in 1917 by the imminent arrival of the Austrian army.

In June 1957, in Sarajevo, I stood on the spot where Gavrilo Princip had fired the fatal shot in June 1914. Even under the Yugoslav Communist regime Princip was hailed as one of the forerunners of national independence. A concrete paving stone was set with two footsteps, commemorating the act which plunged Europe into its four-year conflict. In Belgrade that year I looked across the river to where the Austrians had bombarded the Serb capital on the first day of war. A decade later I went with my father to the Western Front: we stayed at Arras, to the east of which the military cemeteries are the last relics of the battles of 1917 and 1918, and at Ypres, where we listened each evening at eight o'clock to the Last Post, sounded at the Menin Gate by two members of the Ypres Fire Brigade.

While the buglers played under the vast archway of the Menin Gate, all traffic was stopped. The cost of their work was paid for in part by a legacy from Rudyard Kipling, whose only son was killed at Loos. On the walls and columns of the monumental gate are carved the names of 54,896 British soldiers killed in the salient between October 1914 and mid-August 1917 who have no known grave. On the stonework are the shrapnel marks of the fighting there in the Second World War. The last of the stonemasons were still at work engraving the names of 1914–18 when the German armies arrived, as conquerors, in May 1940. The stonemasons were repatriated to Britain.

From the Menin Gate, my father and I walked through the salient, trench maps in hand, reading at each battle site the accounts given in General Edmond's multi-volume official history, the letters and recollections of soldiers, and the poetry. We stood in silence, as all visitors do, at the Tyne Cot Memorial at Passchendaele, on which are carved the names of a further 34,888 soldiers killed in the salient between mid-August 1917 and the end of the war in November 1918, of whom no trace was found sufficient to identify them for burial. In the cemetery in front of the memorial are more than 11,000 individual named graves. Not even the well-mown grass, the carefully tended flower beds and the fifty-year-old trees could lessen the shocking impact of so many names and graves. Not far away, at Menin, which was held by the Germans for all but one month of the war, we visited the military cemetery where 48,049 German soldiers are buried.

Fifteen years after my visit to the site of the assassination of the Archduke Franz Ferdinand in Sarajevo, where the First World War could be said to have started, I made the journey to the woodland clearing near Rethondes in France, to see a replica of the railway carriage in which the Germans signed the armistice in November 1918. It was in the same carriage that Hitler insisted on receiving the French surrender in June 1940. Many links between the two wars are a reminder that only twenty-one years lay between them. Many of those who fought in the trenches in the First World War were leaders in the Second World War, like Hitler, Churchill and de Gaulle, or, like Rommel, Zhukov, Montgomery and Gamelin, became commanders in the second. Others, like Ho Chi Minh, who volunteered to serve with the French as a Vietnamese orderly in the First World War, and Harold Macmillan, who fought and was wounded on the Western Front, rose to prominence after the Second World War.

In 1957 I visited the battle zones on the Russo-Turkish border, and the towns where hundreds of thousands of Armenians were massacred in the first year of the war. Ten years later I was in the military cemetery in Gaza, where the headstones, set specially low because of the possibility of earthquake, record the deaths of the thousands of soldiers who perished in one of the fiercest Anglo-Turkish clashes. I have stood on the spot just outside Jerusalem where two British soldiers, up early one morning in search of eggs, saw approaching them a group of dignitaries, including priests, imams and rabbis, and were offered, instead of food, the surrender of the Holy City. Starting in 1969, I travelled for three consecutive years to the Gallipoli Peninsula, reading aloud from Aspinall-Oglander's two-volume official war history, and from other works, at many of the landing beaches, gullies and hilltops of the peninsula. The contrast between its modern beauty and stillness, and the knowledge of the fighting and suffering there in 1915, has never ceased to haunt me.

During my work on Winston Churchill, I also read aloud, in the courtyards of the farms where he wrote them, the daily letters from Churchill to his wife from the trenches of the Western Front, in which he recognised the endurance of those who could not return, as he could after six months, to the comfort of civilian life in London. Eight years before the outbreak of war in 1914, in a private letter to his wife from German army manoeuvres at Würzburg, to which he had been invited by the Kaiser, Churchill wrote: 'Much as war attracts me and fascinates my mind with its tremendous situations, I feel more deeply every year – & can measure the feeling here in the midst of arms – what vile & wicked folly & barbarism it all is.'

In 1991, a few months after the fall of the Iron Curtain, I was in the newly independent Ukraine, where I wandered through the former Austrian barracks in the former border town of Brody, through which the Russian army marched with such confidence in 1914 during its initial triumph, and out of which it was driven within the year. Despite the decision of Lenin and the Bolsheviks to pull out of the war in March 1918, fighting on the Eastern Front continued, mostly in the form of a civil war, and then as a Russo-Polish war, for two years longer than in the west. Along the road from Brody to Lvov I passed the great bronze cavalry horse and rider who point (or pointed then, before all things Communist were pulled down) with such triumph towards Warsaw. This striking pair commemorated the Bolshevik attempt to overrun Poland in 1920. Like the efforts of their Russian compatriots six years earlier to retain Poland, they had fought and died in vain. In Warsaw I have stood several times over the years at the unknown soldier's memorial: it commemorates not an unknown soldier of the 1914–18 war, as at Westminster Abbey or beneath the Arc de Triomphe, but an unknown victim of the Russo-Polish War of 1920.

During four decades, many soldiers have spoken to me about their experiences on all fronts. As a young soldier myself, in 1954 and 1955, I visited old people's homes where the often shattered survivors of the trenches were living and dying. In the course of my historical researches, which began in 1960, I met many old soldiers, sailors and airmen from all the belligerent armies. Their recollections, and the letters and documents that they had kept, were a window on the past. So too was the personal encouragement of one of the historians of the First World War, Sir John Wheeler-Bennett, and three of my senior colleagues when I went to Merton College, Oxford, as a junior research fellow in 1962, Alistair Hardy, Hugo Dyson and Michael Polanyi, each of whom had seen the noblest and the ugliest sides of that distant war, Hardy and

Dyson as soldiers on the Western Front, Polanyi as a medical officer in the Austro-Hungarian Army.

During my Churchill work I met the eighty-year-old General Savory, who had served at Gallipoli, and who invited me to run my finger along the hollow in his skull caused by a Turkish bullet. He had gone on to serve in Mesopotamia and Siberia. An airman, Richard Bell Davies, who had also fought at Gallipoli, where he won the Victoria Cross, produced from his wallet a piece of wartime toilet paper on which was printed a portrait of the German Kaiser with the words 'Wipe your bottom on me'.

Two other soldiers who had served on the Western Front from the first weeks influenced me by their friendship and by their writings. One was the French painter Paul Maze, DCM, MM with bar, Croix de Guerre, who came to live in England after the First World War, and who escaped from France as the German army entered Paris in June 1940. He had served on the Western Front as a reconnaissance expert for four years, a witness to each of the main British offensives. The second soldier was the British politician Major-General Sir Edward Louis Spears, MC, who entered Parliament after the First World War, and in June 1940 brought General de Gaulle to England. Both Maze and Spears were able, in their books and in their conversation about the First World War, to give a portrait in words of the actions and moods of Flanders, the hopes of the soldiers, and the perils of the four-year journey from the declaration of war in 1914 to the armistice in 1918.

On 3 September 1976, a day still vivid in my memory, I lunched with Anthony Eden (then Earl of Avon) at his home in Wiltshire. He talked about episodes of the Second World War, the outbreak of which had taken place exactly thirty-seven years earlier, and in which his twenty-year-old son Simon, a Pilot Officer in the Royal Air Force, had been killed in action in Burma in June 1945. We spoke of the British decision to go to the aid of Greece in 1941 and the dangers of a Russian collapse, or even a separate Nazi-Soviet peace, in 1942.

There were many echoes in our talk of the First World War, including Britain's decision in 1915 to help Serbia (through the same port city of Salonica that Greece was helped in part in 1941) and the impact of the Russian withdrawal from the war in 1917. One of Eden's most vivid memories was of being told, while he was in the trenches of the Western Front, that his brother Nicholas had been killed in action at the Battle of Jutland in 1916. Nicholas Eden, in charge of a gun turret on the *Indefatigable*, was just sixteen when he died.

Harold Macmillan also helped me in my Churchill work, in correspondence, and in talks at his home and mine, but it was not until I was writing this book that I learned that his spidery handwriting, limpid handshake, and the somewhat ungainly shuffle of his walk, were each the result of wounds sustained in action in 1916.

My travels taught me that there was no area of Europe free from the memories and monuments of the First World War. Cities such as Warsaw and Lille, Brussels and Belgrade knew the full rigours of occupation in two world wars. From Prague and Budapest, Berlin and Vienna, Constantinople and Athens, Paris and Rome, London and New York, Cape Town and Bombay, troops had left for the war zones, and those who returned, after the shock and prolongation of battle, found cities, in Europe at least, where privation and grief had replaced the earlier, brief enthusiasms. In each city monuments recorded the loss.

While travelling, I studied the wording and the iconography of war memorials everywhere. These testified to every form of destruction, from the graves of individual soldiers and civilians to the monuments recording the death of more than half a million horses in the war zones, and a further 15,000 drowned on their way to war: these memorials form a stark, often beautiful, sometimes grotesque reminder of the destruction. Their unveiling and dedication, such as that in 1936 of the Canadian memorial on Vimy Ridge, prolonged the impact of retrospection. Even after the Second World War it was the sight of the bemedalled veterans of the First World War that made the greatest impact at Armistice Day parades. In Boulogne in 1974 I watched the parade of old soldiers of both world wars, led by a stooped survivor of the Battle of the Marne of sixty years earlier, who was given pride of place at the head of the procession.

The battles formed the framework and daily reporting of the war, but mutinies, strikes and revolution echoed the footsteps of the fighting men, as did the work of millions in factories and labour battalions. Mustard gas was an extra hazard for the fighting men. Submarines sent thousands of merchant seamen, soldiers and civilians to unmarked graves. Aerial bombardment added a civilian dimension of terror. Hunger and privation were the lot of millions of citizens behind the lines.

My own researches led to several books in which the First World War had an important place, among them *Sir Horace Rumbold, Portrait of a Diplomat*, which covered the outbreak of the war from the perspective of a British diplomat in Berlin; the third and fourth volumes of the Churchill biography, in which the Dardanelles, the Western Front and the munitions war each had its place; and *The Atlas of the First World War*, covering every front and aspect of warmaking. The impact of the war on Jewish and Arab aspirations in the Middle East was the subject of three chapters in *Exile and Return, The Struggle for a Jewish Homeland*. The impact of the war on the peace treaties and the inter-war years was a feature of the letters and documents that I published in 1964 in *Britain and Germany Between the Wars*.

Also in 1964, shortly after I had given an Oxford typing agency the manuscript of my book *The European Powers 1900–1945*, the head of the agency, Mrs Wawerka, asked to see me. In the book I had ascribed to Austria some of the responsibility for the coming of war in 1914. This had puzzled and distressed her. She had been born and educated in Vienna; as a Jewess she had been forced to leave Austria in 1938 but she knew for a fact that Austria was innocent of any responsibility for the events of 1914.

The blame should be put (and ought to have been put by me) upon the Serbs and Russians.

This episode made a strong impact on me, as did Mrs Wawerka's description of the desperate hunger in Vienna after the war, and the unfairness, as she saw it, of the post-war settlement that dismantled the Hapsburg Empire.

For some it was a war to punish and chastise. For others it became the war to end war. Its name, the Great War, indicated its hitherto unprecedented scale. It was followed, however, by a second even more destructive war, and by other 'lesser' wars throughout the world. In January 1994 there were an estimated thirty-two wars being waged somewhere on earth. The First World War continues to have its place in the discussion of these modern conflicts. On 26 December 1993, while I was writing this book, a British television journalist, commenting on the lack of any Christmas truce in Bosnia, reported, against the background of a deep trench: 'Around Vitez the trench system is a reminder of the First World War, complete with mud.' The trench as shown was not particularly muddy, or waterlogged, nor was it under shellfire. But the imagery of the First World War has remained for eighty years, and through several generations. A relatively short period of time, a war that lasted for four years and three months, has inspired, puzzled and disturbed the whole century that followed.

Some of the political changes that the First World War created were as destructive as the war itself, both of life and of liberty, and were to perpetuate tyranny for more than half a century. Some of the frontier changes of the First World War, intended to put right long-standing wrongs, are still a cause of dispute and conflict today.

In 1923, in the introduction to his book *The Irish Guards in the Great War*, Rudyard Kipling wrote: 'The only wonder to the compiler of these records is that any sure fact whatever should be retrieved out of the whirlpools of war.' Since the first shots were fired eighty years ago, authors have pursued their researches into both the main and the obscure episodes of the war, and into the puzzles. This book is an attempt to convey my own researches, readings, feelings and perspectives on an event that, like the Holocaust in later years, left a searing mark on the western world. It is also an attempt to tell, within the framework of commanders, strategies and vast numbers, the story of individuals.

If each of the nine million military dead of the First World War were to have an individual page, the record of their deeds and suffering, their wartime hopes, their pre-war lives and loves, would fill twenty thousand books the size of this one. Individual suffering is not something that is easily conveyed in a general history, yet all historians try to do it. On 3 December 1993, I was struck by three short sentences in a review by Meir Ronnen of two books on the First World War. The review appeared in the *Jerusalem Post*, where Ronnen wrote: 'Millions died or suffered in the mud of Flanders between 1914–18. Who remembers them? Even those with names on their graves are by now unknown soldiers.'

No single book can redress that balance, though several fine books have tried to do so, among them, most recently, those in Britain by Lyn Macdonald and in France by Stephanie Audouin-Rouzeau (one of the books being reviewed by Meir Ronnen; the other was a biography of the poet Isaac Rosenberg, killed in action on April Fools' Day 1918). In this book, I have tried to give the suffering of individuals its integral part in the narrative of the wider war.

Martin Gilbert
Merton College
Oxford
20 June 1994

Acknowledgements

Many people have encouraged me over the years to explore different aspects of the First World War, or have guided me towards little-known shelves and corners of the vast literature. Charles Mahjoubian, a survivor of the massacre of the Armenians, encouraged me to make the story of the Armenian massacres an integral part of the narrative. Two of my doctoral students, Martin Ceadel and John Turner, chose the First World War as their 'period'. Both have since published books to which all students of the war are grateful, none more so than their former supervisor. Larry Arnn's doctoral thesis, 'Winston S. Churchill as Minister of Munitions', has also been of value to a former boss, and long-standing friend.

My bibliographical and factual knowledge has been enhanced by the help of several friends, among them Clinton Bailey, David Harman, Zena Harman, Jeffrey Siegel, Sarah Meron and Simon Broadbent. As always, Erich Segal has been my guide to all classical allusions. Others who have sent me information are J.W. Bakewell, Dr Vojtech Blodig (Theresienstadt Museum), I.L. Buxton, Andrew Baker, Robert Craig, Sir Brian Fall, Martin Greenwood (Assistant Curator, Kenwood House), Bruce Gaynor, J.P. Gee (Commonwealth War Graves Commission), Julie Kessler, Michael Levine, Len Mader (External Affairs and International Trade, Canada), T.P. Penfold (Commonwealth War Graves Commission), J.P. Rudman (The Archivist, Uppingham School), Colonel William E. Ryan Jr (The American Battle Monuments Commission, Washington DC), Jean Saunders, Dr Harry Shukman, Chris Thomas (Bank of England Reference Library), Sir David Williams, Georgina Wilson, and the Claremont Institute of Claremont, California. I am also grateful for bibliographic help to Professor Oleg Rzheshevski of Moscow and Pauline Underwood (the Macmillan Press Ltd). Like all those who have made use of the British Government archives, I am grateful to the Keeper and staff of the Public Record Office at Kew.

The excerpts from *Testament of Youth* by Vera Brittain are included with the permission of Paul Berry, her literary executor, Victor Gollancz

Ltd (for the British edition) and the Virago Press, London (for the United States edition). I am grateful to the following for permission to reproduce poetry: to George Sassoon, for poems by Siegfried Sassoon (from *Collected Poems 1908–1956*, Faber & Faber); to A. P. Watt on behalf of Crystal Hale and Jocelyn Herbert, for a poem by A. P. Herbert; to Macmillan Publishers Ltd, for a poem by E. Hilton Young (from *A Muse at Sea*, Sidgwick & Jackson); and to David Higham Associates, for a poem by Herbert Read (from *Selected Poetry*, Faber & Faber).

I found all the photographs in this book in the Robert Hunt Library, to whose treasures I was first introduced for my *Second World War* history by Graham Mason, who also let me range freely through the Library's voluminous holdings on the First World War. I have listed the copyright holders for each picture in the list of illustrations. The maps were drawn from my rough drafts by Tim Aspden, who has given them the benefit of his cartographic skills. The typescript was read by my former teacher, Alan Palmer, and gained considerably (as my school essays did forty years ago) from his thoughts and guidance. The expert eye of Dr A.J. Peacock, editor of *Gun Fire, A Journal of First World War History*, has also been of great value. Ben Helfgott made many useful points of style and content. Proof-reading was done by Chris Bessant in Britain and by Arthur Neuhauser in the United States; I am grateful to both of them for their vigilance. Benjamin Buchan at Weidenfeld and Nicolson was helpful on various points of content, as was Ion Trewin. Rachelle Gryn helped in tracking down many elusive facts, as did Kay Thomson, who also helped with the correspondence and revisions. Susie Gilbert has, as with all my work, given the text her scrutiny and guidance.

1

Prelude to war

War between the Great Powers was much talked about in the first decade of the twentieth century, by politicians, writers, novelists and philosophers. Yet the nature of a European war, as opposed to a colonial venture, was little understood. What was known were the many swift forays by superior forces against distant, feeble foes, the victory of machine guns against spears, of massive naval guns against antique cannon. However frightening those conflicts could be for those who took part in them, the general public at home had little sense of anything terrible.

Why should war in Europe be feared? Shortly before the outbreak of war in 1914 a French colonel, who had been a teenager when Germany invaded France in 1870, was listening to a group of young officers drinking to the prospect of war and laughing about the possibility of conflict. He brought their laughter to an abrupt end with the question: 'And do you think that war is always gay, toujours drôle?' His name was Henri-Philippe Pétain. Two years later, at Verdun, he was to witness one of the worst military slaughters of the twentieth century.

The French soldiers whose laughter Pétain brought to an abrupt end were heirs to a tradition of Franco-German enmity that had culminated more than forty years earlier, on 11 May 1871. For on that day, in the Swan Hotel at Frankfurt-on-Main, the German Chancellor Otto von Bismarck signed the agreement transferring all of Alsace and much of Lorraine to Germany. That day, in the German-occupied city of Metz, guns fired in celebration of the triumph. In the classrooms of the French Jesuit College of St Clement, wrote the British historian Basil Liddell Hart in 1931, 'the message of the guns needed no interpreter. The boys jumped to their feet. The superintendent, rising more soberly, cried, "Mes enfants!" – and then, unable to say more, lowered his head and joined his hands as if in prayer. The memory of that terrible moment was not effaced from the minds of the students.' One of those students was the nineteen-year-old Ferdinand Foch, who resented the fact that defeat had come before he could be sent into battle.

Not everyone in the newly-united Germany was satisfied by the victory over France. Other German ambitions were stirred as the Empire gained industrial strength. Aspirations for colonial expansion, for naval power at least as great as that of Britain, for influence over the Muslims of Asia, for a dominant part in the counsels of Europe, intensified the German sense of inferiority. Germany, united only in 1870, had come too late, it seemed, into the race for power and influence, for empire and respect. The need for a further war, and for the overwhelming military strength essential to win it, was the conclusion of the book *Germany and the Next War*, published by a retired German cavalry officer, Friedrich von Bernhardi, in 1912. Bernhardi had ridden as a conqueror through Paris in 1870. In his book he stressed the need for Germany either to make war or to lose the struggle for world power. The 'natural law, upon which all the laws of nature rest', he wrote, was 'the law of the struggle for existence'. War was 'a biological necessity'. German soldiers forty years younger than he were soon to test this confident theory on the battlefield, and to die testing it.

The war of 1870 had been the last war of the nineteenth century between the European powers. Three thousand soldiers had been killed on each side at the Battle of Sedan. In the civil strife that followed in France, more than 25,000 Communards had been executed in Paris, by Frenchmen. Wars, and their aftermath, were known by this example to be costly in human lives and unpredictable, even vicious, in their outcome. After 1870 the German, French, Belgian and British Empires each had its saga of war, defeat and slaughter overseas. Napoleon III's son the Prince Imperial was among the hundreds of British soldiers killed in 1879 by Zulus at and after the Battle of Isandlwana. In 1894 Lieutenant-Colonel Joffre led a French column through the Sahara in the conquest of Timbuctu. At the turn of the century a German Colonel, Erich von Falkenhayn, won a reputation for ruthlessness during the international expedition to crush the Boxer Rebellion in China, the occasion during which the Kaiser William II likened the German troops to the Huns, thus coining a phrase that was eventually to be used against them. 'Just as the Huns a thousand years ago under the leadership of Attila gained a reputation by virtue of which they live in the historical tradition,' he said, 'so may the name of Germany become known in such a manner in China that no Chinese will ever dare again look askance at a German.'[1]

These often distant but always bloody wars offered a warning to those who cared to listen. In 1896 the British poet and classicist A. E. Housman expressed the cruelty of war in his poem 'A Shropshire Lad':

> *On the idle hill of summer,*
> *Sleepy with the flow of streams,*

---

[1] The Huns of antiquity were tribes of Mongolian origin who invaded Europe from the shores of the Caspian Sea in the fourth and fifth centuries, ultimately under Attila. After invading Germany, Attila was defeated on the Marne (!) near Châlons by a combined army of Romans and Goths. It was the Goths who, as a Teuton tribe, were among the German forebears.

2

Far I hear the steady drummer
Drumming like a noise in dreams.

Far and near and low and louder
On the roads of earth go by,
Dear to friends and food for powder,
Soldiers marching, all to die.

East and west on fields forgotten
Bleach the bones of comrades slain,
Lovely lads and dead and rotten;
None that go return again.

Far the calling bugles hollo,
High the screaming fife replies,
Gay the files of scarlet follow:
Woman bore me, I will rise.

Housman's warning sentiments were echoed five years later in the British House of Commons, by Winston Churchill, then a 26-year-old Conservative Member of Parliament. Having experienced fighting in India, in the Sudan and in the Boer War, Churchill found himself when back in London listening to calls for an army capable of fighting a European foe. 'I have frequently been astonished to hear with what composure and how glibly Members, and even Ministers, talk of a European war,' he declared on 13 May 1901, three months after entering Parliament, and he went on to make the point that, whereas in the past wars had been fought 'by small regular armies of professional soldiers', in the future, when 'mighty populations are impelled on each other', a European war could only end 'in the ruin of the vanquished and the scarcely less fatal commercial dislocation and exhaustion of the conquerors'.

Democracy, Churchill warned, would be 'more vindictive' than the courts and cabinets of old: 'The wars of peoples will be more terrible than those of kings.' Ten years later, on 9 August 1911, as German war fever was being whipped up against Britain and France over Germany's claim for a port on the Atlantic coast of Morocco, the German Social Democrat leader August Bebel warned the Reichstag that a European war could lead to revolution. He was laughed at as an alarmist, one parliamentarian calling out: 'After every war things are better!'

The rivalries from which wars sprang could not be assuaged by the logic of anti-war sentiment. The opening decade of the twentieth century saw many such rivalries and resentments among those nations for whom peace, trade, industry and the spread of national prosperity seemed the true necessities, challenges and opportunities. In France, the loss of the territories annexed by Germany in 1871 rankled for four decades. The advice of the French patriot Léon Gambetta, 'Think of it always, speak of it never', rang in French ears. The black cloth which covered the statue of Strasbourg in the Place de la Concorde was a constant visual reminder of the loss of the two eastern provinces. Karl Baedeker's guide for Paris, published in Leipzig in 1900, commented on the draped statue: 'The Strasburg is usually heavy with crape and mourning garlands in reference to the lost Alsace.' For her part Germany had many territorial ambitions, particularly beyond her eastern border. Despising Russia, the Germans hoped to annex the western Polish provinces of the Russian Empire, and also to extend German influence over central Poland, into Lithuania, and along the Baltic coast. It was as if the Empire of William II would redress the balance of power first disrupted by Peter the Great two hundred years earlier, and, forty years after his death, by Catherine the Great.

The Russia of Nicholas II was not without ambitions of her own, particularly in the Balkans, as the Slav champion of a Slav State, Serbia, which was continually struggling to enlarge her borders and to reach the sea. Russia also saw herself as a champion of the Slav races under Austrian rule. Across the Russian border with Austria-Hungary lived three Slav minorities to whom Russia appeared as a champion: Ukrainians, Ruthenes and Poles.

Ruled by Franz Josef since 1848, Austria-Hungary sought to maintain its own large imperial structure by balancing its many minorities. In 1867, in an attempt to balance the conflicting claims of German and Magyar, Franz Josef was made Emperor of Austria and King of Hungary. In the Austrian half of this Dual Monarchy a complex parliamentary system had been devised, the aim of which was to give every minority some place in the legislature.[1] Yet even the Hapsburg desire to change nothing and to disturb nothing clashed with the desire to curb the one irritant to Austrian rule in the south, the ever-growing (or so it seemed) Serbian State.

In Britain, novelists and newspaper writers, as well as Admirals and parliamentarians, reflected British fears of German naval supremacy, heightened in the early summer of 1914 by news of the imminent widening of the Kiel Canal, which would enable German ships to move safely and swiftly from the Baltic Sea to the North Sea. Anti-German feeling was a regular feature of the popular press. There were also repeated calls for the Liberal Government to bring in military conscription, so as not to be dependent in the event of war on the small professional army. The Liberal Cabinet resisted these calls.

The European alliance systems reflected the fears of all States. The two Central Powers, Germany and Austria-Hungary, were linked by formal as well as sentimental bonds. So too, since 1892, were France and Russia, with both of whom Britain had reached agreements to reduce conflicts. Britain and France, though not allied by treaty, had signed an Entente

---

[1] A Law of 26 January 1907 established the following national quotas in the Austrian Parliament of 515 seats: 241 Germans, 97 Czechs, 80 Poles, 34 Ruthenes, 23 Slovenes, 19 Italians, 13 Croats, 5 Roumanians and 3 Serbs. In the elections that followed, the Czech, Polish and Ruthene deputies tended to be on the left-wing. There were also 5 Jewish deputies (4 Zionist and 1 Jewish Democrat). The main left-wing party, the Social Democrats, was made up of 50 Germans, 23 Czechs, 7 Poles, 5 Italians and 2 Ruthenes.

Cordiale in 1904 to settle their overseas disputes in Egypt and Morocco, and since 1906 had been in consultation over military matters. These agreements and habits of consultation created what were known as the Triple Entente: Britain, France and Russia, giving the Central Powers a fear of encirclement. The German Kaiser, William II, was particularly sensitive to this. His dream was to make Germany respected, feared and admired. A grandson of Queen Victoria, he resented the apparent ascendancy in the world of her son Edward VII and her grandson George V, the King-Emperors, ruling the Indian subcontinent with its hundreds of millions of subject peoples.

At his palace at Potsdam, William was surrounded by the memory and ceremonial of his ancestor Frederick William I, founder of the Prussian army. 'To this day,' commented Karl Baedeker in 1912, 'numerous soldiers, especially the picked men of the regiments of guards, form the most characteristic features in the streets of the town.' Also at Potsdam was a bronze equestrian statue of William I, unveiled by William II in 1900, with the goddess of victory seated in front of the pedestal. The goddess, who in Roman times had been the Caesars' presiding divinity, was embellished by reliefs of the prince as a young orderly officer at Bar-sur-Aube in 1814, during the war against Napoleon, and of the triumphal German entry into Paris in 1871.

It was ironic that Potsdam, the symbol of German military might and imperial display, first mentioned in the tenth century, was, in Baedeker's words, 'of ancient Slavonic origin'. No Slav would then claim Potsdam, although in 1945 the Russians were to meet the Western Allies there as victors, occupiers and peacemakers; but the map of post-1900 Europe, with its clearly-drawn borders, many of them unchanged since 1815, others unchanged since 1871, masked strong forces of discontent, many of ethnic origin.

Serbia, landlocked since she first won independence several decades earlier as the first Slav State of modern times, wanted an outlet on the Adriatic, but was blocked by Austria, which in 1908 had annexed the former Turkish province of Bosnia-Herzegovina. This annexation was not only in defiance of the 1878 Treaty of Berlin, to which Britain had been a signatory, but completed Austrian control of more than three hundred miles of Adriatic coastline. Bosnia could also serve as a military base, when need or opportunity arose, for an Austrian attack on Serbia.

Each minority inside Austria-Hungary wanted either to link up with a neighbouring State, such as Serbia, Italy and Roumania, or, in the case of Czechs and Slovaks, Slovenes and Croats, to carve out some form of autonomy, even statehood of its own. The Poles, under German, Austro-Hungarian and Russian rule, had never given up their hopes of independence, which Napoleon had stimulated, but which successive Kaisers, Tsars and Emperors had suppressed for a century.

The danger to Austria-Hungary of the ambitions of the Slavs was explained on 14 December 1912 in a letter from the Austrian Chief of

5

Staff, Baron Conrad von Hötzendorf, to the Heir Apparent of the Hapsburg Empire, the Emperor's nephew Archduke Franz Ferdinand. 'The
unification of the South Slav race', Conrad told Franz Ferdinand, 'is one
of the powerful national movements which can neither be ignored nor
kept down. The question can only be, whether that unification will take
place within the boundaries of the Monarchy – that is, at the expense of
Serbia's independence – or under Serbia's leadership at the expense of the
Monarchy.' Were Serbia to be the leader of Slav unification, Conrad
warned, it would be at the cost to Austria of all its south Slav provinces,
and thus of almost its entire coastline. The loss of territory and prestige
involved in Serbia's ascendancy 'would relegate the Monarchy to the status
of a small power'.

The conflicting fears and desires of many States and peoples did not
create a European war, but they served as a set of multiple fuses waiting
to be ignited, should war begin between two States. War, if it came, would
be an irresistible opportunity to fulfil long-harboured desires or to avenge
long-nurtured hatreds. Germany, so strong industrially, so confident militarily, resented the close alliance between her western and eastern neighbours, France and Russia. As a counterweight, she clung to her southern
neighbour Austria-Hungary, a partner in need, however cumbersome and
divided that partner might be. Germany had also drawn Italy into her
orbit, in 1882, creating a Triple Alliance.

The Kaiser's visit to Sultan Abdul Hamid in Constantinople in 1898,
and his flamboyant pilgrimage to Jerusalem, where the dignitaries of all
three monotheistic faiths erected festive arches for him to ride under,
indicated to the Ottoman Turkish Empire, and to the whole Muslim world,
that they could look to Germany as a friend. By 1914 three impressive
stone buildings stood on the crest of the Mount of Olives overlooking the
Dead Sea: the Russian Church of the Ascension, symbol of St Petersburg's
interest in the Orient since 1888; the private home of an Englishman, Sir
John Gray Hill, purchased that spring by the Zionists for a Jewish university, symbol of nascent national aspirations; and the Augusta-Victoria
sanatorium, built in 1909, named after the Kaiser's wife, and a monument
to the confident assertion of German interests and ambitions.

In 1907 Britain had signed an agreement with Russia. Although the
main aim of this agreement was to settle long-standing Anglo-Russian
disputes in far-off Persia and Afghanistan, it seemed to Germany further
proof of encirclement. As a sign of her own eastern ambitions, Germany
had been pushing forward since 1899 with a railway from Berlin to Baghdad and beyond, using Constantinople as the crossing point from Europe
to Asia. The ferry that took travellers, goods and railway wagons from the
Sirkeci station on the European shore of the Bosphorus to the Haydar
Pasha station on the Asian shore was a symbol of German enterprise.

Plans were being made by the Germans to extend the railway through
Turkey-in-Asia as far south as the ports of Gaza on the Eastern Mediterranean, Akaba on the Red Sea, and Basra on the Persian Gulf. A branch

line running eastward from Baghdad was intended to reach as far as the Persian oilfields, a direct challenge to the influence that Britain and Russia had established in that very region only seven years before. In 1906, in an attempt to counter a possible German railway terminus at Akaba on the Red Sea, Britain, then the occupying power in Egypt, annexed to her Egyptian territories the eastern wastes of the Sinai desert from Turkey. This would enable British guns to be rushed from Egypt to the tiny Bay of Taba, from which they could bombard the rail terminal and port facilities at Akaba if these were used by Germany against British interests.

German fears of encirclement were based upon the gradual drawing together, in agreements and conversations, of France, Russia and Britain. In January 1909 a former Chief of the German General Staff, Alfred von Schlieffen, who had retired four years earlier, published an article on the war of the future in which he warned, about Britain, France, Russia and even Italy: 'An endeavour is afoot to bring all these Powers together for a concentrated attack on the Central Powers. At the given moment, the drawbridges are to be let down, the doors are to be opened and the million-strong armies let loose, ravaging and destroying, across the Vosges, the Meuse, the Niemen, the Bug and even the Isonzo and the Tyrolean Alps. The danger seems gigantic.' Reading this article aloud to his commanding generals, the Kaiser commented: 'Bravo.'

In 1911, five years after the British ensured their ability to destroy at least one of the terminals of the German-dominated Berlin-Baghdad railway, Britain and France acted together to prevent Germany establishing a port at Agadir, on the Atlantic coast of Morocco. A German gunboat having reached the port, the British threatened hostilities if it did not leave. The threat was effective, but the rancour which it left was equally strong.

Public perceptions were not necessarily in line with the facts. British traders could make as much use of the Berlin-Baghdad railway as German traders, and there were eight French directors on the railway board in addition to the eleven German. But the idea of nearly two thousand miles of German enterprise striding across Europe, Anatolia and the Arab provinces of the Ottoman Empire was galling, even threatening, to Britain, with her own imperial interests in the Persian Gulf and Indian Ocean.

Along the route of the railway only Serbia, through which a mere 175 miles ran, was not within the German sphere of influences and alliances. For Germany, the British and French Empires were a source of jealous indignation, even though Germany's own overseas empire included large regions of Africa and wide expanses of the Pacific Ocean, in none of which there was particularly active settlement or exploitation. For Germany, imperial possessions were symbols of power, rather than a significant development of national enterprise and prosperity.

Another cause of Anglo-German friction, exacerbated by determined nationalists on both sides of the North Sea, was the Kaiser's desire to match Britain in naval strength, even though Germany's overseas possessions did not require a navy on the British scale. In 1912 a German naval law, the fourth in twelve years, added 15,000 officers and men to an already substantial naval force. Britain's First Lord of the Admiralty, Winston Churchill, suggested a mutual pause in naval expansion, but this was rejected by Germany. His argument, that a powerful Fleet was a necessity for Britain but a 'luxury' for Germany, while essentially true given Britain's Indian and other widespread imperial responsibilities, offended the Germans, who saw themselves as in every way on a par with Britain, yet expected to take a place of inferiority. For their part the British, fearing an ever-increasing German naval threat in the North Sea, welcomed Russia's naval expansion: on 12 May 1914 the British Cabinet noted with approval that 'the large contemplated increase in the Baltic Fleet of Russia must necessarily ease our position vis-à-vis Germany in home waters.'

Serbia's victory in the First Balkan War against Turkey in 1912 was a set-back to Germany. The military and territorial success of this small Slav State threatened not only Austria's predominance in the Balkans, but also Germany's desire to be the predominant European power in Turkey. The loss of Turkish territory in Europe to Serbia was a victory for Russian sentiment. The Russians, as champions of the Slavs, and as rulers of the Polish and Baltic provinces adjacent to Germany, stimulated German animosity. The racial concept of Teuton against Slav was a force for conflict. Nor did it seem that this conflict was necessarily unwelcome. On 8 December 1912, in a discussion with the Chief of Staff, Count von Moltke, the Chief of the Naval Staff, Admiral von Müller, and the Secretary of State for the Navy, Admiral von Tirpitz, the Kaiser told them, as Müller recorded in his diary: 'Austria had to act vigorously against the foreign Slavs (Serbs), because she would otherwise lose her power over the Serbs in the Austro-Hungarian Monarchy. If Russia were to support the Serbs, war would be inevitable for us.' The German Fleet, the Kaiser added, 'would have to face war against Britain'.

During this meeting, Moltke suggested that 'the popularity of a war against Russia, as outlined by the Kaiser, should be better prepared'. The Kaiser agreed that the newspapers must begin to 'enlighten the German people' as to Germany's 'great national interests' if war were to break out following an Austro-Serbian conflict. According to the instructions passed on by Admiral Müller to the Chancellor, Theobald von Bethmann-Hollweg, who had not attended the meeting: 'The people must not be in the position of asking themselves only at the outbreak of a great European war, what are the interests that Germany would be fighting for. The people ought rather to be accustomed to the idea of such a war beforehand.'[1]

The question of the readiness of the public mind to accept war was one

[1] Imanuel Geiss, a colleague of mine at St Antony's College, Oxford, in 1961, has pointed out in his edition of documents leading up to the war that Admiral Müller's note of this important discussion 'is another of those documents not to be found in the *Grosse Politik* – for obvious reasons'. (*July 1914*, page 42, note 4). *Die Grosse Politik der Europäischen Kabinette 1871–1914* was the 39–volume edition of German documents on the origins of the war published in Berlin between 1922 and 1927.

that Moltke understood, and was concerned about. At the beginning of 1913 he went so far, as did Bethmann-Hollweg, to warn their Austrian opposite numbers not to make war with Serbia, despite the Serbian desire to occupy Albania. Moltke was convinced, he told General Conrad von Hötzendorf, the Austrian Chief of Staff, on 10 February 1913, 'that a European war is bound to come sooner or later, in which the issue will be one of a struggle between Germandom and Slavdom' and that 'to prepare themselves for that contingency is the duty of all States which are the champions of Germanic ideas and culture'. Such a war, however, Moltke warned, 'necessitates the readiness of the people to make sacrifices, and popular enthusiasm'. That time had not yet come.

In June 1913 Churchill repeated, in a private conversation with the German Naval Attaché in London, Captain E. von Müller, the suggestion of a pause in naval expansion on both sides. Müller, who disliked the British and did not want the Foreign Office in Berlin, or the Kaiser, to follow up Churchill's conciliatory suggestion, asked Admiral Tirpitz what he should do. Tirpitz advised him to report the conversation with Churchill as briefly as possible, and in such a way as to give the impression that Churchill was only seeking to delay German naval expansion because he feared that Britain would not be able to maintain her existing naval superiority. Thus Churchill's initiative was twisted in such a way as to prejudice the Kaiser against it. Almost a year later the German Foreign Secretary, Gottlieb von Jagow, complained to the German Ambassador in London: 'Most disagreeable is the tendentious reporting of your naval attaché. Can you not keep him a bit more on leash? This everlasting baiting and calumniation of English policy is extraordinarily disturbing, especially since it is always used in high places in argument against me,' that is, by the Kaiser.

Germany's growing strength was everywhere apparent. In the spring of 1913 her standing army, which a year earlier had been increased to 544,000 men, was increased further to 661,000. That October, the German Chancellor introduced the army increases with the words: 'One thing remains beyond doubt, if it should ever come to a European conflagration which set *Slaventum* against *Germanentum*, it is then for us a disadvantage that the position in the balance of forces which was hitherto occupied by European Turkey is now filled in part by Slav states.'

In the immediate aftermath of the Balkan wars, it was not Germany but her neighbour and ally Austria that defended the needs of *Germanentum* against *Slaventum*. As a result of Austrian pressure, Turkey agreed to the creation of an independent Albania, effectively cutting Serbia off from access to the Adriatic Sea. At the same time Greece, ruled by a King who was married to the Kaiser's sister, denied Serbia access to the Aegean Sea by annexing the coastal region of Thrace from Turkey.

Nations felt aggrieved, unsatisfied, endangered, or confident. Newspapers stimulated the sense of danger and deprivation. Governments beat the drums of racism, patriotism and military prowess. While the deserts

9

and swamps of distant continents seemed to offer prospects of expansion, the competition of rival powers made even a railway across a desert seem a provocation. No single rivalry or disputed place or region caused the war: yet all rivalries and disputes combined to create and whip up the moods and opportunities that made war first thinkable, then possible, and finally desirable. 'I am fed up with war and the clamour for war and with the perennial armaments,' Bethmann-Hollweg told a friend in a moment of vexed truth in June 1913. 'It is high time that the great nations calmed down again and occupied themselves with peaceful pursuits, or there will be an explosion which no one desires and which will be to the detriment of all.'

Territorial greed, and successful conquests, played their part in the continuing concept of a desirable war. After her victory over Turkey in 1912, Italy had annexed Turkey's vast North African province of Libya. A year later Bulgaria, having likewise defeated the Turks, acquired an outlet on the Aegean Sea with access to the Mediterranean. Land-locked Serbia, convinced that the Austrian dominance of Bosnia and the Dalmatian coast was a deliberate attempt to deny her access to the Adriatic Sea, occupied Albania in the Second Balkan War in less than two years. Serbia thus acquired, momentarily, a considerable coastline in the Adriatic.

October 1913 marked the hundredth anniversary of one of Germany's greatest military victories, the defeat of Napoleon at Leipzig, by Prussia, Austria, Russia and Sweden, in the Battle of the Nations.[1] To commemorate this triumph, the Kaiser unveiled a monument to the victory in a ceremony designed to stress Germany's traditional and historic military prowess. Among those at the ceremony was the Austrian Chief of Staff, General Conrad, to whom the Kaiser expressed his support for any Austrian action to force Serbia out of Albania. 'I am with you there,' the Kaiser confided. 'The other powers were not prepared. 'Within a few days you must be in Belgrade. I was always a partisan of peace; but this has its limits. I have read much about war and know what it means. But finally a situation arises in which a great power can no longer just look on, but must draw the sword.'

Serbia's occupation of Albania was a short-lived triumph. On 18 October 1913 the Austrian Government sent an ultimatum to Belgrade, demanding the evacuation of Albania by Serbian forces within eight days. The Serbs complied. That day a British diplomat, Eyre Crowe, noted with truth, and a certain prescience: 'Austria has broken loose from the concert of Powers in order to seek a solution single-handed of a question hitherto treated as concerning all Powers.' On the following day the German Acting

---

[1] One of my Oxford tutors, Karl Leyser, pointed out to me during a tutorial in 1957 that Leipzig (like Potsdam) was originally a Slav settlement. Leipzig, its name derived from the Slav word lipa, a lime tree, was founded before A.D. 1000 by Slav tribes. Leyser, who had left Germany after 1933 because of Hitler's persecution of the Jews, was an expert on the thousand-year struggle between Germandom and Slavdom from its earlier years.

Foreign Minister, Dr Alfred Zimmermann, told the British Ambassador in Berlin, Sir Edward Goschen: 'He had been surprised that the Emperor of Austria endorsed a policy which, under certain circumstances, might lead to serious consequences, but he had done so, and that made it clearer still that restraining advice at Vienna on the part of Germany was out of the question.'

In these final fourteen words lay the seeds of a European war. After the Austrian ultimatum was sent, the Kaiser sent a telegram of congratulations both to the Emperor Franz Josef, and to Franz Josef's Heir Apparent, the Archduke Franz Ferdinand. This German approval, commented Eyre Crowe at the end of October 1913, 'confirms the impression that Germany, pretending to us that she altogether disapproved and regretted the Austrian attitude, has throughout encouraged her ally'. It was noted in Austria that no Russian newspaper suggested that Russia should take any action on behalf of Serbia that might lead to a Russian conflict with Austria.

Austria-Hungary had all the outward trappings of permanence and confidence. 'It is difficult to think without Austria,' Bismarck had said in 1888. 'A State like Austria does not disappear.' On 2 December 1913 High Mass was celebrated in Vienna to mark the sixty-fifth anniversary of the Emperor Franz Josef's succession to the throne. No previous European sovereign had held royal authority for so long. But he could neither curb the national aspirations of his people nor prevent outsiders from encouraging them. Of all the major powers, Russia was most active in stirring the pot. On 19 January 1914 the Austrian Governor of Galicia reported to the Ministry of the Interior in Vienna: 'Recently the agitation of the Russophil party ... has become more lively.... The continuing Russification of Galicia, aided by Orthodoxy, requires greater attention on the part of administrative officers if they are to be able to combat it.'

In the early months of 1914, in the constant search for sources of fuel oil, essential to keep the most modern warships in action, Britain stole a march on Germany by negotiating a predominant share in the Persian oilfields, towards which German railway builders had set their sites and compasses. Yet at the same time, as head of Britain's navy, Winston Churchill, who had twice proposed a pause in Anglo-German naval construction, suggested to his senior Cabinet colleagues that he open secret negotiations with his German opposite number, Admiral Tirpitz. His aim, Churchill explained, was to end 'the unwholesome concentration of fleets in home waters'. The Foreign Secretary, Sir Edward Grey, rejected this suggestion, arguing that if news of the talks leaked out 'the wildest reports will be circulated and we shall be involved in constant explanations to ambassadors at the Foreign Office, and in denials in the Press of the things that will be attributed to us.' Grey's position of seniority prevailed.

Despite this rejection of Anglo-German discussions, war seemed unlikely in the spring and summer of 1914. Disputes between sovereign states could be submitted for settlement to the International Tribunal at The Hague, a tribunal set up in 1900 that was a symbol of the determination of the civilised world not to allow itself to become embroiled in mutually destructive conflicts. Socialists throughout Europe denounced the very concept of war and urged the working class everywhere to refuse to be a part of capitalist war-enthusiasms. Bankers and financiers, like the landed aristocracy with whom they were in competition, felt themselves part of a wider international grouping, which, whether by trade in the one case or intermarriage in the other, had nothing to gain by war, and much to lose. Agreements had been reached that transformed rivalry into co-operation: on 13 August 1913 Britain and Germany had secretly negotiated the creation of potential spheres of influence in Portugal's African possessions. The agreement, for eventual Anglo-German control of Angola and Mozambique, was initialled on 20 October 1913, two days after Austria's 'Albanian' ultimatum to Serbia. There seemed no reason why a Balkan crisis, even one initiated by a European power close to Germany, should inhibit Anglo-German relations.

At the level of political thought, a British writer, Norman Angell, in his book *The Great Illusion*, argued that even a victorious warring power would suffer extraordinary economic and financial loss as a result of war. His warning, first published in 1909, was translated into French, German, Italian and Russian, achieving more than ten English-language printings by 1913. Angell stressed that the great industrial nations, Britain, the United States, Germany and France were 'losing the psychological impulse to war, just as we have lost the psychological impulse to kill our neighbours on account of religious differences'. How could it be otherwise, he asked. 'How can modern life, with its overpowering proportion of industrial activities and its infinitesimal proportion of military, keep alive the instincts associated with war as against those developed by peace?' Even the Prussian Junker 'becomes less of an energumen as he becomes more of a scientist'.

Angell was far from alone in pointing out that the powers whose rivalries made their public opinions so warlike were themselves tied closely together by links of free trade and industrial interdependence. In June 1914 it was a company owned jointly by British and German investors that gained exclusive rights for oil exploration in Mesopotamia. Ships of all the European nations carried in their holds the produce of each other's fields and factories. German, French, British and Russian cars and lorries, which in the event of war would have to transport troops and supplies, functioned thanks to the Bosch magneto, made exclusively in Germany, and imported by the manufacturers of vehicles in every European country. If war came, and supplies of the magneto were cut off, this small but crucial part would have to be reinvented, and then manufactured from scratch.

Acetone, the solvent used in the manufacture of cordite, the explosive component of shells, was another example of the interdependence of the European States. It was produced almost entirely by the distillation of wood. Germany and Austria were two of the main timber-exporting countries, the other two being Canada and the United States. One ton of acetone required at least eighty tons of birch, beech or maple. All Britain's forests would not be able to supply the minimum of a hundred tons needed each year in the event of war. Imported wood was an essential component of warmaking capacity. Within six months of the outbreak of war Britain's need for a synthetic acetone had become urgent, giving science a central part to play, though it took until February 1916 before the synthetic process was in place. One area of total German monopoly was the manufacture of binoculars. In August 1915 Britain was obliged to use a Swiss intermediary in order to acquire 32,000 pairs of German binoculars for the Western Front.

Not only the interdependence of trade, and the growth of travel and tourism since the turn of the century, but the fact that almost every European Head of State was related by marriage to every other, created bonds that seemed unbreakable. The German Kaiser and his cousin by marriage, the Russian Tsar, were in regular and friendly correspondence, addressing each other, in English, as 'Willie' and 'Nicky'. The letters they exchanged breathed neither fire nor brimstone. Yet the continual building up of armies and fleets, the development of the new science of aerial warfare and the national rivalries of the European powers contained ominous overtones that could not be masked by friendly correspondence, Free Trade, or common sense.

In the early months of 1914 the Russians were angered when the Kaiser sent a senior German officer, General Liman von Sanders, to Turkey as military adviser to the Ottoman army. On 12 May 1914, at Carlsbad, the German Chief of Staff, Count Moltke, told his Austrian opposite number, Baron Conrad, that any delay in war with Russia 'meant a lessening of our chances; we could not compete with Russia in masses.' Travelling eight days later by car from Potsdam to Berlin, Moltke told the German Secretary of State, Gottlieb von Jagow, that he was afraid that Russia would in two or three years have built up her maximum war armaments, and that no other way was left to Germany but 'to wage preventive war in order to beat the enemy while we still have some chance of winning'. Moltke's advice to Jagow during their drive was that the Secretary of State should 'orientate our policy at the early provocation of war'.

On May 29 Colonel House, President Wilson's emissary, wrote to the President from Berlin: 'The situation is extraordinary. It is militarism run stark mad. Unless someone acting for you can bring about a different understanding there is some day to be an awful cataclysm.' No one in Europe could bring about that understanding, House warned. 'There is too much hatred, too many jealousies. Whenever England consents, France and Russia will close in on Germany and Austria. England does not want Germany wholly crushed, for she would then have to reckon alone with her ancient enemy, Russia; but if Germany insists upon an ever-increasing navy, then England will have no choice.' Reaching London, House told the British Foreign Secretary how, in Berlin, 'the air seemed full of the clash of arms, of readiness to strike'.

Even as Colonel House wrote and spoke these words of foreboding, Britain and Germany were negotiating the Baghdad Railway Agreement, to share economic opportunities and avoid territorial conflicts in Asia Minor. But the economic benefits of peace were not the only benefits being argued about that summer. Early in June, the German Chancellor, Bethmann-Hollweg, told the Bavarian Minister in Berlin, Count Hugo von Lerchenfeld, that there were circles in Germany which expected war to lead to an improvement in the domestic situation in Germany 'in a Conservative direction'. Bethmann Hollweg thought, however, 'that on the contrary a World War with its incalculable consequences would strengthen the tremendous power of Social Democracy, because they preached peace, and would topple many a throne'.

On June 11, at Caen Wood House in one of the leafier suburbs of North London, an orchestra brought specially from Vienna played to the guests at a spectacular dinner and ball. The host was the Grand Duke Michael, a great-great-grandson of Catherine the Great and the Tsar's second cousin. His guests were the aristocrats and nobility of Europe, headed by King George V and Queen Mary. The guests, and the musicians entertaining them, had no reason to feel anything but a sense of ease and well-being. Yet at any given moment of calm and contentment, terrible disturbances were lurking.

For the Slavs within Austria-Hungary, as well as for the Serbs in their independent kingdom, Tsarist Russia, ruled by the Grand Duke's cousin, was an ever-beckoning patron. In May 1914 a leading Czech member of the Austrian Parliament, Dr Karel Kramar, had sent a Russian friend his thoughts on 'a Slav confederation ruled from St Petersburg' that would be brought into being after a war between Russia and Austria, once the Hapsburg system had collapsed in war.

A sense of instability hung over the whole vast Austro-Hungarian structure. The head of the Dual Monarchy, Emperor of Austria and King of Hungary, Franz Josef, was eighty-three years old. His nephew and heir, the Archduke Franz Ferdinand, was said to dislike the Hungarian predominance in his kingdom intensely, so much so that he had plans to subdivide the whole Empire in such a way that the Hungarian half would cease to be a Hungarian preserve, giving Serbs and Croats much greater autonomy. During the spring of 1914 the Archduke was contemplating, on paper at least, a future 'People's Parliament' for Hungary that would have curbed the Hungarian influence considerably, by increasing the power of the various non-Hungarian minorities within Hungary, including two Slav groups, the Slovaks and the Croats.

On 12 June 1914 the Kaiser went for the weekend to Konopischt, near Prague, to stay with Franz Ferdinand. It was a time of relaxation and hunting. The main topic for serious conversation was the Kaiser's new-found liking for the Hungarian Prime Minster, Count Tisza, whose influence Franz Ferdinand disliked. The Kaiser and the Heir Apparent also discussed the visit that same weekend, by the Russian Tsar, to the Roumanian royal family at Constanta, on the Black Sea. It would seem that the Archduke also asked the Kaiser, but very much in passing, if Germany would still be willing, as the Kaiser had intimated during the Albanian crisis eight months earlier, to give Austria-Hungary her support in destroying the Serbian 'hornets' nest' from which, Austria was convinced, anti-Austrian feeling was being stirred up in Bosnia-Herzegovina. The Kaiser replied that Austria should do something before the situation worsened. He doubted that Austria need fear Russian intervention on behalf of Serbia, as the Russian army was not yet ready for war. Austrian action against Serbia, so it seemed, would have Germany's full support.

The Kaiser left Konopischt for his palace at Potsdam. Nine days later he was at Kiel for the annual Elbe Regatta, Kiel Week, a time of races, dances and enjoyment. Although the newly-opened Kiel Canal represented a German naval threat to Britain, a squadron of British warships was present as honoured guests, its four battleships and three cruisers being moored alongside the German Imperial High Seas Fleet. Officers and men of both navies exchanged enthusiastic compliments as they went on board each other's ships to enjoy the pageantry. Together they stood bareheaded at the funeral of a British pilot killed in an air accident during the festivities.

On board his racing yacht *Meteor V*, the Kaiser was at the centre of the splendour of the regatta. On June 26 wearing his uniform as a British Admiral of the Fleet, he went on board the battleship *King George V*. Technically he was the senior Royal Navy officer present. There was a ludicrous incident during his visit: the Counsellor at the British Embassy in Berlin, Sir Horace Rumbold, had especially put on a morning coat and top hat. The 'Admiral of the Fleet' decided that the diplomat was improperly dressed. Pointing to the top hat he declared: 'If I see that again I will smash it in. One doesn't wear tall hats on board ships.'

On the evening of June 27 the commander of the British squadron gave a reception on board *King George V* for the German officers. Rumbold recalled a few weeks later how then, as throughout the regatta, 'I could not fail to be impressed by the great cordiality which existed between the German and our sailors.' On the following day, June 28 there was a yacht race, watched eagerly by German and British spectators alike. The Kaiser himself was racing, on his yacht *Meteor*. While he was in the Kiel Bay a telegram was brought out to him by launch, put in a cigarette case and thrown on board the yacht. The Kaiser read it: the Archduke Franz Ferdinand, his host at Konopischt two weeks earlier, the heir to the Hapsburgs, had been assassinated in the Bosnian capital, Sarajevo, together with his wife. The race was cancelled, Kiel Week itself brought to an end, and the Kaiser hurried back to his palace at Potsdam.

2

'Wild with joy'

28 JUNE TO 4 AUGUST 1914

The assassination of the heir to the Hapsburgs took place on the anniversary of the defeat of the Serbs by the Turks at the battle of Kosovo in 1349, a humiliating collective memory for all Serbs. There was something particularly tactless in holding a State visit in Sarajevo on 28 June 1914, that day of solemn memories, which was also Serbia's national day. Among those who gathered to watch the Archduke and his wife drive through the city to the Governor's residence was a nineteen-year-old Bosnian Serb, Gavrilo Princip, who had a pistol. He was one of six young conspirators present in the streets that day who dreamed of the moment when Bosnia would be free of the Austrian yoke, and an integral part of Serbia.

That morning one of Princip's accomplices had thrown a bomb at the archducal car. The bomb bounced off the side and exploded against the next car, injuring two officers on the Archduke's staff. Having ensured that the injured men were taken to hospital, and that the would-be assassin had been caught, the Archduke insisted on continuing with his visit to the City Hall. Once there, he remarked with some anger: 'So you welcome your guests here with bombs?' He was then formally welcomed to the city by the Mayor. After the ceremony he asked to be driven to the hospital to visit the two injured officers. During this unscheduled part of the journey the driver, Franz Urban, took a wrong turn into a narrow street in which he could not turn the car round. He therefore slowed down in order to reverse.

Gavrilo Princip, disappointed that his colleagues had ruined their chance of assassinating the Archduke (or even more disappointed that the chance had not fallen to him) was standing, by chance, on the pavement only ten yards from where the car slowed down. Suddenly he saw his 'lost' target coming towards him. Stepping forward, he fired two shots. At first it seemed that no one was hurt, and Urban drove swiftly towards the correct road. But both his passengers had been shot. The Archduke, who had escaped death that morning and been angry at the lack of security provided for him, bled to death during the drive. His wife died with him.

Princip and two of his accomplices had been trained in Serbia by members of the Black Hand terrorist organisation, a fiercely nationalist organisation which the Serb Government itself was even then trying to suppress. The conspirators had been encouraged in their task by the leader of the Black Hand, Colonel Dimitrievic (also known as Apis), a sworn enemy of Austria. Having been given their weapons in Belgrade, the conspirators had been smuggled back across the Austrian border into Bosnia in May. Their aim was to strike a physical blow at Austrian rule. In 1878 the Turks had been driven from Bosnia after ruling there for many centuries, but the subsequent annexation of the province by Austria was a blow to Serb national aspirations. That Franz Ferdinand had come to Bosnia to direct the manoeuvres of two Austrian army corps stationed in the province, troops who could one day be the spearhead of an Austrian attack on Serbia, was a particular incitement to them. The manoeuvres had taken place on the two days preceding the visit to Sarajevo.

Unknown to the conspirators, the victim of their bullets was not unsympathetic to the national aspirations of the nationalities of the Empire, including the Serbs. In court and political circles he had the reputation of wishing to change the Dualism of Austria-Hungary into the Trialism of Austria, Hungary and the South Slavs, giving the Slavs of the Empire the same separate powers and autonomies as had been enjoyed by the Hungarians since 1867. This sympathy to Slav national aspirations, and the Archduke's marriage outside the circle of royalty and aristocracy, had already alienated him from his uncle, the Emperor, whose first comment on his nephew's assassination was said to have been: 'A higher power has re-established the order which I, alas, could not preserve.' For him, apparently, it was not the assassin, but God, who had averted the possible repercussions of his nephew's marriage outside the royal circle.

Franz Josef's remark about the 'higher power' was told by the man who heard it, Count Parr, to his deputy, Colonel Margutti, who wrote up the account ten years later. Franz Josef's most recent biographer writes: 'The harsh comment, with its echo of old worries over the intrusion of a morganatic marriage in what the Emperor regarded as a divinely ordained line of dynastic descent, seems so artificially stilted as to be apocryphal. On the other hand, the news broke on a Sunday, at a time when the unfathomable workings of Providence may have been close to the surface of his shocked mind.'[1]

Fourteen years earlier, to the day, Franz Ferdinand had been forced by his uncle to take an oath barring any children he might have from the throne. The Emperor had always feared that this oath would be abandoned once Franz Ferdinand succeeded him. That danger was now averted. The new heir to the throne, the fifth of his reign, was his great-nephew the

[1] Alan Palmer, *The Twilight of the Habsburgs: The Life and Times of Emperor Francis Joseph*, Weidenfeld and Nicolson, 1994. From 1952 to 1954 Alan Palmer was my history teacher: his enthusiasm for history, then seen only by his fortunate pupils, was later transmitted to a much wider public through more than fifteen published works.

Archduke Charles. 'For me it is a great relief from worry,' he commented.

In the aftermath of the assassination, the Emperor's personal sense of relief was unknown to the public and could have no effect on the repercussions. Indignation at the deed, and fear of a wider Serb conspiracy, led to anti-Serb riots in Vienna and Brünn. From Budapest the British Consul-General reported: 'A wave of blind hatred for Serbia and everything Serbian is sweeping over the country.' The Austrian Foreign Minister, Count Berchtold, and the Chief of the Austrian General Staff, Baron Conrad von Hotzendorf, both saw the assassination as an opportunity to reduce the power of Serbia. They were unclear in their own minds as to whether they should annex some part or all of Serbia, or defeat her in war in order to demand not territory, but a large financial indemnity. Franz Josef was not enamoured of action, fearing that an Austrian attack on Serbia might draw in other powers, in particular Russia, which would be forced by pan-Slav sentiment to come to Serbia's assistance. Equally hesitant was the Hungarian Prime Minister, Count Tisza. On July 1 Conrad noted: 'Tisza was against war with Serbia; he was anxious, fearing that Russia might strike at us and Germany leave us in the lurch.'

Having returned from Kiel to Berlin, the Kaiser was in a bellicose mood. 'The Serbs must be disposed of, *and* that right soon!' he noted in the margin of a telegram from his Ambassador in Vienna on June 30. Against his Ambassador's remark that 'only a mild punishment' might be imposed on Serbia, the Kaiser wrote: 'I hope not.' Yet these comments envisaged nothing more than a swift Austrian victory over Serbia, with no wider repercussions. That day, as the British naval squadron sailed from Kiel, the British admiral signalled to the German Fleet: 'Friends in past, and friends for ever.' Also on June 30, Sir Arthur Nicolson, the senior civil servant at the British Foreign Office, wrote to the British Ambassador in St Petersburg: 'The tragedy which has just taken place in Sarajevo will not, I trust, lead to further complications.'

On July 3 it was announced from Berlin that the Berlin-Baghdad railway would be continued southward to Basra, giving Germany an outlet on the Persian Gulf, and overland access to the Indian Ocean. That summer, however, Britain was within a few months of concluding an agreement with Germany, so that the railway would not be a cause of conflict between them.

The German attitude towards Austria was crucial. On July 4 the German Ambassador to London, Prince Lichnowsky, having just returned from Berlin, told the former British Secretary of State for War, Lord Haldane, that he was 'very worried' about the state of opinion in Germany. 'The general feeling in Berlin', Lichnowsky reported, was 'that Serbia could not be allowed to go on intriguing and agitating against Austria and that Germany must support Austria in any action she proposed to take.' That same day the German Ambassador in Vienna, Count Tschirschky, told a senior Austrian official that Germany would support Austria-Hungary 'through thick and thin', and he added: 'The earlier Austria attacks the better. It would have been better to attack yesterday than today; and better to attack today than tomorrow.'

To this advice the Kaiser added, on July 5, an essential dimension of active German support, telling the Austrian Ambassador to Germany, Count Szogyeny, that Russia was 'in no way prepared for war' and that the Austrians would regret it if, having recognised the necessity of war against Serbia, 'we did not make use of the present moment, which is all in our favour'. The Kaiser added: 'Should war between Austria-Hungary and Russia prove unavoidable', Germany would be at Austria's side.

Later that day, while still at Potsdam, the Kaiser told the German Chancellor, Bethmann-Hollweg, and the Prussian War Minister, General Falkenhayn, that he 'did not believe that there was any prospect of great warlike developments. The Tsar would not side with the Archduke's murderers, and Russia and France were not ready for war.' For this reason, the Kaiser explained, 'there was no need to make special dispositions'. He then returned to Kiel and on the morning of July 6 departed in the imperial yacht *Hohenzollern* for his annual three-week summer cruise in Norwegian waters.

More than a week had passed since the murder of the Archduke. Anger in Vienna, apprehension in Belgrade, and relaxation in Berlin, were the order of the day. With the Kaiser's departure on his cruise, the shock of Europe's latest episode began to subside. In Vienna, however, the secret debates on how to deal with Serbia continued. On July 7 the eight members of the Austro-Hungarian Cabinet met to discuss the Kaiser's offer of German help. Berchtold, who presided, proposed an immediate attack on Serbia, without even a declaration of war.

The overriding mood of the meeting was for war, and for the reduction of Serbia in size, making her dependent on Austria. Only Count Tisza protested to the Emperor, writing to him on the following day that an Austrian attack on Serbia 'would, in human possibility, provoke the world war': a war that Tisza believed would bring not only Russia but also Roumania against Austria-Hungary, exposing the Empire to a 'very unfavourable' prospect.

The Germans ignored Tisza's worries. When the German Ambassador in Vienna, Count Tschirschky, went to see Berchtold, he emphasised the German desire for action against Serbia. 'He told me', Berchtold informed Tisza, 'that he had received a telegram from Berlin according to which his Imperial Master instructed him to declare here with all emphasis that in Berlin an action against Serbia is expected, and that it would not be understood in Germany if we allowed the opportunity to pass without striking a blow.' Fears of Russia continued to influence the Germans. On July 7 Bethmann-Hollweg had commented: 'The future lies with Russia, she grows and grows, and lies on us like a nightmare.' On the following day he informed Prince Lichnowsky that 'not only the extremists' in Berlin 'but even level-headed politicians are worried at the increases in Russian strength, and the imminence of Russian attack.'

On July 8, ten days after the Archduke Franz Ferdinand's assassination, a senior British general, Sir Horace Smith-Dorrien, told his old school association dinner that they should all befit themselves 'for the coming struggle'. He was, he later recalled, 'good-naturedly chafed by my particular friends and asked what had made me so gloomy that evening'. At the Uppingham School speech day three days later, one of those present as a guest, Vera Brittain, whose brother Edward and friend Roland Leighton were both at the school, later recalled 'the breathless silence which followed the Headmaster's slow, religious emphasis on the words: "If a man cannot be useful to his country, he is better dead".'

On July 9, eleven days after the assassination, Edward Grey asked the German Ambassador in London, Prince Lichnowsky, to call on him at the Foreign Office. He then told the Ambassador that Britain had been 'endeavouring to persuade the Russian Government even at the present juncture to adopt a calm view and a conciliatory attitude towards Austria, should the Vienna Cabinet feel obliged in consequence of the Sarajevo murder to take up a stern attitude towards Serbia.' However, there were measures, Grey warned, on which Austria might embark, 'such as to arouse Slav feeling', which might make it impossible for the Russians to 'remain passive'. What these measures might be, Grey did not indicate. That very day his principal diplomatic adviser, Sir Arthur Nicolson, wrote with a certain confidence to the British Ambassador in Vienna: 'I have my doubts as to whether Austria will take any action of a serious character and I expect the storm will blow over.'

This optimistic view might have been confirmed on July 13, had Nicolson known of a secret Austrian report which reached Vienna that day from Sarajevo, stating that there was no evidence to implicate the Serbian Government in the assassination. The Austrian desire to punish Serbia was still strong, however, sustained by the feeling that Germany would support punitive action. When Berchtold finally convinced Franz Josef that Austria could chastise Serbia without any other powers taking Serbia's side, the old man reluctantly agreed to an Austrian ultimatum. Berchtold's successful persuasion was the first step towards war. Nicolson's confidence had been misplaced.

In Vienna, the secret and public debate continued: should action be taken against Serbia? Nicolson's optimistic comment had been written in answer to the warning by one of his subordinates that 'the unwisdom of a blindly anti-Serbian policy is not at all appreciated in Austria, and that is the real point in a rather threatening situation'. The young official was right. His name was Robert Vansittart. Twenty years later he was himself to be the head of the Foreign Office and a strenuous opponent of the appeasement of Germany.

No Austrian ultimatum had been sent to Serbia, and a sense of crisis had begun to wane. On July 16, in a talk in London on the international situation, and the dangers of a 'grand military bonfire', Norman Angell told a largely socialist audience: 'The younger generation are, I believe, increasingly determined not to be the victims of that supreme futility.'

Even as Norman Angell was putting his faith in the 'younger generation', the hesitations in Vienna among the older generation were ending. On July 14 the Austrian Council of Ministers had decided to deliver an ultimatum in a week's time. In London two days later, the German Ambassador, Prince Lichnowsky, commented with some acerbity in a letter to the German Chancellor that the Austrian authorities had only themselves to blame for the assassination of Franz Ferdinand, for having sent him into an 'alley of bomb throwers' at Sarajevo. Even the Serbian Foreign Minister had sent a message to the Austrian Finance Minister in Vienna, who had responsibilities for Bosnia-Herzegovina, that the visit was unwise. But all this was now in the past: under seal of secrecy, the senior authorities in Berlin were informed of the date on which the Austrian ultimatum to Serbia would be delivered, and made no protest. The German army hierarchy was ready for war. On July 17 the Deputy Chief of the General Staff, General Waldersee, wrote to the Foreign Secretary, von Jagow, from Berlin: 'I shall remain here ready to jump; we are all prepared at the General Staff.'

Jagow, like the Kaiser, was confident that Russia would not intervene. On July 18 he informed Lichnowsky in London: 'The more resolute Austria shows herself and the more energetically we support her, the sooner will Russia stop her outcry. To be sure, they will make a great to-do in St Petersburg, but when all is said and done, Russia is at present not ready for war.'

The terms of the Austrian ultimatum were finalised in Vienna on July 19. Linking the Belgrade Government with the assassination, they consisted of a total of fifteen demands, among them Serbian Government condemnation of anti-Austrian propaganda; a joint Austro-Serbian commission to investigate the murder; a Serbian army order condemning the Serbian military involvement with the murders; and a firm promise of no further Serbian intrigue in Bosnia. Serbia would also have to give an undertaking to punish anyone who circulated anti-Austrian propaganda, either in schools or in the various nationalist societies. In addition, Austrian officials would participate in the judicial process, and in the process of punishment, of those connected with the plot.

It was clear to all those at the meeting of the Austrian Council of Ministers on July 19, including General Conrad von Hotzendorf, that Serbia would reject these terms, and that some form of punitive Austrian military action would follow. Conrad was the keenest for war, and determined that Austria would make territorial gains on the Bosnian border as a result of it.

On July 21 Franz Josef agreed to the terms of the ultimatum, influenced by the fact that some groups inside Serbia had been involved in the plot, and by fears of the threat of Serbian expansion. On the following day the Russian Foreign Minister, Sergius Sazonoff, warned Austria against taking drastic action. This Russian warning came too late, and lacked any threat of Russian military action.

The Austrian ultimatum had not yet been delivered. On July 23 the British Chancellor of the Exchequer, David Lloyd George, told the House of Commons that 'civilisation' would have no difficulty in regulating disputes that arose between nations by means 'of some sane and well-ordered arbitrament'. Relations with Germany were better than they had been for some years, he said. The next budget ought to show an economy on armaments. That evening of July 23 the Austrian ultimatum was delivered in Belgrade. An answer was demanded within forty-eight hours.

Reading the Austrian ultimatum to Serbia, Grey called it, on July 24, 'the most formidable document that was ever addressed from one state to another'. That day the Russian Council of Ministers agreed, in strictest secrecy, to mobilise thirteen Army Corps 'eventually' destined to be in action against Austria, while publicly announcing that Russia 'cannot remain indifferent'. On the following day, in a development overshadowed by the Austro-Serbian crisis, but dangerous for Britain, the first German warship sailed through the newly-widened Kiel Canal, marking the first day of Germany's capability to send her ships safely and swiftly from the Baltic Sea to the North Sea.

It was clear that the repercussions for continental Europe of the Austrian ultimatum could be severe. There were those in Britain, however, who saw themselves detached from Europe. The Prime Minister, H.H. Asquith, told King George V that Europe was 'within measurable distance of a real Armaggedon', but that as far as Britain was concerned, 'Happily there seems to be no reason why we should be anything more than spectators.' Britain's First Lord of the Admiralty, Winston Churchill, wrote to his wife that Europe was 'trembling on the verge of a general war' and that the Austrian ultimatum was 'the most insolent document of its kind ever devised'. From Berlin, the British Chargé d'Affaires, Sir Horace Rumbold, wrote to his wife: 'In two hours from now the time limit expires and the Austrians will probably be in Belgrade by Monday. The Lord knows what will happen then and I tell you – between ourselves – that we shall be lucky if we get out of this without the long-dreaded European war, a general bust-up in fact.'

Serbia was reluctant to agree to Austria's wide-ranging demands, but even more reluctant also to provoke an attack from her powerful neighbour. The demands of defence and survival were hard to reconcile. The Emperor Franz Josef had ordered partial Austrian mobilisation that day, yet the process was not to start for three days, and was so cumbersome that it would take sixteen days to complete.

At three o'clock on the afternoon of July 25 Serbia mobilised. Three hours later she replied to the ultimatum, agreeing, as demanded by Austria, that anti-Austrian propagandists would be punished, and that subversive movements would be suppressed. All those connected with the Archduke's assassination would, as also demanded, be brought to justice. As to Austria's insistence on participation in the judicial process inside Serbia, the most drastic point of the ten, Serbia asked only that this demand be submitted to the International Tribunal at The Hague.

Half an hour after the Serbian reply to Austria, which was judged by all outside observers to be conciliatory, even humiliating, the Austrian Ambassador, Baron Giesl, left Belgrade. In an immediate act of self-preservation, the Serbian Government, fearing an immediate attack on the capital, which lay across the Danube from Austria, withdrew southward, to the provincial town of Nis. One unexpected problem for Serbia, which attracted international attention and some amusement, was that the Serbian Army Chief-of-Staff, General Putnik, returning by train from a Bohemian spa where he was taking the waters, was detained in Budapest by the police. Franz Josef, indignant that the General should have been arrested by the Hungarians, ordered him to be given a special train for the journey back to Serbia, with an apology.

Austria and Serbia were not yet at war. Lack of preparedness was a problem: on July 26 Conrad had explained to Berchtold that a full-scale Austrian invasion of Serbia would be impossible for a number of weeks. In Russia, whose preparedness was if anything even more backward than that of Austria, the Tsar, while stressing that Russia could not be indifferent to the fate of Serbia, proposed on July 27 the opening of negotiations with Vienna, on the basis of Serbia's reply to the ultimatum. The Austrians rejected this. A British attempt that same day to convene a four-power conference of Britain, Germany, France and Italy 'for the purpose of discovering an issue which would prevent complications' was rejected by Germany on the grounds that such a conference 'was not practicable'. That day the British War Office instructed General Smith-Dorrien to guard 'all vulnerable points' in southern Britain.

The prospect of a general European war forced those who had a hitherto unchallenged, or untested ideological point of view to work out where they stood in the actual evolution of the crisis. On July 27 the one working class member of Britain's Liberal Government, John Burns, wrote in his diary: 'Why four great powers should fight over Serbia no fellow can understand.' War must be averted 'by all the means in our power'. He held it to be 'my especial duty to dissociate myself and the principles I hold, and the trusteeship for the working classes which I carry, from such a universal crime as the contemplated war will be'.

Burns expressed his feelings at a Cabinet meeting that day. When the meeting was over, Lloyd George informed a leading Liberal journalist that 'there could be no question of our taking part in any war in the first instance. He knew of no Minister who would be in favour of it.' The meeting did agree, however, that the First and Second Fleets, which by chance were concentrated at Portland in the English Channel, at the end of a practice mobilisation that had been agreed upon six months earlier, should not be dispersed to their home ports. Realising that Britain might be drawn into a war by the alliance systems, Churchill obtained Asquith's approval that afternoon to set up special armed guards on ammunition and oil depots, and informed all naval commanders: 'European political situation makes war between Triple Alliance and Triple Entente powers by no means impossible. This is not the warning telegram, but be prepared to shadow possible hostile men-of-war.'

The German High Command was pressing Austria to take military action against Serbia, but to do so quickly, in order to eliminate the danger of pressure to the contrary: the danger of the crisis being resolved before Austrian forces could occupy Belgrade. In Berlin, there was still a feeling that a wider conflict could be averted. 'We are not at war yet,' the Kaiser told a friend on July 27, 'and if I can, I shall prevent it.' In a telegram from Berlin on the following day, the Austrian Ambassador informed Count Berchtold: 'We are urgently advised to act at once and present the world a *fait accompli*.' Serbia would be chastised before war could spread. So keen was the German High Command to see Austria attack before the world could react that they urged Austria not to wait even until the completion of her mobilisation, which still needed almost two weeks.

In the five days following the Austrian ultimatum, Britain took a lead among the European states in pressing Austria not to attack Serbia. She also evolved a formula designed to bring Austria and Russia together. But the Austrian Ambassador in Berlin, in passing on the British proposals for mediation to Vienna, stressed that the German Government 'in no way identifies itself with them, but on the contrary is decidedly opposed to their consideration, and only communicates them in order to satisfy the English.' On July 28 the British Ambassador in Vienna warned London that 'postponement or prevention of war with Serbia would undoubtedly be a great disappointment in this country, which has gone wild with joy at the prospect of war'.

Then came a bizarre episode, which remained secret until after the war. The Kaiser, reading that morning for the first time the full text of the Austrian ultimatum and the Serbian reply, could see no reason at all for Austria to declare war, writing in the margin of the Serbian reply: 'A great moral victory for Vienna; but with it every reason for war is removed and Giesl ought to remain quietly in Belgrade. On the strength of this *I* should never have ordered mobilisation.' He went on to suggest that 'as a visible *satisfaction d'honneur* for Austria, the Austrian Army should temporarily occupy Belgrade as a pledge.' Then negotiations to end the brief military conflict could begin. 'I am convinced', the Kaiser wrote to Jagow, 'that on the whole the wishes of the Danube monarchy have been acceded to. The few reservations that Serbia makes in regard to individual points can in my opinion be well cleared up by negotiations. But it contains the announcement *orbi et urbi* of a capitulation of the most humiliating kind, and with it every reason for war is removed.'

It was too late for such conciliatory counsel: at noon that day, scarcely an hour after the Kaiser penned these unbellicose words, Austria declared war on Serbia, confident of German support if the war widened. The first military conflict of the First World War had begun. Only two nations were as yet combatants: Austria and Serbia. Russia and Germany, for all their preparations, were not inexorably bound to come to blows. Would the war widen? Winston Churchill, on whom the responsibility for Britain's naval war would rest, wrote to his wife on learning of the Austrian declaration of war: 'I wondered whether those stupid Kings and Emperors could not assemble together and revivify kingship by saving the nations from hell but we all drift on in a kind of dull cataleptic trance. As if it was somebody else's operation.'

These were not mere late-night musings without a practical aspect: on the morning of July 29 Churchill proposed to the British Cabinet that the European sovereigns should 'be brought together for the sake of peace'. But despite the Kaiser's belated satisfaction with the Serbian reply, the European sovereigns lacked the will to try to halt the march to war, as each War Office and Admiralty worked to ensure that its preparations should be as advanced as possible. That day, as the German Fleet began to mobilise, the British Fleet was sent to its war stations in the North Sea, putting in place the means whereby Britain could prevent a German naval assault on Britain, or, if war came, could protect British troops should they be sent across the Channel to France.

In Berlin there was a glimmer of hope for British neutrality on July 29, when the Kaiser's brother, Prince Henry, who had been yachting in Britain at the Cowes Regatta and had called on his cousin King George V at Buckingham Palace a few days earlier, reported King George as saying to him: 'We shall try all we can to keep out of this and shall remain neutral.' One of the Kaiser's biographers has commented: 'Although Henry had already shown he was an inaccurate reporter of his English relatives' remarks – probably through a failure to understand linguistic subtleties – the Kaiser gave more attention to this message than to any other reports from London or the assessments of his naval intelligence department.'[1] When Admiral Tirpitz expressed his doubts that Britain would remain neutral the Kaiser replied: 'I have the word of a King, and that is good enough for me.'

With Serbia's border forts under the shadow and imminent bombardment of Austrian guns, on the morning of July 29 Russia publicly called a proportion of its vast population to arms. There was no Russian

---

[1] Alan Palmer, *The Kaiser, Warlord of the Second Reich*, Weidenfeld and Nicolson, London 1978, page 172.

declaration of war on Austria that day, but partial mobilisation of a total force of almost six million men. Russian soldiers and artillery were on the move, setting off towards army camps and fortifications along the border with Austria. The Russian War Minister, General Sukhomlinov, had wanted full mobilisation, but this had been rejected by the Tsar. At least one sovereign still hoped war might be averted. But as the focus intensified upon armies and fleets, authority everywhere was shifted towards War Ministers and General Staffs.

In Berlin, Horace Rumbold found himself on July 29 outside the Crown Prince's Palace at the very moment when the Crown Prince arrived in his car. 'The crowd cheered wildly. There was an indescribable feeling of excitement in the air. It was evident that some great event was about to happen. The olive grey motor cars of the Great General Staff were dashing about in all directions.'

Both Russia and France were pressing Britain to commit herself to the Franco-Russian alliance, to state publicly that a German attack on France would bring Britain in as France's ally and defender. But Grey refused any such commitment, even though the argument put forward by Sazonoff, his Russian opposite number, related not to military action but to deterrence. Sazonoff argued that if Britain took her stand firmly with France and Russia, there would be no war. If she failed to take such a stand, rivers of blood would flow and Britain too would be dragged into the conflict. The Italian Government added its voice in this same sense. But the British Government had no intention of committing itself: on July 29 Grey told the French ambassador in London: 'If Germany became involved and France became involved, we had not made up our minds what we should do; it was a case that we should have to consider.'

Germany now tried to isolate Britain from the conflict, suggesting, in a secret message on July 29, that if Britain were to remain neutral, Germany would take no territory from France except her colonies. This offer was rejected by Grey: when he revealed it later, there was indignation in Britain at what was seen as German cynicism.

In the Russian capital, St Petersburg, rumours were circulating that Austria's designs might extend 'considerably beyond' a punitive occupation of Serbian territory. Serbia's very independence might be in danger. The Russian partial mobilisation of July 29 coincided with the first bombardment of Belgrade by Austrian river monitors. Russian opinion was incensed against Austria. In panic at the prospect of war with Germany, the Tsar appealed directly to the Kaiser, with whom he had been in friendly correspondence for more than twenty years. 'To try and avoid such a calamity as a European war,' the Tsar telegraphed (in English), 'I beg you in the name of our old friendship to do what you can to stop your allies from going too far.' This telegram, signed Nicky, crossed with one (also in English) from the Kaiser to the Tsar, signed Willie: 'I am exerting my utmost influence to induce the Austrians to deal straightly to arrive at a satisfactory understanding with you.'

On the late afternoon of July 29, encouraged by the Kaiser's telegram, the Tsar sent his military chiefs a telegram cancelling general mobilisation and authorising only partial mobilisation. He now proposed to the Kaiser that the 'Austro-Serbian problem' be handed over to the International Court at The Hague. Late that evening the Kaiser proposed to the Tsar that Russia 'remain a spectator of the Austro-Serbian conflict, without involving Europe in the most horrible war she ever witnessed'. The Kaiser went on to offer to help promote an understanding between Russia and Austria. Excited by this, the Tsar tried to countermand the partial mobilisation he had just ordered, but his Foreign Minister, Sazonoff, and the Chief of the Russian General Staff, Yanushkevich, persuaded him that this could not be done: the wheels were already in motion all over the Empire. After midnight the Tsar telegraphed again to the Kaiser: 'We need your strong pressure on Austria to come to an understanding with us.'

Austria had no intention of submitting her dispute with Serbia to The Hague. Nor was the Kaiser able to dissuade his own General Staff from responding to the Russian partial mobilisation by similar German measures. When news of the German partial mobilisation reached St Petersburg, Sazonoff and Yanushkevich prevailed upon the Tsar to sign the order for full mobilisation. Without it, Russia's exposed Polish provinces could be at risk.

It was at four in the afternoon of July 30 that the Tsar signed the order for full Russian mobilisation. Russian popular sentiment applauded the fullest possible solidarity with the beleaguered fellow Slavs of Serbia. Any Russian hope of using the mobilisation not to make war on Austria, but to deter war by the threat of mobilisation, was in vain. Were Austria to mobilise on her Russian front she could confront Russia's six million conscripts with three million of her own. From Berlin, the German Chancellor Bethmann-Hollweg telegraphed to Berchtold in Vienna, on the morning of July 31, urging the Austrians not to mobilise against Russia. But also from Berlin, that same morning, the Chief of the German General Staff, General Moltke, advised his opposite number in Vienna, General Conrad, to mobilise at once. Commented Berchtold: 'Who rules in Berlin: Moltke or Bethmann?' Confident that German support would be forthcoming if Russia declared war, Austria mobilised. That afternoon Germany sent Russia an ultimatum to 'cease every war measure against us and Austria-Hungary' within twelve hours. Russia rejected this demand.

Confident of a swift victory against the lumbering, clumsy Russian war machine, Germany prepared to declare war on Russia. First, however, she asked France to state categorically that she would remain neutral in the event of war between Germany and Russia. France refused. Since 1894 France had been allied to Russia. She immediately called her own men to the colours: nearly three million French soldiers were on their way to the railway stations and crowding into their barracks: a precise total of 4,278 trains had been allocated for this massive preparatory manoeuvre. Yet, despite the order to mobilise, France hesitated to declare war on Germany. 'There is still hope, although the clouds are blacker and blacker,' Churchill wrote to his wife on July 31, and he then gave her a survey of the most recent developments known to the British Cabinet. 'Germany is realising I think how great are the forces against her and is trying tardily to restrain her idiot ally. We are working to soothe Russia.'

Diplomacy, and the hesitations of individuals, were proving powerless to avert the drift to catastrophe. During July 31 the French Ambassador in Berlin, Jules Cambon, and the Belgian Minister, Baron Beyens, appealed to their United States colleague, James W. Gerard, to do something to avert war. Gerard had no instructions from Washington, but he wrote at once to Bethmann-Hollweg: 'Your Excellency, Is there nothing that my country can do? Nothing that I can do towards stopping this dreadful war? I am sure that the President would approve any act of mine looking towards peace.' He received no reply.

In France, the response to the call for mobilisation was overwhelming in its enthusiasm. For ten years the French Socialist Party had preached workers' solidarity across national borders. Its newspaper, *L'Humanité*, and its leader, Jean Jaurès, had striven to create a joint Franco-German socialist policy against war. In vain did Jaurès now appeal for the unity of European working-class interests, for a concerted working class demand that all war measures and mobilisations stop. On July 31, as patriotic fervour mounted among all classes, he was assassinated by a fanatical nationalist.

Jaurès had not been alone in seeing the dangers of war fever. In Berlin on July 31 a leading German industrialist, Walther Rathenau, published an article in the *Berliner Tageblatt* protesting at German's blind loyalty towards Austria. 'Without the protection of this loyalty,' he wrote, 'Austria could not have ventured on the step she has taken.' A question such as the participation of Austrian officials in investigating the Serbian plot 'is no reason for an international war'. Rathenau was not to be assassinated for another seven years, but his article that day sowed the seeds of the accusation of treason that was to be hurled at him when the war was over: a war to which, once started, he gave all his industrial expertise and personal energies.

Those Germans who saw opportunities opening out as a result of a victorious war over Russia, were in a dilemma. If France were to gather her full military strength and declare war on her while the German armies were advancing against Russia in the east, then Germany could be terribly mauled in the west, perhaps even overrun. To avert this, a plan had been devised long before, which every German general knew in detail, to defeat France first, and to do so swiftly, before turning the full German military force against Russia. This plan was the brainchild of Alfred von Schlieffen, Chief of the German General Staff from 1891 to 1905, who had spent twelve years perfecting it, so that it could not fail.

Completed in 1905, the Schlieffen Plan envisaged a German attack through Belgium and Holland into northern France, by-passing the long French fortified frontier, and descending upon Paris in a great sweep from the north. Even after his retirement Schlieffen had continued to improve his plan, the last revision being in December 1912, shortly before his death. His successor as Chief of the General Staff, General Moltke, shortened the line of the sweep by eliminating Holland (which Hitler reinstated in 1940), but as the possibility of war with Russia became imminent, the modified Schlieffen Plan emerged as the essential means of avoiding a two-front war and winning a double victory.

Paris would be occupied, and victory over France achieved, within six weeks. Then Germany could march against Russia. It was a careful, precise and comforting calculation. On July 31 Britain asked both France and Germany if they would respect Belgian neutrality, to the maintenance of which Britain was committed by Treaty. France gave a pledge to do so. Germany made no reply.

No European capital was free from anxiety and activity. 'All the Austrian personnel who were available for mobilisation left at once,' Betty Cunliffe-Owen recalled of August 1 in Constantinople, where her husband was British Military Attaché. 'I was intensely sorry for the Marquise Pallavacini (the Ambassadress); being an Englishwoman, her heart must have been torn in two. Both her sons were in the Austrian Army. She started immediately for Vienna, naturally anxious to see them before they left for the Front.' That day the First Secretary at the German Embassy, Count Kanitz, remarked to Betty Cunliffe-Owen's husband: 'Mon cher, England's whole interest for years has been the Irish question and women's suffrage – of what use then troubling about other people's quarrels? You have got to set your own house in order first.'

In Munich, at a public meeting in the Odeonsplatz on August 1, an exuberant crowd greeted the news of the coming of war. Among those photographed at that moment of public enthusiasm was the Austrian-born Adolf Hitler, then earning a precarious living selling his own watercolours. A French painter, Paul Maze, in Paris on August 1, heard everywhere that day the shouts of 'À Berlin'. At the Place de la Concorde he watched a French cavalry regiment march 'very smartly' across the square, the officers wearing white gloves, 'the tramp of the horses mingled with the shouts of the crowd throwing flowers to the men'. Throughout the day soldiers passed through Paris on their way to the railway stations. 'When artillery passed, the guns were festooned with flowers and women jumped on the limbers to kiss the men.' That day the head of the Russian military mission in Paris, Count Ignatiev, telegraphed to St Petersburg that the French Ministry of War was 'seriously suggesting that Russia invade Germany and advance on Berlin'. Such a request, commented General Golovin, 'was equivalent to asking Russia to commit suicide, in the full sense of the word'.

That day the Tsar sent yet another appeal to the Kaiser to try to prevent a Russo-German war. 'Our long proved friendship must succeed, with God's help, in avoiding bloodshed,' he telegraphed. The Kaiser, however, whose earlier encouragement to Austria had been a factor advancing the crisis, now determined to honour his promise to help Austria, should she be attacked by Russia. At five o'clock in the afternoon he ordered the mobilisation of all German forces. Then, within minutes, he grasped at a straw in the wind that suggested a wider war could be avoided: a telegram from Lichnowsky in London, suggesting that Britain might be willing to remain neutral, and to guarantee French neutrality in a Russo-German war, provided Germany did not attack France in the west. 'So now we need only wage war against Russia, we simply advance with the whole army in the east,' was the Kaiser's enthusiastic, wishful comment to Helmut von Moltke, the Chief of Staff of the German Armies.

Moltke quickly pointed out that no change could be made in the plan to attack France. All was already on the move. A German division, moving westward from Trier, was about to seize the Luxembourg railways, as part of the Schlieffen Plan and an essential preliminary to war in the east, to prevent a two-front war. The Kaiser, unconvinced, ordered a telegram sent to Trier, halting all military operations. Then, at eleven o'clock that night, reversing his stand, he told Moltke that the hoped-for guarantees of British and French neutrality were illusory, and that the war in the west would go ahead. The troops at Trier were ordered to march.

'Three hundred million people today lie under the spell of fear and fate,' a London evening newspaper declared on August 1, and went on to ask: 'Is there no one to break the spell, no gleam of light on this cold dark scene?' Unknown to the newspaper, Britain's King George V, a cousin of both the Tsar and the Kaiser, had telegraphed to the Tsar that day: 'I cannot help thinking that some misunderstanding has produced this deadlock. I am most anxious not to miss any possibility of avoiding the terrible calamity which at present threatens the whole world.'

George V wanted the Tsar 'to leave still open grounds for negotiation and peace'. Sir Edward Grey was hopeful that this royal initiative might have some effect. 'If only a little respite in time can be gained before any Great Power begins war,' he telegraphed to the British Ambassador in Berlin, 'it might be possible to secure peace.' Grey's telegram to Berlin and George V's to St Petersburg reached their recipients on the evening of August 1. They came, as did the Tsar's telegram to the Kaiser, too late. That evening the German Ambassador to Russia, Count Pourtalès, went to the Russian Foreign Ministry in St Petersburg, where he handed Sazonoff the German declaration of war.

'This is a criminal act of yours,' Sazonoff told the Ambassador. 'The curses of the nations will be upon you.' 'We are defending our honour,' the Ambassador replied. 'Your honour was not involved,' Sazonoff declared. 'You could have prevented the war by one word; you didn't want to.' The Ambassador burst into tears and had to be helped from the room by the Foreign Minister.

Germany had declared war on Russia. 'Wives and mothers with children accompanied the reservists from point to point, deferring the hour of parting, and one saw cruel scenes,' the British Military Attaché in St Petersburg, Colonel Knox, later recalled, 'but the women cried silently and there were no hysterics. The men generally were grave and quiet, but parties cheered one another as they met in the streets.' In defiance of Germany, and of all things German, the name St Petersburg, honouring Peter the Great's founding of the city in 1702, was changed to the Russian 'Petrograd' (Peter's Town).[1]

On the night of August 1, the Russian Foreign Minister dined with the British Ambassador, Sir George Buchanan, whose daughter Meriel later recalled: 'Four times that evening Monsieur Sazonoff was called away; the bell of the telephone pealed incessantly, the square outside was a dense crowd of people singing the National Anthem. Till late on in the night crowds besieged the doors of the Embassy cheering for the British Fleet, and always asking the same question: Would England help, would England join them?'

That night, as the first step in the long-prepared strategic moves against France, German troops entered Luxembourg. It was a small-scale operation, scarcely a skirmish. Its objective was to occupy a rail and telegraph junction.

A scramble for war supplies began. In France, fifty monoplanes that were being built for the Turkish Government were seized by the French authorities. In Britain, two battleships being built for Turkey were likewise seized: one of them was under Turkish orders to join the German High Seas Fleet as soon as it was ready to sail. In Danzig, the German authorities prepared to requisition two light cruisers being built for Russia. 'It has been, and still is exciting to the uttermost degree,' Horace Rumbold wrote from the British Embassy in Berlin on the morning of August 2, 'but it is too awful to think what the next few months have in store.'

On August 2 German military patrols crossed the French frontier for the first time since 1871, and there were several skirmishes. At Joncherey, near the German-Swiss border, a French soldier, Corporal André Peugeot, was killed, the first French victim of a war that was to claim more than a million French lives. That day, full British naval mobilisation was put into effect, and orders given to shadow two German warships on their way through the Mediterranean to Turkey. A secret assurance was also given by Britain to France, that if the German Fleet went into the North Sea or English Channel to attack French shipping, the British Fleet

[1] The Bolsheviks changed the name Petrograd to Leningrad, in honour of the founder of the Soviet Union. In 1991 the name was changed back to the original St Petersburg.

would give the French vessels 'all the assistance in its power'.

It was not on a naval victory over France in the North Sea or the Channel, however, but on a rapid overland march through Belgium, that the German war plans depended. It was in order to achieve this goal that, at seven o'clock on the evening of August 2, Germany delivered a twelve-hour ultimatum to Belgium: German troops must be given free passage through Belgium. The Belgians refused. By the Treaty of London in 1839, Britain, Austria, Prussia, France and Russia had agreed that Belgium should form an independent and perpetually neutral State. That Treaty was still in force. 'Were the Belgian government to accept the propositions conveyed to it,' Brussels informed Berlin, 'it would be sacrificing the nation's honour and betraying its engagements to Europe.'

On August 3 Germany declared war on France. As a first step to victory, her troops crossed into Belgium. That day Bethmann-Hollweg told the Reichstag: 'The wrong – I speak openly – that we are committing we will endeavour to make good as soon as our military goal is reached.' When France was conquered, Belgium would be set free. In France, an outpouring of patriotic fervour affected all classes: Alsace and Lorraine would be restored: the humiliations of 1870 and 1871 would be reversed. That day, in Munich, the Austrian citizen Adolf Hitler petitioned the King of Bavaria for permission to enlist in a Bavarian Regiment. On the following day his petition was approved.

Hitherto Britain had stood aside. Among its Cabinet Ministers there was no clear majority for war against Germany, even if Germany attacked France. Britain had no treaty of alliance with France, only the Entente Cordiale signed in 1904 to settle long standing quarrels in Egypt and Morocco. The question of Belgium raised a complication. Belgian neutrality was guaranteed by Britain under a treaty signed in 1839. An ultimatum was sent from London to Berlin: there must be no attack on Belgium.

Germany was unlikely to oblige: her whole two-front war plan was already in action. At a meeting of the Prussian Cabinet in Berlin on August 3, Bethmann-Hollweg told his colleagues that the participation of Britain was now inevitable. To the alarm of those present, Admiral Tirpitz cried out: 'All is then lost!'

In Britain too, there were those who had premonitions of the terrors that were to come. In the village of Rudston a 16-year-old schoolgirl, Winifred Holtby, never forgot an episode that took place as the prospect of war drew nearer. 'Above the counter of the small crowded newspaper shop, large moths flopped clumsily round the swinging paraffin lamp. An old drunken woman wearing a man's cap planted herself in a chair beneath it. "War's bloody hell," she remarked in mild conversational tones. "Ah'm tellin' you God's truth. Two o' my lads went i' South Africa. Bloody hell. That's wha' 'tis".'

The German High Command's confidence in Germany's military prowess was such, that on August 3, even before the march through

Belgium began, German troops in the east crossed the Russian border and occupied three towns in Russian Poland: Bendzin, Kalish and Chenstokhov.[1]

The British Government had demanded that the German army did not cross into Belgium. This was not a bluff. The ultimatum sent from London to Berlin was due to expire at eleven o'clock on the night of August 4. Mines were being laid in the English Channel to prevent the sudden incursion of German warships: among the steamships held up as a result of this minelaying was one coming from South Africa. Its passengers included a 44-year-old Indian lawyer, M.K. Gandhi, who, despite the view of many Indian nationalists that Indians should have nothing to do with their masters' conflict, was to advocate that Indians living in Britain should take 'their share in the war'.

Seven hours before the British ultimatum to Germany expired, German troops entered Belgium. At eleven o'clock that night, Britain declared war on Germany. In Berlin, a crowd quickly gathered outside the British Embassy, smashing windows and hurling both stones and abuse. On the following morning, in apologising for the attack, an emissary of the Kaiser remarked that it would nevertheless show the British Ambassador 'how deeply the people felt the action of England in ranging herself against Germany and forgetting how we had fought shoulder to shoulder at Waterloo'. The emissary added that the Kaiser had been proud of being a British Field Marshal and Admiral of the Fleet, but now he would 'divest himself of these honours'. The Ambassador and his staff prepared to leave Berlin: Horace Rumbold later recalled how, in a final gesture of contempt, the Embassy's three German servants, having been given a month's wages in advance, 'took off their liveries, spat and trampled on them, and refused to help carry the trunks down to the taxi cabs'. A century of diplomatic courtesy, deference and propriety was at an end.

Britain and Germany were to devote to war even greater energies than they had hitherto devoted to trade and industry, imperial expansion, culture and the evolution of a fairer society. Sir Edward Grey, who had laboured to prevent Austria from attacking Serbia, and whose government had refused to make any formal commitment to France, now defended war with Germany on a much wider plane than the violation of Belgian neutrality, telling the American Ambassador in London: 'The issue for us is that, if Germany wins, she will dominate France; the independence of Belgium, Holland, Denmark, and perhaps of Norway and Sweden, will be a mere shadow; their separate existence as nations will be a fiction; all

---

[1] These were their pre-war Russian names, in the transliteration used at the time. Since 1919 they have been better known by their Polish spellings: Bedzin, Kalisz and Czestochowa. In this latter town, a centre of Roman Catholic pilgrimage, my great-grandfather, Dov (David) Fichtencwejg, was among those who saw them enter. Twenty-five years later, as a Jew living in independent Poland, he was to be murdered by the killing squads of a second, far more terrifying German invasion. He was over eighty years old.

their harbours will be at Germany's disposal; she will dominate the whole of Western Europe, and this will make our position quite impossible. We could not exist as a first class State under such circumstances.'

That August, Italy, Portugal, Greece, Bulgaria, Roumania and Turkey remained neutral, watching from the sidelines, but with an eye to future participation if advantage could be gained. Elsewhere in Europe, other nations remained firmly and permanently outside the circle of conflict. Holland, Switzerland, Spain, Denmark, Norway and Sweden took no part in the coming of war, or in its prosecution; nor were they drawn into it as belligerents, though for some it was to prove a lucrative source of revenue and trade. The opening shots of rifle, machine gun and artillery marked a new era for the arms trade, as well as for comradeship, bravery, suffering and torment.

Five Empires were at war by midnight on 4 August 1914: the Austro-Hungarian Empire against Serbia; the German Empire against France, Britain and Russia; the Russian Empire against Germany and Austria-Hungary; and the British and French Empires against Germany. If the war was to be over by Christmas, as many believed, or at the latest by Easter 1915, tens of thousands of soldiers might be killed or wounded before the guns fell silent. Every army believed that it could crush its opponents within a few months. German troops were as confident that they would soon be marching in triumph along the Champs-Élysées in Paris as French troops were that they would parade along the Unter den Linden in Berlin. Of the morning of August 5 in Constantinople, Betty Cunliffe-Owen recalled: 'The Germans left with the light of victory already in their eyes, one of the most truculent being Count Kanitz himself, who promised to send a post card from Paris in a few weeks! – but those few weeks found him a prisoner in Malta!'

As German diplomats left Constantinople, expecting victory, German pacifists were meeting with their European counterparts in the serenity of the south German town of Konstanz, for the founding meeting of the World Alliance for Promoting Friendship Through the Churches. On August 4 the delegates, among them British, French and German church-men for whom war was an abomination, were obliged within hours of reaching their lakeside meeting point to abandon their discussions and hurry home.

3

The opening struggle

AUGUST–SEPTEMBER 1914

Several million soldiers, forming the vanguard of many armies, were gathering in their barracks or on the move on the morning of 4 August 1914. In the east, the Russian troops who had been sent to the frontier of East Prussia were intent on advancing towards Berlin. On the border of Alsace-Lorraine, French troops crossed into Germany with full confidence that they could recover the lost provinces and, in revenge for past defeats and humiliation, reach the Rhine. Further north, on the Belgian-German border, it was a German advance that gathered momentum, threatening to sweep across Belgium into northern France. In 1870 it was a Prussian army, with Bavarian, Saxon and Württemberg regiments at their side, who had fought their way to Paris. In 1914, for the first time since German unification, it was a German army that sought to emulate its Prussian-led predecessor.

Britain, having declared war on Germany on August 4, had no troops on continental Europe. A British Expeditionary Force under the command of Sir John French had yet to be assembled, armed and sent across the Channel to take its place in the front line: but the decision to despatch it had not been made. Aware of British reluctance to become embroiled in Europe, Sir Edward Grey assured Parliament that day that there was no British 'commitment' to send troops at all. The German Admiralty was confident that it could prevent any British troops reaching the Channel ports of France or the North Sea ports of Belgium. But when the German admirals informed the Chief of the German General Staff, General Moltke, that they could take effective action as soon as British troops were crossing the water, Moltke rejected such action with the words: 'This is not necessary, and it will even be of advantage if the Armies of the West can settle with the 160,000 English at the same time as the French and Belgians.'

There was a further sign of the confidence of the German war machine when, in Aachen on August 4, the Kaiser issued an Order of the Day calling on his First Army to 'exterminate the treacherous England, walk over General French's contemptibly small Army'.[1]

From the first night of the German advance into Belgium, Belgian franc-tireurs, or 'free shooters', sniped as best they could from ditches and outbuildings at the German soldiers occupying with such confidence, and apparent ease, the villages of eastern Belgium. This persistent sniping roused the fury of the occupying troops, who felt that having beaten an army back in open combat they ought not then to be harassed further. The Quartermaster-General of the German Second Army, General Erich Ludendorff, later recalled how, on the very first night of the war, he was awakened from his sleep 'by brisk firing, some of which was directed on our house'. This was in the small Belgian town of Hervé. The British historian John Terraine comments, 'Hervé, intact on 4 August, did not long remain so.' A German journalist touring the town a few days later found it 'razed to the ground'. Of about five hundred houses in the town, he reported, 'only nineteen remain. Corpses are lying all over the place; everywhere there is a smell of burning. The church is a broken heap of ruins.'

Hervé had been held collectively responsible for the night-time sniper shootings. The Germans insisted that the Belgians were using civilians for this task, in order to cause havoc behind the front line. The Belgians replied that properly constituted army detachments, or soldiers who were stragglers, or civil guardsmen, were responsible. This, they said, was a legitimate act of war against an invader. International law was on the side of the franc-tireurs. The Fifth Hague Convention of 1907 not only forbade belligerents to move troops across neutral territory, as the Germans were doing in Belgium, but stated that resistance to such movements could not be regarded as itself a hostile act.

After the first few savage German reprisals, the Belgian Government forbade all local resistance. Unable to protect its citizens by an appeal to international law, it tried to do so by keeping them out of harm's way. The Germans, frustrated by the intensity of the Belgian military opposition, quickly came to regard reprisals against Belgian civilians as at least a way of preventing any disruption behind the lines. That they regarded Belgian military resistance as vexatious, but futile, was clear from an outburst by the First Secretary of the German Legation in Brussels, Baron von Stumm, who told his American opposite number, Hugh Gibson, on August 5: 'Oh, the poor fools! Why don't they get out of the way of the steam roller? We don't want to hurt them, but if they stand in our way they will be ground into the dirt.'

A German attack that day on the first serious military obstacle, the Belgian fortress of Liège, with its 35,000 garrison troops, failed to capture

---

[1] In years to come the survivors among these 'old contemptibles', as they proudly called themselves, would be seen in many British towns and villages leading the annual Armistice Day parade. The Kaiser's phrase is often mistranslated 'contemptible little army'.

any of the city's twelve forts. There was even a moment of panic among the attackers, but it was halted on the following day by Ludendorff's energetic leadership. Taking charge of 1,500 men, he penetrated between the forts and entered the city. A day later, on August 7, the central citadel surrendered; but the forts remained and it was necessary for the German troops to overcome them one by one, or be defeated by this obstacle to their advance, and to their plans.

Hitherto, amid the vast armies of conscripts, filled by national systems of compulsory military service, the British alone had a purely professional army, small, highly trained, but lacking the numerical capacity of the European armies. On August 6 the British Cabinet discussed whether this army, altogether only six divisions, should be sent to France at all. The Prime Minister, Asquith, and the Foreign Secretary, Grey, both expressed concern about the vulnerability of Britain herself if the troops were sent to Europe. Grey in particular thought that the Expeditionary Force should remain in Britain. At a meeting of the War Council that evening, Lord Kitchener, who shocked his colleagues by suggesting that the war might prove to be a long one, insisted that two of the six divisions should be kept in Britain for home defence. It was agreed that the remaining four should go to France. The British contribution to the European struggle, even at its greatest extent, could only be a small one: 50,000 men under arms, compared with more than three million Austro-Hungarians, four million Frenchman, four-and-a-half million Germans and nearly six million Russians.

One offer of troops was turned down by the British Government. On the outbreak of war the Irish Nationalist leader, John Redmond, offered to form an Irish army to fight as an entirely Irish force alongside the English, Welsh and Scottish troops. Not wanting to disturb the smooth working of his existing plans, Kitchener rejected this, ignoring the strength of Irish national feeling that might have been channelled into such a force, and, as some Irishmen believed, away from rebellion and terrorism. In the event, 160,000 Irishmen volunteered, and 49,000 were killed, in the ranks of the British Army. But some Irish patriots were outraged by the rejection of Redmond's offer: one of them, Hubert Gough, himself a senior general in the British Expeditionary Force, wrote in the retrospect of forty years: 'Kitchener's refusal added a bloody page to Irish history.'

On August 7, in an attempt to increase the number of British soldiers under arms, Kitchener called publicly for 100,000 volunteers. 'The crowd of applicants was so large and so persistent', *The Times* reported of one recruiting office in London that day, 'that mounted police were necessary to hold them in check, and the gates were only opened to admit six at a time.' According to the newspaper there was no cheering and little excitement, 'but there was an undercurrent of enthusiasm, and the disappointment of those who failed to pass one or other of the tests was obvious'. In peacetime the average recruitment for the regular army had been less than a hundred a day. Volunteers now came forward at a rate of more than 1,500 a day. In London, within four days of the start of the campaign, men were being sworn in at the rate of a hundred an hour, and a special marquee was erected on Horse Guards Parade to cope with the surge in numbers.

Anti-war sentiment, which until the very outbreak of war had been strong in Liberal and Labour Party circles, and in the Trade Union movement, was also dissolving. On August 6, the day before Kitchener's appeal, the journal of the Independent Labour Party, the *Labour Leader*, in an attempt to stimulate anti-war feeling, exhorted its readers: 'Workers of Great Britain, down with war. You have no quarrel with the workers of Europe. They have no quarrel with you. The quarrel is between the ruling classes of Europe. Don't make their quarrels yours.' On August 7, however, the hitherto anti-war editor of the *Manchester Guardian*, C.P. Scott, a leading and influential Liberal, in explaining why he would not attend a public meeting protesting against British participation in the war, wrote to the organisers: 'I am strongly of opinion that the war ought not to have taken place and that we ought not to have become parties to it, but once in it, the whole future of our nation is at stake and we have no choice but to do the utmost we can to secure success.'

A similar attitude of doing one's utmost was evident among all the belligerents. On August 7, in Vienna, the 25-year-old Austrian philosopher Ludwig Wittgenstein, who had just returned from teaching at Cambridge, volunteered as a gunner in the Austrian army, despite a double hernia that entitled him to exemption. 'At first he only succeeded in going to Galicia with a military repair workshop,' his sister Hermione later recalled, 'but he never ceased to worm his way towards the front line.' There were, she said, many comic misunderstandings 'which stemmed from the fact that the military authorities, with whom he was always dealing, always assumed that he was looking for an easier post while he, on the contrary, was after a more dangerous one.'

In every belligerent country the authorities arrested and imprisoned those whom they regarded as dangerous enemy aliens. On August 8, in the West Galician town of Neumarkt[1], forty miles from the Russian border, the Austrian police arrested a Russian exile who had been living there for some years, Vladimir Lenin, fearing that he might be a Russian spy. The leader of the Austrian Social Democrats, Victor Adler, who was in favour with the authorities because his party had declared its support for the war, hastened to assure Vienna that if Lenin were released he would be certain to conduct a vigorous propaganda campaign against the Tsar and against the Allies. Lenin was released, and given permission to travel to neutral Switzerland.

[1] Since 1919, Nowy Targ (in southern Poland).

In Germany Walther Rathenau, the industrialist who had been so despondent in the week before war was declared, went on August 8 to see the Head of the General War Department in Berlin, Colonel Scheüch, to offer his support to the war effort. Pointing out that Germany only had a 'limited number of months' supply of indispensable war materials, Rathenau proposed 'to save Germany from strangulation', and within a few days was put in charge of a specially-created War Raw Materials Department. Metals, chemicals, jute, wool, rubber and cotton were among the raw materials that the Department could commandeer inside Germany, requisition in occupied territory, purchase abroad, or manufacture itself by new and if necessary synthetic methods. Rathenau's task was to help keep Germany at war, yet as a civilian and a Jew he met continual hostility from the army commanders whose fighting abilities he was engaged in helping.

Rathenau realised that the raw material needs of the German army might not be capable of endless fulfilment in a long war. The prospect of a long war was alarming even to the Kaiser, who on August 10 summoned the American Ambassador, Gerard, who later recalled: 'The Kaiser talked rather despondently about the war. I tried to cheer him up by saying the German troops would soon enter Paris, but he answered, "The British change the whole situation – an obstinate nation. They will keep up the war. It cannot end soon." '

Pacifist sentiment did not die with the opening of the cannonades. Socialists who were opposed to war in July remained so in August. In Russia in particular the Menshevik and Bolshevik factions of the Russian Social Democrat Party were both opposed to the war, and in the Russian Parliament, the Duma, voted against war credits. Despite an assurance on August 10 from the French Ambassador in Petrograd, Maurice Paléologue, that 'the collective soul of Holy Russia has never manifested itself so forcibly since 1812', the Entente powers were worried about the spread of anti-war feeling in Russia. On August 11 the Belgian Government prevailed upon its newly appointed Minister of State, the socialist Emile Vandervelde, to send a telegram to the Russian Social Democrat deputies in the Duma, urging them to support the war effort. As Chairman of the International Socialist Bureau, Vandervelde was much respected in Russia: that June he had been in St Petersburg trying to reconcile the different Russian socialist factions. His pro-war telegram was published in the Russian press; type-written copies were circulated in the factories.

Far from stimulating patriotic fervour, the Vandervelde telegram served only to divide the socialist ranks still further, stimulating Lenin, once he had reached Switzerland, to publish and smuggle into Russia his *Theses on the War*, urging Russia's workers to oppose the war. So shocked was Lenin when he read in the Swiss newspapers that the German socialist deputies in the Reichstag had come out in support of the war that he at first disbelieved the reports, believing that they were a fabrication put out by the German General Staff to fool the German working class into acceptance of the war. Bowing to the inevitable force of patriotism in Germany, he now set his sights upon the distant Russian proletariat.

As war began, Austria called upon the national aspirations of its Polish minority to serve the imperial war effort. On August 6 a small force of Polish riflemen, from the Austrian province of Galicia, crossed the Russian frontier and advanced towards the town of Kielce. The cavalrymen among them carried their saddles on their heads, hoping to capture horses from the Russians. As this 'liberation army' drew near to Kielce it was welcomed by Polish women carrying flowers, but the townsfolk, fearing Russian retribution, remained in their homes. After a brief encounter with a Russian patrol they returned, chastened, to Galicia.

Anti-war feeling inside Russia, which Lenin hoped to stimulate from afar in the cause of revolution, was also welcomed, and stimulated, by the Austrians and Germans. Internal unrest of any sort would help them in the struggle against the vast Russian forces. That same August 6 the Austrian Government decided to give money to the Union for the Liberation of the Ukraine, to encourage anti-Russian and separatist agitation. Armenian and Georgian socialists were also encouraged to see the defeat of the Tsar as the way forward to independence.

A racial as well as a political element emerged rapidly in the first weeks of war. On August 11, in a mass meeting at the Town Hall in Berlin, Professor von Harnack, head of the Royal Library, spoke of the threat to western civilisation from 'the civilisation of the Horde that is gathered and kept together by despots, the Mongolian Muscovite civilisation. This civilisation could not endure the light of the eighteenth century, still less the light of the nineteenth century, and now in the twentieth century it breaks loose and threatens us. This unorganised Asiatic mass, like the desert with its sands, wants to gather up our fields of grain.'

Among those living in Berlin was the recently-appointed director of the Institute of Physics, Albert Einstein. 'Europe, in her insanity, has started something almost unbelievable,' he wrote to a friend on August 19. 'In such times one realises to what a sad species of animal one belongs. I quietly pursue my peaceful studies and contemplations and feel only pity and disgust.'

Far from the European conflict, but closely tied up with it, a German officer, Lieutenant-Colonel Kress, sought an interview on August 10 with the Turkish Minister of War, Enver Pasha. Kress told Enver that two German warships, the *Goeben* and the *Breslau*, which had evaded all British naval efforts to catch them, were at the entrance to the Dardanelles and wished permission to enter. Knowing that this would constitute a hostile act to Britain, and draw Turkey into the war orbit of Germany, Enver gave his permission. Kress then asked, if British warships tried to follow the Germans, were they to be fired on? Again Enver said yes. Another German officer who was in the room, Hans Kannengiesser, later recalled: 'We heard the clanking of the portcullis descending before the Dardanelles.... None of us had moved a muscle. Kress took his leave and I proceeded with my report as though nothing had happened.'

To maintain Turkish neutrality, the ships were nominally sold to Turkey, their names were changed to *Javus Sultan Selim* and *Midilli*, and their German commander, Admiral Souchon, ran up the Turkish flag. All British demands that the German military mission in Turkey be withdrawn were rejected by the Turks and Germans alike. But no acts of war took place, only the provocation of the two German warships anchored off Constantinople.

In the North Sea the Germans had a naval setback in the second week of August, when the submarine *U-15* was rammed by a British warship and sank: it was the first German submarine loss of the war, the first of more than 180 that were to be sunk before the end of the war. That same week, on distant Lake Nyasa, in central Africa, a British naval officer, Commander E.L. Rhoades, sailed his gunboat, the *Gwendolen*, with its single 3-pounder gun, across the lake from the British port of Nkata Bay to the tiny German port of Sphinxhaven, thirty miles away. There he opened fire on, and captured, the German gunboat *Wissman*, whose commander, Captain Berndt, had not yet heard that war had broken out between Britain and Germany. 'Naval Victory on Lake Nyasa,' was the headline in *The Times*.

On the battlefields of Europe the fighting had become both continuous and fierce. On August 13 French troops were caught by heavy German artillery fire near Dinant, their movements having been seen by a German spotter plane. Ordered to deny a bridge to the advancing German infantrymen, a French platoon commander led his men forward under fire. On reaching the bridge he was hit in the knee and fell. A moment later his platoon sergeant fell on top of him, dead. The lieutenant later recalled 'the dull thud of bullets entering the bodies of the dead and the wounded that lay about'. With difficulty he dragged himself away. It was the baptism of fire for Charles de Gaulle. He was taken to hospital in Paris, out of action, but eager to return to the front.

On August 12 the Austrian army invaded Serbia. At the town of Sabac, on the Serbian side of the River Sava, there were horrifying scenes: many male civilians were rounded up and shot, children were massacred and women raped. The German advance through Belgium was likewise accompanied by incidents of savagery that were to shock and harden British and French opinion. On August 10 eleven male villagers at Linsmeau had been rounded up and shot. Ten days later it was the village of Andenne, near Namur, that suffered. General von Bülow's printed announcement, dated August 22, and affixed to the walls of Liège, read: 'The population of Andenne, after manifesting peaceful intentions towards our troops, attacked them in the most treacherous manner. With my authorisation the general who commanded these troops has reduced the town to ashes and shot 110 persons.'

At Seilles, fifty villagers were shot, and at the small mining town of Tamines, where German troops had been angered by the vigour of the French soldiers in the area, 384 men were collected near the church, lined up and shot, some by rifle and some by machine gun fire on August 22. The youngest victim was thirteen, the oldest eighty-four. An even larger execution took place on the following day in the town of Dinant. Claiming that German soldiers repairing the bridge had been fired on by Belgian civilians, the Germans shot 612 men, women and children as reprisals, among them a three-week-old baby being held by its mother in her arms.

Two days later, in the early hours of August 25, a German Zeppelin dropped several bombs on Antwerp. In one house, six citizens were killed in their beds. These large, slow-moving, lighter-than-air machines had been seen flying over Europe before the war, when they were as much objects of amazement to the land-bound citizenry as was the aeroplane, perhaps even more so. With the coming of war, it was feared that the Zeppelin would bring death and destruction to any city it attacked. It was, wrote one of its historians, 'the H-bomb of its day, an awesome Sword of Damocles to be held over the cowering heads of Germany's enemies'.[1] In those first months of the war, a French cartoonist, R. Delville, drew the Kaiser riding through the air on a Zeppelin, accompanied by the Angel of Death wearing a German helmet and carrying, on a cushion, the Iron Cross, the reward for the grim, aerial reaping.

The American newspaper correspondent E. Alexander Powell, who was in Antwerp when the first Zeppelin raid took place on the city, wrote in his account, published in Britain three months later, that he had felt 'weak and nauseated' when he entered one house to see the room where a woman had been sleeping. 'She had literally been blown to fragments. The floor, the walls, the ceilings were splotched with – well, it's enough to say that the woman's remains could only have been collected with a shovel.' In a square nearby 'one policeman on duty at the far end of the square was killed instantly and another had both legs blown off'. A woman who was woken up by the first explosion 'and leaned from her window to see what was happening had her head blown off'. The full death toll was ten: two more people died shortly afterwards of their wounds.

Later that day, after the Belgian army launched a successful counter-attack from Antwerp towards Louvain, the German occupation forces in Louvain panicked. The panic had been started by a runaway horse. German sentries, not knowing the reason for the commotion, opened fire. There were shouts of 'The French are here!' 'The English are here!' and, ominously for the city and its citizens, 'The franc-tireurs are here!' Then, not for one day but for five, the German troops stationed in Louvain burned

---

[1] Raymond Laurence Rimell, *Zeppelin! A Battle for Air Supremacy in World War I*, Conway Maritime Press, London 1984, page 31.

buildings and executed civilians. When the American diplomat, Hugh Gibson, visited the town on August 28, a German officer told him: 'We shall wipe it out, not one stone will stand upon another! Not one, I tell you. We will teach them to respect Germany. For generations people will come here to see what we have done!'

About a fifth of Louvain's houses were gutted, and the church of St Pierre was badly damaged by fire. These episodes not only shocked the British and French public, they also gave the Entente propagandists an early triumph. Tales of atrocities were quickly magnified and made as gory as they could be, with phrases such as 'mutilations too horrible to describe', 'rivers of blood' and 'mountains of innocent dead' being followed by exhortations such as 'Humanity cries aloud for vengeance.' The deliberate damage done to Belgian churches enabled an added dimension of guilt to be thrust on the German leaders. An early French picture postcard showed Jesus himself spurning the Kaiser, and walking away from him. The Kaiser, on his knees, seeks the Saviour's hand in vain. In the background is a badly damaged cathedral.

On August 12, as German troops fought to overcome the last Belgian resistance in the forts of Liège, the first troops of the British Expeditionary Force crossed the English Channel, behind a protective shield of nineteen battleships. In ten days, 120,000 men were transported without the loss of a single man or ship. The secrecy of the operation was so well kept that even after ten days of continuous movement the German High Command doubted whether any serious British forces had yet reached France, and the troopships were unmolested by the German navy. Moltke's desire to meet the British army on the battlefield was fulfilled.

On the day that the first British troops did reach France, a senior British nurse in Belgium, Edith Cavell, wrote to *The Times* asking that 'subscriptions from the British public' be forwarded to her medical insti- tute, as 'the Army wounded will have to be dealt with on the Continent and, as far as can be seen at present, mainly at Brussels. Our institution, comprising a large staff of English nurses, is prepared to deal with several hundreds and the number is being increased day by day.' She sought subscriptions 'from the British public'. Her letter was published on August 15 under the heading 'English Nursing in Brussels'.

Neither France nor Britain had any quarrel with Austria-Hungary. The son of one of Austria's wealthiest men was a member of the British Parliament. The Inspector-General of British forces in the Sudan was an Austrian, Sir Rudolph Slatin. The Austrian Ambassador to London, Count Mensdorff, was both a cousin and close personal friend of King George V. But on August 12, eight days after the British declaration of war on Germany, and on the day that the British Expeditionary Force began its cross-Channel movement, Britain and France declared war on Austria- Hungary, claiming that the small contingents of Austrian troops then stationed on the Franco-German frontier were 'a direct menace to France'.

The British Ambassador in Vienna, distressed that two nations that had no cause for quarrel should be at war, asked Count Berchtold to present his 'profound regrets' to the Emperor together with an expression of his hope that the Emperor 'would pass through these sad times with unimpaired health and strength'. The Austrian Ambassador in London was distraught, and in the presence of his American opposite number denounced Germany and the Kaiser and 'paraded up and down the room wringing his hands'. In Brussels, Hugh Gibson noted in his diary on August 15: 'Yesterday's papers announced France's declaration of war against Austria. This morning comes the news that Montenegro has also declared her intention of wiping Austria off the map. Our daily query is now – "Who has declared war to-day?" '

These extra declarations of war, widening the geographic and human scale of the conflict, cost nothing to send, though they were to prove costly to redeem: more costly than anyone imagined. Following the established courtesies, Ambassadors in all the warring States packed their bags, locked their residences and returned to their capitals. In British political and diplomatic circles there was sadness at the departure of the Austrian Ambassador, who had been a much-liked figure, but anger among the populace when the Royal Navy not only put a destroyer at his disposal to convey him across the English Channel, but enabled two hundred Austrian subjects, who might otherwise have been interned, to leave on the same boat. Courtesies, soon to seem old-fashioned, had not yet been abandoned.

Slowly, but with growing emphasis, Britain began to put herself forward as the champion of the Slav minorities inside Austria-Hungary. Above all, she took up the cause of the Czechs. On August 19, from Petrograd, the Russians had published two manifestos, one promising a reborn Poland 'free in religion, in language and in self-government' after the war, the other calling on the subject peoples of Austria-Hungary to rise up and assert their national independence. The Tsar went so far as to tell the Czech leader Karel Kramar, whom he received in audience on August 20, that Russia would look with favour upon the 'free and independent Crown of St Wenceslas' shining, after Austria's defeat, 'in the radiance of the crown of the Romanovs'.

In London, on August 20, in a vivid departure from the truth *The Times* announced that a Czech revolution had broken out in Prague and that the river Moldau 'ran red with Czech blood'. It was also reported, equally wrongly, that some Czech politicians, including the nationalist leader Thomas Masaryk, had been executed in Hradcany Castle. In fact, he was not only a free man, but within five months had made his way to Switzerland. Within two months of the outbreak of war a leading British Conservative newspaper predicted 'that the racial mosaic of the Dual monarchy will be shattered into pieces to form new, and, we may hope, more stable and fortunate combinations in the map of Europe.' In Vienna, however, the prospect of an Austrian victory over Russia excited expansionist reflections. On August 12, the day of Britain's declaration of war on Austria, Austrian diplomats initiated a discussion with regard to the annexation of the Russian provinces of Poland, including Warsaw, to the Hapsburg dominions.

Imperial systems as well as armies were in conflict. Within a week of each other, the Tsarist Empire committed itself to some form of post-war Polish self-rule, and the Hapsburg Empire to some form of political dominion over Poland. To secure this latter aim, on August 16 the Austrian authorities allowed the Polish leader Josef Pilsudski to set up a Supreme National Committee in Cracow, on Austrian soil, to work for the day when Poles and Austrians would march together into Warsaw. Pilsudski's first contribution to his Austrian masters, as well as to his Polish co-patriots, was to form a Polish Legion. He himself led the first brigade, 10,000 strong, against the Russian armies.

In Russia there was still confidence, at least in the mind of the Grand Duke Nicholas, Chief of the General Staff, that the conflict could be won, and won swiftly. On August 21, from Petrograd, Maurice Paléologue informed Paris: 'The Grand Duke is determined to advance with full speed on Berlin and Vienna, more especially Berlin, passing between the fortresses of Thorn, Posen and Breslau.'

Austrian troops were in action on August 23 along a 175-mile front, as General Conrad sent his troops forward across the Austrian border into Russian Poland. The philosopher Wittgenstein was among them, manning a searchlight on a captured Russian river gunboat. Woken up at one in the morning and summoned to man his searchlight, 'I ran to the bridge almost naked,' he wrote in his diary. 'I was certain I was going to die on the spot.' But it was a false alarm. 'I was frightfully agitated and groaned audibly. I felt the terrors of war.'

That morning, in Moscow, the Tsar was present in the Uspensky Cathedral at a solemn service to pray for victory. On the battlefield more than seven hundred miles to the south-west, near the Russo-Polish town of Krasnik, the rapid advance of the Austrian cavalrymen was brought to an abrupt halt by Russian infantry and machine guns. One Austrian soldier who remembered the attack was Friedrich Feuchtinger. His reserve regiment, moving forward three days after the offensive had begun, was being shelled by Russian artillery when the order came to attack. 'On the right the young drummer with his bloodshot feverish eyes, his quivering almost crying mouth and the pale lips, no longer is he that young lad whose vigorous drumrolls brought us once more to our tired feet. I look at him once again, see his eyes widen and his mouth open; blood runs from it and he calls a throaty "Mother," then sinks down dead. We run on with gasping breath; dead and wounded lie all around and we look at them indifferently.'

As Feuchtinger's regiment reached the Russian trenches, the Russians

45

turned to flee. One of them, being closely chased, and apparently without his rifle, stopped all of a sudden, turned round, held out his right hand, and put his left hand into his tunic pocket. As he did so, Feuchtinger plunged in his bayonet. 'I see his blood redden his uniform, hear him moan and groan as he twists with the bayonet in his young body. I am seized with terror. I throw myself down, crawl to him, wanting to help him. But he is dead. I pull my blood-stained bayonet from the dead body. Wanting to fold his hands, I see in the left hand a crumpled photo of his wife and child.'

Austrian troops were also in action near Lemberg, being forced back by the Russians into the fortress. Among the Austrians in this retreat was the violinist Fritz Kreisler. 'For twenty-one days,' he later recalled, 'I went without taking off my clothes, sleeping on wet grass or in mud, or in the swamps.' On one occasion there was a twenty-minute truce when, after shouts across No-Man's Land an unarmed Russian, meeting an unarmed Austrian in the middle exchanged a packet of tobacco for a cigar.

The prospect of serving at the Front was a cause for distress among some who were called up. On August 30 the painter Oskar Kokoschka wrote to a friend from Vienna: 'These simple, starving, bewildered lads and men, who have had nothing but misery all their lives, are being driven to their deaths, or crippled, and nobody gives a tuppenny damn about it afterwards. The streets are filling with pitiful women, who are already pale and ill, but still have the strength of soul not to let their menfolk see how it affects them. Today, in my street, there was a woman who fell on her husband's neck like one demented, because he was having to leave, carrying his few worldly goods in a piece of sacking. Yet the recruits are docile, and grateful for a friendly look.'

There was a further widening of the military conflict on August 23, when Japan declared war on Germany. In Berlin, restaurants refused to serve Japanese customers, and within a few days many Japanese civilians had been interned in Ruhleben camp, a racecourse near Berlin whose buildings had been converted into an internment camp, while others managed to reach Switzerland and safety. With Japan's declaration of war, the Pacific Ocean island groups acquired by Germany in the previous quarter of a century, distant as they were from Germany and its military might, were Japan's for the picking. When Sir Edward Grey tried to restrict the area in which Japan could be active, Churchill wrote to him: 'You may easily give mortal offence – which will not be forgotten – we are not safe yet – by a long chalk. The storm is yet to burst.'

At sea, the war had been full of incident from the first days. On August 6 a British light cruiser, *Amphion*, had struck a German mine and sunk immediately. Those who went down with the ship included both her British crew and the German prisoners they had captured from the minelayer that had laid the fatal mine. In all 150 men were drowned. On August 12, two naval blockades were established, a British blockade to prevent cargo ships reaching the German North Sea ports, and a French blockade to cut off trade to Austria's Adriatic ports.

War had also begun in the air, with each belligerent making use of her tiny air force for reconnaissance and aerial bombardment. The first British, French and German airmen to be killed were all lost on August 12, though none of them in combat. The German, Senior Lieutenant Jahnow, had served as a pilot for the Turks in the First Balkan War of 1912. He was killed in an air crash in northern France. The Frenchman, Sergeant Bridou, crashed on his return to base. Two English airmen, Second Lieutenant Skene and Mechanic Barlow, were killed in their two-seater plane when it crashed near Dover, on its way to France.

On the Eastern Front, German forces were within fifty miles of Warsaw on August 14, driving the Russians before them. On the following day, in the west, Liège finally fell to Ludendorff's assault. 'Liège Falls!' was the triumphal newspaper headline in Germany, the stark, fearful headline in Britain and France. Nor was there much compensation for France when, on the following day, French troops, in punctilious compliance with the pre-war Plan 17, devised in case of war with Germany, crossed into Alsace. They did succeed in capturing the border towns of Thann and Altkirch, but a few days later their attempt to advance to Mulhouse was repulsed.[1] The Germans, by a skilful withdrawal, lured the French to a line where they were exposed to concentrated artillery and machine-gun fire. 'Astonishing changes in the practice of war,' commented General Foch, as the ferocity of the German firepower wreaked havoc on the French attackers, who, 'thoroughly shaken and bewildered by enormous losses, surged back in a retreat which it took the best part of ten days to halt'.

All the regular armies were in action. In every warring State the call went out for volunteers. 'Your King and Country Need You!', the British appeal, first published on August 7, was being reiterated and embellished on a thousand public platforms. In Germany, the Austrian-born Adolf Hitler, who a year earlier had been rejected by the Austrian army on medical grounds, volunteered for service in a Bavarian infantry regiment on August 16, and was accepted. On the Western Front a German reserve officer, Walter Bloem, wrote enthusiastically after his first action: 'It was fabulous, surely a dream. Was the whole war just a game, a kind of sport? Was the Belgian Army just a pack of hares?'

At French headquarters there was laughter at Kitchener's Order of the Day to the British troops then on their way through France. Kitchener advised the men who would be on the soil of their ally: 'Be invariably courteous, considerate and kind. Never do anything likely to injure or destroy property, and always look upon looting as a disgraceful act.'

---

[1] Thann remained in French hands for the rest of the war. The scenic mountain road running south-west from Thann has been known since 1918 as the Route Joffre, after the Chief of Staff of the French Armies in 1914 (later Commander-in-Chief).

Soldiers must be constantly on their guard against 'temptations both in wine and women. You must entirely resist both temptations, and, while treating all women with perfect courtesy, you must avoid any intimacy.' Every soldier was given this advice, to be kept in his Army Service Pay Book. It was 'the joke of the moment', the British liaison officer at French Headquarters, Captain Edward Louis Spears, was told on August 17. 'We were shipping over a girls' school instead of an army.'

German troops were everywhere in the ascendant. On August 17, when two Russian armies, one led by General Rennenkampf (of the German-sounding name), the other by General Samsonov, began their advance into East Prussia. On a 35-mile front, Samsonov was challenged by the commander of the German I Corps (the confusingly named General François), who forced Samsonov to battle, against the orders of his superiors. During the battle, at Stalluponen, François took 3,000 Russian prisoners before retreating to a stronger position.

Despite this German victory on German soil, it was clear to the General Staff that grave danger threatened in East Prussia, which had been effectively denuded of troops to enable France to be defeated before the start of the invasion of Russia. By August 19 Rennenkampf had advanced to Gumbinnen. The German Commander-in-Chief in East Prussia, General Prittwitz, panicked. 'I must withdraw to the Vistula,' he told General François on the telephone. Such a withdrawal would involve the abandonment of the whole of East Prussia. In a hysterical telephone call to the Kaiser's headquarters, Prittwitz even doubted being able to hold the line of the Vistula 'owing to the lowness of the water in the river' at that time of year.

It was a senior Staff officer, Colonel Max Hoffmann, who pointed out that only an initial and successful offensive against the Russian forces would enable the German troops to retreat without being constantly harried by superior forces. To prevent severe fighting at every point of the withdrawal, Hoffmann wanted Prittwitz to move his forces to a point where they could strike equally well at either of the two Russian armies. Prittwitz no longer had the will to fight, however, and on August 22, together with his Chief of Staff, he was recalled. A decisive change now took place in command. To lead the Eastern armies, Moltke brought out of retirement the 67-year-old General Hindenburg. He also appointed as Hindenburg's Chief of Staff the victor of Liège, General Ludendorff. It was in Ludendorff in particular that the German High Command placed its hopes. His having to go to the East pointed up, however, a flaw in the German calculations: the war was having to be waged with the utmost seriousness in the east before there was a decisive German victory in the west.

On reaching East Prussia, Ludendorff found that Colonel Hoffmann's skills had already laid the foundations for victory. But the two Russian armies had advanced deep into the province, threatening the capital, Königsberg. As on the Western Front, the war was much more than one of cavalry dashing forward or infantry plodding behind them. 'There has never been and no doubt will never be again such a war as this – fought with such bestial fury,' Hoffmann wrote in his diary on August 23. 'The Russians are burning everything down.' Among the towns entered by Russian forces on August 26 was Rastenburg, in the very centre of East Prussia.[1]

Battle was begun in the Masurian Lakes, near the villages of Frogenau and Tannenberg, on August 27. At a decisive moment Ludendorff's nerves gave way: so much so that he proposed recalling General François[2] and calling off the encirclement of Samsonov's forces which Hoffmann had devised. Hindenburg, unshaken by the intensity and risk of the battle, supported Hoffmann's plan. The fight continued. On the morning of August 28 Ludendorff urged General François to turn his advancing troops to the support of a weakened sector of the front, but François disobeyed, driving the Russians forward. 'He even made no effort to inform Ludendorff of his action in contravention of a definite order,' a British historian of the battle, General Ironside, has written. 'To the disobedience of Von François, Ludendorff undoubtedly owed the magnitude of his victory on succeeding days.'

By August 30, Samsonov's army was defeated. 'The Emperor trusted me,' he told his Chief of Staff as they struggled to reach the safety of a wood that was, unknown to them, already held by German troops. 'How can I face him again after such a disaster?' Tens of thousands of Russians were in retreat. Men threw down their weapons in order to run faster, but most of them ran into their omnipresent enemy soon enough. After twenty-eight days of turmoil, East Prussia was restored in its entirety to Germany. In triumph the Germans announced that they had taken 30,000 wounded and 95,000 unwounded prisoners, and five hundred guns. The captured horses were also numbered in their thousands. Sixty trains were required to transport the booty of the battlefield back to Germany.

Ludendorff, his nerve recovered, drafted the triumphal dispatch for the Kaiser. He dated it from Frogenau. It was Hoffmann who proposed changing the place to Tannenberg, the scene of a battle five centuries earlier in which the Teutonic Knights, among them a Hindenburg, had been massacred by a vast army of Slavs and Lithuanians. The Battle of Tannenberg, as it became known to history, was described by General Ironside as 'the greatest defeat suffered by any of the combatants during the war'. More than 30,000 Russian soldiers had been killed. In one mound of

---

[1] In 1944 Rastenburg was Hitler's headquarters, and the scene that July of the bomb plot against his life.

[2] Confusing though it might seem to have a German general called François, some have found it even more confusing that the highest German award for bravery was the Pour le Mérite. It had been created by Frederick the Great, King of Prussia from 1740 to 1786, who far preferred French to German as a language (and corresponded in French with Voltaire). He was a nephew of King George I of England, whose native and spoken tongue was German.

corpses a German search party found the dead body of a white-haired general, a bullet wound in his head, a revolver in his hand. It was the Russian First Army commander, General Alexander Samsonov.

Elsewhere on the Eastern Front, the Austrians were less successful than the Germans in facing the Russian attack, not least because of the overwhelming forces ranged against them. When the Russian General, Aleksei Brusilov, broke into Austrian Galicia on August 18, he had thirty-five Russian infantry divisions under his command. The Austrians were also in difficulties in Serbia where, after their initial capture of the town of Sabac, on the Serbian side of the river Sava, and an advance along the Jadar valley, they were confronted by tenacious Serb fighters, determined to drive them out of Serbia altogether. In their fury and frustration, Austrian troops rounded up and shot 150 Serbian peasants at the the town of Lesnica. The atrocities of war were mounting.

The Serbian counter-attack was masterminded by General Putnik, who three weeks earlier had been detained by the Austrians in Budapest. The three-day Battle of the Jadar, culminating in the Austrian retreat on August 19, was the first victory for the Entente powers. 'This war is a grim business for us,' commented one Serb officer, 'but I shook with laughter to see those fellows run.' Within a week the Austrians had evacuated Sabac and retreated across the Sava back into Austria. To explain away their defeat, the Vienna Press Bureau announced that all Austria's forces had to be concentrated on the battle with Russia, that the invasion of Serbia must be considered a 'punitive expedition' only, and that the real offensive would take place on 'a more favourable occasion'.

For a mere punitive expedition it had been costly, with at least 6,000 Austrian soldiers killed, 30,000 wounded and 4,000 taken prisoner. But Serbian losses were not small: 3,000 Serbian soldiers were killed and 15,000 wounded. The figures for the dead, 9,000 in all, are a mere statistic: as with every battle of the war, they reveal nothing about the nine thousand separate points of individual pain and terror in action on the eve of death, or about the suffering of many more thousands of mothers and fathers, sisters and brothers, widows and orphans. *The Times* correspondent who reported on the battle commented: 'The estimation of Austrian losses is somewhat difficult as many of the fallen were not discovered until the penetrating odour of decomposed humanity disclosed the presence of bodies in wood or unharvested field.'

Austria's set-back in Serbia was in strong contrast with Germany's success in Belgium. Following the capture of Liège the German army had moved rapidly through Belgium, forcing the Belgian Government to withdraw from Brussels to Antwerp. On August 17, in an unsuccessful attempt to halt the Germans at Tirlemont, Belgian troops suffered heavy losses: 1,630 men were killed or wounded. Two days later the Belgian fortress of Namur, second only to Liège in size, was besieged. A garrison of 27,000 men faced five German divisions. 'This onslaught caused some anxiety at the

Headquarters of the Fifth Army,' the British liaison officer there, Captain Spears, later recalled, 'but it never entered anyone's head that the town, surrounded by its nine forts, would not hold out for at least a few days, long enough to enable General Lanrezac to cross the Sambre, when, resting his right on the fortress, he could deal a decisive blow at the attackers.'

Strategic hopes and military reality were at loggerheads. In Brussels, the American diplomat Hugh Gibson wrote in his diary on August 19: 'Crowds of people are pouring in from the east in all stages of panic, and some small forces of cavalry have also retreated into the city, looking weary and discouraged. There has evidently been a rout.' That same day, at the southernmost part of the Western Front, at the point where French troops had advanced into Alsace and were approaching the city of Mulhouse, six hundred French soldiers were killed in the villages of Zillisheim and Flaxanden. They had reached to within ten miles of the Rhine but were to get no closer. Among the dead was General Plessier, the first French general to die on the battlefield in 1914.

On the following day, August 20, while the forts of Namur were suffering the impact of the superior German fire power, German troops entered Brussels, the first European capital to be occupied by a conquering army since the fall of Paris in 1870. Brussels itself had not been occupied since the time of Napoleon. That day a military parade celebrated the German victory. Among its features were a hundred motor cars on each of which was mounted a machine gun; cavalry regiments and artillery batteries each headed by its own band; and columns of infantrymen preceded by fifes and drums. 'Some of the regiments presented a very fine sight,' a British newspaper reported, 'the troops were in fine fettle and greatly impressed the citizens.'

In the splendour of conquest, or at rest, troops could try to forget realities of the battlefield, but for those who were at the Front, or even near the front as it moved swiftly forward, a new, harsh world was beginning to impinge upon the accepted conventions of armies at war. For Captain Spears, who had been with the French Fifth Army for the previous two weeks, that moment came on the evening of August 20, as he sat on a hill with a French officer overlooking the fields, towns and villages of the Sambre valley south of Charleroi. 'A dog was barking at some sheep. A girl was singing as she walked down the lane behind us. From a little farm away on the right came the voices and laughter of some soldiers cooking their evening meal. Darkness grew in the far distance as the light began to fail. Then, without a moment's warning, with a suddenness that made us start and strain our eyes to see what our minds could not realise, we saw the whole horizon burst into flame.'

A German artillery bombardment had begun along a wide front. Outlined against the northern sky, innumerable fires were simultaneously burning. 'A chill of horror came over us. War seemed suddenly to have assumed a merciless, ruthless aspect that we had not realised till then. Hitherto it had been war as we had conceived it, hard blows, straight dealing, but now for the first time we felt as if some horrible Thing, utterly merciless, was advancing to grip us.' As the two officers, one British the other French, watched the bombardment continue and the fires spread, it became clear to them 'that to survive it would be necessary to go on beyond exhaustion, to march when the body clamoured to be allowed to drop and die, to shoot when eyes were too tired to see, to remain awake when a man would have given his chance of salvation to sleep. And we realised also that to drive the body beyond its physical powers, to force the mind to act long after it had surrendered its power of thought, only despair and the strength of despair could furnish the motive force.'

This was to become true of all armies, on all fronts, in conditions that were to worsen beyond even what Spears could imagine at that terrifying moment of revelation. A dominating feature of the third week of August, with the armies in rapid movement, was the flight of civilians. As von Bülow's army moved against Charleroi, several thousand Belgians fled from the city and surrounding villages. Spears, witnessing this at Chimay, whither French Fifth Army headquarters had withdrawn, later recalled: 'We were in contact for the first time with the Great Panic. These were the vanguard of a terrified uprooted population, running before some ghastly terror that killed and destroyed and burned all it met.'

That day, August 20, French troops, whose colleagues had marched with such confidence six days earlier into Lorraine, were defeated at Morhange, after one of the first slaughters of the war. The French Second Army was in retreat, many of its troops reported to be nearly at the end of their endurance. One of its Corps, the XX, was commanded by General Foch, who later recalled: 'The roads were blocked by supply columns and by magnificent motor-cars from Nice. On the 21st we had to continue the withdrawal. . . . I went to Nancy. They wanted to evacuate it. I said: "The enemy is two days' march distant from Nancy and XX Corps is there. They won't walk over the XX without protest!" ' Foch was right: his Corps took the offensive three days after the retreat had begun. The German forces having reached almost to Dombasle, eight miles south-east of the city, advanced into a fearful artillery barrage of 75-millimetre guns, forty-eight in all, and were driven back in disorder to Le Léomont, a farm three miles further east.[1] They were also driven out of Lunéville, the town in which the Treaty of Lunéville had been signed in 1801, extending France's eastern border to the left bank of the Rhine.

During the short German occupation of Lunéville, and at Gerbéviller ten miles to the south, atrocities had been committed against civilians. German troops had also crossed the Lunéville-Dombasle road, entering the village of Vitrimont. Although they were driven out after forty-eight hours, they set fire to every house which had not already been destroyed or damaged by their earlier bombardment. Two years later the ruined

---

[1] A monument marking the French victory here was put up after the war, but was destroyed by the Germans after the fall of France in 1940. It was reconstructed by the French in 1950.

houses were still being restored, with the help of two American women, and French Government subsidies for the rebuilding of damaged properties. 'The American lady at the head of the work,' *The Times* reported on 18 January 1917, 'who has taken up her abode in an out-of-the-way corner of the pile of ruins that were once the village of Vitrimont, could probably give us as convincing an answer as anyone as to the reasons why France, at all events, will go on fighting till she has won an unbreakable peace.'

At Sarrebourg, north-east of Lunéville, on what had been the French Second Army front, seven French soldiers were killed on August 21 after they had surrendered. The episode was one of the very few that led to a war crimes trial after the war. The trial was conducted by a German court; the accused were German officers. One of them, Major Crusius, admitted responsibility. 'There lay a Frenchman to all appearance dead,' a German soldier told the court. 'Major Crusius poked him repeatedly with his foot. The third time the man moved and opened his eyes.' Crusius then ordered him to be shot. Several soldiers refused to carry out the order, then one of them 'aimed at the head of the Frenchman and fired'.[1]

At the village of Bleid that day, just inside the Belgian border west of Longwy, a 23-year-old German platoon commander, pushing ahead of his platoon with three men, saw by a farm building at the edge of the village some fifteen to twenty French soldiers, drinking coffee. Without bringing up the rest of his platoon, the young officer opened fire, killing or wounding half the Frenchmen, and extricating himself in time to attack with all his men, and capture half the village. Later that day he attacked again, explaining to his superiors: 'Since I didn't want to remain inactive with my platoon I decided to attack the enemy deployed opposite us.' Thus Erwin Rommel, half a century later the scourge of the British forces in North Africa, first showed his quality of audacity.

On August 21 the citizens of Brussels were spending their first full day under occupation. That day Edith Cavell wrote to the magazine *Nursing Mirror*: 'Some of the Belgians spoke to the invaders in German and found that they were very vague as to their whereabouts and imagined they were already in Paris; they were surprised to be speaking to Belgians and could not understand what quarrel they had with them.'[2] The Germans offered Edith Cavell and the other British nurses in Brussels a safe conduct to Holland, but most of them refused. That night, near the Belgian village of St Symphorien, a British soldier, Private J. Parr, went forward on his bicycle to scout out the land. He did not return. He is buried in the war cemetery in which the Germans later buried both their and the British dead. Parr

---

[1] Major Crusius was sentenced to two years' imprisonment. Following a decision of the Treaty of Versailles in 1920 (Articles 228, 229 and 230), forty-five war crimes trials were held at Leipzig in 1921, in the presence of British and French legal observers, before the Supreme Court of Leipzig.

[2] In 1956 many Soviet troops arriving in Budapest to crush the Hungarian uprising imagined that the Danube was the Suez Canal, and that they were there to fight the British and French forces which had landed at Port Said.

was almost certainly the first British soldier to be killed in the First World War.

By the early hours of August 22, two German armies, one commanded by von Kluck and the other by von Bülow, were positioned in a broad swathe across the centre of Belgium. Their deepest penetration was more than a hundred miles beyond the German frontier, and more than half way to the North Sea ports of Ostend and Dunkirk. Seeking to halt this advance were the troops of three nations: Belgians defending the fortress of Namur, a French army fighting south of Charleroi, and the British Expeditionary Force, which reached the town of Mons at the very moment when the First German Army under von Kluck was driving southward through Mons in a thrust towards the French frontier. The German armies totalled 580,000 men: the French and British less than 336,000, of whom almost 36,000 were British. The size of the German forces had not been estimated correctly by French Intelligence: it was thought that fifteen German corps were advancing, but the real figure was twenty-eight: five complete armies, each of which was thrusting through Belgium.

Reflecting on the nature of the British troops who were at that very moment advancing towards the German troops along a twenty-mile front, Lieutenant Walter Bloem wrote: 'English soldiers? We knew what they looked like by the comic papers; short scarlet tunics with small caps set at an angle on their heads, or bearskins with the chin-strap under the lip instead of under the chin. There was much joking about this, and also about Bismarck's remark of sending the police to arrest the English army.'

That joking was soon ended, as the now khaki-clad British soldiers took up positions along the Mons-Condé canal.

4

From Mons to the Marne

AUGUST–SEPTEMBER 1914

At seven o'clock on the morning of 22 August 1914, just outside the village of Casteau, three miles north-east of Mons, a squadron of British troops of the Royal Irish Dragoon Guards saw a group of German soldiers, distinct in their field grey uniform. Shots were fired: the first shots fired in battle by British soldiers on the continent of Europe for almost a hundred years. The start of the battle is recorded in the British official history. After Corporal E. Thomas fired his rifle, his commanding officer, Captain Hornby, drew his sword and charged. The Germans withdrew. Three hours later, two British airmen, Lieutenant Vincent Waterfall and 2nd Lieutenant George Bailey flew from their air base at Maubeuge on a reconnaissance flight over Mons and Soignies. As they flew above Enghien they were shot down by German artillery fire. Both were killed.

An hour later, at 11.15 a.m., the men of an artillery battery in the British Fifth Army watched as German troops advanced across a ridge to attack an outpost line of British troops. The battery opened fire. 'Our shells fell very short of the German battery which had just come into action,' the Fifth Army commander, General Gough, later recalled. 'I turned to the battery commander and said sharply: "For God's sake hit them!" It was Foreman – a splendid officer – but his reply was damping: "I cannot get another yard out of these guns".' The British guns were thirteen pounders. Neither their range nor the weight of their shells could match the German 77-millimetre field gun with which they were confronted. 'It was not many minutes,' Gough added, 'before the German shells were pitching among us in reply to our fire.'

Throughout August 22 the Germans advanced against the French troops to the east of the British line. At Rossignol an indication of the severity of the fighting survives to this day: the 874 graves in the French military cemetery and, in another cemetery nearby, the remains of 1,108 soldiers whose bodies could not be identified. In an attempt to drive the Germans from Neufchâteau, five French battalions had advanced, with bayonets fixed, against nine German battalions. At the start of the attack, a single German machine-gun burst struck down three French battalion commanders as they conferred at the roadside. Within forty-eight hours of the bayonet charge at Rossignol, Joffre gave the order that 'the attack must be prepared with artillery, the infantry must be held back and not launched to the assault until the distance to be covered is so short that it is certain the objectives will be reached'.

While the French were being mown down at Rossignol, three miles away at Jamoigne a French colonial division was neither under attack nor in action. Its commander, General Leblois, made no effort to go to the help of his neighbours. Joffre later removed him from his command for 'incapacity'. Leblois defended his inaction on the grounds that he had been given no orders to move. Also on August 22, near Virton, the men of the French V Corps panicked, falling back to Tellancourt despite the exhortations of their officers to turn and face the Germans. This precipitate retreat exposed the two adjacent French corps to heavy flank attacks.

Among the French soldiers killed in action on August 22 were Foch's only son, Germain, a twenty-five-year-old infantryman, and Foch's son-in-law Captain Bécourt. Both were buried in a common grave at Yprecourt on the Belgian frontier with others who were killed in the same action.

The French Fifth Army, having been driven from Charleroi, called the British Expeditionary Force to its aid. Late on the night of August 22 General Lanrezac sent a message to Sir John French, asking him to attack, on the following day, the western flank of the German troops that were pushing the French army back southward from the Sambre. The British Commander-in-Chief pointed out that he could not do so. The weight of German troops who were even then approaching his own force was considerable. In order to enable Lanrezac not to be outflanked, however, he intended to hold the British troops on the Mons-Condé canal for twenty-four hours.

On the morning of August 23, at Obourg, north-east of Mons, on the northern bank of the canal, a group of grey-clad soldiers were seen emerging from a wood by British troops of the Middlesex Regiment. Among those watching them was a bugler who had once been a member of the British Legation guard in Shanghai, where the nearby German Legation had been guarded by German troops. He recognised the oncoming soldiers as Germans by their field-grey uniforms and flat caps. The British troops opened fire. Their commanding officer, Major Abell, was killed, shot through the head, the first British officer to be killed. As the rifle fire continued, his second-in-command, Captain Knowles, was also killed, followed by 2nd Lieutenant Hancock. After a prolonged exchange of fire, with many deaths on both sides, the British troops withdrew.

The mood at British headquarters was robust. 'I am now much in advance of the line held by the Fifth Army,' Sir John French informed Lanrezac that afternoon, in justifying his decision to remain on the Mons

Canal, 'and feel my position to be as far forward as circumstances will allow, particularly in view of the fact that I am not properly prepared to take offensive action until tomorrow morning.' This hope for an offensive 'tomorrow morning' was a chimera. During the six hours preceding French's message to Lanrezac, British forces had been under attack by a far larger German force, and were far more likely to have to move back, rather than forward, the next day.

The Battle of Mons had begun. It marked the first serious clash of arms on the Western Front by the British, whose participation had been belittled by von Moltke and mocked by the Kaiser, though that often-contradictory monarch had also said that the British soldiers had staying power. Throughout August 23, in mist and rain, the two armies were in violent conflict.

So unexpectedly had the war descended upon the region, that the inhabitants of the villages near Mons, where the fiercest fighting took place, began the day by setting off for church, in their Sunday best. In many cases they were caught between the two hostile lines. The Germans, numerically a much larger force, were surprised by the intensity of the British rifle fire: so rapid was the firing that the Germans often mistook rifle for machine-gun fire. 'Their losses were very heavy,' General Smith-Dorrien later recalled, 'for they came on in dense formations, offering the most perfect targets, and it was not until they had been mown down in thousands that they adopted more open formations'.[1]

The French painter Paul Maze, who had joined the British forces as an interpreter, later recalled his first sight of the German troops on August 23, in a small village near Binche. 'I focused the telescope on to a railway embankment some 2,000 yards away, and saw in a circle of vivid light a number of little grey figures scrambling down on to the flat. Moving along the railway line more and more were appearing and beyond, from behind a slight rise in the ground, others were coming up.' Maze also recalled how the sight of the Germans had an immediate effect on the villagers. 'Women started to wail, and rushed for home, followed by the men, while the children, torn by curiosity, lagged behind turning to see.' Then the Germans came nearer and firing broke out. 'At once the atmosphere changed – in a few seconds all these civilians were fleeing along the roads while the invasion, creeping up like a tide, steadily gained ground. In their Sunday clothes, carrying in their hands their feathered hats which they had not stopped to put on, they wheeled perambulators, wheelbarrows, bicycles and anything on wheels, and fled with their babies and terrified men.'

For the whole of August 23 the British fought to hold the line. It was a source of pride to them that their numbers, just under 36,000, were

[1] Smith-Dorrien was an expert on heavy losses: in 1879, during the Zulu War, he was one of only forty Europeans out of 800 who survived the Battle of Isandlwana, 110 miles north-west of Durban.

scarcely four thousand more than that of the soldiers commanded by Wellington at Waterloo in 1815, the last time a British army had fought on the European continent. The Germans were impressed by the tenacity of their adversary, even under heavy artillery fire. 'If we thought that the English had been stormed enough to be storm-ripe,' one German captain recalled, 'we were fairly mistaken. They met us with well-aimed fire.' For Walter Bloem the laughter of a few days earlier had disappeared: 'Wherever I looked, right or left, there were dead and wounded, quivering in convulsions, groaning terribly, blood oozing from fresh wounds. They apparently knew something about war, these cursed English.'

A legend started within two weeks of the battle that an angel had appeared 'on the traditional white horse and clad all in white with flaming sword', and, facing the advancing Germans, 'forbade their further progress'. The Angel of Mons was not the only hallucination in those days of battle, marching and exhaustion. 'If any angels were seen on the retirement, as the newspaper accounts said they were, they were seen that night,' Private Frank Richards later recalled of the retreat from Le Câteau three days later. 'March, march, for hour after hour, without a halt; we were now breaking into the fifth day of continuous marching with practically no sleep in between.... Stevens said: "There's a fine castle there, see?" pointing to one side of the road. But there was nothing there. Very nearly everyone was seeing things, we were all so dead beat.'

The local communal cemetery at Mons contains the graves of 330 British soldiers killed in battle on August 23.[1] The British had suffered heavy casualties that day, 1,600 killed or wounded, and had lost ground. The French and Belgian forces had likewise been pushed back after fierce fighting. A French attempt to advance through the Forest of the Ardennes failed. One French Army Corps, the XVII, having lost its artillery to the Germans without it having fired a shot, fell back in panic, stopping only when it reached and fell behind the positions from which it had started on the previous day. In the Bavarian town of Landshut a thirteen-year-old schoolboy noted in his diary: 'The whole city is bedecked with flags. The French and Belgians scarcely thought they would be chopped up so fast.' The schoolboy's name was Heinrich Himmler.

Not every French unit was being 'chopped up' on August 23. At Onhaye, where the German army had managed to cross the river Meuse and was only a mile and a half west of Dinant, General Mangin, in command of a brigade that was in reserve, hurried forward with two infantry battalions and a cavalry regiment and, in a series of bayonet charges, forced the Germans out of the village.

[1] It was not for another four years, on Sunday, 10 November 1918, that the outskirts of Mons rang with artillery and rifle fire again. This time it was Canadian troops who did battle there against the Germans, fighting throughout that night and entering Mons at dawn on Armistice morning. In the same communal cemetery in which the first British dead of the war lie, lie fifty-seven Canadians, killed in action on the last day of the war.

When Sir John French learned on August 23 that General Lanrezac's Fifth Army, faced by the imminent fall of Namur, was falling back, his first instinct was to maintain his position. 'I will stand the attack on the ground now occupied by the troops,' he informed one of his commanders early that evening. 'You will therefore strengthen your position by every possible means during the night.' But it was too late, and too rash, to make a stand. Realising that, with Lanrezac's withdrawal, his troops were in danger of being cut off, at midnight Sir John French ordered the British Expeditionary Force to retreat.

Throughout August 24 and 25 the British Expeditionary Force retreated southward from Mons towards the French frontier, 'the men stumbling along more like ghosts than living soldiers,' one eye-witness wrote, 'unconscious of everything about them, but still moving under the magic impulse of discipline and regimental pride'. A skirmish south of Mons on the 24th saw an early example of what is now known – in a perverse euphemism – as 'friendly fire' when a German unit, penetrating a British trench, was immediately shelled by its own artillery.

As the British Expeditionary Force began its retreat southward, Sir John French learned that Belgium's last defended fortress, Namur, had fallen to the Germans. Shaken by this news, and mindful of the ill-fated retreat of Sir John Moore to Corunna in 1808, he ordered the immediate defence of the port of Le Havre, more than two hundred miles to the south-west. When his order was discussed in London, it was feared that even Le Havre might prove untenable, and that St Nazaire on the Atlantic coast, almost four hundred miles from the battlefield, should be fortified. Not only might the war be over well before Christmas, it seemed, but it might be over with a German victory. Churchill, who saw Lord Kitchener soon after he had learned of Namur's fall, wrote: 'Though his manner was quite calm, his face was different. I had the subconscious feeling that it was distorted and discoloured as if it had been punched with a fist.'

On August 25 the British newspapers broke the story of the struggle. 'The battle is joined and has so far gone ill for the Allies' was the comment in *The Times* that day. There was also a dire warning: 'Yesterday was a day of bad news, and we fear that more must follow.' On the morning of August 26, on the battlefield, General Allenby, commanding the cavalry, feared that the whole Expeditionary Force would be bottled up and captured, as the French army had been at Sedan in 1870, if they did not continue their southward march. Smith-Dorrien warned, however, that his men were virtually overcome with fatigue. 'In that case I do not think you will get away,' said Allenby, to which Smith-Dorrien replied: 'I'll fight it out.' When the Chief of Staff of the British Expeditionary Force learned that the men were going to stand and fight against such heavy odds, he fainted.[1]

The battle that followed, at Le Câteau, was a fearsome one. At one point the German superiority in machine guns was decisive. But the British

---

[1] His name was Sir Archibald Wolf Murray, later known as 'sheep' Murray.

effort was such that the Germans overestimated the size of the forces confronting them. After the battle, which held the line for long enough to enable thousands of men to fall back in relatively good order, the British retreat continued. The extreme tiredness of officers and men was evident even at the top. Allenby himself, overcome by fatigue, was found by a member of his Staff exhausted and disheartened, his elbows on his knees and his head in his hands.

One British battalion, exhausted by its efforts at Le Câteau, and unable to regroup for action, fell back to St Quentin. There, its commanding officer, Lieutenant-Colonel John Elkington, agreed to the request of the Mayor to sign a document surrendering his men, should the Germans enter the town while they were regaining their strength. The Mayor, not wanting St Quentin to become a battlefield, insisted on this. The Germans did not enter the town that day, and Elkington and his men rejoined the main British force, but the surrender document was made public. Elkington was court-martialled and dismissed from the army. Desperate to prove his desire to fight, he joined the French Foreign Legion.

Among the British soldiers killed on August 27 was 2nd Lieutenant Carol Awdry, whose brother recalled seventy-nine years later: 'My father had seen the fulfilment of his own ambition when Carol joined the army. He was prepared to accept the risks of war, which had just been declared three weeks before. To have his son killed on August 27 was absolutely shattering. He and Carol had done everything together.'[1] Each day, for the next four years and more, men and women throughout Europe would dread the arrival of a telegram announcing that they had lost a son, a brother or a husband. Every day those who perused the casualty lists knew that they might find a relative, a friend or a loved one.

The exhaustion of the men on August 27 was remembered by all who fought on that day. One eye-witness recalled: 'The officers roused the sergeants, and the men were hunted out, hustled on to their feet, hardly conscious of what they were doing, and by some means or other formed into a column. Then the column got under way, drivers and troopers sleeping in the saddles, infantry staggering half asleep as they marched, every man stiff with cold and weak with hunger, but, under the miraculous power of discipline, plodding on.'

Plodding on, and also fighting on: the German lieutenant, Walter Bloem, recalled a stand by two British officers and twenty-five infantrymen who, cut off from the rest of their battalion, fought until all but four were killed. These four were taken prisoner. Bloem was an eye-witness of the aftermath of the struggle, writing: 'On the way we stumbled on a dead English soldier in the undergrowth with his skull split open: then another with a bent bayonet in his breast.' On the other side of the retreat on August 27, Paul Maze witnessed the last phase of a British action against a German cavalry

---

[1] Carol Awdry's bother, the Reverend Wilbert Vere Awdry, achieved fame and fortune after the Second World War as the author of the children's book *Thomas the Tank Engine*.

unit. 'As a few Germans were hiding in the corn-stooks, lances and swords were thrust through the hay and I heard fearful yells. The horses were very excited, as were the men, who were showing to each other the blood dripping off their sword blades. Others were busy picking up souvenirs. Meanwhile, I had propped up a wounded German Dragoon, who was vomiting quantities of undigested unripe gooseberries. He had a nasty sword-thrust through his chest. In broken English he told me he had only left the Ritz in London twenty days before, where he had been a waiter.'

As well as the Angel of Mons, another more lasting apparition made its first, tentative appearance on the battlefield in the last week of August. As the British official medical history of the war records: 'During 1914 several men were evacuated from France to England owing to having been "broken" by their experiences in the retreat from Mons.' Within a month, at the base hospitals in France, Lieutenant-Colonel Gordon Holmes, an expert on nervous disorders, 'saw frequent examples of gross hysterical conditions which were associated with trivial bullet and shell wounds, or even with only slight contusions of the back, arms and legs'. By the end of the year more than a hundred British officers and eight hundred men had been treated for nervous diseases, mostly what the official history called 'a severe mental disability which rendered the individual affected temporarily, at any rate, incapable of further service'. By the end of the war, as many as 80,000 officers and men had been unable to continue in the trenches, and many had been invalided out of the army altogether for nervous disorders, including what came to be known as 'shell-shock'.

During a French counter-attack at Richaumont on August 27, the commander of a German Guards' regiment, Prince Eitel Friedrich, watched as his men began to fall back. He immediately took a drum and began to beat on it. The sight of the Kaiser's second son unflinching amid the turmoil halted the panic and the German troops drove back the attackers. This was, however, only a small local success, for on the same day a large-scale counter-attack by General Lanrezac against the German Second Army was so strong that it forced the distant German First Army to turn from its drive around Paris from the north, and to rush to the support of its endangered colleagues. That day, Joffre created a special command for General Foch, carving from elements of other armies a Ninth Army with which to seek to check the German advance. One of Foch's Staff officers was Colonel Weygand.[1] The improvised force was filled with zeal to regain the advantage for France.

The war was gaining a new momentum; the abandonment of fixed, failed plans, and the innovation of improvisation. It was also provoking oppo-

---

[1] In 1940, when he was Commander-in-Chief of the French Army, Weygand supported the opening of armistice negotiations with Germany.

sition. On August 27, in an article in the British Independent Labour Party
newspaper the *Daily Citizen*, a Socialist journalist, Clifford Allen, called
for a widespread Labour protest against the war. Allen declared: 'If by a
great national campaign we denounce unceasingly Britain's participation
in this war – not merely war in general – it will stand for all time that the
voice of Socialism was never stilled for all the specious arguments of
diplomatists in justifying a wicked war.'

The names of the diplomats of every warring nation became known
during August, as each government published the diplomatic telegrams
and memoranda leading up to the war, carefully chosen to show that
responsibility for the conflict lay elsewhere. In publishing his anti-war
article in pamphlet form, Clifford Allen wrote: 'We shall not justify human
suffering by the hours and dates of ambassadorial despatches.'

While anti-war sentiment struggled against the prevailing waves of
patriotic feeling, the 10,000–strong French Foreign Legion, based in North
Africa, was overwhelmed by applications to join, and to fight in Europe.
In the seven months following August 21, when recruiting opened, 32,000
non-Frenchmen enlisted, of whom almost 5,000 were Italians, more than
3,000 Russians, 1,467 Swiss, 1,369 Czechs, a thousand Germans (all of
whom were to fight against Germany) and more than a hundred Americans.
Among those Americans was William Thaw, from Pittsburgh, who wrote
home on August 30 from his base camp: 'I am going to take a part,
however small, in the greatest and probably last, war in history, which has
apparently developed into a fight of civilisation against barbarism. That
last reason may sound a bit grand and dramatic, but you would quite
agree if you could hear the tales of French, Belgian and English soldiers
who have come back here from the front.'

In a letter home, Thaw gave a picture of the variety of Legionnaires who
were training with him, including 'a Columbia Professor (called "Shorty"),
an old tutor who has numerous PhDs, MAs etc., a preacher from Georgia,
a pro gambler from Missouri, a former light-weight prize fighter, two
dusky gentlemen, one from Louisiana and one from Ceylon, a couple of
hard guys from the Gopher Gang of lower New York, a Swede, a Norwegian, a number of Poles, Brazilians, Belgians etc.' It was just like school,
Thaw added, except that instead of getting demerits 'for being naughty,
you get short rations and prison'.

At the end of August the British troops, during their tenacious fighting in
retreat, were helped considerably by a French counter-attack at Guise.
They also had a diversion in prospect when the 3,000 men of the British
Royal Marine Brigade were sent across the North Sea to Ostend, crossing
without incident despite the presence of German submarines. The German
High Command was disturbed by reports that this Marine force was much
larger than it was. It was rumoured, indeed, that these were not British
troops at all, but Russian soldiers who had been brought by sea from
northern Russia to Scotland, then hurried southward by train to the

Channel ports. The figure of 80,000 was mentioned. Then it grew in size to 'little short of a million'.

British travellers, it was said, had spotted these Russians 'with snow on their boots' at various railway stations moving south. As *The Times* reported the rumour, the Russians landed at the Scottish port of Leith, 'and carried at night in hundreds of trains straight to ports on the south coast'. From there they were sent across the North Sea to Belgium. 'It is said in confirmation that belated wayfarers at railway stations throughout the country saw long train after long train running through with blinds down, but still allowing glimpses of carriages packed with fierce-looking bearded fellows in fur hats.'

For seven days, in the vicinity of Ostend, it was not the fictional Russians but the Royal Marine Brigade that gave the Germans the impression of being a much larger force than it was. Then it returned to Britain. The last division of regular soldiers left in Britain had already been sent to France, denuding the British Isles of its professional army in the event of a German invasion. It was a precarious time for Britain. Germany had sufficient troops under arms to land a considerable force on the East Coast. With the help of fog or luck, such an armada might evade a Royal Naval attempt to intercept it. But on August 28, in a naval action in the Heligoland Bight, three German cruisers were destroyed and three others damaged. There were 700 German and 35 British deaths. No British ships were sunk. The danger of invasion receded. 'Everybody quite mad with delight at the success of our first naval venture,' the British admiral who had conducted the action wrote in triumph to his wife. In an incident which seemed to bode well for the survival of chivalry, two hundred German sailors from one of the destroyed cruisers were rescued by the British.

In Germany, the arrival of prisoners-of-war was becoming a familiar sight. On August 30, in Landshut, the schoolboy Himmler wrote in his dairy: 'The whole station was full of curious Landshuters who were crude and almost violent as the *severely* wounded Frenchmen (who are surely worse off than our wounded in that they are prisoners) were given bread, water.'

Also on August 30, in a wartime Sunday edition, *The Times* published a dispatch from one of its most experienced correspondents, Arthur Moore, who had seen the British troops during their retreat from Mons. Writing from Amiens, Moore told of the 'terrible defeat' sustained at Mons a week earlier, and went on to describe 'the broken bits of many regiments' and British soldiers 'battered with marching'. The British public was shocked. The Amiens dispatch, one historian has written, 'broke like a thunderclap on a blissfully confident nation that had been awaiting news of famous victories, and it created consternation in a Cabinet that was already alarmed by its lack of hard news from the front.'[1] That day the British

---

[1] Bernard Ash, *The Lost Dictator, A Biography of Field-Marshal Sir Henry Wilson*, Cassell, London 1968, page 159.

Government, which twelve days earlier had placed an order for 162,000 shrapnel shells, doubled its order.

The Commander-in-Chief, Sir John French, doubted that French forces on the battlefield, far larger than his own, could halt the onward thrust of the German army, which by August 30 had driven the Anglo-French forces southward across the River Aisne. On August 31 French colonial troops attacking east of Gerbéviller were confronted by German machine guns that annihilated them. Nearby, a French Reserve Regiment overran the German defences in half an hour, but as the French battle plan called for a three-hour assault, the German positions which the French troops had occupied continued to be bombarded by French artillery, so severely that the successful troops were forced to fall back to their starting point. Within the course of a few days a 14,500-strong division was reduced to 8,000 fighting men.

On August 31 Sir John French informed London that he intended to withdraw the British Expeditionary Force behind Paris, abandoning the French armies to their fate. Many of the British troops were 'shattered', he wrote to a friend. All of them needed 'to rest and refit'. If London would increase the number of his infantrymen sixfold and his cavalrymen fourfold, he added in caustic vein, 'I would get to Berlin in six weeks without any French help at all.' Without reinforcements on an impossible scale, he intended to separate his force from the French and retire out of the line altogether.

News of French's attitude shocked those whose forces he was supposed to be assisting. On August 31 Joffre appealed direct to the French Prime Minister, René Viviani, to intervene to 'ensure that Field Marshal French did not carry out his retreat too rapidly, and should make up his mind to contain the enemy who was on the British front'. So alarmed was the newly established British War Council at their Commander-in-Chief's attitude that Lord Kitchener was sent to France to explain in person that Britain must continue to render the French armies continuous support. The two men met in Paris on September 1. When the meeting was over, Kitchener was able to telegraph to London with news of a successful mission: 'French's troops are now in the fighting line, where he will remain conforming to the movements of the French army.'

After six days of continuous marching southward, General Lanrezac's Fifth Army had reached Craonne. Captain Spears was an eye-witness to the suffering of the French soldiers. 'Heads down, red trousers and blue coats indistinguishable for dust, bumping into transport, into abandoned carts, into each other, they shuffled down the endless roads, their eyes filled with dust that dimmed the scalding landscape, so that they saw clearly only the foreground of discarded packs, prostrate men, and an occasional abandoned gun. Dead and dying horses that had dropped in their tracks from fatigue, lay in great numbers by the side of the roads. Worse still, horses dying but not yet dead, sometimes struggling a little, a strange appeal in their eyes, looked at the passing columns whose dust covered them, caking their thirsty lips and nostrils.' The heat of the day was intense. Many men, 'utterly worn out, overcome by fatigue or sunstroke, dropped and lay where they had fallen, yet the spark of duty, the spirit of self-sacrifice, survived and bore the Army on'.

One French general, believing all was lost, contemplated suicide, but overcame his despair. Commandant Duruy, who had been in the retreat since the fall of Namur, told Captain Spears that when he came across several hundred men literally running away southward, he stood in the roadway shouting at them to stop, but they paid not the slightest attention. 'Duruy, seeing that fear rode on these men's shoulders and panic reigned in their hearts, drew his revolver and fired; but the men merely stumbled over the prostrate ones and went on, hardly attempting even to dodge the levelled weapon.'

At the village of Néry, on the extreme right of the German line, the German Fourth Cavalry Division, advancing on September 1 through a morning fog, reached the part of the line held by the three regiments of the First British Cavalry Brigade. One of the British artillery units, 'L' battery, was surprised by the unexpectedly rapid German advance. Its horses were still tethered when the attack came. In a few minutes two guns and their crews were overrun. The men operating the remaining gun fought on. The officer in charge, Captain E.K. Bradbury, although mortally wounded, insisted on directing the fire until he died. He, and two of the four others who continued to fire the gun were awarded the Victoria Cross: three Victoria Crosses in almost as many minutes. 'To the cavalryman of the first war,' General Spears has written, 'the tale of "L" Battery at Néry was a shrine concealed deep in his heart where he could pay a proud though secret tribute of affection and respect to his beloved Horse Artillery, his very own gunners who had never been known to let him down.'

As a result of Captain Bradbury's actions at Néry, the German Fourth Cavalry Division was scattered, and could play no significant part in the decisive battle that lay ahead.

While the Anglo-French retreat continued towards the Marne, a German aeroplane appeared over Paris, dropping several bombs, and leaflets announcing the defeat of the French and Russian armies. At the very moment when thousands of Belgian refugees were entering the city from the north, tens of thousands of Parisians began to leave for the south and west, by road, rail and river. Trees were cut down, barricades built, and trenches dug on the main boulevards leading into the city. The government itself, never slow to follow public opinion, departed for Bordeaux on September 2. This departure precipitated an even larger public exodus. Out of the peacetime population of just under three million, more than a million Parisians had fled. The harsh reality of military occupation was made clear that day in Brussels when the newly-appointed German Governor, Field Marshal Baron von der Goltz, issued a proclamation in which he stated: 'It is the stern necessity of war that the punishment for hostile acts falls not only on the guilty, but on the innocent as well.'

Such 'stern necessity' was also evident that day in France, where, twenty-seven miles from Paris, German troops riding through the ancient town of Senlis took the Mayor, Eugene Odent, and six other citizens hostage. They were taken to a field outside the town and shot. As well as the Mayor, the victims of this reprisal were a tanner, a carter, a waiter, a chauffeur, a baker's assistant and a stonecutter. A nineteenth-century painting in the Town Hall shows the execution of four hostages by Armagnacs nearly five hundred years earlier, in 1418, when the town was besieged by the Burgundians. 'Six centuries have elapsed,' commented the 1917 Michelin Guide to the Marne Battlefields, 'but it will be seen that, towards hostages, the Germans still retain the mental attitude of the Middle Ages.'

An hour before midnight on September 1 the French High Command gained a precious piece of military intelligence that gave them, in precise detail, the direction the German First Army was about to take. A German officer, driving in a car from von Kluck's headquarters to the headquarters of his division, had by mistake taken a road that went straight into a French patrol, and was killed. His haversack, containing food, clothing and various papers caked in blood, was brought to a French Intelligence officer, Colonel Fagalde, who found among the papers a map which not only marked the precise dispositions of von Kluck's forces, itself information of great value, but also showed, in pencil, his intended lines of advance on the following day. These were not to the south, towards the French Sixth Army under Maunoury, and Paris, but to the south-east towards the British Expeditionary Force and the river Marne.

The most south-easterly line of the German advance that night was to the village of Longpont, situated at an undefended point between the British Expeditionary Force and the French Fifth Army under Lanrezac. Such points where armies join are always points of weakness. As a result of an accident, the Anglo-French commanders were in possession of a golden key. The French now knew exactly where to direct their Fourth Army, which would not, after all, have to defend Paris from a direct assault.

The British Expeditionary Force reached the Marne on September 2. 'The troops have quite recovered their spirits,' General Smith-Dorrien wrote in his diary, 'and are getting fitter every day, and all they want is the order to go forward and attack the enemy – but that is not possible with the present rearward move of the French Army.' Given the rapidity of the German advance, and its unexpected direction, it was not surprising that on September 2 a German cavalry patrol captured Arthur Moore, the correspondent of *The Times* whose dispatch about the retreat from Mons had so alarmed Britain.[1]

---

[1] Such were the courtesies of war that, as a non-combatant and a journalist, Moore was released within a few days: he later joined the British Army and served both at Gallipoli and Salonica. In the Second World War he was Public Relations Adviser to Lord Mountbatten in South-East Asia (1944–45).

66

On the following day the British Expeditionary Force crossed the Marne, blowing up the bridges behind them. In thirteen days they had retreated nearly a hundred and fifty miles. It was as if the Kaiser's gibe about a 'contemptibly small' army was to be justified. Yet the retreating troops had fought all the way, with dozens of rearguard actions. They had only four hours sleep a night, sometimes less, and were so exhausted that one officer said of them, 'I would never have believed that men could have been so tired and so hungry and yet live.' Another officer, Lieutenant George Roupell, who was later to win the Victoria Cross for bravery, wrote in his diary of the men 'physically weak from long marches and mentally weak from the continual strain of never being out of reach of the enemy's guns'. Roupell added, 'It is scarcely surprising that under these conditions traces of panic and losses of self-control occurred.'

On September 3, in the North Sea, a German submarine, *U-21*, sank a British cruiser, HMS *Pathfinder*, the first warship to succumb to torpedo fire: 259 sailors were killed. The submarine was a new weapon of war, which had the advantage over surface vessels that it could attack and withdraw without being seen. The Germans intended to use their submarine fleet to destroy Allied naval and merchant shipping, impeding the war effort and demoralising the countries whose ships were being sunk. Counter-measures existed, including ramming, surface attack by another vessel, depth charges, minefields, and even air attack. These were helped by the reading of German wireless messages and their decryption, a science in which the British came to excel. But the depredations of the German submarines were to continue until the last days of the war, wreaking havoc on Allied seaborne supplies.

On the very day that the Germans had their first submarine success, a British pilot, Lieutenant Dalrymple-Clark, carried out the first British bombing raid of the war, over land, near the Franco-Belgian border. According to the official report, he 'expended one bomb on about forty Germans – some evidently hurt'. Other pilots, working in close partnership with armoured car squadrons, harassed German motor patrols as they drove along the highways. The British Consul at Dunkirk reported to London that these combined attacks had been 'extraordinarily successful' in disconcerting the Germans as they advanced.

The Belgians also made effective use of armoured car squadrons: when they came up against a similarly armoured German car the similarity was more than in the armoured plating: both the Germans and Belgians had mounted the same weapon, the Lewis machine gun, invented by an American, Major Isaac Newton Lewis (whose father had clearly anticipated his son's inventive turn of mind at birth), which he had sold to Belgium and Germany only after the American War Department repeatedly turned it down. It could fire between 100 and 500 rounds a minute. In the fighting in Belgium, E. Alexander Powell recalled, 'I saw trees as large round as a man's thigh literally cut down by the stream of lead from these weapons.'

*

The German Army was only twenty-five miles from Paris on September 3. That day, at the village of Baron, the 49-year-old composer Albéric Magnard barricaded himself in his house and opened fire on the German soldiers who had called for him to come out, killing one of them. His house was then set on fire with straw and grenades: he perished inside it. The village was then looted. Looting also marked the capture that same day of the nearby village of Ermenonville, where the philosopher Rousseau had died in 1778.

During September 3 several German cavalry patrols rode forward as far as Ecouen, only eight miles from Paris, whose citizens awaited a German assault. To the north-west, it was learned that day, German units had reached the river Seine, blowing up a bridge over the river at Pontoise. Fearful that their city was to be left to its fate, as Brussels had been two weeks earlier, the Parisian mood was grim. But on September 3 it was unexpectedly lifted by a stern proclamation from the city's military governor General Gallieni. 'I have received the order to defend Paris against the invader. This order I shall fulfil to the end.'

To defend Paris, Gallieni had the protection of a newly formed army under the command of General Maunoury. It too awaited a massive onslaught, entrenching itself around the perimeter. But the Germans had fallen into a trap, created by the French withdrawal, that drew them east of Paris and south of the Marne, dramatically extending their lines of supply and communication. By chasing the retreating Anglo-French forces, not to Paris but beyond the river Marne, the Germans lost the chance of taking the capital, for it was south of the Marne, on September 4, that the Anglo-French forces prepared to do battle. 'It was arranged that we are to fall back tonight about twelve miles towards the Seine to take advantage of the dark to cover our movements,' Smith-Dorrien wrote in his diary, 'and also to avoid the piercing heat of the sun, so trying to the men and horses.'

There were other hazards: a retirement, Smith-Dorrien added, 'is always a dangerous operation as regards to discipline, and a good many cases of unnecessary straggling and looting have taken place. Five men are to be tried by court-martial this evening. The losses of officers and non-commissioned officers in certain units make it very difficult to maintain a proper standard of discipline, especially as the temptations are very great, owing to the hospitality of the country-folk and the desertion of so many houses with valuables in.'

More than 1,500 British troops had been killed, wounded or taken prisoner in just over two weeks. Speaking at the London Guildhall on September 4, a month after Britain's declaration of war, Asquith declared that Britain 'would not sheathe the sword until Belgium's wrongs were righted'. These wrongs had been widely publicised. Two weeks after Asquith's speech *The Times* published a letter in which a British Lance-Corporal was quoted as saying, after the battle of Le Câteau: 'The Germans don't like cold steel. They were falling on their knees and praying, but our blood boiled at the way they were treating civilians, and we had no mercy.'

The repercussions of the Amiens dispatch about the British retreat from Mons had continued to reverberate throughout Britain in the week that followed it. 'I think you ought to realise the harm that has been done by Sunday's publication in *The Times*,' Winston Churchill, himself a former war correspondent, wrote to the paper's owner on September 5. 'I never saw such panic-stricken stuff written by any war correspondent before, and this served up on the authority of *The Times* can be made, and has been made, a weapon against us in every doubtful State.' At the Prime Minister's request Churchill himself drafted a special communiqué that was issued that day giving further details of the retreat and seeking to assure the British public that all was well. 'There is no doubt that our men have established a personal ascendancy over the Germans,' Churchill wrote, 'and they are conscious of the fact that with anything like even numbers the result would not be doubtful.' That such 'even numbers' were, under Britain's existing voluntary system, a virtual impossibility, the anonymous communiqué did not say. Yet Churchill, three years before the outbreak of war, had written a paper for the Committee of Imperial Defence in which he set out in detail the sequence of events that were about to unfold: the gradual and then accelerated lack of impetus of the German advance as its fortieth day drew near.

For thirty-three days the German troops had been in continuous advance. They had covered the ground on foot, carrying heavy packs, weapons and ammunition. With time and distance, the impetus of their attack had begun to wane. Logistics were also gradually working against them. To repair the deliberately demolished railway lines in Belgium and northern France was involving 26,000 German railway construction workers, whose work gradually became almost unmanageable. Of the 2,500 miles that made up the Belgian rail network, only three to four hundred miles had been restored by the first week of September. More immediately dangerous for the battles that month, as the First and Second Armies swept forward, the railheads to which ammunition was brought by train had become further and further away from the forward units. On August 25 the distance from the Second Army's railhead to the front line was twenty miles. This had to be covered by road, with much congestion and difficulty, the loads from long trains having to be transferred to individual lorries, vans and horse-drawn transport. By September 2 that distance had increased to ninety-five miles and by September 4 to more than a hundred miles. One part of the rail route was proving particularly difficult: between Liège and Ans the track used by the First Army was so steep that four engines were needed to pull and push each train forward. Liège itself, through which all First and Second Army trains had to pass, was often congested. South of Charleroi the only two lines along which the Second Army's supplies could go were both single-track.

While the problems of supply steadily worsened, German military fervour had also been dampened by the daily resistance with which the troops had been confronted, battles without respite even from men in retreat. They had no inkling, however, that a counter-offensive was imminent. 'The continuation of the French retreat was accepted as certain,' a German officer later wrote. 'Not a sign, not a word from prisoners, not a newspaper paragraph gave warning.'

The Battle of the Marne began on September 5. 'At the moment when the battle upon which hangs the fate of France is about to begin,' Joffre proclaimed to his men, 'all must remember that the time for looking back is past; every effort must be concentrated on attacking and throwing the enemy back.' Troops who could no longer advance 'must at any cost keep the ground that has been won, and must die where they stand rather than give way.' The proclamation ended: 'Under present conditions no weakness can be tolerated.' On the British front there was a similar sense of the crucial importance of the moment. 'I visited the Divisions and found the men very elated at the idea of moving forward rather than backward,' Smith-Dorrien wrote in his diary that day.

The British Expeditionary Force was nearest to Paris, between the Marne and the Seine. The German orders were succinct: 'If any British are met with, they are to be driven back.' But it was the British who drove the Germans back that day, and on eight successive days following that, with cavalrymen advancing rapidly northward, their reconnaissance assisted by cyclist patrols and aircraft. The infantry who followed the cavalry were likewise surprised at the lack of opposition. 'There was cheering evidence of the enemy's demoralisation,' General Edmonds recalled. 'The country near the roads was littered with empty bottles; and the inhabitants reported much drunkenness among the Germans. Indeed, some British artillery drivers while cutting hay discovered German soldiers, helplessly drunk, concealed under the topmost layer of the stack.'

That September 5, as the battle on the Marne began, the magazine *London Opinion* published a graphic drawing of Lord Kitchener, his gloved finger pointing out of the page, with the caption:

YOUR COUNTRY NEEDS
YOU

The poster, drawn by Alfred Leete, had been prepared during the retreat from Mons. It was later to be reproduced ten-thousand fold, though at Kitchener's insistence the words 'God Save the King' were quickly added to it. Peter Simkins, the historian of the recruitment drive which this poster symbolised, has written: 'In view of the fact that it became arguably the best known poster in history, it is perhaps churlish to note that its widespread circulation in various forms did not halt the decline in recruiting.'

Even as Kitchener's appeal for men was being published for the first time, based upon the shock of retreat and heavy losses, the British public was following the new British military successes in France with a rapidly enhanced confidence, pride and moral superiority. This feeling was expressed in verse on September 5, by the much-respected novelist and poet Thomas Hardy:

> *In our heart of hearts believing*
> *Victory crowns the just,*
> *And that braggarts must*
> *Surely bite the dust,*
>
> *Press we to the field ungrieving*
> *In our heart of hearts believing*
> *Victory crowns the just.*

Among the troops confronting the Germans on September 5 were 5,000 native Moroccans, led by 103 French officers. In an attempt to relieve the pressure on the Moroccans, who were at one moment falling back, a nearby battalion of French soldiers was ordered to charge the Germans. The captain in command was killed instantly as he led his men at the double over open ground under continuous German machine-gun fire. His place was taken by Lieutenant Charles de la Cornillière, who led the men forward to where they could lie down and fire back. As his men took what cover they could, he remained standing. As he ordered them 'At five hundred yards, independent fire!' he was shot and fell. A sergeant who tried to help him was killed instantly. The cry went up, 'The lieutenant is killed, the lieutenant is killed' and there was some sign of panic, whereupon the lieutenant managed to raise himself to his knees and shout: 'Yes, the lieutenant has been killed, but keep on firm!' The men advanced. As they did so, de la Cornillière died. His exploit quickly became a rallying point for French patriotic sentiment.

For twelve days the Moroccans, to whose aid Lieutenant de la Cornillière had been going, fought with the other French troops to push back the German forces. Like the other troops engaged in the battle they were successful, but at an exceptionally heavy cost: the death in action of forty-six officers and more than 4,000 men: a death toll of 85 per cent of those in action. It was not loss of life, however, but rapidity of movement that determined the outcome of the battle. On September 6, Admiral Tirpitz noted with alarm: 'We haven't succeeded in entrapping and taking prisoner large masses of troops; in consequence the French army, by means of their network of railways, are constantly taking up new positions.' That day, General Maunoury, who had expected to face the German army in the outskirts of Paris, advanced eastward from his entrenched encampments to attack the German right flank on the River Ourcq. So swift was his move and so fierce his attack that substantial German forces had to be detached from the main Marne battle in order to meet it.

To counter this extra assault, Maunoury appealed to Gallieni for more troops. Two infantry regiments of Zouaves had just reached Paris from Tunis. Requisitioning more than 2,000 Parisian taxi cabs, Gallieni sent the new arrivals by road to the battlefield. Commented the German First Army commander, General von Kluck: 'There was only one general who, against all the rules, would have dared to carry the fight so far from his base; unluckily for me, that man was Gallieni.'

The Battle of the Marne lasted four days. It marked the destruction of the Schlieffen Plan and the end to any chance of a rapid German victory in the west. The number of troops engaged during the battle was enormous: 1,275,000 Germans in action against 1,000,000 French and 125,000 British troops. The ferocity of the actions reflected the determination of the Anglo-French forces to reverse the tide of retreat. In one action, at Guebarré Farm, French troops managed to site a machine gun in such a way that it could, from five hundred yards, fire the length of a German trench that had been dug during the night. Several German attempts to surrender were ignored. When the French eventually ceased firing, six German officers and eighty-seven men emerged from the trench to surrender. More than 450 lay remained in the trench: the dead and the wounded.

On September 7, as the British army advanced, men who had hoped for a brief rest set their faces northward 'in a spirit of cheery resolution', a wartime staff officer, Sir Frank Fox, has written. 'It was an inspiring thought', he added, 'that the time had now come to chase the German.' But as the advance proceeded, death continued to impose its rule of chance. That day an officer who had arrived from Britain a few hours earlier, Second Lieutenant H.A. Boyd, was killed in a skirmish. 'In those early days of the war,' Fox noted, 'this cutting off of a young officer just as he came to realise the dearest ambition of a soldier's life – to go into action in defence of his country – impressed his comrades with a deep sense of tragedy. Later, one's resolution had to be steeled against this, as against the other losses. . . .'

British losses during both the retreat and the advance were severe. A monument at La Ferté-sous-Jouarre records the names of 3,888 British soldiers killed at Mons, Le Câteau, on the Aisne and on the Marne, for whom there were no known graves. The violence of the fighting had destroyed their bodies beyond recognition. Among the names on the monument at La Ferté-sous-Jouarre is that of Private Thomas Highgate. He had not been killed in battle, however, but executed after a Court Martial. He had been found hiding in a barn at Tournan, on the estate of Baron Edouard de Rothschild, just south of the Marne. When found, Highgate was dressed in civilian clothing, his uniform at his side. Questioned by the gamekeeper who discovered him, he said: 'I want to get out of it and this is how I am doing it.' By a remarkable, and for Highgate a most unfortunate coincidence, the gamekeeper was an Englishman and an ex-soldier.

1 The Archduke Franz Ferdinand and his wife in Sarajevo, on the day of their fateful journey, 28 June 1914.

2 The arrest of Gavrilo Princip (being held on the right).

3 Princip in Austrian custody at Theresienstadt military prison.

4 Bethmann-Hollweg, German Chancellor.

5 General Putnik, Chief of Staff of the Serbian Army.

6 Admiral Tirpitz, Commander-in-Chief of the German Navy.

7 Enver Pasha, Turkish Minister of War.

8 The people of Munich welcome the coming of war, among them a 25-year-old Austrian citizen, Adolf Hitler (circled and inset), 1 August 1914.

9 German troops on their way to the front, August 1914. They are travelling 'to Paris' in a wagon originating from Alsace-Lorraine (Elsaß-Lothringen).

10 British troops on their way to the front, 1914.

11 German troops marching through Flanders fields, 1914.

12 Belgian troops take up action stations on the road between Louvain and Brussels, 20 August 1914.

13 The retreat from Mons, British soldiers resting at Gournay, 2 September 1914. The officer standing,
Lieutenant Arkwright, was killed later in the war while flying.

14 Scottish soldiers in retreat across
the Marne, La Ferté sous Jouarre,
10 September 1914.

15 Recruiting poster: Lord Kitchener,
drawn by Alfred Leete.

16 Among the German troops entering Brussels: the German Naval Corps.

17 Belgian refugees fleeing from Ypres.

Private Highgate was handed over to the British military authorities and tried for desertion, by a Court Martial consisting of a colonel, a captain and a lieutenant. He was sentenced to death and shot. In his will in the back of his army paybook he left everything he owned, such as it was, to his girl-friend in Dublin. In the published army records he is listed as 'Died of wounds'. On the day of his execution, Private Highgate was not the only British soldier to die away from the battlefield. 'I am sorry to say', Smith-Dorrien wrote in his diary on September 7, 'that two of our men had to be shot today, one for plundering, and the other for desertion.'

Whatever shell-shock, exhaustion, or fear might have led to Highgate trying to hide from the battle, it was not to serve in his defence. Yet the inability of some soldiers to go on fighting was a feature of every battle. As the German retreat from the Marne gained momentum, some German soldiers also lost the will to fight, one German officer telling his superiors of 'panics behind the line'.

On September 7 the Kaiser was driven towards the battle zone, but the colonel who was escorting him towards it when they came within the sound of artillery fire feared that a French cavalry patrol might break through the already retreating line and capture the Supreme War Lord. The Kaiser left the war zone. That day, a German counter-attack by the Prussian Guard was beaten off by the artillery of Foch's Ninth Army. 'The French artillery had an unexpected effect,' the German official history recorded. 'The intended attack was everywhere nipped in the bud. . . . The 7th September was the worst day in the war so far for troops.' That day, General Moltke, reflecting on the blood that had been spilled during one month of war, wrote to his wife: 'Terror often overcomes me when I think of this, and the feeling I have is that I must answer for this horror.' There was also alarm in Germany on a practical level. 'It is now certain that England is bringing over great numbers of troops from Asia,' Admiral Tirpitz, whose ships had no means of preventing this, wrote home on September 7.

Anglo-French confidence was growing. In a private letter home on September 8, a member of Sir John French's Staff wrote back to London: 'The tide of invasion seems to have ebbed, and without a serious conflict. One is inclined to think that they have shot their bolt and spent their strength within sight of their goal.' The fragility of warfare was also shown that day, however, when an unexpected German infantry attack, unheralded by any preliminary artillery fire, surprised three French divisions of Foch's Ninth Army, together with one of his reserve divisions, all of whom fled to the rear. In their flight they abandoned the village of Fère-Champenoise and left Foch's advanced headquarters at Pleurs almost in the front line. It was only when the French soldiers had retreated six miles behind their overnight positions that they could be persuaded to stop, and to regroup.

The Germans, unaware of how far back the French soldiers facing them had fallen, contented themselves with entering the vacated French front line positions and digging in. A few units entered the deserted streets of Fère-Champenoise. But nothing was done to exploit the morning's success. Commented Liddell Hart, in his biography of Foch: 'The "victorious" Germans, in fact, had merely staggered forward like blind-drunk men, and were unable to give the High Command any light on the situation beyond reports of their own "extreme exhaustion".'

Foch took immediate steps to fill the gap that had been created by the unexpected German advance. The French counter-attack that he ordered caused panic among the Germans, who themselves fell back. Their earlier advance had been part of a strategy designed to facilitate the wider German withdrawal. Realising this, Foch concluded his report to Joffre on the night of September 8: 'The situation is therefore excellent; the attack directed against the Ninth Army appears to be a means to assure the retreat of the German right wing.' This confident message was later 'improved' by legend to the majestic declaration: 'My right is driven in, my centre is giving way, the situation is excellent, I attack.'

That evening, General von Kluck was nearly captured by a squadron of French cavalrymen who penetrated behind the line and, after attacking a German air base south of La Ferté-Milon, moved towards his headquarters there. 'All members of the Staff seized rifles, carbines, and revolvers,' he recalled four years later, 'so as to ward off a possible advance of the French cavalrymen, and extended out and lay down, forming a long firing line. The dusky red and clouded evening sky shed a weird light on this quaint little fighting force.' Learning that the French squadron has been beaten off, von Kluck later reflected: 'These bold horsemen had missed a goodly prize!'

By means of a night attack on September 8 the French Fifth Army, which Lanrezac had commanded during its long retreat from Belgium, captured the village of Marchais-en-Brie. The army's new commander, General Franchet d'Esperey, was determined to force a decision against von Bülow. In order to face d'Esperey, von Bülow abandoned Montmirail and took up a line facing Paris. This new line, which ran from north to south between Margny and Le Thoult, opened the way for the French to move towards the Marne. Cut off from von Kluck and the First Army, von Bülow gave the order to retire behind the Marne.

Amid these German difficulties, Foch's offensive zeal, though in reality often tempered by caution and retrenchment, gained a life of its own. On September 9, while some of his troops were again falling back before a renewed German attack, he issued a proclamation that was truly majestic. 'I ask each one of you to draw upon the last spark of energy which in its moments of supreme trial has never been denied to our race,' he declared. 'The disorder in the enemy's ranks is the forerunner of victory. By continuing with the greatest energy the effort already begun we are certain to stop the march of the enemy and then drive him from the soil of our country. But everyone must be convinced that success belongs to him who holds out longest. The honour and safety of France are in the balance. One more effort and you are sure to win.'

The French retreat continued for several hours. Foch was told by one of his commanders: 'In all ranks there was no question but of retirement.' It was a crisis time, with General Eydoux, the commander of the Ninth Army reserves, telling Foch that it was even too late to expect an orderly retirement. At this Foch replied: 'You say you cannot hold on, and that you cannot withdraw, so the only thing left is to attack.' The attack was to begin within two and a half hours, and was to be carried out 'under any and all circumstances'. In fact, the exhausted French troops were not tested on this occasion. Four hours earlier the advancing Germans had halted, having received an order from General von Bülow to retreat, as four British divisions were even then marching through the open gap between his army and that of von Kluck.

The German retreat brought with it several instances of cruelty for the civilians caught up in it. That day, September 9, when German troops left the villages of Varreddes on the north bank of the Marne, in place of twenty of their own wounded men who remained at the Town Hall they took twenty elderly villagers as hostages. Three escaped. Seven were murdered on the march. The 77-year-old M. Jourdain and the 78-year-old M. Milliardet, both of whom collapsed with exhaustion, were shot at point-blank range. When the 67-year-old M. Mesnil fell down, his skull was smashed in with the butt end of a rifle. During the recapture of Sompuis, where a seventy-year-old Frenchman, M. Jacquemin, was being held captive in his home and repeatedly beaten by a German officer, a shell fell on the house killing the officer. As a result of the ill-treatment he had received, Jacquemin died two days after the town was liberated. These were the incidental cruelties and individual victims of a war that was to claim millions of victims before it had run its course. During the recapture of Sompuis, just south of the Marne, a single German shell killed the commanders of two French brigades, General Barbade and Colonel Hamon.

On September 9 the Germans were driven back across the Marne, and on the 13th across the Aisne, a total retreat of sixty miles since the battle began. Never again were they to get so near to the French capital until, in the summer of 1940, revenge and aerial blitzkrieg succeeded where calculation and strategy had failed, and another French Government, which had likewise fled to Bordeaux, sued for an armistice. In 1914 there was to be no such collapse. As the French Government prepared to return to the capital, the great German flanking movement was itself being outflanked. French and British forces, hurrying northward towards the Channel coast, fought to prevent the Germans from continuing their westward thrust, or from cutting off the British from their cross-Channel lines of supply.

The race to the sea was the second decisive phase of the war in the west.

FROM MONS TO THE MARNE

Sir John French warned London not to underestimate the German military capacity. 'It will never do to oppose them with anything but very highly trained troops led by the best officers,' he wrote to Kitchener on September 7, during the German retreat. 'All their movements are marked by extra-ordinary unity of purpose and mutual support; and to undergo the fatigues they have suffered they must be under an absolutely iron discipline.'

The Germans, for their part, recognised the qualities of their so-recently contemptible adversary. 'From the bushes bordering on the river,' a German officer wrote during the retreat, 'sprang up and advanced a second line of skirmishers, with at least ten paces interval from man to man. Our artillery flashed and hit – naturally, at most, a single man. And the second line held on and pushed always nearer and nearer. Two hundred yards behind it came a third wave, a fourth wave. Our artillery fired like mad: all in vain. A fifth, a sixth line came on, all with good distance, and with clear intervals between the men. Splendid, we are all filled with admiration. The whole wide plain was now filled with these funny khaki figures, always coming nearer.'

'For five solid days we have been pursuing instead of pursued,' Sir John French wrote to a friend on September 10, 'and the Germans have had simple Hell. This very day we have captured several hundred, cut off a whole lot of transport and got ten to twelve guns – and the ground is strewn with dead and wounded Germans. Something like this happened yesterday, and the day before. But that is nothing to what they have lost in front of the Fifth and Sixth French Armies which have been much more strongly opposed. They are indeed fairly on the run and we are following hard.'

When, during the German retreat, Foch entered Fère-Champenoise, he noted that the German troops there had been caught by surprise after a night of hard drinking, 'such a carouse that hundreds of them were sleeping off their wine in their cellars. I saw some of them on the house-tops running like cats and being brought down with a flying shot.' Paul Maze, riding up to the front line on a German cavalry horse that had been abandoned in the retreat, saw two riders coming unexpectedly in his direction. 'Rather startled I waited, my carbine cocked, as I saw they were German soldiers mounted on black horses. They raised their hands on seeing me. They were lost and had been searching for someone to whom to surrender.'

Shortly after this encounter Paul Maze came to a château that was flying a Red Cross flag. 'French surgeons, wearing blood-stained aprons, were smoking cigarettes, contemplating with an air of satisfaction the catch of prisoners below them. German Red Cross men were carrying to waiting carts the wounded who lay on stretchers on every step of a broad marble staircase. There were no ambulances – the medical arrangements seemed very inadequate. A convoy of private motor cars with English wounded passed on the roads, making for Rothschild's château at Chantilly that had been turned into a hospital.'

On the Meuse Front, Fort Troyon, ten miles south of Verdun, was besieged on September 8. For five days the Germans subjected it to an intense artillery bombardment. German emissaries twice called on the fort to surrender 'in the name of the Emperor'. When the defenders answered 'never', the Germans fired 236 shells within half an hour: in all, 10,000 shells were fired. Twenty-two men were crushed to death when a shell blew in the roof of the narrow underground passage through which they were trying to reach the main defenders. The French commanding officer, Commander Toussaint, and a single infantry detachment of 472 men, together with a dozen artillery pieces and two machine guns, held out for five days, but they were overwhelmed in the end. The French High Command decided to withdraw from Verdun altogether, but the local army commander, General Sarrail, ignored the order and remained in possession of the city and its fortresses.

Denied their triumphal entry into Paris, the German army would go on fighting on the Western Front for another four years, as hopeful of victory in August 1918 as they had been in August 1914. But the hopes of a month earlier of being able to defeat France in a knock-out blow and then turn all their military strength against Russia had been dashed. The war of rapid victories had become a strategy of the past, and a dream for the future. Germany was going to have to fight simultaneously, and with constant danger, in both east and west. France was going to have to fight on French soil. Russia was going to have to regain land in the west and Austria to regain land in the east. Christmas was still three and a half months away, but every warring State was going to have to search for new strategies, and even new allies.

5

Digging in: the start of trench warfare

SEPTEMBER–OCTOBER 1914

As the Germans were being driven back from the Marne, with their plan for a swift victory in the west shattered, the Austrians were struggling to avoid being driven back by the Russians across their Galician frontier. On 10 September 1914, the day on which Joffre ordered the pursuit of the Germans north of the Marne with the words 'Victory is now in the legs of the infantry', at Krasnik, just inside the border of Russian Poland, the Russians defeated a substantial Austrian army that had advanced on to Russian soil. Further south, inside Austrian Galicia, a Russian victory led Conrad to order an Austrian retreat. 'Today, very early, we abandoned ship with everything on it,' Ludwig Wittgenstein wrote in his diary on September 13. 'The Russians are on our heels. Have lived through frightful scenes. No sleep for thirty hours, am feeling very weak and can see no external help.'

The war of rapid victories having receded, every warring State sought to enlist the help of disaffected peoples. In the hope of creating difficulties for Britain, the German Military Attaché in Washington, Franz von Papen (who in 1932 became Chancellor of Germany, and in 1933 Hitler's first Vice-Chancellor), talked on September 13 with a former British diplomat, Sir Roger Casement, who wished to enlist German help to achieve the independence of Ireland. Casement suggested to the Germans the setting up of an Irish Brigade that would fight alongside Germany. 'They are keen for it,' he wrote to a friend on the following day, 'keener now than ever as they realise its moral value to their case.' Germany would be fighting the battle for the small nation of Ireland just as Britain was fighting for Belgium.

To further this aim, and to enlist German support for a national uprising in Ireland itself, Casement sailed under a false name from New York to Germany. Three weeks after his arrival he persuaded the German Government to issue a formal declaration that 'Should the fortunes of this great war, that was not of Germany's seeking, ever bring in its course German troops to the shores of Ireland, they would land there, not as an army of invaders to pillage and destroy, but as the forces of a government that is inspired by good-will towards a country and a people for whom Germany desires only national prosperity and national freedom.'

Irish soldiers were never to fight alongside the Germans as patriots or liberators, but from the very start of the war Polish soldiers were fighting alongside the Austrians, hoping that an Austrian victory over Russia would lead to the re-establishment of the Polish nation. The Austrians encouraged the Polish Legion, led by Pilsudski, to regard itself as the precursor to a Polish national army. To counteract the attraction of this force to all Poles, the Russians called on those under their rule to regard a Russian victory as something from which Polish national aspirations could gain. A volunteer Pulawy Legion was set up, of Poles who would fight as a Polish entity in the Russian army. This was followed by a Polish Rifle Brigade. Just as Jew was fighting against Jew (as in the case of Wittgenstein in the Austrian army and the Jewish soldiers among the Russian troops pushing him back), so Pole was set against Pole.

Later in the war, the Germans formed a Polish military force to garrison Polish territory conquered from Russia. On the other side of the conflict, Polish soldiers who fought in the ranks of the German army and were captured on the Western Front formed the basis of a Polish army fighting alongside the Allies. Canada also encouraged recruiting into specially established Polish formations of its army. Later the Americans did likewise. Nearly two million Poles served in the fighting lines, of whom 450,000 were killed. The tragedy of this for Poland was expressed in September 1914 by the poet Edward Slonski:

> *We're kept far apart, my brother,*
> *By a fate that we can't deny.*
> *From our two opposing dug-outs*
> *We're staring death in the eye.*
>
> *In the trenches filled with groaning,*
> *Alert to the shellfire's whine,*
> *We stand and confront each other.*
> *I'm your enemy: and you are mine.*

Slonski was confident, however, that in the long term all was not lost for Poland by this fratricidal tragedy:

> *Now I see the vision clearly,*
> *Caring not that we'll both be dead;*
> *For that which has not perished*
> *Shall rise from the blood we shed.*

The hopes of minorities could be raised in unusual ways. On the Eastern Front the first award of the Cross of St George, the equivalent of the Victoria Cross in Britain, awarded by the Tsar for exceptional bravery on the field of battle, went to a Jewish soldier, Leo Osnas. According to a British newspaper, the *Yorkshire Herald*, by his bravery in action Osnas 'has won freedom for the Jews in Russia; he has gained for his race the right to become officers in the Russian army and navy, hitherto denied them, and he has so delighted the Russian government that it has since proclaimed that henceforth Jews in the Empire shall enjoy the full rights of citizenship.' Commented the newspaper: 'Surely no man's winning of the "V.C." ever resulted in such magnificent results for a subject people as this!' In fact, the Jews of Russia did not receive full citizenship during the war; nor did they escape repeated violent attacks on them by Russian townsmen and villagers looking for scapegoats for Russia's military set-backs.[1]

According to the reports reaching Britain, Osnas was a volunteer. The status of volunteer was one which, as a result of Kitchener's appeal, had suddenly gained in stature. On September 12 it was announced in Britain that the astounding total of 478,893 men had enlisted as volunteers since the outbreak of war six weeks earlier. Without following the continental system of compulsory service, Britain had acquired a substantial army.[2]

Many of these volunteers served in special 'Pals battalions' made up entirely of men from a particular town, or from a professional or work circle. The first of these to be formed was in London, a Stockbrokers' Battalion of whom 1,600 enlisted within a single week. Many cities quickly followed, the Bristol Citizens' Battalion and the Liverpool Pals being among the earliest. In Glasgow it was decided to raise two: very quickly enough men enlisted to form three, one of them entirely drawn from the drivers, conductors, mechanics and labourers of the city's Tramways Department. Known as the Tramways Battalion, they formed the fifteenth battalion of the Highland Light Infantry. The sixteenth was made up almost entirely of past and present members of the City's Boys' Brigade.

This pattern was repeated all over Britain. Even Labour men opposed to the war supported the drive for volunteers: Ramsay MacDonald, under attack for his public anti-war sentiments, supported the call for recruits in his constituency, Leicester. Within a month, fifty Pals battalions had been set up. 'Kitchener's Army' was in being, and was slowly being made ready for war. What its quality would be could only be guessed at. One professional soldier, General Henry Wilson, had no doubts. The volunteers were a 'ridiculous and preposterous army', he wrote in his diary. They would be 'the laughing stock of every soldier in Europe'. It had taken the Germans forty years 'of incessant work' to make their army, with the aid of conscription. 'It will take us an eternity to do the same by voluntary effort.'

*

[1] Osnas had won his medal on 5 September 1914. The report quoted above appeared in the *Yorkshire Herald* of 18 October 1914, and is reprinted in issue No. 28 of *Gun Fire, A Journal of First World War History,* a magazine edited in York by A.J. Peacock, who is also the author of *York in the Great War 1914–1918.*
[2] This figure was only 16,000 less than the total number of men raised in Britain by compulsory service during the whole of 1918.

In France, there was a further reprisal on September 12, after two German cavalrymen had been killed by French soldiers south-west of Reims, near the village of Bouilly. Declaring that the deaths had been caused by the villagers, the Germans destroyed the village. In Belgium, as the German retreat from the Marne gathered momentum, the Belgian Field Army launched a substantial counter-attack, in the hope of forcing the Germans to call troops back from their confrontation with the British and French in the decisive southern battlefield. By September 13 four Belgian divisions had reached the outskirts of the village of Weerde, eighteen miles south of Antwerp, and scarcely twelve miles north of German-occupied Brussels.

The American journalist E. Alexander Powell, having watched the Belgian troops go forward towards Weerde, then witnessed the sequel. 'Back through the hedges, across the ditches, over the roadway came the Belgian infantry, crouching, stooping, running for their lives. Every now and then a soldier would stumble, as though he had stubbed his toe, and throw out his arms and fall headlong. A bullet had hit him. The road was sprinkled with silent forms in blue and green. The fields were sprinkled with them too. One man was hit as he struggled to get through a hedge and died standing, held upright by the thorny branches.' A young Belgian officer 'who had been recklessly exposing himself while trying to check the retreat of his men, suddenly spun around on his heels, like one of those wooden toys which the kerb vendors sell, and then crumpled up, as though all the bone and muscle had gone out of him.' Nearby, a soldier 'plunged into a half-filled ditch and lay there with his head under water. I could see the water slowly redden.'

Weerde remained in German hands. Malines, two miles to the north, was occupied soon afterwards and Louvain regained. German troops and their Austrian siege guns were free to turn their attentions to the last significant Belgian city still in Belgian control, the port city of Antwerp, where the Belgian troops who had so recently gone forward more than half way to Brussels now reinforced the defenders of the forts around the perimeter.

Despite the violent surprises of the battlefield, the optimism of the Allied commanders survived. On September 13, the day of the Belgian defeat at Weerde, a conference of French and British generals met at Joffre's headquarters. The dominant feature of the conflict was the continuing German retreat from the Marne. There was a discussion about how many days it would take before the German armies would be pushed back across the German border. A British general, Henry Wilson, said four weeks. Some of the French generals thought it might be three. Victory could still come by Christmas.

'Defeat' and 'victory' were becoming familiar words. So too was 'casualty', a word that, with the statistics that came with it, blended together 'killed', 'missing' and 'wounded'. The phrase 'heavy casualties' associated with almost every victory or retreat could mean hundreds, even thousands of deaths. The newspapers of all the warring States were publishing obituary notices of officers, and casualty lists, on a daily basis. There were few readers who did not know someone at the front. On September 13, General Foch learned of the death both of his son-in-law and of his only son. They had been killed in action on the Belgian border three weeks earlier. When he was brought the news, Foch asked his staff to leave him for a while. Half an hour later he called them back with the words: 'Now let's get on with our work.' Later he wrote to his lifelong friend General Millet: 'I have discreetly broken the news to my wife, who is still at Plougean. One ought to disregard everything, and yet I quake as I think of the disturbance which is bound to occur there, to the grief of my poor women folk. For my part I am steeling myself on this subject so as not to fail in my duty.' In this letter Foch also commiserated on Millet's own 'desolation', for his son-in-law had also been killed and his daughter had died of grief on hearing the news. Millet himself died within a month of these tragedies.

On September 14, General Moltke was removed from his post as Chief of the German General Staff. The Battle of the Marne had been his nemesis, a mere six weeks after the start of the war. One historian has described him as 'a cultured, sensitive soldier who, in his spare time, liked to play the cello, read Goethe and Maeterlinck, and was interested in the faith-healing teachings of the Christian Scientists'.[1] Failure had claimed its first scapegoat among the mighty. Moltke had found the casualty lists unbearable.

September 14 saw the death of the first British Public School master to be killed in action, Alexander Williamson, then serving as a lieutenant in the Seaforth Highlanders.[2] That day also saw the death of Percy Wyndham, a grandson of one of Britain's wealthiest men, the 1st Duke of Westminster. Three days earlier Wyndham had written to his mother: 'Supply me with socks and chocolates which are the two absolute necessities of life.' He was killed leading his men at Soupir, shot in the head at close range.

There were individual soldiers in all the warring armies who could not face the intensity of battle. On September 16, on only the third day of his active service, a twenty-year-old British soldier, Private George Ward, had left the battlefield after two companions had been wounded, telling his sergeant-major that he too had been hit. Six days later, Ward reported back to his battalion, where he was found to be unwounded, and was court-martialled. His Corps Commander, General Sir Douglas Haig, wrote on the court-martial file, 'I am of the opinion that it is necessary to make an example to prevent cowardice in the face of the enemy as far as possible.' Ward was shot, then buried on the banks of the Aisne. Like Private

[1] Alan Palmer, *Who's Who in Modern History*, Weidenfeld and Nicolson, London 1980, page 234.
[2] Williamson had taught at Highgate School, in North London, where he had earlier been a pupil. His was one of 113 names on the school war memorial, which was my first realisation of the scale of the death toll in the First World War.

Highgate, executed three weeks earlier, he is commemorated on the memorial at La Ferté-sous-Jouarre to those who were killed in action but had no known grave.[1]

Execution was not always the penalty for desertion. On the same day that Ward was sentenced to death, at the same place and for the same offence, Corporal N. Prior was reduced to the rank of private and given two years hard labour.

The severe morality of the battlefield was matched at home by a growing sense of sacrifice, and sternness of outlook, expressed on September 19 by the British Chancellor of the Exchequer, David Lloyd George, when he told a vast audience at the Queen's Hall in London: 'A great flood of luxury and of sloth which had submerged the land is receding and a new Britain is appearing. We can see for the first time the fundamental things that matter in life, and that have been obscured from our vision by the tropical growth of prosperity.' In Russia this sentiment had already been expressed, if in a more prosaically political way, by a declaration of the Social Democrat Party in the Duma after the outbreak of war that 'through the agony of the battlefield the brotherhood of the Russian people will be strengthened and a common desire created to free the land from its terrible internal troubles'.

This high moral tone, whether of 'fundamental things' or of 'brotherhood', required to be backed by an ability to win on the battlefield. Yet within seven weeks of the outbreak of the war, the first warning bell was being sounded: in the French army a shortage of ammunition had begun to impede the ability of the gunners to exploit the German retreat. On September 19 Joffre wrote direct to the Minister of War, Alexandre Millerand, asking for at least 50,000 rounds a day to be sent to him, if he was to continue the advance. Millerand replied two days later that this figure could not be reached, though he 'did not despair' of achieving a rate of 30,000 rounds a day in three weeks' time. He went on to tell Joffre, 'on your side' to do everything possible to prevent waste. 'Please see that fatigue parties gather up the cartridge cases left on the battlefields, or else offer to pay the inhabitants for all they bring in.'

In search of untapped sources of shells, Joffre scoured the gun batteries behind the lines, including those of Paris and Dunkirk. These were improvised, even desperate measures, far from the triumphant cry of 'À Berlin!' of seven weeks earlier. But the difficulties of waging war did not necessarily create doubts about its outcome. 'Here the feeling is absolutely united; and running breast high for a prolonged and relentless struggle. There will I think be no difficulty in putting a million men in the field in the spring

---

[1] Privates Highgate and Ward were the first two of more than three hundred British soldiers shot for cowardice or desertion during the First World War. With the opening of the court-martial records in 1988, a campaign was mounted for a posthumous pardon for them all, on the grounds that those executed had been suffering from shell-shock and other battle stresses. In 1993 the British Government rejected the plea for pardon.

of 1915,' Churchill wrote from London on September 20 to a friend in the country, and he added: 'Doom has fallen upon Prussian military arrogance. Time and determination are all that is needed.' On the following day the sense of loss for the many thousands already bereaved was expressed in *The Times*, when the paper published a poem, 'For the Fallen', written by Laurence Binyon, a 45-year-old art historian. Binyon, who is said to have written the words sitting on a cliff at Polzeath, in Cornwall, had volunteered as a Red Cross nursing orderly in France. After the war four of his lines became the single most recited verse in Britain during commemoration of the war dead:

> *They shall grow not old, as we that are left grow old,*
> *Age shall not weary them, nor the years condemn.*
> *At the going down of the sun and in the morning*
> *We will remember them.*

On September 22 the British made their first air raid on Germany, attacking Zeppelin sheds at Cologne and Düsseldorf. 'The surprise was complete,' the senior British pilot reported, 'and the numerous Germans in the vicinity ran in all directions.' That day, however, a German submarine, the *U-9*, torpedoed three British cruisers, the *Aboukir*, *Cressy* and *Hogue*, within the space of an hour: although 837 men were rescued, 1,459 were drowned. It was to be the worst British naval disaster of the whole war. A week later Asquith instructed the Admiralty to mine the North Sea 'without stinting, and if necessary on a Napoleonic scale'.

In the Indian Ocean on September 22 the German raider, the light-cruiser *Emden*, which had already sunk or captured a dozen British merchant ships, bombarded the Burma Oil Company depot at Madras, igniting 50,000 tons of naval fuel oil. Commented a relative of the Kaiser, Prince Joseph of Hohenzollern, who was serving on board: 'It was very lucky for Madras that the wind was westerly so that the flames from the oil tanks stood out seawards. If the opposite had been the case part of the town might easily have been destroyed by the flames.'

Across the globe the incidents of war proliferated. Newspaper readers in all lands were confronted by a plethora of daily incidents, some important to one region or people, some to another. No day passed without the range and scale of the war being evident. For a brief moment on September 23, for example, Serbian troops threatened to overrun Sarajevo, but were driven off by Austrian troops. That same day, in the Far East, British, Australian and Japanese troops were moving against the many scattered German ports and islands, acquired by Germany during the previous three decades. German ports in Africa were likewise being seized.

In the search for allies against the Turks, should Turkey enter the war, Britain was trying to enlist the help of the Sherif of Mecca's son Abdullah, and offering the Arabs control of vast regions of the Turkish Empire in return for Arab participation. In neutral Washington, President Wilson was protesting to the British Government that Britain's naval blockade of Germany would have 'evil effects' on American public opinion. Also in North America, Canadian troops were preparing to embark on the Atlantic crossing, intent on participating in the war before it ended.

Whether the war would end by Christmas, as so many had earlier imagined, was being questioned. A German soldier taking part in the race to the sea wrote home: 'I have the impression that the war will last a long time. Well, I shall hold out even if it goes on for another year.' He was killed shortly after writing his letter.

On September 26, at St Mihiel, between Verdun and Toul, the Germans besieged the French fortress of Camp des Romains. Despite being cut off, and subjected to heavy artillery and grenade attacks, the garrison refused repeated demands to surrender. A smoke attack finally forced them out. According to a report published a month later in the *New York Times*, 'When the survivors of the plucky garrison were able to march out, they found their late opponents presenting arms before them in recognition of their gallant stand. They were granted the most honourable terms of surrender, their officers were allowed to retain their swords, and on the march to honourable captivity they were everywhere greeted with expressions of respect and admiration.' Five officers and three hundred men were taken prisoner.

The Germans were intent on reaching the Belgian and French coastline. On the day of the fall of Camps des Romains, German artillery began the bombardment of the forts defending Antwerp. With Liège and Namur having fallen, Antwerp possessed Belgium's last great ring of forts. In London, Kitchener and Grey recognised the importance of as long a resistance as possible at Antwerp. They were afraid that once the German troops who were attacking the city had conquered it, they would move rapidly towards the Channel ports, forcing the British army to retreat into western France, and possibly threatening Britain herself. Even one week's resistance would enable the British army to form a defensive line in Flanders, from which an attack could then be launched to liberate Belgium, and then drive the Germans back to Germany.

Determined to stiffen the ability of Antwerp to hold out for a few more days, Kitchener at once sent British heavy artillery and personnel to the city, and asked the French army to do likewise. On September 30 Asquith wrote to his friend Venetia Stanley: 'The Belgians are rather out of "morale", and are alarmed at the bombardment of Antwerp which has just begun. They are sending their archives and treasure over here, and talk of moving the seat of government to Ostend. Kitchener has given them some good advice – namely not to mind the bombardment of their forts, but to entrench themselves with barbed wire etc. in the intervening spaces, and challenge the Germans to come on.'

On October 1 the British Cabinet decided to send to Antwerp a whole division then on its way to Sir John French in northern France. On the following morning, the Germans penetrated two of the city's forts. Summoning Churchill that evening, Kitchener and Grey stressed the importance for the battle in France of a continued Belgian resistance in Antwerp. Churchill offered to go to Antwerp himself and report on the situation. He left London that night, and spent the next three days in the trenches and fortifications of the city, and in discussions with the Belgian Government, which had moved to Antwerp after the fall of Brussels, hoping to stiffen its resolve. But, he telegraphed to Kitchener on October 4, the Belgian troops were 'weary and disheartened', especially as the ground between the forts and the city was so waterlogged, partly as a result of deliberate flooding, that they were unable to dig trenches for their protection.

In an attempt to prolong the defence of the city long enough to enable the British Expeditionary Force to reach the coastal region before the Germans, the Belgian Government appealed to Britain for troops. Such troops as were available were sent at once, 2,000 men of the Royal Naval Division on October 4, and a further 6,000 on the following day. Among these troops was the poet Rupert Brooke, who, with hundreds of others, had recently volunteered to serve in the division, which had been set up by Churchill on the outbreak of war. Brought straight from their barracks in Britain, where two-thirds of them had just begun training, some had never fired a rifle or used an entrenching tool. They arrived from Ostend in London buses whose sides still bore their peace-time routes and destinations: Bank, Holborn, Piccadilly, Shepherd's Bush and Strand.

It was not intended that the men of the Royal Naval Division, which included one fully trained Marine Brigade, would be on their own for long. Twenty-two thousand professional British troops, a full division, were at that very moment on their way from Britain, crossing by sea to Ostend. 'It is most necessary', Kitchener telegraphed to Churchill on October 5, 'that the Belgians should not give way before the forces now on the sea arrive for their support.' For the citizens of Antwerp, with 8,000 British soldiers already in the city, it seemed that deliverance had arrived. Cries of 'Vive les Anglais!' and 'Vive Tommy Atkins!' resounded through the streets.[1]

Louise Mack, an Australian woman who was in Antwerp on October 5 noted in her diary that day: 'Haggard, hollow-eyed, exhausted, craving the rest they may not have, these glorious heroes revive as if by magic under the knowledge that other troops are coming to help theirs in this gargantuan struggle for Antwerp. The yellow khaki seems to sweep along with the blue uniforms like sunlight.' The presence of British troops even seemed to give a different perspective to the distant noise of the guns. 'The boom of the cannon is growing fainter and fainter,' Louise Mack wrote

---

[1] The original Tommy Atkins, who gave the name 'tommy' to the British soldier, was a private in the Royal Welch Fusiliers who fought in the American War of Independence. In 1829 the Duke of Wellington chose the name as an example for the Soldiers' Account Book.

on October 5, 'as the Germans appear to be pushed further and further back.' This was an illusion. Although on the following day the much larger British force of 22,000 men reached Ostend, the decision of the French Government not to send any troops of its own, as previously promised, caused the British to hesitate and hold back.

Late on the evening of October 7, using their 17-inch Austrian howitzers, the Germans, who had hitherto concentrated on the forts, began the bombardment of Antwerp itself. The first shell fell near the cathedral. 'As it exploded,' wrote Louise Mack, 'I shut my eyes, clenched my hands, and sank on the floor by my bedside, saying to myself, "God, I'm dead!" And I thought I was too. The enormity of that sound-sensation seemed to belong to a transition from this world to the next. It scarcely seemed possible to pass through that noise and come out alive.' The first person to be killed inside the city was a fourteen-year-old boy. The second to be killed was a street sweeper decapitated as he was running for shelter.

The ferocity of the bombardment was such that the defenders had no means of counter-attack. Against the Austrian 17-inch guns the British 6-inch naval guns and 4.7-inch howitzers were outmatched. Nor would the British division still at Ostend move forward without the French, who, having halted at Ghent, refused to do so. 'The French having failed us,' Asquith wrote to Venetia on October 8, 'and the Belgian field army being quite untrustworthy, there is alas! nothing to be done but to order our naval men to evacuate the trenches tonight.' Asquith, one of whose sons had been present at the siege, later elaborated on this remark about the Belgians, telling Venetia: 'The Belges ran away and had to be forced back at the point of the bayonet into the forts, while the Germans at a safe distance of five or six miles thundered away with their colossal howitzers.' The siege guns continued to bombard the city throughout October 9. On the following morning, after two days and nights of destruction, Antwerp could hold out no more. The King of the Belgians (who was married to a daughter of a Bavarian duke) was said to have fired the last shot before the surrender.[1]

Antwerp's prolonged resistance gave the British Expeditionary Force time to complete the move from its positions north-east of Paris, following the Battle of the Marne, to Flanders and the Channel ports. Inside Antwerp, E. Alexander Powell witnessed the march past of the victors in a parade that lasted five hours and in which 60,000 German soldiers took part, passing in review before the Military Governor, Admiral von Schroeder, and their commander, General von Beseler. After the massed ranks of the cavalrymen, riding with their lances held high, came the sailors of the German naval division, 'then the Bavarians in dark blue, the Saxons in light blue, and the Austrians – the same who had handled the big guns so

[1] Another pre-war dynastic link across the war lines: Queen Elisabeth of the Belgians was named after her father's favourite sister, Elisabeth, Empress of Austria, who had been assassinated by an anarchist at the turn of the century.

effectively – in uniforms of a beautiful silver grey.'

Fifty-seven British soldiers had been killed during the siege of Antwerp, 936 were taken prisoner-of-war and sent to camps inside Germany, and 1,600 retreated into neutral Holland, where they were interned for the rest of the war. Among those who managed to return to Britain was Rupert Brooke, who had celebrated the coming of war with the words:

> *Now, God be thanked Who has matched us with His hour,*
> *And caught our youth, and wakened us from sleeping.*

'This war is really the greatest insanity in which white races have ever been engaged,' Admiral Tirpitz wrote to his wife on October 4. 'We are exterminating each other on the continent for England to reap the benefit. Moreover perfidious Albion succeeds in holding us up before the world as the guilty party.' For the citizens of occupied Belgium, it was German rule that was proving onerous that autumn. On October 5 the Military Governor, Field Marshal Baron von der Goltz, issued a proclamation in which he stated: 'In future, villages in the vicinity of places where railway and telegraph lines are destroyed will be punished without pity (whether they are guilty or not of the acts in question). With this in view hostages have been taken in all villages near the railway lines which are threatened by such attacks. Upon the first attempt to destroy lines of railway, telegraph or telephone, they will be immediately shot.'

This was German ruthlessness, known in Britain as 'frightfulness': it was contrasted five days later in a private letter from Walter Rathenau to the Chancellery, in which, amongst all the madness generated in two months of war, the man who was charged with finding the raw materials essential to make war proposed 'a real peace'. It should be based, Rathenau believed, on the German evacuation of Belgium, reconciliation with France, and the creation of a European economic system that would bring together Germany, Austria, France and Belgium. Such a system would represent 'an internal victory far surpassing all external achievements'. Rathenau went on to point out that 'economic alliance with a neighbouring country included future political alliance also'. Eight years later Rathenau was to make these ideas the basis of his policy as Foreign Minister: they were to lead, also, to his assassination at the hands of anti-Semitic ultra-nationalists.

In Galicia, the Russian army continued to advance deep into Austria, and some Russian cavalrymen even crossed into Hungary. 'It looks bad for the Austrians,' was General Max Hoffmann's comment on September 26. 'They have saved money over their army for twenty years, and now they are paying for it.' But the Russian provinces of Poland, which had been annexed by Russia in the eighteenth century, were being slowly overrun, with Hoffmann's own strategic help, by the Hindenburg-Ludendorff combination, and battles of great intensity were opening up for Poland the prospect of an end to nearly 150 years of Russian rule. The question of whether the new rulers, the Germans, would grant Poland autonomy or independence was still unresolved. Extreme German nationalists were calling for the creation of a permanent buffer zone between Germany and Poland, carved out of Russian territory, from which sixteen million Poles would be deported into Russia, to make way for German settlers.

The neutral States, watching the daily progress of the war with their own national interests and ambitions in mind, could not see what its outcome would be, and remained spectators. The Entente powers, in their search for new allies and new armies, were finding great reluctance among the neutrals to participate. Italy, with her common border with Austria, and her territorial aspirations in the Adriatic, was an obvious Entente prize. Yet the Italian Government clung tenaciously to neutrality. It was challenged on October 10, when the future Italian Fascist leader, Benito Mussolini, then a leading socialist, published an article in a Socialist newspaper calling for a reversal of his party's anti-war stand and urging Italian participation on the side of the Entente. His hope was that war would lead to revolution and the fall of the monarchy. For the French Government, anxious to have Italy as an ally, the ultimate goal was unimportant: what mattered was to have an influential voice calling for war. To enable Mussolini's pro-war views to have the widest possible circulation, the French Government financed his first independent newspaper, *Popolo d'Italia*, providing him with funds on a monthly basis. The first payment was taken to him by a French Socialist politician.[1]

It was not payment, but patriotism, that led a German naval lieutenant, Karl Lody, to undertake an espionage mission in Britain immediately after the outbreak of war. Travelling from Berlin under a false American passport, he went first to Edinburgh, then to Rosyth, then to Liverpool, reporting by telegram to neutral Sweden on Britain's naval preparations and dispositions. Lody also reported on London's anti-aircraft defences. His telegrams were read by the British censor, seemed suspicious, and were stopped. The only one that was allowed through was his report of the rumour that Russian soldiers were on their way through Britain to France.

Lody was arrested on October 2, while on his way to the British naval base at Queenstown. He was tried by Court Martial at the Westminster Guildhall and sentenced to death by firing squad at the Tower of London. On the morning of his execution he said to the officer guarding him, 'I suppose you will not shake hands with a spy?' to which the officer replied, 'No, but I will shake hands with a brave man.' After Lody's execution, a British Intelligence chief wrote: 'He never flinched, he never cringed, but he died as one would wish all Englishmen to die – quietly and undramatically, supported in his courage by the proud consciousness of having done his

---

[1] The first issue of *Popolo d'Italia* appeared on 15 November 1914. Six months later the Russian Government discussed giving Mussolini similar financial support to urge the immediate entry of Italy into the war. In October 1917, after the Italian defeat at Caporetto, British Intelligence provided him with funds to combat anti-war sentiment in Italy.

duty.' In Berlin there was less praise. 'One must confess', wrote Lody's spymaster, 'that his capabilities for such important work were practically nil.'

On October 3, in the race to the sea, German forces entered the Belgian town of Ypres. Two days later the first air combat took place above France, when two French aviators shot down a German plane, whose crew of two was killed. On October 8, the first of sixteen German Zeppelins to be destroyed by British aircraft was bombed in its shed at Düsseldorf by a British pilot, Flight-Lieutenant Reginald Marix.[1]

On October 10, in an intensification of the drive north, the German Fourth Army was ordered 'to cut off the fortresses of Dunkirk and Calais'. That day a German cavalry detachment entered the northern French city of Lille. While they were in discussion with the Mayor, French cavalrymen arrived. There was a brief skirmish, and the Germans rode off. A few hours later German artillery fell on the city, and a German aeroplane dropped a bomb, killing a boy and a horse.

On October 11 the German bombardment of Lille began in earnest. Within two days more than 5,000 shells had been fired into the city and eight hundred buildings were destroyed. On October 13, Lille surrendered. The German troops who then occupied it were so exhausted by their previous exertions that many lay down on the pavements and slept.

The race for the sea was slowly being won by the British and French. On October 14, British troops drove the Germans out of Bailleul. They discovered that in the few weeks it had been under German occupation a war tax had been imposed on the farmers, and fourteen Frenchmen of military age had been rounded up and shot. Before leaving, the Germans had opened the doors of the local lunatic asylum, leaving hundreds of its inmates to wander about the countryside unaided. Many were later found dead by the roadsides or in the woods.

Violent death had become commonplace, calling forth different emotions. After one of his closest friends was killed by a chance shell on October 14, General Smith-Dorrien wrote in a private letter: 'Those who go to eternity before the task is completed are heroes, and must be thought of as such and not mourned.' Among those for whom a grave had been dug on the previous day was the 26-year-old Lieutenant Bernard Montgomery, who had been so seriously wounded that it was assumed that he would die. While leading his platoon of thirty men against the village of Méteren, a German rifle bullet had passed through his chest. A soldier who was trying to put a dressing on the wound was hit, and fell across him. As the two men lay there, both unable to move, the Germans continued firing. Montgomery was hit again in the knee. The soldier was killed. It was not for another four hours that stretcher bearers were able

---

[1] In 1916 Marix lost a leg while test flying an aeroplane near Paris. Between 1939 and 1945 he served in Coastal and Transport Commands, retiring with the rank of Air Vice-Marshal in 1945.

to bring Montgomery out. He was unconscious and believed to be dying. Comments one of his biographers: 'With characteristic lack of co-operation he declined to die and when the time came for the unit to move they had to take him with them.'[1]

On October 15 the Germans succeeded in entering the Belgian port of Ostend. 'It really is extraordinary how very unpopular we are,' Admiral Tirpitz wrote to his wife that day, after visiting Antwerp. Almost all of Belgium was now under occupation, and tens of thousands of Belgian refugees had arrived in England, stimulating anti-German feeling. On October 17 the London *Evening Standard* had a headline: 'Ridding London hotels of the enemy,' and listed those hotels 'today officially declared clear of Germans and Austrians'. On the following day Thomas Hardy wrote of his pastoral dream that the Belgian refugees would arrive in Britain with their bells and music:

> *Then I awoke; and lo, before me stood*
> *The visioned ones, but pale and full of fear;*
> *From Bruges they came, and Antwerp, and Ostend,*
>
> *No carillons in their train. Foes of mad mood*
> *Had shattered these to shards amid the gear*
> *Of ravaged roof, and smouldering gable-end.*

By the utmost exertions of British, French and Belgian troops, the limit of the German advance had been reached. At several points the most westerly German units were being driven eastward, back across the Franco-Belgian border. The French town of Armentières was retaken by the British. Among those killed at Armentières on October 18 was Churchill's cousin Norman Leslie. 'The ever widening conflagration of this war devours all that is precious, and the end is far away,' Churchill wrote in condolence to his cousin's mother, Leonie Leslie. 'The British army has in a few weeks of war revived before the whole world the glories of Agincourt and Blenheim and Waterloo, and in this Norman has played his part.'

Also on October 18, Ypres was recaptured from the Germans. From there, the British planned to push the Germans back through Belgium at least as far as Menin and Roulers. A few miles up the Menin Road, however, and along the railway line to Roulers, the Germans halted the British advance. During October 19, General Rawlinson, who had been instructed to 'move on Menin', hesitated: British pilots and Belgian refugees had reported that German reinforcements were being hurried forward. Menin, a mere twelve miles from Ypres, remained in German hands.

Hopes were high among the German soldiers, in particular those still behind the lines, for further victories. A German private just off to the

[1] Alun Chalfont, *Montgomery of Alamein*, Weidenfeld and Nicolson, London 1976, page 62. In the Second World War, Montgomery commanded the 8th Army in North Africa (defeating Rommel at Alamein) and then the 21st Army Group, from Normandy to Lüneburg Heath, where he took the surrender of all German forces in Belgium, Holland and north-west Germany.

front wrote to his pre-war landlord on October 20: 'Once we have arrived at our destination, I shall write to you straight away and send you my address. I hope we shall get to England.' That soldier was Adolf Hitler. Nine days later he was to be in action.

Determined to prevent German soldiers reaching England, and fearful of the reluctance of British sailors to open fire on troop transports, on October 22 Churchill informed his Admiralty officials: 'A precise order should be given that all transports believed to be conveying German troops to England are to be sunk by torpedo or gunfire. No parley with or surrender by a transport on the high seas is possible.'

German troop transports which, after reaching the British coast, surrendered 'wholesale and immediately' could be dealt with 'as mercifully as circumstances allow', but British officers would be 'held responsible that the enemy gains no advantage by any exercise of humanity'. Only when the fighting had stopped altogether could Germans swimming in the water be made prisoners-of-war 'in the regular way provided the fighting efficiency of the ships is not affected'. The possibility of invasion prompted harsh measures: in the event, these measures were never put to the test, in either World War.

On the morning of October 21, British and French cavalrymen at the Belgian village of Passchendaele, on a ridge half way between Ypres and Roulers, left the village and fell back towards Ypres. They had not been attacked, but sought the greater security of proximity to the larger town. Both sides began to dig trenches, linking them in a continuous line, with machine-gun emplacements, dug-outs, communication trenches leading to the rear, and saps going forward as close as possible to the enemy front line. Artillery observation posts, balloons and air patrols kept an eye on any distant movement. The trench lines established between Ypres on the British side, and Menin and Roulers on the German side, the Ypres Salient, became the scene over four years of some of the harshest fighting of any war in history. At the time, however, it seemed that the skirmishes east of Ypres were but a passing moment in the struggle. 'In my opinion,' Sir John French telegraphed to Lord Kitchener on the evening of October 21, 'the enemy are vigorously playing their last card and I am confident they will fail.'

That 'last card' proved to be far more than a series of cavalry skirmishes. What became known as the First Battle of Ypres (or 'First Ypres') was a determined German attempt to drive the British out of the salient altogether, as part of a wider strategy aimed at breaking through to the North Sea and Channel coast.

Not only against Ypres, but further south at Messines and Neuve Chapelle, German units sought to push the British back, singing patriotic songs as they advanced. But the German grand design was nowhere within sight of success. The war of rapid movement was over. The struggle had become one for villages, hills, copses and roads. On October 21, a German artilleryman, Herbert Sulzbach, who was in action for the first time, wrote in his diary: 'We pull forward, get our first glimpse of this battlefield, and have to get used to the terrible scenes and impressions: corpses, corpses and more corpses, rubble, and the remains of villages.'

German infantrymen had just captured the village of Premesque. 'The bodies of friend and foe lie tumbled together', Sulzbach wrote. 'Heavy infantry fire drives us out of the position which we had taken up, and this is added to by increasingly heavy British artillery fire. We are now in an area of meadowland, covered with dead cattle and a few surviving, ownerless cows. The ruins of the village taken by assault are still smoking. Trenches hastily dug by the British are full of bodies. We get driven out of this position as well, by infantry and artillery fire.'

That night, Sulzbach reflected on his first day in action. 'A dreadful night comes down on us. We have seen too many horrible things all at once, and the smell of the smoking ruins, the lowing of the deserted cattle and the rattle of machine-gun fire makes a very strong impression on us, barely twenty years old as we are, but these things also harden us up for what is going to come. We certainly did not want this war! We are only defending ourselves and our Germany against a world of enemies who have banded together against us.'

On October 23, after two days of hand-to-hand fighting near Langemarck, in the Ypres Salient, 1,500 German dead were counted on the battlefield. At the hamlet of Kortekeer more than seven hundred Germans were taken prisoner. With them were liberated fifty British soldiers who had been captured by the Germans at the start of the battle.

The line of trenches was beginning to acquire a fatal, static logic of its own. Although the British success at Kortekeer was reported to headquarters as a 'break-through', no attempt was made to follow it up. At the same time German high-explosive shells, known to the French as 'marmites', to the British as 'coal-boxes' and 'Jack Johnsons', were blowing in trenches and causing continual Allied casualties.[1] The German hopes of reaching the sea were as vain as the British hopes of pushing deep into Belgium. The battle in the Ypres Salient had become a battle for the salient itself, for an area no more than eight miles wide at its widest. At Reutel, just north of the Menin Road, a battalion of the Wiltshire Regiment was all but wiped out on October 25, the few survivors being taken prisoner.

South of Ypres, Indian troops went into action for the first time on the Western Front when, on the night of October 25, between Wytschaete and

---

[1] Jack Johnson was the Black American world heavyweight boxing champion from 1908 to 1915. Both British nicknames derived from the black smoke of the explosion of these 15-centimetre shells, whose arrival was preceded by a deep roar. The 77-millimetre field-gun shell was known as a whizz-bang.

Messines, they drove off a German attack. The Official History of the
Indian Corps in France records how one of them, Sepoy Usman Khan,
having been shot twice by rifle fire, refused to leave his position. Only
when 'a large piece of flesh was blown away from both legs by a shell
splinter' was he carried back. For his 'grand example' he was awarded the
Indian Distinguished Service Medal. The Indians had left the subcontinent
almost exactly two months earlier.

On October 26 the Indian Corps carried out its first attack on the
Western Front. Their first British officer to be killed, Captain P.C. Hampe-
Vincent, was lost that day, as were nine of his men. Within four days, four
more British officers and four Indian officers, and more than two hundred
Indian soldiers, had been killed. In the Ypres Salient that day, many British
troops holding the village of Kruiseecke, just south of the Menin Road,
were killed or buried alive as British artillery fired into the village from
afar, unaware that it was being held by their own men. German artillery
fire had been almost continuous for fifty-six hours. A military historian,
Anthony Farrar-Hockley, who was himself in action in Korea in 1950, has
written: 'Gradually, from every one of the four battalions, men began to
fall back: fit men blown out of their trenches who were searching for the
remains of their units; wounded men walking painfully to the rear; men
recovering from the dreadful experience of being buried alive – the lucky
ones traced and dug out by their comrades; men broken by exhaustion
and the continual shock of seeing friends killed and wounded and the
rising conviction that they themselves were about to die.'[1]

Alarmed at reports of 'units in disorder', Sir Douglas Haig, commanding
I Corps, wrote in his diary of how 'I rode out at about 3 p.m. to see what
was going on, and was astounded at the terror-stricken men who were
coming back'. Still, he added, 'there were some units in the Division
which stuck to their trenches'. Sir John French was even more sanguine,
telegraphing to Kitchener that evening that the Germans were 'quite
incapable of making any strong and sustained attack'.

At German headquarters, von Moltke's successor as Chief of the General
Staff, General Falkenhayn, was deeply disappointed that the British line
had not been broken. Substantial reinforcements would be needed, he told
his commanders on October 27, before any decisive offensive action could
be carried out, but they were on their way. Would reinforcements be
enough? Bitterly the dismissed Moltke was to write to the Kaiser about
Falkenhayn that he 'does not possess the inner forces of spirit and soul to
draft and carry through operations of great scope'.

Falkenhayn was still hopeful, however, of breaking through the British
lines. A German attempt at Neuve Chapelle that day to fire shrapnel
containing an irritant substance was unsuccessful.[2] But after the commanding officer and the adjutant of the British battalion holding the line

[1] Anthony Farrar-Hockley, *Death of an Army*, Arthur Barker, London 1967, page 122.
[2] The substance was dianisidine chlorsulphonate.

94

just south of Neuve Chapelle were killed, German troops drove a gap through the British line.

It was distant fighters, in one of those Indian battalions so recently brought across the Indian Ocean, through the Red Sea and across the Mediterranean, who answered the urgent appeal to fill the breach. Darkness had fallen. The Indian soldiers, unused to the marshy ground and its intersection by barbed-wire defences, had difficulty in reaching the gap. When they did so, they were subjected to German machine-gun fire directed by brilliant searchlights.

At first light on October 28 the Indians attacked, breaking into Neuve Chapelle village, fighting house-by-house and hand-to-hand. One German, fearful as he surrendered that he would be bayoneted nevertheless, was comforted by a Sikh who patted him on the back with the exhortation, 'Be not afraid!' Within hours of this success, however, a sustained German counter-attack drove the Indians out of the village. On their way back they were savaged by German artillery and machine-gun fire. Of the 289 men who managed to extricate themselves from Neuve Chapelle, only sixty-eight reached the road from which the attack had started. For his courage during the retreat Subadar Malla Singh was awarded the Military Cross, the first Indian officer to receive it during the war. In the ensuing six days of fighting, more than twenty-five British officers and five hundred Indian officers and men were killed, and 1,455 wounded.

That day, when the Cabinet met in London, it was decided to keep secret the fact that one of Britain's most modern battleships, the *Audacious*, had been sunk by a German mine off the northern coast of Ireland. The main argument for secrecy, Asquith's wife later wrote in her diary, was that the British troops were 'very exhausted' on the Western Front, 'and that the news of the sinking, had it reached the Germans, 'would have cheered them up dangerously'.[1]

German reinforcements were now being hurried forward to the whole British sector of the front. The German offensive began at 5.30 on the morning of October 29. A German wireless message had been intercepted two days earlier giving the precise time of the attack, but the British artillery, restricted because of shell shortages to nine rounds per gun per day, was unable to take advantage of this intelligence. During the battle, Herbert Sulzbach, whose artillery battery was camouflaged to prevent it being seen from the air, noted in his diary, 'British planes drop leaflets saying that we ought to surrender. The other way round would be more sensible!' At the Front, he added, 'A Saxon company tries an extremely daring assault entirely on its own, which costs the lives of nearly every man in the company.'

Among the German units in action for the first time that morning was

[1] The Germans did not learn of the sinking of the *Audacious* for another two weeks, when on 14 November 1914 an American newspaper, the *Philadelphia Public Ledger*, published a photograph of the ship going down. The photograph had been taken by a passenger on board the ocean liner *Olympic*.

the List Regiment, which during the day's fighting outside Gheluvelt lost 349 men. 'I can proudly say that our Regiment fought like heroes,' Adolf Hitler wrote to his landlord. 'I was made lance-corporal and was saved by a near miracle.'

For General Falkenhayn, the battle for Gheluvelt was the essential, and as he hoped brief, prelude to the capture of Ypres and the march to the sea. That night a new Order of the Day was issued by General von Fabeck to the German troops who were to fight when battle was renewed on the morning of October 30: 'The breakthrough will be of decisive importance. We must and therefore will conquer, settle for ever the centuries-long struggle, end the war, and strike the decisive blow against our most detested enemy. We will finish the British, Indians, Canadians, Moroccans, and other trash, feeble adversaries, who surrender in great numbers if they are attacked with vigour.'

Such was the exhortation with which General von Fabeck sought to inspire the troops who had been put under his command for the crucial assault. For four days they took part, Hitler among them, in the battle for Gheluvelt. The fighting was savage: one British battalion, shelled at close range for twenty minutes, lost its commanding officer and 275 men: the fifty-four men who survived were all taken prisoner. Every one of them was wounded. Gheluvelt remained in British hands.

During the afternoon of October 30, German troops broke through the British line towards Klein Zillebeke. Irish Guards were sent to hold the new line. On their way to the Front, during a brief halt, a company officer recorded in his diary: 'In the centre of the road lay a dead trooper of some British cavalry regiment, his horse also half dead across him. A woman passed. She had all her household treasures strapped on her back and held the hands of two very small children. She took no notice of any one, but I saw two little children shy away from the dead man.'

That night Irish Guardsmen on patrol could see their German adversaries 'in their spiked helmets' silhouetted against the glare of a burning farmhouse, moving to their positions for the next morning's attack. 'Two years later,' their historian has written, 'our guns would have waited on their telephones till the enemy formation was completed and would then have removed those battalions from the face of the earth. But we had not those guns.'[1] That evening Foch agreed to send French troops to reinforce the British line, his advice to Sir John French being: 'Hammer away, keep on hammering away, and you will get there.'

On the morning of October 31, the renewed German attack drove the British out of Gheluvelt. 'To add to the horrors of the day,' Farrar-Hockley has written, one British battalion learned that their German opponents 'had clubbed to death and bayoneted some of the wounded and stripped all the prisoners of clothing, watches, wallets and trinkets'. There was an

---

[1] Rudyard Kipling, *The Irish Guards in the Great War*, Macmillan, London 1923, volume I, page 38.

'occasional savage reprisal', but in the main such barbaric behaviour was uncommon. Shortly after midday a shell hit British headquarters in the salient, killing one general and several Staff officers. By mid-afternoon Gheluvelt was once more in British hands. But the Commander-in-Chief had almost lost his nerve, having seen hundreds of wounded British soldiers falling back. 'There is nothing left for me to do but go up and be killed with I Corps,' Sir John French told Foch that afternoon, but the indomitable Frenchman replied without hesitation: 'You must not talk of dying but of winning.'

Having promised to send six battalions of French soldiers to the British line, Foch wrote out for the British Commander-in-Chief his own strategic thoughts: 'It is absolutely essential *not to retreat*; therefore the men must dig in wherever they find themselves and hold on to the ground they now occupy.' Any movement to the rear by 'any considerable body of troops would lead to an assault on the part of the enemy and bring certain confusion among the troops. Such an idea must be utterly rejected.'

Of the eighty-four British infantry battalions under Sir John French's command, with an original strength three months earlier of thirty officers and between 966 and 977 men, only nine now had between 350 and 450 men. Twenty-six had been so mauled as to have between 200 and 300 men, thirty-one were down to between 200 and 100. Eighteen of the British battalions had less than a hundred soldiers. Despite this drastic reduction in its fighting strength, the British Expeditionary Force, with Canadian, Indian and French support, held the Ypres Salient. Among the British officers killed in the salient on the last day of October was Prince Maurice of Battenberg. He was leading his battalion across an open space when a shell exploded near him. Wishing his men goodbye, he was taken by stretcher towards a field dressing station, but died before reaching it. Like the Kaiser, Prince Maurice was a grandson of Queen Victoria.

On the evening of November 1, on the right flank of the British force, where it linked with the French, the Irish Guardsmen holding the line were driven back by heavy shelling and machine-gun fire to the fringe of Zillebeke Wood. Officers, orderlies, batmen, even cooks, seized rifles and joined the front-line troops. ' 'Twas like a football scrum,' one man later recalled. 'Every one was somebody, ye'll understand. If he dropped there was no one to take his place.' Of the 400 men in that battalion, more than 130 were killed, 88 of them when their trench was completely blown in by German shellfire.

On November 2 the right flank of the British line was taken over by French troops. The town of Ypres, though now under German shellfire, remained in Allied hands. Three days later the Germans made one further attempt to push through to the coast, attacking to the south of Ypres, along the Wytschaete Ridge. But a shortage of artillery shells forced a reduction in the scale of the preliminary bombardment that Falkenhayn would have liked. Among the German soldiers in action near Wytschaete on November 5 was Hitler. For his part in the fighting he was later awarded the Iron Cross, Second Class. 'It was the happiest day of my life,' he wrote to his landlord. 'True, most of my comrades who had earned it just as much were dead.' More than 700 of the 3,600 men of the List Regiment had been killed during its first ten days in action.

On November 6, a week after his cousin Prince Maurice of Battenberg's death in action fighting against the Germans, the Kaiser himself went to Warneton, south of Ypres, to encourage his forces. He was the first sovereign of the war to feel that his presence might inspire his men. During his visit, however, he made a bad impression on a German division who saw him talking amiably, in English, to some British prisoners-of-war whom they were escorting back from the battlefield.

That battlefield was becoming the graveyard of thousands of young Germans and Britons. A nineteen-year-old British officer, Eric Dorman-Smith, who had been wounded at Mons in August, returned to his battalion in the first week of November. He was shocked by what he found. 'The catalogue of loss was almost too much to take in,' his biographer Lavinia Greacen has written. Dorman-Smith's first company commander had been killed on the Aisne on September 15. A close friend, a brilliant Cambridge athlete, had been killed by a sniper five days later. Another friend was also dead, 'killed on 27 October at Neuve Chapelle after fourteen days of continuous fighting; he too had been picked off by a well-positioned sniper'. In the fighting at Neuve Chapelle, shellfire had killed nine soldiers in his company. 'The most recent nightmare was the disappearance of Captain Fletcher, the boxing specialist, who was known to have been killed with others on November 1 but whose body could not be found.'

On November 11 the Prussian Guard were ordered to take Ypres itself. Their attack was preceded by the heaviest artillery bombardment of the war thus far, made possible by the deliberate stockpiling of shells over the previous week. For a short while the German troops broke through the British front line, but were beaten back. At one moment in the battle, a British battalion saw what appeared to be a wave of German troops coming towards them in the fog and smoke. For some minutes the grey figures did not seem to be moving. Then, as the fog began to clear, they saw that it was not a line of enemy advancing, but a bank of German dead lying across their front.

At Dixmude, north of Ypres, a battalion of the Third Guards Field Artillery regiment, composed almost entirely of German students, overran the French machine-gun posts facing them but was virtually annihilated. Among the students who survived that ordeal was the nineteen-year-old Richard Sorge, later a German journalist in Japan and one of Stalin's most successful spies.[1]

---

[1] Sorge's success was to have warned Stalin of Germany's preparations to attack the Soviet Union in June 1941. He was subsequently caught, and executed by the Japanese. Stalin himself took no part in the First World War, having been exiled by the Tsarist authorities to a distant and remote Siberian village.

The First Battle of Ypres was coming to an end. In its last hours a senior British officer, Brigadier-General FitzClarence, who had won the Victoria Cross during the Boer War, and who was disappointed that a renewed attack on the much-fought-over Polygon Wood seemed out of the question, went forward to see for himself if something might be done. As he did so he was shot, one of the last casualties of the battle.

More than 5,000 British and 5,000 German soldiers had been killed, in an area less than ten miles from north to south and five miles from east to west. The German breakthrough to Calais had failed. The British remained in Ypres and the Germans in Menin, pressing upon Ypres from three sides, shelling it and hoping, in vain, to make it untenable. Both armies set to work building front-line trenches, communication trenches, dug-outs and strong points. Between the two armies, stretching from the sea to the Alps, the shell-pitted, fought-over waste of No-Man's Land was the scene of continual skirmishes. Both armies were supported by a growing artillery force, their respective depredations inhibited only by the shortage of shells.

6

Towards the first Christmas: 'mud and slime and vermin'

NOVEMBER–DECEMBER 1914

As the armies on the Western Front settled down to deepen their trenches and extend their fortifications, all the while sniping and raiding and subjecting each other to spasmodic artillery fire, the gap between the dangers and burdens of the front line, and the perceptions of the capitals, was growing. Returning briefly to London in November 1914, General Smith-Dorrien later recalled: 'I was struck by the fact that people in England didn't in the least realise the strenuous nature of the fighting at the front, or that we were a long thin line without reserves which might be broken through at any time. Their minds seemed set on what appeared to me to be a ridiculous fear of an invasion of England.'

Recruitment in Britain for Kitchener's Army, the much publicised New Armies that were intended to join the battle in the spring of 1915, continued throughout the winter of 1914. On October 21 a *Punch* cartoon, later made into a poster, showed Mr Punch saying to a professional footballer: 'No doubt you can make money in this field, my friend, but there's only one field today where you can get honour.' On November 7 a Labour Member of Parliament, J.H. Thomas (fifteen years later Secretary of State for the Colonies), told a London audience that, if thousands of young men who were eligible for the army found it possible to go to football matches, 'either those young men did not understand the situation or they were cowards and traitors.' A month later the first of two Football Battalions was raised in London by a Conservative Member of Parliament, William Joynson-Hicks. It served as the 17th Battalion, the Middlesex Regiment.

In Germany that October, the Imperial Government decided to counter the hostile sentiment stirred up among neutrals and belligerents by the invasion of Belgium. The form chosen was a 'Manifesto to the Civilised World' signed by ninety-three German artists, poets, historians, philosophers, scientists, musicians and clergymen. 'We shall wage this fight to the very end as a civilised nation,' the manifesto declared, 'a nation that holds the legacy of Goethe, Beethoven and Kant no less sacred than hearth and home.' The signatories included Wilhelm Roentgen, the discoverer of

X-rays, and Max Reinhardt, a pioneer of modern theatre. In the title of the manifesto, the German word used for 'civilised world' was 'Kulturwelt'. This was immediately taken up with zeal by Germany's enemies, who mocked at the reality of German 'Kultur', ascribing it to every act of violence and atrocity, to every bombardment of a town or destruction of a church, and to every individual act of savagery.[1]

A counter manifesto, entitled 'Manifesto to Europeans', was immediately drafted by a leading German pacifist, Georg Friedrich Nicolai, Professor of Physiology at the University of Berlin and a distinguished cardiologist, in which he appealed for a united European intellectual response which might lead, after the war, to a united Europe: 'The first step in this direction would be for all those who truly cherish the culture of Europe to join forces – all those whom Goethe once prophetically called "good Europeans". We must not abandon hope that their voice speaking in unison may even today rise above the clash of arms, particularly if they are joined by those who already enjoy renown and authority.'

Nicolai sought signatories among a large number of Berlin university professors. Only three agreed to sign it. One of them, the eighty-year-old Wilhelm Forster, head of the Berlin Observatory, had also signed the official manifesto. The other two signatories, both scientists, had only recently arrived in Berlin, Otto Buek from Heidelberg and Albert Einstein from Switzerland. It was Einstein's first published foray into the world of politics. 'Alas,' Buek later recalled, 'we had overestimated the courage and integrity of German professors.'

The Kaiser himself had joined the campaign for the assertion of German cultural values, writing on November 25 to the British-born racialist philosopher Houston Stewart Chamberlain, who had become a German citizen: 'It is my unspeakable conviction that the country to which God gave Luther, Goethe, Bach, Wagner, Moltke, Bismarck and my grandfather will yet be called upon to fulfil great tasks for the benefit of mankind.'

While the land war in northern France was turning into the confrontation of trenches and barbed wire, at sea the tyranny of the torpedo was establishing itself in all waters. On October 15 a German submarine, the *U-9*, which had sunk three British cruisers in September, torpedoed the British cruiser *Hawke* in the North Sea: 525 British sailors were drowned and only twenty-one saved. Two days later, in the South China Sea, a German torpedo sank a Japanese cruiser *Takachiho* and 271 Japanese sailors were drowned. On October 26, in the English Channel, a French steamship, the *Amiral Ganteaume*, mistaken for a troopship, was torpedoed by the German submarine *U-24* and forty Belgian refugees were drowned.

The power of the German submarines, particularly against merchant

[1] While travelling in 1980 in Poland, I found the words 'Deutsch Kultur' painted in large white letters on the ruins of one of the crematoria at Auschwitz.

ships and ocean liners, was considerable. But in the growing battle of wits between the German submarine commanders and their Royal Navy adversaries, a precious advantage was gained by the British that October. On October 13, the Russian Imperial Navy sent to London a German naval signal book from the German cruiser *Madgeburg*, which had gone aground in the Gulf of Finland and come under Russian naval gunfire. The German signalman who was about to destroy the book was killed by a bursting shell. When the Russians came to take his body for burial they found the book. As a result of this find, British cryptographers were able to begin work painstakingly decoding the German naval wireless messages and locating their adversaries.

In the Pacific Ocean, the German Far Eastern Squadron, commanded by Admiral Maximilian von Spee, was wreaking havoc among British merchant ships. On November 1, off Coronel, von Spee was confronted by British warships led by the cruisers *Good Hope* and *Monmouth*. He sank them both, and 1,500 British sailors were drowned, including their admiral, Sir Christopher Cradock. It was the first serious British naval defeat for a hundred years: since the nascent United States navy had defeated a British fleet on Lake Champlain in 1814. Among the dead was a neighbour of the Callaghan family of Portsmouth. 'It took a few days for the news to filter back to Portsmouth,' recalled the then $2\frac{3}{4}$-year-old James, 'and when it did I have a very clear memory of clutching my mother's hand as she walked down the street to visit and comfort the widow. I was conscious of the grief in that room. What engraved it indelibly on my memory was the sight of the young widow suckling her new baby at her breast.'[1]

Since the second day of the war, the Imperial German Navy had laid mines in the North Sea. This minelaying, outside an enemy's three-mile limit, was illegal under the Second Hague Convention of 1907: it led on November 3 to a declaration, strongly advocated by the British Prime Minister, that the whole of the North Sea must be regarded as a British 'military area' and that parts of it would be mined. Neutral ships would enter the North Sea 'at their own peril'. If they put in to British ports, where they could be searched for any supplies on their way to Germany, they would then be escorted through the minefields, any 'illegal' cargo having first been removed.

The neutral States most affected by the blockade, Norway and Sweden, protested at this British breach of international law. But the British were convinced that it was 'necessary to adopt exceptional measures appropriate to the novel conditions in which this war is being fought', and the blockade remained in force, steadily denying Germany essential war supplies and

---

[1] James Callaghan (born in March 1912) was Prime Minister from 1976 to 1979, the last British Prime Minister who could recall the First World War. His predecessor Harold Wilson (born in March 1916) remembered his mother answering some of his persistent questions by telling him that what he wanted would happen 'when the war is ended'.

foodstuffs. The United States, although asked by the Norwegian Government to join the protest against Britain, refused to do so.

There was an essential difference between British and German practice in the North Sea. Whereas the German minelaying policy resulted in many hundreds of neutral ships being blown up, the British blockade was only dangerous to those ships which declined to put in to British ports. In two years, only five American ships were sunk, and four American lives lost, as a result of American-registered merchant ships refusing to comply with the British blockade.

On the Eastern Front, German troops pressed forward inside Russian Poland, and Russian troops pushed deeper into Austrian Galicia. As the Germans moved into Russia's Polish provinces, the local population turned savagely against the Jews who had lived in their midst for several centuries. Shops, homes and synagogues were looted. In the zone of the Russian armies, according to the French Ambassador to Russia, Paléologue, Jews were being hanged every day, accused of being secretly sympathetic to the Germans and wanting them to succeed. The fact that a quarter of a million Jews were serving in the Russian army did not help to combat prejudice. Hundreds of thousands of Jews were driven from their homes in Lodz, Piotrkow, Bialystok and Grodno, and from dozens of other towns and villages. They took to the road, carrying what possessions they could put on carts or into bundles, and moved eastwards, eventually finding sanctuary deep inside Russia, far from the hysteria of the war zones.

On the battlefields of the Eastern Front, the casualties were on an even greater scale than in the west. On October 12, Stanley Washburn, special war correspondent of *The Times* with the Russian armies, wrote from the hospital base at Rovno: 'As one wanders about these limitless wards of the stricken, one is increasingly impressed with what the human being can stand and yet, with modern medical treatment, recover from. So delicate is the human body that it seems incredible that it can stand such dreadful usage and still recuperate and eventually be as good as new. One man that we saw had been shot through the head. The wound was clean and in two weeks he was nearly well.' Other soldiers, shot through the stomach, bladder and lungs, 'were recovering as easily as though to be shot were a part of the ordinary man's day of work'.

Ten days later, from the battlefield in Galicia, Washburn sent *The Times* an account of the field of battle. 'In every direction from each shell hole is strewn the fragments of blue cloth of the Austrian uniform, torn into shreds and ribbons by the force of the explosive; and all about the field are still bits of arms, a leg in a boot, or some other ghastly token of soldiers, true to discipline, hanging on to a position that was alive with bursting shells and flying shrapnel.'

On what had been the battlefield a short time earlier, Washburn came upon a wooden cross and crucifix. One arm of the figure of Christ had been 'carried away by a shrapnel fragment'. Nailed to the cross was a rough wooden sign with the words: 'Here lie the bodies of 121 Austrian warriors and four Russian warriors.'

On October 17 the German forces in southern Poland, confronted by vastly superior Russian numbers, were forced to withdraw. Individual units retreated as much as sixty miles in a single day. The Russians were now in a position to threaten the German industrial heartland of Silesia. By a supreme effort of logistical skill, Ludendorff and Hoffmann moved the German Ninth Army, which was then facing north-east from Posen to Cracow, to a new position, facing south-east from Posen to Thorn, in order to threaten the Russian city of Lodz, forcing the Russian troops then poised to enter Silesia to defend the threatened city. This was the moment when, on October 21, Polish troops, fighting under Austrian orders, took part in their first battle against the Russians.

That week, a rumour swept through the Austro-German forces on the Eastern Front that Paris had fallen to the Germans. When the rumour was dispelled, the philosopher Wittgenstein was led to thoughts of despair about the outcome of the war, and about the future for all Germans. From his river gunboat on the Russian front, he wrote on October 25: 'It makes me feel today more than ever the terribly sad position of our race – the German race. Because it seems to me as good as certain that we cannot get the upper hand against England. The English – the best race in the world – *cannot* lose. We, however, can lose and shall lose, if not this year then next year. The thought that our race is going to be beaten depresses me terribly, because I am completely German.'

These pessimistic thoughts did not seem borne out by the next development of the war, for in the early hours of October 29, far from the Eastern Front, there was a considerable success for Germany, and an added burden for Russia, when the two German warships, the *Goeben* and the *Breslau*, that had lain off Constantinople since mid-August, bombarded two of Russia's Black Sea ports, Nikolayev and Odessa, and dropped mines in the Russian shipping lanes. A Russian minelayer was also sunk. The two warships then proceeded to bombard Sebastopol, Feodosia and Novorossisk, setting fire to some fifty petrol storage tanks and granaries. Because the two German ships were flying the Turkish flag, by this brief bombardment Germany and Austria acquired an ally against the Entente. The German admiral commanding the action, Admiral Souchon, wrote to his wife: 'I have thrown the Turks into the powder keg.'

The bombarding of the Black Sea ports led to an immediate widening of the war, which the German High Command were convinced would be to their advantage. Such retaliation as was possible seemed small, even trivial: on November 1 the British attacked a Turkish minelayer in Smyrna harbour.[1] On the following day, a British light cruiser bombarded the

---

[1] Two British destroyers took part in this attack. One of their commanders, Captain A.B. Cunningham, became First Sea Lord in the Second World War (1943–46). The other, Captain Prentis, was killed in action at the Dardanelles on 28 April 1915.

Turkish Red Sea port of Akaba. After the Turkish garrison had fled, a Royal Naval party went ashore and blew up the post office. On November 3, British and French warships bombarded the Turkish forts at the Dardanelles. The fortress on the northern shore, Sedd-ul-Bahr, was hit and its powder magazine blown up. That same day, Russian troops crossed Turkey's eastern border.

Turkey responded by declaring war on the Entente powers. She was not entirely unprepared. At the Dardanelles, a German officer, Colonel Erich Weber, had for more than a month been in charge of the Turkish fortifications, sealing the waterway and organising the laying of mines. Following the brief British naval bombardment, four more German officers and 160 German soldiers were sent to accelerate the strengthening of the Turkish defences. Mines were laid, including Russian mines which the Turks had recovered from the Black Sea, French mines recovered off Smyrna, and even Bulgarian mines left over from the second Balkan War. The minelaying was done by a German naval officer, Captain Gehl. German gunners manned the forts at Chanak and Kilid Bahr, the Narrows through which any invading fleet must pass. At Chanak a German artillery officer, Lieutenant-Colonel Wehrle, set up eight howitzer batteries overlooking the Dardanelles.

With Turkey's declaration of war, one more Empire had become a hostage to the fortune and ill-fortune of war. However much the Germans might see Turkey as a gain for the Central Powers, the British treated the widening of the war against them with a certain contempt. 'It is the Ottoman Government and not we', Asquith declared at the Guildhall on November 5, 'who have rung the death knell of Ottoman dominion not only in Europe but in Asia.' Two days later 4,500 British and Indian troops, who had sailed from Bombay three weeks earlier, landed at Fao, at the head of the Persian Gulf, in the distant Turkish province of Mesopotamia. 'I *loathe* the Turk,' Asquith's wife wrote in her diary that week, 'and really hope that he will be wiped out of Europe. Germany blackmailed Turkey till it went over, but except for threatening Egypt I doubt if it will bother us much.' Churchill wanted 50,000 Russian troops to be brought by sea from Archangel or Vladivostok to attack the Turks on the Gallipoli Peninsula. 'No other military operations are necessary,' he wrote to Sir Edward Grey. 'The price to be paid in taking Gallipoli would no doubt be heavy, but there would be no more war with Turkey. A good army of 50,000 men and sea power – that is the end of the Turkish menace.'

No military action was taken at Gallipoli that winter. Enquiries of the Russians led to alarming reports of 800,000 recruits ready to go to the front but having no rifles to equip them, and of Russian officers complaining that their men 'could live on what they picked up locally – frozen potatoes and turnips – they could stick the frost but ammunition did not grow in the fields.' Churchill suggested that Greece might 'undertake an attack on Gallipoli on behalf of the Allies', but the Greeks, despite their own long-cherished designs on Constantinople, were unwilling to commit troops against Turkey, being torn between the pro-Entente sympathies of their Prime Minister, Venizelos, and the apparent pro-German inclinations of their King, Constantine, whose wife Sophie was the Kaiser's sister. Only in Mesopotamia did the Turks face a military attack that month: the British and Indian troops who had landed at Fao on November 7 occupied Basra and, two weeks later, reached Kurna, at the confluence of the Tigris and the Euphrates. Five British, sixty Indian and three hundred Turkish soldiers had been killed. More than a thousand Turks, known to the British as 'Catch 'em alive'o's' had been taken prisoner. One of the remotest parts of the Ottoman Empire was under British control, and any Turkish threat to the British oilfields at Abadan had been averted.

In Constantinople, where the British Embassy constituted, and still constitutes today, an impressive monument to Victorian power and influence, Betty Cunliffe-Owen, wife of the Military Attaché, watched an unprecedented scene: 'In the Embassy garden a huge bonfire was burning – the documents and records of British achievements in Turkey for over one hundred years were slowly burning before the eyes of the Ambassador and his Secretaries. It was the funeral pyre of England's vanishing power in the Ottoman Empire.'

In neutral Switzerland, the exiled Russian Bolshevik leader Vladimir Lenin watched the conflict spread. 'The epoch of the bayonet has begun,' he wrote. From it, he predicted, a civil war between the classes would emerge, the prelude to revolution and the triumph of the working class. A one-day strike in Petrograd on November 12 was a tiny forecast of Bolshevik aims. More sinister for the stability of Russia, the Tsarist police discovered Bolshevik cells in several army units, especially among the railway battalions on which the protection of the Russian army's communications depended.

In Germany, the small group of intellectuals led by Georg Nicolai launched, on November 16, a New Fatherland League, appealing for 'the prompt achievement of a just peace without annexations' and for the establishment after the war of an international organisation that would have as its aim the prevention of future wars. Einstein was a founder and active supporter of the League. One of those who attended the League's meetings, Dr Franziska Baumgartner-Tramer, recalled fifty years later that when Einstein spoke 'it was always with great pessimism about the future of human relations'. She remembered how 'I managed to get to him on one occasion, when I was depressed by the news of one German victory after another and the resultant intolerable arrogance and gloating of the people of Berlin. "What will happen, Herr Professor?" I asked anxiously. Einstein looked at me, raised his right fist, and replied: "This will govern!" '

On November 18 the redeployed German forces on the Eastern Front reached and almost surrounded the city of Lodz: the 150,000 Russian troops defending the fortress were confronted by 250,000 Germans. When

the senior Russian general ordered a retreat, to prevent complete encirclement, the Tsar's uncle, the Grand Duke Nicholas, Commander-in-Chief of
the Russian forces, countermanded the order.

The battle for Lodz was on a gigantic scale. At one point three German
divisions that were themselves in danger of encirclement broke out from
the Russian trap, taking with them 16,000 Russian soldiers whom they
had taken prisoner earlier, and sixty-four captured heavy guns. In the
course of the breakout, 1,500 German soldiers were killed. German
reinforcements, summoned urgently from the Western Front, arrived too
slowly to take advantage of the Russian discomfiture. Germany, excited
by the prospect of a victory even greater than that of Tannenberg, was
unable to achieve it. 'The colossal mass which they had tried to roll back
only retired a short stretch and then stood still in immobility,' one historian
has written. 'The energies of both armies flagged, worn out by defeats,
fighting, and the vileness of the swampy country; the frost was becoming
more severe, with icy winds, and the temperature at night fell to within
ten degrees (Fahrenheit) of zero. The approach of winter laid its paralysing
hand on the activity of German and Russian alike.'[1]

For the victory at Lodz, Hindenburg was made a Field Marshal. Further
south, the British Military Attaché with the Russian armies, Colonel Knox,
was despondent, writing in his diary on November 25: 'The necessity for
rapid refilling of casualties owing to the enormous losses of modern war
has been, I fear, lost sight of in Russia, and if we have to advance in the
winter, our losses will be three times as great.' Winter was bringing terrors
of its own to all the contending armies. 'We have lost several men frozen
to death in the trenches at night,' Knox noted. A captured Austrian officer's
diary 'revealed the fact that one officer and six men in his company had
been frozen to death in a single night'. In the Russian lines orders had been
given to keep the men supplied with hot tea, but a Russian commander
told him: 'Such orders are easy to write, but difficult to carry out, when
not a day passes without one of the orderlies who carry the officers'
lunches to the trenches being wounded.'

On the Austrian front, Russian troops crossed briefly into Austrian
Silesia, and for the second time entered Hungary. General Conrad, aware
of the desire of the national minorities of the Empire to take advantage of
Austria's weakness, proposed on November 26 the imposition of military
rule in Bohemia, Moravia and Silesia. This was rejected, however, by Franz
Josef, who was confident that the turmoil of war would not undermine
his multinational empire. But Conrad, in making his military plans, had
always to take into account that Slav units, whether Poles, Czechs, Slovaks,
Slovenes or Croats, could not always be counted upon to give of their best
when confronting Russian troops.[2]

[1] John W. Wheeler-Bennett, *Hindenburg, The Wooden Titan*, Macmillan, London 1936, p. 44.
[2] One racial minority scattered throughout the Hapsburg lands was the Jews. During the First
World War three Austro-Hungarian Field Marshals and eight generals were Jewish. One of

There was a moment of panic in Vienna on November 28, when news arrived that Russian troops were within eight miles of Cracow, the capital of Austrian Poland. But in a seventeen-day battle near Limanowa, the Austrian Fourth Army defeated the Russians and drove them eastward. As the battle of Limanowa began, the Austrian Third Army drove the Russian troops from the northern Hungarian town of Bartfeld, pushed the Russians from the Carpathians, and within two weeks had retaken the strategic Dukla Pass. The military threat to Austria-Hungary was over.

Russia began to look for more troops, and to seek help from the British for guns and munitions. Such help only came on a commercial basis: in the course of two years Britain was to sell Russia a thousand aeroplanes and aeroplane engines, 250 heavy guns, 27,000 machine guns, a million rifles, eight million grenades, 64,000 tons of iron and steel, 200,000 tons of explosives and 2,500,000,000 rounds of ammunition.

The mobilisation of Russian students, ordered on December 1, while adding to the number of soldiers under arms, also gave Bolshevik student organisers access to the army. Later that month the eastern Siberian police reported to Petrograd that soldiers travelling by the Trans-Siberian Railway were being subjected to anti-war propaganda. In Petrograd itself, reported the Chief of Staff of the Russian Sixth Army, wounded soldiers brought back from the Front to the capital were being approached by unidentified civilians who 'on the pretext of sympathy conduct conversations and at the end of them attempt to hand over leaflets which on examination turn out to be proclamations calling for an end to the war'. On December 21 the commander of the Russian First Army reported that with the arrival of reservists 'signs of socialist propaganda have been observed': he was taking steps to stamp out such propaganda.

In search of allies against the Turks, the Tsar visited the Caucasus front on December 30, telling the head of the Armenian Church that 'a most brilliant future awaits the Armenians'. With these words, the fate of hundreds of thousands of Armenians was endangered, as Turkey saw in its own large Armenian minority a source of fifth column activity, treachery and disloyalty, and did nothing to dampen anti-Armenian feeling. Another minority that was in danger in two war zones was the Jews. In October, Russian townsfolk, seeking scapegoats for the German successes in Russian Poland, had turned savagely against Jews in Vilna, Grodno and Bialystok, and Russian soldiers were assured 'that were it not for the Yids – traitors – the Prussian army would have been utterly routed'. In December, the newly appointed Turkish military commander in Palestine, Jemal Pasha, rounded up five hundred Russian immigrant Jews and ordered them to be deported by sea from Jaffa to Egypt. The German-born Zionist Arthur Ruppin tried to intercede on their behalf but was unsuccessful, writing in his diary: 'At

them, Field Marshal Johann Georg Franz Hugo Friedlander, was deported by the Germans in 1943 from Vienna to the Theresienstadt Ghetto, and from there, in 1944, to Auschwitz, where he perished.

the harbour that evening I had to watch whole families with their hurriedly collected belongings – old people, mothers and babies – being driven on to the boat in infinite disorder.'

Jemal Pasha's Turkish patriotism led him to neglect potential allies. On his way from Constantinople he had passed through Beirut, where he hanged a number of the leaders of the Arab national movement. In Jerusalem he found a number of Zionists who, having joined the local Ottomanisation Committee, had obtained permission to recruit a Jewish militia to help defend Palestine against the Entente. Ignoring this gesture, Jemal disbanded the militia, announced that anyone found with a Zionist document on him would be put to death, and expelled from Palestine two of the leading Zionist supporters of the Ottomanisation Committee: David Ben-Gurion and Yitzhak Ben-Zvi. Both were manacled and put on board ship at Jaffa with a note from the Governor of the port: 'To be banished forever from the Turkish Empire.' Within a few weeks they were on their way to America, to rally the Zionists to the Entente and to help raise troops for a specifically Jewish Legion within the Entente forces.[1]

The United States was preserving strict neutrality in the European conflict. But the commercial and profit-making aspects of war were not impeded by neutrality, indeed they were stimulated by it. In London on November 3, Churchill arranged with Charles Schwab, the head of Bethlehem Steel, that Britain would buy eight 14-inch guns needed for the newly commissioned monitors. These guns were being manufactured by Bethlehem Steel for a Greek battlecruiser then under construction in Germany. Four days later two American companies accepted an order from the British Admiralty for twelve flying boats, four to be built in Buffalo and eight on Long Island. The first of a swelling tide of war materials had begun to make its way across the Atlantic to Britain and France. Submarines were to be next, ordered by Britain and transported by boat across the Atlantic in strictest secrecy.

There was no respite in the war at sea. On November 9, in the Indian Ocean, in the first wartime action ever fought by an Australian warship, the cruiser *Sydney* sank the German raider *Emden*. During her seven week voyage the *Emden* had captured eight unarmed Allied merchant ships and sunk fifteen, sending to the bottom cargoes of coal, tea, rubber, cattle and even racehorses. In Penang harbour she had sunk a Russian cruiser and a French destroyer. Reaching Diego Garcia Island in October she had been welcomed by a French resident with gifts of fresh eggs and vegetables: he had no idea that war had broken out two months earlier, and was satisfied by the explanation for the ship's warlike appearance that she was part of German-French-British 'world naval manoeuvres'.

---

[1] Both men later played a leading part in establishing Jewish national institutions in Mandate Palestine. In 1948 Ben-Gurion became the first Prime Minister of the State of Israel; in 1952 Ben-Zvi became the State's second President.

In the engagement that destroyed the *Emden*, 134 of her crew were killed. Her captain, Karl von Müller, was praised in the British newspapers for having shown 'chivalry in his treatment of the crews and passengers of the captured ships'. 'If all the Germans had fought as well as the Captain of the *Emden*,' wrote *The Times*, 'the German people would not today be reviled by the world.'

On November 26, while loading ammunition at Sheerness, the British battleship *Bulwark* was destroyed by an internal explosion, and 793 sailors were killed. There were only twelve survivors. On December 8, in the southern Atlantic, Admiral von Spee prepared to raid the Falkland Islands. British naval forces led by Admiral Sturdee drove him off: in the naval battle four German warships were sunk and 2,100 German sailors killed. There were only ten British deaths. Eight days later, four German cruisers bombarded the British east coast towns of Scarborough, Whitby and Hartlepool, killing forty civilians and wounding several hundred.

The German bombardment of the three British coastal towns provided a propaganda victory for Britain. Henceforth, the Germans were portrayed as the 'baby killers of Scarborough'. It was also a shock for Britain, the first occasion on which civilians had been killed in Britain by enemy action since 1690. An account of the raid was written at the time by a sixteen-year-old schoolgirl, Winifred Holtby, who was in school when the first shells fell. 'Just as we got through the gate another shell burst quite near', she wrote to a friend, 'and "Run!" came the order – and we ran. Ran, under the early morning sky, on the muddy, uneven road, with the deafening noise in our ears, the echo ringing even when the actual firing stopped for a moment – it never stopped for more; ran, though our hastily clad feet slipped on the muddy road. Over the town hung a mantle of heavy smoke, yellow, unreal, which make the place look like a dream city, far, far away. Only the road was real, and the tight pain that caught us across our breast – it was not fear, but something inexplicable that hurt, and yet in some strange way was not wholly unpleasant.'

Looking back a few moments later, Winifred Holtby 'heard the roar of a gun, and the next instant there was a crash, and a thick cloud of black smoke enveloped one of the houses in Seamer Road; a tiny spurt of red flame shot out'. Rumours from the town said that the Germans had landed. Returning there two hours later, Winifred Holtby added her 'earnest hope that never again will England suffer as she did on that awful December 16th, 1914 – but if she does, may I be there to see it'.

The emerging war in the air, though on a small scale, saw several important developments as 1914 drew to a close. On November 21 three British aircraft carried out the first long-distance bombing raid of the war when they flew from the French town of Belfort to the German Zeppelin sheds at Friedrichshafen, on Lake Constance, each carrying four bombs. One Zeppelin was damaged and a hydrogen tank destroyed. One British aviator who had to make a forced landing was attacked by German civilians and badly injured: he had to be rescued by German soldiers. Two days after the Friedrichshafen raid the first French bombing group was formed. On December 1 the first German aircraft were fitted with radio equipment, to enable them to fly over the front line and report back on the location of enemy artillery units and troop movements. Such reconnaissance duties became a major feature of the war in the air. There were also new devices to be tested: on December 6 a metal arrow dropped from a French plane mortally wounded a German general on horseback.

In the Balkans, on December 1, Austria achieved its goal of occupying Belgrade. What might five months earlier have been Europe's sole war-making objective was now accomplished. The Serbs continued to fight tenaciously, however, and two weeks later Belgrade was recaptured. More than 40,000 Austrian soldiers were taken prisoner and 133 heavy guns captured. On entering Belgrade the Serbs found 10,000 Serbian prisoners of war, and a thousand horses, left behind by the Austrians in the retreat.

That winter an American war correspondent, John Reed, travelled through Serbia. His journey began in the southern town of Nis, where he saw 'soldiers in filthy tatters, their feet bound with rags – soldiers limping, staggering on crutches, without arms, without legs, discharged from the overcrowded hospitals still blue and shaking from typhus. For the typhus had swept the town, where people were living six and ten to a room, until everywhere the black flags flapped in long, sinister vistas and the windows of the cafés were plastered with black paper death notices.' Travelling to Belgrade, he visited the university, which was 'a mass of yawning ruins', and he explained: 'The Austrians had made it their special target, for there had been the hotbed of pan-Serbian propaganda, and among the students that formed the secret society whose members murdered the Archduke Franz Ferdinand'.

Reed made the journey to Sabac, where he and an artist companion were told of the atrocities committed by the Austrians during their brief occupation. 'The soldiers were loosed like wild beasts in the city, burning, pillaging, raping. We saw the gutted Hotel d'Europe and the blackened and mutilated church where three thousand men, women and children were penned together without food or water for four days, and then divided into two groups – one sent back to Austria as prisoners of war, the others driven ahead of the army as it marched south against the Serbians.' Reed was shown a photograph taken in the village of Leknica, 'showing more than a hundred women and children chained together, their heads struck off'. His book, published in 1915, confirmed for its Allied readers the barbarism of the Central Powers.[1]

Towards the end of November, while in London, Winston Churchill

[1] Reed later became famous for his book *Ten Days That Shook the World*, his eyewitness account of the Bolshevik revolution. He died in 1920 and is buried in Moscow's Red Square. His report from Serbia was reprinted in 1994, an article in *The Times* being headed: 'Sketches of 1915 foretell horrors of modern Bosnia' (*The Times*, 26 March 1994).

learned that his close friend, Hugh Dawnay, had been killed in action. He also received a letter from a close friend and fellow Member of Parliament, Valentine Fleming, who was serving on the Western Front, and sought to describe the scene. 'First and most impressive,' Fleming wrote, 'the absolutely indescribable ravages of modern artillery fire, not only upon all men, animals and buildings within its zone, but upon the very face of nature itself. Imagine a broad belt, ten miles or so in width, stretching from the Channel to the German frontier near Basle, which is positively littered with the bodies of men and scarified with their rude graves; in which farms, villages and cottages are shapeless heaps of blackened masonry; in which fields, roads and trees are pitted and torn and twisted by shells and disfigured by dead horses, cattle, sheep and goats, scattered in every attitude of repulsive distortion and dismemberment.' In this zone both day and night were made 'hideous by the incessant crash and whistle and roar of every sort of projectile, by sinister columns of smoke and flame, by the cries of wounded men, by the piteous calls of animals of all sorts, abandoned, starved, perhaps wounded'.

Along this 'terrain of death' stretched two more or less parallel lines of trenches, some 200 to 1,000 yards apart. In these trenches, Fleming explained, 'crouch lines of men, in brown or grey or blue, coated with mud, unshaven hollow-eyed with the continual strain, unable to reply to the everlasting run of shells hurled at them from three, four, five or more miles away and positively welcoming an infantry attack from one side or the other as a chance of meeting and matching themselves against *human* assailants and not against invisible, irresistible machines, the outcome of an ingenuity which even you and I would be in agreement in considering unproductive from every point of view'. Fleming ended his letter: 'It's going to be a *long war* in spite of the fact that on both sides every single man in it wants it stopped *at once*.'[1]

On November 23, Churchill sent this letter to his wife Clementine. 'What would happen I wonder,' he asked, 'if the armies suddenly & simultaneously went on strike and said some other method must be found of settling the dispute! Meanwhile however new avalanches of men are preparing to mingle in the conflict and it widens every hour.' That evening, in the Ypres Salient, German troops broke into the trenches being held by Indian troops at Festubert. There was much hand-to-hand fighting and several trenches were lost. What the Official History of the Indian Corps in France calls 'uncompromising orders' were then received from the corps commander, Lieutenant-General Sir James Willcocks, 'that the original line must be restored before dawn and held at all costs'.

These orders were obeyed, although a fall of snow in the night made

---

[1] Fleming, a major in the Queen's Own Oxfordshire Hussars, and a Conservative Member of Parliament since 1910 (Churchill was then a Liberal) was killed in action on the Western Front on 20 May 1917. His son Peter was later a distinguished traveller and travel writer, his son Ian the author of the 'James Bond' novels; both were young children at the time of their father's death.

the Indians an easy target for German rifle and machine-gun fire. At one point, the official history records, where very heavy machine-gun fire was making the men hesitate to advance, two Indian soldiers, both Gurkhas, 'earned the Indian Distinguished Service Medal by rushing on and carrying the company forward'.

On November 24 the Indians recaptured the trenches that had been lost, taking a hundred German prisoners. When the battle was over, it was discovered that an Indian corporal, Darwan Singh Nedi, had continued fighting although twice wounded in the head. Only when his company lined up after the action did his commanding officer see 'that he was streaming with blood from head to foot'. He was awarded the Victoria Cross. That day, in a nearby sector of the front, a British officer, Lieutenant F.A. De Pass, led two of his Indians soldiers into the sap of a German trench that had been pushed out to within ten yards of the Indian line. The sap was destroyed. De Pass made an even more dangerous foray on November 25, when he and an Indian soldier faced German machine-gun fire for two hundred yards, to bring in a badly wounded Indian lying in No-Man's Land.

The next day, De Pass again went forward to a sap-head in the front line, to repair a parapet that had been damaged. Seeing a German sniper at work, he tried to shoot him, but was himself shot through the head and killed. The Official History of the Indian Corps in France wrote of him: 'He was the very perfect type of British officer. He united to singular personal beauty a charm of manner and a degree of valour which made him the idol of his men. He was honoured in death by the Victoria Cross. No one in war earned it better.' Although the history did not say so, Lieutenant De Pass, a Londoner, was also a Jew.

On November 25, French artillery bombarded the village of Arnaville, on the east bank of the river Moselle, only ten miles south of Metz. The action marked what a French military spokesman called 'the beginning of a new invasion of German territory'. But no territorial gains were made. Further west, French civilians were evacuated from the village of Sampigny for fear that the Germans might try to destroy the house of President Poincaré there, or even capture the President if he were to visit the village. They did succeed in destroying the house, Le Clos, and much of the town, using the long-distance heavy Austrian siege guns that had been so effective in August against the Belgian forts.

Elsewhere on the French sector of the Western Front, among the French Foreign Legion volunteers fighting that month was the American, William Thaw. 'Wish I were back dodging street cars on Broadway for excitement,' he wrote home on November 27. 'Am that tired of being shot at!' He had already been hit 'in the cap and bayonet' and had not washed 'for twenty days'.

The British troops in the Ypres Salient were now instructed by Joffre to make a limited attack on the German trenches. There was no strategic aim in this, or hope of breaking through the trench lines, but the more limited desire, in conjunction with a series of French attacks further south, to help the Russian armies. The French and British Governments hoped that pressure on the Russians in the east would be reduced if as many German soldiers as possible were tied down in the west. One of those soldiers was Hitler, who on December 2 received his Iron Cross. Writing to his landlord two days later, he said: 'It is a sheer miracle that I am hale and hearty, what with the tremendous exertions and the lack of sleep.'

Following its declaration of 20 November 1914 in favour of 'national prosperity and national freedom' for Ireland, the Germans encouraged Irish soldiers who had been taken prisoner-of-war to form an Irish Brigade, to fight alongside the German army. A special camp was set up at Limburg in which to bring these Irishmen together. On December 3, and again on the 4th and 6th, Sir Roger Casement visited the camp in order to encourage the 2,000 soldiers there to join the Irish force. He was accompanied by a German prince, Emich von Leiningen, who had been educated (like Churchill) at Harrow School, and who had received the Grand Cross of the Royal Victorian Order in 1898. The Irish soldiers were not impressed. 'I will not return to Limburg to be insulted by a handful of recreant Irishmen,' Casement wrote rather peevishly to a friend after a fourth visit early in January.

Casement succeeded in enlisting fifty-five men, of whom only ten were regarded as reliable enough to be considered for an eventual landing on Irish soil. Despite his impassioned appeal to the Irish nationalists in the United States, only a single Irish-American volunteer crossed the Atlantic to join the force. Casement did, however, achieve a diplomatic success when, in Berlin on December 27, he signed a secret treaty with the German Secretary of State, von Jagow, whereby, in the event of a German naval victory over Britain, the troops of his minuscule brigade would be landed on the Irish coast with a supporting unit of German officers and men.

Visiting the front line that winter, General Pétain reported that deep mud was delaying the French advance. In the British sector, 20,000 men were invalided during the winter on account of 'trench feet' alone. The British Commander-in-Chief, Sir John French, found the ground 'only a quagmire' when he visited it on December 10. 'In that part of the world,' General Smith-Dorrien later recalled, 'there appeared to be no stones or gravel, and rain converted the soil into a sort of liquid mud of the consistency of thick porridge without the valuable sustaining quality of that excellent Scots mixture. To walk off the roads meant sinking in at once.' As the protective parapets were built 'they gradually subsided and the trenches filled with water, so to retain any cover at all meant constant work'.

The fighting continued but with no advantage to either side. 'We took five trenches last night,' General Wilson wrote that December, 'but we have been put out of four of them, chiefly by bombs, and we lost some

1,500 I'm afraid. The movement was good, but the expense was great.' On December 16 the Indian Corps, which had already suffered 2,000 men killed, was sent forward near Givenchy to capture the German front-line trench: fifty-four men were killed in an attempt that failed. Two days later the Indians were ordered to attack again, but 'only on such objectives as are reasonably favourable'. It was during this attack, which was initially successful, that, in the words of the Official History of the Indian Corps in France (written in 1917): 'The enemy, having failed to turn our men out by fair means, attempted one of the many ruses peculiar to the children of "Kultur". A party of Germans advanced up a communication trench with their hands up in token of surrender. As they got nearer, we discovered that behind them were machine guns ready to fire on any of our men who might show themselves. This enterprising party met with a suitable reception.'

Conditions on the Western Front were worsening with the approach of winter. During the attack on Givenchy on December 18, a group of Highlanders adjacent to the Indian Corps were unable to fire, because most of their rifles had become clogged with mud, and were then captured by the Germans. That day, in the part of the line held by a battalion of Scots Guards, an attack on the German trenches in what their official historian, C.T. Atkinson, called 'a not very happily conceived enterprise' led to half the battalion being killed or wounded. The orders for the attack, Atkinson commented, showed 'an optimism which did not indicate any close acquaintance either with the state of the ground or with the general conditions of the front line, or any very accurate appreciation of the difficulties of attacking entrenched positions defended by modern rifles and machine-guns and protected by belts of barbed wire'. What had prompted the order for the attack was the information that several German divisions had been moved from the Western to the Eastern Front. But they had not taken their barbed wire with them!

At Givenchy, a German counter-attack on December 20 won back the few saps that had been taken two days earlier. These saps, narrow trenches that extended forward from the main trench line, often to within a few yards of the enemy trench, were frequently the locations of fierce hand-to-hand fighting. Other dangers were posed by the weather. The Official History of the Indian Corps in France commented: 'The elements were warring on the side of the enemy, for torrential rain during the night had made the trenches almost untenable. In many places the fire-step had been washed away, and the men were consequently unable to stand high enough to fire over the parapet.' In addition, the trenches were knee-deep 'and in some places waist deep in mud and icy water, which clogged a large number of rifles and rendered them useless'. Owing to the 'thick and holding mud', the trenches had become 'veritable death-traps'. Only the slowest movement was possible: 'men had their boots, and even their clothes, pulled off by the mud'.

A retreat was ordered. While it was being carried out, the Germans exploded a mine under one of the Indian trenches. This was one of the first examples of what were to become frequent attempts to blow up a section of the enemy's trenches from below, having dug beneath them deep underground from one's own lines. The history of the Indian Corps in France commented, of the effect of the mine: 'Of E Company, under Captain Yates, not a trace has ever been found.'

The savagery of the conflict was to arouse great indignation when details of German treatment of wounded men, after they had been captured, became known in the Allied capitals. A German soldier's diary, found by the French, was passed on to the British and reproduced in the daily bulletin of the First Army. 'The sight of the trenches and the fury, not to say bestiality, of our men,' this German soldier had written on December 19, 'in beating to death the wounded English affected me so much that, for the rest of the day, I was fit for nothing.' Within a few days of the failure of the attack of December 18 on Givenchy by the Scots Guards, there was anger in the British lines when news spread of how a wounded British soldier, crawling painfully back, was then shot twice in the thighs by the Germans, and then deliberately killed, as he reached the British parapet.

The daily incidents of trench warfare could be extremely cruel. On December 22, two men who had been lying wounded right up against the German parapet for two days, since the German counter-attack, reached their own front line. Both of them had gangrene. One of them had gone mad. On the following day, after an attack by the Liverpool Scottish Regiment, the Colour Sergeant, R.A. Scott Macfie, wrote to his father of the messages sent back from a trench just captured from the Germans by F Company: 'Vance, a recently promoted corporal, killed; an F Company piper badly wounded; Beach, one of my men, shot through the knee; etc.'

Stretcher bearers arrived, on their way to the front, and Macfie challenged them:

'Halt, who goes there?'
'Liverpool Scottish stretcher-bearers.'
'Is Faulkner there?'
'No.'
'Citrine?'
'Yes.'
'How are you doing, Citrine?'
'Fine, Colours!'

Citrine was the sole euphonium player in the regimental band. 'He had wanted to go out as an ordinary private but, being intelligent, the doctor had persuaded him to be a stretcher bearer.' Fifteen minutes later, the stretcher bearers returned:

'Well, who have you got?'
'Citrine, shot dead.'

Macfie was concerned about the wounded piper. 'The stretcher bearers were sent for and arrived some time before dawn. The officer refused to allow them to proceed because it was too late. The poor piper died of bleeding & exposure during the forenoon, in a trench full of water, and without anything to eat or drink, and another wounded man had to lie on his corpse.'

Amid these terrors of war, there was an added danger to troops in combat. On December 22, Churchill informed his Admiralty officials that Sir John French had ordered 'instant fire' to be made on any German white flag on the Western Front, 'experience having shown that the Germans habitually and systematically abuse that emblem'. Consequently, 'any white flag hoisted by a German ship is to be fired on as a matter of principle'. An 'obviously helpless' ship would be allowed to surrender but in cases of doubt the ship should be sunk. In any naval action, 'white flags should be fired upon with promptitude'.

That Christmas, a spontaneous outburst of pacific feeling took place in the war zones, as the troops of every European army celebrated their Saviour's birth. For nearly five months the war had been fought with mounting severity. Suddenly, as darkness fell on Christmas Eve, there was, in sections of the front line, a moment of peaceable behaviour. 'We got into conversation with the Germans who were anxious to arrange an Armistice during Xmas,' a 25-year-old lieutenant with the Scots Guards, Sir Edward Hulse, wrote in his battalion's war diary. 'A scout named F. Murker went out and met a German Patrol and was given a glass of whisky and some cigars, and a message was sent back saying that if we didn't fire at them they would not fire at us.' That night, on a front where five days earlier there had been savage fighting, the guns were silent.

On the following morning, German soldiers walked across towards the British wire and British soldiers went out to meet them. 'They appeared to be most amicable and exchanged Souvenirs, cap stars, Badges etc.,' noted Hulse. The British gave the German soldiers plum puddings 'which they much appreciated'. Then arrangements were made between the two sides to bury the British dead who had been killed during the disastrous raid on the night of December 18, and whose bodies were still lying between the lines, mostly at the edge of the German front-line wire where they had been shot down. 'The Germans brought the bodies to a half way line and we buried them,' Hulse wrote in the battalion diary. 'Detachments of British and Germans formed a line and a German and English Chaplain read some prayers alternately. The whole of this was done in great solemnity and reverence.'

That Christmas Day, fraternisation between the Germans and their enemies took place almost everywhere in the British No-Man's Land, and at places in the French and Belgian lines. It was almost always initiated by German troops, through either messages or song. Near Ploegsteert a German-speaking British officer, Captain R.J. Armes, having listened with his men to a German soldier's serenade, called for another and was treated to Schumann's 'The Two Grenadiers'. Men from both sides then left their trenches and met in No-Man's Land, when there was 'some conviviality', as Captain Armes called it, followed by two final songs, 'Die Wacht Am Rhein' from the Germans and 'Christians Wake!' from the British.

'Most peculiar Christmas I've ever spent and ever likely to,' Sapper J. Davey wrote in his diary. 'One could hardly believe the happenings.' Davey, also on the Western Front, exchanged souvenirs with the Germans in the trenches opposite his. Other British soldiers joined with their fellow German infantrymen in chasing hares. Some kicked a football about in No-Man's Land. One British officer, 2nd Lieutenant R. D. Gillespie, was taken into the German lines and shown a board which had been put up to honour a British officer who, in an earlier attack, had reached that trench before being killed.

Bruce Bairnsfather, whose book of trench tales, *Bullets & Billets*, was among the most popular British wartime volumes, recalled going into No-Man's Land on Christmas Day to join 'the throng about half-way across to the German trenches. It all felt most curious: here were these sausage-eating wretches, who had elected to start this infernal European fracas, and in so doing had brought us all into the same muddy pickle as themselves.' It was his first sight of German soldiers close up. 'There was not an atom of hate on either side that day; and yet, on our side, not for a moment was the will to war and the will to beat them relaxed.' At one point Bairnsfather used his barbed-wire cutters to swap two coat buttons with a German officer. 'The last I saw of this little affair', Bairnsfather recalled two years later, 'was a vision of one of my machine gunners, who was a bit of an amateur hairdresser in civil life, cutting the unnaturally long hair of a docile Boche, who was patiently kneeling on the ground while the automatic clippers crept up the back of his neck.'

'I think I have seen one of the most extraordinary sights today that anyone has ever seen,' Second Lieutenant Dougan Chater wrote to his mother from his trench near Armentières. 'About 10 o'clock this morning I was peeping over the parapet when I saw a German, waving his arms, and presently two of them got out of their trenches and some came towards ours. We were just going to fire on them when we saw they had no rifles so one of our men went out to meet them and in about two minutes the ground between the two lines of trenches was swarming with men and officers of both sides, shaking hands and wishing each other a happy Christmas.'

Chater told his mother that this fraternisation continued for about half an hour, until most of the men were ordered back to the trenches. But then it resumed. 'For the rest of the day nobody has fired a shot and the men have been wandering about at will on the top of the parapet and carrying straw and firewood about in the open. We have also had joint burial parties for some dead – some German and some ours – who were lying out between the lines.'[1]

The French Foreign Legion was also in a part of the line where the fighting stopped, burial parties went to work, and cigars and chocolate were exchanged. Among the Legionnaires was Victor Chapman, an American who had graduated from Harvard in 1913. 'No shooting was interchanged all day, and last night absolute stillness,' he wrote to his parents on December 26, 'though we were warned to be on the alert. This morning Nedim, a picturesque, childish Turk, began again standing on the trenches and yelling at the opposite side. Vesconsoledose, a cautious Portuguese, warned him not to expose himself so, and since he spoke German made a few remarks showing his head. He turned to get down and – fell! a bullet having entered the back of his skull: groans, a puddle of blood.'

Sir John French later recalled that when he was told of the fraternisation, 'I issued immediate orders to prevent any recurrence of such conduct, and called the local commanders to strict account, which resulted in a good deal of trouble.' One of those who has made a study of the 1914 Christmas truce, A.J. Peacock, has noted that on Boxing Day the General Staff of the British 7th Division 'issued orders saying that such unwarlike activity must cease'.[2]

In the air, the war had continued even on Christmas Day, when nine British seaplanes attacked German Zeppelin sheds at Cuxhaven. Dense frozen fog made it impossible for the pilots to locate the sheds, but the flight of the seaplanes above two German cruisers so alarmed one of them that she tried to move out of her moorings and struck the other, damaging both. That same day, a German seaplane dropped two bombs on the village of Cliffe, near Gravesend. No one was hurt.

There was no Christmas truce among the French Foreign Legionnaires in Alsace. On Christmas Day they, unlike their fellow Legionnaires elsewhere in the line, were ordered to continue fighting. Led by Lieutenant-Colonel Giuseppe Garibaldi, a grandson of the Italian patriot, they launched an attack on German positions. Among those killed was the Colonel's cousin, Captain Bruno Garibaldi. West of Mulhouse, at the southern extremity of the Western Front, French troops were in action on Boxing Day against the village of Steinbach. Fighting for the town, which in the final phase was street-by-street, lasted five days, with seven hundred German and six hundred French soldiers being killed before the French were finally driven back.

Far from the front line, Christmas 1914 saw the first deaths among Russian prisoners-of-war being held at a camp at Wittenberg, thirty miles south-west of Berlin. These were men who had been captured at the Battle of

[1] A facsimile of Second Lieutenant Chater's letter was chosen in 1993 as the illustration on the Christmas card of the Imperial War Museum, London.
[2] *Gun Fire, A Journal of First World War History*, no. 28, 1994, page 30, edited by A.J. Peacock.

Tannenberg four months earlier. Their daily rations at Wittenberg consisted of a one-kilogramme loaf of black bread to be shared between ten men, and a thin soup made from potato flour and beans. There was little fuel to heat their barracks, in which a single narrow mattress had to serve for three men, who took it in turns to use it. Unlike the British and French prisoners-of-war, the Russians received no food parcels from home. A British officer who tried to help described them as 'gaunt, of a peculiar grey pallor, and verminous'.

Hunger, cold and physical weakness took their toll, compounded by an outbreak of typhus. A German doctor who arrived in the camp during the epidemic took some bacteriological specimens for his research work at Magdeburg, and then left. Six captured British medical officers did what they could to help. Three of them contracted the disease and died.

In England, in the week after Christmas, more than a hundred anti-war Christians met at Trinity Hall, Cambridge, for four days of discussion about the doctrinal challenge of war. Among the debaters was the Reverend Richard Roberts, a Presbyterian who was soon forced to leave his North London church because of his pacifist views. The dilemma that confronted those at the conference was the dual, conflicting loyalty of international morality, as in the defence of France against invasion, and Christian morality. After four days of debate the participants concluded: 'Firstly, that Britain was bound in honour to help France; secondly, that war was unchristian.'

The 'unchristian' nature of war was not generally accepted. In answer to the Christian pacifists of Cambridge, one of Oxford's leading classicists, Alfred Zimmern, wrote scathingly in the introduction to a book of essays linking the Allied war effort with the struggle to uphold democracy: 'Those who hold that Christianity and war are incompatible would seem to be committed to a monastic and passively anarchist view of life, inconsistent with membership in a political society.' The leading clergy of Europe supported the war and blessed the soldiers going to it. On December 26 an Irish poet, Katharine Tynan, published a poem in the *Spectator*, subsequently much quoted by the Bishop of London, A. Winnington-Ingram, in which death on the battlefield had a divine motivator:

> Lest heaven be thronged with grey-beads hoary,
>   God, who made boys for His delight,
> Stoops in a day of grief and glory
>   And calls them in, in from the night.

God 'calls them in': on the Caucasian front two different faces of God were in conflict as Russian Christian and Turkish Muslim troops faced each other in a bitter struggle in the mountain passes of eastern Turkey. Slowly the Russians were driven from Turkish soil, back across the frontier which Russia had established, at Turkish expense, in 1878. It was during the struggle on the Caucasus Front, at Sarikamis, that the two armies became locked in a ferocious battle. Desperate for Russian troops not to be driven back further, the Grand Duke Nicholas appealed to Britain for some British action against Turkey that might draw Turkish troops away from the east. The British response, initiated by Kitchener and supported by Churchill, was for a naval attack on the Turkish forts at the Dardanelles.

The arguments in favour of action at the Dardanelles were convincing. British warships could gather unmolested in the Aegean. If needed, Australian troops already on their way to Egypt, destined for the Western Front, would be available, assuming that troops were to be put ashore at all, to fight what Kitchener regarded as an inferior Turkish enemy. At Sarikamis, the Russians were forcing the Turks back, but their need for a diversion, though no longer acute, was still urgent. Russian troops from Siberia, who might have tilted the balance in the Caucasus, were needed for the defence of Warsaw. British help for the Russians could be provided without taking a single soldier from the Western Front.

Within the British War Council, it was the stalemate on the Western Front that offered another reason for an attack on Turkey, assuming that such an attack could lead to a swift victory. 'Are there not other alternatives than sending our armies to chew barbed wire in Flanders?' Churchill asked Asquith on December 29. Three days later Lloyd George expressed the same view when he urged 'bringing Germany down by knocking the props from under her'. Lloyd George suggested that some action might be taken against Austria-Hungary, perhaps a landing somewhere along the Dalmatian coast. Within a few weeks, after considerable discussion, the British War Council, headed by Asquith, decided that Turkey was to be the prop that would be knocked down. 'Steps will be taken to make a demonstration against the Turks,' Kitchener informed the Russian Government on the second day of 1915.

Another war zone was about to be created. The capacity to kill and destroy was spreading. Hundreds of towns and villages that had known many decades of tranquillity, some even centuries of tranquillity, had become the meeting points of armies and the scenes of devastation and pain. 'A huge, cumbrous mechanism had cast a blight of paralysis on human endeavour,' one of the war's historians, John Buchan, has written. 'The fronts had been stricken by their vastness into stagnation. Already a man could walk by a chain of outposts from Switzerland to the Vosges, and in a ditch from the Vosges to the North Sea.'[1]

Each corps, regimental and regional history told the same story of peril and failure that December. The historian of the London County Council war effort, Vincent Weeks, himself later a veteran of fifteen months on the

[1] John Buchan, *The King's Grace, 1910–1935*, Hodder and Stoughton, London 1935, page 130. Buchan, who wrote a history of the South African forces on the Western Front, a history of the Royal Scots Fusiliers, a 24-volume 'Nelson Library' history of the war as it was taking place, and a one-volume *History of the Great War*, is best known for his novels and thrillers. His brother Alastair died in 1917 of wounds received in action at the Battle of Arras.

Western Front, described trench warfare at this time 'with its mud and slime and vermin, with its patrols in No-Man's Land, with its nightly ration parties. Working parties and burying parties, with its continual casualties from shell, bomb, mine and sniper, with its sudden bombardments and raids and minor attacks, with its hours of cold and wet, boredom and discomfort, punctuated by minutes of deadly peril.'

From the London County Council alone, in two weeks of static trench confrontation in December 1914, six members were killed. They had served, in civilian life, in the tramways, parks, education and asylums departments. Arthur James Webb had worked as an orderly at the Bexley Mental Hospital. A private in the Grenadier Guards since August, he was killed in action on 29 December 1914 near La Bassée, not far from a French mental hospital. He was one of the last fatalities of 1914. That day Churchill wrote to Asquith: 'When Kitchener declared that there was nothing in front of us but "boys and old men", he was wrong; and when you and I agreed there was a fine and terrible army in our front, we were right. It has taken 5,000 men and more, in killed and wounded, to prove the simple fact.' Yet more deaths were to mark the closing of the year: at a Court Martial on December 30, two British soldiers who had been found hiding in a barn were sentenced to death: they were shot two weeks later standing side by side.

In the trenches and in the capital cities doggerel reflected the growing realisation that the war was going to be a long one, and that trench life was to be a feature of it. A popular tongue-twister that winter in London was:

> *Sister Susie's sewing shirts for soldiers*
> *Such skill at sewing shirts our shy young sister Susie shows*
> *Some soldiers send epistles,*
> *Say they'd rather sleep on thistles*
> *Than the saucy, soft, short shirts for soldiers sister Susie sews.*

In Flanders the British soldier sang (to the tune of 'My Little Grey Home in the West'):

> *I've a little wet home in a trench,*
> *Where the rainstorms continually drench,*
> *There's a dead cow close by*
> *With her feet towards the sky*
> *And she gives off a terrible stench.*
>
> *Underneath, in the place of a floor,*
> *There's a mass of wet mud and some straw,*
> *But with shells dropping there,*
> *There's no place to compare*
> *With my little wet home in the trench.*

Many accounts of the soldiers at the front were published as the war went on, some romantic, some witty, some sad. The reader far from the war zone could only glimpse at reality, gain a certain impression, pick up a certain mood or image. Among those whose notes from the front were published during the war was a French interpreter with the British forces, Captain Philippe Millet, who had been wounded at Charleroi in August 1914. In his book he recalled a conversation with a British soldier that December. 'Twenty-two days in the trenches, sir – yes, *twenty-two*. The regiment has lost five hundred men. As for me, I have only had a scratch on the nose, but the bullet which did that killed my pal outright.'

The pain and casualties of trench warfare, and the calm discussion of territorial aspirations, were part of different worlds, yet they went side by side. On December 3 the Japanese Government, which was fighting the Germans in the remote islands and ports of the Pacific Ocean, obtained a promise from Britain that Japan could occupy all German territory north of the Equator. This agreement caused much anger to the Australian Government, which had hoped to acquire these large colonial possessions for Australia. In neutral Italy there were voices urging participation in the war in order that Italy should not be left out when the time came to divide the spoils of victory. Through the columns of his French-subsidised newspaper, and in his public speeches, Benito Mussolini was arguing that the Italian Government should enter the war. 'Neutrals never dominate events,' he declared in a speech in Parma. 'They always sink. Blood alone moves the wheels of history.'

It was not so easy to be lyrical about 'blood' and 'history' when the war impinged upon one's personal life. When Betty Cunliffe-Owen, who had left Constantinople in August with other Entente diplomats and diplomatic wives, finally reached Athens, she recalled how 'we saw Home papers – had the Home letters – heard the Home news! Sad news, alas! for some of us. It was here Lord Gerald Wellesley heard of his gallant brother's death in France, and here, in the Roll of Honour, we saw the names of friends known long ago in the happy days of Peace. To me, their names seemed to stand out as though printed in letters of gold. Yes, "stronger than Death, and above Life," and never to be effaced – but – *how* it hurt. How horribly it hurt – the aching thought that never again should we clasp their hands – never smile a greeting to one another. A shadow fell over my soul, and somehow the world had grown darker.'

That darkness was reflected most starkly in the French casualty figures since the start of the war five months earlier: 300,000 dead and 600,000 wounded, captured or missing. As one historian has pointed out, the French death toll in those five months was more than the total number of British war dead in the whole of the Second World War.[1]

---

[1] Alistair Horne, *The Price of Glory, Verdun 1916*, Macmillan, London 1962, page 19.

7

Stalemate, and the search for breakthroughs

JANUARY–MARCH 1915

The year 1915 opened with blood being poured out without respite. On the Serbian Front at the beginning of 1915, typhus struck the soldiers in both the Austrian and Serbian Armies. As a gesture of support for Serbia, British women volunteers took more than a hundred tons of hospital stores and medicine to Serbia. For Britain, the year 1915 opened with a naval disaster, the sinking of the battleship *Formidable* by a German submarine: 547 sailors were drowned. On the Western Front, trench warfare saw vast armies unable to move forward more than a few hundred yards without heavy loss. Near Perthes, in Champagne, after twelve attacks and twenty counter-attacks, French troops advanced less than a mile. At Xon, south of Metz, where they were driven off the high ground but then regained it, the official French communiqué announced: 'We found dead bodies belonging to five different regiments.'

The struggle for trenches, slopes, woods and copses seemed to offer an endless prospect of chests against bullets. In London, however, Asquith received a letter from a colleague stating that 'it would be quite easy in a short time to fit up a number of steam tractors with small armoured shelters, in which men and machine guns could be placed, which would be bullet-proof. Used at night, they would not be affected by artillery fire to any extent. The caterpillar system would enable trenches to be crossed quite easily, and the weight of the machine would destroy all barbed-wire entanglements.' The letter-writer was Winston Churchill. His letter marked the first step in the practical evolution of the tank.

Every warring State searched for new allies and new war zones. On January 5, Lord Kitchener told the British War Council that, as the official minutes of the meeting recorded, 'the Dardanelles appeared to be the most suitable objective, as an attack here could be made in co-operation with the Fleet'. If successful, it would re-establish communication with Russia; settle the Near Eastern question; draw in Greece and, perhaps, Bulgaria and Roumania; and release wheat and shipping now locked up in the Black Sea. The War Council's secretary, Colonel Hankey, went even further.

Success at the Dardanelles, he said, 'would give us the Danube as a line of communication for an army penetrating into the heart of Austria, and bring our sea power to bear in the middle of Europe'.

The Entente Powers hoped to draw not only Greece, Bulgaria and Roumania, but also Italy into their orbit. Germany and Austria were likewise looking for allies, particularly against Russia. One small but active group waiting to be wooed was the Russian Bolsheviks, many of whose leaders were in exile in Switzerland. The Bolsheviks had not expected the Austrian and German Governments to be sympathetic to their revolutionary cause, but policy-makers in both Berlin and Vienna were eager to support the spread of Bolshevism in the hope, not all that far fetched, that the Bolsheviks would undermine stable government in Russia and destroy the warmaking powers of the Tsar.

On January 7 a Bolshevik group in Petrograd distributed leaflets to soldiers, workers and peasants, calling on them not to pay their monthly rents. That same day, in Constantinople, a wealthy Bolshevik, Alexander Helphand, approached the German Ambassador to Turkey with the words: 'The interests of the German Government are identical with those of the Russian revolutionaries.' The aim of the Bolsheviks, Helphand explained, was the total destruction of Tsarism and the division of Russia into smaller states. Germany would not be able to defeat Russia in battle if it were not possible to kindle a major revolution inside Russia. Helphand's conversation marked the start of a growing German interest in stimulating revolution in Russia: an interest that was to be intensified by the stalemate on the battlefield, and to find its culmination in facilitating the return of Lenin to Russia, across German soil. Within three months the German Government gave money to an Estonian intermediary to give to Lenin, to encourage him to pursue his anti-war activities. In fact, he needed no encouragement.[1]

Germany's own power to continue the war was noted on January 15 by Stanley Washburn, correspondent of *The Times* with the Russian armies, who wrote, after speaking to several German prisoners-of-war near Warsaw: 'The more one sees of the Germans, and these are far below the average in type, the more one begins to feel that there is a long, long road ahead of the Allies before these determined people are broken.'

On the night of January 19 the Germans launched their first bombing raid on Britain, when two Zeppelins crossed the North Sea to the Norfolk coast. Four civilians were killed, two at Yarmouth and two at King's Lynn. On the Western Front, the Germans captured 5,000 French prisoners during the Battle of Soissons. In the Ypres Salient, German troops kept up their pressure on the British lines, making Ypres itself virtually uninhabitable. Despite renewed assaults, Messines, to the south of Ypres,

---

[1] The sum paid over to Lenin was between 200,000 and 250,000 Marks, worth at that time between $50,000 and $62,000 dollars. When the Bolsheviks came to pay it back in 1923 the inflation of the Mark was such that it was worth less than $1.

remained in German hands. 'We are still in our old positions, and keep annoying the English and French,' Hitler wrote to his landlord on January 20. 'The weather is miserable and we often spend days on end knee-deep in water and, what is more, under heavy fire. We are greatly looking forward to a brief respite. Let's hope that soon afterwards the whole front will start moving forward. Things can't go on like this for ever.'

As Germany increased its military influence in Turkey, there were those who increasingly saw the Near East as the area in which Britain could be most effectively struck, and harmed. On January 21 an enthusiastic pro-Turkish professor, Ernst Jackh, told the Kaiser that Prussian officers then in Turkey would soon be looking out across the Suez Canal, Britain's lifeline to India. The Kaiser flared up in anger: 'You must be mad. My troops are not there for that purpose.' To a German admiral who was present, the Kaiser seemed 'obviously terrified by the thought of a long war'.

In the skies above the German-occupied North Sea coast, British aviators were learning the new art of aerial bombardment. On January 23 two young pilots, Richard Bell Davies and Richard Peirse, each dropped eight bombs from a low altitude on German submarines lying alongside the Mole at Zeebrugge. Davies, severely wounded at the start of his attack with a bullet in his thigh, carried on despite loss of blood and extreme pain. For his bravery he was awarded the Distinguished Service Order.[1]

On the Western Front daily skirmishes and artillery bombardments caused a steady toll. But the German soldiers were hopeful of a swift victory in due course. 'Here we shall hang on until Hindenburg has softened Russia up,' Hitler wrote to his landlord on January 26. 'Then comes the day of retribution!' Victory over Russia was not, however, to come that year or the next.

Each action on the Western Front had a story of its own. In a letter to his parents, Second Lieutenant Preston White reminded them that January 27 was 'Bill II's birthday'. In 'honour' of the Kaiser, the British artillery on White's sector 'fired twenty-one rounds at the Germans' trenches shortly after daybreak. Some of the artillery commanders on our side seem to have a certain sense of humour. So have the Germans. They started signalling the "miss" with a flag from their trenches after every shell, but finally a shell landed fairly on the top of the flag and the signaller went out of business.'

On January 29, in the Argonne, where French and German troops faced each other, a German lieutenant, Erwin Rommel, led his platoon in the capture of four French block-houses. Having crawled through the French wire, he shouted for his platoon to follow, but none of them did so. After further shouting, Rommel had to crawl back and warn the commander of

[1] Davies and Peirse had been among Churchill's flying instructors in 1913 and 1914. In 1940 Peirse was made Commander-in-Chief of Bomber Command.

his leading platoon: 'Obey my orders instantly or I shoot you.' The whole company then crawled through the wire. Having captured the block-houses, they then beat off a French counter-attack, but outflanked and under heavy fire, they were forced to withdraw. For his bravery in the action Rommel was awarded the Iron Cross, First Class, the first officer in his regiment to be honoured in this way. It soon became a regimental saying, 'Where Rommel is, there is the front.'

On January 30, in another German attack in the Argonne, seven hundred French soldiers were taken prisoner.

At sea, the death toll was determined not by the intensity of the fighting, but by the size of the ship and how quickly it sank. On January 13, all but one of the crew on board the German submarine *U-7*, commanded by Captain Koenig, were drowned when their submarine was torpedoed, by mistake, by *U-22*, commanded by Captain Hoppe. Koenig was Hoppe's best friend. A third submarine that left Wilhelmshaven that day, *U-31*, disappeared: it was assumed that it had struck a mine.[1]

On January 24, off the Dogger Bank, the British made use of the captured German code book sent to them earlier by the Russians to intercept the German Cruiser Squadron. It was a British victory which gave a boost to national morale. Fifteen British sailors were killed, but on the German flagship *Seydlitz* the death toll was 192. On the *Blucher*, 782 German soldiers were drowned: an episode captured on film. A still from it, of hundreds of sailors sliding off the sinking hull into the sea, was engraved on the side of silver cigarette cases, as a British souvenir.

In the English Channel, the first British merchant ship to be torpedoed without warning was sunk by a German submarine on January 30. This submarine success was quickly followed up. On February 1 an American diplomat in Paris, John Coolidge, noted in his diary: 'Another little merchant ship has just been sunk by the Germans, just at the mouth of the Mersey, which gives us all a horrid feeling. The Germans are so angry at not getting ahead that they leave nothing undone.'

That day, the German Chancellor agreed to the Imperial Navy's request to launch submarine warfare against all ships, including neutral ships, that were bringing food or supplies to the Entente Powers. This decision was made public on February 4 in the form of a declaration by Germany of an 'area of war' in the waters around Britain and Ireland. The declaration stated that 'even though the German naval forces have instructions to

[1] Of the 199 German submarines sunk between 1914 and 1918 (out of 300 that saw active service) the fate of more than fifteen was never ascertained. It was assumed that they, like forty others, were destroyed by mines. Not so, however, the *U-31*, which drifted ashore six months later on the East Coast of Britain. All her crew were dead: six months earlier, while on the bottom of the sea for the night, they had apparently been overcome by poisonous gases. After the submarine's tanks had blown one by one, she had become buoyant enough to drift to the surface.

avoid violence to neutral ships in so far as they are recognisable', in view of the contingencies of naval warfare the torpedoing of neutral ships 'cannot always be avoided'.

The reason given by the Germans for embarking upon this widening of the submarine war was 'retaliation' against the British 'hunger-blockade' of Germany: the British mining of the North Sea established the previous November. Even the United States was chided by the Germans for having 'generally acquiesced' in the British measures. Five days after the German declaration, the United States warned the German Government that the proposed submarine warfare constituted 'an indefensible violation of neutral rights', and that Germany would be held to 'strict accountability' if an American vessel or the lives of American citizens were lost as a result of the new policy. The United States would take 'any steps it might be necessary to take' to safeguard American lives and property. What those steps might be was not explained.

In the Eastern Mediterranean, a 130-mile Turkish march across the Sinai desert, using wells dug secretly in advance by German engineers, reached its objective, the Suez Canal, on the night of February 3. On the following morning, 5,000 Turkish troops, commanded by a German officer, Lieutenant-Colonel Kress, tried to cross the canal. Three pontoon bridges were thrown across, and about sixty men succeeded in reaching the western side of the canal, but they were driven off by Indian troops, supported by British warships bombarding from the sea, and the guns of an armoured train. The Turkish hopes of throwing a further 20,000 troops across the canal were dashed, as were the German hopes of stimulating an anti-British uprising in Egypt once Ismailia was captured. Two hundred Turks were killed and more than seven hundred taken prisoner.

The growing numbers of prisoners-of-war had led all warring governments to establish special departments to seek information about them, try to arrange exchanges of severely wounded men, and protest about ill treatment. A Dutch visitor to three camps in Germany, Ruhleben, Doberitz and Burg, reported on February 4 that the camp at Burg 'was simply awful – the hatred towards England in Germany is simply incredible and I am afraid the poor prisoners have to suffer for it'. The American diplomat who was looking after Britain's interests was not, however, impressed. 'An angel from heaven could not satisfy the prisoners at Ruhleben,' he wrote to his British opposite number after a further complaint, 'unless he opened the gate and told them to leave.' Yet the complaints continued: at Gutersloh camp, prisoners were angered when they were only allowed to write one letter and three postcards a month. Cricket and theatrical performances helped them pass the time, but could not lessen the burden, frustration and monotony of captivity. At Zossen, a section of the prisoner-of-war camp was set aside for Muslim, Indian and black prisoners. In the centre of the camp a mosque was built 'at the Kaiser's command'.

Those British subjects who had been living in Germany when war broke out came from almost every corner of the Empire. There were also many merchant seamen whose ships had been seized in German ports on the outbreak of war, or who had been captured at sea by German commerce raiders. Sikhs, Black Africans and Malays were among their number. At Ruhleben, where most of them were interned, these internees were kept separate. For a small fee they would carry out menial tasks for the other inmates, one of whom, Percy Brown, a British free-lance photographer, who on an assignment in Holland had inadvertently crossed the German border, later described the non-White barracks as 'the happiest and cleanest in the camp. Most of the coloured men played, sang and danced. Their life was a continuous concert. . . . West Indians and Malays played lullabies in undertones, quiet, soothing music with no banging or discord. In the centre of the barracks was a laughing laundry firm of five Africans. As they ironed out the wash they hummed lilting spirituals to the strokes of the irons. At the back entrance our cobbler danced a queer little rhythmic dance to the singing tone of the ukelele while half a dozen customers waited patiently for their clogs.'

Russian prisoners-of-war in Germany were less fortunate. A Canadian private, Mervyn Simmons, at a camp at Parnewinkel, was present when some of the 'cadaverous, exhausted' Russians, who were being forced to work seventeen hours a day at hard labour, refused to go to work. On the day after the revolt, German soldiers arrived. New working parties were called for, and all those Russians who would not join them were ordered to run in a circle. 'In an hour they were begging for mercy, whimpering pitifully as they gasped out the only German word they knew – "Kamerad, O Kamerad" – to the NCO who drove them on. They begged and prayed in their own language; a thrust of the bayonet was all the answer they got. Their heads rolled, their tongues protruded, their lips frothed, their eyes were red and scalded – and one fell prostrate at the feet of the NCO, who, stooping over, rolled back his eyelid to see if he were really unconscious or was feigning it. His examination proved the latter to be the case, and I saw the Commandant's motion to kick the Russian to his feet. This he did with a right good will, and the weary race went on.'

On February 10, five hundred French soldiers were taken prisoner during a German counter-attack in Champagne. That same day, 10,000 Russians were surrounded and captured near Kovno, on the Eastern Front, where the scale of the battles and of the casualties was enormous. Four days later, at Lyck, a further 5,000 Russians were taken prisoner, followed by the unprecedented number of 70,000 at Augustow during the following week. This coincided with a French military success in Champagne, the capture of three yards of German trenches and four German soldiers.

The wounded of all armies were being tended in Casualty Clearing Stations and, where their wounds were severe, but capable of treatment, sent back to military hospitals. Hospital trains had become a regular sight far behind the lines. In one such train, travelling from the Western Front to Le Havre via Boulogne, Sister K. Luard, of the Queen Alexandra's Imperial Nursing Service, noted in her diary on Saturday February 13: 'Still on the way to Havre! And we loaded up on Thursday. This journey is another revelation of what the British soldier will stick without grumbling. The sitting-ups are eight in a carriage, some with painful feet, some with wounded arms, and some with coughs and rheumatism, etc., but you don't hear a word of grousing. It is a mercy we got our bad cases off at Boulogne – pneumonia, enterics, and some badly wounded with only rifles for splints, including an officer dressed in bandages all over. He was such a nice boy. When he was put in clean pyjamas and had a clean hankie with Eau-de-Cologne, he said, "By Jove, it's worth getting hit for this, after the smells of dead horses, dead men and dead everything." '

In the air, hopes for the effectiveness of bombing outstripped the reality. Continuous Russian bombing of German-controlled railway stations in Poland could not halt the German advance. On February 12 the Kaiser expressed his hopes that the air war against England 'will be carried out with the greatest energy'. A target list was drawn up: military bases and dumps, barracks, oil and petrol stores, and the London docks. At the Kaiser's specific command, attacks on the royal palaces and residential areas were forbidden. Three Zeppelins set off within a week of the Kaiser's order, but were caught in a snowstorm off the Jutland coast and wrecked. During a further attempt early in March to raid Britain, the Zeppelin concerned was blown back across the North Sea by a gale, and shot down by an anti-aircraft battery at Nieuport on the Belgian coast.

On the day that the Kaiser was advocating bombing raids on Britain, a British agent was interviewing a French refugee in Britain, Mademoiselle de Bressignies, who was willing to return to her home town of Lille and transmit information to Britain. Returning to Lille, she lived in a convent disguised as a nun. The radio equipment she needed was smuggled to her in sections, using the regular commercial ferry between Folkestone and the Dutch port of Flushing. Because the generator needed to power the equipment was so noisy, it was decided that, while she would have to receive her tasks by radio, she would have to send her answers by pigeon post. This she did, working steadily for two months, but then she was arrested. She managed to swallow the report that was on her when she was caught. Sentenced to life imprisonment, she died in prison two months before the Armistice.

On February 15, Indian soldiers in barracks at Singapore mutinied, and thirty-nine Europeans were killed. It was the first large-scale mutiny of the war. It was intended by its organisers as part of a general uprising by Sikh militants against the British in India. The uprising had been encouraged by the Germans, who hoped that India was ripe for revolution, just as, two weeks earlier, they had expected the Egyptians to be ready to overthrow the British once the Turks crossed the Suez Canal. A German ship, the *Bayern*, which had earlier been interned by the Italians, was found to be carrying half a million revolvers, 100,000 rifles, and 200,000 cases of ammunition, possibly for the uprising in India. The Sikh militants had certainly expected German help of this sort.

In Singapore, British soldiers were called upon to carry out the executions of the ringleaders. Thirty-seven of them were shot. In India, the uprising was betrayed by a police spy and the ringleaders were arrested before they could give the signal for revolt. Eighteen of them were hanged. From across the subcontinent, Indians continued to volunteer to serve in France, where the first Indian Victoria Cross for bravery had been bestowed at the end of January. As Gandhi later wrote, in support of Indian participation in the war: 'If we would improve our status through the help and co-operation of the British, it was our duty to win their help by standing by them in their hour of need.'[1]

In that 'hour of need' a tactic was being tried that was to introduce a permanent element into trench warfare: underground tunnels, dug beneath the enemy's trenches, where explosive charges would blow up on the eve of an attack, killing, concussing and confusing the defenders. On February 17 a British mining engineer and Conservative Member of Parliament, John Norton Griffiths, having persuaded the War Office to establish special Tunnelling Companies to take the war beneath the trenches, enlisted his first volunteers. They were all peacetime miners, willing to submit to the dangers of digging in the war zone. Within a week the first volunteers were in France. On being led towards the trenches by a guide, they had their first taste of war when a sniper's shot rang out and their guide fell dead. Their own efforts were to be a noted feature of future offensives: in 1917, after a German dug-out had been half buried by one of their explosions, four German officers were found inside it, comfortably seated and outwardly unhurt. They made no move when the British soldiers entered. They were dead from concussion.

At the Dardanelles, on February 19, the British renewed their single day's naval bombardment of the previous November. The two outer forts at Sedd-ul-Bahr and Kum Kale were smashed by the 15-inch guns, against which there was no defence. A German naval officer, Lieutenant Woermann, was killed. Covered with a Turkish flag, his face towards Mecca, he was buried that evening on the peninsula. Six days later there was another bombardment, and Sedd-ul-Bahr and Kum Kale ceased to exist, except as ruins. They were ruins, however, in which artillery pieces and machine gunners, could, and would be sited.

On the Eastern Front, the scale of battle remained a formidable one. When

[1] In 1942 Gandhi took a different view, launching the Quit India movement at a time when Japanese forces were approaching the Indian border. He was immediately interned.

the Germans captured Przasnysz on February 22 they took 10,000 Russian prisoners. When they were driven out of the town three days later, 5,400 Germans were taken prisoner. The fighting on the Western Front, though not with such dramatic changes of fortune, knew no abatement: on February 26 the Germans used flame-throwers for the first time, against French trenches near Verdun: this was the first of an estimated 653 flame-thrower attacks. But the trench system, with it deep protection, gave flame-throwers little more than the element of surprise. On the day after this first attack, a conventional French counter-attack was successful, and two days later, on March 1, French troops were issued with grenades for the first time. That day a seventy-strong German infantry detachment, advancing behind armoured shields for the first time, lost half its men killed or wounded, without piercing the French trenches. Among the French troops in action was the newly promoted Captain de Gaulle. On March 10 he was wounded in the hand by shrapnel: the wound, though superficial by the standards of trench warfare, turned septic, forcing de Gaulle to spend two months in hospital.

On March 10 the British tried to break through the German trenches at Neuve Chapelle and to capture the village of Aubers, less than a mile to the east. At the start of the battle, 342 guns launched a thirty-five minute barrage on the German trenches, the artillery fire being directed in part by eighty-five reconnaissance aircraft. More shells were fired in that short opening barrage than in the whole of the Boer War, an indication of the terrifying transformation of the nature of war within a period of fifteen years.

Following this barrage, the British and Indian divisions attacked along a 4,000-yard front. At the centre of the attack, after four hours of often hand-to-hand fighting, Neuve Chapelle village was captured and four lines of German trenches were overrun. But on the northern sector, nearest to Aubers, a 400-yard length of the German front line was not bombarded. The guns allocated to that sector had not reached the front. The men who advanced on that sector, in three successive waves, crossed No-Man's Land towards an intact German wire. 'It was thought at first that the attack succeeded in reaching the German trenches,' the Official History recorded, 'as no one behind could see and not a man returned.' Every one of the attackers, almost a thousand, had been killed.

The chain of command during the battle at Neuve Chapelle was such that considerable time was taken to ascertain what should be done at each stage of the fighting. Telephone lines having been cut by German shellfire, messages, often long-winded and sometimes unclear, had to be sent back and forth by messenger. Sometimes crucial messages crossed in mid-journey, requiring new messages and creating an added muddle. Errors of Intelligence were made: the initial German strength was overrated, and the German position in certain places was exaggerated. A British attack shortly after midday on March 11 took place five minutes after the supporting artillery fire had stopped, leading to heavy casualties. When one officer asked his colonel, 'Have we got to advance, will you give the order?', the colonel replied: 'No, it is a mere waste of life, impossible to get twenty yards, much less two hundred. The trenches have not been touched by artillery. If artillery cannot touch them the only way is to advance from the right flank. A frontal attack will not get near them.'

Yet Haig ordered a frontal attack, and almost all those who took part in it were killed. That evening he gave the order for a renewed advance on the following day.

On the third day of the battle, the British repelled a German attack in the morning, then launched their own attack just after midday. This effort was forced to a halt within two hours: many units had been wiped out. Haig looked, however, to troops who had not yet seen action to carry the day. 'Information indicates that enemy on our front are much demoralised,' he informed them. 'Indian Corps and the 4th Corps will push through the barrage of fire regardless of loss, using reserves if required.' When this order reached those who would have to put it into effect that evening, there was some dismay. One of the Indian Corps commanders, Brigadier-General Egerton, informed his superior, General Willcocks, 'that the attack ordered was not likely to succeed'. Willcocks cancelled the attack, telling Haig, who had just arrived at Indian Corps headquarters, that 'he did not consider it feasible to make an attack with such a large body of troops by night over unreconnoitred ground'.

Haig accepted Willcocks's decision, but it was by then too late to stop units of 4th Corps from moving forward further north. The official history wrote, of these 4th Corps attacks, the last of the battle, that the confusion was heightened by the exhaustion of the men who, after three days and nights under fire, had fallen asleep and 'could only be aroused by the use of force – a process made very lengthy by the fact that the battlefield was covered with British and German dead, who, in the dark, were indistinguishable from the sleepers'.

The battle was over. A small salient 2,000 yards wide and 1,200 yards deep had been taken, and 1,200 German soldiers captured. The cost of these gains was high: 7,000 British and 4,200 Indian casualties. A senior member of Haig's Staff, General Charteris, wrote: 'I am afraid that England will have to accustom herself to far greater losses than those of Neuve Chapelle before we finally crush the German Army.' From the Ypres salient, Captain Colwyn Philipps wrote to his mother on March 12: 'People out here seem to think that the war is going to be quite short, why, I don't know; personally, I see nothing to prevent it going on for ever.'[1]

The casualties did not end with the end of the battle. Lieutenant Preston White wrote to his parents of the journey to the front line shortly after Neuve Chapelle: 'There were, of course, no communication trenches of any kind, and the Germans peppered us good and proper as we came up.

[1] Philipps was killed in action in the Ypres Salient on 15 May 1915.

One bullet passed through the head of a man from the company that we were relieving, and went on and lodged in one of our men's jaws.' There was also 'rather a gruesome experience' when his men were digging out earth to fill sandbags: 'They brought to light the stiffened arm and hand of a man in khaki, only a few inches below the surface. We knocked up a mound and stuck a cross on top, to prevent anyone else digging him up.' The Company Sergeant-Major's 'latest effort was to crawl out in front of the breastwork to get those dead Indians and lift any loot they might have on them.'

White, like many of those who wrote home, gave details of the villages and hamlets at which the fighting was taking place. In his case he also gave their names. 'I can just imagine you,' he wrote, 'in Henley dining room, sprawling over a table with a large scale map, and the magnifying glass,' his mother laying on the sofa saying at intervals to his father: 'Dear! Dear! what a concern Harry! Do you think it's worth while?' White gave no answer to his mother's imagined question. On the following day he wrote home again: 'Such a day of news for us, good and bad. Wood-Martin, three pals of mine, and four men I knew, killed, loss of two English battleships, forcing of the Dardanelles, and intervention of Italy, all in one day.'[1]

The attempt to force the Dardanelles took place on March 18, less than a week after the end of the battle at Neuve Chapelle. It was intended by the Allies to be a turning point of the war, ending, if successful, the stalemate on the Western Front of which Neuve Chapelle, itself intended to be a breakthrough, had proved such a costly example. The intention on March 18 was for an Anglo-French naval force to break through the Narrows into the Sea of Marmara, and then to sail across the Marmara to Constantinople.

In the British War Council there had been long and detailed discussions about how the attack at the Dardanelles should be followed up. Not only Churchill, whose Royal Navy ships made up the main component of the attack, but also his colleagues on the British War Council expected a swift push through the Dardanelles, followed by panic in the Turkish capital when so many warships appeared off its shoreline. Lord Kitchener was confident that, once the Fleet had forced its way through the Narrows, the Turkish garrison on the Gallipoli Peninsula would evacuate its position without any British troops having to go ashore, and that, without any further fighting, 'the garrison of Constantinople, the Sultan, and not improbably the Turkish army in Thrace, would also decamp to the Asiatic shore'.

This triumph would be achieved by ships alone: Kitchener also believed that with patience and wise negotiations the remaining Turkish forces in Europe 'would probably surrender'. Edward Grey told the War Council

---

[1] The Dardanelles were not forced that day (nor were they ever to be), nor had Italy yet entered the war on the Allied side.

that once the naval success was achieved at the Dardanelles 'we might have a coup d'état in Constantinople', with Turkey abandoning the Central Powers and returning to its former neutrality. Churchill even wondered if the Turkish soldiers might not then agree to serve as mercenaries with the Allied armies. Other Ministers looked to the naval victory as a means of persuading Greece, Bulgaria and Roumania to enter the war on the side of the Entente. It was thought that once the British navy was in control of the Sea of Marmara it could link up with the Russian navy in the Black Sea, and make a combined assault up the Danube, into the very heart of Austria-Hungary.

For every member of the British War Council, the attack on the Dardanelles had emerged as the most obvious and promising strategy for by-passing the stalemate on the Western Front, opening a new front on the Danube, and helping Russia. Lloyd George summarised the benefits in a memorandum circulated to the War Council. 'To bring Bulgaria, Roumania and Greece in with Serbia means throwing an aggregate army of 1,500,000 on to the Austrian flank. This will not only relieve the pressure on Russia, but indirectly on France. It will tend to equalise things, and thus give us time to re-equip the Russian Army.'

From India came enthusiasm from the Viceroy, Lord Hardinge, who believed that victory at the Dardanelles would have 'a strong effect' on the hitherto pro-German sentiments of the Muslims of Persia and Afghanistan. It would also liberate Russian grain, he pointed out, so that India's ability to obtain foodstuffs would be 'much alleviated'. Finally, there were the territorial gains that victory conjured up in the minds of those for whom a naval triumph was imminent. Lord Kitchener wanted Britain to annex the Ottoman Syrian towns of Aleppo and Alexandretta. The Admiralty were intent upon annexing the whole of the Euphrates valley, from Urfa to Baghdad and down to Basra, to prevent Russia reaching the warm waters of the Persian Gulf. Lewis Harcourt, the Colonial Secretary, wanted Britain to annex the southern Anatolian port of Marmarice. Herbert Samuel wanted Britain to establish a Jewish National Home in Turkish Palestine.

The territorial benefits to be gained as a result of a victory at the Dardanelles were attractive to many nations, encouraging them to look with favour on the Anglo-French plan. With the defeat of Turkey, Russia would receive the eastern province of Armenia, and also the capital, Constantinople, which had been promised to her by Britain in secret conversations as far back as 1908. Greece, denied Constantinople because of this prior British promise to Russia, would be given the western Anatolian province of Smyrna, with its large Greek population. Italy, if she joined the Entente, would be given the southern Anatolian province of Adana. France, whose warships were ready for action alongside those of Britain, would receive the Turkish province of Syria, including the Lebanon. Bulgaria, in return for joining the Entente, would retain the port of Dedeagatch, on the Aegean Sea, which she had seized from Turkey a year earlier.[1] Greece and Roumania, as well as Bulgaria, might be given ports on the Sea of Marmara.

Many national aspirations, and many territorial changes, depended upon the success of the naval attack at the Dardanelles which began on the morning of March 18. It was nearly successful. Six British and four French battleships took part. The Turkish forts at the entrance to the Straits had been put out of action by naval bombardment in the preceding days. Within three hours the forts covering the minefields inside the Straits had been incapacitated. The lines of mines laid across the entrance to the Dardanelles were swept clear as the warships advanced.

Only nine more lines of mines, all identified by the British and ready for sweeping, lay between the advancing warships and the fort of Chanak at the Narrows. But an unexpected line of twenty mines, which had been laid parallel to the shore by a small Turkish steamer, the *Nousret*, ten days earlier, wreaked havoc. Three of the ten Allied battleships were sunk, the British losing the *Irresistible* and the *Ocean* and the French the *Bouvet*. A second French battleship, the *Gaulois*, was badly damaged and had to be beached. The British battleship *Inflexible* also struck a mine and was put out of action. On the *Bouvet*, 620 men were drowned; on the British warships, only forty-seven. Both the British and French admirals regarded this as an acceptable risk of war.

For the German officers who had supervised the Turkish artillery, the Allied attack of March 18 had been near to success, as their own ammunition had run low. 'We've been very lucky,' was the comment of Lieutenant-Colonel Wehrle. His batteries had fired 1,600 rounds and scored 139 direct hits on the Allied warships. Only three of his men had been killed. Dummy batteries, with metal pipes pointing to the sky, had served to deceive the Allied gunners.

The British Admiral was eager to renew the attack on the following day, and was encouraged to do so by Churchill. Both men were confident that if the warships could force their way past the Narrows and into the Sea of Marmara, the artillery batteries on the peninsula would be outflanked, and the impact of an Anglo-French Fleet in the Sea of Marmara would demoralise the Turks and cause them to give up the fight. But a sudden spell of bad weather, and then a growing desire among the senior British in particular to see the army put on shore to attack the remaining forts from the rear, led to postponements.

On the morning of March 19, in the immediate aftermath of the naval set-back, the British War Council continued to discuss the fruits of victory over Turkey. Grey suggested making a good impression on Britain's Muslim subjects, especially the sixty million Muslims of the Indian Empire, by

[1] In 1945, at the Potsdam Conference, Stalin asked for Dedeagatch as Russia's Aegean port.

setting up a British-sponsored Muslim state in Arabia, Syria and Meso-potamia. With the future relations of Britain and the Muslim world in mind, Kitchener proposed the transfer to British control of Mecca, the centre of the Islamic world. The India Office insisted that the Turkish province of Basra 'must form part of the British Empire'. Lloyd George went so far as to suggest the possibility of giving Germany herself 'a bone of some sort' in the Turkish Empire, to act as a counterweight to Russia's future growing predominance. A single day's set-back had not dampened the territorial hopes of the would-be victors.

Lord Kitchener's choice as commander of the Allied forces to land on the Gallipoli Peninsula, or to be taken through the Dardanelles by ship to Constantinople itself if the initial, solely naval, attack of March 18 succeeded, was General Sir Ian Hamilton. Reaching the Dardanelles in time to witness the naval attack from on board ship, Hamilton heard the Admiral say, after the attack was called off, that he was ready to try-again. Hamilton now envisaged putting his troops ashore in conjunction with the next naval attack. As he wrote to Kitchener that evening: 'Certainly it looks at present as if the Fleet would not be able to carry on at this rate, and, if so, the soldiers will have to do the trick.' Hamilton added: 'It must be a deliberate and progressive military operation.'

Kitchener now planned to put a large army ashore. Churchill, while still believing that a second naval assault could be successful, failed to persuade his naval advisers of this, and was forced from that moment to take a back seat, the military planning being Kitchener's responsibility, and Kitchener being secretive in the extreme. Any chance of a swift and spectacular naval triumph on the Dardanelles was over, despite an attack ten days later on the Bosphorus forts by the Russian Black Sea Fleet. Five Russian battle-ships, two cruisers and ten destroyers took part in this attack. A second day of Russian activity was made impossible because of fog. Then two Russian destroyers were sunk by the German-officered *Goeben*, and the Russian Fleet withdrew. At the Dardanelles, gales were preventing even the simplest minesweeping operations. Both the Dardanelles and the Bos-phorus remained firmly under Turkish control.

The prospect of a sudden disintegration of the Ottoman Empire was over. The Greek, Bulgarian and Italian governments, each of which had been as excited as the British War Council at the prospect of the sudden surrender of Constantinople, maintained their cautious neutrality. The Roumanian Government allowed 150 German naval mines to pass through Roumania on their way to Turkey. As British, Australian, New Zealand and French troops gathered in Egypt and on the Aegean islands, only the Russians took advantage of what could still be a British land victory over the Turks. On March 20 the British government signed a secret understanding whereby, in return for Russian benevolence towards British desires elsewhere in the Ottoman Empire and in the neutral zone in central Persia, Russia would annex Constantinople and the Bosphorus, more than half of Turkey-in-Europe, and the European and Asian shores of the

Dardanelles, including the Gallipoli Peninsula itself. Britain would capture Gallipoli; Russia would rule it.

It was to prevent Russia from being the master of Constantinople and the Straits that Britain had gone to war with her in 1854, sending an army to fight in the Crimea. In 1878 Disraeli had sent a British fleet through the Dardanelles to warn the Russians away from the Turkish capital. Now Britain agreed that, if its troops then gathering for an assault on the Gallipoli Peninsula were to be militarily victorious, Russia would be the territorial victor.

Among the soldiers preparing for the land battle was the poet Rupert Brooke. While still in training, however, he was taken ill with dysentery, and having taken part in an exercise on the Aegean island of Skyros, he died after a mosquito bite on his lip became poisoned. He was buried on the island, in an olive grove. Four hours later his colleagues sailed for Gallipoli.

On the Eastern Front, the Russians under Brusilov continued to push the Austrians back in the Carpathians: on March 20, the day on which Russia was secretly promised Constantinople and the Straits, Brusilov took 2,400 Austrian prisoners near Smolnik. At Okna, on Easter Day, March 22, in a surprise Russian attack, Circassian cavalrymen overran an Austrian position. A Croatian sergeant, Josip Broz (later, as Tito, the communist ruler of Yugoslavia), was pierced in the back by a lance. 'I fainted,' he later recalled. Then 'the Circassians began to butcher the wounded, even slashing them with their knives. Fortunately, Russian infantrymen reached the positions and put an end to the orgy.' Broz was taken prisoner. That same day, the Austrian fortress of Przemysl surrendered. Amid ferocious blizzards, hundreds of wounded men had frozen to death in the fields before they could be treated; the senior Austrian commander escaped by aeroplane. The spoils of victory were astonishing: seven hundred heavy guns were captured, and 120,000 Austrian soldiers were taken prisoner, including nine generals, and 700 artillery pieces were captured.

'Some of us are a little sceptical about the number of prisoners taken at P...,' Lieutenant Preston White wrote home from the Western Front on hearing of the capture of Przemysl, and he added, 'oh, damn it, I shan't try to spell the beastly word.'[1] On White's sector of the trenches it was a time of relative quiet. 'We had only one man killed,' he wrote. 'He was shot through the head while looking up to see how many dead bodies were lying between the two lines of breastworks. He died just as we were bandaging him up.'

At the Kaiser's headquarters at Charleville, the fall of Przemysl was a blow, countered only by the British naval set-back at the Dardanelles. 'The one will lessen the effect of the other,' wrote Admiral Tirpitz from

[1] The pronunciation as well as the spelling of Przemysl was to trouble the British soldier, for whom the following explanatory rhyme was devised: 'A damp *chemise'll* make you sneeze.'

Charleville. 'But everywhere the Russians are attacking ruthlessly and the Austrians are always beaten, and we too are getting nervous. Hindenburg is coming to the end of his resources.' Brusilov was quick to follow up his success at Przemysl: on March 25 he retook the Lupkow Pass, capturing a further 8,200 Austrian soldiers.

In Petrograd and Vienna, in Paris, London and Berlin, the drums of patriotism beat all the more loudly as the stalemate and bloodshed of the battlefield intensified. That day Albert Einstein wrote from Berlin to the French writer and pacifist, Romain Rolland: 'When posterity recounts the achievements of Europe, shall we let men say that three centuries of painstaking cultural effort carried us no farther than from religious fanaticism to the insanity of nationalism? In both camps today even scholars behave as though eight months ago they suddenly lost their heads.'

On the Eastern Front, the German advance was creating similar anti-Jewish feeling in Lithuania to that which it had created six months earlier in Poland. The Jews were again accused of being secretly supportive of Germany, and waiting to welcome in the German troops. Once again there was widespread looting of Jewish homes and shops. Russian Cossacks, the traditional enemies of the Jews since the seventeenth century, forced them out of their homes and drove them through the snow. As many as half a million Jews were forced to leave Lithuania and Kurland, yet more refugees in search of a safe corner, their livelihood and their security destroyed.

Further south, the Austrian high command appealed to Germany for help against the continuing Russian offensive. Before a special German mountain corps could arrive, however, a further 11,000 Austrians were taken prisoner by Brusilov. At Austrian headquarters the morale of their front-line troops was described as 'below zero'.

Turkey, too, had appealed for German help. On March 26, General Liman von Sanders arrived at the Gallipoli Peninsula to take command of the Turkish Fifth Army, as an Anglo-French army gathered on the nearest Aegean islands for an assault on the peninsula. Under pressure from Germany, Bulgaria as well as Roumania was allowing German weapons to pass through her territory on the way to Turkey: a diplomatic protest by Britain was in vain. At Chanak, German aircraft arrived to provide the Turks with aerial reconnaissance.

For the British policymakers, a sense of impending victory still prevailed at the Dardanelles. On March 25 the Colonial Secretary, Lewis Harcourt, sent the members of the War Council a memorandum headed 'The Spoils', in which he suggested that, on the defeat of Turkey, Britain should annex Mesopotamia 'as an outlet for Indian immigration', and should offer the

Holy Places[1] as a mandate to the United States. At the Dardanelles itself, General Hamilton was also confident, informing Admiral de Robeck on March 30 that the 'wisest procedure' would be to renew the naval attack. 'It is always possible that opposition may suddenly crumble up,' Hamilton wrote. 'If you should succeed be sure to leave light cruisers enough to see me through my military attack in the event of that being after all necessary.'

It was only three and a half weeks before that military attack was to take place, yet Hamilton still envisaged a possible naval victory that might make a military landing unnecessary. Meanwhile, both sides prepared their troops, arms and munitions for the land battle in what Asquith described as the 'glorious Orient'. A warning note was sounded by Colonel Hankey, who wrote to Asquith on April 12 that the military landings at Gallipoli were 'a gamble upon the supposed shortage of shells and inferior fighting qualities of the Turkish armies'. There seemed to be confirmation, however, of the British view of Turkish military incompetence that very day when, in Mesopotamia, a Turkish attack on the British and Indian troops holding Kurna and Basra was driven off. At Shaiba, south-west of Basra, the British and Indian force of 6,000 routed more than 10,000 Turks, stimulating the sense of superiority. Six days later a British aircraft dropped six 100-pound bombs on the German aircraft hanger at Chanak, destroying the aircraft inside.

Not only could the Turks be defeated and hurt with apparent ease, it seemed, but as news of the battle at Shaiba reached England a sense of moral superiority was also possible. At one point in the action a British cavalry officer, Major Wheeler, and his senior Indian officer, Jemadar Sudhan Singh, galloped forward towards the main Arab force supporting the Turks. Having reached the Arab standard, they found that they were cut off from the rest of their colleagues. Wheeler was shot dead while still on his horse. Sudhan Singh was pulled to the ground, had oil poured over him, and was set on fire: his still-smouldering body was recovered by the British later in the day. Both men received posthumous awards, Wheeler the Victoria Cross, Sudhan Singh the Indian Order of Merit.

Throughout March and April, British forces and supplies were being assembled in the Eastern Mediterranean for a military landing on the Gallipoli Peninsula. The Turks were also busy. Labour battalions, made up of Greeks, Armenians and Jews from the town of Chanak, were being put to work to strengthen the defences of the peninsula. From Cape Helles at its tip to Bulair at its narrow waist, work was begun and progess made.

Five hundred German officers and men were helping the Turks with these preparations. Two of the six Turkish divisions on the peninsula were

---

[1] Jerusalem, Bethlehem and Nazareth: in effect, Palestine. Churchill had suggested giving Palestine to Belgium, as compensation for her suffering under German occupation. Samuel wanted it acquired by Britain for a Jewish homeland. Kitchener wanted Haifa to become a British port and oil pipeline terminal, linking the Eastern Mediterranean with the oilfields of Northern Mesopotamia (Mosul).

commanded by German officers. British air attacks by day forced most of the defences to be prepared at night. 'The Gallipoli Peninsula is being fortified in frantic haste,' Admiral de Robeck reported to General Hamilton. 'Thousands of Turks work all night like beavers, constructing trenches, redoubts and barbed wire entanglements. It is true that we have never seen any of them, but every dawn brings fresh evidence of their nightly activities.' Those nightly activities included, at Cape Helles, laying barbed wire on the beaches where the Allies might land, and digging machine-gun emplacements on the cliffs overlooking those beaches.

With so many battlefronts and preparations, each warring nation focused on the news of its own soldiers and citizens. Individual stories often made the greatest impact. On March 28 the first American citizen was killed in the eight-month-old European war: Leon Thrasher, a mining engineer. He was drowned when a German submarine, the *U-28*, torpedoed the cargo-passenger ship the *Falaba*. The *Falaba*, which was on its way from Liverpool to West Africa, sank in eight minutes. Of its 242 passengers and crew, 104 were drowned. There was also a success that day against the German submarine, when the captain of a British steamer, Captain Charles Fryatt, saved his ship, the Great Eastern Railway steamer *Brussels*, by turning towards an attacking submarine and attempting to ram it. The submarine fled, and Fryatt was awarded a gold watch by the Admiralty.

Despite the risk of alienating neutral America, the German Navy intensified its submarine campaign against merchant ships. On March 31 more ships were sunk in a single day, twenty-nine, than in the war up to that time, and 161 British lives were lost.

Anti-war feeling was evident that March, at the Front and behind the lines, with a British provocation and Communist agitation seeking the same goals. In neutral Switzerland, a British agent, George Pollitt, who in civilian life had been an industrial chemist, set up a network of agents in Germany, to exploit German anti-war feeling and made good use of it. One of his informants was 'an idealistic socialist Russian-German Jew' who thought that a German victory would 'put back the socialist clock', so he was willing to help the British. He had made contact with the editor of a socialist newspaper who was working secretly to launch an anti-war coup, and who was 'in correspondence with socialists all over Germany who send him military information which they hope will enable him to judge his opportunity for the coup. They have no idea that they are helping the enemy or doing anything like spying.'

In Berlin, an anti-war protest was held on April 1, led by Rosa Luxemburg. She was imprisoned. Other German anti-militarists prepared to travel to neutral Holland for the opening on April 18, at The Hague, of the International Women's Peace Congress. More than a thousand delegates gathered, from twelve countries, but twenty-five British women were prevented from going by the simple government device of suspending the ferry service between Britain and Holland, the same route by which British espionage equipment had been sent across the North Sea to be smuggled to Mademoiselle de Bressignies in Lille.

France also knew the pullulation of anti-war feeling. On April 8, on the Western Front, a French anti-militarist story writer, Louis Pergaud, was accidentally killed by his own artillery fire after his unit had advanced into the German lines. A regiment of the French Foreign Legion was disbanded when discipline broke down. The dissatisfied volunteers, Russians, Belgians and Italians, were not allowed to stay in France, but were sent to their own armies. There they fought, and many of them died, under the strict discipline, and special comradeship, of national armies. That Easter a British poet, Edward Thomas, recently enlisted but still in training in Britain, wrote about the growing number of war dead in his poem 'In Memoriam':

> *The flowers left thick at nightfall in the wood*
> *This Eastertide call into mind the men,*
> *Now far from home, who, with their sweethearts, should*
> *Have gathered them and will do never again.*

Still preserving her neutrality, Italy was looking for the best territorial inducement to enter the war. On April 8 she offered to join the Central Powers if Austria would cede to Italy the Trentino, the Dalmatian Islands, and the towns of Gorizia and Gradisca on the Isonzo river, and recognise Italian 'primacy' in Albania. A week later, Austria declined these terms. The Italians then asked the Entente for even greater gains in return for entering the war. The Entente agreed to negotiate, leading a French diplomat to comment: 'The Italians are rushing to the aid of the victors.'

Continuing Russian successes on both the Carpathian and Armenian Fronts contributed to a sense of well-being among the Entente powers. To encourage the Russian war effort, a British Member of Parliament and Middle Eastern traveller, Sir Mark Sykes, proposed the establishment, once Turkey was defeated, of a 'special Russian administration' in Palestine, in the region of Jerusalem, Bethlehem and Jaffa. After one month's fighting in the Carpathians, General Brusilov was in control of seventy miles of the Carpathian crest, from the Dukla to the Uszok Pass, threatening the Hungarian plain.

On the Caucasus Front, the continuing Russian advances led to tragedy. The Turks, bitter at their losses of men and land, blamed the local Armenian population for co-operating with the Russian invaders. Starting on April 8, tens of thousands of Armenian men were rounded up and shot. Hundreds of thousands of women, old men and children were deported southward across the mountains to Cilicia and Syria. On April 15 the Armenians appealed to the German Ambassador in Constantinople for formal German protection. This was rejected by Berlin on the grounds that it would offend the Turkish Government. By April 19 more than 50,000 Armenians had been murdered in the Van province. On April 20 the predominantly

Armenian city of Van was surrounded by Turkish forces: there were 1,300 armed Armenians in the city defending 30,000 civilians. For thirty days they resisted repeated attempts to break into the city, until saved by the arrival of Russian forces that brought with them the congratulations of the Tsar for their courage in holding out.

Elsewhere in the Ottoman Empire the killings and expulsions of Armenians continued. Even as those in Van were resisting the siege, tens of thousands were deported from Erzerum and driven southward over the mountains into northern Mesopotamia. April 24 was declared Armenian Day of Mourning. That day the head of the Armenian Church, Catholicos Kevork, appealed to President Wilson to intervene, but in vain. In Constantinople, the German Ambassador went to the Turkish Foreign Ministry and expressed his hope that anything that 'might look like Christian massacres' would be avoided. He was told that the Turkish garrison in the Province of Van consisted of poorly trained conscripts and that 'excesses' might not be entirely avoidable.

The news of the killings at Van became widely known and publicised throughout Europe and the United States. On April 28 the German Vice-Consul at Erzerum, Max Erwin von Scheubner-Richter, was instructed by Berlin to intervene against 'massacres'. He was warned, however, not to do so in such a way as to create the impression 'as though we want to exercise a right of protection over the Armenians or interfere with the activities of the authorities'. This effectively tied his hands.[1] The killings continued.

The stalemate on the Western Front did not prevent daily British raids into No-Man's Land, continual shelling by both sides, and daily casualties. On April 13, Lieutenant William Gladstone, grandson of the 'great' Gladstone, three times Prime Minister, was killed in action. There were also moments of philosophic reflection. On April 18, the 22-year-old Lieutenant Robert Sterling, who at Oxford a year earlier had won the Newdigate Prize for his poetry, wrote to a friend of how, some three weeks earlier, he was in the trenches as the Germans were shelling them, and suddenly saw a pair of thrushes building a nest a few yards behind his line. 'At the same time, a lark began to sing in the sky above the German trenches', Sterling wrote. 'It seemed almost incredible at the time, but now, whenever I think of those nest-builders and that all but "sightless song", they seem to represent in some degree the very essence of the Normal and Unchangeable Universe carrying on unhindered and careless amid the corpses and the bullets and the madness.'

Among those on the Western Front on April 20, just south of the Ypres Salient, at Ploegsteert Wood, was the 20-year-old Lieutenant Roland Leighton, who had gone straight into the army from school. On April 24

---

[1] After the war Scheubner-Richter became one of the earliest supporters of Adolf Hitler. He took part in the Munich Putsch of 9 November 1923, when he was killed, marching at Hitler's side.

he wrote to his friend Vera Brittain, who noted in her diary that he had 'found the body of a dead British soldier hidden in the undergrowth a few yards from the path. He must have been shot there during the wood-fighting in the early part of the war. The body had sunk down into the marshy ground so that only the tops of the boots stuck up above the soil'.

In the third week of April the stalemate on the Western Front was marked by a new and unpleasant phase: one that was intended by the Germans to end the stalemate and lead to victory. It was on April 22 that gas was used for the first time in the First World War. That evening, near Langemarck in the Ypres Salient, the Germans discharged, within five minutes, 168 tons of chlorine from 4,000 cylinders against two French divisions, one Algerian, the other Territorial, and against the adjacent Canadian Division, over a four-mile front.

The effect of the gas was devastating. 'Hundreds of men', Sir John French informed Kitchener, 'were thrown into a comatose or dying position'. The Algerian troops fled, leaving an 800-yard gap in the Allied line. Wearing respirators, the Germans advanced cautiously, taking 2,000 prisoners and capturing fifty-one guns. But no reserves had been brought forward to exploit the success by driving through the gap. The attack had been experimental, not tactical: nor had the possibility of eliminating the Ypres Salient altogether been in the German military minds.

On the following day, a second German gas attack was made on the Canadians near Langemarck. They were overrun, their bravery in defence being commemorated by the first award of the Victoria Cross to a Canadian, Lance-Corporal Frederick Fisher. Having covered with his machine gun the retreat of an artillery battery under heavy fire, Fisher went forward again into the firing line and was killed 'while bringing his machine-gun into action under heavy fire, in order to cover advance of supports'.

Among the British in action in the Ypres Salient on April 23 was Lieutenant Sterling, who five days earlier had written to a friend about the thrushes and larks in the war zone. Throughout the day, with fifteen men, he held his section of the trench against repeated German assaults, before he was killed.

As the battle continued on April 24, German artillery and machine-gun fire destroyed hundreds of British and Indian troops as they counter-attacked across No-Man's Land, before they could even reach the first line of German trenches. Another Canadian won the Victoria Cross that day: Company Sergeant-Major Frederick Hall, who twice left his trench under continuous German machine-gun fire to pull back wounded men whom he had heard crying out for help. As he was lifting the second man into the trench he was caught by a machine gun burst and killed. Hall's Victoria Cross, like his fellow-Canadian, Fisher's, was posthumous.

That evening General Smith-Dorrien, who had been on the Western Front since the Battle of Mons eight months earlier, drove to Sir John French's headquarters to urge him not to order any further attacks. His mission was in vain. On the following morning, April 25, 15,000 British and Indian troops were ordered into action. Yellow flags, issued to the advancing troops so that they could show their position to the British artillery, served as guidance for the German gunners.

As the Indian troops in the centre of the attack began to falter, some seeking shelter in the shell holes, the Germans released gas, making any further advance impossible. French colonial troops, blacks from Senegal, were ordered to make a diversionary attack on the British flank, but were so terrified by the gas that they shot their own officers (who had orders to shoot them if they turned away from the line of advance) and hurried back through the French lines to the supply dumps and casualty stations in the rear, where for several hours they looted the stores and raped the nurses. A British cavalry brigade was summoned by the French to restore order, and did so.

A third Canadian won the Victoria Cross on April 25, Captain Francis Scimager, who throughout the four days of battle had been working as a doctor in an advanced dressing-station, located in a farm. When the farm buildings came under heavy fire, he directed the removal of the wounded, and himself carried a severely wounded man to safety. When he was unable to carry this wounded man any further, he stayed with him under fire until help could be found.

Although 2,000 Canadians were killed in these attacks, the Germans experienced considerable difficulties in combining a gas attack with an infantry advance. Without a favourable wind, the gas was a danger to the advancing troops, who found themselves moving forward into their own poison cloud. With a sudden unfavourable wind it became a positive danger, blowing back into the trenches where men waiting to go over the top to exploit the success of the gas were themselves affected by it, and incapacitated. As for the Allied forces, within a few days they were issued with a simple but effective respirator, linen soaked in chemical or, in emergency, moistened by the wearer's own urine. The immediate danger was over. Angrily, Kitchener declared, 'Germany has stooped to acts which vie with those of the Dervishes,'[1] but on the following day he obtained the Cabinet's permission to use gas himself against the German lines.

A new weapon had become a part of the accepted method of warmaking. 'The horrible part of it is the slow lingering death of those who are gassed,' General Charteris wrote in his diary six days after the first attack. 'I saw some hundred poor fellows laid out in the open, in the forecourt of a church, to give them all the air they could get, slowly *drowning* with water in their lungs – a most horrible sight, and the doctors quite powerless.'

---

[1] In 1898 Kitchener had defeated a Dervish army at Omdurman, in the Sudan (and took as his title, Lord Kitchener of Khartoum).

8

The Gallipoli landings

APRIL–MAY 1915

On 25 April 1915, a day of gas and demoralisation for British and French alike on the Western Front, the Anglo-French military landings, from which the Allies expected so much, took place on the Gallipoli Peninsula. Like the naval attack on the Narrows five weeks earlier, the troop landings were carried out in the hope of a swift victory. No victory, however, either swift or slow, resulted. As with the naval attack, there were moments when it seemed that success was within grasp. Opportunities for success existed, but were cast away by mistakes and mischance.

Two separate landing areas were chosen on the Gallipoli Peninsula, one at Cape Helles, at the southern tip of the peninsula, and one further north, opposite the town of Maidos. It was intended that the advance from the southern landings would push the Turks back to the northern landing, trapping them between the two forces. The first landing took place on the northern beach, codenamed Z Beach, shortly before dawn. Two months earlier the low British estimate of Turkish fighting abilities had led Kitchener to comment caustically that Australian and New Zealand troops would be quite adequate for the task of what he called 'a cruise in the Marmara'. It was therefore Australians and New Zealanders, who had reached Egypt on their way to the Western Front and been diverted for the quick and easy battle against the Turks, who were put ashore on Z beach. Possibly because of a navigational error, they were put ashore not at their original landing place, Gaba Tepe, from where they might have advanced on almost level ground across the central part of the peninsula at its narrowest point, but at Ari Burnu, a smaller cape further north, below the precipitous heights of Chunuk Bair. 'Tell the Colonel,' Commander Dix, in charge of the first landing, called out, 'that the damn fools have landed us a mile too far north!'

The landing itself was virtually unopposed. Shortly before midday a Turkish battery near Gaba Tepe began to shell the soldiers on the landing beach. Many men pushed inland, where the Turks began to inflict heavier casualties. Still, the Australians pushed forward, up a steep terrain, towards the high ground. In the late afternoon, the company of Turkish troops holding the crest of Chunuk Bair ran out of ammunition and began to withdraw. As a small group of Australians approached the crest, the commander of one of the six Turkish divisions on the peninsula, Mustafa Kemal, who was at that moment reconnoitring the area ahead of the main body of his troops, reached the men who were pulling out. In his memoirs he recalled the dialogue that followed: 'Why are you running away?' 'The enemy, sir.' 'Where?' 'There.'

Kemal looked across to the hill. The Australians had just reached it. Unless something stopped them, they could quickly move on to the higher ground. 'One doesn't run away from the enemy,' Kemal told his retreating troops. 'We have no ammunition,' they replied. 'If you haven't any ammunition, at least you have your bayonets.' Kemal then ordered the Turkish detachment to halt, fix bayonets and lie down facing the enemy. 'As soon as the men lay down, so did the enemy,' he later recalled. 'This was the moment of time that we gained.' One of the Australians, Captain Tulloch, later recalled a Turkish officer standing under a tree less than a thousand yards away, giving orders. Tulloch fired at the officer, who did not move.

Kemal's own best regiment was at that very moment engaged in routine practise manoeuvres on the eastern slopes of Chunuk Bair. Ordering it forward, he took two hundred men and led them to the crest. He reached it ahead of most of them, and saw, four hundred yards below, an Australian column advancing. Pushing his men forward, he organised each group as it arrived, keeping the Australians from the crest. A battery of guns arrived. Wheeling the first gun into position himself, and under fire, Kemal knew that if the crest was not held the whole position on the peninsula could be lost.

An Australian scout, returning from the high ground, found a group of Australians sitting in the sun 'smoking and eating as if on a picnic'. When he told them that the Turks were coming on 'in thousands', the officer in charge replied, 'I didn't dream they'd come back.' The Turkish line of retreat along the Bulair Peninsula was denuded of men in order to reinforce the counter-attack. One more Turkish and two Arab regiments were thrown in. Throughout the day the fighting continued. The Australians were held two-thirds of the way up the slope.

Successive waves of Turks, hurling themselves on their adversary, were killed by machine-gun fire as they clambered over the bodies of the previous wave. More and more Australian wounded were falling back to the narrow breach. 'There was no rest, no lull,' one Australian soldier wrote, 'while the rotting dead lay all around us, never a pause in the whole of that long day that started at the crack of dawn. How we longed for nightfall! How we prayed for this ghastly day to end! How we yearned for the sight of the first dark shadow!'

By nightfall both the Australians and the Turks were exhausted. The two Arab regiments were at the end of their ability to fight on. Throughout the night Kemal tried to get his tired soldiers to drive the Australians into the sea. The Australians held on to the western slopes of Chunuk Bair and could not be dislodged. Many, however, were falling back from the front line, 'and cannot be collected in this difficult country', their commanding officer, General Birdwood, reported. Birdwood added that the New Zealand Brigade, which had lost heavily during the day, 'is to some extent demoralised'. He wanted to evacuate the beachhead. When this request was conveyed by ship to the Commander-in-Chief, General Sir Ian Hamilton, whose original orders had been confidently headed 'Constantinople Expeditionary Force', he replied: 'Your news is indeed serious. But there is nothing for it but to dig yourselves right in and stick it out.'

Hamilton added that the southern force would be advancing the next morning, 'which should divert pressure from you'. This was a remarkably over-optimistic assessment of what would be possible in the south, as the events there during April 25 had made clear.

There were five separate landing beaches at Cape Helles on April 25, codenamed S, V, W, X and Y Beaches. At V Beach 2,000 troops, two Irish battalions and a Hampshire one, were hidden in a collier, the *River Clyde*, which was deliberately run aground. A bridge of lighters was prepared so that the men could rush from the ship to the shore. As they tried to do so, they were caught by fierce machine-gun fire from the cliff above, and by artillery fire of one of Colonel Wehrle's batteries, located in the ruins of the Sedd-ul-Bahr fort that had been blasted during the naval bombardments two months earlier. Further along V Beach, more men were landed from naval cutters, small wooden boats propelled with oars. These men, too, were mown down, many of them sinking in the water and drowning under the weight of their packs. So many men were lost in the first hour that a halt was called until nightfall, when the remaining troops in the *River Clyde* were put ashore. By the time the Turks were beaten back, more than half those who had landed were killed or wounded. A Royal Naval commander, a sub-lieutenant, two midshipmen and two seamen were each awarded the Victoria Cross for their bravery at V Beach that morning.

At W Beach it was men of the Lancashire Fusiliers who were to be put ashore. In 1811, during a Spanish Peninsula War battle against Napoleon's army, it was said of their predecessors: 'Nothing can stop this astonishing infantry!' Put into cutters, they were towed in flotillas of six by steam picket boats, then rowed the final distance. On reaching their beach, they found that the preliminary naval bombardment had failed to inflict serious damage on the barbed-wire entanglements along the shore. Many Turks had also survived the naval bombardment, hiding in their dug-outs, and awaited the invader in silence, their machine guns ready for action. 'It might have been a deserted land we were nearing in our boats,' one British officer, Captain Raymond Willis, later recalled. 'Then, crack! The stroke oar of my boat fell forward to the angry astonishment of his mates, and pandemonium broke out as soldiers and sailors struggled to get out of the sudden hail of bullets that was sweeping the beach and the cutters from end to end.'

The men were so tightly packed in the cutters that some continued to sit upright after they had been shot dead. From the cutters, the men jumped into deep water. With seventy pounds weight of kit, and their rifles, many of those who were hit drowned under the weight of their equipment. Others were killed outright. Many, reaching the shore, were killed as they struggled to surmount the barbed wire. Several men were killed by a British naval shell falling short. Captain Clayton, reaching the shelter of the cliff with a few of his men, recalled how 'I shouted to the soldier behind me to signal, but he shouted back "I am shot through the chest." I then perceived they were all hit.' In all, 950 men had landed at W Beach. By the time the beach was secured, six officers and 254 men had been killed, and 283 wounded.

Six Victoria Crosses were awarded to the Lancashire Fusiliers, including Captain Willis, for their bravery that morning at W Beach. One of the six, Private W. Keneally, died afterwards of his wounds, in hospital at Malta. The phrase 'Six VCs Before Breakfast' became a proud boast in Lancashire.[1] Henceforth W Beach was to be known as Lancashire Landing.

Three of the six beaches at Cape Helles, S, X and Y, were hardly defended. Troops landing at S Beach were virtually unopposed. When told by a Turkish prisoner that there were only one thousand men in the area, they dug in, assuming that the Turk was referring to the immediate area. In fact, he meant the whole of the peninsula south of Gaba Tepe. When other prisoners confirmed this figure later in the day, and made it clear that the thousand men referred to those in the whole of the Cape Helles area, including the village of Krithia and the heights of Achi Baba, they were not believed. Yet what they said was true: at that moment the Turks were far less able to repel a serious advance than they had been at Chunuk Bair. Had those who landed known the actual situation, they might have entered Krithia and reached the heights of Achi Baba without serious opposition.

On X Beach the small guard of twelve Turkish defenders surrendered without firing a shot, and the attackers reached the cliff top without a single casualty. They then turned back to W Beach to help in the battle there. A chaplain who was with them later described the sight that confronted them: 'One hundred corpses lay in rows upon the sand, some of them so badly mauled as to be beyond recognition. . . . Some of the Lancashires lay dead half-way up the cliffs, still holding their rifles in their cold, clenched hands.'

The Turks on W Beach were outflanked by men from the other beaches, and beaten back by the surviving Lancashires and a steady stream of reinforcements that eventually outnumbered them ten to one. At Y Beach

---

[1] 'Six VCs Before Breakfast' is also the title of one of the chapters in Geoffrey Moorhouse's book *Hell's Foundations*.

those who landed reached the cliff top without opposition at all. As the different beachheads were linked up, it seemed possible that, despite the terrors of that first day's fighting at V and W, the strategic plan might still come to pass, with the Turks driven so far northward that Allied troops would be able to capture all the forts on the European shore. Once this had been achieved, the object of the landings would be secured: the Fleet would sail through the Narrows and on to Constantinople.

For the men who had landed amid such carnage at V and W, the main thought was of digging in, and tending the wounded. At W Beach the task of attending to the wounded was a battle in itself. 'It was difficult to select the most urgent cases,' one medical orderly later wrote. 'Men had lost arms and legs, brains oozed out of shattered skulls, and lungs protruded from riven chests; many had lost their faces and were, I should think, unrecognisable to their friends.... One poor chap had lost his nose and most of his face, and we were obliged to take off an arm, the other hand, and extract two bullets like shark's teeth from his thigh, besides minor operations. It was really a precious hour or more wasted, for I saw him next morning being carried to the mortuary.' By nightfall on April 26 more than 30,000 Allied troops were ashore. The number of dead and wounded in the first two days of battle exceeded 20,000. Hospital ships, soon to be as familiar a sight in the Eastern Mediterranean as warships, took the wounded back to Egypt.

At Cape Helles, the Turks rushed reinforcements forward. Unable to drive the British off the beaches, they withdrew on April 27 to a position across the peninsula in front of the hill of Achi Baba. To command the southern front, Liman von Sanders sent a German officer, Hans Kan-nengiesser. He reached the peninsula on April 29, followed a few days later by a German naval officer, Lieutenant Bolz, with eight machine guns and thirty-two German Marines. The British had already attempted to reach Achi Baba on April 27 and been driven off by Turkish soldiers sent down from Maidos. Even the first British objective, the village of Krithia, only four miles from the landing beaches, proved an impossible objective: of the 14,000 men who attacked the Turks that day, 3,000 were killed or wounded.

A few days later, as four battalions of Lancashire Fusiliers were approaching the peninsula by sea, to reinforce those already there, they passed a hospital ship carrying the wounded back to Egypt. The newcomers called out enthusiastically, 'Are we downhearted? No!' to which those leaving replied: 'But you bloody soon will be!'

One group of soldiers landed at Cape Helles not only to fight against the Turks, but to fight for their own national ideal. On the day after the naval attack of March 18, the Zionist leader Vladimir Jabotinsky, determined to contribute towards a victory over the Turks that might advance the nationalist aspirations of the Jews, had been present at the establishment of an entirely Jewish military unit, the Zion Mule Corps, drawn from

Palestinian Jews who had fled from Palestine to Egypt. Commanded by a British officer, Lieutenant-Colonel Patterson, with five British and eight Jewish officers, the five hundred served on the Gallipoli Peninsula from first to last.

The senior Jewish officer in the Zion Mule Corps, Captain Joseph Trumpeldor, had fought in the Russian army against Japan in 1904, when he lost an arm. In 1912 he had settled in Palestine. A year after the Gallipoli landings Colonel Patterson wrote: 'Many of the Zionists whom I had thought somewhat lacking in courage, showed themselves fearless to a degree when under heavy fire, while Captain Trumpeldor actually revelled in it, and the hotter it became the more he liked it, and would remark: "Ah, it is now *plus gai*!" '

From first to last, the Narrows remained under Turkish control, not even threatened by infantry assault. There were moments when incompetent and confused leadership at Gallipoli made a mockery of the bravery and tenacity of the Allied troops. The British Commander-in-Chief, General Sir Ian Hamilton, who had been as dashing an officer as could be imagined on the North-West Frontier of India, remained for the duration of the landings, and for much of the subsequent fighting, on board ship, watching the battle from offshore, or studying his commanders' reports at his headquarters on the distant island of Mudros.

The Turks, under German generals, but inspired and cajoled by their own Mustafa Kemal, were able to keep the invading force pinned down to its two beachheads. The Anglo-French landings had succeeded, however: tens of thousands of men were ashore, and the prospect of an Allied victory remained sufficiently alluring for the Italians to sign a secret treaty on April 26, committing themselves to the Entente.

Just as, in its own secret treaty on March 20, Russia was to acquire Constantinople and the Straits once the Ottoman Empire was defeated, so under the secret treaty by which Italy agreed to join the war, she too would acquire substantial territory. Italy's territorial gains would come both from a defeated Austria-Hungary and a defeated Turkey. They were spelt out with precision in the text of the treaty. From Austria-Hungary, Italy would acquire the Trentino, the South Tyrol, Trieste, the counties of Gorizia and Gradisca, the Istrian Peninsula, Northern Dalmatia and numerous islands off the Dalmatian coast. From Turkey she would acquire a substantial 'sphere of influence' in Anatolia. She would also be given additional colonial territory in North Africa and, from Albania, would receive the Adriatic port of Valona, and Saseno Island.

The prospect of gaining these considerable territories depended, for both Russia and Italy, upon victory at the Gallipoli Peninsula. At first there seemed to be a real hope of a speedy success. On April 28 a force of 14,000 men advanced two miles inland from Cape Helles, almost to the heights of Achi Baba, from which they would have been able to look down on, and fire on, the Turkish forts on the European shore. But despite repeated assaults, those heights remained in Turkish hands, as did the village of Krithia below them. Since the initial landings, Turkish reinforcements had been brought up uninterruptedly from the Constantinople region, and from Anatolia.

On April 30 the Turkish Minister of War, Enver Pasha, confident that he could eliminate these Allied two toeholds on Turkish soil, ordered General Liman von Sandars to 'drive the invaders into the sea'. This proved impossible to fulfil. When, on May 3, Kitchener assured the British War Council that there was 'no doubt that we shall break through', he too was mistaken. That night a ferocious attack by the Turks at Cape Helles was thrown back by the French.

At Gallipoli, as on the Western Front, trenches and even ridges were to change hands again and again, but on a normal-size map there would be no perceptible change of the line. The war at sea also continued at the Dardanelles, but without a conclusion: on the night of April 30, firing more than fifty of its massive 15-inch shells the whole length of the Dardanelles waterway, the British battleship *Lord Nelson* set part of the town of Chanak on fire. It was to do so again four weeks later. On May 1 a British submarine, penetrating beneath the defences of the Narrows, sank a Turkish troop transport, the *Guj Djemal*, with 6,000 troops on board. But neither the flames of Chanak nor the British submarine presence in the Sea of Marmara could affect either Turkish morale or the ability of the Allies to break the stalemate.

On May 6, in a second attempt to capture the flat-topped hill of Achi Baba, or at least the village of Krithia at its base, a force of 25,000 British and French troops, supported by 105 heavy guns, pressed forward six hundred yards, but the village and the crest eluded them. Among the British troops were the two Naval Brigades that had fought at Antwerp in October 1914. There they had lost fifty men: at Krithia half their number, 1,600 men in all, were killed or wounded. During the battle a 26-year-old New Zealand lieutenant, Bernard Freyberg, whose commanding officer was killed in the attack, suffered a severe abdominal wound. Two months later he was wounded in the stomach again. After a distinguished military career in two World Wars, and several more serious wounds on the Western Front, Freyberg died in 1963, when his Gallipoli wound opened up.

The German officer commanding the Turkish troops south of Achi Baba, who drove the British off, was Major-General Erich Weber. Six months earlier, as Colonel Weber, he had supervised the closure and mining of the Dardanelles.

The attempt to end the stalemate on the Western Front by a rapid and decisive victory elsewhere was over. Fighting would continue on the peninsula for the rest of the year. But the element of surprise had been lost, and the battles on the Western, and Eastern Fronts, which the blow against Turkey was intended to help, continued without respite or amelioration.

The naval hopes of March, and the military hopes of April, had both been dashed. Ill-luck and error, followed by the unexpected vigour of the Turkish defenders, shattered the Allied dream of a turning point that would bring them both victory in the field and territory on the map.

9

The Entente in danger

MAY–JUNE 1915

On 1 May 1915 a combined Austro-German force began its offensive to drive the Russians out of the Carpathians. It was a German commander, General August von Mackensen, who led the troops, and a German artillery expert, Colonel Bruchmüller, who devised the artillery tactics. The main attack was preceded by a 610-gun bombardment, the largest barrage yet attempted on the Eastern Front, which included gas shells. It lasted for four hours, and 700,000 shells were fired.

Within twenty-four hours the Russians were driven out of Gorlice; five days later they were driven out of Tarnow. Thousands of Russian soldiers lay dead on the battlefield. Nine months of victorious Russian advances were over. One by one the Carpathian passes were regained by the Austro-German armies. Within a week more than 30,000 Russian soldiers had been taken prisoner. After the battle for the mountain town of Sanok, the Russian commander reported that his army had been 'bled to death'.

A British nurse, Florence Farmborough, who was serving in a medical unit with the Russian forces, was a witness to the Russian suffering. Reaching a monastery in the village of Molodych, the retreating doctors and nurses set up an emergency operating theatre. 'To enquire as to how and when the wounds had been inflicted was impossible; in the midst of that great wave of suffering, the acuteness of which was plainly visible and audible, we could but set our teeth and work.' A dozen ambulances were taking the less gravely wounded men to the rear. But however many were taken away, more were brought in. The wounds she saw were such 'as to set one's heart beating with wonder that a man could be so mutilated in body and yet live, speak and understand'. One man to whom she turned had his left leg and side saturated with blood. 'I pushed the clothes back and saw a pulp, a mere mass of smashed body from the ribs downwards; the stomach and abdomen were completely crushed and his left leg was hanging to the pulped body by only a few shreds of flesh.' A priest, passing by at that moment, shielded his eyes in horror and turned away. 'The soldier's dull eyes were still looking at me and his lips moved, but no words

154

came. What it cost me to turn away without aiding him, I cannot describe, but we could not waste time and material on hopeless cases, and there were so many others waiting.'

Two days later Florence Farmborough was in torment when orders were given to retreat further, and for the most seriously wounded to be left behind. 'Those who could walk, got up and followed us; running, hopping, limping, by our sides. The badly crippled crawled after us; all begging, beseeching us not to abandon them in their need. And, on the road, there were others, many others; some of them lying down in the dust, exhausted. They, too, called after us. They held on to us; praying us to stop with them. We had to wrench our skirts from their clinging hands. Then their prayers were intermingled with curses; and, far behind them, we could hear the curses repeated by those of our brothers whom we had left to their fate. The gathering darkness accentuated the panic and misery. To the accompaniment of the thunder of exploding shells, and of the curses and prayers of the wounded men around and behind us, we hurried into the night.'

In Vienna, the Austrian Foreign Minister, Count Czernin, believed that the time had come to seek peace with Russia on 'a policy of renunciation' of all Austrian and German conquests. As he told the Parliament in Vienna immediately after the war, this was the 'one point only' in the whole conflict when peace could have been made with Russia on good terms, 'with the Russian army in flight and the Russian fortresses falling like houses of cards'. In Berlin, however, the belief that the triumph at Gorlice was but a prelude to the total destruction of the Russian armies made any such peace talk premature. That month a petition was sent to the Chancellor by the six most powerful German economic and industrial groupings, demanding a series of territorial annexations and changes once the war was won.

The demands of the German industrialists and manufacturers included, in the west, Belgian military and economic dependence on Germany, taking away from France her English Channel coastline as far as the mouth of the River Somme, annexation of the coal-producing region in northern France, and control of the fortresses of Verdun, Longwy and Belfort. The petitioners also asked for the establishment of a 'colonial empire adequate to satisfy Germany's manifold economic interests', presumably at the expense of Britain and France; and in the east, the annexation of 'at least part' of Russia's Baltic provinces and the Russian territory 'to the south of them', so that the 'great addition' to Germany's manufacturing resources that would be acquired in the west would be counterbalanced 'by an equivalent annexation of agricultural territory in the east'. The total area being demanded contained a population of eleven million people. One of the main forces behind these demands was the chief director of Krupp's, Alfred Hugenberg.[1]

*

[1] In 1929, when leader of the German National Party, Hugenberg provided Hitler with funds to

The Germans had a sense of being in the ascendant in both east and west. On the Western Front, repeated German gas attacks on May 1 drove the British back almost to the suburbs of Ypres. Many of the gassed men were brought to a field dressing station at Essex Farm, near Boezinge. More than a thousand British soldiers, nine Canadians, and eighty-three unknown soldiers are buried in the cemetery next to the dressing station. Among those who tended the wounded and dying men at Essex Farm was a 42-year-old Canadian doctor, John M. McCrae. An author of a book on pathology, he had volunteered as a gunner on the outbreak of war, but then transferred to the Royal Canadian Army Medical Corps. After two days surrounded by the human wreckage of the German attack, he wrote one of the most frequently quoted English-language poems of the war:

> *In Flanders fields the poppies blow*
> *Between the crosses, row on row,*
> > *That mark our place; and in the sky*
> > *The larks, still bravely singing, fly*
> *Scarce heard amid the guns below.*
>
> *We are the Dead. Short days ago*
> *We lived, felt dawn, saw sunset glow,*
> > *Loved and were loved, and now we lie*
> > *In Flanders fields.*
>
> *Take up our quarrel with the foe:*
> *To you from failing hands we throw*
> > *The torch; be yours to hold it high.*
> > *If ye break faith with us who die*
> *We shall not sleep, though poppies grow*
> > *In Flanders fields.*[1]

At sea on May 1, that day of German success on both the Western and Eastern Fronts, a German submarine sank an American merchant ship, the *Gulflight,* off Sicily. Three Americans were killed. That day also, the principal New York newspapers published an advertisement sent to them by the German Embassy in Washington, which contained the following warning: 'Travellers intending to embark on the Atlantic voyage are reminded that a state of war exists between Germany and Great Britain and her allies; that the zone of war includes the waters adjacent to the British Isles'; and that vessels flying the British flag or a flag of her allies 'are liable to destruction in those waters and that travellers sailing in the war zone on ships to Great Britain or her allies do so at their own risk'. This warning was published next to a British Cunard Line advertisement

---

campaign against the Versailles Treaty. He later put his party's votes (some three million) at Hitler's disposal, giving Hitler a majority in the Reichstag shortly after coming to power. Hitler had already given Hugenberg two ministries, Economics and Agriculture. In 1934, when Hitler no longer had need of him, Hugenberg was pushed aside.
[1] McCrae's poem was first published, anonymously, in *Punch*, on 8 December 1915.

for the sailing, at ten that morning and again on May 29, of the *Lusitania*, 'Fastest and Largest Steamer now in Atlantic Service'.

The *Lusitania* sailed that day, as planned, but left her berth two and a half hours late. Six days later, on May 7, she was torpedoed off the southern coast of Ireland. Had she left on time, she might not have been sighted by the German submarine. On May 6 the *U-20*, commanded by Captain Walther Schwieger, had already sunk without warning two British merchant ships, the *Candidate* and the *Centurion*. Four torpedoes had been fired; three were left. That evening the Captain of the *Lusitania*, William Turner, received a wireless message from the British Admiralty: 'Submarines active off south coast of Ireland.' Four further warnings were sent that night and early the following morning.

The *Lusitania* received a sixth Admiralty warning at 11.52 on the morning of May 7. The guidelines under which all British captains were sailing advised them to 'Avoid headlands, near which submarines routinely lurked and found their best hunting'. Turner was steaming off three headlands: Brownhead, Galley Head and the Old Head of Kinsale. The instructions also stressed: 'Steer a midchannel course'. Turner was twelve miles off the Irish coast at a point where the distance from land to land was about 140 miles. The guidelines were to operate 'at full speed'. Turner had dropped his speed. The guidelines were to steer a zigzag course. Turner was steaming on a straight course. The guidelines had been in force since February 10. The zigzag instruction had been elaborated on April 16.

At noon on May 7, *U-20* sighted the cruiser *Juno*, but as she was zigzagging and going at full speed, Captain Schwieger gave up the chase. An hour and a half later he sighted the *Lusitania*. A single torpedo was fired, without warning. The *Lusitania* sank in eighteen minutes. Of the 2,000 passengers on board, 1,198 were drowned, among them 128 Americans. When the American Ambassador in Berlin, expecting (wrongly) that he would be recalled in protest, asked a leading German banker to take his valuables for safekeeping, the banker replied through a secretary, 'Tell Judge Gerard I will take care of his valuables for him, but tell him also that if the *Mauretania* comes out tomorrow we shall sink her too.'

The sinking of the *Lusitania* shocked American opinion, but President Wilson had no intention of abandoning neutrality. Six days after the sinking, in an official rebuke of the German Embassy newspaper warning of May 1, Wilson stated that 'no warning that an unlawful and inhumane act will be committed' could be accepted as a legitimate excuse for that act. In due course, as with the *Gulflight*, the Germans apologised. The German newspapers were less apologetic. According to one Catholic Centre Party paper, the *Kölnische Volkszeitung*, 'The sinking of the giant English steamship is a success of moral significance which is still greater than material success. With joyful pride we contemplate this latest deed of our Navy. It will not be the last. The English wish to abandon the German people to death by starvation. We are more humane. We simply sank an English ship with passengers, who, at their own risk and responsibility, entered the zone of operations.'

In Britain, the sinking of the *Lusitania* was, for the rest of the war, a powerful symbol of the conflict between right and wrong, the Kaiser being portrayed as the real murderer of Captain Schwieger's victims. Anti-German riots took place as far afield as Victoria, British Columbia, and Johannesburg. Captain Turner survived, having been washed off the bridge. Captain Schwieger continued to seek out British vessels.

Despite the sinking of the *Lusitania*, the United States preserved its neutrality. But there were those in America who questioned the concept, and the morality, of standing aside from the European conflict. That Spring, a former American President, Theodore Roosevelt, published a book in which he argued, with examples drawn from the German occupation of Belgium, that the American Government should not hesitate to denounce 'such wrong' as that committed by the Germans there. Those of German descent in the United States he warned were 'in honour bound to regard all international matters solely from the standpoint of the interest of the United States, and of the demands of a lofty international morality'. Dante reserved 'a special place of infamy in the inferno', Roosevelt pointed out, 'for those base angels who dared side neither with evil nor with good'. The only peace of permanent value 'is the peace of righteousness'.

Roosevelt argued that the much-advertised sending of food from America, to help the Belgians under German occupation, had enabled the Germans to take money and food from the Belgians and permit Belgium to be supported by outsiders. 'The professional pacifist would do well to ponder the fact that if the neutral nations had been willing to prevent the invasion of Belgium, which could only be done by willingness and ability to use force, they would by this act of "war" have prevented more misery and suffering to innocent men, women and children than all the organised charity of all the "peaceful" nations of the world can now remove.'

In urging a rapid American rearmament, intensified military training, and a vastly increased naval construction programme, Roosevelt expressed the view that 'there would probably have been no war' if Britain had followed the peacetime advice of those who wanted introduce conscription, 'for in that case she would have been able immediately to put in the field an army as large and effective as, for instance, that of France.' He was convinced that a more fully armed Britain could have deterred Germany in August 1914, and he went on to warn that 'what befell Antwerp and Brussels will surely some day befall New York, San Francisco, and may happen to many an inland city also', if adequate preparations were not made for the nation's defence.

As to America's role in the conflict, Roosevelt poured scorn on those who argued that the United States must act as a neutral mediator. If the nations of Europe wanted peace, and America's assistance in securing it, he wrote, 'it will be because they have fought as long as they will or can. It will not be because they regard us as having set a spiritual example to them by sitting idle, uttering cheap platitudes, and picking up their trade, while they have poured out their blood like water in support of the ideals in which, with all their hearts and souls, they believe.'

On May 9, on the Western Front, French troops launched an attack on the German positions on Vimy Ridge. It was part of the first combined Anglo-French attempt to break through strongly fortified trench lines. For five hours before the attack French artillerymen fired shrapnel shells. Then, after a two-minute silence, buglers sounded the advance, and the troops left their trenches to advance across No-Man's Land. After a thousand yards they reached the first German wire. The artillery bombardment had failed to break it. With their wire-cutters the troops struggled to make the necessary breaches, as the German machine gunners opened fire on them. Those who survived moved on to the next line of wire. Eventually the objectives were reached, the Germans withdrawing to better lines. Some men advanced three miles, to the villages of Vimy and Givenchy. There they were hit by their own artillery. Among the French troops was a regiment of the French Foreign Legion, 3,000 strong: during the attack they lost their commanding officer, shot in the chest by a sniper, and all three battalion commanders, as well as 1,889 soldiers.

The British also attacked on May 9, opposite Fromelles and La Bassée, in an attempt to capture the Aubers Ridge that had been denied them during the Battle of Neuve Chapelle two months earlier. In the crucial preliminary bombardment fewer than 8 per cent of the artillery shells fired were high-explosive, and the total time during which a sustained artillery barrage was possible was only forty minutes, severely limiting the amount of damage that could be done to the German barbed wire and trench defences. Many of the shells were too light to do serious damage to the German earthworks. Others were defective. One German regimental diary reported that shells falling on its front were duds, made in the United States, and filled with sawdust instead of explosives. Some shells, fired from over-used and worn-out guns, fell far short of the German lines.

As a result of the failures of the preliminary bombardment, when the British soldiers attacked they were unable to get through the relatively undamaged German defences. The German regimental diary also described how, as the British artillery bombardment lifted and the smoke of the exploding shells cleared away, 'there could never before in war have been a more perfect target than this solid wall of khaki men, British and Indian side by side. There was only one possible order to give – "Fire until the barrels burst." '

May 9 was not only a day of gloom for the British army, short of shells and pinned down by German machine-gun fire, at Aubers Ridge. It was also a day of expectation: the day on which the first men of Kitchener's Army left for active service in France. The first to embark for France was the 9th (Scottish) Division, one of the many New Army's volunteers who had been recruited during the previous nine months with such zeal all over

Britain. The 9th Division was followed within two weeks by the 12th (Eastern) Division, which also went to the Western Front. Three more New Army divisions were being made ready for Gallipoli.

As the eager volunteers of Kitchener's Army made their way to France, the Battle of Aubers Ridge saw a series of tragedies for the British and Indian troops involved. After the first assault had failed to breach the German line, men who had been wounded in No-Man's Land were killed by a forty-minute British artillery bombardment of the very shell holes in which they had found shelter. The official history of the Rifle Brigade reported the following conversation:

General Rawlinson: 'This is most unsatisfactory. Where are the Sherwood Foresters? Where are the East Lancashires on the right?'

Brigadier-General Oxley: 'They are lying out in No-Man's Land, sir, and most of them will never stand again.'

After the failure of the first assault, British troops running back to the safety of their own lines were being fired on by the Germans as they ran, but as they had with them a number of German prisoners, they were thought by the British to be an enemy counter-attack, and were fired on from the British trenches as well. Few could survive the cross-fire. In an attempt to restore order, Brigadier-General Lowry-Cole, a 'veteran' of the Battle of Neuve Chapelle, stood on the British parapet, where, as he was exhorting the retreating men to make a stand, he was shot dead.

That afternoon Haig ordered a second attack, despite the reports of air force reconnaissance of the steady forward movement of German reinforcements. The commander of the Indian Corps, General Willcocks, protested at the order to attack again, as he had protested earlier, and successfully, at Neuve Chapelle. General Gough, commanding the 7th Division, also reported to Haig that, after a 'personal reconnaissance' of the ground, he was convinced of 'the certainty of any further attempt to attack by daylight being a failure'. Only General Haking, commanding the 1st Division, had confidence in a further assault. Haig accepted Haking's judgement.

Led by the kilted pipers of the 1st Black Watch, playing their bagpipes, the British forces attacked again. They were savaged by German machine-gun fire. When Haig ordered the attack 'to be pushed in with bayonet at dusk' the commanders on the spot made it known that they regarded such orders as mistaken. Haig cancelled them, then told the commanders that they must succeed on the following day. But at a further conference with Haig on the morning of May 10 the three commanders, Haking, Gough and Willcocks, each made it clear that they did not have enough artillery ammunition to start a second day's offensive.

The losses in the first, and as it emerged the only, day of the Battle of Aubers Ridge were 458 officers and 11,161 men. Individual bravery had been in evidence throughout the day. Three Victoria Crosses had been won. But the means to break the German line did not exist, and Haig agreed that the battle should not be renewed. 'Our attack has failed,'

General Charteris wrote in his diary on May 11, 'and failed badly, and with heavy casualties. That is the bald and most unpleasant fact.'

Among those in the Ypres Salient on May 13, when the Germans began a heavy artillery bombardment, was Captain Julian Grenfell, who had been in action in the Salient the previous November, and been twice mentioned in dispatches for bravery. Two weeks earlier he had written one of the most quoted British poems of the war, 'Into Battle', the last four stanzas of which read:

> *In dreary, doubtful, waiting hours,*
> > *Before the brazen frenzy starts,*
> *The horses show him nobler powers;*
> > *O patient eyes, courageous hearts!*
>
> *And when the burning moment breaks,*
> > *And all things else are out of mind,*
> *And only joy of battle takes*
> > *Him by the throat, and makes him blind,*
>
> *Through joy and blindness he shall know,*
> > *Not caring much to know, but still*
> *Nor lead nor steel shall reach him, so*
> > *That it be not the Destined Will.*
>
> *The thundering line of battle stands,*
> > *And in the air death moans and sings;*
> *But Day shall clasp him with strong hands,*
> > *And Night shall fold him in soft wings.*

During the German shelling on May 13, Grenfell was hit by a shell splinter. 'I stopped a Jack Johnson with my head', he wrote to his mother from the Casualty Clearing Station, 'and my skull is slightly cracked. But I'm getting on splendidly.' He was taken to a military hospital at Boulogne. His parents came from England to be at his bedside. His sister Monica did not have so far to travel: she was a nurse at the nearby military hospital at Wimereux. Within ten days Grenfell was dying. 'Hold my hand till I go,' he asked his mother on May 25. On the following day he was dead.

Not only the Western Front, but also the Gallipoli Peninsula, gave the lie to any pretence that might have survived of an early or easy victory. From Gallipoli, Winston Churchill's brother Jack wrote to him on May 9: 'It has become siege warfare again as in France.' As on the Western Front, small gains were made at heavy cost, as when on May 12, near Cape Helles, Gurkha troops captured Cape Tekke. On the following day all plans for a renewed naval assault through the Narrows were abandoned: early that morning 570 British sailors had been drowned when the battle-ship *Goliath* was torpedoed by a Turkish torpedo boat commanded by a German naval officer, Lieutenant Firle.

In the autumn of 1914 the Angel of Mons had served as a source of inspiration for battle-weary troops. In the early summer of 1915 a different image became a feature of Allied emotions. On May 15, *The Times* reported a story that had gained wide currency at the front: during the battle at Ypres in April, counter-attacking troops had discovered the body of a Canadian soldier, crucified on a Belgian barn door. German bayonets, piercing his hands and neck, made it clear who his murderers had been.

The story was never verified, and was almost certainly untrue, but it quickly grew in the telling. Four days after the report in *The Times* a Canadian private wrote to his wife that it was not one but six Canadians who had been crucified, their bodies being marked with a plaque telling Canadians 'to stop in Canada'. Another Canadian private was told that, after a stretch of trench had been retaken, a Canadian soldier had been found with 'large nails through the palms of his hands'. The next time the unit was in combat, 'our officers told us to take no prisoners, "shoot the bastards or bayonet them".'

An artist's representations of the scene elaborated on it further: a bronze frieze exhibited at the Royal Academy in London just after the Armistice showed German soldiers beneath the crucifix smoking and throwing dice. The sculptor, Derwent Wood, called his work *Canada's Golgotha*.[1]

At Aubers Ridge, the failure of the British artillery barrage, and the inability to launch a second day's attack as a result of a lack of sufficient or adequate artillery shells angered Sir John French, whose men were being slaughtered on an unequal battlefield. He himself had earlier given the order for artillery ammunition to be in the proportion of 75 per cent shrapnel and only 25 per cent high explosives. Making no mention of this, he decided to give detailed information about the shell shortage at Aubers Ridge to Colonel Repington, the war correspondent of *The Times*. Repington used his knowledge to devastating effect, publishing a series of articles critical of the government's warmaking abilities. This was the first serious challenge to the Liberal Party's exclusive control of war policy.

Sir John French also sent two officers back to London to give details of the shell shortage to the Conservative leader, Andrew Bonar Law, and the most discontented of the Liberal Cabinet Ministers, David Lloyd George. By this stratagem, Asquith was put under immediate pressure to abandon his all-Liberal administration, to give senior places to his Conservative rivals, and to establish a Ministry of Munitions. It was being widely asserted among politicians of both parties that the war could no longer be fought as a party political venture, or without long-term planning and production. Of the six million shells that ought to have been delivered to the army by the beginning of May, only about a third had actually been supplied.

[1] In the Second World War, Nazi propaganda cited *Canada's Golgotha* as an example of British lies in claiming German atrocities.

Repington's first dispatch on the shell shortage in France was published on May 14. Two days later, the First Sea Lord, Admiral Fisher, resigned, alerting the Conservative Leader to his dissatisfaction over the conduct of the Dardanelles campaign. The shell shortage on the Western Front and the naval failure at the Dardanelles thus combined to force Asquith, on May 19, to form a coalition government, bowing to Conservative pressure for an equal place in the highest warmaking counsels. As a price of joining the coalition, the Conservatives insisted that Churchill be removed from the Admiralty. This was done, despite his pleas, and those of his wife Clementine that her husband alone had the 'deadliness' to fight Germany.

The new head of the Admiralty was Arthur Balfour, a former Conservative Prime Minister. Kitchener remained at the War Office, committed both to the land battle on the Gallipoli Peninsula and to the growing war of attrition on the Western Front. On May 19, at Gallipoli, above the northern landing beach, a massive assault by 40,000 Turks was beaten back by the 17,000 Australian and New Zealand troops then ashore. What had been envisaged less than a month earlier as a continually forward movement until the peninsula was overrun had become a defensive struggle to retain two tiny footholds in inhospitable terrain. On May 22, several thousand miles from Gallipoli, 214 soldiers setting off for the peninsula by train from Scotland were killed in a three-train collision at Gretna Green, the worst railway accident in 150 years of British railway history.[1]

Three days later, at Gallipoli itself, more than a hundred sailors were drowned when a German submarine, the *U-21*, the first to reach the Dardanelles from the Baltic Sea, torpedoed the British battleship HMS *Triumph*. The submarine's commander was Otto Hersing, who eight months earlier had sunk the first British warship to be destroyed by torpedo. A German naval officer, Wilhelm Tägert, who was then serving with the Turks on the peninsula, later recalled: 'The sinking of the *Triumph* was so tremendous a sight that for the moment warfare was forgotten on shore. The soldiers in both lines of the trenches on the Gallipoli hills stood up in plain sight of each other, forgetting everything in their intense excitement. They watched, fascinated, until the *Triumph* had taken her last plunge, then jumped back into the trenches and began shooting at each other again.'

Hersing's exploit caused grave alarm among the Allies at the Dardanelles. Nor had he finished his spectacular work. His second victim, only a day later, was another British battleship, HMS *Majestic*. The six other battleships whose 14- and 15-inch guns had been pounding the Turkish trenches from the hitherto safe waters off the peninsula withdrew at once to the security of distant harbours. The official British naval historian, Julian Corbett, commented: 'Hundreds of thousands of Turkish troops, depressed by loss and failure, and demoralised by the heavy shell fire from the sea, had seen the stampede of the ships they most dreaded;

---

[1] In all, 226 people died in the train crash.

thousands of our own men had seen the loss of the ships as well, and they knew there was nothing now but the cruisers and destroyers to support them in their daily struggle in the trenches.'[1]

The Central Powers had cause for rejoicing at Hersing's exploit. In Constantinople, however, there was consternation when a British submarine, which two days earlier had sunk a Turkish torpedo gunboat off Seraglio Point, torpedoed a Turkish troopship. On the peninsula itself the continuing slaughter was such that on May 24 the Australian and New Zealand forces agreed to a ten-hour truce, to enable the Turks to bury 3,000 of their dead.

On the Western Front, despite the British shortage of shells which had led to the failure and calling off of the Battle of Aubers Ridge, gas was proving ineffective in breaking the trench stalemate to Germany's benefit. A four-and-a-half-mile-wide German gas attack in the Ypres Salient on May 24 against three British divisions led to no German breakthrough. That day Private J. Condon, of the Royal Irish Regiment, was killed: he is believed to have been the youngest soldier to die in the salient during the war. According to the headstone on his grave, he was fourteen years old. On the following day, when the Second Battle of Ypres came to an end, the British and Canadian forces had pushed the line of trenches forward 1,000 yards over a 3,000-yard front. They had also taken eight hundred German prisoners. But the cost had been high: 16,000 casualties, as against 5,000 German casualties.

In No-Man's Land near Loos an enormous flowering cherry tree had blossomed with stunning beauty that spring. After the blossoms had fallen a young British officer went out on night patrol and, climbing to the top of the tree, fixed a Union Jack to the trunk. As he was climbing down the tree, the Germans sent up a flare, and the officer was seen. A machine-gunner opened fire and he was hit. His body hung there: the attempts by two British patrols to get his body down on the following two nights were unsuccessful. Then the British artillery was asked to fire on the tree in the hope of bringing the body, and the tree, down. Gradually all the branches were blown off, and the body fell to the ground, but the tree stump remained.[2]

At the end of May, in London, the *Labour Leader* published a letter from the pacifist Clifford Allen. 'The country has now ceased to fight for the causes of the war,' he wrote, 'and merely continues to fight, even more intensely and madly, because of the results of warfare.' The longer peace was delayed, he argued, 'the more bitter becomes the war, and the harsher and therefore more temporary the ultimate peace'. Whatever truth this

[1] The British offered a reward of £100,000 for the capture of Commander Hersing, but he continued to torpedo Allied shipping until 1918. After the war he became a potato farmer in northern Germany, living at Rastede, fifteen miles from the sea.
[2] Alan Clark, who recounts this story in his book *The Donkeys* (page 162, note 2) adds that the tree flowered again in 1920.

argument contained, it made no impact on the course of the war.

On May 31 a single Zeppelin flew over London, dropping ninety small incendiary bombs and thirty grenades. Seven people were killed and thirty-five injured. Commented Colonel A. Rawlinson, who was later to be put in charge of the defence of London against air attack: 'Having at that time just reached home from Flanders, after making a somewhat too close acquaintance with a "Jack Johnson" (a large-calibre high-explosive German shell) on the Aubers Ridge on May 9th, the damage done by the number of bombs which had been dropped on London appeared to me, I remember, to be absolutely negligible.' Of the nine aircraft that went up, in vain, to try to attack the Zeppelin, one crashed, and its pilot was killed.

On the Western Front, the stalemate was complete: small raids into No-Man's Land, spasmodic shelling, sniping, and the creation of ever-deeper barbed wire and trench defences became the daily pattern. In the fighting at Notre Dame de Lorette that month, many thousands of French soldiers were killed. Today, from the top of a lighthouse tower on the crest of the hill, a searchlight shines each night, rotating 360 degrees, as a memorial. A perpetual flame burns nearby. In the Ossuary lie the bones of 20,000 unknown soldiers, gathered from the surrounding battlefields. In the grave-yard next to the Ossuary are 20,000 individual graves.

On the Eastern Front, a war of movement had begun, with the Austro-German forces regaining the Carpathian passes and the Galician lands beyond them. In contrast to the eight hundred Germans captured by the British in the last days of Second Ypres, the Germans announced on May 25 that they had taken 21,000 Russians prisoner east of the river San. Within a week the Russians were being pushed back towards Przemysl. The Viennese painter, Oskar Kokoschka, then a cavalryman in the Austro-Hungarian army, was among those who were, at that very moment, preparing to leave for the Front. 'When we left Hungary', he later recalled, 'girls in colourful costumes brought us Tokay wine and cheered us; I lifted one girl on to my saddle. How proud I was to be on horseback! People in Galicia . . . threw flowers and rejoicing in our coming; we were welcomed like liberators.'

After Austrian forces had re-entered the East Galician town of Stryj, it was announced that their gains on the Carpathian Front included 153,000 Russian prisoners and three hundred guns. Russia's hopes of gaining Austrian territory were rapidly dissolving. It was now her own territory that, for the first time since the Napoleonic Wars, was seriously at risk. On the Polish Front, where Russia had already been driven back almost to Warsaw, German troops using gas caused more than a thousand Russian casualties near Bolimow and, in a second gas attack two weeks later, drove the Russians back four miles on the river Bzura.

A seventh war front opened on May 23, when Italy declared war on

Austria-Hungary.[1] The main battle was to be waged in the two mountain regions claimed by Italy from Austria, in the South Tyrol and along the Isonzo river. Some Italian advances were made, some mountain peaks secured, but the Austrian General Staff, whose armies were moving forward at that very moment on the Eastern Front, ordered a strong defence. 'The troops should construct positions, place obstacles in front of them, and remain there', was the Austrian order of the day on May 27.

The search for munitions was everywhere becoming urgent. In France, on June 1, more than a million conscripts ready to be sent to the front line were diverted to munitions factories. That day, in Britain, the first women were employed as munitions workers. On June 3, Lloyd George declared that it was the absolute duty of every citizen to place his life and labour at the disposal of the State. On the following day Churchill echoed this declaration with the words: 'The whole nation must be organised, must be socialised if you like the word, and mobilised.' The Government had to acquire 'a reserve power to give the necessary control and organising authority, and to make sure that every one of every rank and condition, men and women as well, do, in their own way, their fair share'. The making of munitions, first under Lloyd George and then under Churchill, was to become the main task of female labour, and, before the war was over, the main source for the assertion of women's rights.

Parallel with the increase in the production of munitions came new inventions: that June, General Dumézil designed a trench mortar that was to be used in the French, Italian, Russian, and, in due course, American armies. From the United States came ten new submarines, made for Britain by Bethlehem Steel of Pennsylvania, smuggled across the Canadian border to avoid breaching America's neutrality laws, and then, after being assembled in Montreal, brought across the Atlantic.

On May 24, on the initiative of the Russian Government, Russia, France and Britain issued a public denunciation of the Turkish killing of Armenians, calling it an act which was 'against humanity and civilisation'. For these 'sub-human crimes', the declaration warned, 'all members' of the Ottoman Government would be held personally responsible. On June 4, having consulted with the German Ambassador in Constantinople, the Turkish Government replied to the Allied declaration that it was merely exercising its sovereign right of self-defence, and that the responsibility for anything that happened in the Armenian districts must be borne by the Entente powers, who had 'organised and directed the revolutionary movement' in the first place.

In a broad belt more than five hundred miles behind the Russian front, from the former Ottoman capital of Bursa to the crusader city of Aleppo,

---

[1] The other six fronts were the Eastern Front, the Western Front, the Southern (Austro-Serbian) Front, the Caucasus Front, the Gallipoli Front and the Mesopotamian Front. Fighting was also taking place, though more spasmodically, in East Africa, Central Africa (the Cameroons), South-West Africa, and Persia.

the killings continued. In a massacre at Bitlis that began on June 17 and continued over eight days, 15,000 Armenians were killed. At nearby Sirt, hundreds of Armenian, Nestorian and Jacobite Christians were murdered. In July both the German and Austrian Governments decided to protest. The Turks brushed their protests aside. When the German consul in Aleppo, Walter Rossler, urged Berlin to raise with the Turkish authorities the cruelties of the deportations in his area, he was told that, despite the reprehensible 'machinations' of the Armenians themselves, efforts on their behalf had already been made.

In a humanitarian act, five French warships took 4,000 survivors of the massacres from the Syrian coast to Port Said. It was a gesture which, however welcome in itself, could have no impact on Turkish action. Within seven months, more than 600,000 Armenians were massacred. Of the 500,000 deported during that same period, more than 400,000 perished as a result of the brutalities and privations of the southward march into Syria and Mesopotamia. By September as many as a million Armenians were dead, the victims of what later became known as genocide, later still as ethnic cleansing. A further 200,000 were forcibly converted to Islam. 'So great is the anguish and suffering of the Armenians,' their own lyric poet Avetik Isahakian wrote the following February, 'so hideous and unprecedented, that the infinity and fathomlessness of the universe must be considerate in gauging it; there are no words in the dictionaries to qualify the hideousness of the terrors. Not a single poet can find words....'

In the fight against the Turks, the British and Indian troops in Meso-potamia, commanded by General Townshend, a veteran of the fighting on the North-West Frontier of India, moved northward on June 2 from their base at Kurna up the river Tigris. When a tiny advance force of a hundred British sailors and soldiers reached Amara, the Turkish garrison there surrendered, fearful that the much larger force was near, which it was not. The 2,000 Turks in Amara, including a whole battalion of the Con-stantinople Fire Brigade, were equally if not more fearful of the anger of the 20,000 Arab inhabitants of the town, and all too glad to surrender. Much glee was caused among the British when a Turkish officer asked permission to telegraph to his wife in Anatolia: 'Safely captured.' Per-mission was granted.

On June 3 the Austro-German forces retook the Galician fortress of Przemysl. Russia's control of Galicia was all but over. A British observer with the Russian Third Army wrote: 'This army is now a harmless mob.'

At Gallipoli, in an offensive launched on June 4, the Anglo-French forces tried for a third time to reach the hill of Achi Baba. More than 30,000 British and French troops took part in the attack. At one point the Turks had built a dummy trench. The British bombarded it, then the men advanced, only to find that the real trench beyond was intact and fully manned. Nevertheless, at heavy loss, they captured it, driving the Turks out and capturing six Turkish machine guns. Then they were shelled, deliberately by the Turks and accidentally by their own artillery, which had at last discovered the error of the dummy trench. Seeking to escape this double bombardment, the men abandoned their guns and returned, under continual Turkish fire, to their own lines. Most of their officers were killed.

Immediately opposite Krithia, the advance by men of the Lancashire Fusiliers was successful, and the Turks were driven back to within half a mile of the village of Krithia. But when Colonel Kannengiesser wanted to move a Turkish battalion from another part of the line to hold the line there a senior Turkish officer told him: 'For God's sake, Colonel, don't order a single man to retire. If the others see that, they will all retire and run as far as Constantinople.' This was the opportunity for the British General, Aylmer Hunter-Weston, to exploit the Turkish weakness, but he decided instead to send his reserves to that sector of the line where the French had failed to push the Turks back, and where a battalion of the Royal Naval Division had almost been destroyed. 'It was a hard decision, and a wrong one,' one historian has written.[1] As a result of it, the men who had advanced almost to Krithia had to fall back, and accept new positions only five hundred yards in front of their starting-off trenches of the morning.

Between 250 and 500 yards of Turkish-held trenches were captured that day, on a mile-long front, but Achi Baba remained well behind the Turkish lines. To bring the British and French wounded back to the beaches for evacuation that day was an arduous task, under continual Turkish sniping and artillery fire. 'As I made my way along the trench,' a member of the Royal Naval Division, Chief Petty Officer Johnston, wrote in his diary, 'I passed many heaps of dead upon which the great ugly flies were feasting. Wounded by the dozen were huddled in side trenches waiting for the time when it would be possible to get stretchers along to convey them to the base.' Indian mule-cart drivers, and men of the Zion Mule Corps, after bringing ammunition from the beaches to the trenches, would return with a new cargo, the wounded.

As for the dead, the need to consolidate the new positions meant that there was at first no time for burials. On the front of one Scottish regiment, the Scottish Borderers, writes the official British historian, the dead 'were piled up on each side of the communication trench to the captured position, where they made a ghastly avenue. By an unfortunate mistake in psychology a Territorial battalion of the Scottish Borderers, arriving shortly afterwards on the peninsula, had to bury these corpses as their first task on shore. It was not a good beginning.' When burials did take place, they could be sickening. 'The flies crawled in their millions over the dead,' Chief Petty Officer Johnston wrote, 'and rose in clouds when a corpse was lifted to the grave and then descended to their feast before the spadeful of earth was placed.'

[1] Robert Rhodes James, *Gallipoli*, B.T. Batsford, London 1965, page 214.

18 Baluchi troops enter the line, Wytschaere, Flanders, October 1914.

19 A French poster, after the execution of Nurse Edith Cavell in Brussels on 12 October 1915.

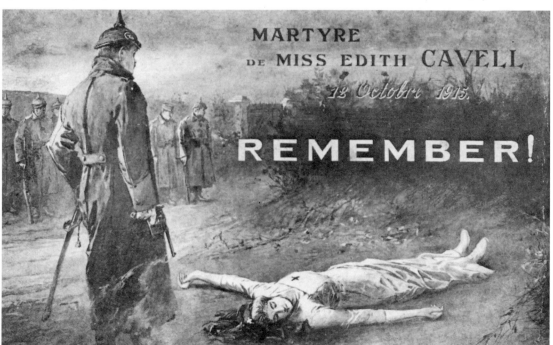

20 The Cunard ocean liner *Lusitania*, a pre-war postcard.

21 Survivors of the *Lusitania*, after her sinking on 7 May 1915.

22 The Eastern Front: German soldiers and Jewish refugees watch, while a village burns.

23 Jewish refugees flee the battle area as the Germans advance into Russian Poland.

24 Russian soldiers man a trench, bayonets at the ready.

25 Dead Russian soldiers in a trench in Galicia, looked at by their Austrian adversaries who have overrun them.

26 British troops prepare for a gas attack, Flanders, 1915.

27 British dead on the battlefield at Neuve Chapelle, 10 March 1915: a German photograph.

28 Gallipoli: horses picketed on the beach between Cape Helles and Gully Ravine, troops resting.

29 Gallipoli: a wounded man is carried by stretcher along a commmunication trench to the rear.

30 Gallipoli: Australian dead at Lone Pine, Anzac.

31 Gallipoli: a photograph taken during the 10-hour truce of 24 May 1915, when the Turks gathered up 3,000 of their dead from the battlefield for burial.

32 Gallipoli: frost-bitten soldiers at Suvla Bay lying on straw in a shelter built of biscuit crates, after the severe frost of November 1915.

33 Wounded men being taken off the Gallipoli Peninsula by barge, to a hospital ship.

Among the dead on June 4 was Private Jim Scotson, who was standing next to his father in the trenches when he was shot dead by a Turkish sniper. His father fainted with the shock and was sent by hospital ship to Egypt suffering from a nervous breakdown. Two brothers were also in the trenches that day, Fred and Harry Tennant. Harry was killed that morning. Fred wrote to their mother: 'He fell with his face to the enemy, and I am sure no man could wish for a more glorious death.' A few days later Fred was badly wounded: before the end of the month he too was dead.

The Turks had been exhausted by the attack of June 4. 'I felt that another energetic attack by the English would have the worst results,' Colonel Kannengiesser recalled. 'Had the British continued their attack the next day with the same violence,' a Turkish officer wrote, 'all would have been lost.' But neither the British nor the French had the strength to attack the next day. The Hood Battalion of the Royal Naval Division, which had arrived on the peninsula with thirty officers, and lost twenty in the attack on May 6, lost a further six on June 4. Among them was Lieutenant Oscar Freyberg, whose brother Bernard was then in Cairo recovering from his stomach wound. Oscar was last seen alive in action in a Turkish trench, a pistol in both hands. His body was never found.

Another of the soldiers killed on June 4 was Private T. Eardley, from Manchester. Eardley had been serving on the peninsula since the landings in April. In civilian life he was an avid autograph collector. After his death a postcard was found in his trench which read: 'A man who goes on calmly hunting autographs with all civilisation crumbling around him, and the Turkish enemy not far below the horizon, really deserves to succeed. So here goes. G. Bernard Shaw.'

Among those who fought in the battle of June 4 and survived was A.P. Herbert, whose book about life and death on Cape Helles, and about a brave man shot for cowardice, *The Secret Battle*, was called by Churchill in his introduction 'one of those cries of pain wrung from the fighting troops by the prolonged and measureless torment through which they passed; and like the poems of Siegfried Sassoon should be read in each generation, so that men and women are under no illusion about what war means.' A.P. Herbert also wrote a poem about the battle:

> This is the Fourth of June
>   Think not I never dream
> The noise of that infernal noon,
>   The stretchers' endless stream,
> The tales of triumph won,
>   The night that found them lies,
> The wounded wailing in the sun,
>   The dead, the dust, the flies.
>
> The flies! oh God, the flies
>   That soiled the sacred dead.

> *To see them swarm from dead men's eyes*
> *   And share the soldiers' bread!*
> *Nor think I now forget*
> *   The filth and stench of war,*
> *The corpses on the parapet,*
> *   The maggots in the floor.*

The Turks counter-attacked on June 6, their preparatory planning having been done by Kannengiesser and two German staff officers. When the Turks advanced into No-Man's Land they came across one of the German Marines who had been part of a machine gun team captured by the British on June 4. This sailor, Leading Seaman Peters, when being led back through the British trenches, had broken free, and then rushed forward in the confusion to the front line. As he jumped up and ran across No-Man's Land, the British soldiers marvelled at what they thought was the keenness and bravery of one of their number. Unfortunately the Turks, seeing a man rushing forward in naval uniform, assumed that he was British and opened fire. He had to shelter in a shell hole, hiding there for two days and nights without food or water. He was saved when the Turks reached him during their counter-attack. Shortly afterwards, in a counter-attack, the British pushed the Turks back to the original British lines.

The second Battle of Krithia was over. The toll of dead and wounded on both sides was massive: 4,500 British, 2,000 French and 9,000 Turks. On the hospital ships going to Egypt, stops were made to bury at sea those whose wounds had been too severe to mend. The Assistant Director of Medical Services in Alexandria wrote: 'I used to wake in the morning and see the ships waiting to enter the harbour, and wonder where we would put all the people.'

As on the Western Front, so at Cape Helles, the line of trenches was deepened and strengthened, the two armies facing each other with daily sniping and artillery fire. At Cape Helles the Turks were able to shell not only from the direction of Achi Baba, to the north, but also from the south, firing across the Dardanelles from the Asiatic shore, from the very plain of Troy that had seen the ancient drama of the Trojan War. Among the British officers at Cape Helles was Patrick Shaw-Stewart, an Oxford scholar and a poet:

> *I saw a man this morning*
> *   Who did not wish to die:*
> *I ask, and cannot answer,*
> *   If otherwise wish I.*
>
> *Fair broke the day this morning*
> *   Against the Dardanelles;*
> *The breeze blew soft, the morn's cheeks*
> *   Were cold as cold sea-shells.*
>
> *But other shells are waiting*

Across the Aegean Sea,
Shrapnel and high explosive,
Shells and hells for me.

O hell of ships and cities,
Hell of men like me,
Fatal second Helen,
Why must I follow thee?

'Nowadays we who are alive have the sense of being old, old survivors,' Shaw-Stewart wrote home from Gallipoli. Two years later he was killed in action on the Western Front, having refused to go back to a casualty clearing station after his ear had been torn off by shrapnel a few minutes before.

On June 6 a German attempt was made to co-ordinate a naval and air attack on Britain. Three Zeppelins set off that night from their sheds in German-occupied Belgium. One, in technical difficulties, landed almost as soon as it took off. Two others crossed the North Sea, but were forced by fog to turn back before they reached the East Coast. One of those that returned was spotted near Ghent by a young pilot, Flight Sub-Lieutenant Rex Warneford, who managed, despite intermittent gunfire from the Zeppelin, to fly above it. He then released three bombs, the third of which exploded, destroying the Zeppelin. Nine of the ten Zeppelin crew members were killed. The tenth, Coxswain Alfred Mühler, survived an 8,000-foot fall in the Zeppelin's gondola, which crashed through the roof of the Convent of St Elisabeth in Ghent after throwing him out at a hundred feet. The convent caught fire. Two young nuns, a child, and a man trying to save the child, lost their lives. 'In spite of our mourning,' Mother Thérèse later recalled, 'there was in all our hearts a fierce joy for the intrepid daring and victory of Lieutenant Warneford. After the war a plaque was fixed on the wall of our convent in memory of the young airman, and a nearby street was named after him.'

The force of the explosion on the Zeppelin had turned Warneford's plane over and over, and for a while it was upside down, losing all its remaining fuel. It glided down to a field near Ghent and broke a petrol feed pipe. There was still some petrol in the reserve tank. Repairing the pipe and managing to restart the engine after thirty-five minutes behind German lines, Warneford saw a group of German cavalrymen approaching the plane. He jumped into it and took off, calling out to the cavalrymen as he left the ground, 'Give my regards to the Kaiser.' His exploit was given massive coverage in the British press and, his cousin Mary Gibson has written, 'took some of the darkness out of the war's other gloomy bulletins'. The King took the extraordinary step of sending a personal telegram to Warneford on the day after the action 'conferring upon you the Victoria Cross'. In a covering note to the Admiralty, the King's Private Secretary added: 'His Majesty feels that if this is to be sent the sooner the better.'

The King's prescience was better than he knew. Ten days later Warneford was taking an American journalist, Henry Needham, for a flight from Buc aerodrome, near Paris. At 2,000 feet the aircraft went into a spin, and in coming out of the spin, its tail broke off. Falling to about 700 feet, the plane turned upside down and, to the horror of the onlookers, Warneford and Needham were thrown out, and fell to the ground. Needham was killed instantly. Warneford died an hour later in hospital. His public funeral was followed by a public recruiting drive using him as the focus of the appeal 'not to let young Warneford be the last of the heroes'. He was twenty-three years old. A memorial erected by the *Daily Express* in the Brompton Cemetery showed his plane attacking the Zeppelin.

Those who attended Warneford's funeral in London were not to know that the Germans had succeeded in establishing a spy ring of seven agents in British ports. On June 15 the head of French military cryptography, Colonel Cartier, passed on to British Intelligence a number of intercepted German top-secret wireless messages that gave the identification of these agents. All were arrested, and at least two were executed in the Tower of London. German espionage was virtually at an end, mostly carried out by neutrals. Two of these, a Peruvian and a Norwegian, were also shot after being captured.

In German-occupied Belgium a new Governor, Baron von Bissing, was making it clear that, once the war was over, Germany intended to keep some form of control over the land she had conquered. In a speech on June 19 he explained why his policy would be to care for the 'welfare and prosperity' of Belgium. 'I am of the opinion that a squeezed lemon has no value and that a dead cow will give no milk. It is, therefore, necessary and important that a country which has such importance for Germany economically and otherwise, is kept alive, and that the wounds of war are healed as much as possible.' Later in the year Bissing wrote a memorandum in which he drew attention to Germany's failure before 1914 to assimilate or to satisfy her French and Polish minorities. 'For years to come we must maintain the existing state of dictatorship,' he wrote. 'Belgium must be seized and held, as it now is, and as it must be in the future'; and on the Kaiser's birthday seven months later he declared: 'What has been entrusted to us, we want to hold on to.'

On the Western Front, the British launched no offensive that June. In his letters home, the nineteen-year-old Robert Graves gave a picture of the daily shelling and sniping of the 'static' line. On June 8 seventeen of the men in his battalion were killed or wounded by German bombs and grenades. The German front-line trench was only, on average, thirty yards away from where Graves was. On the following day, in a section of the line that was only twenty yards from a German-occupied sap, 'I went along whistling "The Farmer's Boy", to keep up my spirits,' Graves wrote, 'when suddenly I saw a group bending over a man lying at the bottom of the trench. He was making a snoring noise mixed with animal groans. At my feet lay the cap he had worn, splashed with his brains. I had never seen human brains before; I somehow regarded them as a poetical figment. One can joke with a badly-wounded man and congratulate him on being out of it. One can disregard a dead man. But even a miner can't make a joke over a man who takes three hours to die, after the top part of his head has been taken off by a bullet fired at twenty yards' range.'

French troops were fighting in Artois, attempting to push through the German trenches, but in vain. On June 18, after savage hand-to-hand fighting, many small advances, ridges captured and then lost, and after 18,000 casualties, the battle was called off. On the Meuse-Argonne front, a further 16,000 French soldiers were killed or wounded in repulsing a German attack. Thousands of men on both sides were simply obliterated by the intensity of the artillery bombardments and the severity of trench combat: among those who 'disappeared' in Artois was the French novelist Jules Leroux. He was thirty-four years old.

On June 27, Vera Brittain began her first day's work as a nurse in a British hospital, tending wounded men brought back from the Western Front. That day she heard a Scottish sergeant in the hospital remark: 'We shall beat them, but they'll break our hearts first!' In a memorandum written on June 29, General Pétain told his superiors that the war of attrition on the Western Front would go 'to the side which possesses the last man'. In London that day the British Government introduced a National Registration Bill, the first step on the road from voluntary to compulsory military service. Kitchener's Army of volunteers, the New Armies even then joining the regular troops on the Western Front and at Gallipoli, were to reach more than two million men, but by the end of June 1915 it had become clear that even this would not be enough. That week the number of French troops under arms reached five million. To protect the men at the front, new devices continued to reach all armies: most important for the individual French soldier was the steel helmet, but there were never enough: in July 180,000 were produced, in August only 55,000. British steel helmets followed soon afterwards.

The war on the Western Front focused on raids into the the enemy trenches, spasmodic bombardments, and occasional small-scale attacks. One such attack, by the 1st London Rifle Brigade, pushed the British line forward seventy-five yards along a 300-yard front. Among the attackers was Rifleman Ernest Jones. His nephew, Nigel H. Jones, revisited the scene sixty-seven years later, noting that, according to the British official history, the captured trench was 'choked with German dead and littered with letters and parcels. Evidently the mail had just arrived. Some kind of meal had been in progress, for there was an abundance of hot coffee which was eagerly consumed by the raiders who in addition fortified themselves with cigars.' A German counter-attack was beaten off, but at a heavy cost. By the end of the day more than eighty British soldiers had been killed, among them Ernest Jones.

*

In Mesopotamia, where after the capture of Amara at the beginning of June there had seemed a prospect of a series of British victories, grave difficulties were beginning to emerge. On June 27 a British and Indian force attacked the Turkish garrison at Nasiriyeh. The heat, bearable three weeks earlier, had become unbearable, reaching 115 degrees Fahrenheit (45 degrees Celsius). Fierce-biting mosquitoes appeared in profusion. The Turkish field-guns, as at Gallipoli, kept up an unexpectedly steady and accurate fire. Nasiriyeh was captured, but there were warning signs to be seen. The Turkish forces withdrew, but quickly began to prepare a new defensive position at Kut. As the British and Indians prepared to follow them, sickness began to decimate the fighting abilities of the troops. As one historian of the campaign has written, with sunstroke and heat-stroke came 'restlessness, anxiety, shortness of temper and a feeling of utter depression'.[1] One British officer later recalled a burial party: 'We started out for the cemetery, about a mile away at 6 p.m. Before we had gone half the distance a man went down with heat-stroke and was carried back, limp and twitching, to hospital. As the corpse was lowered into the grave, one of the men on the ropes stumbled forward and fell limply into the grave on top of the dead body. And as we fell in to march back, another man went down. Luckily we had brought a spare stretcher, and with one man on this, and one man on the stretcher on which the dead man had been carried to the grave, we returned. We had buried one man and lost three others over the job.'

As the men suffered from the heat, from lack of medical supplies, and even from lack of fresh vegetables, despite a glowing report in *The Times* that fresh vegetables were being brought regularly from Bombay, plans were being made to march on Kut.

At Gallipoli, Mustafa Kemal was confident that he could drive the Australian and New Zealand forces off Chunuk Bair and into the sea. On June 28, ten days after the arrival of a new Turkish regiment, fresh for battle, he led the attack. The attack was repulsed and the new regiment wiped out. Kemal offered his resignation, but was persuaded by General Liman von Sanders to remain. His courage had become an inspiration to the defenders of Turkish soil. On one occasion, as an Allied battery was shelling systematically along the Turkish trench line, the shells coming ever closer to where Kemal was standing, he refused to move, but lit a cigarette instead and remained in the trench with the men. The shelling turned elsewhere. A legend was born.

Also on the Gallipoli Peninsula on June 28, the British forces at Cape Helles attacked, hoping to drive the Turks out of Krithia. Although the village was not reached, the left flank of the British position, along Gully Ravine, was pushed forward a thousand yards. One British battalion, on

[1] A.J. Barker, *The Neglected War, Mesopotamia 1914–1918*, Faber and Faber, London 1967, page 97.

entering the Turkish trenches, found a breakfast of biscuits and hard-boiled eggs waiting to be eaten. There was also a store of cigars. 'A more gruesome find', a regimental historian noted, 'was of the bodies of some Royal Dublin Fusiliers killed on April 27 and still unburied.'[1]

Several Turkish counter-attacks were driven off, one group of Turkish soldiers breaking through the line and digging in between the British front line and support trenches. They seemed to be making signs that they wanted to surrender, but when some British soldiers went up to them, to bring them in, the Turks opened fire. They were then attacked from both sides and overrun.

The fighting on the Gallipoli Peninsula, from which the Entente Powers had expected so much, had become another stalemate: a replica in minia-ture of the trench warfare on the Western Front, which it had been intended to bring to a rapid end, but terrors of which were now being duplicated in a distant war zone.

[1] Sir Frank Fox, *The Royal Inniskilling Fusiliers in the World War*, Constable, London 1928, page 187.

10

The Central Powers in the ascendant

JUNE–SEPTEMBER 1915

On 13 June 1915, on the Eastern Front, Polish cavalrymen, fighting under Austria's orders, but fired by Poland's national aspirations, won a victory over the Russians at Rokitna. Nine days later, Austrian troops retook the most important of the East Galician cities, Lemberg, and were poised to cross into the Russian province of Volhynia. On the Polish front, the German army was making continuous gains: on July 18 more than 15,000 Russians were taken prisoner at Krasnostaw.

The painter Oskar Kokoschka, reaching Lemberg on July 22, wrote to a friend: 'Off to join the regiment tomorrow morning – three days' journey. It's now part of a German cavalry force ordered to Russia! No trenches, but reconnaissance, thank God, and – the wonderful thing about Russia – the chance of an Iron Cross. All along the way, many villages destroyed by gunfire, cemeteries, all the famous battlefields, cholera....'

In the last week of July, the Russian General Staff circulated all Russian commanders with a secret report about Bolshevik anti-war propaganda. This propaganda, it was explained, was being hidden in gifts sent to the troops from home. A Russian army report stated: 'Super-human efforts were required to keep the men in the trenches.' The Germans recognised, in this Russian discontent, a means of disrupting their adversary's fighting abilities. On July 27 the American Ambassador in Berlin, James W. Gerard, reported to Washington that the Germans were 'picking out the revolutionists and Liberals from the many Russian prisoners of war, furnishing them with money and false passports and papers, and sending them back to Russia to stir up a revolution'. In Petrograd on July 30 the Minister of War, General Poplivanov, warned his ministerial colleagues: 'Demoralisation, surrender and desertion are assuming huge proportions.'

It was not only in Russia that the continuation of war was raising the spectre of unwelcome change. On July 15, two weeks before Poplivanov's warning, Sir Edward Grey had met the Canadian Prime Minister, Robert Borden. 'He spoke with great gravity as to the burdens imposed by the War,' Borden wrote in his diary. The continuation of the war, in

Grey's opinion, 'must result in the overthrow of all existing forms of government'.

That July, the Italians fared badly on their fronts with Austria. In the Dolomites, the Austrians repulsed fifteen separate Italian attacks. On the Isonzo, after five days of fighting on a 21-mile front, the Italians, despite a six-to-one numerical superiority, suffered heavy casualties and gained less than a mile. In the heights above Gorizia, the Austrians drove them back, taking 1,500 Italian prisoners. In the Adriatic, two Italian cruisers were sunk by Austrian submarines.

The Allies were also in difficulties at the Dardanelles. On the Gallipoli Peninsula that July, British troops twice refused to advance. In the Narrows, a French submarine was lost in the Turkish net defences.

On July 25, with a German assault imminent, the Russians evacuated the factories in Warsaw.[1] In Turkish Armenia that July, Turkish troops pushed back the Russian advance while, behind the lines, at Trebizond on the Black Sea, between July 7 and 23 as many as 15,000 Turkish troops, rampaging through the predominantly Armenian town, massacred its 17,000 Armenian inhabitants: there were only a hundred survivors. At the same time, further south, on the upper Euphrates, thousands of Armenians were massacred in the villages around Mus. News of these massacres caused indignation when it reached the Entente powers: in London, the House of Lords debated and denounced them on September 6. But as the war continued, earlier restraints were abandoned. Britain was preparing to use poison gas in the next offensive, and on July 20 the Kaiser, under pressure from the Chief of the German Naval Staff, von Bachmann, rescinded his earlier order not to bomb residential areas in London. Henceforth, only buildings of 'historic interest' were to be spared.

A distant Entente victory took place in German South-West Africa on July 9, when South African forces received the surrender of the Germans there. Sixteen days later South Africa annexed the territory. Less than a year after the outbreak of war, its spoils were being distributed. In Europe, without entering the war on the side of the Central Powers, Bulgaria signed a secret treaty with Germany and Austria on July 17 by which she secured a promise of six hundred square miles of Turkish territory in Thrace. She then began to press for further gains, including the Serbian and Greek provinces of Macedonia, and the Roumanian coastal region of Silistria.

In Berlin, on July 27, the New Fatherland League gave its support to a declaration by ninety-one prominent German intellectuals, opposing all territorial annexations and pressing for a compromise peace. Einstein was again among the signatories. He also supported the League when it

---

[1] In July 1941, as the German army swept once more into Russia, Stalin ordered the evacuation of eight hundred factories in western Russia to the Urals, Siberia and Soviet Central Asia, thereby preserving the Soviet Union's industrial war making capacity.

distributed in the post an anthology of statements by a number of British pacifists, among them Bertrand Russell and George Bernard Shaw. This was too much for the German authorities. The League's offices were raided, it was prohibited from any further publishing, its members were forbidden to communicate with one another, and two of its women secretaries were imprisoned. This was the prelude to a complete ban on the League's existence.

Following the failures at Neuve Chapelle in March and Aubers Ridge in May, the new all-party Government in Britain, still headed by Asquith, was determined to renew the offensive on the Western Front. The senior Conservatives, out of office since 1905, were now members of the inner councils of war which decided to seek a breakthrough that autumn. At an Anglo-French meeting in Calais on July 6, at which the French Minister of War, Alexandre Millerand, and the British Prime Minister, Asquith, were the senior politicians present, this strategy was co-ordinated. On the following day, at Joffre's headquarters at Chantilly, Sir John French agreed with Joffre's view, as recorded by the official minutes of the meeting, 'that the general strategic situation demanded the offensive, and pledged himself to the utmost of his means'. Yet Kitchener, who was present at the Calais conference, wrote scathingly to the Chief of the Imperial General Staff, Sir William Robertson: 'Joffre and Sir John told me in November that they were going to push the Germans back over the frontier; they gave me the same assurances in December, March and May. What have they done? The attacks are costly and end in nothing.'

Without offensives there could be no quick victory, and yet, Lloyd George declared on July 17, 'a victory which tarries means a victory whose footprints are footprints of blood'. As the recently appointed Minister of Munitions, he was urging women to work in the munitions factories, to hasten the day when that victory would be possible. In the Ypres Salient, even before the new plan of attack agreed upon at Calais and Chantilly could be devised, ferocious struggles took place between the confronting armies. One was for the mine crater at Hooge, created during a British assault on the German trenches. A crater such as this was a prized objective, giving as it did an element of shelter to the troops whose army captured it, and a relatively protected spot from which to fire on the enemy. In an attempt to keep the British from the crater, which lay in the German front line, the Germans made use of their dreaded heavy mortar shell, the *minenwerfer*, known to the British as 'Minnie' or 'Moaning Minnie'.

One of the British officers present at Hooge when the attack began on July 29, Lieutenant G.V. Carey, later recalled: 'This was the most alarming frightfulness that our fellows had as yet knocked up against. Apart from the number of people it had blown to bits the explosions were so terrific that anyone within a hundred yards' radius was liable to lose his reason after a few hours, and the 7th battalion had had to send down the line several men in a state of gibbering helplessness.'

None of the troops involved in the attack from Zouave Wood to Hooge Crater had been in that part of the line before. They were in worse disarray on July 30, when the Germans used flamethrowers for the first time, sending jets of burning petrol against them. 'There was a sudden hissing sound,' Lieutenant Carey later recalled, 'and a bright crimson glare over the crater turned the whole scene red. As I looked I saw three or four distinct jets of flame – like a line of powerful fire-hoses spraying fire instead of water – shoot across my fire trench.' The men caught in the blast of the fire 'were never seen again'.

The German trenches were to be attacked again that same afternoon. 'It is only charitable to assume that the staff, from their position fifteen miles back, were imperfectly informed of the real position,' Carey commented. 'At 3 o'clock the four battalions duly went over the top and were swept out of existence by an enemy whose machine guns there had been no time to locate, and on whom our meagre artillery preparation had made no impression. Many of the men were caught on our own wire, and I believe that none got more than fifty yards beyond the edge of the wood.'

That summer, the stalemate in the west was in contrast to movement in the east. There is a graphic picture of the fighting in a letter from Koko-schka, sent from the Galician Front to a friend, describing what happened to him on August 5. 'I was really lucky to escape with my life yesterday,' the painter-turned-cavalryman wrote, 'because the Cossacks show no mercy if they catch you! I and a patrol were ambushed in the endless forest and swamp hereabouts. We lost more than half our men. Hand-to-hand fight-ing, with all of us thinking our last hour had come. It was pure chance that two or three of us got away, me last because my horse is weak and, to crown it all, went lame!!!! Then a life-or-death chase, with the first of the brutes only ten paces behind me, firing all the time and shrieking "Urrah-Urrah". I kept feeling his lance in my liver. I used my sabre to flog my horse to its limits and just made it back to my unit. You should see how they respect me!'

On August 5 the German army entered Warsaw. After almost exactly a year of war, another great European city had been overrun. For the first time since 1815, Russia was denied control of the Polish capital. It was a signal triumph for the Central Powers. The Germans now set their long-term sights on Finland, Russia's province since the Swedes had been driven out in 1808. On August 8 the Kaiser authorised the formation of a battalion 2,000-strong to be recruited entirely from Finns, which would fight against Russia on the Eastern Front. 'The recruiting for this battalion now began,' the Finnish national leader, Gustav Mannerheim, later recalled, 'and forms one of the most thrilling chapters in recent Finnish history. Everything, of course, had to be done with the utmost secrecy: and in a country honeycombed with the Russian police.' The recruits were smuggled out of Finland to Germany. Hundreds of Finns, accused of helping the recruits to escape, were imprisoned in Petrograd. But within nine months the battalion was in action.

As the German forces advanced east of Warsaw, the Russian army fell back, leaving only the fort of Novo-Georgievsk, at the confluence of the Vistula and the Bug, to slow down the German advance. But as soon as its garrison of 90,000 men had been surrounded and besieged, the German army continued its eastward sweep. To contain Novo-Georgievsk, 80,000 German soldiers from essentially non-front-line units were assembled. To destroy the fort, whose bulwarks and outlying fortifications had been strengthened in 1891, the Austrian howitzers that had been so effective against Antwerp in October 1914 were again deployed, including six 16-inch guns, under the command of the victor of Antwerp, General von Beseler.

The siege of Novo-Georgievsk began on August 10, the bombardment a few days later. The fortress surrendered on August 20, when the Germans took all 90,000 of the Russian defenders prisoner, including thirty generals.

Amid the terrifying struggles on the battlefield, the danger of daily life in the trenches, and the harsh privations of the prisoner-of-war camps, most serving officers were still able, in all armies, to call upon comforts from home. British officers on the Western Front could subscribe to special hampers made up by Harrods in London, to bring them extra food and other comforts on a regular basis. Friends could be persuaded to help. Oskar Kokoschka tried to obtain some extras that autumn by asking his artistic patron in Vienna to send out to him on the Eastern Front:

> 6 prs thick brown socks, not wool
> 300 good cigarettes (strong)
> 1 set silk underwear or similar
> 1 bottle brandy or whisky (and glass)
> 1 large tin Köstens' wafers
> 5 tins sardines
> 1 good flashlight and 5 spare batteries
> 6 jars assorted savouries
> 3 jars preserves
> 1 clothes brush
> 1 tin dubbin
> 1 box Sarotti bonbons

'If they won't all fit into one standard parcel,' Kokoschka added, 'please make two or three. I need everything. Again, please be as quick as you can.'

On August 6, the day after the Germans entered Warsaw, in an attempt to break the Turkish defences at Gallipoli, and to enable Allied ships to force their way through the Narrows, substantial British forces landed at a new beach on the Gallipoli Peninsula, at Suvla Bay. The aim of the new landing was to link up with Anzac positions to the south, and to drive the Turks off the heights of Chunuk Bair and the even higher Koja Chemen Tepe, linked to it by a spur.

As a means of drawing Turkish troops away from this high ground, two diversionary attacks were planned. The first was on the precipitous terrain above Anzac Cove, where the Australians penetrated the Turkish trenches at Lone Pine in one of the fiercest battles on the peninsula. Seven Victoria Crosses were awarded for gallantry on Lone Pine, and 1,700 of the attackers were killed and wounded. When the Australians consolidated their new trenches, more than a thousand Turkish corpses had to be lifted out for burial. A further 4,000 Turks were killed or wounded.

In the second diversionary attack, at Cape Helles, the village of Krithia and the heights of Achi Baba were once more the objectives, but the attack on them was beaten off by the Turks, whose total casualties that day, in dead and wounded, were 7,510. There were 3,480 British casualties. Among the British in action that day was Second Lieutenant George Horridge, who had been shot through the ribs in the June battle, while trying to rescue a wounded man. Returning from hospital in Egypt in time for the August battle, he went over the top with a walking stick in one hand and a pistol in another, and returned unharmed. That night a shell landed in his trench, and he was wounded again.

The Cape Helles attack was intended as a diversion for the new landing to the north, at Suvla Bay. This landing was successful. Australian, New Zealand, Indian, Gurkha and British troops, coming ashore and over-coming the Turkish defenders, crossed the coastal plain towards the hills. Then the generals hesitated: surprised by such a swift advance. Their minds, fashioned by the warfare on the Western Front, were attuned to 'victories' of a hundred yards. A virtually unopposed advance of half a mile bewildered them. The hesitation was decisive and disastrous. The bulk of the force stayed close to the beach, where many men enjoyed an unexpected and relaxing swim.

Further south, from the Australian lines at Anzac Cove, 16,000 men advanced northward through the night of August 6, along the beach towards Suvla Bay and then inland, intent on seizing the summit of Koja Chemen Tepe. At this moment Colonel Kannengiesser reached Koja Chemen Tepe. He had earlier been summoned with a Turkish division from Cape Helles to help repel the attack on Lone Pine, but having found out that he was not needed there, had gone further north, to the very section of the battlefield where he was most needed. From there he saw, in the dawn light, an Australian column three hundred yards below, moving up the steep slope. Having hurried forward ahead of his men, Kannengiesser had only twenty soldiers with him. He ordered them to lie down and open fire. The attackers, believing this to be a substantial force, lay down, took cover, and prepared to defend their position on the slope.

The heights remained in Turkish hands. During the day Liman von Sanders ordered two reserve regiments to the summit. Koja Chemen Tepe was held. Further south, along the saddle, a New Zealand battalion reached the summit of Chunuk Bair. There had been no opposition. When they reached the ridge, the New Zealanders found a single Turkish machine gun and its sleeping crew. But Turkish troops on the spur on either side of them, Hill Q and Battleship Hill, opened fire, preventing reinforcements from arriving, and driving off the New Zealanders who tried to dislodge them. A Maori contingent, unable to face the intensity of the Turkish fire, sought shelter in a nearby gully.

On August 9 the attack on Koja Chemen Tepe was renewed. A small force of British and Gurkha troops reached the crest, repelling a Turkish counter-attack with a bayonet charge. They were about to drive the Turks back down the far slope when British naval gunners, not knowing that the summit was in Allied hands, opened fire, blasting the attackers and forcing them back.

During the day, the New Zealand troops holding the summit of Chunuk Bair were attacked by Turks commanded by Mustafa Kemal. They counter-attacked, and the Turks were momentarily in disarray. Kemal's Staff advised withdrawing down the eastern slope, but Kemal, recently promoted to Colonel and awarded by the Germans the Iron Cross First Class, urged them, and his men, to defend their native land.[1] 'Don't rush it, my sons,' he said as he walked along the Turkish trenches. 'Don't be in a hurry. We will choose exactly the right minute, then I shall go out in front. When you see me raise my hand, look to it that you have your bayonets sharp and fixed, and come out after me.' The men waited.

Facing the Turks on Chunuk Bair were the men who had just relieved the New Zealanders: two battalions of Kitchener's New Army, the 6th Loyal North Lancashires and the 5th Wiltshires. They had never been in action before. There were six Turkish battalions forming up on the other side of the hill. The situation was clear to Kemal as a result of personal reconnaissance. At 4.45 on the morning of August 10, Kemal gave the signal by raising his hand and walking forward. The Turks rushed at the defenders with their bayonets. The Loyal North Lancashires were bayoneted to a man. The Wiltshires, who by incredible ill-luck were at that moment resting in a valley just below, having put down their rifles and equipment, could only turn and run.

The Turks now rushed down the slope, intent on forcing the British off the hill altogether. But at that moment New Zealand machine gunners on a nearby spur opened fire, and the left wing of the Turkish advance was halted. The right wing, reaching a small plateau known as The Farm, was engaged in hand-to-hand fighting by other New Army troops, men of the

---

[1] On 15 September 1915 Kemal narrowly escaped injury or death when a Royal Naval Air Service plane bombed the Staff car in which he was travelling. A similar incident took place in 1944 when Field Marshal Rommel, then commanding the German forces in Normandy, was seriously injured when his Staff car was hit by machine-gun fire from an Allied fighter.

38th Brigade. Among those killed was Brigadier-General A.H. Baldwin, commander of the brigade, and his brigade-major. They had fallen in the front line. After more than half of the British troops had been killed or wounded, the survivors fell back. The British official historian writes: 'The Turks, too exhausted to follow, and too weak even to stay where they were, had retreated to the main ridge. The Farm plateau, forsaken by both sides, was held by the dying and the dead.'

Retreating to the crest, the Turks remained in possession of Chunuk Bair. The British line was now much deeper than it had been before the August battle, but still confined to the western side of the peninsula. For a few moments, the troops who had reached the top of Chunuk Bair had seen the waters of the Narrows glinting far below. They were never to see them again. The British objectives of August 6 were never gained. Kemal was promoted to General.

At Suvla Bay, the successful landings of August 6 had been followed by three days of inertia and uncoordinated fighting. Twenty-five British battalions were ashore by the morning of August 7. 'Heavy fighting has been going on since yesterday at the Dardanelles,' Admiral von Tirpitz wrote in his diary that day. 'The situation is obviously critical. Should the Dardanelles fall, the World War has been decided against us.'

During the morning of August 7, only three Turkish battalions were on their way to reinforce the small Turkish units that were still in action at Suvla. Most of the Turkish artillery and machine guns had been withdrawn to avoid capture. Half a mile from where one small action was taking place, six British battalions were sitting doing nothing. 'We all had the feeling', General Liman von Sanders later wrote, 'that the British leaders had delayed too long on the shore instead of advancing from the landing place at any cost.'

The judgement of the British official historian, Brigadier-General Aspinall-Oglander, who himself landed at Suvla Bay on the third day, was even more severe. By the 'hesitation and delay of the 7th and 8th August', he wrote, 'the advantages gained by the surprise landing at Suvla had all been thrown away. The IX Corps had trifled too long with time. The chance of gaining the high ground on very easy terms had disappeared. It was now to be a fight between forces of equal numbers, with the British troops in the open, sun-baked plain, and the Turks in possession of every point of vantage. The Turks, moreover, were definitely superior in skirmishing and in the use of their rifles to these young New Army troops straight out from England; and once surprise had gone there was little chance with anything approaching equal numbers of scoring a British success.'

On August 9, British troops at Suvla succeeded in capturing Scimitar Hill, in the foothills of the Chunuk Bair range, but they were driven off, and fell back in confusion towards the shore, 'like a crowd streaming away from a football match' as one officer described them in his diary. The

Turks advanced rapidly down to the plain. One senior officer, Lieutenant-Colonel H.G.A. Moore, was bayoneted by a Turk after he surrendered, and died soon afterwards. Another, Major F.W. Brunner, who was shot in the ankle on the way down from the hill, was also killed in cold blood.

Among the soldiers killed at Suvla Bay was the first Newfoundlander to be killed in action in the First World War. The most recent historian of Newfoundland's contribution to the war, David Macfarlane, has written: 'Private Hugh McWhirter mounted no gallant attack. He uttered no brave last words. He had simply been standing, deafened by the screech and explosion of artillery – a terrified boy in an ill-fitting uniform in a front-line trench near the ridge of Karakol Dagh. Then, from out of nowhere, he had been blasted to red bits of khaki and flesh by a Turkish shell. Suddenly he was gone, and those beside him in the shallow firing-trench were stunned. Sprayed by bits of shrapnel, dirt and intestine, they knew just as suddenly what this war was going to be about.'

In the four-day battle for Suvla Bay and Chunuk Bair, 50,000 British and Anzac troops had been engaged, of whom 2,000 were killed and 10,000 wounded. More than 22,000 sick and wounded were taken off the Peninsula and sent by sea to hospitals in Egypt and Malta. On August 13 the military hospitals in Egypt and Malta were reported full. That day the assault was renewed. Troops advancing from the beach head at Suvla Bay reached the Anafarta Ridge below the 882-foot Tekke Tepe, part of the Chunuk Bair ridge. There they halted, unwilling, as they had been a week earlier when they landed, to continue the advance as far as they might have done.

A staff officer went forward to see what had happened. 'I found the 53rd Division in a line of lightly dug trenches, with men standing about on the parapet and even cooking in front of the trenches,' he later reported. 'No work was going on, and there was a general air of inaction. I was astonished to find that this was the front line. There were no Turkish trenches or Turks in sight, and only some occasional desultory shelling and sniping. While I was there it was discovered that some troops in trenches in bushes on our left, which for some days had been thought to be Turks, were in reality British.'

Within twenty-four hours the newly constituted Turkish 5th Division, commanded by a German officer, Major Willmer, counter-attacked, and the British were driven back.

On August 14, in London, Kitchener read General Hamilton's report on the Suvla Bay landings. He was indignant at Hamilton's account of the the reluctance of the commanders to move boldly in the initial stages, and at the deficiencies revealed, such as the 53rd (Welsh Territorial) Division having landed without any artillery, no stores and only a single Field Ambulance. 'I am taking steps to have these generals replaced by real fighters,' Kitchener wrote to Churchill that day. Two days later, General

Stopford, commanding IX Corps, and two of his divisional generals, General Hammersley, commanding the 11th Division, and General Lindley, commanding the 53rd Division, were relieved of their commands. General Mahon, commanding the 10th (Irish) Division resigned: he was later sent to command the Salonica Army.

'We are all trying to understand what on earth has happened to these men and why they are showing such extraordinary lack of enterprise', Churchill's brother Jack, who was on Ian Hamilton's Staff, wrote to him when the battle was over. 'They are not cowards – physically they are as fine a body of men as the regular army. I think it is partly on account of their training. They have never seen a shot fired before. For a year they have been soldiers and during that time they have been taught only one thing, trench warfare. They have been told to dig everywhere and have been led to expect an enemy at 100 yards range. From reading all the stories of the war they have learnt to regard an advance of 100 yards as a matter of the greatest importance.'

Jack Churchill went on to explain: 'They landed and advanced a mile and thought they had done something wonderful. Then they had no standard to go by – no other troops were there to show them what was right. They seemed not to know what they should do. Was it right to go on so far – might they be cut off or suddenly walk into a trap? Was an occasional bullet only a sniper or was a hidden trench bristling with rifles waiting for them?... The 10th and 11th had nothing to go by. They showed extraordinary ignorance. A shell burst near a working party – at least half a mile away. Officers and men stopped work, rushed to the low beach cliffs and lay down taking cover! A land mine exploded and the men near all lay flat and remained there thinking they were being shelled! I have just heard that the 53rd are no better. A few shots sent them retreating pell mell from Chocolate Hill! Blaming the senior officers must be left to the people who can give effect to their opinions. But there is no doubt that these divisions were completely out of hand.'

John Hargrave, who was serving with a Field Ambulance Unit at Suvla, recalled the mood of the men when news of the sacking of the generals reached them, just as a new assault was ordered on the Kiretch Tepe ridge, overlooking the Gulf of Saros. They were, he wrote, 'leaderless and lost in the midst of battle – and dreaming about packing up and going home.' Most of these troops, he added, 'were now in a state of acute dejection – many seemed vacant and shell-shocked – and were unfit for further service under fire. But, of course, they had to "soldier on".'

As the Turkish forces denied victory to the Allies on the Gallipoli Peninsula, their allies continued to wreak havoc on sea and land. On August 13 a German submarine sank the 11,000-ton Allied troop transport, the *Royal Edward* near the Italian Dodecanese island of Kos: 1,865 soldiers were drowned. On the Eastern Front, on August 17, after a 1,360-gun bombardment including the use of 16-inch naval guns, and the firing of 853,000 shells, German forces captured the fortress city of Kovno.[1]

The Russian commandant of the fortress, General Grigoriev, who had failed to blow up the only railway tunnel between Ostend and Petrograd, had left the bridge over the river Niemen intact, was said never to have left his dug-out except at night, and who had left the fortress before its fall without telling his chief of staff, was Court-Martialled and sentenced to eight years hard labour. In the military store houses at Kovno the Germans captured several millions tins of preserved meat, the main Russian front line supply, on which their own troops could now be fed. Further south the German-Austrian forces approached the fortress of Brest-Litovsk, driving the Russian forces back to the river Bug.

News of the suffering of the Russians as they retreated to the Bug were reported to General Gourko, who was then in Galicia: 'Men who had fought in several wars and many bloody battles told me that no horrors of a field of battle can be compared to the awful spectacle of the ceaseless exodus of a population, knowing neither the object of the movement nor the place where they might find rest, food and housing. Themselves in an awful condition, they increased the troubles of the troops, especially of the transport who had to move along roads filled with the disorganised human wave. Many a time our forces had to stop and fight a rear-guard action just to allow this crowd to make room for the troops.... God only knows what sufferings were endured here, how many tears were shed and how many human lives were given as victims to the inexorable Moloch of war.'

The plight of Russia's soldiers was spreading grave discontent among all its armies. It was also swelling the prisoner-of-war camps throughout the German-conquered lands. On August 17, the day of the fall of Kovno, the number of Russian prisoners-of-war was 726,694 in German prison camps, and a further 699,254 were held by the Austrians: a total of 1,425,848 Russians in captivity.[2] Conditions in captivity could be severe. In the spring and summer of 1915 there had been a typhus epidemic among the Russians being held in a prisoner-of-war camp at Gardelegen. Of 11,000 prisoners there, three hundred died. By August 1915, typhus in the camp at Wittenberg had become so rampant that the German camp administration abandoned the 15,000 Russian, British and French prisoners-of-war there to their fate, surrounding the perimeter fence with machine guns and dogs. Only an outpouring of neutral criticism led the German staff to return to the camp and improve conditions in it.

On August 18, Lord Kitchener visited First Army headquarters in France. Exactly a month earlier he had been scathing about the prospects for success of any British offensive on the Western Front. Now he told Haig

---

[1] Twenty-six years later the Ninth Fort at Kovno was the site of the mass murder by the Gestapo of tens of thousands of Jews from Kovno itself and from several cities in western Europe.
[2] By August 1915 the Germans also held 330,000 British, French and Belgian prisoners-of-war.

that the Russians had been 'severely handled' on the Eastern Front. Wlodawa, on the river Bug, fell to the Germans that day, part of the seemingly daily loss of a fortress, a city or a town. To come to Russia's aid, Kitchener told Haig, Britain and France must both 'act vigorously' on the Western Front. Just as the Russian appeal for help at the very end of 1914 had been a catalyst for the Anglo-French attack at the Dardanelles at the beginning of 1915, so the Russian losses on the Eastern Front that August were to be the catalyst for a new offensive in the west. Kitchener told Haig, who underlined his words in his diary that day, that 'we must act with all our energy, and do our utmost to help the French, even though, by doing so, we suffered very heavy losses indeed'.

The continuing Russian losses in the east, culminating on August 19 with the surrender of 90,000 officers and men at Novo-Georgievsk, made Kitchener's call for a renewed offensive in the west seem all the more justified, and urgent. Winston Churchill, who saw Kitchener at the War Office in London that week, later recalled: 'He looked at me sideways with a very odd expression on his face. I saw he had some disclosure of importance to make, and waited. After appreciable hesitation he told me that he had agreed with the French to a great offensive in France. I said at once that there was no chance of success. He said that the scale would restore everything, including of course the Dardanelles. He had an air of suppressed excitement like a man who has taken a great decision of terrible uncertainty, and is about to put it into execution.'

The British attack was planned for late September, at Loos. On August 21 Churchill was present at a conference in Margate, attended by the Canadian Prime Minister, Robert Borden, during which Borden asked 'when the supply of munitions would be ample'. Opinions differed: Bonar Law answered that it would be in 'about five months', but Churchill believed it would not be until 'the middle of the following year'. Despite this warning, the conference decided that the offensive, on which Kitchener was set, would go ahead.

War strategies were sustained both by practical necessity on the battlefield, and by patriotic fervour at home. This was true in all the belligerent lands. 'I must confess that I am bitterly disappointed at the narrow nationalist bias to be found even among men of great stature,' Einstein wrote that August from Berlin to a fellow physicist in Holland. 'If, in addition, one recognises that those who are well informed and possess the power to act lack human compassion, it becomes apparent how sad is the thing that is worshipped as the "fatherland". Frontiers make little difference; it is much the same everywhere.'

In Berlin, the Reichstag voted on August 20 to give the Government whatever extra money it needed for war purposes. Only one deputy voted against, Karl Liebknecht, who also demanded immediate peace talks. Unknown to Liebknecht, the German Government had itself proposed making peace with Russia, though on the basis of German territorial gains in the east carved out of the land already captured, and leaving Germany free to concentrate all her war powers on the defeat of Britain and France in the west. The Russian Government replied that there could be no peace while a single German or Austrian soldier was on Russian soil. Two million more men were about to be called into the Russian army.

Yet the onward march of the Austro-German armies was inexorable. By the end of August the Russians had been forced to abandon the fortress of Brest-Litovsk, the industrial city of Bialystok, and the Volhynian market town of Lutsk, where 7,000 Russian soldiers were taken prisoner. Among the German officers killed in the fighting was the war poet, Captain August Stramm.[1]

In the United States there had been a series of angry protests about the loss of American lives on the *Lusitania*, but these had not led to a declaration of war on Germany. Nor did the deaths of three American citizens on board the unarmed White Star liner *Arabic*, torpedoed without warning by the German submarine *U-24* in the Irish Sea on August 19, with the loss of forty-four passengers, bring America's entry into the war any nearer.[2]

There was another incident at sea later that day, after the German submarine *U-27* shelled and halted the cargo steamer *Nicosian*, bringing a cargo of mules from New Orleans to England. A British armoured merchant ship, the *Baralong*, pretending to be an American merchantman flying the Stars and Stripes, approached the *U-27*. The disguised *Baralong* had on board two concealed guns and a platoon of Royal Marines. Lowering the Stars and Stripes, and raising the British colours, she opened fire on the *U-27*. Twelve of the submarine's crew jumped into the water. Believing, wrongly, that these crewmen were those who had sunk the *Arabic* earlier in the day, the Marines opened fire. Six of the Germans were killed while they were in the water. The surviving six managed to reach the engine room of the *Nicosian*, where they took refuge. All six were hunted down and killed by the Marines, and their bodies thrown overboard. The German Ambassador in Washington protested at the misuse of the American flag in 'murdering German sailors', an act which the American Secretary of State, Robert Lansing, described privately as 'shocking'.

On August 15 there was a further British assault on the Turkish-held hills at Suvla Bay. After eight hours, in which the Turks were driven back, a Turkish counter-attack forced the assaulting troops to return to their trenches. One of those in the attack was Lance Corporal Francis Ledwidge, an Irish poet serving in the Royal Inniskilling Fusiliers, who wrote to a friend after the battle: 'A man on my right who was mortally hit said: "It

---

[1] Six days later the German song writer Fritz Jürgens was killed on the Western Front, in the French sector (Champagne).
[2] On 22 November 1915 the American Government rejected a German offer of £1,000 for every American who had been lost on the *Lusitania*.

can't be far off now", and I began to wonder what is was could not be far off. Then I knew it was death and I kept repeating the dying man's words: "It can't be far off now". But when the Turks began to retreat I realised my position and, standing up, I shouted out the range to the men near me and they fell like grass before a scythe, the enemy.' Ledwidge added: 'It was Hell! Hell! No man thought he would ever return. Just fancy out of "D" Company, 250 strong, only 76 returned.'

Ledwidge's letter reflected the clash between 'Hell!' and exhilaration. 'By Heavens, you should know the bravery of these men,' he wrote. 'Cassidy standing on a hill with his cap on top of his rifle shouting at the Turks to come out; stretcher-bearers taking in friend and enemy alike. It was a horrible and a great day. I would not have missed it for worlds.' Some months later, Ledwidge recalled that day, and his fellow Irishmen, most of them Roman Catholics, who were killed during it, when, having been wounded on the Salonica Front, he was taken to hospital in Cairo. A Church of England clergyman 'seemed to be taking a great interest in me and promised me a book of poetry, but suddenly he saw on my chart that I was an RC and hurried from me as if I were possessed. He never came over to me since although he has been in the ward many times. I wonder if God asked our poor chaps were they RCs or C of Es when they went to Him on August 15th.'

A final British assault was launched at Suvla Bay on August 21, but the Turks were by then in position, well dug in, well armed and determined not to give ground. The main objectives were the lowest foothills of the Chunuk Bair range, Hill 60 and Scimitar Hill, against which the earlier attack on August 9, when the Turks were not so well dug in, had failed. One officer detailed to lead the preliminary attack on Scimitar Hill, Lieutenant-Colonel Sir John Milbanke, had won the Victoria Cross during the Boer War. After receiving his orders at divisional headquarters, Milbanke went back to his men and told them: 'We are to take a redoubt, but I don't know where it is and don't think anyone else knows either, but in any case we are to go ahead and attack any Turks we meet.' The men advanced up the hill, with Milbanke leading them. He was killed at their head.

During the attack on Hill 60, one Australian unit of 150 men was caught in Turkish machine-gun fire and 110 men were killed or wounded. A second unit was likewise brought to a halt with heavy casualties. As the wounded men lay in the scrub, Turkish shelling set it on fire. The scrub burned out of control, the soldiers' clothes caught fire, and many died before help could reach them. Two men, a Presbyterian chaplain, the Reverend A. Gillison, and a stretcher bearer, Corporal R.G. Pittendrigh, who had been a Methodist clergyman in civilian life, went forward to pull the men from the flames. In attempting a similar act of rescue the following morning, both men were killed.

In the attack on Scimitar Hill, the commander of the 87th Brigade, Brigadier-General Lord Longford, led his men in person, but was killed with his brigade-major. Their bodies were never found. Some troops, reaching a position just below the crest, could look back across the plain below almost to the mouth of the Dardanelles. But the crest remained under Turkish control. Captain William Pike, of the Royal Inniskilling Fusiliers, who was in reserve that day, was so determined to reach the crest that he called for volunteers and rushed forward. Neither he nor those who followed him returned. Another Inniskilling officer, Captain Gerald O'Sullivan, who had won the Victoria Cross at Krithia less than two months earlier for a daring bombing raid into the Turkish trenches, called for another attempt to reach the crest: 'One more charge for the honour of the regiment.' Fifty men responded to his call. Only one, a wounded sergeant, survived. The bodies of Pike and O'Sullivan were never found.

One of those severely wounded in the attack on Scimitar Hill, Private F.W.O. Potts, remained on the hill for forty-eight hours rather than abandon a friend who was too badly wounded to move, but whom Potts could not carry. Eventually, using a shovel as an improvised sledge for his friend, and pulling him along, while being fired at all the way by the Turks, he reached the British lines. For this act of courage he was awarded the Victoria Cross.[1]

The attack on Scimitar Hill was the last, and in proportion to the numbers involved the most costly, as well as one of the least successful of the Allied offensives on the Gallipoli Peninsula. Of the 14,300 men who took part in it, more than 5,000 were killed or wounded. The Turkish casualties were half those of the British. General Liman von Sanders later wrote of the 'severe and bloody fighting'.

Four British divisions, supported by gunfire from four cruisers, had failed to break through the Turkish defences. 'It is only possible for me to remain on the defensive,' a chastened General Hamilton telegraphed to Kitchener on August 23. Six days later even a planned assault on Hill 60 was given up. But Kitchener told his ministerial colleagues that day that 'the Turks could not last much longer'. It was wishful thinking of a very costly sort. But it came only nine days after Italy declared war on Turkey: the Italians hoping, like Kitchener, that the defeat of the Ottoman Empire was not only imminent, but full of territorial promise for the victors.

A new general was sent out to take command at Suvla, Sir Julian Byng, a veteran of the Western Front. The official historian of the Gallipoli campaign, Brigadier-General Aspinall-Oglander, commented: 'The experienced pilot had arrived. But the ship to be steered into port was already hard on the rocks.' Aspinall-Oglander, who served on the peninsula throughout the campaign, also recalled a problem that August which even the most zealous commander could not remedy. 'The principal scourge

---

[1] The British official historian writes: 'Countless gallant deeds, never reported to headquarters, have faded into oblivion. But as a tribute to all brave men, known and unknown, who especially distinguished themselves this day, the story may here be quoted of Private F.W.O. Potts....' Aspinall-Oglander, *Military Operations, Gallipoli*, William Heinemann, London 1932, volume II, page 354, note 1.

from which the troops were suffering', he wrote, 'was a peculiarly violent form of diarrhoea. Broadly speaking, the whole force, from the Commander-in-Chief downward, was affected by this complaint, and the men were so weak from it that few could walk at a quicker pace than a crawl.'[1]

The Allied positions at Suvla were overlooked by the Turks on the high ground from which they had resisted all Allied efforts to dislodge them. On August 29 a single Turkish shell killed 113 mules. Two days later Byng's Chief of Staff, Captain Basil Brooke, wrote home: 'We are shelled all day as there is no room back, which is rather upsetting to one's nerves. Thank goodness they have not got as much as the Bosch, or as big, but quite enough to be unpleasant.' Byng himself, having examined the situation, told General Hamilton that there were far too few high-explosive shells available on the peninsula to justify a further British offensive. Hamilton dismissed Byng's 'French standards for ammunition', commenting: 'His sojourn on the Western Front has given him inflated standards as to the numbers of guns and stocks of HE shell which are essential to success, especially with troops who have suffered heavy losses.' Byng did not yet realise, Hamilton added, 'that if he is going to wait until we are fitted out on that scale, he will have to wait till doomsday'.

Another contrast at Gallipoli with attitudes on the Western Front was pointed out by Basil Brooke in a letter home. 'The old Turk is a great gentleman. He never shoots at the hospital ships in the bay, or at the hospitals, very different from our friend the Bosch.' Yet even at Gallipoli a wound did not necessarily mean a hospital ship, adequate medical help, and recovery. Early that September, Vera Brittain recalled, 'we heard of the first casualty to happen in our family. A cousin from Ireland, we learnt, had died of wounds after the landing at Suvla Bay; the original bullet wound behind the ear had not been serious, but he had lain untended for a week at Mudros, and was already suffering from cerebral sepsis when operated on, too late, by an overworked surgeon on the crowded *Aquitania*. I had hardly known my cousin, but it was a shock to learn that lives were being thrown away through the inadequacy of the medical services in the Mediterranean.'

Following the sinking of the passenger steamer *Arabic*, British passenger ships were armed for their own defence. The first of these to be attacked was the liner *Hesperian*, which was sunk on September 4. Thirty-two passengers were drowned. Her adversary was the *U-20*, commanded by Captain Schwieger. He was not to know that the *Hesperian* was carrying on board the corpse, only recently recovered from the sea, of a traveller on one of the earlier victims of his torpedoes, the *Lusitania*.

On the Western Front, the $4\frac{1}{2}$-month lull between the Battle of Aubers Ridge and the Battle of Loos was a lull only in a comparative sense. Each day saw

[1] Brigadier-General Aspinall-Oglander, *Military Operations, Gallipoli*, William Heinemann, London 1932, volume II, page 368.

shelling, courage, fear and death. The diary of Captain F. Hitchcock, of the Leinster Regiment, recorded that August the scenes of the 'static' front line in the Ypres Salient. The line was newly established where earlier fierce fighting had taken place. Hitchcock wrote of khaki figures of the previous battle hanging on strands of barbed wire 'in hideous attitudes', of British dead on No-Man's Land, of German dead in the British trenches, of any grass that remained 'burnt up by liquid fire', and of men who were hit by spasmodic German artillery fire having to wait until stretcher bearers could reach them and being 'hit for a second time and killed'.

On August 16 Hitchcock's trenches were inspected by the brigadier-general. 'The brigadier said the battalion had done splendidly, and that the place was thoroughly consolidated: he, however, objected to a German's leg which was protruding out of the parapet.' Hitchcock was told to have the limb buried. 'I called Finnegan, and told him to remove the offending limb. As it would have meant pulling down the whole parapet to bury it, he took up a shovel and slashed at it with the sharp edge of the tool. After some hard bangs, he managed to sever the limb. I had turned away and was standing in the next fire bay, when I overheard Finnegan remarking to another man: "And what the bloody hell will I hang me equipment on now?" '

This episode is an example of the outer reaches to which men's sensibilities – and their humour – were driven. The alternative was to pull down the parapet, risking further lives. Later that day a wounded British soldier was found 'in a dying condition', as Hitchcock noted, in a nearby dug-out. 'He appeared to have been there for days without any help.' On the following day, August 17, Hitchcock recorded in his diary how three dead men were discovered in a hollow. 'This was a sad sight, as the trio consisted of a patient lying on a stretcher and the two stretcher bearers lying across him, with the slings of the stretcher still across their shoulders. All had been knocked out by the same shell.'

The British soldiers on Belgian soil were not entirely among friends. This aspect of the war appears in a brief diary entry by Private Edmund Herd on August 30: 'Belgian civilians caught signalling to German 'plane by means of a windmill. Court-martialled and shot. Rained in evening.' On penetrating the German trenches after one attack, Herd was shocked to find Belgian civilians there, including women, who had fraternised with the Germans. He and his fellow soldiers were even more shocked to find the German trenches full of items that certainly did not exist in their own trenches: wine, cheese, coffee and cigars. Even the German prisoners, he noted some months later, were 'in splendid condition and wearing good uniforms'.

From the wings, the anti-war movement continued to agitate for an end to the war. Between September 5 and 11 an International Socialist Conference met at Zimmerwald in Switzerland. Among the Russian delegates was the Bolshevik leader Vladimir Lenin and the Menshevik leader

Leon Trotsky. The conference issued a manifesto demanding immediate peace and, in pursuit of their more revolutionary goals, civil war 'between the classes' throughout Europe.

The Zimmerwald deliberations and the call for peace coincided with an intensification of the air war. During a German air raid on Lunéville, on market day, forty-eight civilians were killed and fifty injured. On the night of September 7, in the middle of the Zimmerwald Conference, a German Zeppelin started a large fire in the City of London. Six men, six women and six children were killed and thirty people injured. On the following night a second Zeppelin, dropping its bombs on Holborn and Bloomsbury, hit two motor buses, and killed twenty-two people (Lenin had earlier lived in exile in nearby Clerkenwell). On the day after the raid, as Colonel Rawlinson recalled, 'citizens of all classes, from the Lord Mayor downwards, took steps to insure their participation in the general demonstration of dissatisfaction'.

Londoners insisted on an anti-aircraft defence system. Rawlinson was sent to Paris, where General Pellé, Chief of the French General Staff, agreed to provide without delay a French 75-millimetre auto-cannon mounted on an armoured car. This weapon reached London within two days. Thirty more were then ordered. To accommodate the new anti-aircraft units, the Grand Duke Michael, great-great-grandson of Catherine the Great, put Caen Wood House, scene of the magnificent ball scarcely a year earlier, at Rawlinson's disposal. Anti-aircraft barrages were eventually set up all around the capital, enabling incoming Zeppelins, and later aeroplanes, to be tracked from barrage to barrage. Each barrage was given a name: raiders coming in from the north crossed Dickens, then Potsdam, then Amethyst, then Pot Luck. Eastern raiders came first to Jigsaw, then to Knave of Hearts, then to Zig Zag.

As Londoners reacted to their second aerial attack by demanding an adequate defence, the International Socialists at Zimmerwald were calling for an immediate peace. Five days after the Zimmerwald Conference ended, Albert Einstein was in Switzerland visiting the French pacifist Roman Rolland at Vevey. Einstein was not hopeful of a speedy end to the war. 'The victories over Russia have revived German arrogance and appetite,' he told Rolland, who recorded in his diary: ' "Greedy" seems to Einstein the word that best characterises the Germans. Their power drive, their admiration of, and belief in, force, their firm determination to conquer and annex territories, are everywhere apparent.' Einstein added that the German Government was more moderate than the people. 'It has wanted to evacuate Belgium but could not do so; the officers threatened revolt. The big banks, industries and corporations are all-powerful; they expect to be repaid for the sacrifices they have made.' As for the Kaiser, he was 'merely the tool' of big business and the officers. 'He is decent, weak and in despair over a war which he never wanted and into which he was forced because he was so very easy to manipulate.'

*

On the Austrian Front that September, where the Russians had briefly been able to reverse the pattern of defeats when General Denikin, commanding Brusilov's 4th Division, recaptured Lutsk. But the town was lost ten days later. There was a much more serious Russian reverse on September 18, when German forces entered Vilna, the largest city in Russian Lithuania, taking 22,000 Russian soldiers captive. Two weeks later the German High Command East moved its headquarters to the city of Kovno, where in 1812 Napoleon had watched his troops cross the river Niemen on their march to Moscow.

For Ludendorff, the move to Kovno was more than a military one. In pre-war years Germany had harboured a sense of grievance at being excluded by Russia from the Baltic regions. Now that balance could be redressed. 'I determined to resume in the occupied territory that work of civilisation at which the Germans had laboured in those lands for many centuries,' Ludendorff later wrote. 'The population, made up as it is of such a mixture of races, has never produced a culture of its own and, left to itself, would succumb to Polish domination.' His idea was that, once the war was won, Lithuania and Kurland would be ruled by a German prince and colonised by German farmers. Poland, ever it would seem the plaything of its neighbours, would become 'a more or less independent state under German sovereignty'.

Germanisation of the conquered eastern lands was begun at once. General Ernst von Eisenhart-Rothe was appointed the Intendant General overseeing six administrative areas which, independent of army control, organised financial, judicial, agricultural and forestry systems in the occupied areas. The German nature of these efforts was paramount. Poles, Lithuanians and Letts lived under martial law. Political activity was forbidden. No public meetings were allowed. Newspapers were censored. Courts were presided over by German judges. All schoolteachers had to be German, and to teach in German. A Polish request for a university in Vilna was turned down, by Ludendorff himself.

At sea, the German submarine sinkings continued: on September 19, when U-boat gunfire sank the British troop transport *Ramazan* in the Aegean Sea, 311 Indian troops were drowned; a month later 140 British troops were drowned when a German submarine torpedoed their troopship, the *Marquette*. The heaviest naval toll that autumn, however, was the death of 672 German sailors on the *Prinz Adalbert*, sunk by a British submarine in the Baltic: there were only three survivors. On September 27, at the Italian port of Brindisi, Austrian saboteurs destroyed the Italian battleship *Benedetto Brin*: 456 sailors were killed.

Behind the lines, four French citizens were shot by the Germans in Lille on September 22, for having helped French prisoners-of-war to reach the Allied lines. In Russia, discontent in the army found an outlet in whatever cause of protest was open to it. On September 24 five hundred reservists attacked the police at a railway station in Petrograd in protest against the suspension of the Russian parliament, the Duma. Other protests took place far behind the lines, in Rostov-on-Don and Astrakhan. This was followed five days later by rioting in Orsha among 2,500 convalescing soldiers. Even the wounded were raising their voices against the war, to which, once mended, they would be returned.

At the Front, news of the disturbances cast a pall. In the village of Chertoviche, in White Russia, Florence Farmborough, the British nurse with the Russian army, wrote in her diary on September 25 of the previous few days: 'The news which reached us from Russia was far from good; rumours of internal disturbances were wafted to us as on an ill wind. Bread, it was said, was growing scarce; in some parts famine already threatened to engulf the masses. The thousands of refugees swarming into the cities and towns were followed by pestilence and crime.'

11

The continuing failure of the Entente

SEPTEMBER–DECEMBER 1915

The Allied offensive on the Western Front, intended to relieve Russia's military distress on the Eastern Front, began on 25 September 1915, two weeks after the end of the Zimmerwald Conference calling for an immediate end to the war. The needs of an ally in danger could not be ignored: the defeat of Russia would enable the Germans to transfer enormous forces from the east to fight against Britain and France.

The offensive was launched in two separate regions. The French attacked the German trench lines in Champagne, the British at Loos. These were the offensives agreed by the British and French leaders at the Calais and Chantilly Anglo-French conferences in July. In Champagne, the French made a two-mile dent in the German line along a fifteen-mile front and took 1,800 Germans prisoner. The capture of the German strongpoint of La Courtine was reported with particular enthusiasm in Paris, the depth and intricacy of its communication trenches and underground tunnels being remarkable.

Also in Champagne, awaiting the order to go forward, an American volunteer in the French Foreign Legion, the poet Alan Seeger, wrote home enthusiastically on September 25: 'I expect to march right up the Aisne borne on an irresistible élan. It will be the greatest moment of my life.' Another American volunteer, the nineteen-year-old Edmond Gênet (a great-great-grandson of Citizen Gênet who had been sent to America in 1792 by revolutionary France as its representative, and settled in New York State), also wrote home that day, telling his parents of the German prisoners-of-war he saw on his way to the front: 'Some of them, mere boys of sixteen to twenty, were in a ghastly condition. Bleeding, clothing torn to shreds, wounded by ball, shell and bayonet, they were pitiable sights. I saw many who sobbed with their arms around a comrade's neck.' Nearer the front line Gênet saw 'one poor fellow who must have been totally blinded for he walked directly into the barbed wire and had a most trying and painful time to get out.'

Gênet and five hundred of his fellow Legionnaires were in action on

196

September 28 at the battle for the German strongpoint known as Navarin Farm, east of Reims, where more than three hundred were killed or wounded. Gênet and Seeger survived. Among those killed was Henry Weston Farnsworth, a graduate of Harvard, class of 1912, who had gone straight from university to the First Balkan War as a newspaper correspondent, and who, when war broke out in Europe, hurried to be part of it. Joining the Foreign Legion, he revelled in its diverse characters, writing to his parents of 'a Fijian student at Oxford, black as ink', 'a Dane, over six feet', 'another Dane, very small and young', 'a Swiss carpenter, born and bred in the Alps, who sings – when given half a litre of canteen wine – far better than most comic opera stars' and 'the brigadier Mussorgsky, cousin descendant of the composer'. Most of those killed that September 28 are forgotten. Farnsworth is remembered because the letters he wrote to his parents survive.[1]

Among the Legionnaires who were severely wounded at Navarin Farm was John Elkington, the British officer who had been court-martialled and dismissed from the British army for his 'surrender document' a year earlier. For his bravery in action the French army awarded him the Médaille Militaire and the Croix de Guerre. When his award became known in London, his British commission and rank were restored to him on the personal initiative of King George V.

While the French were attacking in Champagne, the British attacked at Loos. The initial bombardment was along a six-and-a-half mile front. Using poison gas for the first time, the British released 150 tons of chlorine across No-Man's Land, from 5,243 gas cylinders. As a direct result of the gas, six hundred German soldiers were killed. British troops advanced at one point more than 4,000 yards. One battalion was led in its assault by men dribbling a football across No-Man's Land.

On the sector of the line held by the 15th (Highland) Division, the British gas failed to blow forward into the German trenches. As the men hesitated to go forward through their own gas cloud, Piper Peter Laidlaw rallied the men of his battalion by striding up and down the British parapet playing 'Scotland the Brave' on his bagpipes, ignoring both the gas fumes surrounding him and the German machine-gun fire. He was wounded, but continued to play. The Scotsmen went forward, overrunning the first two lines of German trenches. Laidlaw was awarded the Victoria Cross.

Frank Cousins, one of the men of the Special Company who released the gas that day, wrote in his diary: 'One poor lad fainted at the parapet and then went over. In came a lad with a pierced vein which we turnequed.[2] He was still there at 2 o'clock. He too wanted to go over again. Then a

---

[1] Farnsworth's parents endowed the Farnsworth Room in the Widener Memorial Library at Harvard, 'for the leisurely reading of such standard books as Henry Farnsworth loved', and supplied the room with books, pictures and furniture.
[2] Cousins's version of 'applied a tourniquet'.

fellow came in gassed. Then we got a man in who was shot thru' the stomach and gradually bled to death. Then came a man with a smashed leg. We helped all these. One Black Watch officer came in with a shattered leg. We got him across our trench and his remark was typical: "What a damned mess there is in this trench!" We were busy in the trenches till 11.30. Then I went over the top and I worked between the two trenches making men comfortable and giving water.'

Another of those whose task was to release the gas was Donald Grantham, who found himself, like Cousins, attending to the injured. Garside, Harris and Aldridge were all members of a special Brigade, responsible for the gas cylinders and pipes. 'Heard a man gassed,' he wrote in his diary, 'and found Garside unconscious, brought him round and got him into a dugout nearby.... Then into fire trench where I found Harris dead with a bullet hole clean through his head. Helped drag him into a dugout. This was about nine and I did not get his blood washed off my hands for over ten hours. Did a few bandages and helped wounded down. Carried a man with wounded foot right out, then carried another part way. Helped others. Returned to our dugout then went and fetched Aldridge (badly gassed) from fire trench and carried him right out to the Dressing Station.'

The death toll at Loos exceeded in intensity that of any previous battle. On September 25 the 'Roll of Honour' notices in *The Times* filled four columns.[1] The soldiers made great efforts to keep up their spirits. Harold Macmillan, a future British Prime Minister, moving up to the front line at Loos with his regiment on the following day, wrote to his mother: 'A stream of motor-ambulances kept passing us, back from the firing line. Some of the wounded were very cheerful. One fellow I saw sitting up, nursing gleefully a German officer's helmet. "They're running" he shouted.' For three hours Macmillan's regiment waited, and sang 'almost ceaselessly, "Rag-time" – and music hall ditties, sentimental love-songs – anything and everything. It was really rather wonderful.'

The next day, September 27, saw Macmillan's regiment in action. His commanding officer was gassed, and both the second-in-command and the adjutant were killed. Macmillan himself was slightly wounded in the head, and shot through the right hand.[2] He had been 'more frightened than hurt', he wrote to his mother from hospital, but it had been 'rather awful – most of our officers are hit'. The words 'rather awful' masked a deep well of suffering.

Pushing through Loos to the Lens-La Bassée Road on the second day of the battle, British troops crossed the road at two points, opposite Hulluch, and opposite the Bois Hugo. Their numerical superiority was considerable, but several dozen German machine guns faced them in both places. 'Ten

---

[1] Two days later, when a Gallipoli list was published, including Australian casualties, the 'Roll of Honour' covered five columns.
[2] 'Which accounts for the spidery handwriting of later age as well as for the limp handshake of which critics occasionally made jest.' Alistair Horne, *Macmillan, 1894–1956*, Macmillan, London 1988, vol. I, page 38.

columns of extended line could clearly be discerned,' recorded the German regimental diary of the men defending Hulluch. Each advancing column was estimated at more than a thousand men, 'offering such a target as had never been seen before, or thought possible. Never had the machine gunners such straightforward work to do nor done it so effectively. They traversed to and fro along the enemy's ranks unceasingly.'

It was five months since Haig had told the British War Council: 'The machine gun is a much over-rated weapon and two per battalion is more than sufficient.' He was once again being proved terribly wrong. The German regimental account continued: 'The men stood on the fire-steps, some even on the parapets, and fired triumphantly into the mass of men advancing across open grass-land. As the entire field of fire was covered with the enemy's infantry the effect was devastating and they could be seen falling literally in hundreds.' Further south, as the British troops approached the Bois Hugo, a similar slaughter was taking place. Again the German regimental diary gave a stark picture, describing how 'dense masses of the enemy, line after line, appeared over the ridge, some of the officers even mounted on horseback and advancing as if carrying out a field-day drill in peacetime. Our artillery and machine guns riddled their ranks as they came on. As they crossed the northern front of the Bois Hugo, the machine guns caught them in the flank and whole battalions were annihilated.'

Hundreds of men have left descriptions of the Battle of Loos, some in letters, some in recollections. Fourteen years later, Robert Graves, who was just twenty at the time of the battle, gave an account in his book *Goodbye to All That* of one episode, and of one officer's story: 'When his platoon had run about twenty yards he signalled them to lie down and open covering fire. The din was tremendous. He saw the platoon on the left flopping down too, so he whistled the advance again. Nobody seemed to hear. He jumped up from his shell-hole and waved and signalled "Forward." Nobody stirred. He shouted: "You bloody cowards, are you leaving me to go alone?" His platoon-sergeant, groaning with a broken shoulder, gasped out: "Not cowards, sir. Willing enough. But they're all f——g dead." The Pope's Nose machine gun traversing had caught them as they rose to the whistle.'[1]

So appalled were the Germans at the effect of their machine guns that they called the battle the 'Field of Corpses of Loos' (Der Leichenfeld von Loos). Near the Bois Hugo, when the fifth British attempt to push past the wood had failed, and when wounded men began to work their way back to the British lines, one German regimental diary commented: 'No shot was fired at them from the German trenches for the rest of the day, so great was the feeling of compassion and mercy for the enemy after such a victory.'

After that fifth attempt to push past the Bois Hugo, the attack was called

---

[1] One of Robert Graves's five sons was killed in action in Burma in the Second World War.

off. Among the officers reported 'missing' after he had been caught by German machine-gun fire and shellfire from the wood was Second Lieutenant John Kipling, the only son of Rudyard Kipling. Some years later Rudyard Kipling was told by a soldier who had witnessed the attack: 'Jerry did himself well at Loos and on us innocents. We went into it, knowing no more than our own dead what was coming, and Jerry fair lifted us out of it with machine-guns. That was all there was to it *that* day.' After the war, Rupert Grayson, who had been wounded in the hand by the same shell splinter that killed John Kipling, became almost a surrogate son for the writer, and a prolific writer himself. He died in April 1991, at the age of ninety-three.

John Kipling's body was never found. The officer who went forward with him, 2nd Lieutenant Clifford, was also shot: either killed outright or fatally wounded. His body was found only later. Captain Cuthbert, who led the detachment, was also killed that day. His body was never found. Twenty-seven of those whom they led were also killed.[1] Rudyard Kipling wrote of his son's death, and the death of so many sons:

> *That flesh we had nursed from the first in all cleanness was given …*
> *To be blanched or gay-painted by fumes – to be cindered by fires –*
> *To be senselessly tossed and retossed in stale mutilation*
> *From crater to crater. For this we shall take expiation.*
> *But who shall return us our children?*

With an outpouring of anger, another of the young officers who fought at Loos, Roland Leighton, wrote to his fiancée, Vera Brittain: 'Let him who thinks War is a glorious, golden thing, who loves to roll forth stirring words of exhortation, invoking Honour and Praise and Valour and Love of Country with as thoughtless and fervid a faith as inspired the priests of Baal to call on their own slumbering deity, let him but look at a little pile of sodden grey rags that cover half a skull and a shin-bone and what might have been its ribs, or at this skeleton lying on its side, resting half crouching as it fell, perfect but that it is headless, and with the tattered clothing still draped round it; and let him realise how grand and glorious a thing it is to have distilled all Youth and Joy and Life into a foetid heap of putrescence!' Leighton went on to ask: 'Who is there that has known and seen, who can say that Victory is worth the death of even one of these?'

For the French, the Champagne offensive was declared to be a success, with Joffre announcing at its close that 25,000 German soldiers had been

---

[1] Among the Irish Guardsmen killed that day (27 September 1915) at Loos were Lance-Sergeant George Lewis, Lance-Corporals Michael Docherty, William Hutchinson, Horace Lawson and Peter O'Rourke, and twenty-two Privates: Michael Cahill, Michael Doyle, James Green, John Guilfoyle, Thomas Jolly, John Higgins, John McIntosh, Horace Keogan, Charles Lewis, Alexander Morrow, John V. Murray, Patrick Murray, John McCallum, James McLennan, Patrick McHugh, James McMahon, Patrick Neafson, James Rogers, William H. Sherwood, Eugene Sullivan, Michael Sutton and Richard Tabsley. Such lists could be compiled for every day of the war, and for every war front, and multiplied 200-fold for each day.

captured, as well as 150 heavy guns. For the British, Loos was a set-back that caused much heartsearching and distress. Of nearly 10,000 British soldiers who attacked at Loos, 385 officers and 7,861 men were killed or wounded. To General Haking, who on the afternoon of the second day asked the survivors 'What went wrong?', the official history recorded the men's answer: 'We did not know what it was like. We will do it all right next time.' But moods were changing: in the House of Lords, a bastion of propriety and patriotism, the Battles of Neuve Chapelle and Loos were being described as 'defeats'. On October 8, after a visit to Sir John French's headquarters, Haig noted in his diary: 'Some of the wounded had gone home and said that they had been given impossible tasks to accomplish and that they had not been fed.'

During and after the Battle of Loos, Captain W. Johnson, serving with a field ambulance, noticed a phenomenon that had not been widely seen on the battlefield since the retreat from Mons. Many of the younger members of Kitchener's New Armies, the volunteers of eighteen and nine-teen, were patients sent to him from the front line with what the official medical history of the war describes as 'definite hysterical manifestations (mutism and tremors)'.

On the Eastern Front, the eastward flight of refugees from the war zone continued to add to the chaos and hardship behind the lines. Reaching the station at Brest-Litovsk, on October 5, on her way back to Moscow, Florence Farmborough noted in her diary: 'All was disorder and confusion. The town had been lately raided by a German Zeppelin and near the station two or three houses had been entirely destroyed, while, in the town itself, considerable havoc had been caused by incendiary bombs.'

On October 10 the German poet Rilke wrote in a private letter from Munich, 'Can no one prevent it and stop it?' But in a lodging house in neutral Switzerland the war offered a prospect of future triumph. 'News from Russia testifies to the growing revolutionary mood' was Lenin's comment in a private letter, on the day of Rilke's questioning.

That September, an energetic naval officer, Commodore Roger Keyes, the Chief of the Naval Staff at the Dardanelles, submitted a new plan for forcing the Straits by ships alone. He was overruled by the admiral. Sixteen years later Churchill commented bitterly: 'I marvelled much in those sad days at the standard of values and sense of proportion which prevailed among our politicians and naval and military authorities. The generals were so confident of breaking the line in France that they gathered masses of cavalry behind the assaulting troops to ride through the huge gaps they expected to open on the hostile front. To sacrifice a quarter of a million men in such an affair seemed to them the highest military wisdom. That was the orthodox doctrine of war; even if it did not succeed, no error or breach of the rules would have been committed. But to lose one hundredth part as many sailors and a dozen old ships, all of which were in any case to be put on the Mother Bank in a few months' time, with the possibility of gaining an inestimable prize – there, was a risk before which the boldest uniformed greyhead stood appalled. The Admiralty and Generals had their way. The fleet continued idle at the Dardanelles. The armies shattered themselves against the German defence in France. The Bulgarians carried an army of 300,000 men to join our enemies; and Serbia as a factor in the war was obliterated.'

In Mesopotamia, the British advance along the Tigris had continued, with an assault on Kut being launched on September 26, as the battles at Loos and in Champagne were at their height. Kut was taken, though not without some alarms when Indian troops seemed reluctant to storm the Turkish trench lines, and with hardships brought on by a thirst so intense that men were incapacitated. There was an additional cause for fear: on the first night of the battle, wounded men who could not be found in the intense blackness of the night were robbed by marauding Arabs, mutilated and murdered. Yet the aftermath of the capture of Kut seemed hopeful, the Turks still not seen as formidable enemy. Among the captured Turkish weapons was a Persian cannon from the time of Napoleon: it was dated 1802. The British had come 380 miles from the sea. The way seemed clear for a renewed advance in November, through Ctesiphon where the Turks were reported to be digging in, and on to Baghdad, only a further twenty-two miles away.

Behind the lines in Europe, the punishment of those who helped the other side was continuous. In German-occupied Brussels, on the morning of October 12, following her Court Martial, the 49-year-old British nurse Edith Cavell was being led to her execution for having helped British and French prisoners-of-war, and Belgians who wanted to serve with the Allies, to escape to neutral Holland. At the execution posts a Belgian, Philippe Baucq, was being shot with her. She asked the guards for some large pins, which they gave her. She then pinned her long skirt tightly round her ankles, so that her dress would not flare up after she had been shot. She was struck by four bullets: one pierced her heart and killed her instantly.

During her trial, Edith Cavell had admitted the offences of which she had been charged. Protests by the American diplomats in Brussels, who were in charge of British interests, had no effect, despite Hugh Gibson's appeal to the head of the German Political Department in Belgium, Baron von der Lancken, to telephone the Kaiser and seek his direct intervention. Once sentence had been passed, Lancken said, 'even the Emperor himself could not intervene'. When this emphatic statement was published later in the war, the Kaiser was understood to have been greatly displeased.

On the night before her execution, Edith Cavell told the American Legation chaplain, the Reverend Horace Gahan: 'They have all been very kind to me here. But this I would say, standing as I do in view of God and eternity: I realise that Patriotism is not enough. I must have no hatred or bitterness towards anyone.' Despite this Christian sentiment, her execution led to an upsurge in anti-German feeling in Britain and the United States. This feeling was inflamed by the wide circulation of a false story that she had fainted on the way to the execution post, and had been shot while lying on the ground by the officer in charge of the firing squad. This imagined episode was depicted in the *New York Tribune* in a drawing of the prostrate and bleeding body of Edith Cavell, lying on her back, with a tall German officer, wearing a spiked helmet, standing over her and holding an enormous smoking revolver. The caption read 'GOTT MIT UNS', God is with us.

In Flanders, the Battle of Loos continued. Among those killed on October 13, in an attack on the Hohenzollern Redoubt, was the twenty-year-old poet Charles Sorley, who had written shortly before his death:

> *Earth that blossomed and was glad*
> *'Neath the cross that Christ had,*
> *Shall rejoice and blossom too*
> *When the bullet reaches you.*
> > *Wherefore, men marching*
> > *On the road to death, sing!*
> > *Pour gladness on earth's head,*
> > *So be merry, so be dead.*
>
> > *On marching men, on*
> > *To the gates of death with song.*
> > *Sow your gladness for earth's reaping,*
> > *So you may be glad through sleeping.*
> > *Strew your gladness on earth's bed,*
> > *So be merry, so be dead.*

Sorley's body was never found. His name is carved in stone on the Loos Memorial to the Missing. A poem that was found in his kit after he was killed spoke of 'millions of the mouthless dead' and warned those who said that they would remember:

> *... scanning all the o'ercrowded mass, should you*
> *Perceive one face that you loved heretofore,*
> *It is a spook. None wears the face you knew.*
> *Great death has made all his for evermore.*

On the night Charles Sorley died at Loos, the Germans carried out their heaviest air raid of the war over Britain. Five Zeppelins took part, dropping 189 bombs on London and the Home Counties. Seventy-one civilians were killed.

On the front in Champagne, the French poet Auguste Compagnon was killed that month. On the Eastern Front, the painter Oskar Kokoschka was among the Austrian soldiers wounded in action and henceforth a civilian in all but name. 'My wounds proved more decorative than lethal,' the 29-year-old Second Lieutenant wrote to a friend. 'A bullet in the head and a hole in the chest. My engagement is broken, my studio resolved, and a big silver medal in exchange. I am a pensioner!!!!!!' His food parcel, made up as he had asked with the comforts he most wanted while campaigning, arrived after he had been wounded, and was returned to Vienna. He followed it shortly afterwards.

Russia, Britain, France and Italy each suffered set-backs that autumn. On the Isonzo Front a cholera epidemic forced the Italian commanders to isolate whole units. Paratyphoid fever was also a hazard. Among those who were laid low by it was Private Benito Mussolini, the socialist editor who had welcomed Italy's entry into the war, and whose son, born that autumn while his father was in the trenches, he named Vittorio Alessandro, in joint honour of the eventual victory and an English naval captain who had recently distinguished himself by his bravery. 'Rain and lice, these are the two enemies of the Italian soldier,' Mussolini wrote in his diary. 'The cannon comes after.' His own trenches were more than 6,000 feet above sea level, on Monte Nero. 'We do not take fortresses by force,' he noted, 'we must take the mountains.' But those mountains were defended by the Austrians with every defensive skill.

The lack of success of the Entente continued to be contrasted with the successes of the Central Powers. On October 5 a massive artillery bombardment, including 170 heavy guns and 420 heavy mortars, was the prelude to an Austro-German invasion of Serbia. At last, and despite the set-backs of the autumn of 1914, the murder of Franz Ferdinand was going to be avenged, and with a terrible vengeance. That same day, 13,000 French and British troops landed at Salonica, intent on hurrying northward to Serbia's defence. Among the forces facing the Austrians and Germans as they crossed the Danube to attack Belgrade were four Anglo-French naval guns. But the Austro-German forces overwhelmed all opposition. The Serbs, weakened by a typhus epidemic, evacuated their capital on October 9. That same day the Austrians invaded Serbia's ally and neighbour, Montenegro. Bulgaria, eager to annex the southern Serb region of Macedonia, attacked the Serbs two days later. The Central Powers had gained a new partner.

The Entente rushed to the defence of Serbia, as in 1941 Britain was to rush to the defence of Yugoslavia. On October 14, as the first French units reached the Greek-Serbian frontier, a further 18,000 French troops landed at Salonica. But it was the ordeal on the Western Front that continued to dominate French thought. On October 19, in Champagne, 815 French soldiers were killed, and more than 4,000 made seriously ill, when the Germans used a mixture of chlorine and phosgene in a gas attack along a ten-mile front.[1] For the Italians, too, the Austro-German-Bulgarian

---

[1] Phosgene (carbonyl chloride) had been discovered by John Davy in 1811. It is a colourless, heavy gas, and very poisonous. It is used today in the preparation of polyurethane plastics and some insecticides.

advance into Serbia was completely overshadowed on October 18 by the opening of the third battle of the Isonzo. The numerically superior Italian forces, nineteen divisions as against eleven, 1,250 guns as against 604, failed to capture the two objectives, Mount Sabotino and Mount San Michele.

On October 21 the Bulgarians, who had set their sights on the annexation of Serbian Macedonia, entered the Macedonian city of Skopje. The first shots fired by the French on the Salonica Front were against Bulgarian troops, when they beat off a Bulgarian attack on Strumica railway station, twenty miles from the Bulgarian border. A new war zone had opened, the twelfth at that moment in the war.[1] It was in a region with few roads, rough mountains, narrow defiles and rushing torrents. When French troops, continuing northward from Negotin, approached the river Vardar on their way to Veles, they headed for the road bridge marked on the map. When they reached it, they discovered it had been destroyed in the First Balkan War.

For one of the leading combatants, the Austrian General Conrad, the rapid success of this new attack on Serbia led to hopes that, once Serbia was defeated, it might somehow be possible to make peace with Russia, and end the war, while the existing structure of Europe was still intact. He put this to Franz Josef in a memorandum on October 22, but it was to be almost exactly three years before peace came, and with it the complete disintegration of the Hapsburg Empire. The imminence of victory was a time for boasting and advancing, not for reflection and compromise. At Potsdam, on October 22, at a meeting with the American Ambassador James W. Gerard, the Kaiser spoke angrily of United States financial help for Britain and France and protested that 'a number of submarines' built in America had been escorted to Britain by ships of the American navy. 'America had better look out after this war,' he warned the Ambassador. 'I shall stand no nonsense from America after the war.' He was careful, however, to distance himself from the sinking of the *Lusitania*, telling Gerard that he would 'not have permitted' the ship to be torpedoed if he had known about it, and that 'no gentleman would kill so many women and children'.

In the war zones, suffering and privation were everywhere evident. By October 24 the Bulgarians had driven a wedge between the Serb forces and the French who were trying to come to their aid. Three days later the German forces entered Knjazevac, taking 1,400 Serbian soldiers prisoner. As German, Austrian and Bulgarian forces were overrunning Serbia, two

[1] The other main war fronts at that time were the Western and Eastern Fronts, the Gallipoli and Mesopotamian Fronts, the Caucasus Front, the Serbian Front (where there was heavy fighting around Kragujevac until November 23, when the Serb retreat into Albania began), the Italian-Austrian Front, and the Salonica Front. Fighting was also taking place, though spasmodically, in East Africa, Central Africa (the Cameroon) and Persia. In Egypt, 100,000 British and Dominion soldiers were awaiting a possible German-led Turkish attack on the Suez Canal.

Entente war zones were becoming cursed by mud and rain. On the Gallipoli Peninsula, the troops who were huddled together in crowded, wet, constantly shelled trenches had no possibility of driving the Turks off the high ground. On the Isonzo and Dolomite Fronts, Italian forces still battling for the peaks were repeatedly driven off, or made the smallest gains for the heaviest of costs.

With the ending of the Third Battle of the Isonzo on November 4, more than 20,000 Italian soldiers had been killed and a further 60,000 wounded. In the Dolomites there had been a moment of Italian rejoicing on October 30 when a grandson of Garibaldi, General Peppino Garibaldi, captured the mountain village of Panettone. After capturing the 4,662-foot mountain pass of the Col di Lana on November 7, however, his forces were driven off two nights later.[1]

On the Western Front, in Champagne, German troops, many of whom had just been brought back from the Russian Front, drove the French from La Courtine, which had been captured with such plaudits a month earlier. They also drove the French out of a 900-yard section of their front-line trenches north of Massiges on November 4, killing most of their occupants and taking twenty-five prisoners. In a French counter-attack, however, mostly with grenades, the Germans were driven back.[2]

The fighting in Champagne was severe: in the region of La Courtine and Massiges, within a radius of only five miles, five villages were totally destroyed: Hurlus, Perthes-les-Hurlus, Le Mesnil-les-Hurlus, Tahure and Ripont. Ten miles to the west, beyond Navarin Farm, are two more ruined villages, Moronvilliers and Nauroy. On the modern Michelin maps these eighty-year-old relics of the devastation of the war zone are shown with the symbol 'ruines'.

The Entente was faring worst on the Eastern Front, where the whole of Russian Poland had fallen under German control. The number of Russian soldiers taken prisoner-of-war in the twelve months of conflict had reached 1,740,000. At Helsinki, Russian sailors on the battleship *Gangut* and the cruiser *Rurik* protested against the bad food and the severity of their officers. Fifty were arrested. The Russian Finance Minister, Peter Bark, hurried to France, travelling by sea from Archangel via Britain, to seek extended financial credits to shore up Russia's warmaking abilities. A million pounds sterling had been borrowed in the second week of war. That sum had reached £50 million, with a further £100 million promised.

---

[1] These battles were taking place on the main Dolomite route from Bolzano to Cortina, now a region of ski resorts. The 1930 Baedeker guidebook for Northern Italy refers to the Col de Lana as 'famous for the sanguinary battles fought here during the War'. Modern guide books omit this fact.
[2] Ten miles south-east of the battlefields of La Courtine and Massiges was the village of Valmy, where in 1792 a Prussian army was defeated by troops of the French Republic. General Kellermann, the victor of Valmy, later served under Napoleon as commander of the French forces on the Rhine.

Bark wanted even more, but President Poincaré was not helpful. 'I could remind Mr Bark', the protocol of their discussion read, 'that neither the text nor the spirit of our alliance led us to foresee that Russia would ask us at some time to lend our credit.' Bark produced his trump card: not gold reserves or the collateral of raw materials, but the threat that Russia would be unable to continue the war without French economic assistance. Poincaré gave way. The prospect of the German and Austrian armies being freed to move against the west was an overpowering argument. Russia remained at war, its indebtedness growing by the day.

With the new credits, Russia could import war materials on a larger scale, even from Japan, her enemy of a decade earlier. A mass of stores came in, through the Russian port of Archangel and then by railway over vast distances. Within a year Russia owed Britain £757 million and the United States £37 million. The British goods that reached Russia under this credit system included 27,000 machine guns, one million rifles, eight million grenades, 2,500 million bullets, 300 aeroplanes and 650 aeroplane engines. Among Russia's needs was barbed wire. At the outbreak of war she possessed just over 13,000 tons in store. In the following year she manufactured a further 18,000 tons. But in that same year 69,000 tons had been purchased abroad and brought to Archangel. The problem, as with all war supplies reaching that remote northern port, was to get them to Petrograd and then on to the front. When Colonel Knox passed through Archangel that October he found 'an enormous accumulation of stores at the port – copper, lead and aluminium, rubber and coal, and no less than 700 automobiles in wooden packing-cases. Much of this material was lying out in the open.' Only 170 railway wagons were able to leave the port each day. A British firm was working to improve the railway line.

In an attempt to increase their ability to bring western war supplies to the front, the Russians were also trying to link the port of Murmansk with Petrograd. More than 30,000 Russian labourers were brought on six-month contracts to the cold, inhospitable region from provinces on the Volga, and 5,000 from Finland. But it was not enough, as hundreds and then thousands deserted, and almost none agreed to renew their contracts. Recourse was eventually had to German and Austrian prisoners-of-war, of whom 15,000 were brought to the railway, as were 10,000 Chinese labourers. The railway took a year and half to complete. Even then its carrying capacity developed only slowly.

At Gallipoli the daily ravages of gales and illness had created havoc with the fighting abilities of the Allied forces. As many as three hundred men were being evacuated sick every day. Shortage of ammunition was limiting artillery fire to two rounds per gun per day. A new British commander, Sir Charles Monro, was sent out to retrieve the situation. Hardly had he arrived than he received, on October 28, a telegram from Kitchener with the bluntest of messages: 'Please send me as soon as possible your report on the main issue at the Dardanelles, namely, leaving or staying.' Monro immediately sought the opinion of each of his commanders, at Helles, Anzac and Suvla, about the possibility of a new offensive against the Turkish positions. They were unanimous: their men were capable of no more than twenty-four hours' sustained battle.

On October 31, Monro replied to Kitchener's telegram, recommending withdrawal. He was supported by General Byng, commanding at Suvla, who wrote: 'I consider evacuation advisable.' General Birdwood, the Anzac commander, disagreed, fearing that a withdrawal not only would be used by the Turks to claim a complete victory, but would have an adverse effect on Muslims everywhere, including in India. No decision was reached, and the troops remained on the peninsula.

At Salonica, British forces, some from Gallipoli, had landed to join the French effort on behalf of Serbia. Their progress was slow. 'You'll probably ask why we don't get on,' G.H. Gordon, a captain in the 10th Irish Division, wrote on November 1, 'but there's a very good reason, their strong position and our not enough men.' The conditions at Salonica made him wish he was back in France. 'All our moves here have been done in inky blackness and usually under rain and on very ill-defined tracks in the hills.'

On November 5, Bulgarian forces captured Nis, giving the Germans a direct rail link from Berlin to Constantinople, and ending the Serbian-controlled section of the Berlin-Baghdad Railway.[1] The Serbian armies fought tenaciously, regaining villages and holding up the advancing armies, but being steadily driven back. For every fifty shells in Austria's advancing artillery, the Serbs had only one with which to reply, and their gunners received a stream of orders not to waste them, and then only to use them in emergency.

Burning their last motorised vehicles and heavy guns, 200,000 Serbian soldiers and civilians retreated a hundred miles across the mountains to find sanctuary in Albania. But the three-week march over rough terrain exacted a terrifyingly heavy toll: the death of 20,000 Serbian civilian refugees. 'People who shared in the retreat', Miss Waring wrote in her wartime history of Serbia, 'tell a confused story of cold, hunger, gorgeous scenery, Albanian ambushes, of paths covered with the carcasses of horses, of men dying at the wayside. We hear of the Ministers of Russia and Great Britain laying on straw next to the Serbian Foreign Minister, his wife and son, while in the next room lay the Italian and French Ministers, secretaries, consuls, dragomans, servants, pele-mele. We hear of the King, lying on a stretcher, drawn by four bullocks, sharing the difficulties of the road with the common soldier.'

The march across the mountains was a saga of distress, with hunger, privation and disease adding to the difficulties of the harsh terrain. Among

[1] The rail link between Germany and Turkey (Berlin-Constantinople) was formally reopened on 15 January 1916. Three days later, in the occupied Serbian city of Nis, the Kaiser, who had come from Berlin, made King Ferdinand of Bulgaria (who had come from Sofia) a Field Marshal in the German army.

those who had travelled from Britain to help the Serbs was Mabel Dearmer, a pioneer film-maker and successful novelist, playwright and illustrator. 'What chance would Christ have today?' she wrote in a public appeal, as the march continued. 'Crucifixion would be a gentle death for such a lunatic.' Shortly after sending her appeal, she died of enteric fever, while trying to help sick women and children.

As the marchers moved slowly westward, there was another grim hazard. Albania had declared itself for the Entente and offered help to the Serbs. But Albanian tribesmen who had suffered at Serb hands in 1912 and 1913 attacked the columns and killed hundreds of the marchers.

Although they were fleeing for their lives, the Serbs took with them into the mountains of Albania more than 24,000 Austrian prisoners-of-war. When the marchers reached the Albanian coast, these Austrians were interned in Italy and Sardinia. Many of them also died, of typhus and cholera. The Serb soldiers who reached the sea, more than 260,000, went mostly to the Greek island of Corfu, where they awaited in exile the day when they might liberate Serbia from the Austrian yoke. The evacuation had involved 1,159 escort voyages by forty-five Italian, twenty-five French and eleven British steamers. As well as the men, 10,000 horses were also taken away to safety. It was, writes one historian, the 'largest sea evacuation in history until Dunkirk'.[1]

Sick and wounded Serb soldiers were sent to a quarantine camp on the small island of Vido, where so many hundreds died that it became known as the Island of Death. Of the 30,000 Serb boys who set off to cross the mountains, only half survived the march. Hundreds more were killed by Austrian air bombardment while waiting in the harbour of San Giovanni di Medua for ships to take them to Corfu. Once on Corfu, a hundred boys died each day for lack of food. The survivors of this terrible saga were sent for their safety, and their schooling, to England and France. Those children who were consumptive were sent to a sanatorium on Corsica. The war of embattled armies had also become a war of prisoners-of-war, of forced marches, of refugees, and of orphans.

Serbia's two military allies, the French and the British, withdrew into Greece, while Bulgarian troops took up positions along the former Serb border. This war zone, like that on the Italian-Austrian Fronts, was one of mountain passes, rugged terrain, few roads, and steep gorges. For the Entente soldiers it was also very far from home. There was no way in which these small forces could intervene in the fate of occupied Serbia, where hundreds of Serbs were executed and others imprisoned for the slightest manifestation of nationalist sentiment. Yet south Slav nationalism,

[1] Randal Gray and Christopher Argyle (editors), *Chronicle of the First World War*, volume I, 1914–1916, Facts on File, Oxford 1990. At Dunkirk 224,318 British and 111,172 French troops were evacuated, a total of 335,490.

the hope of a larger south Slav kingdom, could not be crushed by Austrian persecution. In the words of the Serb poet Zmay Yovanovitch:

> And what the power that drove thee on, and bore
> Thee up, and lent thee wings? It was the hope
> Within the brain. Without it there had been
> No flight beyond the darkening clouds.

On November 7, off Sardinia, an Austrian submarine shelled and then torpedoed an Italian ocean liner, the *Ancona*, on its way to New York with many Italian immigrants on board: 208 passengers were killed, including twenty-five Americans. As with the previous German submarine sinkings, the American Government protested, found the Austrian reply unsatisfactory, but took the matter no further. On November 17 a British hospital ship, the *Anglia*, struck a German mine off Dover and sank: 139 among its crew and the wounded men on board were drowned.

On November 14 a new war zone was opened, one of the least remembered of the war. On that day, in the deserts of Italian Libya, which before 1912 had been part of the Ottoman Empire, the Senussi tribesman rose up in revolt against the Allies. Supported by the Turks, the Senussi opened fire at a British-Egyptian border post at Sollum. Two days later, three hundred tribesmen occupied the Zaura monastery at Sidi Barrani. British troops were sent into action, but the tribesmen, with the desert as their hiding place, continued to cause considerable aggravation.

Captain Jarvis, a British officer based in Egypt, who was an expert on desert warfare, later wrote: 'In some respects this was the most successful strategical move made by our enemies of the whole war, for these odd thousand rather verminous Arabs tied up on the Western Frontier for over a year some 30,000 troops badly required elsewhere and caused us to expend on desert railways, desert cars, transport etc. sufficient to add 2d to the income tax for the lifetime of the present generation.'

Five days after the outbreak of the Senussi revolt in what had earlier been one extremity of the Turkish Empire, an act of heroism took place behind the Turkish lines in European Turkey when two British pilots, Richard Bell Davies, who in January had been injured in an attack on Zeebrugge, and G.F. Smylie, bombed a railway junction at Ferrijik on the Gulf of Enos. Smylie's machine was hit by Turkish anti-aircraft fire: he made a forced landing, could not start up his plane, and disabled it. Davies, seeing this from the air, landed nearby, grabbed hold of Smylie as a group of Turkish soldiers approached, hauled him on board and flew off with him to safety. For this 'feat of airmanship that can seldom have been equalled for skill and gallantry' Davies was awarded the Victoria Cross.

Since May, in a minor Ministerial position, Churchill had continued to impress on his Cabinet colleagues the possibility of victory at Gallipoli, if the planning and execution of the land campaign was improved, and the naval attack re-activated. His advice had not been heeded. On November 4, General Monro, dispatched to the Salonica Front, was replaced at Gallipoli by General Birdwood, who wanted to try one more military assault on the Turkish positions. He was overruled by Kitchener, who made a surprise visit to the peninsula on November 11 and insisted that evacuation be carried out speedily. That day, the inner Cabinet was reduced to a five-man War Council, from which Churchill was excluded. He at once resigned from the Government and went to the Western Front, with the rank of Lieutenant-Colonel, to become a battalion commander.

At Gallipoli, a thunderstorm on November 27, with hail and torrential rain, swept men and animals along the gullies and trenches. At least a hundred men were drowned. Among the British officers at Suvla during the blizzard was Captain C.R. Attlee, who described in his memoirs how the heavy rain 'turned our trenches into moats'.[1] There followed two days of ferocious blizzard with driving snow, when another hundred men froze to death or died of exposure. At Suvla alone 12,000 men were treated for exposure. For the Australians and Indians in particular, the sub-zero temperatures were a torment. The only welcome deaths were those of the millions of flies that had gorged themselves on the corpses: when the storm passed they had disappeared.

Evacuation had become inevitable: the only question was, when? But on December 2, having returned to London, Kitchener asked the commanders at Gallipoli whether a renewed attack might not be possible after all, if the four British divisions at Salonica were to be sent to Suvla Bay (from which some of them had earlier come). General Byng was sceptical, pointing out that the landing piers at Suvla were being repeatedly washed away by storms, that the rain had made such roads as there were almost impassable, and that there was not enough existing shelter from the storms for the troops already there. Once more, evacuation was back at the top of the agenda.

Not evacuation, but a renewed advance was the unchanging British plan of campaign in Mesopotamia. There, on November 21, General Townshend attacked the Turkish defences of Ctesiphon, as a prelude to what was intended to be a rapid march on Baghdad, a mere twenty-two miles away. But the earlier good fortune of Basra, Kurna, Amara and Kut was over. Of the 8,500 British and Indian troops who went into battle at Ctesiphon, more than half were killed or wounded. Despite almost twice that number of casualties, the Turkish defenders, far from panicking and fleeing as they had in earlier battles, not only stood their ground but counter-attacked. The British, four hundred miles from the sea, could expect no reinforcements of any sort; the Turks could, and did call on the resources of Baghdad, only a few hours' march away.

Having come so far, the British were forced to retreat. The humiliating

---

[1] From 1940 to 1945 Attlee was a member of Churchill's War Cabinet and Deputy Prime Minister. In 1945 he became Prime Minister of Britain's third Labour Government.

journey back to Kut began on November 25. The survivors of the battle were exhausted and demoralised: the lack of facilities for the wounded made every mile of the retreat a torment. Shortly after the retreat began, a Turkish gun battery managed to immobilise the river flotilla, exposing those who were marching along the river bank to continual fear of attack. When the wounded continued by river south from Kut to Basra, Arab brigands, firing from both banks, killed many as they lay helpless in the ships taking them back.

At Kut, the defences were strengthened and preparations made to resist a Turkish attack. It was known that a senior German officer, Field Marshal von der Goltz, was on his way to take command, with 30,000 Turkish reinforcements. The British public, hitherto confident that the capture of Baghdad was imminent, suddenly faced the prospect of one of its armies being cut off and trapped, as Gordon had been at Khartoum three decades earlier. When the War Cabinet in London advised General Townshend to leave Kut and withdraw further down river, they received the reply that he was already besieged.

In the trenches on the Western Front, winter had brought wet and cold to plague the troops. The 36-year-old Raymond Asquith, the son of the British Prime Minister, and himself a Member of Parliament, wrote to a friend on November 19 of another 'unpleasant feature' of daily life in the trenches, 'the vast number of rats which gnaw the dead bodies and then run on one's face making obscene noises and gestures.' The Prime Minister's son added: 'Lately a certain number of cats have taken to nesting in the corpses, but I think the rats will get them in the end; though like all wars it will doubtless be a war of attrition.'

In London, on November 27, pacifists from all over Britain gathered to establish a No-Conscription Fellowship, with the declared aim of refusing to do any form of military service. Many of them were Quakers. What united them, their President, Clifford Allen, declared, was 'a belief in the sanctity of human life'. On December 4, Henry Ford despatched a 'Peace Ship', *Oscar II*, across the Atlantic with leading American women and journalists on board. Their instruction was: 'Get the boys out of the trenches and back to their homes by Christmas.'

In Berlin that month, a prominent banker told the American Ambassador, James W. Gerard, that 'the Germans were sick of the war; that the Krupp's and other big industries were making great sums of money, and were prolonging the war by insisting upon the annexation of Belgium'. Prussian landowners were also in favour of continuing the war, the banker told the Ambassador, 'because of the fact that they were getting four or five times the money for their products, while their work was being done by prisoners'.

The fate of the Armenians was the harshest of all outside the war zones. A 25-year-old Jewish girl, Sarah Aaronsohn, who had set out from

Constantinople to her home in Palestine, travelled that December through the Taurus mountains to Aleppo. Her biographer has written: 'She saw vultures hovering over children who had fallen dead by the roadside. She saw beings crawling along, maimed, starving and begging for bread. From time to time she passed soldiers driving before them with whips and rifle-butts whole families, men, women and children, shrieking, pleading, wailing. These were the Armenian people setting out for exile in the desert from which there was no return.'[1]

As the second winter of the war arrived, its impact was felt in all the war zones. But cold weather on the Eastern Front did not deter nine hundred Cossack troops from a three-day, 24-mile march, in fourteen degrees of frost, through the Pripet marshes to the headquarters of a German division. There, on November 28, they captured the eighty-strong Staff including the divisional general, who later shot himself. The front line in the east was stabilising. The Germans had driven as far east as Dvinsk and Vilna, the Austrians had regained Brody and Czernowitz. Russian Poland was entirely under German occupation. To feed the captive population, the Germans opened talks on December 2 with a United States diplomat, Dr Frank Kellogg.

At the Dardanelles, the new British admiral, Wester Wemyss, argued that a renewed naval attack, like that of March 18 by ships alone, would enable the Straits to be opened and kept open. In two telegrams to London he outlined his plan and expressed his confidence that it would succeed. His proposal for action was rejected. Instead, he was put in charge of all naval arrangements for the total evacuation of the Gallipoli Peninsula. The evacuation of the troops from Anzac and Suvla began on December 8. At Suvla, Captain Attlee was in command of a rearguard holding the perimeter around the evacuation beach. In twelve days 83,048 troops, 4,695 horses and mules, 1,718 vehicles and 186 heavy guns were taken off. The year-long effort to reach Constantinople by sea and defeat Turkey by an overwhelming show of naval strength in the Sea of Marmara was over. All that remained was to evacuate the troops at Cape Helles.

The Turkish triumph of late 1915 was not confined to Gallipoli. In Mesopotamia, at one of the southern extremities of the Ottoman Empire, 25,000 British and Indian troops were besieged by 80,000 Turks in Kut. The siege began on December 5. The defenders held out for 147 days, waiting in vain for reinforcements to reach them from Basra. The relief force was itself under constant attack as it tried to reach Kut: in a battle at Sheikh Sa'ad more than 4,000 of the relieving force were killed or wounded. So bad were the medical arrangements that even eleven days after the battle a newly arrived Indian Field Ambulance unit found two hundred British and eight hundred Indian wounded still lying in the open, on muddy ground,

[1] Anita Engel, *The Nili Spies*, Phoenix, Jerusalem 1989, page 62.

without shelter, and with their first dressings still unchanged.

The set-back in Mesopotamia did not weaken the attraction to the British of a renewed effort to undermine the Central Powers, and make substantial territorial gains, by breaking the Ottoman Empire. Many national aspirations were at stake. As the Russian-born Jewish nationalist Vladimir Jabotinsky wrote, while the outcome of the war was still uncertain: 'The only theatre where "decisive blows" can be imagined is Asiatic Turkey. On that theatre warfare seems to have kept its old character: smaller numbers of men and material, smaller losses as price of victory, and incomparably quicker territorial advance in the case of victory. This truth cannot be obscured by the two failures of Gallipoli and Kut: the causes of the melancholy results of the Dardanelles and Mesopotamian campaigns are sufficiently known, and these results do not prove anything except the danger of either negligent or half-hearted warfare.'

It was not until the very last phase of the war in Europe that Jabotinsky's pointers to victory in Asia were to be followed, and proved true, opening up vast areas of the hitherto closed confines of the Ottoman Empire to partition and spheres of influence. Not only Jewish but also Arab aspirations had been stimulated by the prospect of an Allied victory on the Gallipoli Peninsula. On July 14, while the fighting there was still undecided, the Sherif of Mecca, Sherif Hussein, had written to the British authorities in Cairo to request British acknowledgement of 'the independence of the Arab countries'. If this did not come within thirty days, he had warned, the Arabs 'reserve to themselves complete freedom of action': a scarcely veiled threat to throw their desert resources behind the Turks.

Sherif Hussein's request had reached Cairo after the second Gallipoli landings. Even the hanging of eleven Arab leaders in Syria by the Turkish Governor, Jamal Pasha, on August 21, had not stimulated a more favourable British attitude to Arab aspirations, even though one of those hanged, Abd al-Karim al-Khalil, had hoped to organise an anti-Turkish revolt along the Eastern Mediterranean coast between Beirut and Sidon, which could well have cleared the way for an Allied landing there, cutting the Turkish lines of communication with Gaza, Sinai and the Suez Canal.

The immediate British response to Hussein's search for independence was a cynical one. 'I should personally recommend the insertion of a pious aspiration on the subject of the Sherif's ideal of an Arab Union,' the Governor-General of the Sudan, Sir Reginald Wingate, advised. 'Something might be added to ensure his remaining definitely on our side until our success at the Dardanelles enables us to give more authoritative expression to our views.'

Before that hoped-for British success at Gallipoli, an Arab staff officer in the Ottoman army, Muhammad Sharif al-Faruqi, deserted from the Turkish forces at Gallipoli and crossed into the British lines. He was, he told those who questioned him, a descendant of the Prophet and wished to be taken to the Holy City of Mecca to see the Sherif Hussein. Taken by boat to Cairo, he was interrogated there on October 11 by Colonel Gilbert

Clayton of the Arab Bureau, to whom he revealed that he was a member of a secret Young Arab Society opposed to Turkish rule. The society's leaders, he said, in both Syria and Mesopotamia, wished to collaborate with the British in return for Arab independence.

According to al-Faruqi, both the Turks and the Germans were willing to grant the Arabs their territorial demands. This was not true, but Clayton and his colleagues in Cairo had no means of checking it. On the very day of al-Faruqi's interrogation, Bulgaria mobilised against the Allies. The situation on the Gallipoli Peninsula was suddenly endangered by the prospect of Bulgarian troops joining the conflict. Al-Faruqi told Clayton that if an immediate British declaration was made supporting Arab independence, with specific territorial lines, the anti-Turk revolt would begin at once: in Syria, Mesopotamia and Palestine. On the following day, October 12, Clayton telegraphed the Foreign Office in London advising acceptance of the terms implicit in Al-Faruqi's report. To reject the offer, Clayton warned, would 'throw the Young Arab Party definitely into the arms of the enemy.' The Arab 'machinery' would at once be asserted against Allied interests throughout the Ottoman Empire.

Clayton's reasoning was decisive: eleven days after he sent his telegram to London the British Government made the commitment to Arab independence that Sherif Hussein had earlier sought in vain. In a letter sent to the Sherif from Sir Henry McMahon, Britain agreed 'to recognise and support the independence of the Arabs within the territories included in the limits and boundaries proposed by the Sherif of Mecca'. These included Mesopotamia and much of Syria. They excluded, at McMahon's insistence, 'portions of Syria lying west of the districts of Damascus, Hama, Homs and Aleppo'. Whether or not they excluded Palestine was to be a matter of subsequent dispute, since that was not mentioned in the exchange of letters. Six years later McMahon was to explain, in a letter to the Colonial Office: 'It was as fully my intention to exclude Palestine as it was to exclude the more northern coastal tracts of Syria.'

The siege of Kut had begun on December 5. On December 7 the British Cabinet made its decision to evacuate Suvla and Anzac, but not, as yet, Cape Helles. A week later McMahon wrote again to Hussein to inform him that the latest Arab request, for neither Aleppo nor Beirut to be excluded from the area of future Arab independence, would have to be taken up with the French. As for the part the Arabs must play in the future, 'it is most essential', McMahon wrote, 'that you spare no effort to attach all the Arab people to our united cause and urge them to afford no assistance to our enemies. It is on the success of these efforts, and on the more active measures which the Arabs may hereafter take in support of our cause, when the time for action comes, that the permanence and strength of our agreement must depend.'

The British had failed to secure victory either at Gallipoli or in Mesopotamia. These distant failures were to prove a strong deterrent to further distant campaigns, putting off the time when an Arab revolt against the

Turks would become an integral part of Allied war strategy. The Arabs in 1916, like the Italians and Bulgarians in 1915, wanted to see some prospect of victory and territorial gain before committing themselves to battle. For the British, the frustrations of each of the set-backs of 1915 were considerable, with Gallipoli and Mesopotamia the most depressing. On December 20, Lloyd George expressed these feelings when he spoke in the House of Commons: 'Too late in moving here, too late in arriving there. Too late in coming to this decision, too late in starting with enterprises, too late in preparing! In this war the footsteps of the Allied forces have been dogged by the mocking spectre of "too late", and unless we quicken our movements damnation will fall on the sacred cause for which so much gallant blood has flowed.'

As 1915 came to an end, it was clear that the war that was to have ended by Christmas 1914 was certainly not going to be over by Christmas 1915. The British Government did not want it, however, to continue in the Balkans. On December 4, at a conference in Calais, the British, led by Asquith, insisted that the Allied forces at Salonica should withdraw. Now that Serbia was defeated they could serve no purpose there. The French bowed to this logic. But two days later, at a further inter-Allied conference, this time at Chantilly, the Russians, Italians and Serbs prevailed upon the French to agree to keep the Salonica Front open. In support of this view, the Tsar himself sent Asquith a telegram regretting the Calais decision. Less than a week after Calais, Kitchener and Grey returned to France, and agreed that the Salonica Front should remain in place, Kitchener reporting back to his colleagues that 'good feeling had been restored'.

Plans were also laid at Chantilly for an Allied victory on the Western Front in 1916, when Joffre obtained British agreement for a joint and simultaneous Anglo-French offensive in the summer of 1916. It would take place both north and south of the river Somme, on a forty-mile front. What Joffre described as the 'brilliant tactical results' of the Champagne and Artois offensives of 1915 would be repeated and surpassed. Germany, his experts reported, was running out of reserves. With Kitchener's New Armies on the British front, with sufficient guns for an overwhelming preliminary bombardment and sufficient ammunition for a sustained advance, the Battle of the Somme would be decisive.

On December 19, Sir Douglas Haig took over from Sir John French as Commander-in-Chief of the British army in France. That same day, an ominous day for millions, he wrote scathingly in his diary of the fate of the telegram he had sent to the War Office at noon, asking who was to succeed him as commander of the First Army. 'Up to 11 p.m. no reply reached me. Then Sir Wm Robertson arrived from England and telephoned from St Omer that the Prime Minister and Lord K had gone out of London for the weekend, and nothing could be settled until Monday! And this is war-time!'

That day, December 19, the Germans released phosgene gas, ten times more toxic than chlorine, against the British forces in the Ypres Salient. Their aim was to cause panic and a mass retreat. But the British troops, who had been surprised by the new weapon in April, were now well trained in gas drill and well equipped with gas helmets. A thousand soldiers were gassed, and 120 killed. The wind was a strong one that day, blowing the gas cloud southward across the British lines and far to the rear: because of a curve in the line, some of the gas was blown along the German trenches on the Wytschaete Ridge.

The hoped-for British panic did not take place, and the line held. In London, Vera Brittain received a pencilled note from her fiancé, Roland Leighton, on the Western Front: 'Shall be home on leave from 24th Dec.– 31st. Land Christmas Day. R'. She contemplated with excitement the possibility of getting married during that brief leave, even of having a baby, 'Roland's very own, something of himself to remember him by if he goes.' Throughout Christmas Day she awaited him, then went to bed knowing that he would be with her on the following day. 'The next morning I had just finished dressing, and was putting the final touches to the pastel-blue crepe-de-Chine blouse, when the expected message came to say that I was wanted on the telephone. Believing that I was at last to hear the voice for which I had waited for twenty-four hours, I dashed joyously into the corridor. But the message was not from Roland . . . it was not to say that he had arrived home that morning, but to tell me that he had died of wounds at a Casualty Clearing Station on December 23rd.'

Roland Leighton had not been killed in the thick of battle. Like so many of the war's dead, his life was destroyed far from the violence of a massive onslaught or the onrush of armies. His platoon had taken over a section of the trenches where the front-line wire was badly in need of repair. He had gone to inspect the area where the wiring party would have to work. His way should have led through a communication trench, but it was flooded, so he had taken a concealed path through a gap in the hedge. The previous British occupants of that sector of the front had not passed on the message that the communication trench had been flooded for some time and that the Germans were accustomed to open fire now and again at the gap in the hedge with a machine gun. The moon was nearly full that night, and the German machine gun was a mere hundred yards from the hedge. As Leighton reached the gap, the Germans opened fire and he was hit in the stomach. Two men risked their lives to carry him back to the trench. The next day an operation could not save him. One machine-gun bullet had injured the base of his spine. That night, as his fiancée later wrote, 'Uppingham's record prize-winner, whose whole nature fitted him for the spectacular drama of a great battle, died forlornly in a hospital bed.'[1]

---

[1] Of the sixty-six boys who entered Uppingam School with Leighton in September 1909, seventeen were killed during the First World War or died of wounds received in action. One boy, Frank Hodgkinson, was a civilian prisoner in Ruhleben camp throughout the war; another,

On the Western Front, the conditions of warfare at the end of 1915 were appalling, described immediately after the war by a former front-line correspondent, Phillip Gibbs, in his book *Realities of War*. 'Our men were never dry,' he wrote. 'They were wet in their trenches and wet in their dug-outs. They slept in soaking clothes, with boots full of water, and they drank rain with their tea, and ate mud with their "bully", and endured it all with the philosophy of "grin and bear it!" and laughter, as I heard them laughing in those places, between explosive curses.' Hardly had the trenches been drained after one rain storm than another undid the work 'and the parapets slid down, and water poured in; and spaces were opened for German gun-fire, and there was less head cover against shrapnel bullets which mixed with the rain drops and high explosives which smashed through the mud'.

During November the rain was so intense that many trenches were knee high, and even waist high in water. Gibbs recalled how, in one sector of the front, 'reckless because of their discomfort, the Germans crawled upon their slimy parapets and sat on top to dry their legs, and shouted, "Don't shoot! Don't shoot!" Our men did not shoot. They, too, sat on the parapets drying their legs, and grinning at the grey ants yonder until these incidents were reported back to GHQ – where good fires were burning under dry roofs – and stringent orders came against "fraternisation". Every German who showed himself – owing to a parapet falling in – would be shot too. It was six of one and half a dozen of the other, as always, in this trench warfare, but the dignity of GHQ would not be outraged by the thought of such indecent spectacles as British and Germans refusing to kill each other on sight. Some of the men obeyed orders, and where a German sat up and said, "Don't shoot!" plugged him through the head. Others were extremely short-sighted ... Now and again Germans crawled over to our trenches and asked meekly to be taken prisoner.'

An episode took place that winter that was spoken of throughout the Western Front. Above a German parapet, Gibbs has narrated, 'appeared a plank on which in big letters was scrawled these words: "The English are fools." "Not such bloody fools as all that!" said a sergeant, and in a few minutes the plank was smashed to splinters by rifle-fire. Another plank appeared with the words: "The French are fools." Loyalty to our Allies caused the destruction of that board. A third plank was put up. "We're all fools. Let's all go home." That board was also shot to pieces, but the message caused some laughter, and men repeating it said, "There's a deal of truth in those words. Why should this go on? What's it all about? Let the old men who made this war come and fight it out among themselves at Hooge. The fighting men have no real quarrel with each other. We all want to go home, to our wives and our work." But neither side was prepared to "go home" first. Each side was in a

Brian Horrocks, became a distinguished general in the Second World War, helping to defeat Rommel in North Africa and commanding 30th Corps in the Normandy landings.

trap – a devil's trap from which there was no escape.'

In his book, Gibbs described that 'devil's trap' as follows: 'Loyalty to their own side, discipline, with the death penalty behind it, spell words of old tradition, obedience to the laws of war, or to the caste which ruled them, all the moral and spiritual propaganda handed out by pastors, newspapers, generals, staff officers, old men at home, exalted women, female furies, a deep and simple love for England, and Germany, pride of manhood, fear of cowardice – a thousand complexities of thought and sentiment prevented men, on both sides, from breaking the net of fate in which they were entangled, and revolting against that mutual, unceasing massacre, by a rising from the trenches with a shout of, "We're all fools! . . . Let's all go home!" '

A particular source of agony that winter, adding to the torment of lice and rats, was 'trench foot'. 'Men standing in slime for days and nights in field boots or puttees lost all sense of feeling in their feet,' Gibbs wrote. 'These feet of theirs, so cold and wet, began to swell, and then go "dead" and then suddenly to burn as though touched by red hot pokers. When the "reliefs" went up scores of men could not walk back from the trenches, but had to crawl, or to be carried pick-a-back by their comrades. So I saw hundreds of them, and as the winter dragged on, thousands.' Battalions lost more men from the fighting line from trench foot than from wounds. 'Brigadiers and Divisional Generals were gloomy, and cursed the new affliction of their men. Some of them said it was due to damned carelessness, others were inclined to think it due to deliberate malingering at a time when there were many cases of self-inflicted wounds by men who shot their fingers away, or their toes, to get out of the trenches. There was no look of malingering on the faces of those boys who were being carried pick-a-back to the ambulance trains at Rémy siding near Poperinghe with both feet crippled and tied up in bundles of cotton-wool. The pain was martyrizing like that of men tied to burning faggots for conscience' sake. In one battalion of the 49th (West Riding) Division there were over 400 cases in that winter of 1915.'

A cure was eventually found: rubbing feet with oil two or three times a day. But while the malady lasted it wreaked havoc with the fighting strength of the battalions. Nevertheless, Gibbs wrote, 'The spirit of the men fought against all that misery, resisted it, and would not be beaten by it.'

The Christmas Truce that had broken out so spontaneously on the Western Front in 1914 was not repeated in 1915. 'Nothing of the kind is to be allowed on the Divisional front this year,' one British Infantry Brigade was informed five days before the festive season was to begin. 'The Artillery will maintain a slow gun fire on the enemy's trenches commencing at dawn, and every opportunity will as usual be taken to inflict casualties upon any of the enemy exposing themselves.'

These orders were, in the main, obeyed. The historian Lyn Macdonald has written of how 'in the trenches close to Plugstreet Wood a tremendous voice entertained the trenches of both sides with a selection from *La Traviata*, stopping abruptly in mid-aria as if a door had been slammed shut'. Near Wulverghem the Germans set up a tree on the parapet of their front trench on Christmas Eve, ablaze with candles. 'For a few moments the tiny pinpoints of flame flickered uncertainly in the dark until a British officer ordered rapid fire and the Tommies shot it down.'[1]

Christmas Day was no different. 'We hailed the smiling morn with five rounds fired fast, and we kept up slow fire all day,' Corporal D.A. Pankhurst of the Royal Artillery noted. 'Those were our orders. Some batteries sent over as many as three hundred shells. It was a Christmas present to Fritz, they said. But I do believe myself that it was intended to discourage fraternising.' The shelling and shooting continued that day. Second Lieutenant W. Cushing was a witness when a private was killed in his battalion, a shell fragment having severed his femoral artery. 'Stretcher-bearers attempted to deal with this mortal wound by using a tourniquet,' Cushing wrote, 'but this caused the poor chap pain, and the MO told us on the field telephone to remove it and let him die in peace.' The Medical Officer had apparently been 'about to risk his own life by coming to us across the open – there were no communication trenches left – but the CO ordered him to stay where he was at battalion HQ. It was just as well. We couldn't afford to lose a Medical Officer in a fruitless effort to save life. He couldn't possibly have arrived in time.'

Thus died Private W.G. Wilkerson on Christmas Day. He was buried in New Irish Farm Cemetery at St Jan, near Ypres. As the precise location of his grave could not be found when the cemetery was put in order at the end of the war, he is commemorated on a special memorial headstone bearing the inscription 'Known to be buried in this cemetery.' Near him lie 4,500 other dead.[2] On the Gallipoli Peninsula, where the men at Cape Helles were expecting to be evacuated within a few weeks, Christmas Day saw further deaths from Turkish shelling and sniper fire. Among those killed that day was the twenty-nine-year-old Arnold Thompson, a captain in the Royal Army Medical Corps, who had graduated from New College, Oxford, eight months earlier.[3]

On the Eastern Front, the Central Powers were confident of their power. In Galicia, a two-week Russian offensive that ended on December 27,

[1] Lyn Macdonald, *1915, The Death of Innocence*, Hodder and Stoughton, London 1993, page 592. The sources that Lyn Macdonald has assembled in her various books on the First World War are the envy of many historians, including this one.

[2] Among them 4,272 British soldiers, 254 Canadians, sixty-five Australians, twenty-three New Zealanders, six South Africans, five Indians, three Newfoundlanders and one West Indian. Also buried in New Irish Farm Cemetery are twelve unknown soldiers, six Chinese labourers and one German soldier.

[3] Of the 1,223 members of New College who served during the First World War, 217 were killed in action. A further thirty-eight schoolboys who had gained admission to the college, but had volunteered for military service as soon as they left school, were also killed.

although supported by a thousand guns, each with a thousand shells, failed to break the Austrian line: 6,000 Russian soldiers were taken prisoner. That day the British Cabinet decided to evacuate Cape Helles, ending any Entente presence on the Gallipoli Peninsula.

At the end of 1915 the Central Powers were in the ascendant. Serbia was entirely under Austrian and Bulgarian occupation. Russian Poland and Belgium were under German control. At sea, the sinking of Entente shipping had been continuous and destructive. The German plans for victory in 1916 included unlimited submarine warfare, and an attack on the French forces defending Verdun and its ring of forts. The aim of this attack was to wear down the French army by the attrition of numbers. General Falkenhayn looked to an attack on Verdun to create a 'breaking point' in French morale. 'If we succeeded in opening the eyes of her people to the fact that in a military sense they have nothing more to hope for,' he wrote to the Kaiser on December 15, 'that breaking point would be reached, and England's best sword knocked out of her hand.' If the French were determined to defend Verdun to the last, as Falkenhayn was convinced they would, then, he told the Kaiser, 'the forces of France will bleed to death' whether the Germans captured Verdun or not.

'Never through the ages', comments the historian Alistair Horne, 'had any great commander or strategist proposed to vanquish an enemy by gradually bleeding him to death. The macabreness, the unpleasantness of its very imagery could only have emerged from, and was symptomatic of, that Great War, where, in their callousness, leaders could regard human lives as mere corpuscles.' In his history of Verdun, Horne quotes two other comments with regard to the attitude of the commanders to the losses, that of Haig's son, that the British Commander-in-Chief 'felt that it was his duty to refrain from visiting the casualty clearing stations because these visits made him physically ill', and that of Joffre who, after pinning a military decoration on a blinded soldier, said to his Staff: 'I musn't be shown any more such spectacles.... I would no longer have the courage to give the order to attack.'[1]

As he put forward his reasons for the Verdun offensive, General Falkenhayn was dismissive of Russia's power to intervene to take the pressure off France, or to threaten Germany in the east. 'Even if we cannot expect a revolution in the grand style,' he told the Kaiser in his memorandum of December 15, 'we are entitled to believe that Russia's internal troubles will compel her to give in within a relatively short period.' To weaken Russia internally, on December 26 the authorities in Berlin handed the Russian Jewish Bolshevik, Alexander Helphand, a million roubles to spread anti-war propaganda throughout Russia. The money was paid over after the German Ambassador to Denmark persuaded Berlin that Russia could only be detached from the Entente by revolution, and that the

[1] Alistair Horne, *The Price of Glory, Verdun 1916*, Macmillan, London 1962, page 36.

Bolsheviks had it in their power to undermine the authority of both the Tsar and the Russian generals.

The year 1915 ended as it had begun, with a disaster at sea. On December 30, in the North Sea, an accidental internal explosion blew up the British cruiser *Natal*, with 304 fatalities. That same day, in the eastern Mediterranean, a German submarine torpedoed without warning a Peninsular and Oriental steamship company liner, the *Persia*: 334 passengers were drowned, among them the United States Consul in Aden and one other American citizen. Three days after the sinking an American diplomat in Paris, John Coolidge, wrote scathingly in his diary: 'An American consul on his way to his post at Aden was on board, so probably Mr Lansing will buy a new box of note-paper and set to work.' He was right: America's neutrality was still a fixed feature of the war scene. Robert Lansing, the Secretary of State, issued a formal protest, but no more.

On December 29, in Paris, the French National Assembly passed a Law which gave the land on which the British war cemeteries were located on French soil as 'the free gift of the French people for a perpetual resting place of those who are laid there'. The cemeteries are still there eighty years after the war began: more than 2,000 cemeteries, tended by nearly five hundred gardeners. Even as the war was being fought, the future of its most poignant monuments was being enshrined in Law.

After twelve months of fighting, the line of trenches along the Western Front had not been broken by either side. It was Germany that stood along the line as the conqueror and occupier of French and Belgian soil, far from her own borders. Several French villages in the fighting line had been destroyed so completely that they were never rebuilt: east of St Mihiel are two such villages, Regniéville and Remenauville, taken in April from the Germans. At their entrance today is the road sign: 'Village détruit'. Yet the nature of confrontation was such that the British in the Ypres Salient were emphatic that they had secured a great victory by holding Ypres at all. The town itself, regularly shelled by the Germans, was a ruin, but that too could be shown to have its virtuous aspect.

'Only the methodical and painstaking Boche could have reduced a town of such size to such a state,' commented Ian Hay, himself a soldier and one of the most popular British writers on the war. 'But – the main point to observe is this. We are inside, and the Boche is outside! Fenced by a mighty crescent of prosaic trenches, themselves manned by paladins of an almost incredible stolidity, Ypres still points her broken fingers to the sky – shattered, silent, but inviolate still; and all owing to the obstinacy of a dull and unready nation which merely keeps faith and stands by its friends.'

Hay told his readers that there was a further lesson to be learned: 'Such an attitude of mind is incomprehensible to the Boche, and we are well content that it should be so.' One could stand on 'certain recently won eminences', Wytschaete Ridge, Messines Ridge, Vimy Ridge and Monchy, and look back 'not merely from these ridges, but from certain moral ridges – over the ground which has been successfully traversed, and you can marvel for the hundredth time, not that the thing was well or badly done, but that it was ever done at all.' In contrast with a sense of moral superiority were the men awaking 'grimy and shivering, to another day's unpleasantness'. That 'unpleasantness', however, had hardly any place in Hay's narrative. The dead in his account had 'gone to the happy hunting-grounds'.

What was clear, as 1915 came to an end, was that a mood of greater resignation prevailed than six months earlier. 'We no longer regard War with the least enthusiasm,' Hay wrote. 'We have seen It, face to face. Our sole purpose now is to screw our sturdy followers up to the requisite pitch of efficiency, and keep them remorselessly at that standard until the dawn of triumphant and abiding peace.' An experienced writer could still deploy the words and concepts 'efficiency', 'standard' and 'triumphant'. Equally experienced soldiers could use a different language, a different perspective. Returning to the Western Front from their Christmas leave, the soldiers at Victoria Station were heard to sing a new refrain:

> *I don't want to die,*
> *I want to go home.*
> *I don't want to go to the trenches no more,*
> *Where the whizz-bangs and shells do whistle and roar.*
>
> *I don't want to go over the sea,*
> *To where the alleyman will shoot at me,*
> *I want to go home*
> *I don't want to die.*

12

'This war will end at Verdun' (the Kaiser)

JANUARY–APRIL 1916

The ascendancy of the Central Powers on the battlefield at the beginning of 1916 was reflected in the treatment of the national minorities inside Austria-Hungary. That January the German language was declared to be the only official language in Bohemia. In the streets of Prague the police used truncheons against people whom they heard speaking Czech. But in the policy-making centre, Vienna, the Austrian leaders recognised the enormous problems that the war was creating, especially as the Russian army, for all its setbacks, continued to fight with tenacity. 'There can be no question of destroying the Russian war machine,' General Conrad warned Count Tisza on January 4, and he added: 'England cannot be defeated; peace must be made in not too short a space, or we shall be fatally weakened, if not destroyed.'

Britain and Canada, alone of the combatants, still had entirely volunteer armies. On the day of Conrad's warning there were 2,675,149 Britons under arms, all volunteers. In Canada, the volunteer system had raised 150,000 men since the outbreak of the war, and had seen the participation of four divisions on the Western Front, but the Canadian Prime Minister, Sir Robert Borden, having visited Britain and gained some idea of the magnitude of the task, called in his New Year's message on January 1 for 500,000 Canadians to join the fight, out of a population of eight million.

In Britain itself, pressure was mounting for the introduction of conscription, which would add at least two million more men to the armed forces. On January 5 the Prime Minister, Asquith, introduced the first Conscription Bill to the House of Commons. On the Western Front, one of Asquith's former political colleagues, Winston Churchill, was spending his first days as a battalion commander. On January 17 he was summoned to the town of Hazebrouck to hear a lecture by his friend Colonel Tom Holland, on the Battle of Loos. He described the scene in a letter to his wife Clementine: 'The theatre was crowded with generals and officers.... I could not even get a seat, but stood at the wings of the stage. Tom spoke very well but his tale was one of hopeless failure, of sublime heroism

utterly wasted and of splendid Scottish soldiers shorn away in vain ...
with never the ghost of a chance of success. 6,000 killed and wounded out
of 10,000 in this Scottish division alone. Alas, alas. Afterwards they asked
what was the lesson of the lecture. I restrained an impulse to reply "Don't
do it again". But they will – I have no doubt.'

Going forward with his battalion to its front-line positions near the
village of Ploegsteert, Churchill shared with his men the hazards of war.
One morning, as he was going up to the front-line trenches , a shell burst
in the cellar of a ruined convent that he was passing. 'A fountain of
brickbats went up into the air', he wrote to his wife, 'and I watched them
carefully from fifty yards away, to dodge if any fell near me. Suddenly I
saw, almost instantaneously with the explosion, five or six black objects
hurtling towards me – You know how quick thought is. I had no time to
think they were splinters, to argue that they could not belong to the same
explosion, and to reach out for a another solution, before I saw that they
were frightened birds!'

Churchill served on the Western Front for six months. On several
occasions he was nearly killed when German shells burst nearby. Once,
when he was in reserve billets, a shell entered his bedroom, passed right
through it, penetrated the cellar where many of his men had taken shelter,
and then failed to explode. On another occasion, going up to the trenches,
he watched as a German gun systematically shelled the front-line, its shell-
bursts coming ever closer. 'One could calculate more or less where the
next one would come,' he wrote three days later to his wife. The path to
the trenches led alongside the ruined convent, 'and I said, "the next will
hit the convent". Sure enough just as we got abreast of it, the shell arrived
with a screech and a roar and tremendous bang and showers of bricks and
clouds of smoke and all the soldiers jumped and scurried, and peeped up
out of their holes and corners. It did not make me jump a bit – not a pulse
quickened. I do not mind noise as some very brave people do. But I felt –
twenty yards more to the left and no more tangles to unravel, no more
anxieties to face, no more hatreds and injustices to encounter ... a good
ending to a chequered life, a final gift – unvalued – to an ungrateful
country – an impoverishment of the war-making power of Britain which
no one would ever know or measure or mourn.'

The Austrian conquest of Serbia having been completed before the end of
1915, a new war front opened on 8 January 1916, when 45,000 Austrian
troops and 5,000 Bosnian Muslims, as well as 3,000 Italians, attacked
Montenegro, Serbia's neighbour and ally. A 500-gun artillery barrage, as
well as air and sea attacks, opened the campaign. Within forty-eight hours
the Montenegrins were driven from the 4,850-foot Mount Lovcen, 'the
Gibraltar of the Adriatic', and forced back to their capital, Cetinje. On
January 11, Cetinje fell. Six days later Montenegro surrendered. 'It is all
over with poor little Montenegro bar the shouting,' the American diplomat
John Coolidge wrote in his diary on January 16. 'When her emergency

came, there was no one to help her, so she had to go.' The war had lasted nine days. Those Montenegrin troops who managed to escape joined the Serb escapees on Corfu.

Unknown to the Austrians until after the event, the day of their attack on Montenegro was the day on which the last British troops left Cape Helles on the Gallipoli Peninsula. During eleven days 35,268 troops had been taken off, without any casualties. In a final effort to challenge the Turks, they left behind booby traps, land mines, dummy sentinels, and 'clockwork' rifles which would fire when water dripping through a tin of sand dropped through to a lower tin that would then fall on the trigger mechanism. One of the last British soldiers to leave, Sergeant Mannion, later described how 'When we were a mile out from the beach, we were all ordered to go below. At this moment a big magazine on shore was blown up, and we could hear the pieces of scrap-iron falling on the roof of the lighter. The sea was very rough and our lighter pitched and tossed about like a cork on the waves. We were all very sea-sick. There was a rumour that we had broken adrift, and the sailors confirmed this. Our cable had parted and we were drifting, in a rough sea, off a hostile shore. But nobody seemed to worry much. We had got safely off Gallipoli, a thing which none of us had expected.'

As well as the men, 3,689 horses and mules were taken off the peninsula. But 508 mules were shot, and 1,590 vehicles abandoned. The human cost of the effort is recorded in the statistics of each army. More than 66,000 Turkish soldiers had been killed, and 28,000 British, 7,595 Australian, 2,431 New Zealand, and 10,000 French. Two memorials, one at Helles and one at Anzac, record the names of those British and Commonwealth soldiers with no known grave. Thirty-three Commonwealth war cemeteries on the peninsula contain the graves of those whose bodies were found. On the grave of Gunner J.W. Twamley his next of kin caused the lines to be inscribed:

> Only a boy but a British boy,
> The son of a thousand years.

A bereaved Australian sent the following lines:

> Brother Bill a sniping fell:
> We love him still,
> We always will.

From parents whose grief could not find comfort in religion came the question:

> What harm did he do Thee, O Lord?

The Turks, relieved at the disappearance of their enemy from Gallipoli, transferred 36,000 troops from there to Mesopotamia. But on the Caucasus Front, the Russian commander, General Yudenitch, despite ferociously cold weather that cost him 2,000 men incapacitated by frostbite,

drove back the Turks to the city of Erzerum, during the battle for which
many Arab troops fighting with the Turks deserted. Finally entering
Erzerum in mid-February, the Russians took 5,000 Turkish soldiers prisoner, but lost the fighting capacity of 2,000 more of their own men from
frostbite. In pursuit of the Turks west of Erzerum, the Russians took a
further 5,000 prisoners. Russian morale at home was boosted, momentarily at least, by these distant successes.

Germany continued to look to anti-war agitation in Russia as a way to
lessen the burdens on the Eastern Front, and perhaps to end them altogether. On January 11 more than 10,000 Russian workers went on strike
at the Black Sea port and naval base of Nikolayev. Within two weeks the
strike spread to Petrograd, where as many as 45,000 dock workers went
on strike. Both the Russian discontent with the war and the national
aspirations of Russia's subject peoples stimulated German attention. On
January 18, Berlin was informed by one of its agents that contact had been
made with an Estonian revolutionary, Keskula. Not only intrigue but also
the realities of the battlefield seemed to point to German victories. That
week the Chief of the German Naval Staff, Admiral Holtzendorff, expressed his confidence in the ability of his submarines to knock Britain out
of the war altogether well before the end of the year. The new Commander-
in-Chief of the German High Seas Fleet, Admiral Scheer, appointed on
January 24, was also confident that he could bring the British main fleet
to action in the North Sea, and defeat it.

Britain was preparing for a long war, with equal confidence. On January
27, the first step was taken towards compulsory military service. The
continued financial goodwill of the United States was enabling Britain to
raise money for the purchase and manufacture of arms.

In Germany, an anti-American campaign had begun, typified by a cartoon
showing President Wilson releasing the dove of peace with one hand while
pouring out munitions to the Allies with the other. On the Kaiser's birthday,
January 27, an American flag, draped in black, was placed on the statue
of Frederick the Great in Berlin with the words attached on a silk banner
in letters of gold: 'Wilson and his Press are not America'. Photographs of
the wreath were sent all over Germany. One German newspaper declared:
'Frederick the Great was the first to recognise the Independence of the
young Republic after it had won its freedom from the yoke of England, at
the price of its very heart's blood through years of struggle. His successor,
Wilhelm II, receives the gratitude of America in the form of hypocritical
phrases and war supplies to his mortal enemy.'

At the front, the Kaiser's birthday was anticipated by German troops
who a few days earlier had shouted at the British opposite them: 'We are
Saxons, and after the 29th you can have our trenches and the f—— Kaiser
too.' Somewhat more enthusiastic German soldiers, seeking a birthday
present for the Kaiser, attacked French positions south of the Somme on
the night of January 28, overrunning the village of Frise, and capturing or

killing all the French troops there. Early on the following morning the Germans attacked a part of the British line, near Carnoy, being held by the Liverpool Pals, one of the first of Kitchener's Pals battalions to have reached the front. They were driven off, the Pals being excited to find that one of the wounded German officers they captured, Lieutenant O. Siebert, was wearing the ribbon of the Iron Cross, Second Class. He died of his wounds later that day.

There was no pause in the warmaking efforts of the Entente. In Mesopotamia the British were fighting a steady and harsh battle against the Turks, seeking to reach the besieged garrison at Kut, almost unnoticed amid the more accessible war news of the Western Front. The relief force Kut so desperately waited for was fighting its way northward, encountering continual Turkish resistance, masterminded by the 72-year-old German officer, Field Marshal von der Goltz. At the Battle of Wadi on January 13, more than two hundred British and Indian troops were killed and 1,400 wounded. Casualties were even higher at the Battle of Hanna eight days later, where 2,600 of the attackers were killed or wounded. The forty-six guns available to the British proved inadequate to dislodge or demoralise the Turkish defenders before the assault.

Among the British officers in action at Hanna was the future British Prime Minister, Captain C.R. Attlee, who, carrying a large red flag to alert the British artillery as to the advancing infantry's whereabouts, led his men out of their trench. The artillery barrage was effective and there was little Turkish opposition, either in the first or second line of trenches. Attlee then reached the third Turkish line. 'Just as I got there, and was sticking my flag in the ground', he later recalled, 'a shrapnel got me from behind, lifting me up like a big kick. I found myself sitting opposite Private O'Neill. Two lads came up and asked if I was hit. I said I did not know, but when I stood up I found that I was, and could not move.' In his memoirs Attlee recalled how 'a shell – fired, as I found out years later – by one of our own batteries – caught me with a bullet through the thigh and a piece of nose-cap in the buttocks and I had to be carried off the field'.

On a hospital ship on the Tigris that night, a Second Lieutenant, looking at the torment of those wounded who had been brought on board, but for whom, even there, no medical help was forthcoming, is said to have remarked to his sergeant: 'I suppose this is as near hell as we are likely to see?' Drawing himself up, as in answer to a parade-ground question, the sergeant replied: 'I should say it is, sir.'

Among those killed at Hanna was Robert Palmer, a grandson of the turn-of-the-century Prime Minister, Lord Salisbury, and a cousin of the Foreign Secretary Sir Edward Grey. Three months earlier *The Times* had published Palmer's poem 'How Long, O Lord?' which included the lines:

> *From sodden plains in West and East the blood*
> *Of kindly men streams up in mists of hate,*
> *Polluting Thy clean air: and nations great*

In reputation of the arts that bind
The world with hopes of Heaven, sink to state
Of brute barbarians, whose ferocious mind
Gloats o'er the bloody havoc of their kind,
Not knowing love or mercy.

On the morning after the Battle of Hanna, the British asked for a six-hour truce to bury their dead and collect their wounded. As soon as the white flag was raised to signal its start, a number of Arabs rushed out from the Turkish lines and began to rob the disabled and the dead. The injured were stripped of their clothes. Those who tried to resist had sand stuffed in their mouths and a tight grip held their mouths shut until they expired. Turkish officers, appalled at the sight, came to the rescue of the survivors.

The Battle of Hanna was being fought in the hope of relieving the men besieged in Kut. In Kut itself, in contrast to the terrible heat of summer, sleet and an icy wind worsened the plight and morale of the attackers, and of the many wounded for whom no medical treatment was immediately available. 'Lying in ankle-deep pools amidst a sea of mud,' one of their historians has written, 'they must have plumbed the depths of agony; in any history of sufferings endured by the British Army the collective misery of that night of 21st January 1916 is probably without parallel since the Crimea.'[1] 'A black-letter day for Kut in general and myself in particular,' E.O. Mousley wrote in his diary. 'About 6 a.m., in the pitch dark, the water burst into our front line by Redoubt D and flooded the trenches up to one's neck. All the careful and dogged efforts of our sappers could not stop it.' The Turks had also been flooded out of their defences and had to go back. 'It was a queer sight to see them running over the top where we had previously seen only their pickaxes and caps. . . . We shelled his ragged masses with great glee.'

General Aylmer, in command of the force that had been sent to relieve Kut, was no longer confident that he could succeed. 'I am very doubtful of morale of a good many of the Indian troops,' he telegraphed to General Townshend on January 24, 'especially as I have the gravest suspicions of extent of self-mutilation amongst them.' Even with reinforcements he did not think he could break through to Kut. Townshend replied that he could hold out 'for eighty-four days'. But he was likewise dismissive of the Indians. 'One or two all-British divisions are all we want,' he telegraphed to Aylmer. 'There now is time to demand good white troops from overseas, and Army Corps to save and hold Mesopotamia if the Government considers it worth holding.'

New techniques and inventions were adding an extra dimension to war-making. On January 29 the first British tank began its trials. More than a year earlier, Churchill had encouraged the inventors and technical experts

[1] A.J. Barker, *The Neglected War, Mesopotamia 1914–1918*, Faber and Faber, London 1967, page 218.

to work out an effective design, and when the War Office blew cold, had provided money from his Admiralty funds to start experiments. He had also encouraged those who believed, as he did, that the tank could be an effective weapon in ending the stalemate of trench warfare, and in substantially lessening the casualties which had become the terrible hall-mark of every Western Front offensive.

In the air, Germany retained the ascendancy. Here too, while at the Admiralty, and in his letters from the trenches, Churchill had urged the importance of building up a strong air force, with a view to giving the soldiers on the ground the protection of both air reconnaissance and air cover. For the British public, it was German air activity that still created alarm. On January 31, nine Zeppelins flew across the North Sea to Britain: 389 bombs were dropped on the Midlands.[1] One of the Zeppelins crashed into the sea on its return, and all sixteen of its crewmen were killed.

In the war at sea, the first merchant ship was sunk by aerial bombs on February 1. It was the British cargo ship *Franz Fischer*, destroyed by a German plane two miles off the Kentish Knock. Thirteen of her crew were killed. A week later, off Beirut, 374 French sailors were drowned when a German submarine torpedoed the French cruiser *Amiral Charner*, which went to the bottom four minutes after being hit. There was only one survivor. The German submarine was the *U-21*, commanded by Otto Hersing, who had already sunk one British battleship off Scotland and two off Gallipoli.

Two plans, one German, one Anglo-French, both aimed at securing victory on the Western Front, were being devised in mid-February. The Germans were in the final stages of planning what they believed would be a successful war of attrition, centred upon a massive, sustained attack on the French fortress of Verdun. Chosen by Vauban in the eighteenth century as the vital fortress on the road to Paris, in 1792 Verdun had surrendered after only two days of battle to a Prussian army. News of its fall had caused panic in Paris and was the immediate cause of the September massacres there. In 1870 Verdun had capitulated to the Germans after a six-week siege. In September 1914 Joffre had ordered General Sarrail to withdraw from Verdun as part of his wider strategy. Sarrail had refused to do so. Throughout 1915 the German front-line trenches had been only ten miles from the centre of the town. Now it was to be the German Army's main objective for 1916.

As the Germans made plans to attack at Verdun, the British and French were making preparations for a breakthrough that summer on the Somme. Confident of success, the British and French Governments issued a dec-laration at Le Havre, on February 14, stating that there could be no peace with Germany until Belgian independence was restored and financial reparations paid for the damage done inside Belgium during the German occupation.

*

[1] By the end of May 1916, 550 British civilians had been killed in German airship attacks.

On February 21 the Germans launched their attack on Verdun. Two months earlier, Falkenhayn had impressed upon the Kaiser that French determination to hold the historical citadel on the road to Paris from the east would 'compel the French General Staff to throw in every man they have' rather than give up the fortress and find another, less costly line to hold. The city of Verdun, which in 1870 had held out longer than Sedan, Metz or Strasbourg, was defended by two principal fortresses, Fort Douaumont and Fort Vaux, and by 500,000 men. The Germans threw a million men against them. The battle was to continue for ten months, described by one historian as 'the greatest battle of attrition in history'.[1]

It began with a nine-hour German artillery bombardment, by 850 heavy guns, along an eight-mile front. The first shot, fired by a Krupp 15-inch naval gun from almost twenty miles away, hit the cathedral. After an intense nine-hour bombardment, unprecedented in warfare, 140,000 German infantrymen advanced towards the French defences. The pounding of the shells had wreaked havoc with the front-line trenches and dugouts, burying many men under an inescapable weight of earth. 'We shall hold against the Boche although their bombardment is infernal,' one front line unit reported back that night. Of its 1,300 men, more than half were dead or wounded. Of every five men, one corporal remarked, 'two have been buried alive under their shelter, two are wounded to some extent or other, and the fifth is waiting'.

The Germans had used gas shells on February 21. On the following day the French countered with a phosgene gas shell of their own. They also opened a road for supplies from Bar-le-Duc, soon known as La Voie Sacrée, the Sacred Road, the defence of which became a central feature of the struggle for Verdun. For their part, the Germans deployed 168 aircraft to maintain constant artillery-reconnaissance patrols over the fortress.

On the second day of the attack, the Germans made use of their surprise armament, flamethrowers, ninety-six in all. By the third day they had advanced two miles and captured 3,000 French soldiers. That day, February 23, French troops holding out in the village of Samoneux were the victims of a rumour that the village had fallen to the Germans: as soon as the rumour was believed, a heavy and accurate French bombardment was directed on to the village by artillery that had just reached Verdun. For two hours the defenders were pounded by their own side, then, as the bombardment ended, the Germans moved in to take advantage of it. The village was theirs. One of those taken prisoner, Lieutenant-Colonel Bernard, who had obeyed his orders to hold the village 'at all costs', was brought before an august visitor who had come to the area to be present at the fall of Verdun and was watching the battle through a periscope: the Kaiser. 'You will never enter Verdun,' Bernard told him.

On February 24 the Germans advanced another mile and took a further

[1] John Laffin, *Brassey's Battles, 3,500 Years of Conflict, Campaigns and Wars from A-Z*, Brassey's Defence Publishers, London 1986.

10,000 prisoners. French troops were fleeing from the front line in panic, or shattered. A North African division, consisting largely of Moroccan and Algerian tribesmen, was thrown into the battle that day. They turned and fled when they came up against a mass of Germans advancing towards them. Some of those who fled did not get very far. A French officer tried in vain to halt them by his word of command. Then, as a French Staff officer later wrote, 'a section of machine guns fired at the backs of the fleeing men, who fell like flies'.

On February 25 the Germans captured Fort Douaumont. The French defenders had failed to appreciate the speed of the German advance, and many of the guns that might have prolonged the defence were unmanned, or had been taken away for use elsewhere. It was a disaster for France, a triumph for Germany. Two German officers were awarded the Pour le Mérite. The Kaiser was at hand to give them his own congratulations. The Germans were poised to abandon Falkenhayn's idea of using the attack on Verdun to bleed France white, and instead to take advantage of French weakness and chaos to advance to the city itself. The French, too, might have decided that night to give up Verdun altogether, abandon the salient, and fall back to a more easily defensible line. But it was not to be: that midnight command of the defence of Verdun was given to General Pétain. He was determined not to allow the fortress to fall into German hands. 'Retake immediately any piece of land taken by him,' he insisted, and on the following day he issued the famous order: 'They shall not pass.'

After five days of battle, and much slaughter, the battle was to go on. Douaumont remained in German hands, but continued ferocious German shelling and daily assaults, while they savaged the French defenders, failed to give the Germans their entry into the city. In the week beginning on February 27, the French brought to Verdun, along the Voie Sacrée, 190,000 men and 23,000 tons of ammunition. That same week an unexpected spring thaw turned the battlefield and the road into a sea of mud, but mud was no deterrent to the continued fighting, or to the intensity of the artillery barrages. In the first five weeks of conflict at Verdun, German soldiers were killed at the astounding rate of one every forty-five seconds. French deaths were even higher. The Kaiser's biographer, Alan Palmer, has written: 'Ultimately on this one sector of the Western Front the Germans suffered a third of a million casualties in occupying a cratered wasteland half the size of metropolitan Berlin.'

That February, the Austrians, conquerors of Serbia and Montenegro, turned their forces against Albania. Durazzo was occupied on February 27, the Italians having killed 900 mules and donkeys on the eve of their forces and the Albanians evacuating the town. Their leader, Essad Pasha, moved to Naples, where he set up a provisional Albanian government. The Serbian Government-in-exile remained on Corfu. The British and

French, determined not to allow the Austrian and Bulgarian forces unchallenged control of the Balkans, continued to land troops at Salonica. On February 26, when the French troop transport *Provence II* was sunk by a German submarine off Cerigo, 930 soldiers were drowned, but 1,100 survived to join the Salonica force, and to face the hazards not only of the Austro-German army, but of disease. On February 29, a British doctor wrote to the chief British medical officer at Salonica: 'You still have about two months grace before General Malaria comes into the field.'

At Verdun, the high daily death toll led on February 28 to an emergency conference of the German Crown Prince, commanding the German Fifth Army, and General Falkenhayn. Although surprise had been lost, the Crown Prince commented, the prospects of a 'considerable moral and material victory' remained. What was needed to secure this was the necessary quantity of men and materials to continue the offensive 'not by driblets, but on a large scale'. This was agreed. Then, on March 2, French forces threw back a German assault on Vaux. Among the Frenchmen captured that day was Captain Charles de Gaulle. He had been wounded by a bayonet thrust through his thigh. There were also many German wounded. One German general described them as 'like a vision of hell' as they streamed back past his headquarters. The German Expressionist painter Franz Marc wrote on March 3: 'For days I have seen nothing but the most terrible things that can be painted from a human mind.' On the following day Marc was killed by a French shell.

On March 6, during a driving snowstorm, the Germans launched an attack on the high ground of Mort-Homme, on the left bank of the Meuse. The preliminary artillery bombardment was as intense as that of February 21. Crossing the river at Brabant and Champneuville, and supported by the heavy gun fire from an armoured train, German troops gained an unexpected advantage when many of the shells fired at them by the French failed to explode in the soft, swampy ground. Mort-Homme held, but in the course of two days' fighting 1,200 French soldiers surrendered. To keep the others in the line, the commander of the forces on the left bank, General de Bazelaire, warned that artillery and machine guns would be turned on any unit that retreated further.

On the second day of the battle for Mort-Homme, the Germans captured the nearby Bois des Corbeaux. The French counter-attack was led by Lieutenant-Colonel Macker, who entered the legends of the war by leading his men forward 'brandishing his cane and calmly smoking a cigar'.[1] Advancing through machine-gun and shellfire to a hundred yards of the wood, Macker ordered his men to fix bayonets and charge. The German force, its own commander having been killed, fell back. Within an hour the wood was once more in French hands. Later that day another French unit drove the Germans from a smaller wood nearby. When Macker went

[1] Alistair Horne, *The Price of Glory, Verdun 1916*, Macmillan, London 1962, page 158.

forward to congratulate its commander, both were killed by fire from a German machine gun. Macker's men were demoralised by his death, and in a German counter-attack the Bois des Corbeaux was again lost. The struggle for Mort-Homme continued for more than a month. Thousands died on both sides, but the heights were never overrun.

Thousands were also being killed on the right bank of the Meuse in the struggle for Fort Vaux. The village of Vaux changed hands thirteen times during March, but the fort remained in French hands. When the German commander, General Guretzky-Cornitz, was told that the fort had finally been taken, he immediately passed the news back to German headquarters, which announced the victory to the world. The Kaiser awarded the General the much-prized Pour le Mérite, but the General's men, marching in columns of four to take over the fort, were shot down. Fort Vaux had not been captured after all. Joffre, in triumph, issued an Order of the Day to the defenders: 'You will be those of whom it is said – "they barred the way to Verdun!"'

On March 20, in a German attack on the western extremity of the Verdun Salient, between the villages of Malincourt and Avocourt, the 11th Bavarian Division was led by General von Kneussel, who in 1915 had won the Pour le Mérite for his capture of the Russian-held fortress of Przemysl. At first the attack went badly, with many German infantrymen being buried alive in the deep jumping-off points they had dug facing the French front line, which the French had spotted and blown in. But the French troops in front of them had been in the trenches too long and their morale was low. Deserters, reaching the German lines, gave details of the passages through the French wire. Within four hours of the German attack, the French position was captured, a whole French brigade being surrounded and surrendering: 2,825 men, twenty-five machine guns and, to the amusement of the German war correspondent who broke the story, a full box of medals – the Croix de Guerre – ready for distribution.

Two days later the Germans tried to follow up their success, but French machine gunners, firing at them from three sides, led to 2,400 German casualties and no further gains. President Poincaré, who had been ashamed of the deserters at Avocourt, could breathe more freely, at least for a while.

As the torment of Verdun continued, de Gaulle was taken to a German military hospital in Mainz, then to the first of several prisoner-of-war camps further east from which he tried, with great ingenuity, to escape. On one occasion he got within sixty miles of the Swiss frontier, but he was still in captivity when the war ended. Among his prison activities was to teach French to a fellow prisoner-of-war, the 23-year-old Tsarist officer, Mikhail Tukhachevsky. Created by Stalin a Marshal of the Soviet Union in 1935, Tukhachevsky was executed by Stalin two years later. As a prisoner-of-war he was more successful than de Gaulle. At his sixth escape attempt he managed to get back to Russia, and to active service.

In an attempt to help relieve the pressure on the French at Verdun, the

Italian army launched its fifth battle on the Isonzo Front on March 11. Five days of fighting were brought to an unexpected halt, however, when snow and rain made the mountain battlefield impassable. The few gains that the Italians did make were lost when, after the battle ended, Austrian gas shells forced them to evacuate their new positions.

On the Voie Sacrée, whose name was coined during the battle by the writer Maurice Barrès, the French were managing to send up to Verdun 6,000 trucks a day, totalling 50,000 tons of stores and 90,000 men a week: a sustaining and feeding of a battlefield, and of the greedy guns, unprecedented in warfare. The equivalent of a whole division of men was employed to maintain the road, shovelling an estimated three-quarters of a million tons of metal to keep it firm. 'All the colourful components of France's Colonial Empire were to be found at work keeping the Verdun lifeline open,' one historian has written, 'powerful Senegalese ... wielded picks next to industrious little Annamites, clad in yellow uniforms.'[1]

At the end of March, a British officer, Lieutenant Bernard Pitt, who before the war had held classes in English literature at a Working Men's College in London, was in reserve billets north of Arras. A poet and lover of the English countryside, he wrote to a friend: 'Do you wonder that, reading Wordsworth this afternoon in a clearing of the unpolluted woodlands, and marking the lovely faded colours on the wings of hibernated butterflies, and their soft motions, I felt a disgust, even to sickness, of the appalling wickedness of war.' Though several times in action, he had 'so far' escaped injury. 'Now I am in command of a Trench Mortar Battery, and I find the work as interesting as any war-making can be. You know we all long for the war to end, whether by peace, or by that furious slaughter that must lead to peace. Verdun, no doubt, has shortened the war by months.'

Daily attacks and counter-attacks around Verdun were decimating defenders and attackers alike, but the French were as determined not to relinquish the fortress as the Germans were to make them bleed there. During a month of fighting the front line between Fort Douaumont and Fort Vaux fluctuated no more than a thousand yards. Not only men but horses were the victims of this war of attrition. In one of his last letters home before he was killed, Franz Marc had exclaimed: 'The poor horses!'. In only one day, 7,000 horses were killed by long-range French and German shelling, ninety-seven from a single shell fired by a French naval gun.

On the Caucasus Front, the Russians were continuing to make swift advances. On the night of March 3, during a bayonet charge at the height of a snow blizzard, the town of Bitlis was captured and 1,000 Turks taken prisoner. On the Black Sea shore, Russian forces moved steadily westward,

[1] Alistair Horne, *The Price of Glory*, page 148. The Annamites were the inhabitants of the coastal region of Indo-China (today's Vietnam), which had been a French protectorate since 1884.

occupying the port of Rize. A political gain for Russia during that first week of March was Britain's agreement to allow a southward extension of the Russian sphere of influence in Persia, first demarcated in 1907.

After the evacuation of Gallipoli, the Turkish colonel Mustafa Kemal was sent to the Caucasus Front and promoted to general's rank, with the title Pasha. He was thirty-five years old. Other Turkish troops had been sent from Gallipoli to Mesopotamia, where, on March 7, the British tried once more to break through to the besieged soldiers in Kut. The relief force had steadily worked its way forward to within sight of the minarets of the besieged town. But the attack, at Dujaila, only two miles from Kut, failed: 3,500 of the attackers were killed or wounded, and General Aylmer was sacked. The relief force fell back. The siege of Kut continued.

In their attempt to tie down British and Italian troops in North Africa, the Turks had continued to help the Senussi tribesmen in Libya in their revolt against the British. A special Western Desert Force had been set up, based in Alexandria, to protect Egypt from attack, and to try to beat the Senussi back. An armoured car detachment, headed by the Duke of Westminster, was sent out. Together with the South African Scottish Brigade it drove into the desert to seek out the 7,000-strong Turco-Senussi division. A principal task was to liberate ninety-two British prisoners-of-war held by the Senussi: the officers and crew of the Royal Naval patrol boat *Tara*, formerly the Irish mailboat *Hibernia*, who had been torpedoed by the Germans in the eastern Mediterranean and handed over by the Germans to the Senussi. They were being held prisoner in a remote desert encampment at Bir Hakeim.

On March 17 the armoured cars reached Bir Hakeim. The prisoners-of-war were so amazed to see them that for some moments they stood in bewildered silence. Most of them were suffering from dysentery. They had lived for weeks on desert snails and tiny roots. To prevent a surprise reversal of fortune, the Duke ordered their former Senussi guards to be executed.[1]

At sea, on March 22, the British had success with a new weapon, a depth charge, which was dropped by a ship off the south-west coast of Ireland and destroyed a German submarine. But the balance of naval sinkings still lay with Germany. On March 23 a German submarine torpedoed and sank the Folkestone-Dieppe ferry *Sussex*, which it believed, wrongly, to be a troopship: fifty passengers were drowned, including the Spanish composer Granados, and three Americans. An American appeal to the Allies, sent two months earlier, not to arm merchant ships or passenger liners was rejected by Britain and France that same day, March 23.

The war at sea had become one with few restrictions on either side. On March 28 the Reichstag in Berlin voted for immediate unrestricted

---

[1] From 26 May to 10 June 1942 Free French troops held the fortress of Bir Hakeim against German infantry, tank and air assault. A Paris métro station commemorates that heroism.

submarine warfare. Two days later a German submarine in the Black Sea sank the Russian hospital ship *Portugal*, stating that she had mistaken her for a troop transport: 115 patients, nurses and crew were drowned. When the United States-bound liner, the *Cymric*, was sunk five weeks later, with five deaths, she was the thirty-seventh unarmed liner to be sunk by German submarines since the *Lusitania*.

Not only submarine warfare, but occupation, was pitiless. At dawn on April 1, in German-occupied Belgium, the occupation authorities executed a Belgian woman, Gabriel Petit, who had been among the distributors of the clandestine newspaper *Libre Belgique*. At her trial she confessed to another of her activities, helping to smuggle across the lines would-be Belgian recruits to the Belgian army. After her sentence she had been kept in prison for two weeks in the hope that the prospect of death would lead her to betray her colleagues, but she refused to break under mental or physical duress.

Inside the Ottoman Empire there were also those who regarded opposition to the regime as patriotic. Not only Armenians, but also Arabs, were suffering from Turkish fears of the national aspirations of their subject peoples. In Beirut, a Maronite Christian, Yusuf al-Hani, had sought French support for an independent Lebanon even before the war. He, and sixty others who thought as he did, decided to invite the French to enter the Levant as Lebanon's protector. Before they could do much more than discuss their idea, they were arrested. When a British agent contacted them in Aley prison, one of them asked him: 'Where are the English? Where are the French? Why are we left like this?' On April 5, Yusuf al-Hani was hanged in Beirut.

Throughout April, British troops were in action on the Western Front, but it was at Verdun that the main battle continued. By the end of March, the toll of dead and wounded there had reached 89,000 French and 81,607 Germans. On April 1 the Kaiser declared: 'The decision of the War of 1870 took place in Paris. This war will end at Verdun.' Eight days later, in a further attempt to capture Mort-Homme, the Germans were driven back, leaving 2,200 men dead and wounded on the battlefield. That day Pétain exhorted his troops: 'Take courage, we'll get them.'

On the Eastern Front, the Russians had been beaten back around Lake Naroch, suffering 12,000 deaths from frostbite, but on April 14, the day on which the Naroch battle ended, General Brusilov put forward a plan to attack on a broad front within the coming month, and began to make his plans, at the very moment when the British were planning their Somme offensive for June. The intensity of the German involvement at Verdun seemed a hopeful augury for both these offensives.

How far the Russian troops were capable of a strong offensive was unclear. During the Russian Orthodox Easter on April 10 there had been truces on the Austrian Front, with soldiers from four Russian regiments crossing into the Austrian lines to fraternise on that solemn and festive day. The Austrians took more than a hundred of the Russians prisoner. On April 18, Brusilov felt obliged to issue a strong directive: 'I declare once and for all that contact with the enemy is permitted only by gun and bayonet.'

Among those who faced the Russians that month was Richard Sorge, who had survived the baptism of fire of the Student Battalion at Dixmude in October 1914 and been wounded in the leg in Galicia in June 1915. Both his legs were now broken by shrapnel. Taken to hospital at Königsberg, he was left with a permanent limp. For his gallantry in action he was awarded the Iron Cross, Second Class. Returning to his studies, he turned to Marxism, Communism, and the career of spying that was to lead to his execution in the Second World War.

That April saw fighting and the preparation for more fighting on all the war fronts. Churchill, in the trenches on the Western Front for the fourth month, wrote with foreboding to his wife on April 14: 'I greatly fear the general result. More than I have ever done before, I realize the stupendous nature of the task; and the unwisdom with which our affairs are conducted makes me almost despair at times of a victorious issue. The same leadership that has waited on public opinion and newspaper promptings for so long, will readily be the exponent of an inclusive peace – if that mood is upward in the nation.'

Churchill went on to ask his wife: 'Do you think we should succeed in an offensive, if the Germans cannot do it at Verdun with all their skill and science? Our army is not the same as theirs; and of course their staff is quite intact and taught by successful experiment. Our staff only represents the brain power of our poor little peacetime army – with which hardly any really able men would go. We are children at the game compared to them. And in this day-to-day trench warfare – they lose half what we do in my opinion.'

Among those killed in the Ypres Salient, on April 18, was a Canadian volunteer, Sergeant Major S. Godfrey. He was 47 years old. The inscription on his gravestone reads: 'Past the military age he responded to the Mother Country's call.' With similar words of fact, and affection, hundreds of thousands of parents, widows and children perpetuated a loved one's memory.

During April, the German airship raids on Britain intensified. Sunderland was bombed on the night of April 1, Leith and Edinburgh on the following night, East London five times in the month. The targets were docks and naval facilities, but most of the casualties were civilians. Death also came by accident to those who were helping the war effort. On April 2, an accidental explosion at a munitions factory at Faversham in Kent killed 106 munitions workers, many of them women. By April 1916 almost 200,000 women were being employed in war industries.

On April 20, in France, a special air squadron was formed, centred upon 180 American citizens who had volunteered to fight against Germany in the air. Called the Lafayette Escadrille (Squadron), after the French aristo-crat who had fought against Britain in the Revolutionary War of 1776, its pilots were to shoot down as many as two hundred German aircraft, for the death in action of fifty-one of their volunteers.

Training for the planned Anglo-French offensive on the Somme was con-tinuous. On April 25 Siegfried Sassoon was among the recipients of a lecture by a Major on the bayonet. He later recalled the Major's phrases:
'If you don't kill him, he'll kill you.'
'Stick him between the eyes, in the throat, in the chest, or round the thighs.'
'If he's on the run, there's only one place; get your bayonet into his kidneys; it'll go in as easy as butter.'
'Kill them, kill them; there's only one good Bosche and that's a dead un!'
'Quickness, anger, strength, good fury, accuracy of aim. Don't waste good steel. Six inches are enough – what's the use of a foot of steel sticking out of a man's neck? Three inches will do him, and when he coughs, go find another.'
During his training, Sassoon wrote a poem, 'The Kiss', to the bullet and the bayonet: the lead and steel with which the soldier fought, and on which his life depended.

> To these I turn, in these I trust –
> Brother Lead and Sister Steel.
> To this blind power I make appeal,
> I guard her beauty clean from rust.
>
> He spins and burns and loves the air,
> And splits a skull to win my praise;
> But up the nobly marching days
> She glitters naked, cold and fair
>
> Sweet Sister, grant your soldier this:
> That in good fury he may feel
> The body where he sets his heel
> Quail from your downward darting kiss.

Among those in England who heard of the sufferings on the Western Front that April was Winifred Holtby. She was then nearly eighteen. A friend of her had been wounded in the shoulder and sent back to England to recuperate. Through him, she later wrote, she had endured at second hand 'all the enormities he had seen at the front – the mouthless mangled faces, the human ribs whence rats would steal, the frenzied tortured horse, with leg or quarter rent away, still living; and rotted farms, the dazed and hopeless peasants; his innumerable suffering comrades; the desert of No-Man's Land; and all the thunder and moaning of war; and the reek and freezing of war; and the driving – the callous, perpetual driving by some great Force – which shovelled warm human hearts and bodies, warm human hopes and loves, by the million into the furnace.'

On April 28, Second Lieutenant Bernard Pitt was out of the trenches for twenty-four hours. 'I have earned a day of rest', he wrote to a friend, 'and am sitting under a walnut tress on the edge of this half-ruined village, blossoming cherry and pear trees near me in the broken closes, a field of dandelion and daisies at my feet, with swallows wheeling across it.' Flowers and birds in profusion delighted Pitt's eye. 'Gaudy butterflies fan themselves in splashes of sunlight, and bronze and black beetles creep about on their errands. Yet the woods are defiled by war.'

On April 30 the Germans launched their third gas attack in four days against British units on the Western Front, along a 3,500-yard front. With a wind of more than nine miles an hour, it blew 11,000 yards behind the British line. A contemporary report, kept secret at the time, described how grass and other vegetation 'were turned yellow by the gas as far back as 1,200 yards from the front line. Rats were killed in the trenches in large numbers. Eleven cows, twenty-three calves, one horse, one pig and fifteen hens were killed in the fields behind the lines....' The soldiers had been given sufficient warning to put on their respirators, but, as the report noted, 'the speed with which the cloud reached the trenches, and the concentration of gas, were such that a man was bound to fall victim if he hesitated in the slightest in putting on his respirator or fumbled in adjusting it'.

Eighty-nine British soldiers were killed that day by gas, and a further five hundred incapacitated. Those who 'died rapidly in the trenches', the report noted, showed 'copious frothing ... paroxysmal coughing, too, was a prominent feature in the early stages'. Some men, 'either experiencing some slight irritation of the eyes or lungs owing to a little gas penetrating the helmet, or under the misapprehension that the smell of the chemicals with which the fabric was treated signified it was defective, and admitting gas, tore off their helmets and fell victims to the cloud'.

Among the dead on April 30 was Second Lieutenant Bernard Pitt, in charge of a trench mortar battery. 'Your husband was observing his fire from the front trenches', Pitt's commanding officer wrote to his widow, 'and had just sent the man with him back to his mortars, when the Germans exploded a mine close to the spot, and we have been unable to find a trace of him since.'

In mid-April the Entente gained a new influx of strength at Salonica, when the first of 125,000 Serbian troops were taken there on Anglo-French troopships, escorted by French and British warships, from Corfu to Salonica. There they joined the 42,000-strong Army of the Orient. French,

British and Serbian forces were to be in action together. During the four-day voyage, none of the French or British transports was sunk. Off Malta, however, when the British battleship *Russell* struck a mine, 124 sailors were drowned.

On the Italian Front, the Italians made small gains amid the mountain peaks, and thick snow, for heavy losses. On April 14 one of Garibaldi's grandsons, Captain Menotti Garibaldi, retook the 9,715-foot Punta Serauto in the Dolomites after it had been taken, then lost. In Mesopotamia, the Indian soldiers in the besieged British garrison at Kut were reduced first to eating their horses, then to taking opium pills to assuage the pangs of hunger. The force that had been coming to their relief since January was still unable to break through: it was noted that the Turks confronting them were now being led by German officers. Nor were the Russians able to come down from the north to effect a rescue from the rear, despite their further victories over the Turks on the Caucasus Front, and the capture of the Black Sea port of Trebizond on April 18. In a brave attempt to push food supplies through, fifteen men volunteered to take 270 tons of food by paddle steamer, the *Julnar*. Led by a former Tigris and Euphrates Navigation Company employee, Lieutenant-Commander Cowley, and Lieutenant H.O.B. Firman, the expedition was within eight and a half river miles of Kut before being caught in the Turkish steel-wire defences, and being taken prisoner. Cowley was executed by the Turks, and Firman died in Turkish captivity: both were posthumously awarded the Victoria Cross.

It was clear that the garrison at Kut could not hold out much longer. On April 27 three British officers, among them Captain T.E. Lawrence ('Lawrence of Arabia'), offered the Turks £1 million in gold if the besieged troops were allowed to leave in peace and rejoin the British forces in the south. 'Your gallant troops will be our most sincere and precious guests,' was the Turkish commander's reply. The garrison at Kut continued to hold out, the Turks waiting patiently for its inevitable and imminent collapse. Russian troops in Persia, driving westward from the Paitak Pass, were approaching the Mesopotamian border, but were still more than a hundred miles from Baghdad.

Even further from the main European war zones, a continual battle was being fought in East Africa by the British, the Belgians and the South Africans against the German forces there. Despite long marches, and many fierce encounters, the Germans, led by the intrepid General von Lettow-Vorbeck, were not willing to give up.

The war was in its twenty-first month. That April, in the Reichstag, the leader of the German Social Democrats, Karl Liebknecht, enraged the patriotic mass of members by interrupting the Chancellor to declare that Germany was not free, and that the German people had not wished for war. At Kienthal, in neutral Switzerland, the Second Socialist International met on Easter Monday to find a common attitude. Both French and

German socialists attended, and denounced the war as a capitalist conspiracy, fought for the benefit of arms profiteering and territorial gain. In such an atmosphere it was not surprising that the Russian exile, Lenin, failed to convert the delegates to his view that the war was to be welcomed, as a necessary and inevitable prelude to the fall of capitalism through civil war. Ten days before the conference met, the Russian secret police had reported that a revolutionary mood existed among some 2,000 drivers at the Petrograd Military Drivers School.

On the day that the socialist anti-war leaders gathered at Kienthal, an anti-British uprising broke out in Dublin. Since the outbreak of war, the Irish nationalist Sir Roger Casement had been pressing the Germans to take the potential of Ireland's rebellion seriously. Following Casement's efforts, on April 2 a small German merchant ship, the *Aud*, had been sent with 20,000 rifles and a million rounds of ammunition to the Atlantic coast of Ireland. Three weeks later a German submarine, the *U-19*, brought Casement himself from Germany to Tralee Bay on the same coast. But a Royal Navy sloop, the *Bluebell*, intercepted the *Aud*, which scuttled herself before she could land her cargo. Casement, put ashore on an inflatable raft, was arrested four days later, tried, and executed for treason.[1]

Despite Casement's arrest the Easter Monday uprising went ahead, but a last-minute uncertainty led one of its leaders, Eoin MacNeill, to cancel the mobilisation orders on the Saturday. The result was that instead of 5,000 men only 1,000 marched from their headquarters at Liberty Hall to the centre of Dublin. There they seized the Post Office, the Law Courts, St Stephen's Green and several other locations. An Irish Republic was declared from the steps of the Post Office, and a proclamation read out, in which the Germans were described as the Republic's 'gallant Allies' in Europe, 'thereby blandly dismissing the fact', one historian had written, 'that the flower of Ireland's manhood had been fighting those allies in Europe for the past twenty months'.[2]

The first troops sent against the Post Office were Irish men of the two Irish regiments most recently recruited, the 3rd Royal Irish Rifles and the 10th Royal Dublin Fusiliers. Firing from the sea, the gunboat *Helga* destroyed the rebels' headquarters at Liberty Hall. Despite the hopes of the rebels, there was no popular uprising to support them, and after a week they were crushed. During the fighting sixty-four of the rebels were killed, and at least 220 civilians caught in cross fire and the artillery attacks on rebel-held buildings; 134 troops and policemen were also killed crushing the rebellion. Fifteen of the rebel leaders were executed. A sixteenth,

[1] Casement had been knighted in 1911 for his work in the British Consular Service, investigating charges against a British company in South America. He was sentenced to death on 29 June 1916, and on the following day was deprived of his knighthood. He was executed at Pentonville Prison, London, on 3 August 1916.
[2] Robert Kee, *The Green Flag*, London 1972, vol. II, page 253.

Eamon de Valera, a mathematics professor, was saved from execution because he was an American citizen.[1]

That spring the British Government had introduced two new medals for bravery, the Military Cross, for officers, and the Military Medal, open to men and women. The Military Medal was intended principally for private soldiers, but among the first recipients were two nurses, who were awarded it for their 'bravery under fire' during the Easter Rising.

As Britain's experience in Ireland had shown, conflict, which had broken out in the autumn of 1914 on the battlefronts and oceans, and had come to focus, in 1915, on parallel lines of trenches, could no longer be restricted to the confrontation of opposing armies. Ideologies, national and political, were also capable of violent exertions.

[1] Imprisoned in several English gaols for the rest of the war, de Valera was Prime Minister of Eire throughout the Second World War, maintaining his country's status as a neutral State, and even sending condolences to the German Embassy in Dublin on Hitler's death in April 1945.

13

'Europe is mad. The world is mad.'

APRIL–JUNE 1916

As Britain was crushing the Easter Rising in Dublin, her diplomats were dividing up Asia Minor in a secret agreement with France. In the Levant, France would control the Lebanese littoral, with its capital at Beirut. An Arab sovereign State in Syria, based on Damascus, would be under French protection. Britain would be sovereign over the port city of Haifa and the crusader city of Acre, thus controlling the bay that would serve as the Mediterranean terminal for oil pipe lines coming from Mesopotamia. Palestine would be under the triple protection of Britain, France and Russia. An Arab State under British protection would go from the Mediterranean to the Red Sea.

It was a substantial partition, but Turkey was far from defeated. The agreement, negotiated in Paris by Sir Mark Sykes and Georges Picot, who gave it the name by which it became known, was signed on 26 April 1916. Three days later, at Kut, the British and Indian forces surrendered. It was as great a victory for the Turks as the evacuation of the Gallipoli Peninsula had been three months earlier. On the previous day the Turks had been offered £2 million in gold, and a promise that none of the men who were allowed their freedom would be sent to fight the Turks, but this was rejected. After surrendering, Townshend's army was led away into captivity.

More than 9,000 troops surrendered to the Turks on April 29. In Britain the shock was considerable: more men had surrendered to the despised Turk at Kut than had surrendered to the Americans at Yorktown.[1] More than 2,500 badly wounded and sick men were allowed their freedom, in return for the release from British captivity of an equal number of Turkish prisoners-of-war. On April 30 the Kut garrison was marched into captivity towards distant Anatolia.

Too late to save the garrison at Kut, on May 3 a detachment of Russian

[1] An estimated 7,000 men, under Cornwallis, surrendered to the American revolutionary forces under Washington at Yorktown in 1781.

troops reached the Mesopotamian border, where they learned on the radio of Kut's surrender. They continued across the border, capturing the Mesopotamian town of Khanikin, but were to get no further. Russian troops were never to achieve their pre-war masters' goal of reaching the warm waters of the Persian Gulf.

In the fighting on the Western Front during 1915, more than 7,000 Indian soldiers had been killed. At Gallipoli, 1,700 died. In Mesopotamia, the Indians losses exceeded 29,000. This was the theatre in which they suffered most. From Mesopotamia, thousands of wounded Indian soldiers were brought back by sea to Bombay. The editor of *The Times of India*, Stanley Reed, indignant at the sight of 'a dreadful stream of broken men', published an editorial on the failure of the authorities. 'The sick and sorry who ought to have been treated as convalescents were returned in ordinary troopships; thousands who ought to have been regarded as hospital cases were moved in ill-found transports.'

Of the 850,000 Indian soldiers who left the subcontinent during the First World War, 49,000 were killed in action. India also made her contribution to the material aspects of the Allied struggle, including the manufacture of 555 million bullets and more than a million shells. Over 55,000 Indians served in the Indian Labour Corps, as butchers, bakers, carpenters, shoemakers, tailors and washermen. Many did menial work within range of the enemy guns. In Delhi, a monumental arch records the Indian losses, India's contribution in blood to the Allied war effort.

Turkey's determination not to relinquish control of her Empire was seen in Syria on May 6, when on the orders of the Governor, Jamal Pasha, twenty-one Syrian Arabs, leading advocates of an 'Autonomous Syria', were hanged: fourteen in Beirut and seven in Damascus. One of those hanged in Damascus was a senator in the Ottoman Parliament in Constantinople, Abd al-Hamid al-Zahrawi. As he was being hanged the rope broke under his weight. The hangman did not hesitate, but tried a second time, with success. Later that month two more Arab leaders were hanged, this time in Jerusalem: the Mufti of Gaza, Ahmed Arif al-Husseini, and his son Mustafa. Both had been caught while leaving Gaza to join the Arab revolt in the Hedjaz.

The executions obtained for Jamal Pasha the name 'The Bloodthirsty'. Anti-Turkish feeling intensified throughout the Levant. Many of those executed had wanted to separate Syria and Lebanon from the Ottoman Empire, some had wanted to invite the French to take over the littoral. Several had already tried to stimulate revolt. But the Allies were in no position to take advantage of such activities: the Gallipoli expedition had ended in ignominy four months earlier, the Mesopotamian expedition was in disarray, and the Salonica Front was a not-so-distant reminder of the difficulties of exploiting any landing from the sea. A vast army was ashore at Salonica, more than a quarter of a million men, but apart from a few skirmishes, it made no move against the well-entrenched Bulgarians. What were they doing, Clemenceau asked in ridicule: 'Digging! Then let them be known to France and Europe as "The gardeners of Salonica".'

At Charleville, the German Army Headquarters in eastern France, the American Ambassador to Germany, James W. Gerard, protested on May 1 direct to the Kaiser about the continued German submarine sinkings of merchant ships. The Kaiser replied by denouncing the British naval blockade of Germany, and America's compliance with it. Before he would allow his family and grandchildren to starve, he said, he would 'blow up Windsor Castle and the whole Royal family of England'. On behalf of the United States, Gerard pressed the Kaiser to authorise submarine attacks only on warships. American policy, the Ambassador explained, was that submarines could exercise 'the right of visit and search, but must not torpedo or sink any vessels unless the passengers and crew are put in a place of safety'.

Within a week the German Government gave these assurances. It could not risk American belligerency. But in a letter to the State Department, the Ambassador expressed his belief that the rulers of Germany would 'at some future date, forced by public opinion, and by the von Tirpitz and Conservative parties, take up ruthless submarine war again, possibly in the autumn, but at any rate about February or March, 1917'.

At Verdun, the French and German armies remained in daily conflict. After one small German success on May 5, a French sergeant wrote: 'How could anyone cross the zone of extermination around us?' Three days later 350 Germans soldiers were killed in Fort Douaumont when a munitions magazine exploded. On May 19 the Germans introduced a liquid-gas shell in the bombardment of Chattancourt, but though the gas added to the horror of shelling, the line itself held. General Pétain, watching 21-year-old troops returning from the battlefield at Verdun, wrote: 'In their unsteady look one sensed visions of horror, while their step and bearing revealed utter despondency. They were crushed by horrifying memories.'

On the British sector of the Western Front, Lieutenant Harold Macmillan (a future British Prime Minister) wrote to his mother in mid-May, after a German attack was driven back: 'The most extraordinary thing about a modern battlefield is the desolation and emptiness.' Macmillan was convinced that the Allied cause was right, and that it was this moral aspect that made it possible for the British soldier to go on fighting. In his letter he criticised all talk of peacemaking. 'If anyone at home thinks or talks of peace,' he told his mother, 'you can truthfully say that the army is weary enough of war but prepared to fight for another 50 years if necessary, until the final object is attained.' The British daily newspapers were, he felt, 'so full of nonsense about our "exhaustion" and people at home seem to be so bent on personal quarrels, that the great issues (one feels) are becoming obscured and forgotten'. Many of the soldiers 'could never stand the strain and endure the horrors which we see every day, if we did not feel that this was more than a War – a Crusade.'

Macmillan told his mother that all the Allied soldiers at the Front had the same conviction, 'that our cause is right and certain in the end to triumph'. It was because of this 'unexpressed and almost unconscious faith' that the Allied armies had a 'superiority in morale' which would one day be the deciding factor.

Behind the lines, the tyranny of occupation was all-pervasive, and widely publicised among the Allies. On May 12, in German-occupied France, the Germans deported 25,000 men and women as farm labourers in Germany. They were given a mere hour and a half to pack their belongings. Three days later, in Belgium, the German Governor-General ordered all unemployed to accept work in Germany.

The use of foreign labour enabled the Germans to release yet more of their own able-bodied men to fight. Occupation was providing a means of prolonging the war.

In Mesopotamia, a veritable death march had begun, foreshadowing the Gestapo-organised death marches of Jewish concentration camp prisoners at the end of the Second World War. The soldiers captured at Kut, nearly twelve thousand in all, British and Indian alike, were marched northward without any concern whatsoever for their well-being, or for their helpless status as prisoners-of-war.

The march started from Kut on May 6. On the second day, the captives, many of whom had had their boots stolen in the night, were forced to cover fifteen miles without water or shade. Those who stumbled and fell were beaten with whips and sticks by their Arab guards. An officer who had been sent on to Ctesiphon by boat watched the prisoners being driven along the opposite bank. 'The eyes of our men stared from white faces drawn long with the suffering of a too tardy death and they held out their hands towards our boat. As they dragged one foot after another, some fell and those with the rearguard came in for blows from cudgels and sticks.'

In Ctesiphon itself, this officer, Captain E.O. Moulsey, saw marchers 'dying with a green ooze issuing from their lips, their mouths fixed open, in and out of which flies walked'. On May 18 the marchers reached Baghdad, where the American Consul, Mr Brissell, paid money to the Turkish authorities to have five hundred men sent to hospital and, in due course, back to Basra. More than 160 died of privation on the journey back. To protect the thousands who were still being marched northward, those who reached the safety of Basra were forbidden to speak of what they had been through at the hands of the Turks and the Arabs.

After being kept for three days in a compound without either shade or sanitation, the prisoners-of-war were forced to continue on their march.

At Tekrit they were stoned as they trudged northward through the town.[1] Officers, who had been separated from the men, and saw them on the march, noted that those who were sick were stoned when they crawled out of the hovels in which they were trying to rest. These men 'were afraid to go any little distance to relieve themselves for fear of being murdered for their clothes'. Another officer recorded coming across a British soldier who had been left by the Turks in a cave 'and had evidently not eaten anything for days but had crawled down to the river. He was delirious and jabbering, and thought he was a dog'. Finding, among seven naked corpses lying in a yard, one man who appeared to be alive, a fellow prisoner asked an Arab guard to give the man some water. 'At that he picked up a water bottle and asked me to show him the man. Suspecting nothing, I did so, and the Arab walked round to his head, and forcing open his mouth, inserted the neck of the bottle inside. A few bubbles, a convulsive twist, and the poor fellow was dead, deliberately choked to death.'

General Townshend was taken by train from Mosul to Constantinople, along the completed Anatolian section of the Berlin-Baghdad railway. Also on the train was the body of Field Marshal von der Goltz, who had died in Baghdad as the siege of Kut was ending. While his men were being forced to submit to the indignities and horrors of a forced march, Townshend was given a residence on the island of Prinkipo, off Constantinople, where he remained until the end of the war.

Of the 2,500 British soldiers captured at Kut, 1,750 died on the northward march or in the appalling conditions of the prisoner-of-war camps in Anatolia. Of the 9,300 Indian soldiers captured at Kut, 2,500 died: a total death toll of 4,250. Their saga of pain and death was one of the most evil aspects of the war.

On May 15 the Austrians launched a massive offensive on the Trentino Front, with nearly four hundred guns participating in the opening bombardment. After a fierce resistance the Italians were driven off the mountain peaks. Heavy snow nine days after the offensive began forced it to a halt before it could capture the 4,000-foot Mount Pasubio, but within a week the offensive was resumed, and one by one the peaks and passes fell. By the last day of May the Austrians had captured 30,000 Italian prisoners. But the advance, across mountainous, craggy terrain, had exhausted the attackers. A gain of twelve miles, so small an area on the map, was, for those who had carried it out, a major success.

On the Western Front there was as yet no offensive: all was being prepared for the Battle of the Somme. Daily British raids across No-Man's Land into the front-line German trenches kept the soldiers on both sides of the line at constant readiness for action. On May 16, during one such

[1] Tekrit was later the birthplace (in 1937), and a subsequent centre of power, of Saddam Hussein, against whom American and British troops marched in 1991.

raid, Private David Sutherland was wounded. His platoon commander, Lieutenant Ewart Mackintosh, carried him back a hundred yards through the German trenches, while under fire. As Sutherland was being lifted out of the trench, to be carried across No-Man's Land, he died. He had to inform Sutherland's parents of their son's death. He also wrote a poem:

> So you were David's father,
> And he was your only son,
> And the new-cut peats are rotting
> And the work is left undone,
> Because of an old man weeping,
> Just an old man in pain,
> For David, his son David,
> That will not come again.
>
> Oh, the letters he wrote you,
> And I can see them still,
> Not a word of the fighting
> But just the sheep on the hill
> And how you should get the crops in
> Ere the year get stormier,
> And the Bosches have got his body,
> And I was his Officer.
>
> You were only David's father,
> But I had fifty sons
> When we went up in the evening
> Under the arch of the guns,
> And we came back at twilight -
> O God! I heard them call
> To me for help and pity
> That could not help at all.
>
> Oh, never will I forget you,
> My men that trusted me,
> More my sons than your fathers',
> For they could only see
> The little helpless babies
> And the young men in their pride.
> They could not see you dying,
> And hold you while you died.
>
> Happy and young and gallant,
> They saw their first born go,
> But not the strong limbs broken
> And the beautiful men brought low,
> The piteous writhing bodies,
> They screamed 'Don't leave me, sir,'

> *For they were only your father*
> *But I was your officer.*

Mackintosh won the Military Cross for his attempt to save Private Suth-
erland. He himself was wounded and gassed at High Wood, during the
Battle of the Somme. A year and a half later he was killed in action at
Cambrai. Sutherland's body was never found: his name appears on the
Arras memorial, one of 35,928 soldiers killed in the battles around Arras
with no known grave.[1]

In Parliament, the British Government was seeking further funds for the
prosecution of the war. Churchill, who had returned from six months in
the trenches, told the House of Commons: 'I say to myself every day, what
is going on while we sit here, while we go away to dinner or home to bed?
Nearly 1,000 men – Englishmen, Britishers, men of our race – are knocked
into bundles of bloody rags every twenty-four hours, and carried away to
hasty graves or to field ambulances.' It was the men in the front-line
trenches, he said, not those with jobs in the rear echelons, in supply or
garrison duty, or at home, 'who pay all the penalties in the terrible ordeal
which is now proceeding'.

Those penalties were being paid without respite. At Verdun, on May
23, another French attempt to take Fort Douaumont appeared, momentarily, to have succeeded. 'Two companies of the 124th carried the German
trenches by assault,' an eye-witness, Company-Commander Charles
Delvert, wrote. 'They penetrated there without firing a shot.' But they had
only their rifles and bayonets. 'The Boche counter-attacked with grenades.
The two companies, defenceless, were annihilated.' The 3rd Battalion,
coming to their aid, was 'smashed up by barrage fire in the approach
trenches.' Nearly five hundred men were killed or wounded. 'The dead
were piled up as high as the parapet.'

One of those serving with the 124th Regiment was Second Lieutenant
Alfred Joubaire. He was twenty-one. A few days earlier he had marched
up to Verdun behind his regimental band, listening to the strains of
'Tipperary'. On May 23 he jotted down in his diary: 'Humanity is mad! It
must be mad to do what it is doing. What a massacre. What scenes of
horror and carnage! I cannot find words to translate my impressions. Hell
cannot be so terrible. Men are mad!' This was Joubaire's last diary entry.
That day, or the next, he was killed by a German shell. One projectile
from the 2,200 artillery pieces that the Germans had concentrated on the
salient. The French, inflicting their daily casualties, had 1,777 artillery
pieces with which to reply: steel against flesh and blood.

The French war effort was focused on defending Verdun and its forts. The
British in Picardy faced the Germans across deep, heavily wired lines of
trenches. On the night of May 25, Siegfried Sassoon watched as twenty-seven

---

[1] The Arras memorial also lists all the 'missing' of the Royal Flying Corps and the Royal Air
Force who fell anywhere on the Western Front.

men went forward on a raiding party near Mametz, their faces blackened and 'with hatchets in their belts, bombs in pockets, knobkerries'. But they were unable to get through the German wire. Then, rifle shots being heard, and bombs thrown by both sides, the wounded began to come back. Sassoon went forward, finding one wounded man who pointed him to a deep crater with the words: 'O'Brien is somewhere down the crater badly wounded.' Sassoon entered the crater. The Germans opened fire again. 'The bloody sods are firing down at me from point blank range,' Sassoon thought, imagining that his time had come. After minutes that passed 'like hours' he found O'Brien, twenty-five feet down in the crater. 'He is moaning and his right arm is either broken or almost shot off: he's also hit in the leg.' It turned out later that he had been hit in the body and head as well.

Sassoon went back to the British trench for help. Other badly wounded men were being brought in. One had his foot blown off. 'I get a rope and two more men and we go back to O'Brien, who is unconscious now. With great difficulty we get him half way up the face of the crater; it is after one o'clock and the sky beginning to get lighter. I make one more journey to our trench for another strong man and to see to a stretcher being ready. We get him in, and it is found he has died, as I had feared.'

Corporal Mick O'Brien had served on the Western Front since November 1914. He had fought at Neuve Chapelle, Festubert and Loos. As Sassoon prepared for the next battle, on the Somme, he could not get the episode out of his mind, recalling two days later 'O'Brien's shattered limp body propped up down that infernal bank – face ghastly in the light of a flare, clothes torn, hair matted over the forehead – nothing left of the old cheeriness and courage and delight in any excitement of Hun-chasing. Trying to lift him up the side of the crater, the soft earth kept giving way under one's feet: he was a heavy man too, fully six feet high. But he was a dead man when we lowered him over the parapet on to a stretcher. . . .'

On the night of May 31 forty-two German warships left their North Sea anchorage to attack Allied shipping off the Norwegian coast. They were also hoping that they might come into contact with the British Grand Fleet, which the twenty-four German battleships, five battle cruisers, eleven light cruisers and sixty-three destroyers could bring to action, breaking, if victorious, the ever-tightening British blockade.

By two o'clock in the afternoon of June 1 a British naval force of twenty-eight battleships, nine battle cruisers, thirty-four light cruisers and eighty destroyers was bearing down on them. Two formidable forces were about to clash, bringing into sharp focus the training, experience, abilities and ambitions of four leading admirals: Hipper and Scheer on the German side, Jellicoe and Beatty on the British. The first engagement began shortly before four o'clock, when Hipper and Beatty's ships came within sight of each other. During the action, the British battleship *Indefatigable* was sunk and 1,017 men drowned. Then the battleship *Queen Mary* was blown up and 1,266 men killed.

At six o'clock, off the coast of Jutland, a second engagement began, in which Hipper and Jellicoe were in contention, with ninety-six British ships placed between fifty-nine German ships and their base. Hipper's flagship, the battle cruiser *Lützow*, was disabled by twenty-four direct hits, but despite her injuries was able to sink the British battleship *Invincible*, from which there were only six survivors. More than 2,000 of her sailors perished beneath the waters. Jellicoe's flagship, the *Lion*, was also damaged. Then, at just after half-past six, Scheer carried out a previously practised withdrawal back to base, losing only a single battleship, the *Pommern*.

For the Germans, despite having fewer losses than the British, the Battle of Jutland was a mauling. After it they decided not to risk a major naval battle again. Britain had lost three battleships, three cruisers and eight destroyers. The Germans lost one battleship, four cruisers and five destroyers. The Kaiser's boastful comment was 'The spell of Trafalgar is broken.' But the German Fleet never again sought battle with the Grand Fleet, and Scheer, in his report to the Kaiser, stated that victory could only be achieved by the submarine war against British trade.

The outcome of the battle of Jutland was also a blow for Britain, which had hoped in any such major naval engagement to use its superiority in numbers to break the power of the German Fleet. A somewhat depressing Admiralty communiqué was followed by a second one, drafted at the British Government's request by Churchill, putting the battle in a more confident light. The question asked in her London hospital, Vera Brittain recalled, was: 'Were we celebrating a glorious naval victory or lamenting an ignominious defeat. We hardly knew; each fresh edition of the newspapers obscured rather than illuminated this really quite important distinction. The one indisputable fact was that hundreds of young men, many of them midshipmen only just in their teens, had gone down without hope of rescue or understanding of the issues to a cold, anonymous grave.'

On the British warships 6,097 sailors had drowned, on the German ships, 2,551.

On the day after Jutland, German forces launched a massive attack on the British lines in the Ypres Salient, advancing seven hundred yards through the British trenches on a 3,000-yard front. One British general was killed and another taken prisoner. Within forty-eight hours, however, some of the captured ground was retaken by the British. That same day, on the Eastern Front, General Brusilov launched a massive Russian offensive. This was Russia's chance to avenge the defeats of the previous year in Poland, and the reverses in the Carpathians. Brusilov had originally intended that the offensive would begin in July, but with Austria's continuing stubborn defence on the Italian Front, it was moved forward to June in order to try to help the Italians by forcing Austria to transfer troops from the west to the east.

The Brusilov offensive began with an incredible 1,938-gun barrage along a 200-mile front from the Pripet marshes to the Bukovina. The numerical superiority of the Austrian army defending Lutsk, 200,000 men as against 150,000 Russians, was not, as one historian has written, 'of much moment in a war of fire-power'.[1] After a few hours the barrage had wreaked havoc on the Austrian front-line trenches, and made more than fifty breaches in the barbed wire. 'Apart from the bombardment's destruction of wire obstacles,' an Austrian inquiry reported to Vienna two weeks later, 'the entire zone of battle was covered by a huge, thick cloud of dust and smoke, often mixed with heavy explosive gases, which prevented men from seeing, made breathing difficult, and allowed the Russians to come over the ruined wire obstacles in thick waves into our trenches'. Sweeping forward, the Russians captured 26,000 Austrian troops in a single day.

On June 5, the second day of the Brusilov offensive, when the Austrian defenders of Lutsk fled and the city was occupied by the Russians, an unexpected event caused a deep shock throughout Britain, and even among the British troops on the Western Front. In the ice-cold waters of the North Sea, a British cruiser on its way to Russia, the *Hampshire*, was sunk by a German submarine north-west of Scapa Flow. On board was the Secretary of State for War, Lord Kitchener, on a mission to Russia. As the ship went down, Kitchener was drowned. Although his Cabinet colleagues had long regarded him as ineffective, for the public he was the man who had constituted the strength and stability of the governing, warmaking instrument. Legend had it that he had not been drowned at all, but had been taken to Russia to conduct the new offensive in greatest secrecy.

Also on June 5, the news overshadowed by Kitchener's death, the philosopher Bertrand Russell was brought to trial, at the Mansion House in London. Despite his impassioned appeal for 'respect for the individual conscience', he was fined £100 for publishing a leaflet supporting conscientious objection to military service. That very day his friend and Cambridge protégé, the philosopher Wittgenstein, was in action on the Eastern Front. At Okna, which Brusilov's forces were attacking, his gun battery held its ground. As a result of his bravery, Wittgenstein, then a lance corporal, was recommended for the Silver Medal for Valour, Second Class, a rare honour for someone of such a low rank. The citation read: 'Ignoring the heavy artillery fire on the casemate and the exploding mortar bombs, he observed the discharge of the mortars and located them. The battery in fact succeeded in destroying two of the heavy-calibre mortars by direct hits, as was confirmed by prisoners taken.' Ignoring the shouts of his officer to take cover, Wittgenstein continued to observe the effect of the gunfire. 'By this distinctive behaviour', the officer reported, 'he exercised a very calming effect on his comrades.'

Two philosophers, who three years earlier had sat together deep in

[1] Norman Stone, *The Eastern Front*, Hodder and Stoughton, London 1975, page 247.

discussion of truth and logic, had taken diametrically opposed attitudes to the war.

On June 7, even as Brusilov was bringing comfort to the Allies on the Eastern Front, there was a blow to Allied fortunes in the west when, after holding out for three months, Fort Vaux fell to the Germans. The defenders had fought in subterranean passages, amid the stench of decomposing bodies that could not be buried, under massive bombardment including gas shells, for almost a week. Pulverised by German artillery, they had been reduced to their last twelve gallons of water. A carrier pigeon, which had been badly affected by gas on its previous flight, took out the fort's last message, 'We are still holding out ... relief is imperative ... this is my last pigeon', and then dropped dead. It was awarded the Légion d'Honneur. Of the many thousands of carrier pigeons who flew with daily messages through the war zones, in all the contending armies, it was the only one to be honoured by a military decoration.

The six hundred survivors of the garrison of Fort Vaux were taken into captivity. So impressed was the German Crown Prince at the courage of the fort's commander, Major Raynal, that he not only congratulated him but presented to him the captured sword of another French officer, Raynal's sword having been lost. Such courtesies after the grim battle were part of an ancient chivalry, but elsewhere the battle went on. As the struggle continued west of Fort Vaux, about twenty French soldiers, with their bayonets fixed ready for action, were buried alive in a trench.[1]

As Pétain had insisted, Verdun itself would not fall, despite the continuing and mutual slaughter. On the Eastern Front, Brusilov continued to advance. On June 9 the Austrian general commanding on the Czernowitz Front, Pflanzer-Baltin, ordered the retreat. Many Austrian artillerymen fled, either leaving their guns untended, to fall into Russian hands, or taking their guns with them, so that the infantrymen who remained in their positions were without any artillery protection. Wittgenstein later recalled how, during the long retreat, 'he sat utterly exhausted on a horse in an endless column, with the one thought of keeping his seat, since if he fell off he would be trampled to death'.

On June 12, Brusilov announced that in the advances that his men had made since the start of his offensive eight days earlier, they had captured 2,992 Austrian officers, 190,000 Austrian soldiers, 216 heavy guns, 645 machine guns and 196 howitzers. One third of the Austrian forces facing him had been taken captive. Within another five days the Russians had occupied Czernowitz, the most easterly Austro-Hungarian city, and a centre of culture and commercial enterprise.

A further Allied success that June was the entry of Arab forces into the

[1] Shortly after the war the tips of some of their bayonets were discovered sticking out of the ground. The trench became a French national monument.

conflict. Headed by Sherif Hussein of Mecca, the Arab Revolt had begun on June 5, outside the Turkish-controlled city of Medina. Its initial actions, though enthusiastic, were premature and unsuccessful. An Arab force of 50,000, of whom only 10,000 had rifles, was driven off by the Turks. That day, half a dozen British advisers, including Captain T.E. Lawrence ('Lawrence of Arabia'), landed secretly at Jeddah, on the Red Sea.

Far from the massive, destructive conflicts on the Western and Eastern Fronts, a new land front had opened, the tenth front then operational.[1] On June 7, Hussein declared the independence of the Hedjaz from the Turks. Four days later two British cruisers, *Fox* and *Hardinge*, shelled Turkish positions north of Jeddah. Three British seaplanes flew bombing raids on Turkish positions in the port. Arab forces having learned the lesson of their first encounter at Medina, in the next encounter a week later the Turks were outnumbered and outgunned. Mecca fell to the Arabs on June 13, and Jeddah three days later.

The war in the air had become a daily feature of the war zones. Flying from the French city of Nancy, a French aviator, Lieutenant Marchal, dropped leaflets over Berlin denouncing the war guilt of the German Kaiser and the Austrian Emperor. He then flew on to Kholm, in Austrian-occupied Poland, where he was taken prisoner, but later escaped. On June 22, French bombers flew on a raid to Karlsruhe, causing more than two hundred civilian casualties. At Verdun, Lieutenant Balsley, an American volunteer fighter pilot, the first in Europe, was shot down by a German fighter pilot, but escaped unharmed.

The last major German attempt to capture Verdun took place on the evening of June 22, when a German artillery bombardment was launched, using a new phosgene gas: Green Cross. Men and horses were caught and killed by the terrible fumes. Doctors treating the wounded were themselves struck down. For several hours the rain of death continued, then 30,000 Germans attacked. Near Fleury a whole French division, 5,000 men, was wiped out, and Fort Thiaumont, two miles north of Verdun, was captured. Among the German attackers was Lieutenant Friedrich Paulus, who, twenty-six years later, was to surrender a whole German army at Stalingrad after being surrounded and outnumbered.

A German university student, then serving in the army, Hans Forster, later recorded some of the scenes of the advance to Fleury. 'To the front of us a railway embankment; to the right a curve in it. There forty-five Frenchman

---

[1] The other fronts being the Western and Eastern Fronts, the Caucasus Front (also known as the Armenian Front), the Persian Front (Russian troops on the border of central Mesopotamia), the southern Mesopotamian Front, the Salonica Front, the Italian Front, the East African Front (where Belgian troops had just invaded the Urundi area of German East Africa, and Northern Rhodesian police had just occupied the German East African border town of Bismarckburg), and the Sinai Front, where the Turks had renewed their attacks into the British-held peninsula, overrunning El Arish.

are standing with their hands up. One corporal is still shooting at them – I stop him. An elderly Frenchman raises a slightly wounded right hand and smiles and thanks me.'[1] Fleury was taken, but the Germans were halted before they could enter Fort Souville, the last but one fort between them and Verdun itself. The Germans did not have enough Green Cross gas for a second gas attack.

'They shall not pass!' was the last line of an Order of the Day from General Nivelle. Fearful that, if Fort Souville fell, Verdun would become untenable, the French sought British help. Haig was committed to launching a British offensive on the Somme on June 29. The French Prime Minister himself, Aristide Briand, went to see Haig on June 24 to ask him to attack sooner. Haig said it was too late to do so, but that the artillery barrage would be begun as planned, and kept up until the assault in five days' time. Thus began the longest concentrated artillery bombardment in modern warfare.

In Germany, anti-war feeling was growing. Deaths from starvation as a result of the Allied blockade were becoming a daily occurrence. In 1915 some 88,232 deaths had been attributed to the blockade. In 1916 the number rose to 121,114.[2] There were food riots in more than thirty German cities. On June 28 a three-day protest strike began, in which 55,000 German workers took part. The one anti-war member of the Reichstag, Karl Liebknecht, was expelled from the Reichstag and sentenced to two years' hard labour for continuing to urge soldiers not to fight. Two months later his sentence was increased to four years.

The Entente had begun to make a little progress. On the Italian Front, a third of the Austrian advances made during the Trentino offensive were steadily recovered, despite a terrifying Austrian bombardment on the night of June 28, when hydrocyanide gas shells were fired, causing grave injury to more than 6,000 sleeping Italians. On the next day, however, the Italians retook the trenches they had been forced to abandon, helped by the blowing back of the gas on to the Austrian troops, more than a thousand of whom were injured, and took 416 Austrians prisoner. On the Russian Front the Austrians were mauled at the Battle of Kolomea, when the Russians took more than 10,000 prisoners, entering Kolomea on June 29.

At Verdun, the French held Fort Souville, and the threat to the city was averted. A second test for the Entente was imminent: the planned British breakthrough on the Somme. It was Haig's hope, he wrote to the General Staff on June 16, that 'the advance was to be pressed eastward far enough to enable our cavalry to push through into the open country beyond the

---

[1] Forster was killed near Verdun later in 1916.
[2] That is, 241 deaths a day in 1915 and 331 deaths a day in 1916. In 1917 the number rose to 712 a day (259,000 in the year) and in 1918 to 802 a day (293,760 in the year): a total civilian death toll of 762,106. The German civilian death toll from Allied bombing in the Second World War was almost exactly the same (approximately 800,000).

enemy's prepared lines of defence'. A British officer, Major Robert Money, wrote in his diary in late June: 'It appears that in about a week's time we shall be required to prance into the Hun trenches – well cheerio and I hope the Huns will like it.' Money was impressed by the fact that, as he noted, 'nothing seems to have been spared to make this show a success – nothing seems to have been overlooked'.

The preliminary artillery barrage, opened at the French request on June 24, was sustained along a twelve-mile front. More than 1,500 guns and howitzers fired 1,732,873 shells. Although many of this enormous number of shells merely churned up the already battered surface, causing less damage than hoped to the deep dug-outs of the German defenders, and although many were duds, the impact of the bombardment on the mood and morale of the attackers was considerable. During brief pauses in the bombardment raids were made across No-Man's Land to report on the situation in the forward German trenches. An Intelligence summary for June 25/26 reported, somewhat ominously in retrospect: 'Raids attempted all along the Corps Front were unsuccessful, in some sectors owing to intense machine gun and rifle fire.' On the night of June 28, men of the Newfoundland Regiment entered No-Man's Land to raid the German trenches opposite theirs but, according to one observer, 'turned tail'.

It was the scale of the bombardment that gave the waiting British and Canadian troops their confidence. 'Very hot stuff here,' Second Lieutenant George Norrie wrote to his mother on June 29, 'and I am enjoying myself. Talk about "shell-out" this show beats it – I think I was made for it.' That evening men of the Newfoundland Regiment again raided the German trenches opposite theirs, finding it 'full of Huns'. According to the same observer: 'They slew a lot but lost heavily themselves.' In another raid that night, Scottish infantrymen brought forty-six German prisoners back with them. The offensive had been due to begin on June 29. Heavy rain, and a realisation that the bombardment had not been as effective as intended, forced its postponement for forty-eight hours, lessening the stunning and surprise aspects of the pounding. But when the order to attack was finally given on July 1, one of the potentially decisive battles of the war was begun.

In the South Atlantic Ocean, the explorer Ernest Shackleton, after two years of isolation in the remote Antarctic, finally reached the small island of South Georgia. In his memoirs he recalled his first question to Mr Sorlle, the manager of the tiny British whaling station there, and Sorlle's reply:

'Tell me, when was the war over?' I asked.

'The war is not over,' he answered. 'Millions are being killed. Europe is mad. The world is mad.'

14

The Battle of the Somme: 'It is going to be a bloody holocaust'

JULY–AUGUST 1916

Opening on 1 July 1916, the Battle of the Somme was the Anglo-French attempt to break through the German lines by means of a massive infantry assault, to try to create the conditions in which cavalry could then move forward rapidly to exploit the breakthrough, perhaps even ride to victory. As they moved up into position the British soldiers sang:

> We beat them on the Marne,
> We beat them on the Aisne,
> We gave them hell
> At Neuve Chapelle
> And here we are again!

Among the tens of thousands of men gathering for the battle was Lieutenant William Noel Hodgson, a Cambridge contemporary of Rupert Brooke. He was twenty-three years old, and known by his fellow-soldiers as 'Smiler'. On the eve of the battle he wrote a poem, 'Before Action':

> I, that on my familiar hill
> Saw with uncomprehending eyes
> A hundred of Thy sunsets spill
> Their fresh and sanguine sacrifice,
> Ere the sun swings his noonday sword
> Must say goodbye to all of this!
> By all delights that I shall miss,
> Help me to die, O Lord.

The battle began on the morning of July 1, when nearly a quarter of a million shells were fired at the German positions in just over an hour, an average of 3,500 a minute. So intense was the barrage that it was heard on Hampstead Heath, north of London. At 7.28 a.m. ten mines were exploded under the German trenches. Two minutes later, British and French troops attacked along a 25-mile front.

As they went over the top, most British soldiers carried with them about sixty-six pounds' weight of equipment: a rifle, ammunition, grenades, rations, a waterproof cape, four empty sandbags, a steel helmet, two gas helmets, a pair of goggles against tear gas, a field dressing, a pick or a shovel, a full water bottle and a mess tin. General Edmonds has written, in his official history, that the weight of this equipment made it 'difficult to get out of a trench, impossible to move much quicker than a slow walk, or to rise and lie down quickly.' A British military historian, Peter Liddle, comments: 'In the event, many thousands of men offering so bulky and slow-moving a target would crumple to the ground quickly enough but would not rise at all, never mind quickly.'[1]

Early in the battle, a young Scottish drummer, Walter Ritchie, stood on the parapet of a captured German trench and, as all around him men were beginning to fall back, repeated the 'charge' again and again. He was awarded the Victoria Cross. One British battalion, the Accrington Pals, left behind a few of its signallers as it went over the top. They watched the attack from behind a mound of earth. 'We were able to see our comrades move forward in an attempt to cross No-Man's Land, only to be mown down like meadow grass,' Lance Corporal H. Bury later recalled. 'I felt sick at the sight of this carnage and remember weeping. We did actually see a flag signalling near the village of Serre, but this lasted only a few seconds and the signals were unintelligible.'

As many as a hundred German machine guns, most of them hidden in armoured emplacements which had protected them during the bombardment, opened fire as the infantry moved forward from their trenches. Many of the attackers were killed as they bunched together to push through the unexpectedly small gaps in their own barbed wire. One officer, Second Lieutenant Eric Miall-Smith, wrote home three days later of the 'glorious victory' on that first day of the battle. 'I know I accounted for four Germans so I have done my bit.' Miall-Smith added: 'I saw parties of Germans during the attack fire on our fellows until they were within a few yards of them; then, as soon as they found out that there was no hope for them they threw down their arms and rushed forward to shake our men by the hands. Most of them got their desserts and were not taken prisoners. Some of the wounded Germans were shooting men in the back after they had been dressed by them. They are swine – take it from me – I saw these things happen with my own eyes.'

Another officer, Lieutenant J. Capper, later recalled a German soldier clasping his knees and thrusting a photograph of his wife and children at him. 'I remember feeling inward amusement at adopting a "tough guy" approach towards so comparatively harmless and frightened an individual when I was myself having to make a great effort at disguising my own "windiness".' A British medical officer, Captain G.D. Fairley, himself wounded, wrote in his diary of how, as he made his way along the trenches

[1] Peter H. Liddle, *The 1916 Battle of the Somme, A Reappraisal*, Leo Cooper, London 1992, page 39.

with stretcher bearers, looking for wounded, 'We came across a case of "shell-shock". An emotionally distraught soldier was going back, cowering, cringing and gabbering with fright at the shell fire.'

Vera Brittain's brother Edward was on the Somme on July 1. While waiting for orders to go over the top, in the second wave, his men had been unnerved by the large numbers of wounded from the first wave coming back and crowding into the trench. Then a battalion in front of them in No-Man's Land had panicked. 'I can't remember just how I got the men together and made them go over the parapet,' Brittain told his sister a few weeks later. 'I only know I had to go back twice to get them, and I wouldn't go through those minutes again if it meant the V.C.' Finally, as the men followed him and he was about seventy yards into No-Man's Land, he was hit in the thigh. After trying to continue to lead his men forward, but unable to do so, he found refuge in a shell-hole. There a shell fragment pierced his arm. In the shell-hole were two other men. 'One was badly wounded,' he told his sister, 'but the other wasn't hurt at all – only in a blue funk.'

Brittain managed to crawl back to the British trenches. 'I don't remember much about it except that about half way across I saw the hand of a man who'd been killed only that morning beginning to turn green and yellow. That made me feel pretty sick and I put on a spurt.' For his courage that morning, Second Lieutenant Brittain was awarded the Military Cross.

Two German-held villages, Mametz and Montauban, were captured on July 1, as well as a German strongpoint, the Leipzig Redoubt. The human cost of the day's attack was higher than on any other single day of battle in the First World War. Just over a thousand British officers and more than 20,000 men were killed, and 25,000 seriously wounded.

In the battle for Mametz, 159 men of the Devonshire Regiment who attacked Mansel Copse were killed by a single German machine gun, built into the base of a crucifix at the edge of the village, four hundred yards from their starting point. The British officer who led the attack on the copse, Captain D.L. Martin, had predicted that the machine gun at the crucifix would be a fatal hazard if it survived the preliminary British artillery fire. He was killed with his men as they advanced into the uninterrupted fire. They were buried in a trench in the copse, and a notice was put above their grave: 'The Devonshires held this trench. The Devonshires hold it still.' Among the officers buried in that trench was William Noel Hodgson, 'Smiler', the battalion's Bombing Officer. When bringing up a supply of bombs up to the trench, he was killed by a bullet in the throat. His body was found with that of his batman lying at his side.

Reaching the front line ten days after the Battle of the Somme, a British officer recorded in his diary the information he was given by the Padre of the attack on Mametz. 'His news was ghastly – everyone I care for gone: all four officers of my company killed: dear Harold died most splendidly before the German lines. He was shot through the stomach and Lawrence killed behind him by the same shot. Iscariot was shot through the heart below Mansel Copse and all his staff killed around him; Smiler killed about the same place, getting his bombs up. No single officer got through untouched. The men did grandly – going on without officers and reaching all objectives.'

Among those in action on July 1 was Second Lieutenant Henry Field. 'Thank God I don't flinch from the sound of the guns,' he had written to his mother four months earlier. His 800-strong battalion, the 6th Royal Warwicks, reached their objective near Serre, but after coming under unbroken German machine-gun fire from both flanks were forced to fall back to their original line. Of the 836 who set out, 520 were killed and 316 wounded. Lieutenant Field was among the dead. On the first Christmas of the war he had written:

> *Through barren nights and fruitless days*
> *Of waiting when our faith grows dim*
> *Mary be with the stricken heart,*
> *Thou hast a son, remember him.*
>
> *Lord Thou hast been our refuge sure,*
> *The Everlasting Arms are wide,*
> *Thy words from age to age endure,*
> *Thy loving care will still provide.*
>
> *Vouchsafe that we may see, dear Lord,*
> *Vouchsafe that we may see,*
> *Thy purpose through the aching days,*

Field never finished the final line. Of his battalion's destruction near Serre, it's official historian wrote: 'July 1st – Ill-fated day. Wounds and death were the fruit of it, and to those who outlived it an accursed memory of horror. Imperishable courage inspired every fighting man, but, where, where was Victory?'

In an attack on the village of Serre itself, John Streets, a company sergeant in the Sheffield Pals, and another of those who found solace in poetry, was hit. As he went back for medical help he was told that a soldier in his platoon was too seriously wounded to return to the Dressing Station on his own. Streets returned towards the front line to bring the soldier back, and was never seen again. He could not even be the beneficiary of a funeral such as he had earlier described in his poem 'A Soldier's Funeral':

> *No splendid rite is here – yet lay him low,*
> *Ye comrades of his youth he fought beside,*
> *Close where the winds do sigh and wild flowers grow,*
> *Where the sweet brook doth babble by his side.*
> *No splendour, yet we lay him tenderly*
> *To rest, his requiem the artillery.*

Streets' brother Harry was serving that day with a Field Ambulance Unit, at a Dressing Station in Albert. He later described how the wounded

'flooded in on foot, or were brought by stretchers, wheelbarrows, carts –
anything. Their wounds were dressed and then they were laid out on the
floor to await evacuation'. Those who were not expected to survive were
put on one side and left. 'It was very hard to ignore their cries for help',
he wrote, 'but we had to concentrate on those who might live.'

On that first day, the only Dominion force then on the Somme, a
Newfoundland battalion, was almost wiped out. Of the 810 soldiers in
action, 710 were either killed, missing or wounded. 'It was a magnificent
display of trained and disciplined valour,' one of Haig's divisional commanders, General de Lisle, informed the Newfoundland Prime Minister,
'and its assault only failed of success because dead men can advance no
further.'

Elsewhere during the first day of battle on the Somme, more than five
hundred of the attackers were taken prisoner by the Germans. One British
objective, Bapaume, less than ten miles from the starting point, was never
reached, neither that day, nor after five months of renewed assaults.

The scale and intensity of the British attack on July 1 had an immediate
effect on the Germans, causing the transfer of sixty heavy guns and two
infantry divisions from Verdun to the Somme, and an end to the German
search for victory at Verdun.

The first day of the Battle of the Somme was the 132nd day of the Battle
of Verdun, for whose tormented defenders it drew off tens of thousands
of German troops. French attacks on the Somme further south made larger
gains than the British, but they too failed to get anywhere near their first
day's objective, the town of Péronne. They did, however, take 3,000
German soldiers prisoner and capture eighty German guns.

On the second day of the Battle of the Somme, July 2, a young South
African soldier, Hugh Boustead, was among the infantrymen who went
into the attack. 'Our brigade crossed the scarred fields through the stricken
squadrons,' he later wrote. 'Dead and dying horses, split by shellfire, with
bursting entrails and torn limbs, lay astride the road that led to battle.
Their fallen riders stared into the weeping skies. In front, steady bursts of
machine-gun fire vibrated on the air. Caught by a barrage, these brave men
and fine horses had been literally swept from the Longueval road.'

A German attempt to recapture Montauban on July 2 was driven off.
On the following day British forces attacked, but failed to capture the
villages in the German line, Ovillers and La Boiselle. South of the Somme,
the French made greater progress, so much so that a German general's order
that day stated directly: 'I forbid the voluntary evacuation of trenches.' But
by nightfall on July 4 the French had taken 4,000 Germans prisoner and
broken through the German line on a six-mile front.

Among the troops sent forward on the following day were detachments
of the Foreign Legion. In their ranks were several dozen Americans,
including the Harvard graduate, and poet, Alan Seeger (Legionnaire No.

19522). He was with a unit led by a Swiss baron, Captain de Tscharner, in an attack on the strongly fortified village of Belloy-en-Santerre. During the attack they were caught in the enfilade fire of six German machine guns. Lying mortally wounded in a shell-hole, Seeger was heard crying out for water, and for his mother. In his poem 'Rendezvous' he had written earlier that year:

> *I have a rendezvous with Death*
> *On some scarred slope of battered hill,*
> *When Spring comes round again this year*
> *And the first meadow-flowers appear.*
>
> *God knows 'twere better to be deep*
> *Pillowed in silk and scented down,*
> *Where love throbs out in blissful sleep,*
> *Pulse nigh to pulse, and breath to breath,*
> *Where hushed awakenings are dear....*
> *But I've a rendezvous with Death*
> *At midnight in some flaming town,*
> *When Spring trips north again this year,*
> *And I to my pledged word am true,*
> *I shall not fail that rendezvous.*

By nightfall Belloy-en-Santerre was in the Legion's hands, but twenty-five officers and 844 men had been killed or seriously wounded, a third of the attackers' total strength.

Going forward on July 4 along a former German communication trench, Siegfried Sassoon passed 'three very badly-mangled corpses lying in it: a man, short, plump, with turned-up moustaches, lying face downward and half sideways with one arm flung up as if defending his head, and a bullet through his forehead. A doll-like figure. Another hunched and mangled, twisted and scorched with many days' dark growth on his face, teeth clenched and grinning lips.' Then, at noon, closer to the front line, he passed 'thirty of our own laid out by the Mametz-Carnoy road, some side by side on their backs with bloody clotted fingers mingled as if they were handshaking in the companionship of death. And the stench undefinable.'

The British war correspondent Philip Gibbs, going forward on July 4 to the German trenches at Fricourt that had earlier been overrun, recalled how 'It looked like victory, because of the German dead that lay there in their battered trenches and the filth and stench of death over all that mangled ground, and the enormous destruction wrought by our guns, and the fury of fire which we were still pouring over the enemy's lines from batteries which had moved forward. I went down flights of steps into German dug-outs astonished by their depth and strength. Our men did not build like this. This German industry was a rebuke to us – yet we had captured their work, and the dead bodies of their labourers lay in those dark caverns, killed by our bombers who had flung down hand-grenades.

I drew back from those fat corpses. They looked monstrous, lying there crumpled up, amidst a foul litter of clothes, stick bombs, old boots, and bottles. Groups of dead lay in ditches which had once been trenches, flung into chaos by that bombardment I had seen. They had been bayoneted. I remember one man – an elderly fellow – sitting up with his back to a bit of earth with his hands half raised. He was smiling a little, though he had been stabbed through the belly, and was stone dead.'

Gibbs commented: 'Victory! ... Some of the German dead were young boys, too young to be killed for old men's crimes, and others might have been old or young. One could not tell because they had no faces, and were just masses of raw flesh in rags of uniforms. Legs and arms lay separate without any bodies thereabouts.'

The first of the wounded from the Battle of the Somme had begun to arrive in London on July 4. Vera Brittain, at a hospital in Camberwell, later recalled 'the immense convoys which came without cessation for about a fortnight, and continued at short intervals for the whole of that sultry month and the first part of August'. The distance from the battlefield was no protection against extreme distress. 'Day after day I had to fight the queer, frightening sensation – to which, throughout my years of nursing, I never became accustomed – of seeing the covered stretchers come in, one after another, without knowing, until I ran with pounding heart to look, what fearful sight or sound or stench, what problem of agony or imminent death, each brown blanket concealed.' Among the wounded who reached Vera Brittain's hospital was, by complete chance, her brother Edward. He was to remain in England, and in intense pain, for many months.

The battle on the Somme became a daily struggle for small woods and even smaller villages. On July 6, the village of La Boiselle was captured. The village of Contalmaison, captured by the British on the morning of July 7, was lost that evening. That same day, a British attack on Mametz Wood was driven off. On July 8, British forces captured most of Trones Wood, but heavy German shelling, followed by a German counter-attack, forced them out. Hundreds were killed in these attacks, and thousands wounded. Hugh Boustead later recalled the moment when he and his men were caught in a German shell barrage. 'Although a shell pitched practically in the middle of the section,' he later recalled, 'the three of us in the centre escaped any hurt other than a tremendous shock and blast which blew the equipment off our shoulders, our steel hats away, and poured tear gas in great clouds all over the trench. Coughing and spitting and weeping and blinded by the tear gas we could hear those of our comrades who were wounded moaning under the debris. Six of the section, three on either side of us, were utterly destroyed, torn to pieces, and six more were wounded.'

On the Somme, as in each of the great battles where artillery tore up the bodies and then the corpses of the dead, proper identification was impossible for hundreds of thousands, those who are recorded on the monuments of these battles as having 'no known grave'. Four years after the Battle of

34 Serbian refugees flee southward through Macedonia, autumn 1915.

35 Armenian refugees reach the safety of Baku.

36 Serbian Headquarters
Staff cross the river
Drin, in Albania, during
their retreat to the
Adriatic, October 1915.

37 German troops on
guard on the Eastern
Front, winter 1915–16.

38 German soldiers escort Russian prisoners-of-war to the rear.

39 A corridor in the University of Vienna, used as a hospital for wounded Austrian soldiers.

40 The first day of the Battle of the Somme, going over the top on 1 July 1916, a still from a British war film.

41 An ammunition limber on the Somme, near Flers, November 1916.

42 The Somme: two British soldiers with two German prisoners-of-war, La Boisselle.

43 Senegalese troops en route to the Western Front, 18 June 1916.

44 The Somme: British soldiers resting, Thiepval, August 1916.

45 Two British nurses with a wounded soldier.

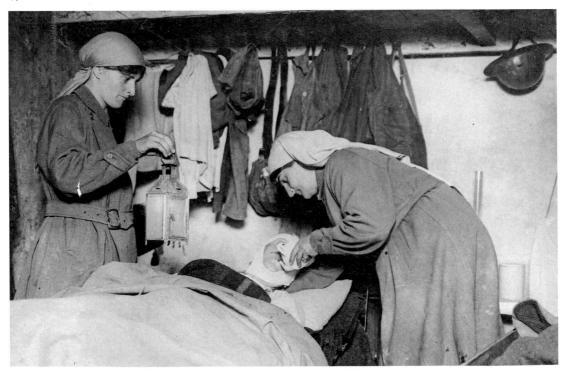

46 On the outskirts of Berlin, German citizens inspect a dummy trench. An officer
with the Iron Cross instructs in the use of a minethrower.

47 A trench on the Somme: German dead behind a destroyed machine-gun post, near Guillemont,
September 1916. A British soldier looks on.

48 Verdun: a machine-
gun crew in action,
Fort Vaux, 22
November 1916.

49 Verdun: the graves of
the six members of a
French gun battery,
Fort Vaux.

the Somme, Boustead received a letter from the War Office in London 'asking if I could throw any light on the grave of Number 5100, Private Hugh Boustead of the South African Scottish, the cross of which had been erected in Montauban valley in 1916 during the Somme Battle'. He was able to assure the authorities that he was alive and well.

After nine days of battle, the Germans had been pushed back a mile in some places, nearly two miles in others. On July 10 the British recaptured what was left of Contalmaison village. That night, at Verdun, the Germans launched their final attempt to break through the French defences, take Fort Souville, and reach the city. As on June 23, the attack began with shelling with Green Cross gas shells. But in the two-and-a-half weeks that had elapsed since then, the French soldiers had been issued with gas masks that were effective against the new gas. Later in the attack, the German use of flamethrowers eliminated a whole battalion. Thirty-three of its officers and 1,300 men were either killed or captured.

By nightfall, 2,400 French soldiers had been taken prisoner, and Fort Souville's garrison knocked out by artillery fire. On the following day a small group of German soldiers, no more than thirty, reached the outer wall of the fort and raised their flag. Just over two miles away they could see the twin towers of Verdun cathedral. Sheltering in the fort were sixty French soldiers, and a lieutenant, Kléber Dupuy. Leading his men out of the fort, Dupuy regained the walls, taking ten of the Germans prisoner. The rest were either killed, or fled. Verdun was secure.

On the Somme, the British advance had continued. On July 12, Mametz Wood was finally taken. The number of Germans captured had risen to more than 7,000. A further 2,000 prisoners were taken during a push through the German lines on July 14, when both Longeuval and Bazentin were captured, and Trones Wood was secured for the second time. In an effort to use this success to demoralise the Germans, a British aeroplane was ordered to fly over the front line and to radio back, in a message that it was known the Germans would intercept: 'Enemy second line of defence has been captured on a front of 6,000 yards. British cavalry is now passing through in pursuit of the demoralised enemy.' Comments the official Royal Air Force historian, H.A. Jones: 'Although this message, which was flashed out at 10.30 a.m., deliberately exaggerated the situation at that time, the turn of events later in the day was to give it a measure of truth. Cavalry went through in the evening.'

Air power also played its part on the Somme on July 14. A Royal Flying Corps Observer, Lieutenant T.L.W. Stallibrass, noted in his log book that day: 'A large force of Hun infantry were entrenched in a road running S.S.E. from High Wood. Fortunately a British aeroplane from No. 3 Squadron spotted the infantry and descended to 500 feet and flew up and down the line strafing them with a Lewis gun.'

On July 15, the fight for Delville Wood began, the first of fifteen days' hand-to-hand fighting and ferocious artillery bombardments. The battle

started when the 3,000 strong South African Brigade, of which Hugh
Boustead was a part, was ordered to capture the wood. 'We moved forward
through an orchard in single file, led by the platoon officer,' he later
recalled. 'Smith, the Second Lieutenant, got through but the next seven
who followed him were shot dead in a circle of a few yards, picked off by
clean shooting without a murmur.'

On the second night of the battle, Boustead wrote, 'We nearly suffered
complete annihilation from our own "steel footballs" – circular bombs
with a long stick on which the charge is propelled. They went on pitching
among us for hours on end, curiously causing no casualties, but they added
to our terror.' On the third day he went forward with a party of snipers
to try to pin the Germans down at Waterlot Farm. 'Three of us spent the
afternoon there,' he wrote. 'There were already six South African Scottish
lying dead in their firing places ahead of us, but we were able to effect quite
a good shoot on the Germans moving from Waterlot and after a number of
hits they stopped.' A few hours later, Boustead was wounded and left the
battlefield. 'My main relief was a chance to get some sleep,' he later recalled.
'For five days and nights we had hardly slept at all and at times I was
conscious of a longing to get hit anywhere to be able to sleep.'

To the left of Delville Wood on July 15 the British managed to reach
High Wood. At one point in the action a front-line carrier pigeon flew into
the British artillery headquarters with a message requesting that heavy
artillery be turned on a German machine-gun emplacement in the wood.
A Royal Flying Corps reconnaissance later in the day showed that the
wood had been only partly overrun: on the west side British troops waved
flags in reply to the aeroplane's signal, but on the east side the Germans
opened rapid fire. On the following day, the British evacuated their part
of the wood. In the cemetery to the south of the wood are 107 British, 37
New Zealand and 36 Australian graves, an incomplete but permanent
reminder of the cost of one day's battle.

On July 16 a heavy artillery bombardment was launched against the
German defences along the ridge dominated by the village of Pozières.
Rain and mist made any aerial spotting impossible, however, and far from
the defences being broken up, the Germans, who realised that an attack
was imminent, were able to build new machine-gun emplacements. The
preliminary British infantry attack on the following morning was driven
off by machine-gun fire so intense that the next day's attack was cancelled.
On July 18, Harold Macmillan was injured. 'The pair of spectacles which
I was wearing must have been blown off by the force of the explosion,' he
wrote to his mother the next day, 'for I never saw them again. Very luckily
they were not smashed and driven into my eye.' A grenade had exploded
in his face, stunning him. When he came to, and asked his corporal what
had happened after the grenade went off, the corporal replied: 'Well, sir, I
saw the German trying to run away. So I 'it 'im, and 'is 'elmet came off.
Then I 'it 'im again and the back of 'is 'ead came off.'

*

A diversionary attack north of the Somme, at Fromelles, was being planned for July 19, to be carried out by Australian troops. The Australians, many of whom had fought the previous summer, autumn and winter at Gallipoli, treated their harsh new tasks with characteristic irreverence, singing, to the tune of 'The Church's One Foundation':

> *We are the Anzac Army,*
> *The A.N.Z.A.C.,*
> *We cannot shoot, we don't salute,*
> *What bloody good are we.*
> *And when we get to Ber-lin*
> *The Kaiser he will say,*
> *'Hoch, Hoch! Mein Gott, what a bloody odd lot*
> *To get six bob a day!'*

This was the Australians' first offensive action on the Western Front. Its aim was to prevent the Germans from moving reinforcements to the Somme. On the eve of the battle, General Elliott, the senior Australian officer at Fromelles, alarmed by the strength of the German position, asked a British Staff Officer, Major H.C.L. Howard, for his estimate of how the attack would go. Howard replied: 'If you put it to me like that sir, I must answer you in the same way as man to man. It is going to be a bloody holocaust.'

General Elliott asked Howard to report his view back to Haig. He did so, his report coinciding with Intelligence information that there was no longer any urgency for an attack, as German troops were not being transferred to the Somme, and did not therefore need to be pinned down. Haig's corps commander, General Sir Richard Haking, wanted the attack to go on, however, the headquarters record noting that 'he was quite confident of the success of the operation, and considered that the ammunition at his disposal was ample to put the infantry there and keep them in'. Pressed to agree to a delay in the attack, Haking was emphatic: 'The troops are worked up to it, were ready and anxious to do it, and he considered that any change of plan would have a bad effect on the troops now.'

Two miles south of Fromelles was the high ground of Aubers Ridge, the objective of the attack. The attack itself lay across a low, wet No-Man's Land towards a strongly fortified German salient, the Sugar Loaf, which overlooked the attackers' approach. 'I know you will do your best for the sake of our lads who are fighting down south,' Haking told them on the eve of battle. In the church tower at Fromelles, reinforced by a concrete stairwell, with a loophole specially designed for an observer, the Germans could see, throughout July 18, the preparations being made for the attack both in the front-line trenches and those behind them. The assault began on the late afternoon of July 19, preceded by a day-long artillery barrage. The first Australian casualties were caused by their own shells falling short, and by some heavy German artillery fire. When the attack began, the

German machine guns in the salient opened fire: the artillery had failed to silence them.

An hour after the first men had gone over the top, General Elliott reported: 'Every man who rises is being shot down. Reports from the wounded indicate that the attack is failing from want of support.' The wounded were streaming back. A British attack on the other side of the salient was also beaten back with heavy British casualties. Then, at a point in the line a little way from the Sugar Loaf, the Australians reached a main German trench. 'The enemy was caught in the act of manning his parapets, and some bitter hand-to-hand fighting followed,' the battalion's historian, Captain Ellis, later wrote. 'It terminated, as all such hand-to-hand fighting terminated throughout the war, in the absolute triumph of the Australians and the extinction or termination of the Germans.'

The Sugar Loaf Salient, which General Haking had ordered to be attacked 'throughout the night', eluded its attackers. As dawn broke, more wounded tried to get back to the Australian lines. Many of them lay out in No-Man's Land, 'trying to call back to us', Sergeant H.R. Williams later wrote, 'and in doing so made of themselves a target for the German machine gunners'. Those who managed to get back were like men 'awakened from a nightmare', Williams recalled. 'The ordeal of the night was plainly visible on all faces, ghastly white showing through masks of grime and dried sweat, eyes glassy, protruding and full of that horror seen only on the face of men who have lived through a heavy bombardment.'

During the night, one group of Australians and some British soldiers had reached the outer wire of the Sugar Loaf, but were unable to push through it. The Australian official war historian, C.E.W. Bean, visiting the battlefield in November 1918, shortly after the Armistice, wrote: 'We found the No-Man's Land simply full of our dead. In the narrow sector west of the Sugar Loaf Salient, the skulls and bones and torn uniforms were lying about everywhere. I found a bit of Australian kit lying fifty yards from the corner of the salient, and the bones of an Australian officer and several men within a hundred yards of it. Further round, immediately on their flank, were a few British – you could tell them by their leather equipment.'

Amid the hundreds of cemeteries on the Western Front, one, a mile north of Fromelles, contains the graves of 410 Australians, and the names of 1,298 more 'missing' amid the mud and detritus of the battlefield. The battle at Fromelles was a brief interlude, far from the Somme, during that vaster battle. Yet its casualties were high: 1,708 Australian dead and nearly 4,000 wounded. The British dead were at least four hundred. The German dead and wounded were less than 1,500 in all. Four hundred Australians were taken prisoner: they were marched by the Germans through Lille.

The aim of the attack at Fromelles, to keep German troops back from the Somme, was a failure. A successful counter-attack on July 20 showed the Germans that their line was not in any serious danger. That day, on the Somme, an unprecedented, and perhaps unrepeated incident took place, recalled later by a British army chaplain: 'The only occasion when we have heard troops in battle break into a spontaneous and whole-hearted cheer was when after a half-hour's single combat on July 20, 1916, a German aeroplane crashed behind our lines, with the full glory of a blood-red sky in the background. The excitement had been so intense that on both sides the gunners had stopped firing to watch.'[1]

On the Somme, the attack on Pozières was about to be renewed. 'Why go to war with one another? With these men we have no quarrel,' a young Australian schoolteacher, Private Jack Bourke, wrote in a letter home four days before the battle began. A German soldier, writing home on July 21, headed his letter 'In Hell's Trenches' and added: 'It is not really a trench, but a little ditch shattered with shells – not the slightest cover and no protection. We have lost fifty men in two days and life is unendurable.'

The attack on Pozières was renewed on July 22. German troops had used the six days since the previous attack to place a network of machine-gun posts in shell-holes in front of their main defences. The British night-time artillery bombardment, seen from afar, turned the whole skyline into 'one flickering band of light'. As the newly arrived Anzac Corps went into action, there was little time or mood for mercy. One Australian officer, Lieutenant E.W.D. Laing, later recalled a German soldier who 'tried to give himself up as soon as he saw our chaps on him. "Come out, you ...", yelled one of my men. I heard him, rushed back shouting at the chap to shoot the swine or I would – so he got him.'

Six Germans were killed in that sweep and eighteen captured. 'The men had great sport chucking bombs down any hole they saw,' Laing remembered. In the corner of one dug-out, Private Bourke found some gift boxes of cake addressed in a child's handwriting. 'In another corner was a coat rolled up,' he wrote in a letter home. 'I opened it and found it stained with blood. Right between the shoulders was a burnt shrapnel hole, telling a tragic tale. The owner of the coat was a German and some might say, not entitled to much sympathy. Perhaps he was not, but I could not help thinking sadly of the little girl or boy who had sent him the cakes.'

This was the second Australian baptism of fire on the Western Front in three days. Contemporary letters and later recollections all testify to the severity and cruelty of the fighting. Lieutenant-Colonel Iven Makay recalled how, as the Australians advanced, many Germans 'remained in their dugouts, terrified and had to be bombed or bayoneted out. Some never came out. A number of the German prisoners would not, through pure fright, cross No-Man's Land. They had to be killed.' In the Pozières military cemetery is a memorial to 14,691 soldiers killed while attacking the ridge in 1916, 1917 and 1918, but who have no known grave. There are also 690 named Australian headstones.

On July 25 the assault at Pozières was renewed again. Lance Corporal E. Moorhead later recalled how, after his company had entered a deserted

---

[1] Rev. E.C. Crosse, *The Defeat of Austria as seen by the 7th Division*, London 1919, page 35.

German trench, a captain 'filled to the neck with rum' ordered the men to continue 'and dashed ahead again. Finally the survivors came back in a panic, calling out we must retreat, were all cut up, the Germans were on us etc etc. The Captain had been shot through the heart on the barbed wire.' Not long afterwards the Germans attacked, the impetus of their thrust broken by the Australian artillery. 'When the Huns came into view over the crest in twos and threes or singly, some with packs, probably filled with bombs, others with fixed bayonets, we lined the parapet like an excited crowd and blazed like hell at them, knocking them over like rabbits, not a man getting away so far as I could see. The range was about 400, and as each man appeared he got 100 bullets in him. One officer appeared and waved his men forward in a lordly way, and then collapsed like a bag, filled with our lead. I fired about 30 rounds and did my share.'

A little while later there was a moment of black humour. 'One unfortunate Boche,' Moorhead recalled, 'having run the gauntlet of our rifle fire was getting away apparently only slightly wounded when one of our shells burst on him as though aimed, and he went up blown to pieces. Well, we cheered and laughed at the happening as though it was the funniest thing in the world.'

Not so funny was the experience of an Australian officer, Captain W.G.M. Claridge, who was wounded that day and sent to hospital in England. 'I am not going to tell a lie and say I wasn't afraid,' Claridge wrote to his parents two weeks after the battle, 'because I was and who wouldn't be with Death grinning at you from all around and hellish 5.9 inch shells shrieking through the air and shrapnel dealing death all round. I don't know how long I stood it without breaking.' He had been buried three times, and was 'very thankful to get my wound as it got me out of the firing line for a rest.'

That night, July 25, Haig wrote in his diary: 'The situation seems all very new and strange to Australian HQ. The fighting here and the shell-fire is much more severe than anything experienced at Gallipoli. The German, too, is a very different enemy to the Turk! The hostile shelling has been very severe against Pozières today.' General Rawlinson, commenting in his diary that night on the film of the battle that had just been compiled, wrote: 'Some of it very good but I cut out many of the horrors in dead and wounded.'

Writing to his parents on July 28, a young infantryman, George Leigh-Mallory, described life in the trenches as 'as harrowing as you can imagine when one sees the dead and the dying and hears of regiments being cut up by machine guns'. Leigh-Mallory added: 'I am not one of the optimists about the war and shall be quite surprised if it ends before Xmas. I suppose we may at any moment hear very good news from Russia – but it's a very long time coming and the German war machine must be far from run down if he can put up the fight he has done.'[1]

[1] George Leigh-Mallory survived the war. He disappeared while climbing Mount Everest in

On July 29, a day after this infantryman's pessimistic, or at least realistic, letter home, Haig received a letter from London, written by General Sir William Robertson, Chief of the Imperial General Staff, warning him that 'The powers-that-be are beginning to get a little uneasy in regard to the situation.' This concern was, Robertson explained, 'Whether a loss of say 300,000 men will lead to really great results, because, if not, we ought to be content with something less than we are doing now.' These same powers-that-be, Robertson added, 'are constantly enquiring why we are fighting and the French are not. It is thought that the primary object – relief of pressure on Verdun – has to some extent been achieved.'

Haig had no doubt that the Somme offensive should continue. 'In another six weeks,' he replied, 'the enemy should be hard put to find men. The maintenance of a steady offensive pressure will result eventually in his complete overthrow.' That 'steady offensive pressure' continued, but with no decisive result, and a steady mounting up of British casualties. On July 30 four British battalions, among them three Liverpool Pals battalions, attacked the village of Guillemont, which had resisted a similar attack a week earlier. The dense fog made the preliminary British artillery preparations almost valueless, as many German soldiers left their trenches unseen, and took shelter in No-Man's Land. As the attackers went forward the fog did not protect them, however, as the German machine gunners knew in which direction the attack must come, and fired into the advancing men, who could not see from where their adversary's fire came. One group of Pals, reaching the German front line, found more than sixty Germans in the bottom of a trench, apparently sheltering from the bombardment. Only one prisoner was taken, 'presumably for intelligence purposes', comments the historian of the Liverpool Pals.[1]

Letters that survive, written by the attackers immediately after the battle for Guillemont, give a picture of the randomness of death. Lance-Corporal H. Foster described how 'Our sergeant had just given us our rum ration and gone to the shell hole where the gun team were, and here, unfortunately, one gas shell found its mark, landing in the centre of the gunners. Poor lads, it wiped the whole of them out.' Corporal G.E. Hemingway wrote an account of the death of his friend Lance-Corporal J. Quinn, in one of the many hundreds of thousands of letters sent home during the war to describe to a wife or parent the fate of his or her loved one: 'About half way across No-Man's Land, whilst waiting in a shell-hole for one of our own barrages to lift, I became aware of the fact that Joe was in the next hole to mine, and we smiled encouragement to each other. Enemy machine guns were sweeping the whole place with explosive bullets, and there was a fearful noise, and speech was impossible. The streams of death whistled over our shell-holes, coming from the left flank, and Joe's hole

1924. His brother Trafford, a pilot in the First World War and a leading airman (including Commander-in-Chief Fighter Command) in the Second World War, was killed in an air crash in November 1944.
[1] Graham Maddocks, *Liverpool Pals*, Leo Cooper, London 1991, page 116.

being to the left of mine, he received the bullet in his side. He slipped away quietly – just a yearning glance, a feeble clutching at space, and then a gentle sinking into oblivion, with his head on his arm.'

Among the members of the Liverpool Pals killed at Guillemont on July 30 was Lance-Corporal S. Atherton, who for fifteen years had been a player and then groundsman for the Oxton Cricket Club in Birkenhead. Although a married man, he had been among the very first to volunteer. He left a widow and four daughters, the eldest seven years old, the youngest two-and-a-half. On his behalf the Club made a special appeal for funds 'to tide the Widow over the next six years' or until her children 'are in a position to assist her by their own earnings'.

Five hundred men of the 2,500-strong Liverpool Pals battalions were killed that day, plunging Merseyside into mourning. Many of the bodies of the dead lay out in No-Man's Land until they were reduced to skeletons by the intensity of the August sun. Some, submerged and buried under the continually shell-shattered earth, were not discovered until more than a decade after the war.

From central and eastern Turkey, the great flight of Armenians, driven from their homeland amid scenes of brutality and terror, had continued throughout the early months of 1916. Armenian refugees became a feature of many Mediterranean ports. On July 1, a British officer in Egypt, Ronald Storrs, wrote home: 'Port Said is swamped by Armenian refugees, dumped upon us from Cilicia by French battleships. They are fighting the Turks very bravely. Which reminds me, disabuse your pen of the phrase, Good Old Turks, etc. If the massacres of Urfa and Adana were not enough, let the present horrors suffice to erase from our political vocabulary the false and foolish legend of the "First Gentleman in Europe".'

In the literature of the war, the novel *The Forty Days*, by Franz Werfel, was to become the monument to the epic flight of the Armenian people.

On the Eastern Front, the Russians had continued to push the Germans and Austrians westward. In the first week of July more than 30,000 Germans were taken prisoner. Once more, the British nurse Florence Farmborough was a witness to the ugly aftermath of the battle, for victor and vanquished alike. Her field hospital was then at Barish. 'As the fighting became more intense, the wounded lay massed outside our temporary dressing station, waiting for attention – countless stretcher cases among them. A few would crawl inside, beseeching the care they so urgently needed. We were working day and night, snatching a brief hour here and there for sleep. In the evening the dead would be col-lected and placed side by side in the pit-like graves dug for them on the battlefield. German, Austrian, Russian, they lay there, at peace, in a "brothers' grave". Swarms of flies added to the horror of the battle-fields and covered the dead brothers, waiting in their open ditches for burial, as with a thick, black pall. I remember the feeling of horror when I first saw that black pall of flies *moving*.'

On July 8, Russian troops reached Delatyn, less than thirty-two miles from the Jablonitsa Pass over the Carpathians, and the Hungarian border. 'Terrible weather,' Ludwig Wittgenstein wrote in his diary on July 15. 'In the mountains, bad, quite inadequate shelter, icy cold, rain and mist. An excruciating life.' On the 16th Florence Farmborough, on the other side of the line to Wittgenstein, wrote in her diary: 'The mud is so thick that high boots get sucked off the owners' legs.' Two nurses had been killed by Austrian bombs four days earlier, and one on the previous day. On the following day, seventy badly injured men were brought in. 'A young Tatar, heavily wounded, was carried to the operating table. He could speak no Russian and vainly tried to whisper something to us which we could not understand. One of our Tatar drivers was sent for; he stooped low over the prostrate form, but no answer came to his eager questioning. "He's gone!" said a voice. The weather-beaten face of the older tribesman stiffened with emotion as he walked away.'[1]

By the end of the month, the East Galician border town of Brody had fallen to the Russians, and 40,000 Austrians had been taken prisoner within two weeks. Russian losses were also heavy. Florence Farmborough's field hospital received eight hundred wounded men in twenty-four hours. Stomach wounds were in the majority. Amputations were also common. 'One leg was so heavy I could not lift it from the table,' she wrote. 'Someone helped her carry the leg 'to the tiny shed where a stack of amputated limbs awaited burial. I had not been in that shed before and I turned away hastily; I went to our room, drank some water and swallowed two aspirins; the choking feeling disappeared and I was myself again. But my thoughts would not adjust themselves so easily: after the war, what would happen to those limbless men?'

To try to bring Brusilov's offensive to a halt, Hindenburg and Ludendorff took over a large section of the Austrian Front in the last week of July. A German commander, General Bothmer, took over much of the front in East Galicia. Pflanzer-Baltin was forced to accept a German officer, Hans von Seeckt, as his Chief of Staff.[2] German troops were dispatched to the battle line, and Austrian and German companies joined to create mixed battalions. Even Turkish troops were sent for. 'The fact that the arrival of the Turks in Galicia, even before they got there, has been so loudly proclaimed', General Hoffmann wrote in his diary on July 27, 'is surely rather humiliating for the Austrians.'

Behind the German lines, in occupied Belgium, the strongest efforts had been made by the German occupation authorities to prevent the celebration of the eighty-fifth anniversary of Belgian independence on July 21. 'I warn

[1] The Tatars (also known as Tartars) were a Turkic-speaking, Muslim people living in the Crimea and along the Volga. They had been annexed to Russia by Catherine the Great in 1783. In the Second World War, Stalin deported them to Central Asia.
[2] From 1920 to 1926 von Seeckt was the German Army Chief of Staff, when he laid the foundations for the rebuilding of the German Army.

the population that it must refrain from all demonstrations,' the Governor of Brussels and Brabant, General Hurt, declared nine days earlier, and he listed as punishable 'public reunions, parades, assemblies, harangues, and speeches, academic ceremonies, the placing of flowers before certain monuments etc., the decoration of public or private buildings, the closing of stores, cafés etc., at unusual hours.' Commented the head of the American Legation in Belgium, Brand Whitlock: 'By one of those mysterious and tacit understandings that no one could trace to their source, everybody that day appeared wearing a green ribbon, green being the colour of hope, and while it was no doubt discouraged it was not yet forbidden the Belgians to hope.'

The Germans were not amused by this demonstration of patriotic zeal, or by a brief popular demonstration of support for Cardinal Mercier, the Archbishop of Malines, when, that evening, he was seen leaving Brussels by car for Malines. A fine of a million marks was imposed on the citizens of Brussels, and was collected. Mercier had won popular esteem for his public letters of protest against the excesses of the occupation.

Six days after the Belgian national day there was an episode in Belgium that confirmed the British view of German savagery. On July 27, in Bruges, the Germans executed Captain Charles Fryatt, formerly the commander of the Great Eastern Railway steamer, the *Brussels*. Fryatt had been found guilty by Court Martial of trying to ram a German submarine. He had been seized when the *Brussels* was intercepted by the Germans during one of its regular twice-weekly crossings from Harwich to the Hook of Holland, ten weeks after the exploit that won him so much praise in Britain. He and his crew were taken to Ruhleben prison camp just outside Berlin. At the Court Martial the Germans accused Fryatt of being a 'pirate' for attacking the vessel that was attacking him. A Canadian civilian internee at Ruhleben, John Ketchum, who had been studying music in Germany when war broke out, later recalled: 'The judicial murder of a man who had lived at Ruhleben, if only for a month, caused deep shock and anger, and brought the war home to the camp as nothing had done before.'

Inside Britain, the same patriotism that found Fryatt's execution repugnant also found repugnant the refusal of men to serve in the army. For some time, conscientious objectors had been abused as cowards and traitors. In the last week of July more than two hundred of these 'COs', as they were known, were sent to a stone quarry at Dyce, near Aberdeen, to break stones. A Tribunal set up by the Government found, however, more than 4,000 cases of genuine conscientious objectors. Alternative service was made available to them: including agricultural and medical work. Those who refused alternative service were frequently imprisoned. Repeated refusal led in many cases to repeated imprisonment, and hard labour, breaking stones in the quarries at Princetown Prison on Dartmoor.

In the United States, still tenaciously neutral, a Preparedness Day Parade was held in San Francisco on July 22. During the parade a bomb was thrown at the city's Stock Exchange by Thomas J. Mooney, a socialist-anarchist opposed to the war. Nine people were killed and wounded forty. Mooney was sentenced to death, but his sentence was commuted to life imprisonment. He was released in 1939.

During the autumn of 1916 there was violent activity on almost every war front, but no decisive change in the battle lines. On the Somme, as at Verdun, the German army, far from marching from triumph to triumph, was being bled to death. Haig's conviction that continued assaults would lead to the enemy's 'overthrow' led him to continue to try to reach the objectives that he had set for the first day of battle on July 1. On July 23, Australian troops had entered Pozières, two of them being awarded the Victoria Cross. Slowly, despite repeated counter-attacks, the Germans were being pushed back across the Somme battlefield. On July 31, at his desk in Berlin, Walther Rathenau wrote in his diary that the 'delirious exaltation' he had witnessed in the streets two years earlier had seemed to him even then 'a dance of death'; an overture to a doom that would be 'dark and dreadful'.

On the Somme the weather was the most gorgeous summer sunshine: 'not the weather for killing people', Harold Macmillan wrote to his mother on August 2. Six nights later the Germans raided the British trenches in the Ypres Salient, and preceded the raid with a preliminary discharge of gas. One 19-year-old private soldier, John Bennett, who panicked at the sudden and startling noise of the 'gas gong', fled from the trench to the rear. When he returned a few hours later to his battalion's support trenches, he found that seven men had been killed and forty-six wounded as a result of the gas attack. He was at once arrested and charged with 'misbehaviour before the enemy'.

At Bennett's trial his commanding officer intimated that Bennett, who had enlisted six weeks before the outbreak of war, went to pieces when under shellfire. He was sentenced to death, but during the review procedure a brigadier-general recommended that the sentence be commuted. The Corps commander, Lieutenant-General Sir Aylmer Hunter-Weston, a veteran of the fighting at Gallipoli, disagreed. Cowards, he said, 'constitute a serious danger to the war effort, and the sanction of the death penalty was designed to frighten men more than the prospects of facing the enemy'. Bennett was shot. Two other men were also executed that day for desertion.

As the fighting on the Somme continued, thousands of men left the battlefield with their nerves shattered. Reporting sick and being asked what had happened, most would answer, 'Shell-shock.' With some, this was clearly the case, but for the medical authorities it was not necessarily so. The official medical history writes: 'To explain to a man that his symptoms were the result of disordered emotional conditions due to his rough experience in the line, and not, as he imagined, to some serious disturbance of his nervous system produced by bursting shells, became the most frequent and successful form of psychotherapy. The simplicity of its character in no way detracted from its value, and it not infrequently ended in the man coming forward voluntarily for duty, after having been given a much needed fortnight's rest in hospital.'

Still, the genuine cases of shell shock were also growing, reaching more than 50,000 by the end of the war. It was during the Battle of the Somme that, because of the intensification of nervous breakdowns and shell-shock, special centres were opened in each army area for diagnosis and treatment. The view of the military authorities, as the official medical history emphasises, was that the subject of mental collapse was 'so bound up with the maintenance of morale in the army that every soldier who is non-effective owing to nervous breakdown must be made the subject of careful enquiry. In no case is he to be evacuated to base unless his condition warrants such a procedure.'

On August 8, British forces on the Somme launched a further attack against the village of Guillemont. The attack, planned at the last moment, lacked adequate artillery preparation. As the soldiers left their trenches, they found that the German artillery was hitting No-Man's Land with great accuracy. As they continued their advance along Death Valley they were met by intense German machine-gun fire. On the sector being fought over by the Liverpool Scottish Battalion, ten of their twenty officers, and ninety-six of their six hundred men, were killed or missing. The battalion attacked three times before being forced to fall back. That evening, in search of wounded men lying out on the battlefield, the battalion's medical officer, Captain Noel Chavasse, led a group of volunteers into No-Man's Land. 'We collected a lot of identification discs,' he wrote home, 'and so cut down the tragic missing list.' The word 'missing' meant, in virtually every case, killed without any identifiable trace being found.

Among those whom Chavasse brought back were three badly wounded men who had been lying only twenty-five yards from the German front line. Two of them died later. 'The amazing thing about this rescue exploit', one soldier recalled, 'was that he carried and used his electric torch as he walked about between the trenches, whistling and calling out to wounded men to indicate their whereabouts, and so be brought in. Ignoring the snipers' bullets and any sporadic fusillade, he carried on with his work of succour throughout the hours of darkness.' At one point the group of rescuers found themselves right up against a German trench. The Germans opened fire, and Chavasse was wounded in the thigh. For his work that night, he was awarded the Victoria Cross.

On the Eastern Front, General Brusilov was approaching the westward limit of the Russian advance, capturing the city of Stanislau (Stanislawow) in Eastern Galicia on August 7, and taking 7,000 Austrian and 3,500 German prisoners, but failing to threaten German-occupied Poland, Western Galicia or Hungary. The carnage was considerable. Florence Farmborough and her fellow Russian nurses had, on their way to the front one morning, to pass through what had been a battlefield. 'The dead were

still lying around,' she wrote in her diary, 'in strange, unnatural postures –
remaining where they had fallen: crouching, doubled up, stretched out,
prostrate, prone.... Austrians and Russians lying side by side. And there
were lacerated, crushed bodies lying on darkly-stained patches of earth.
There was one Austrian without a leg and with blackened, swollen face;
another with a smashed face, terrible to look at; a Russian soldier, with
legs doubled under him, leaning against the barbed wire. And on more
than one open wound flies were crawling and there were other moving,
thread-like things.'

Ten days later, Florence Farmborough reported 'several groups of desert-
ing men' in the vicinity of her dressing station. They were rounded up and
sent back to the trenches. Two days later a dying soldier with a severe
stomach wound begged her for water. It was known on all fronts that for
such wounds water was a grave danger. 'His eyes challenged mine; they
were dying eyes, but fiercely alight with the greatness of his thirst. I
reasoned with myself: if I give no water, he will die tormented by his great
thirst; if I give him water, he will die, but his torment will be lessened. In
my weakness and compassion, I reached for the mug; his burning eyes
were watching me; they held suspense and gratitude. I put the mug to his
lips, but he seized my arm and tilted the mug upwards. The water splashed
into his open mouth, sprayed his face and pillow, but he was swallowing
it in noisy gulps. When I could free my arm from his grasp, the mug was
empty. I was deeply distressed and knew that I was trembling. I wiped his
face dry and he opened his eyes and looked at me; in them, I saw a great
thankfulness, an immense relief. But, before I could replace the mug, a
strange, gurgling sound came from him, and, out of his mouth, there
poured a stream of thick, greenish fluid; it spread over the stretcher-bed
and flowed on to the floor. His eyes were closed ... he had stopped
breathing.'

On August 22, Brusilov's army was confronted, along a twelve-mile sector
of the front, by two divisions of Turkish troops, who a year earlier had
been fighting at Gallipoli. But still the Austrian forces were driven back.
'The officers on the active list occupy comfortable chairs in the higher Staff
appointments,' General Hoffmann, who was now controlling the battle in
Galicia, wrote in his diary on August 27. 'Besides, there are all these
different races mixed up together – no less than twenty-three distinct
languages. No one understands anyone else.'[1]

The Turks were active that August not only against the Russians in

[1] The nine main languages spoken in the Hapsburg Dominions (and recognised in the Austro-
Hungarian Army regulations), were German, Hungarian, Czech, Slovak, Slovene, Croat, Serb,
Ruthene, Italian, Polish and Roumanian. Other languages spoken by small minority groups
included Ukrainian, two types of Albanian, Yiddish (German-Jewish), Ladino (Spanish-Jewish),
Greek, Turkish, Romany, Vlach and Armenian. There were also some Lithuanian, Latvian,
Estonian and Finnish troops serving on the Eastern Front, alongside, but not part of, the Austro-
Hungarian army.

Galicia, but against the British in Sinai, renewing their attempt to reach the Suez Canal. Behind the Turkish lines, however, ten British seaplanes, flying from a carrier off the port of Haifa, bombed Turkish military stores and railway junctions at Afula, on the Haifa-Damascus railway, and at Adana, on the Berlin-Baghdad line. The Turks, not without air resources of their own, bombed Port Said, injuring nearly fifty civilians, and damaging a Royal Navy aircraft carrier.

On the Salonica Front, the line remained static along the Greek-Serbian border, despite the arrival of 5,000 Russian and 11,000 Italian troops at the beginning of August. Early that summer the Greeks, still neutral, handed over to the Bulgarians the strong Fort Rupel, commanding the deep gorge along which the River Struma led into Bulgaria. The Allies regarded this as an act of treachery. The Greeks claimed that they had already agreed with the Allies neither to help nor hinder the Central Powers. Handing over the fort was, in the Greek perspective, a neutral act. The British continued to try to win over the Greeks, on whose soil they were fighting, to a more active pro-Allied stance. To this end a stream of propaganda was deployed. A young British historian, Llewellyn Woodward, who had visited Germany several times before the war, was employed at Salonica distributing information from London to the Greek newspapers. 'I remember a disgusting sentence,' he later wrote, 'transmitted by wireless from the propaganda office: "Our men are enjoying killing Germans in the spring sunshine."'

British and French troops, in action that month on the Salonica Front, captured an abandoned wayside station and two hills. On August 17, however, a force of 18,000 Bulgarians attacked the Allied line near Florina, at the point where it was being held by Serb forces. The Bulgarian commander, a general in his seventies, had fought alongside the Prussians in 1870. 'We shall be in Salonica in a week,' was the Bulgarian boast, and in Athens there were visions of a triumphal German entry into the capital itself. The Bulgarians captured Florina on the second day of their offensive, securing a small Bulgarian toe-hold in northern Greece. But further Bulgarian advances were driven back, Serb reinforcements being brought to the front on British lorries. On the eastern flank of the front, where a year earlier Bulgaria had occupied a fifty-mile-deep wedge of the Greek region of Thrace, the Royal Navy monitor *Picton* shelled Bulgarian positions near Kavalla, while British aircraft bombed Bulgarian-controlled railway bridges near the inland town of Drama.

On the Italian Front, the Italians had launched their sixth offensive on the Isonzo Front on August 4, driving the Austrians back, capturing several mountain peaks, and entering their objective, the town of Gorizia. Among the Italian soldiers prominent in this offensive was Colonel Badoglio, Chief of Staff of an army corps, who on one occasion led six battalions into action.[1] When the offensive was called off two weeks later, the Italians had

---

[1] At the end of the battle Badoglio was promoted to Major-General, at the age of forty-four. In

gained between three and four miles along a fifteen-mile front, and had taken nearly 50,000 Austrians prisoner, but the cost of this success had been extremely high. As many as 20,000 Italian soldiers had been killed and a further 30,000 wounded.

On the Caucasus Front, Russian troops suffered a setback on August 6, when Turkish forces commanded by Brigadier-General Mustafa Kemal retook the eastern Anatolian towns of Bitlis and Mus. This ended all prospect of a Russian-sponsored Greater Armenia.

In German East Africa, the British, Belgians and South Africans made only slow advances on the periphery, a high point being a successful Royal Naval attack on Dar es Salaam. The German forces, unwilling to give up their remarkable operations, despite having lost two-thirds of the territory, continued to inflict defeats on both the Belgians and the South Africans, leading General Smuts to inform his wife: 'We are having a terribly hard time.' In two months he was to lose 33,500 of his pack animals on whom he was dependent for moving supplies across country.

At sea, German submarines continued to wreak havoc among the merchant ships which carried Allied war and food supplies. A single submarine, the *U-35*, during a 25-day tour of duty in the Mediterranean, sank, mostly by shellfire, a total of fifty-four merchant ships, including thirty-two Italian ships carrying 50,000 tons of coal. The death toll in naval disasters continued to be high: when, early that August, Austrian saboteurs entered Taranto harbour and blew up the Italian battleship *Leonardo da Vinci*, 248 Italian sailors were killed. But the war at sea did not always favour the Central Powers: during an attack on a Russian naval patrol in the Gulf of Finland three months later, seven German destroyers were sunk in a minefield off Reval in one night, and more than a thousand sailors drowned.

The war at sea was in many ways the forgotten war. The fighting sailors and the merchant seamen were in daily danger. One of their chroniclers, E. Hilton Young, wrote of the mine-sweeping trawlers, whose crews were also virtually unsung warriors:

> *We sift the drifting sea,*
> *   and blindly grope beneath;*
> *obscure and toilsome we,*
> *   the fishermen of death.*

Every Allied warship, and every Allied and neutral merchant ship that plied its way across the Atlantic or through the Mediterranean with war supplies or food was vulnerable to German submarine attack. During four years of war more than 2,000 British naval and merchant vessels were sunk, and more than 12,000 sailors and merchant seamen drowned. The

1936 he led the Italian forces in the conquest of Abyssinia. In September 1943 he formed an anti-Fascist government in Italy and negotiated an armistice with the Allies. In April 1944 his Government declared war on Germany.

number of German submarines that were destroyed by Allied action was also considerable, more than two hundred, with the loss of 515 German naval officers and 4,849 men. By the scale of the battles on the Eastern and Western Fronts these losses were small, but for those who fought at sea, or sailed the seas, they were the high cost of a dangerous war.

On the Somme, attrition rather than breakthrough had become the grim pattern of fighting for the Anglo-French armies. It was a war of woods, copses, valleys, ravines and villages taken and lost, then retaken and lost again. On August 17 the British poet and painter Isaac Rosenberg wrote to a friend: 'We are kept pretty busy now, and the climate here is really unhealthy; the doctors themselves can't stand it. We had an exciting time today, and though this is behind the firing line and right out of the trenches there were quite a good many sent to heaven and the hospital. I carried one myself in a handcart to the hospital (which often is the antechamber to heaven).'

On August 18, German troops counter-attacked from their positions in Leuze Wood. The war correspondent Philip Gibbs saw them advance towards the British trenches, 'shoulder to shoulder, like a solid bar'. It was 'sheer suicide', he wrote. 'I saw our men get their machine-guns into action, and the right side of the living bar frittered away, and then the whole line fell into the scorched grass. Another line followed. They were tall men, and did not falter as they came forward, but it seemed to me they walked like men conscious of going to death. They died. The simile is outworn, but it was exactly as though some invisible scythe had mown them down.'

Gibbs noted that in all the letters written by German soldiers during those weeks of fighting 'and captured by us from dead or living men, there was one cry of agony and horror'. 'I stood on the brink of the most terrible days of my life,' wrote one of them. 'They were those of the battle of the Somme, it began with a night attack on August 13 to 14. The attack lasted till the evening of the 18th, when the English wrote on our bodies in letters of blood: "It is all over with you". A handful of half-mad, wretched creatures, worn out in body and mind, were all that was left of the whole battalion. We were that handful.'

The losses of many of the German battalions were, Gibbs wrote, 'staggering, but not greater than our own, and by the middle of August the morale of the troops was severely shaken.'

At an army barracks at Warley, in Essex, a Court Martial took place on August 18, not of a soldier charged with desertion but of a pacifist charged with refusing to agree to any form of military or non-combatant service. This was the 26-year-old Clifford Allen, the President of the No-Conscription Fellowship, who told the officers trying him: 'I believe in the inherent worth and sanctity of every human personality, irrespective of the nation to which a man belongs.' He was sentenced to three months' hard labour, then released for a few hours, court-martialled, and sentenced again, for longer periods each time.

In the third week of August, the Australians were in action beyond Pozières. 'When you get this, I'll be dead; don't worry,' a former bank clerk, Sergeant D.G.J. Badger, wrote to his parents before the attack. He was killed on August 21. Three days later Lieutenant Bert Crowle, who had been wounded on the 21st, wrote to his wife and son: 'Just a line you must be prepared for the worst to happen any day. It is no use trying to hide things. I am in terrible agony. Had I been brought in at once I had a hope. Now gas gangrene has set in and it is so bad that the doctor could not save it by taking it off as it had gone too far and the only hope is that the salts they have put on may drain the gangrene out otherwise there is no hope.'

Crowle had been brought back more than four miles by the stretcher bearers, starting the journey across open ground in front of the German trenches. One stretcher bearer walked in front, waving a Red Cross flag. As often happened in such instances, the Germans did not open fire. Crowle told his wife this, then continued: 'The pain is getting worse. I am very sorry dear, but still you will be well provided for I am easy on that score. So cheer up dear I could write a lot but I am nearly unconscious. Give my love to dear Bill and yourself, do take care of yourself and him. Your loving husband Bert.' A few hours later Lieutenant Crowle was dead.

15

War on every front

A new war front was about to open. Since July 1914, Roumania had tenaciously preserved its neutrality, while allowing German and Austrian military supplies and personnel to pass through her territory on their way to sustain the Turkish war effort against the Allies. On 18 August 1916 the Roumanian Government decide to take advantage of what it hoped would be the continuing Russian success against Austria. That day a secret treaty was signed between the Allies and Roumania, whereby Roumania would acquire three long-sought-after pieces of territory: the Austro-Hungarian province of Transylvania up to the river Theiss, the province of Bukovina up to the river Pruth, and the Banat region in its entirety.

Nine days later, on August 27, a new war zone opened: Roumania, its dreams of expansion now gratified, at least on paper, declared war on Austria. That day Roumanian troops crossed the Austro-Hungarian border into Transylvania. King Ferdinand, a German by blood, told the Roumanian Crown Council that day: 'Then I have conquered the Hohenzollern who was in me, I fear no one.'

Another Hohenzollern, the German Kaiser, momentarily panicked as Roumanian troops advanced into the heartland of the Hapsburg Empire, telling those closest to him: 'The war is lost.' The Central Powers were confronted by Russia's continuing advance in the east, by daily British pressure on the Somme, and by Roumania's belligerency. On August 28, in an attempt to strengthen Germany's warmaking capacities, the Kaiser replaced his Chief of the General Staff, General Falkenhayn, by Field Marshal Hindenburg. Appointed as Hindenburg's deputy, Ludendorff was given a new and impressive-sounding title, that of First Quartermaster-General.

Hindenburg and Ludendorff were summoned to the Kaiser on August 29 to learn of their elevation. They urged him to begin unrestricted submarine warfare without delay, irrespective of the effect that it might have on the United States or the Scandinavian countries. That same day, Hindenburg also wrote to the Minister of War insisting that munitions production must be doubled, and artillery and machine-gun production trebled, by the spring of 1917.

Within two weeks, with the creation of a Supreme War Command, Hindenburg obtained effective command of all the armies of the Central Powers. This was agreed at a conference with the Kaiser at which the Turkish War Minister, Enver Pasha, and the Bulgarian Tsar Ferdinand were present. To strengthen the Salonica Front, Enver had already sent a Turkish Division, 12,000 strong, to take over the Drama-Kavalla sector of the Bulgarian line. German troops were also serving on the Salonica Front: in an attempt to seize a small village held by the Germans, British troops captured seventy German soldiers.

The Central Powers, despite the many war zones in which they were engaged, and despite the bloodletting on the Somme, remained in the ascendant. The Kaiser's panic had been unnecessary. Roumania's advances in Transylvania against the Austrians, advances which might have greatly assisted the Russian forces in the Carpathians, were short-lived. On September 1 the Bulgarians declared war on their Balkan neighbour and prepared to join the German army gathering to attack across the Danube from the south. The former Chief of the Army Staff, General Falkenhayn, was given command of the main army attacking from the north, with help on his flank from the Austrians. Roumania was geographically vulnerable to such a two-pronged attack.

On September 3, the first troops of the Central Powers moved against Roumania in the south. As they advanced, Bulgarian aircraft bombed Bucharest. The Roumanians had appealed to London and Paris for help. In an attempt to take pressure off the Roumanian Front, the French and British launched a new offensive on the Somme on the very day of the Central Power attack. The village of Guillemont, so long an objective of the British forces, was captured, but High Wood, and the Schwaben Redoubt, two much-fought-over features of the desolate battlefield, remained in German hands. On the banks of the river, the villages of Cléry and Omiecourt fell to the French.

Fighting continued throughout September 4. Among the officers in action that day was a leading Irish nationalist, the 36-year-old Tom Kettle, a Professor of National Economics in Dublin, and former Member of Parliament, who had joined the British army on the outbreak of war. He had done so, he wrote, to fight 'not for England, but for small nations': that is, for Belgium. In a letter to his brother on September 4 he wrote: 'I am calm and happy, but desperately anxious to live. If I live I mean to spend the rest of my life working for perpetual peace. I have seen war, and faced modern artillery, and know what an outrage it is against simple men.' A few weeks earlier Kettle had written to his wife: 'I want to live, too, to use all my powers of thinking and working, to drive out this foul thing called War and to put in its place understanding and comradeship.'

On September 5, on the Somme, the British captured Leuze Wood, three miles east of the July 1 front line. In a further attack that day, Irish troops captured the village of Ginchy. On going up to the line, the stench of the dead in the communication trenches had been so strong that some of them used foot powder on their faces. Before the attack the officers were given pieces of green cloth to be stitched on the back of their uniforms, a symbol of Irish patriotism. Touching his patch, Tom Kettle told his soldier servant: 'Boy, I am proud to die for it!' Leading his men into the village that day, Kettle was killed. His soldier servant, in a letter of condolence to Kettle's wife, wrote: 'He carried his pack for Ireland and Europe. Now pack-carrying is over. He has held the line.'

One of those who was near Kettle when he was killed later wrote: 'I was just behind Tom when we went over the top. He was in a bent position and a bullet got over a steel waistcoat that he wore and entered his heart. Well, he only lasted about one minute, and he had my crucifix in his hand. Then Boyd took all the papers and things out of Tom's pockets in order to keep them for Mrs Kettle, but poor Boyd was blown to atoms in a few minutes.'

Four days before his death Kettle had written a poem to his daughter, for that future time when she might ask why her father had 'abandoned' her to go to 'dice with death':

> *And oh! they'll give you rhyme*
> *And reason: some will call the thing sublime,*
> *And some decry it in a knowing tone.*
> *So here, while the mad guns curse overhead,*
> *And tired men sigh with mud for couch and floor,*
> *Know that we fools, now with the foolish dead,*
> *Died not for flag, nor King, nor Emperor,*
> *But for a dream, born in a herdsman's shed,*
> *And for the secret Scripture of the poor.*

Had Kettle survived the attack of September 5, he would have taken up the post of Base Censor, away from the daily dangers of the front line, and the assault. In his last letter to his brother he had written: 'Somewhere the Choosers of the Slain are touching, as in our Norse story they used to touch, with invisible wands those who are to die.'

On the French sector on September 4, the village of Bouchavesnes, more than four miles from the July 1 starting point, was captured. At Verdun, however, where the French had succeeded in holding the inner ring of forts, more than five hundred French soldiers were killed that evening when the Tavannes railway tunnel, being used for the accommodation of troops, blew up. The disaster was an accident, caused by fire breaking out in an ammunition store. One of the few eye-witnesses later described how, after the explosions, 'a shattered body flew into me, or rather poured over me. I saw, three metres away, men twisting in the flames without being able to render them any help. Legs, arms, flew in the air amid the explosion of the grenades which went off without cease.' Those men who managed to reach the exit of the tunnel were caught in a German bombardment, and several killed. Among the dead inside the tunnel was a brigade commander and his staff, and almost the whole of two companies of territorials. The fire burned for three days. When finally men could enter it, they found only the dead.

The French were preparing to counter-attack at Verdun. The disaster in the Tavannes Tunnel could not deter them from that. On the Somme, the battle seemed to be coming to a close. 'It is nice to think that our heavy fighting is coming to an end,' Noel Chavasse wrote home on September 7. 'The Huns are beaten to a frazzle in front of us. We are feeling top dogs. There is nothing like the losses we had at first.'

After Roumania's initial successes in crossing into Hungary, the new Roumanian war zone became the scene of a swift German advance. On September 5, in an attack on the Danube fortress of Tutracaia, General Mackensen captured 25,000 Roumanian soldiers and 115 heavy guns. On the Eastern Front, where the Russians had continued to advance, taking tens of thousands more Austrian prisoners, the Russian General Staff were warned by General Averyanov on September 11: 'We are close to complete exhaustion of the manpower reserves.' The Brusilov offensive was nearing its end. On the Somme, a new offensive was in preparation. 'The flies are again a terrible plague,' Harold Macmillan wrote to his mother from his front-line dug-out, 'and the stench from the dead bodies which lie in heaps around is awful.' Paul Maze, going into trenches with a roll of maps tied in a red band, heard a soldier call out: 'For God's sake let him pass, it's a bloke with the Peace Treaty.' Returning from the trenches one evening, he 'came past a quarry where a heavy bombardment with gas shells had caught the day casualties lying out in rows ready for transportation at night. The shouts and groans of the men made me give a hand in helping get them away from the gas area.' As a result, he too was affected by the gas.

On September 12, General Sarrail opened the first offensive on the Salonica Front. French, Russian, Serb, British and Italian troops took part in it. In the foothills the advance was successful, but reaching the higher mountains it came to a halt. The Serbs briefly recovered a few hundred yards of Serbian soil, but were then driven back. The French, too, were in difficulties, their actual position in no way made easier by Sarrail's barrage of telegrams: 'Press forward with all your forces.' 'Go forward on your flank, I count on it.' 'March ahead. March ahead. March ahead.'

Another area of continual offensive action by the Entente was the Italian Front. On September 14 the Italians launched their seventh offensive on the Isonzo river. Once again, several mountain peaks, including the 7,723-foot Mount Cardinal, were captured. Once again, the Austrians held the line.

On the Somme, a potentially dramatic turn in the Entente fortunes took place on September 15, when tanks were used for the first time in battle. Forty-nine tanks took part in the attack, moving forward on a wide front. Ten of the tanks were hit by German artillery fire, nine broke down with mechanical difficulties, and five failed to advance. But those that did manage to go forward were able to advance more than 2,000 yards, capturing the long-sought High Wood, and three villages, Flers, Martinpuich and Courcelette. Churchill wrote to Admiral Fisher, both of them then out of office and out of power: 'My poor "land battleships" have been let off prematurely and on a petty scale. In that idea resided one real victory.' Recognising the potential of the new weapon, Haig asked the War Office for a thousand of them. The Germans were far behind in their tank experiments.

Among the troops taking advantage of the tank during their own advance was the Guards Division. During the division's move forward that day, those killed included Raymond Asquith, the Prime Minister's son, shot through the chest as he led his men forward. In order that his men should not know that he was mortally wounded, he lit a cigarette after he fell. He died on the stretcher while being taken to a Dressing Station.

A future Prime Minister, Harold Macmillan, who was also serving with the Guards, was badly wounded on September 15. He survived throughout the morning in No-Man's Land, in a shell-hole which was twice blown in on top of him by German shells exploding a few yards off. At first he read from a pocket edition of Aeschylus's *Prometheus*, in Greek; then, as afternoon drew on, 'I took 1/2 grain morphia,' he wrote to his mother, 'and succeeded in sleeping till 3.30 p.m.,' when a sergeant-major, reaching him in the bottom of the shell-hole, asked, as if on the parade ground, 'Thank you, sir, for leave to carry you away.' Making his own way back, after a while, to the field hospital, Macmillan was caught by a sudden and severe bout of shelling. 'Then I was very frightened,' he wrote. First at hospital in Abbeville, then in England, surgeons decided that it would be too risky to try to remove the bullet fragments in his pelvis: this gave him, for the rest of his life, a shuffling walk. He remained on crutches, with a tube in the wound, until the end of the war.

During the day on which he was wounded, Macmillan recalled seeing a tank, one of 'these strange objects', bogged down in a shell-hole. The ungainly vehicle was quickly to prove its worth, even when used in small numbers, for eleven days after its first use a British attack with thirteen tanks captured the village of Thiepval, which had held out since the first day of the Somme offensive. That same day, Combles fell to an infantry attack supported by two tanks, while at Guéudecourt, where the tanks went forward assisted by air reconnaissance, five hundred Germans were taken prisoner for only five British casualties.

On September 16 the Canadians were sent forward into the line. When they attacked at three o'clock that afternoon, Private John Chipman Kerr led a charge that was to enter the annals of Canadian military history. As Lieutenant-Colonel G.R. Stevens, chronicler of the military service of soldiers from Edmonton, has written: 'Although his finger had been blown off he sprang from shelter and raced along the top of the trench, shooting down the enemy bombers from traverse to traverse. His astonishing onslaught proved the last straw for the badly-shaken Germans and sixty-two unwounded prisoners surrendered. Having delivered his captives at a support trench, Kerr returned to action without troubling to have his wound dressed.' For this episode, Kerr was awarded the Victoria Cross. He was one of fourteen volunteers from a single family. In order to enlist, he and his brother had walked fifty miles in midwinter from their remote farmstead to the nearest railhead.

Forty-two Canadians had been killed in the attack on September 16. Among those killed on the Somme six days later was a nineteen-year-old British soldier, E.W. Tennant. Having left school at the age of seventeen in order to enlist, he had been in the trenches since shortly after his eighteenth birthday. His poem 'The Mad Soldier' opened with the lines:

> I dropp'd here three weeks ago, yes – I know,
> And it's bitter cold at night, since the fight –
> I could tell you if I chose – no one knows
> Excep' me and four or five, what ain't alive.
> I can see them all asleep, three men deep,
> And they're nowhere near a fire – but our wire
> Has 'em fast as can be. Can't you see
> When the flare goes up? Ssh! boys; what's that noise?
> Do you know what these rats eat? Body-meat!

Not the Somme, but Roumania, became the main focus of military endeavour for the new German High Command that month. On September 15, Hindenburg issued the order: 'The main task of the Armies is now to hold fast all positions on the Western, Eastern, Italian and Macedonian Fronts, and to employ all other available forces against Roumania.' Not only military manpower, but civilian labour was to be conscripted into the German war effort: a newly devised Hindenburg Industrial Programme involved the recruitment of German labourers and the forcible deportation of 700,000 Belgian workers, to be transported to Germany. On September 16 the German-Jewish industrialist Walther Rathenau, who had been urging European reconciliation and the mitigation of hatred, wrote a public letter to Ludendorff supporting the Belgian deportations. Among those who protested was Cardinal Farley of New York, who declared: 'You have to go back to the times of the Medes and the Persians to find a like example of a whole people carried into bondage.'

President Wilson, reflecting American indignation at the Belgian deportations, instructed his Ambassador in Berlin, James W. Gerard, to raise the matter with the German Chancellor. 'There are Belgians employed in making shells, contrary to the rules of war and The Hague Conventions,'

Gerard told him. 'I do not believe it,' the Chancellor replied. 'My auto-mobile is at the door' was Gerard's riposte. 'I can take you in four minutes to where thirty Belgians are working on the manufacture of shells.' The Chancellor declined this invitation for a drive.

On September 16, on the Eastern Front, the recently arrived Turkish troops beat off a Russian gas attack. On the Western Front that day, while visiting Cambrai, Hindenburg gave orders for a 'semi-permanent' defence line to be constructed five to thirty miles behind the front: the Hindenburg Line, a deep fortified zone that would halt any Allied military breakthrough before it could approach the Belgian or German frontier. Among those killed that day on the Western Front was Dillwyn Parrish Starr, a 32-year-old American lieutenant in a British Guards regiment. Born in Philadelphia and educated at Harvard, Starr had volunteered in 1914 as an ambulance driver with the French, served with the British armoured cars at Gallipoli, and then transferred to the Guards, with whom he went to the Somme. Starr was one of 32,000 Americans who had circumvented the British army regulations that listed, among the categories of those 'not to be allowed to enlist or re-enlist under any circumstances', the category: '(vi) A foreigner'.

Among the thousands of soldiers ordered into action on September 16 was Private Henry Farr, but he refused to go forward to the front line trenches. 'I cannot stand it,' he said. He was then dragged forward scream-ing and struggling, but broke away and ran back. He had only recently been released from hospital after treatment for shell-shock, having been at the front since 1914. Court-martialled for cowardice, he was executed.[1]

On the Salonica Front, French and Russian troops recaptured Florina from the Bulgarians on September 17, although the Serbs, having taken the 7,769-foot Mount Kajmakcalan on the following day, were driven off it. They finally captured the mountain's two peaks, which lay just inside the Serbian border, two weeks later.

Behind the Turkish lines on September 17, German aircraft shot down two British seaplanes attacking the Turkish base at El Arish, but then withdrew sixty miles eastward across the desert to Beersheba. As Hind-enburg wished, the main thrust of the Central Powers was against the new belligerent, Roumania.

On September 26 Falkenhayn's army crossed the 11,555-foot Rotenturm Pass into Transylvania, capturing the city of Hermannstadt and taking 3,000 Roumanian prisoners. Only a month after the Roumanian decision to enter the war, her leaders' hopes of expanding into Hungary had

---

[1] Private Farr's granddaughter, Janet Booth, hoped that a Private Member's Bill introduced by Andrew Mackinlay into the House of Commons on 19 October 1993, on behalf of all those executed for cowardice and desertion in the First World War, would lead to a posthumous pardon, but the bill was unsuccessful.

been dashed. On October 1 the Germans reached Petrosani, driving the Roumanians back to the frontier. Further east, they were driven out of the city of Kronstadt a week later, then back through the Transylvanian Alps to the Roumanian border, then, on October 13, through the Torzburg Pass to the town of Rucar, six miles inside Roumania.

From mid-October, the fate of Roumania hung in the balance. On October 19, Mackensen's army broke through the Dobrudja defence lines, and three days later entered the port city of Constanta, capturing large quantities of oil and grain. On the Transylvanian Front, a month later, Lieutenant Rommel won distinction during the capture of the 3,937-foot Mount Lesculiu.

In the war against Britain, the Germans were gaining in confidence, despite the risks. On September 2, sixteen German naval and army airships set off in a joint-attack over eastern England. It was the largest raid ever mounted. Ten of the airships succeeded in crossing the North Sea, reaching London shortly before midnight. One of them, having dropped its bombs, was chased by several aircraft and forced to weave its way through a fierce anti-aircraft artillery barrage, before being shot down by Lieutenant Robinson over Cuffley, in Hertfordshire. It was the first victim of a new incendiary bullet. It fell to the ground in flames, its destruction seen by thousands of people who gathered on roofs and in the streets to watch it.

So bright was the glow of the burning airship that it was seen as far away as Reigate, thirty-five miles to the south. 'This was the moment that so many Londoners had waited to see for so long', writes the historian of the Zeppelins, R.L. Rimell, 'and they made the most of it. Complete pandemonium broke out as people rushed out on the streets. Singing, clapping and cheering seemed to go on and on echoing over the rooftops. Many groups patriotically launched into "God Save the King", while children and women danced in the streets. Railway engine whistles and factory hooters added to the cacophony of delirium. Excited parents held toddlers up to the windows to witness the event, and for many it would be a lasting impression even over sixty years later.'

Rimell added: 'Just no one could tear his eyes from the blazing hulk as it hung motionless, for several seconds, 11,500-feet up, before finally sinking nose-down in a shallow dive. An acrid smell of burnt fabric and wood was reported to have remained in the air long after the awesome wreck had vanished from view.' Among thousands of eyewitnesses was 10-year-old Henry Tuttle. 'We opened the front door and there it was', he later recalled. 'It was a fantastic sight like a big silver cigar and it seemed to be going very slow by this time. A lot of people came out of their houses and then all of a sudden flames started to come from the Zeppelin[1] and then it broke in half and was one mass of flames. It was an incredible

---

[1] Technically, Robinson's victim (SL 11) was not a Zeppelin but a Schütte Lanz, a similar dirigible, designed and built by a different manufacturer.

sight: people were cheering, dancing, singing and somebody started playing the bagpipes. This went on well into the night. The Italian in our house was walking in the centre of the road shouting at the sky in Italian and waving a big boot knife. All the children (and I was one of them) marched up and down with him, cheering like merry hell. What a sight, which I shall never forget. We were told afterwards, at school, that the "Zepp" was shot down by Lt Robinson, RFC.'

When, at the moment of his triumph, Lieutenant William Leefe Robinson, Royal Flying Corps, had fired green and red cartridge flares to signal his success, the vast crowd that was watching the airship's destruction realised what the flares were and had given a mighty cheer. Robinson was awarded the Victoria Cross for his exploit, the only Victoria Cross to be awarded for an exploit on (or above) British soil. There was a certain bitterness among the pilots on the Western Front. 'I would rather attack one of those gas bags than a couple of fighting Huns any day,' was one pilot's comment. But Robinson's feat, a triumph in itself, was also a boost for national morale. When he received his Victoria Cross from King George V at Windsor Castle, an enormous crowd was there to greet and cheer him.

In the forty eight hours after the airship had been brought down, 10,000 people went by train from King's Cross to visit the scene and search for souvenirs. Inside the local church, the bodies of the sixteen crewmen were placed in coffins. A girl who peered through the keyhole saw several policemen playing 'ball' with their helmets over the coffins. The military funeral a few days later, at Potters Bar cemetery, at which buglers of the Grenadier Guards sounded 'The Last Post' in honour of the dead airmen, caused some distress to a public shocked by the loss of life caused during the raid, during which 371 bombs had been dropped and four civilians killed.

Leefe Robinson became a British hero for his exploit on September 2. Two weeks later a German hero, Baron Manfred von Richthofen, entered the legends of the war, when he shot down his first plane over the Western Front. Richthofen, who had already been in action bombing Russian military formations and railway junctions on the Eastern Front, found himself in aerial combat with a British pilot, Second Lieutenant Lionel Morris, and his observer, Lieutenant T. Rees. 'My Englishman twisted and turned, flying in zig-zags', Richthofen wrote immediately after the combat. 'I was animated by a single thought: "The man in front of me must come down, whatever happens." At last a favourable moment arrived. My opponent had apparently lost sight of me. Instead of twisting and turning he flew straight along. In a fraction of a second I was at his back with my excellent machine. I gave a short burst of shots with my machine-gun. I had gone so close that I was afraid I might dash into the Englishman. Suddenly I nearly yelled with joy, for the propeller of the enemy machine had stopped turning. Hurrah! I had shot his engine to pieces; the enemy was compelled to land, for it was impossible for him to reach his own lines.'

Richthofen watched as his adversary descended from the sky. 'The English machine was swinging curiously to and fro. Probably something had happened to the pilot. The observer was no longer visible. His machine-gun was apparently deserted. Obviously I had hit the observer, and he had fallen from his seat. The Englishman landed close to the flying ground of one of our squadrons. I was so excited that I landed also, and my eagerness was so great that I nearly smashed up my machine. The English flying machine and my own stood close together. I rushed to the English machine and saw that a lot of soldiers were running towards my enemy. When I arrived I discovered that my assumption had been correct. I had shot the engine to pieces, and both the pilot and observer were severely wounded. The observer died at once, and the pilot while being transported to the nearest dressing station. I honoured the fallen enemy by placing a stone on his beautiful grave.'

After the Zeppelin raid of September 2, Londoners in the vulnerable East End of the capital took the underground trains each evening to seek the greater safety of the West End.[1] On October 1, seven Zeppelins dropped more than two hundred bombs on Britain. One of the Zeppelins was shot down at Potters Bar by a Royal Flying Corps pilot, Lieutenant W.J. Tempest, and all nineteen of its crewmen were killed.

At sea, the German submarines continued their depredations. On September 22 the main German news agency reported: 'One of our U-boats hit in the Mediterranean on 17 September a packed enemy troopship. This ship sank within forty-three seconds.'[2] On October 1, the Kaiser congratulated his submarine service on the sinking of one million tons of Allied shipping, much of it British. A week later the first German submarine attack on the eastern seaboard of the United States, by U-53, led to the sinking of five merchant ships, three British, one Dutch and one Norwegian, off Nantucket Island. The American Ambassador in Berlin was even then on board ship on his way back to New York, steaming in the very vicinity of the sinkings. 'I imagined that the captain slightly changed the course of our ship,' he later wrote, 'but the next day the odour of burning oil was quite noticeable for hours.' A few days later, in a four-hour talk, President Wilson told Gerard that he wanted 'both to keep and to make peace'.

In the distant Mediterranean, the war of torpedo against liner continued. On October 4 a German submarine struck twice, each time with success,

[1] My mother, who was then five years old, recalls travelling on the underground with her mother and two sisters to escape the bombardment. It was not until 1940, however, that her mother's Whitechapel home was damaged by German bombs.
[2] This news item was reprinted in a satirical broadsheet by Karl Kraus, a Viennese who opposed the war, and who gave it the headline: 'With watch in hand.' Twenty-two British lives were lost that September as a result of German submarine sinkings in the North Sea and the Mediterranean.

sinking first the Cunard liner *Franconia*, on which twelve died, and then the French troop transport *Gallia*, on which six hundred men were drowned.

On the Salonica Front, malaria was reducing the fighting abilities of the British troops, three hundred of whom died of the disease in one month. On October 14, despite the use of gas shells, a major Allied offensive against the Bulgarian lines was unable to capture even the first line of trenches. At sea, German submarine sinkings were continuous: on October 28 the British liner *Marina* was torpedoed without warning off the Fastnet Rock. Eighteen passengers were drowned, among them six Americans. A United States steamer, the *Lanao*, was also sunk by a German submarine that day, off Portugal. Many observers wondered how long it would be before these sinkings forced the United States to declare war on Germany. Two days earlier President Wilson had told the Cincinnati Chamber of Commerce: 'I believe that the business of neutrality is over. The nature of modern war leaves no State untouched.'

On the Somme, the British were still trying to reach their first day's objective. But rain and mud were impeding every effort. On October 2 the recently captured village of Le Sars was lost to a German counter-attack. The official British historian, General Edmonds, commented: 'Rain fell in torrents, and the battle area became a sea of mud. Men died from the effort of carrying verbal messages.' Le Sars was recaptured five days later. On that day, a British platoon sergeant, Leslie Coulson, who had earlier fought at Gallipoli and been wounded, was killed in action. Earlier in the battle he had written, in his poem 'From the Somme':

> *I played with all the toys the gods provide,*
>   *I sang my songs and made glad holiday.*
> *Now I have cast my broken toys aside*
>   *And flung my lute away.*
>
> *A singer once, I now am fain to weep.*
>   *Within my soul I feel strange music swell,*
> *Vast chants of tragedy too deep – too deep*
>   *For my poor lips to tell.*

On October 11, four days after Leslie Coulson's death, a Canadian private, Earl Hembroff, who was serving with the Canadian Field Ambulance, described in his diary a trench being used as part of an Advance Dressing Station to which the wounded were being brought. It had been the scene of a desperate struggle not long before. 'Dead lying all over, especially in pieces as shells persist in bringing them to the surface. Bodies in chamber all blackened from smoke bomb. One Tommy with arms around Boche as in a deadly struggle.' Preachers buried the dead at night. The troops were exhausted 'and some of the biggest cried like babies'.

*

That day, a British visitor, Viscountess D'Abernon, reached the town of Albert, writing in her diary: 'I left Paris full of eagerness and excitement to see the British Front, where, up to the present, no women visitors had been allowed.' Looking over the battlefield with her military escort, General Davidson, 'we saw the whole Pozières-Thiepval horizon come under a barrage of German fire'. For more than an hour she watched the bombardment. 'Several of our aeroplanes came over, making for hangars, many miles behind, and tales were told of gallant deeds and especially of the prowess of a young fellow, named Albert Ball, who has just brought down his thirtieth Boche aeroplane, is aged nineteen, and lives to tell the tale.[1] We stood for a long while riveted by the strange Satanic scene – but, at last, it was a relief to turn away. The ground which we were treading, the shell-holes we avoided, are broken patches of the battlefield of only a short month ago. It was here and then that Raymond Asquith's brilliant promise was extinguished and my dear nephew, Charles Feversham, was killed, and on the grey horizon beyond Albert there are, at this moment, thousands of fellow-countrymen, their trenches the playground for shells bursting so thickly and continuously that General Davidson thought they must herald an impending attack. The scene had a Lucifer, Prince of Darkness kind of splendour, but uppermost in my mind was a sense of the wickedness and waste of life, the lack of any definite objective commensurate with all this destruction, desolation and human suffering.'

Lady D'Abernon visited a Casualty Clearing Station. 'The beds are very small,' she wrote, 'and have only one regulation blanket on the top of the coarsest of unbleached sheets. In the officers' tent the only difference made (but religiously observed) is that a coloured cotton quilt instead of a white one covers the regulation blanket. Except for this mark of somewhat chilly, comfortless distinction, everything is identical. In the officers' tent the faces were, almost without exception the faces of mere boys. Special tents are set apart for abdominal wounds, for chest wounds, for eyes, for gas-gangrene, etc., and of course separate tents for the Boches. Amongst these one lonely figure, still on a forgotten stretcher, was lying with his face turned to the wall. Unlike others he did not speak nor even look round as we passed through, and remains in memory a lonely pathetic figure.'

On October 12, on the Somme, Newfoundland soldiers were in action at Guéudecourt. The British were experimenting with a creeping barrage, whereby the men advanced behind a curtain of explosions designed to pulverise the German wire and to stun the German soldiers. More than one in ten of the attackers was killed as they moved forward too quickly, or as shells fell short. Among the Newfoundlanders was Lance-Corporal Raymond Goodyear. It was his first battle. As he ran forward he seemed

[1] Ball was killed in action on 7 May 1917. He was awarded a posthumous Victoria Cross for his conspicuous bravery during the previous eleven days.

to stumble and fall: his captain turned to help him up, then saw that Goodyear had been hit by a shell-burst just below the waist. The historian of the Goodyear family, David Macfarlane, writes: 'For a moment his round, blackened face looked puzzled beneath his oversized tin hat. He didn't seem to realise what had happened. He'd been ripped open as if he'd run into the full swing of an axe.'

Even as winter approached, the generals tried to find a balance between what could be done, and what they felt ought to be done. 'The bad weather which has forced us to slow down', General Rawlinson wrote in his diary on October 14, 'has given the Boche a breather. His artillery is better organised, and his infantry is fighting with greater tenacity, but deserters continue to come in; and, the more we bombard, the more prisoners and deserters we shall get. I should like therefore to be more or less aggressive all the winter, but we must not take the edge off next year.' A week later, on the Somme, the British captured a thousand German prisoners.

At Verdun, on October 24, the French took their first offensive action of the year, recapturing Fort Douaumont and taking 6,000 German prisoners. On the Italian Front the Italians launched the eighth battle of the Isonzo, capturing more than 5,000 Austrian soldiers, and in the Trentino regained the northern slopes of Mount Pasubio. But the Russian offensive had reached its limit, and ended that October, when nearly 200,000 Russian workers were involved in an estimated 177 political strikes. Whether any further Russian military initiative might be possible was cast in doubt that month, when the Tsar was warned by General Alexeyev that there were only sufficient reserve troops for a further five months' fighting. At the end of the month a Russian army censorship bureau reported that soldiers were saying: 'After the war we'll have to settle accounts with the internal enemy.'[1]

Inside Austria, through Karl Kraus's satirical broadsheet *Fackel,* anti-war opinions were circulated even to the troops. One of those who contributed to the broadsheet, Wittgenstein's friend Paul Engelmann, was convalescing from illness in the town of Olmütz. While lying sick in bed he saw a group of Czech soldiers being taken into the Church of St Maurice, opposite his house, for Mass, as was the custom before being sent to the front. Leaving his sick bed, Engelmann went into the church and addressed the men, urging them in the name of the Holy Spirit not to fight. A historian of this episode comments: 'This, naturally, he did in German and it is unlikely that the Czech troops understood it. In a kindly way the officer in charge simply told Engelmann to be off and took no further action. Engelmann, back in bed, was greatly relieved.'[2]

Wittgenstein visited Engelmann in Olmütz and expressed his pessimism

[1] On the last day of October 1916, Russian losses were estimated at 4,670,000 killed and wounded, more than 1,000,000 missing, and 2,078,000 taken prisoner-of-war.
[2] Brian McGuinness, *Wittgenstein, A Life*, Duckworth, London 1988, page 248.

about the outcome of the war as far as Austria-Hungary was concerned. He nevertheless made the Austrian Treasury a gift of a million crowns, his private income over three years, for the purchase of a 12-inch howitzer, one of the more formidable Austrian artillery pieces. Equally patriotic, on the Russian side of the line, was a young cavalryman, Georgi Konstantinovich Zhukov, who had already won the St George's Cross for capturing a German officer on the Roumanian front. That October, while on a reconnaissance patrol, he was blown from his horse by an exploding mine, and his hearing impaired. Sent to hospital in Kharkov, he later recalled how 'delighted' he was when posted to a combat regiment.[1]

On November 3, on the Italian Front, the ninth battle of the Isonzo was called off after three days because of deep mud: during those three days, 9,000 Austrian soldiers were taken prisoner. But there was no shortage of new men to fill the gap.

On the Eastern Front, other shortages were impeding any hope of a renewed Russian success. 'The plain truth is', wrote Colonel Knox in his diary on November 5, 'that without aeroplanes and far more heavy guns and shell and some knowledge of their use, it is butchery, and useless butchery, to drive Russian infantry against German lines.' In the previous five months, Knox was told by General Dukhonin, the Quarter-Master General, Russian losses 'may well have exceeded a million men' killed and wounded.

For two years and three months of war, the conflicts on the battlefield had been severe but essentially inconclusive. The confidence of the Central Powers in any decisive breakthrough, or even in wearing down the enemy's will to fight, had been ended by French and British perseverance on the Western Front, by Brusilov's advance in the east, and by Italian tenacity in the mountains. The Kaiser concluded that a stroke of political genius, or at least realism, was needed: the winning over of Polish national opinion and feeling to the German cause. Ludendorff was already an enthusiast. 'Let us found a Grand Duchy of Poland with a Polish army under German officers,' he had written that summer to the Foreign Minister, von Jagow. 'Such an army is bound to come one day, and at the present moment we can make use of it.'

By November 1916 the encouragement and moulding of Polish nationalism created, in the German-occupied Polish provinces of Russia, an ally and bastion against further Russian inroads, leaving Germany more free to concentrate on the Western Front. On November 5 the German-sponsored Kingdom of Poland was proclaimed, with Warsaw as its capital. The Poles,

[1] In 1941 Zhukov became Chief of Staff of the Soviet Army. The most successful Soviet Marshal of the Second World War, he led the counter-offensive at Stalingrad in 1942, the offensive at Kursk in 1943, and in 1945 was responsible for the capture of Berlin, where he accepted the German surrender. From 1955 to 1957 he was Soviet Minister of Defence.

sensing German weakness in making the offer at all, pressed for political power as well as the military status offered them. 'No army without a government to direct it' was Josef Pilsudski's ungracious yet pragmatic comment. When a government was denied him, Pilsudski withdrew his 10,000-strong Polish brigade from Ludendorff's command.

The decision of the Kaiser and Ludendorff to proclaim a Kingdom of Poland backfired even more seriously in the wider sphere of Germany's interest, for the Chancellor, Bethmann-Hollweg, was even then exploring the possibility of a separate peace with Russia. Whatever its territorial arrangements might have been, one thing was certain, the Tsar could not accept an independent Polish Kingdom carved out of his western provinces. Secret talks for a Russo-German peace, which had already taken place informally in neutral Stockholm between the German industrialist, Hugo Stinnes, and the Vice-President of the Duma, A.D. Protopopov, were not resumed. One person who was relieved at this was Lenin, who, from his Swiss exile, had been worried that the conclusion of peace between Russia and Germany would prevent the outbreak of revolution in Russia.

Not the possibility of peace, but the certainty of continuing war, marked the reality of the coming of winter in 1916. In Ruhleben internment camp more than 5,000 civilians had been buoyed up for two years by the hope of the camp's early dissolution, but after the British and German Governments agreed to exchange all civilian prisoners over the age of forty-five, those who remained realised that they would remain captive for a long time. One of the British returnees, Israel Cohen, commented on November 6, in his preface to the first published history of the camp: 'Hundreds of tragedies are being slowly and secretly enacted behind the brick walls and barbed wire fence of Ruhleben, tragedies that will never be known beyond the immediate circle of those whom they concern – of men torn from their families, reft of their livelihood, and tormented daily by gnawing anxiety about the future struggle for which physical privation and mental depression are rendering them more and more unfit.'

The deprivation of liberty at Ruhleben was offset, if such a basic loss can ever be offset, by music concerts, theatrical and operatic performances, debating societies, a library, a cinema, church and synagogue services, and sport. Cricket was played in blazers and flannels. Education classes were organised, by the prisoners, within the framework of an Arts and Science Union which boasted seventeen departments and 247 teachers. It was believed in the camp that Einstein was among those who donated scientific apparatus for laboratory courses in heat, light and sound. History lectures were given by an Oxford don, J.C. Masterman, who in 1939 was to be in charge of 'turning' all German spies in Britain into British agents, the Double-Cross System.[1]

[1] Masterman lectured unbrokenly from June 1915 until 3 August 1918, when he failed to meet his class, and was found to have escaped. He was recaptured two days later.

There was even a mock Parliamentary Election (held on 3 August 1916). The result was: Women's Suffrage candidate 1,220, Liberal 924, Conservative 471. This result was immediately publicised by the Germans as a protest against the British Government for entering the war. However, the 3,000 men who would remain in the camp after the exchange were, Israel Cohen wrote, far from anti-war: they were indeed, as he expressed it, 'all men who have been denied any of the glories or compensations of war, and who have to resume the battle of life with crippled constitutions'.

The 'glories and compensations of war' were a feature of many books and articles published in all the belligerent capitals. On the Salonica Front, however, the joint Serbian-French assault which started on November 10, in freezing rain, held all the usual terrors and perils of warmaking. As a strategic exercise it was a success, the Bulgarians being pushed back across the Serb border, and the Allies almost reaching the southern Serb town of Monastir. Among the thousand prisoners taken during the advance were many German soldiers who had only recently arrived to reinforce the Bulgarian line. On November 19, Serbian, French and Russian cavalry units entered Monastir. The French cavalry officer who entered the town at the head of a Franco-Russian division, as the last German artillery battery was leaving, was a Captain Murat, a descendant of Napoleon's Marshal who had entered Moscow in 1812. It was four years to the day since the Serbs had wrested the town from the Turks, during the First Balkan War. Elated by his success, General Sarrail called it the first French victory since the Battle of the Marne.

One final offensive was launched on the Somme battlefield that November, against the villages of Beaumont Hamel, Beaucourt and St Pierre Divion on the river Ancre, villages that had resisted all assaults since July 1. The attack began in thick fog. As the British advanced, groups of Germans were left intact and continued firing. Paul Maze, going towards Beaumont Hamel to report on the situation, 'wandered about a good deal before I found the old German front line, but, once I did, I followed in their wake, as I recognised their dead.' At one moment a friend passed in the other direction. 'He looked exhausted and dishevelled in contrast with the two carrier-pigeons he had in a basket, whose eyes glittered with eagerness.' The only effective communications between the forward troops and their headquarters was by pigeon.

Five thousand German prisoners were taken on that first day of the renewed battle. Beaucourt was captured on the second day, the day on which the novelist 'Saki', 46-year-old Lance-Sergeant H.H. Munro, was killed by a German sniper. In 1915 Munro had deliberately falsified his age in order to be allowed into the army. Six days after the battle, one of the British company commanders, Captain 'Cardy' Montague, a veteran of Gallipoli, recalled that when he reached the ruins of Beaucourt 'the Germans could not face our men and were surrendering in hundreds. It was an amazing sight, they came out of their holes, tearing off their equipment.'

Montague himself was wounded, as was the battalion's commanding officer, Lieutenant-Colonel Bernard Freyberg, hit by shrapnel in the neck after having led a decisive attack through the German trenches. 'There was a bang, a curious ringing note in my ear, and I lost consciousness,' Freyberg later recalled. 'When I came to, my head gave me a great deal of pain, and as I lay face downwards hot blood was dropping from my nose and chin. I thought at first my head had been smashed, but I located the wound in my neck with two dirty fingers. I looked at the man on my left; he was curled up. I moved his head, and found he was grey and dead.'

For having 'inspired all with his own contempt of danger', Freyberg was awarded the Victoria Cross. The official history of his division, the 29th Division, stated, eight years later: 'By his initiative, fine leading and bravery, Lieutenant-Colonel Freyberg won the battle of Ancre. Probably this was the most distinguished personal act in the war.' It was nearly Freyberg's last act: on being taken back to the casualty clearing station with his head and eyes covered in blood-soaked bandages, and his colour gone through loss of blood, he was put in the tent with those who were expected to die, and who were given no treatment except pain-killing drugs. Later he heard a quiet voice giving orders for him to be moved to the tent for those expected to live, where treatment was given. He could not find out who his saviour was. A quarter of a century later, while in a hotel foyer in Cairo, he heard that same voice and asked the man if he had been on the Ancre in November 1916. It was the medical officer who had saved his life, Captain S.S. Greaves, then commanding a hospital ship.

An account of the last battles of the Somme offensive appeared in the *Daily Mirror* and the *Paris Daily Mail* (which the troops read). It was written by W. Beach Thomas, who wrote, of the dead British soldier: 'Even as he lies on the field he looks more quietly faithful, more simply steadfast than others.' Commenting on Thomas's account of the battle, one officer wrote home: 'He has drawn well on his imagination, as half of it is not true, but just what he thought it would be like.' The reality was not described in the newspapers, and usually only glimpsed in letters home. One diarist, Lieutenant Guy Chapman, caught that reality in his curt entry on the night of November 16: 'No. 1 Coy is badly knocked out. Lauder and Young both badly wounded, Sergeant-Major Dell wounded. Far-rington killed. Sgt Brown not expected to live. Sgt Baker wounded. Westle, poor fellow, killed. Foley – the last of his family – killed, a lot of other good men, too many to speak of.'

Near Beaucourt station, Chapman wrote, lay 'the skeleton of five wagons and their team, the grisly evidence of the tragedy of a Bosche ration convoy. There is a sickly stench, the mixed smell of exploded picric acid, gas, blood, putrefying corpses and broken bricks. Here and there lie the bodies of the fallen.' Burial parties were working without ceasing: '800 English-men and forty Germans were buried yesterday – evidence of what price the assaulting parties must pay for some few yards of ground. Damn Germany!'[1]

On the night of November 17 the first snow fell on the Somme battlefield. On the following night the final assault of the campaign took place, an advance of a thousand yards along the Ancre. It was much hampered by mist and snow. Among those killed that night was Sergeant Alexander Macdonald, a British sniper. In his memory, his friend Ewart Macintosh wrote a parody of the soldiers' favourite tongue twister, 'Sister Susie's sewing shirts for soldiers', the chorus of which went:

> *Sniper Sandy's slaying Saxon soldiers,*
> *And Saxon soldiers seldom shew but Sandy slays a few,*
> *And every day the Bosches put up little wooden crosses*
> *In the cemetery for Saxon soldiers Sniper Sandy slew.*

After four-and-a-half months of struggle, suffering and advance there was no concluding victory, or even coda: one divisional history recorded that two companies which had taken part in the assault on November 18 had disappeared 'entirely, being overwhelmed by machine-gun fire'.

As the battle on the Somme drew to an end, each side was already making plans for a new offensive in 1917. They were also announcing the cost of the Somme offensive. On November 1 the British and French announced that, since the start of the battle on July 1, they had taken 72,901 German prisoners and captured 303 artillery pieces, 215 mortars and nearly a thousand machine guns.

The statistics of death were also being calculated by both sides, reaching unprecedented levels. The British dead on the Somme in the four months since July 1 amounted to 95,675. The French 'Somme' toll was 50,729. The total number of Allied dead on the Somme was 146,404. The German death toll was even larger: 164,055. The 70,000 and more prisoners were the fortunate ones, sent to the rear, and to prisoner-of-war camps, where the International Committee of the Red Cross supervised their conditions.

At Verdun, the French recaptured Fort Vaux on November 3. When the battle ended on the Somme that November, the British line had moved forward six miles, but was still three miles short of Bapaume, the first day's objective. In this massive exercise of human effort, several hundred thousand soldiers had been killed.

In five months, more than twenty-three million shells were fired by the two contending armies at Verdun, on average more than a hundred shells

---

[1] Guy Chapman was awarded the Military Cross in 1918. He was later a distinguished historian of France, and subsequently Professor of Modern History in the University of Leeds (1945–53). This quotation, the comment of Major Montagu, and the Divisional History record that follows, are taken from *The 1916 Battle of the Somme, A Reappraisal*, by another Leeds historian, Peter Liddle, Keeper of the Liddle Collection in the Library of the University of Leeds, whose work in collecting soldiers' writings and testimonies has put all historians of the First World War in his debt.

a minute. Verdun itself remained in French hands, but the death toll there was 650,000 men. When added to that of the Somme, this made a five-month death toll of 960,459 men: almost a million. It was an average of more than 6,600 men killed every day, more than 277 every hour, nearly five men every minute.

On the Western Front, after all the savagery of the Somme and Verdun, 127 German divisions faced 106 French, 56 British, six Belgian and one Russian division: 169 divisions in all. The British Expeditionary Force, which in August 1914 had consisted of 160,000 men, was 1,591,745 strong by the end of 1916.[1]

The statistics of the confrontation reflected the intention, and the determination, of all the opposing armies to continue to fight. As 1916 came to an end, the German army possessed 16,000 machine guns on the Western Front, the Russian army 16,000 machine guns on the Eastern Front. Three years earlier this weapon, with its rapid, uninterrupted, stuttering fire, had been the symbol of European dominance over distant, alien and despised peoples:

> *Whatever happens, we have got*
> *The Maxim gun, and they have not.*

Maxim's invention had now become a means whereby those who shared the highest values of civilisation, religion, science, culture, literature, art, music and a love of nature, were to continue to bleed each other to death or victory. A British writer, Israel Zangwill, a pre-war novelist of wit and charm, summed up the year 1916 with a different tone:

> *The world bloodily-minded,*
> *The Church dead or polluted,*
> *The blind leading the blinded,*
> *And the deaf dragging the muted.*

[1] This included 125,517 Australian and New Zealand (Anzac) troops and 104,538 Canadians.

16

The intensification of the war

NOVEMBER 1916–JUNE 1917

On 7 November 1916, Woodrow Wilson was re-elected President of the United States. Twelve days later, on November 19, he sent a note to all the warring powers, proposing that a means be found to end the conflict. On the previous day, the 85-year-old Franz Josef had expressed his 'keen satisfaction' that talk of peace was in the air. On November 20, despite a bout of bronchitis, he was at work as usual on official files. In the afternoon the doctors persuaded him to go to bed, but he gave instructions to be woken early the next day. 'Tomorrow morning at half past three,' he said to his valet. 'I am behindhand with my work.' Early on the morning of November 21, as he had wanted, he was at work on his official papers. Then, just after nine o'clock that evening, he died.[1]

The new Emperor of Austria and King of Hungary was Franz Josef's 29-year-old great nephew, Archduke Charles. The first reports that reached him as Emperor were of the imminent Austro-German conquest of Roumania. On November 23, General Mackensen crossed the Danube near Zimnicea, the passage of his army being swiftly accelerated by a pontoon bridge built by Austrian engineers. Two days later the Roumanian Government began to evacuate Bucharest for the northern city of Jassy.

There were German successes in the air and at sea that November. On November 21 the ocean liner *Britannic*, then being used as a hospital ship, was torpedoed in the Aegean. Twelve of those on board were drowned as the liner went down, some in a lifeboat when it was cut in half by the ship's propeller. Among those saved was a stewardess who had been on the fateful pre-war voyage of the liner's sister ship, the *Titanic*. Two days later, above the Western Front, Manfred von Richthofen shot down a British air ace, Major Lanoe Hawker, a winner of the Victoria Cross. It was Richthofen's eleventh 'kill'. On November 25, in the Atlantic off

---

[1] There was another death of note that November, three days after Franz Josef, that of Sir Hiram Maxim, the inventor (in 1889) of the machine gun. He died in London at the age of seventy-six.

Lisbon, the German submarine *U-52* sank the French battleship *Suffren*. There were no survivors.

On November 27 seven Zeppelins raided England, dropping more than two hundred bombs. Two of the raiders were shot down: in one of them, hit by the incendiary bullets fired by a British pilot, all twenty crewmen were killed. On the following day a single German seaplane flew over London, dropping six bombs on Kensington. 'I heard the explosions from the Foreign Office and thought they were practising with rifles at Wellington Barracks,' one senior diplomat, Lord Hardinge, later recalled. No one was killed, but six civilians were wounded. The raid marked the first aircraft as opposed to Zeppelin attack on the capital.

That November, on board a Swedish ship in Dieppe harbour, two men in civilian clothes were arrested and handed over to the British military authorities. Their names were Albert Ingham and Alfred Longshaw. Both were private soldiers from a Machine Gun Company who had been about to go into the trenches in October when they deserted. In civilian life they had been railway clerks together at Salford Goods Yard. Both were court-martialled and then shot, on December 1. Ingham's parents were told that he had 'died of gun shot wounds' and Longshaw's that he had 'died of wounds'. Both men appear on the roll of honour of dead railwaymen at Salford Station. After the war, when Ingham's father discovered what had really happened, he asked the War Graves Commission to put a unique inscription on his son's grave in France:

SHOT AT DAWN
ONE OF THE FIRST TO ENLIST
A WORTHY SON
OF HIS FATHER

*

To prevent oil from the Roumanian oilfields at Ploesti falling into Austro-German hands, on December 5 a British Member of Parliament, Colonel Norton-Griffiths, organised a spectacular act of sabotage, blowing up or releasing from their tanks more than 800,000 tons of petrol. It was a dramatic gesture, but it could not affect the outcome of the campaign. On December 6, German troops, followed by General Mackensen on his white horse, entered Bucharest. The Kaiser celebrated the victory with champagne. The Central Powers were now the conquerors of five capitals: Brussels, Warsaw, Belgrade, Cetinje and Bucharest. The Entente held no Central Power capitals in their grasp.

The only capital in which Entente troops were in action was Athens. The King of Greece having refused to allow the Entente to make use of his capital for the movement of supplies up to the Salonica Front, on November 30, French and British troops had landed at Piraeus and on December 1 were in action with the King's forces. About forty Greek soldiers were killed, and there were several French and British deaths.

Then the Entente forces agreed to withdraw. To ensure control of the Eastern Mediterranean telegraph cables, on December 6 the British occupied Syra Island, and within two months were in occupation of all the Cyclades islands. In Salonica, the pro-Entente Greek forces, under Venizelos, set up a Provisional Government and declared war on Germany and Bulgaria. But when the Venizelists tried to take control of Athens they were routed by forces loyal to the King, and to neutrality.

In Britain there was a change in the central direction of the war on December 6. Ageing and demoralised, Asquith was replaced as Prime Minister by David Lloyd George, the one person in the Government, Churchill wrote to a friend, who possessed 'any aptitude for war or knowledge of it'. Churchill went on to warn that the difficulties before the new Government were enormous 'and only disasters lie ahead for many months'.

On December 12 the German Chancellor, Bethmann-Hollweg, in a speech in the Reichstag, offered to open negotiations with the Entente in a neutral country. Three days later the French launched a massive attack on the German stranglehold around Verdun, pushing the line back almost to where it had been nine months earlier and capturing more than 11,000 German soldiers and 115 heavy guns. In triumph the new French commander, General Nivelle, told his men, 'I can assure you that victory is certain.' One of the historians of Verdun, Alistair Horne, has written, with greater truth, and no little bitterness borne of deep study: 'Neither side "won" at Verdun. It was the indecisive battle in an indecisive war; the unnecessary battle in an unnecessary war; the battle that had no victors in a war that had no victors.'

Would the war end, now the combatants were in correspondence about possible talks? On December 20, before the Entente had replied to Bethmann-Hollweg's suggestion for negotiations, President Wilson asked each of the Allied powers to formulate its own peace conditions. 'Did the President realize', asked the British diplomat, Lord Hardinge, in retrospect, 'that to support peace at that moment was to support militarism with all the horrors it had entailed?' A phrase in Wilson's letter, about the United States 'being too proud to fight', caused particular offence among those who had been fighting for more than two years. The official British answer came on the day after Wilson's note, and was made by Lloyd George, who had become Prime Minister twelve days earlier. 'We shall put our trust rather in an unbroken army than in broken faith,' he declared. He had been made Prime Minister by those in both main political parties who believed he would be by far the best person to prosecute the war with vigour. He would not let them down. On the day after his speech, and in direct response to it, General Ludendorff urged upon his superiors the immediate start of unrestricted submarine warfare.

Despite President Wilson's intervention, the intensification of the war was clearly in prospect. On the day of Lloyd George's rejection of the American note, a National Service department was set up in Britain, to co-ordinate the calling up of more men to active service. In charge of the new department was a local politician and businessman, Neville Chamberlain, whose cousin and close friend Norman was then serving on the Western Front.[1]

As Christmas 1916 drew near, and throughout the festive season, there was every indication that the war would be continued on all fronts. On the Sinai Front, Australian and New Zealand forces had pushed the Turks back to El Arish, a mere twenty miles from the border of Palestine, occupying the desert town on December 21. In Roumania, on December 23, Falkenhayn's army took 10,000 Roumanian prisoners: Germany could now obtain much-needed food from one of the granaries of Europe. The Tsar's rejection of Wilson's note was made in an Order of the Day to his armed forces on December 25. Two days later, in the Aegean Sea, a German submarine sank the French battleship *Gaulois*. On December 30 the Entente powers formally rejected Bethmann-Hollweg's suggestion for negotiations as 'empty and insincere'. Three days later the Kaiser told those closest to him that, when the war was over, 'the coast of Flanders must be ours'.

The Christmas Truce of 1914 was a thing of the past. No such fraternisations were allowed on the Western Front in 1916. A French front-line newspaper described the soldiers' activities just south of the Somme: 'On Christmas Day about twenty of us were crowded in a rotten sap captured from the Germans near Ablaincourt. We went in there twenty-four hours earlier, to organise that particular sector. Our men had covered nearly 40 kilometres on foot and had just spent four hours in the nauseating air of motor-buses. They had brought three days' supply of food with them which was supposed to last over Christmas night. For the evening meal, therefore, we ate what was left at the bottom of our bags ... those bags which still had something in them.' In that area of the Somme, 'covered in mud – there was no water to be had. These two army corps – the relievers and the relieved – had a truly wretched Christmas night, distressing too.... For this third Christmas of the war there were certainly – at the front – several other thousands of squads who had nothing but shells to help them celebrate Christmas.'

The hopes of many, that President Wilson's involvement would bring peace, were strong. 'Apparently the war is gradually coming to a close,' the German-born Arthur Ruppin, a Zionist then in Constantinople, wrote in his diary on the last day of 1916. 'Probably, it will still take some time, but 1917 will bring us peace.' This was a chimera: despite the killing, the wounding and the capture of so many hundreds of thousands of men, despite Wilson's peace note, the armies were still burgeoning. The war would go on, after two years and five months of slaughter. Russia's ability

[1] Neville Chamberlain was British Prime Minister from 1937 to 1940.

to make war was enhanced in the last month of the year by the opening of the Murmansk-Petrograd railway. As 1916 ended, Russia had more than nine million men under arms. Germany had seven million. Austria, although an estimated 800,000 of her soldiers had already been killed and a million badly wounded, had nearly five million.

The year 1917 opened with a maritime loss, when a German submarine sank the British troop transport *Ivernia* off Cape Matapan and 121 troops were drowned. They had been on their way to Egypt, to form part of the force that was pushing the Turks back across the Sinai desert towards Palestine. Nine days later a British force drove the Turks out of the border town of Rafah, taking 1,600 prisoners. The whole of the Sinai Peninsula, hitherto an outpost of the Ottoman Empire, was now under British control.

In London that winter, Alex Aaronsohn, a Roumanian-born Palestinian Jew, offered his services to the British to help find a way to drive the Turks from Palestine. His family had already established a spy ring inside Palestine: he now put this at Britain's disposal. Their knowledge of the wells and springs in the desert between Gaza and Beersheba was to be a crucial factor in guiding the British forces when the time came to advance. Aaronsohn, whose services were accepted after a searching interview, returned to Cairo.

In addition to the Turks, whose main land Empire was in Asia, eleven European nations were at war as 1917 began. The most recent power to become a belligerent was Portugal, whose troops had yet to join the Allied line on the Western Front. The Allied side now consisted of the Russians, the British, the French, the Italians, the Japanese, the Portuguese, the Serbs (with a tiny toe-hold in the south of their country), the Belgians (likewise clinging to a fragment of their soil), and the Roumanians (just driven out of their capital). The British forces included contingents from Australia, New Zealand, India, South Africa, the West Indies and Canada. As well as the Turks, the Central Powers consisted of Germany, Austria-Hungary and Bulgaria.

National aspirations were playing a larger part in the war. In Arabia, the Arab revolt was gaining momentum, with British officers, including T.E. Lawrence, participating in a series of raids on Turkish positions near Yenbo, on the Red Sea, and three British warships assisting the Arab leader, the Emir Feisal, in the capture of Wejh three weeks later. Czechs, Slovaks and Poles were also looking towards some fulfilment of their respective national aspirations, should Austria-Hungary collapse. Many Jews hoped that the defeat of Turkey would lead to some form of Jewish autonomy in Palestine. That January a member of the Jewish spy ring led by the Aaronsohn family inside Palestine made contact with an Australian military patrol on the Sinai border.

Only the United States among the great powers maintained its neutrality, despite the earlier loss of many of its citizens to German submarine warfare.

'There will be no war,' President Wilson assured his fellow-countrymen on January 4. 'It would be a crime against civilisation for us to go in.' Wilson learned, however, from a conversation between his Ambassador in Berlin and the Chancellor two days later, that the Kaiser's peace offer of the previous month was not what it seemed. While Germany was prepared to 'withdraw from Belgium', the 'guarantees' she had mentioned in general terms were clearly unacceptable when spelt out: according to the Chancellor, Germany would require the permanent occupation of Liège and Namur and of 'other forts and garrisons throughout Belgium', the 'possession' of the Belgian railways and ports, and a German military presence, with Belgium denied an army of its own.

Ambassador Gerard told the Chancellor: 'I do not see that you have left much for the Belgians, excepting that King Albert will have the right to reside in Brussels with an honour guard', to which the Chancellor replied: 'We cannot allow Belgium to be an outpost of Great Britain.'

All discussion of the future of Belgium was about to become academic. The Kaiser was on the verge of the step that would bring America into the war. On January 9 he presided over a Crown Council at which the long-debated question of unrestricted submarine warfare was to be resolved. The first person to speak was the Chief of the Naval Staff, Admiral von Holtzendorf, who assured the Kaiser that, with the introduction of unrestricted submarine warfare England would sue for peace in six months. The Kaiser asked the Admiral about the effect of the sinkings on the United States. 'I will give Your Majesty my word as an officer that not one American will land on the Continent' was Holtzendorf's reply. Hindenburg, who spoke next, cited a decrease in supplies of munitions going to the Allies as the great benefit. Bethmann-Hollweg, ever an opponent of the measure, warned that it would bring the United States into the war, but then, with the military and naval chiefs against him, asked to withdraw his opposition.

The Kaiser hesitated no longer. Unrestricted German submarine warfare, against all shipping, whatever flag it flew and whatever cargoes it carried, would begin 'with the utmost energy' from February 1. The aim of the decision, the German submarine leader, Commodore Bauer, explained to his commanders, 'is to force England to make peace, and thereby decide the whole war'. In January 1917, the last month in which restrictions were in force, German submarines had sunk fifty-one British, sixty-three other Allied, and sixty-six neutral ships. This came to more than 300,000 tons, of which a third was British. With American merchant ships as acceptable targets, those figures could now be substantially increased.

In Austria there was less confidence that an outright victory could be secured by the new war measure: on January 12, in Vienna, Count Czernin told the Austrian Council of Ministers that it was necessary to look for a compromise peace. This was made all the more urgent, as far as maintaining the unity of the Hapsburg Empire was concerned, by an Allied declaration that day, issued in Rome, promising to strive for the national liberation of all the subject people of the Hapsburg dominions, chief among them the Poles, Czechs, Slovaks, Slovenes, Croats, Serbs and Roumanians. An appeal by President Wilson on January 21, in his State of the Union Address, that a 'united Poland' should emerge from the war a sovereign State, with access to the Baltic Sea, was given public support by the Russian Tsar in the last week of January. In search of support in the military struggle, Poland's century-long captors were offering to become her liberators. In a prisoner-of-war camp in southern Russia, Roumanians who had been captured while fighting in the Austrian army signed an oath to fight against their former Hapsburg masters.

On the Western Front that January, the confrontation between the contending armies, though not marked by any offensive, was a continual struggle against shelling, sniping and mud. On January 12 the poet Wilfred Owen was among those who went forward into the line for a four-day stint near Beaumont Hamel. Four days later, on his return to his battalion's reserve billets, he wrote to his mother: 'I can see no excuse for deceiving you about these last four days. I have suffered seventh hell. I have not been at the front. I have been in front of it. I held an advanced post, that is, a "dugout" in the middle of No-Man's Land.' The dugout held twenty-five men 'packed tight,' he explained. 'Water filled it to a depth of 1 or 2 feet, leaving say 4 feet of air. One entrance had been blown in and blocked. So far, the other remained. The Germans knew we were staying there and decided we shouldn't.'

For fifty hours Owen's dugout was under shellfire, sometimes intense, sometimes intermittent. On the Sunday, he told his mother, 'I nearly broke down and let myself drown in the water that was now slowly rising over my knees. Towards 6 o'clock, when, I suppose, you would be going to church, the shelling grew less intense and less accurate; so that I was mercifully helped to do my duty and crawl, wade, climb and flounder over No-Man's Land to visit my other post. It took me half an hour to move 150 yards.' In the platoon to Owen's left, 'the sentries over the dugout were blown to nothing'.

A sentry guarding Owen's dugout was also hit by shellfire. In his poem 'The Sentry', Owen wrote:

> . . . down the steep steps came thumping
> And splashing in the flood, deluging muck –
> The sentry's body; then, his rifle, handles
> Of old Boche bombs, and mud in ruck on ruck.
> We dredged him up, for killed, until he whined
> "O sir, my eyes – I'm blind – I'm blind, I'm blind!"
> Coaxing, I held a flame against his lids
> And said if he could see the least blurred light
> He was not blind; in time he'd get all right.
> "I can't," he sobbed. Eyeballs, huge-bulged like squids',

307

Watch my dreams still; but I forgot him there
In posting next for duty, and sending a scout
To beg a stretcher somewhere, and floundering about
To other posts under the shrieking air.

As Germany moved towards an intensification of the war at sea, the recently appointed German Foreign Minister, Dr Alfred von Zimmermann, worked out a scheme whereby, if unrestricted submarine warfare were to bring the United States into the war, Germany could win the support and active alliance of Mexico. With Germany's 'generous financial support', he explained in a coded telegram to the German Minister in Mexico City on January 19, Mexico would 'reconquer' the territories it had lost seventy years earlier: Texas, New Mexico and Arizona. Germany and Mexico would 'Make war together, make peace together.'

On January 23, while the Zimmermann telegram was still a closely guarded secret, the German Ambassador in Washington, Count Bernsdorff, still hoping to keep the United States out of the war, asked Berlin for $50,000 to influence individual members of Congress.[1] As a result of skilful British cryptography, his telegram was deciphered in London two days before it was received in Berlin. But on February 3, less than two weeks after this attempt to buy American neutrality, the German submarine, U-53, in one of the very first actions of unrestricted submarine warfare, sank an American cargo ship, the *Housatonic*, off the Scilly Islands. Although a British ship rescued the crew of the *Housatonic*, its cargo of grain was lost. In Berlin, Zimmermann told the American Ambassador that evening: 'Everything will be alright. America will do nothing, for President Wilson is for peace and nothing else. Everything will go on as before.'

Zimmermann was wrong. That day President Wilson announced to Congress that he was breaking off diplomatic relations with Germany. He had not declared war, but he had brought two-and-a-half years of wartime diplomacy to an end. News of the break did not reach Berlin until the following morning. At that moment there were just over a hundred German submarines available for action, and a further forty undergoing repairs. Fifty-one had been sunk since the outbreak of war.

During February 3, as the possibility of America entering the war increased, the Portuguese Expeditionary Force arrived in France. Here were 50,000 more men committed to trench warfare, and to the hope of a breakthrough. On the following day, however, in a brilliant defensive move, the Kaiser ordered the withdrawal of his troops on the Western Front to the recently fortified Hindenburg Line, known to the Germans as the Siegfried Line. By removing his troops from the many kinks and salients that had been created during the fighting of 1916, this reduced by twenty-five miles the length of the line that had to be defended, releasing thirteen divisions for service in reserve.

---

[1] The 1994 value of this sum is approximately $420,000 (£280,000).

Between the old front line and the Hindenburg Line, the Germans had systematically devastated the area, blowing up houses, burning farms, uprooting orchards, mining the few remaining buildings, and obliterating roads, so that the Allies would find nothing but useless ruination. When Crown Prince Rupprecht of Bavaria, a Field Marshal and an army group commander, protested at the extent of the devastation, he was overruled by Ludendorff. As the Allied troops moved forward, unopposed, they were amazed by the scale of the destruction. At the Town Hall in Bapaume, two French deputies were killed when the mined building blew up. Several members of a British divisional Staff suffered the same fate elsewhere in the evacuated zone.

Germany now prepared to face the might of the United States. The danger of America's entry into the war was offset, however, as far as the German High Command was concerned, by the continual news from Russia of military weakness and anti-war feeling behind the lines. On February 16 General Hoffmann noted in his diary: 'There is very encouraging news from the interior of Russia. It would seem that she cannot hold out longer than the autumn.' Ten days later, as many as five hundred Russians were protesting against the war in the streets of Petrograd. The British Military Attaché with the Russian Army, Colonel Knox, had already sent London his estimate of Russia's dwindling military capacity. More than a million men had been killed. A further two million were either missing (that is to say, dead) or prisoners-of-war. More than half a million were in hospital. Nearly a million and a half were on extended leave or had been excused all further service. A further million men had deserted. 'These men were living quietly in their villages, unmolested by the authorities, their presence concealed by the village communes, who profited by their labour.' The number of troops at the front, and those available to be called up, was insufficient to meet the demands of 1917 if the losses continued as before.

Nearly two years earlier the Allies had promised Russia that she could annex Constantinople and the Straits once Turkey was defeated. On February 12 the Russian Government sought a further secret assurance with regard to its western frontier. It proposed doing so by giving France a free hand with regard to her German frontier. At an audience with the Tsar, the French Ambassador in Petrograd transmitted the French desire to secure for herself 'the restoration of Alsace-Lorraine and a special position in the valley of the river Saar, as well as to attain the political separation from Germany of her trans-Rhenish districts, and their organisation on a separate basis in order that in future the river Rhine might form a permanent strategical frontier against a Germanic invasion.'

The Tsar 'was pleased to agree to this in principle,' the Ambassador reported to Paris and London, and with this imperial authority behind it, negotiations for an agreement began, based on a Russian formula that had been expressed almost a year earlier, that 'while allowing France and England complete liberty in delimiting the western frontiers of Germany, we expect that the Allies on their part will give us equal liberty in delimiting our frontiers with Germany and Austria-Hungary'. As Russia's armies and peoples plunged towards turmoil, its rulers were still looking forward to the territorial advantages of an imminently victorious power.

Franco-Russian agreement with regard to the western frontier of Germany was reached on February 14. On that day the Russian Government accepted, in strictest secrecy, that Alsace-Lorraine would be 'restored to France'. It also agreed that the French frontier with Germany would be drawn up 'at the discretion of the French Government', that France would acquire 'the entire coal district of the Saar valley', and that the German towns and regions west of the river Rhine would be 'entirely separated from Germany and freed from all political and economic dependence upon her'. All that remained was to finalise Russia's frontiers in the east: these negotiations continued in Petrograd throughout February and into March.

On February 22, on the Isonzo sector of the Italian Front, the accidental explosion of a mortar bomb wounded Sergeant Mussolini in his trench. Four of those with him were killed. He was in hospital for six months, during which time forty-four fragments and splinters of shell were removed from his body. To stimulate national morale, the King, to whose monarchy Mussolini had once been opposed, visited the patriotic editor in hospital. When he was discharged from hospital, he returned not to the front but to journalism, and to the five-year road to Fascism and power.

On the Salonica Front, the ferocity of the winter made any Allied advance beyond Monastir impossible. But the Germans were always seeking a means to bring the war to this remote region. On February 27 fifteen German aircraft, triple-engined machines each carrying four machine guns, caused many casualties in the Allied ranks. Some of the wounded British soldiers were taken to a hospital which was bombed five days later, and were killed in their beds. A week after the second bombing attack, a third hospital was bombed. Two British nurses were among the dead.

The Balkan Front provided a considerable focus for British nursing activity. Sympathy for the Serbs was widespread in Britain, and volunteers were not hard to find. In addition, the Royal Army Medical Corps had provided more than 6,500 beds for Serbian soldiers. One of those super-intending the distribution of food for the Serbian Relief Fund in Monastir, Mrs Harley, was a sister of Field Marshal Sir John French. She was killed by shrapnel during an artillery barrage.

With all German submarine restraints ended, death at sea was increasingly an almost daily feature of the war. In the last week of January, 350 sailors drowned when the armoured merchant cruiser *Laurentic*, a former ocean liner, hit a mine off the coast of Ireland. On February 15 an Italian troop transport on its way to Salonica, the *Minas*, was torpedoed by the German submarine *U-39*. Of the thousand troops on board, 870 were drowned.

Two days later a British anti-submarine ship, the *Farnborough*, sank the *U-83*. There were only two survivors from the German submarine. The captain of the British ship, Commander Campbell, was awarded the Victoria Cross. On February 24 a French liner, the *Athos*, was torpedoed in the Mediterranean.

Among those drowned on the *Athos* were 543 Chinese labourers, recruited in China to work as part of a large labour force on the Western Front. When the news of the sinking reached China it acted as a deterrent to recruiting, but by the end of the war almost 100,000 Chinese were employed on menial tasks throughout the zone of the armies. The French Government allowed private firms to employ Chinese labourers throughout France. Their contract, signed before they left China, obliged them to work ten hours a day and seven days a week, with 'due consideration' made for Chinese festivals. Such consideration was not always given. Labourers were paid between one and two francs a day. Trickery was always suspected, a correspondent of *The Times* warning that the Chinese labourer 'has his own little tricks and dodges. As one Chinaman is, to the Western eye, indistinguishable from another, there is always a danger that Ah Lung may try to draw the pay of Weng Chow, who is on the sick list or has gone home. Consequently every coolie has his fingerprints taken and registered under the supervision of Scotland Yard.'

Although the Chinese labourers on the Western Front were excluded from combat duties and worked behind the lines, they were not immune from danger. In a German air raid on a British army base at Dunkirk, eight Chinese were killed and fifteen injured by a single bomb. After further air raids in that area, a group of Chinese employed by the French went on strike. French armed guards were sent to force them back to work. In the ensuing struggle two Chinese were killed. There is a passage in Lloyd George's memoirs about these men, the graves of 1,612 of whom are scattered around northern France, in more than twenty British war cemeteries. 'At times, of course,' Lloyd George wrote, 'these Chinese coolies came under aerial bombing or long-distance shelling. That did not greatly perturb them; they were far less nervous under fire than the British West Indian Auxiliaries, who were similarly engaged on Labour Corps duties. But it tended to disorganise their work in another way, because if they suffered any fatal casualties, they would all break off work to attend the funeral, and neither threats nor cajolery had the least effect on them, nor would bombing or shelling by the enemy scatter their cortege, until the obsequies had been duly completed.'

Those in charge of Chinese labourers were given a phrase book, written by a British major. The phrases included 'Less talk and more work', 'The inside of this tent is not very clean', 'You are very undisciplined, and if you are not more careful I will be compelled to punish you', and 'This latrine is reserved for Europeans and is not available for Chinese'. What was available in one instance was a jetty made of logs, built out over a river. The 'latrine' was the space between the logs.

On February 19, a month after it had been sent, Zimmermann's telegram urging the Mexicans to enter the war against the United States, and to 'recapture' Texas, Arizona and New Mexico was decyphered in London, and immediately transmitted to the American Government. The first reaction of the American diplomat who was shown it in London was 'Why not Illinois and New York while they were about it?'

The Zimmermann telegram was published in the United States on March 1. Those in America who were alarmed at the prospect of war denounced the telegram as a forgery, but two days later Zimmermann announced that it was genuine. One more nail had been knocked into the coffin of American neutrality.

The Allied war against the Turks, which had received such a set-back a year earlier with the evacuation of Gallipoli and the fall of Kut, gained momentum on several fronts in the opening months of 1917. In Mesopotamia, British and Indian troops, steadily moving up river again, reached Kut on February 24, taking 1,730 Turkish prisoners. It was ten months since nearly 12,000 British and Indian troops had been captured there, and sent northwards on their cruel march.

In Persia, Turkish forces were pushed back from Hamadan to Kermanshah. In Arabia, on the Hedjaz railway, the first serious raid was carried out on the line, at Toweira, by fifty Arabs under the guidance of a British officer, Captain Garland. Off Palestine, a Royal Navy yacht, the *Managam*, brought money to the Jewish spy ring working for Britain, handing it over at the crusader port of Athlit. On the Sinai-Palestine border, British troops overran two Turkish border posts, at Nakhl and Bir-el-Hassana. The Allied aim, that year, was to drive the Turks from Jerusalem. Three days after British troops in Mesopotamia occupied Ctesiphon, the scene of Britain's defeat a year earlier, bringing British troops once more to within twenty-five miles of Baghdad, the British orientalist Gertrude Bell commented: 'That's the end of the German dream of domination in the Near East. Their place is not going to be in the sun.' On the day after her letter was written, the Turks began to evacuate Baghdad: 9,500 Turkish soldiers moving out as 45,000 British and Indian troops drew near.

As the Turks left Baghdad, the Germans blew up the radio station. But seven new aeroplanes, still in their crates, remained intact, awaiting the conqueror. After marching more than a hundred miles in fifteen days, British forces entered the city on March 11. 'To the British troops, knowing nothing of the background', one historian has written, 'it was a bewildering reception. Persians dressed like Joseph in long silken coats of many colours; red-fezzed oriental Jews in misfit European clothing; handsome Armenian refugees who had spent the night huddled in Christian churches, fearful of their fate if any of the fleeing Turks learned of their existence; lordly turbaned Muslims in black flowing robes – all turned out to cheer them as they tramped in through the Southern Gate. It was a gala display, a fiesta – something that had *not* taken place when Townshend's men had tottered painfully through the same streets.'¹ Those men were still captives in Anatolia, far to the north.

Behind the lines, the severity of occupation continued. The 700,000 able-bodied men who had been deported from Belgium to Germany were working in farms and factories. In Serbia, a rebellion near Nis was suppressed by Austrian and Bulgarian troops with great brutality, more than 2,000 Serbs being executed. Anti-war propaganda was also spreading, not only in Russia, but in France, where at the end of February, General Nivelle told the authorities that pacifist propaganda was reaching his soldiers.

The conditions of trench warfare were also demoralising. On March 26, a front-line newspaper written and produced by French soldiers on the Western Front commented, on the mud that had become a curse of the trench system: 'At night, crouching in a shell-hole and filling it, the mud watches, like an enormous octopus. The victim arrives. It throws its poisonous slobber out at him, blinds him, closes round him, buries him. One more "*disparu*", one more man gone.... For men die of mud, as they die from bullets, but more horribly. Mud is where men sink and – what is worse – where their soul sinks. But where are those hack journalists who turn out such heroic articles, when the mud is that deep? Mud hides the stripes of rank, there are only poor suffering beasts. Look, there, there are flecks of red on that pool of mud – blood from a wounded man. Hell is not fire, that would not be the ultimate in suffering. Hell is mud!'.

On the Eastern Front, it was becoming almost impossible for many Russian officers to maintain military discipline. Early on the morning of February 17 a number of front-line cavalry squadrons were issued with live ammunition and ordered to ride to cavalry headquarters some distance behind the line. They were not told of the purpose of this manoeuvre. 'Soon', one of their number, Georgi Zhukov, later recalled, 'everything became clear. From around a street corner appeared a demonstration carrying red banners. Spurring on his horse, our squadron commander, followed by other squadron commanders, galloped towards regimental headquarters, from which a group of officers and factory workers had emerged.'

A 'tall cavalryman' then addressed the assembled soldiers, telling them that the working class, peasants and soldiers no longer recognised the Tsar. 'The Russian people', he said, 'wanted an end to the slaughter of an imperialist war; they wanted peace, land and liberty.' The cavalryman ended his short speech with a call for an end to Tsarism and an end to the war. 'Though there had been no command,' Zhukov wrote, 'the soldiers knew what they should do. They shouted and cheered, mingling with the demonstration.'

Throughout the Eastern Front the Bolsheviks were appealing to the

¹ A.J. Barker, *The Neglected War, Mesopotamia 1914–1918*, Faber and Faber, London 1967, page 377.

soldiers not to fight, and to join soldiers' committees to uphold and propagate revolutionary demands. From the front the agitation spread to the cities, and to the capital. In Petrograd a strike broke out on March 3 in the Putilov munition works, the army's main provider of weapons and ammunition. That evening, recalled the British Ambassador's daughter, Meriel Buchanan, 'a bread shop in the poorer quarter of the town was looted, and the first little band of Cossacks patrolled the Nevsky'. For the next three days there were riots in the streets by citizens demanding bread. By March 8 there were an estimated 90,000 factory workers on strike. That day, at Mogilev, the Tsar wrote to his wife that he was greatly missing his half-hour game of patience every evening, and he added, 'I shall take up dominoes again in my spare time.' In his diary he wrote: 'In all my spare time I am reading a French book on Julius Caesar's conquest of Gaul.' Even more than the Kaiser, the Tsar had become isolated from his country's moods and changes. On March 10, as a general strike began in Russia, Martial Law was declared in Petrograd.

The United States was not yet in the war, and Russia was in turmoil: it was a crisis moment for the Allies. But how long the United States could remain neutral was an open question. Another serious challenge to that neutrality had come on February 25, when a German submarine sank the Cunard liner *Laconia* off the Fastnet Rock. Twelve passengers were drowned, among them four Americans. The American government's reaction was not very swift, however, or decisive. On March 5, as the Red flag of revolution was being held aloft in the streets of Petrograd, Woodrow Wilson told the United States Congress: 'We stand fast on armed neutrality.' The sinking of the American steamship *Algonquin* a week later, torpedoed without warning, followed by three more sinkings in four days, was a further provocation, but still led to no declaration of war.

On March 10, in Petrograd, the power of the Duma, Russia's hitherto weak but now assertive Parliament, was being challenged by the Petrograd Soviet of Workers', Soldiers', and Peasants' Deputies. Led by Prince Tseretelli, a member of the Menshevik Party, the Soviet derived its authority from the popular vote, and from popular discontent with the war. Yet despite the existence of the rival authorities of both Duma and Petrograd Soviet, the Tsar, from his military headquarters near the front, at Mogilev, 450 miles away from the capital, still sought to carry out the duties of a sovereign, and to uphold his country's national interest. On March 11 he authorised the final phase of the Franco-Russian agreement on the future frontiers of Europe. Almost a month earlier Russia had agreed to a virtual free hand for France in the west. Now, on March 11, following further negotiations in Petrograd and Paris, the French agreed, again in the strictest secrecy, to recognise Russia's 'complete liberty in establishing her western frontiers'.

That 'liberty' was of short-lived duration. On March 12, as the Tsar left Mogilev to return to his capital, the soldiers of the Petrograd garrison, 17,000 men, joined the crowds in the streets of the capital demonstrating against him. There was street fighting when soldiers loyal to the Tsar, together with the police, sought to maintain order, but they were massively outnumbered. At eleven in the morning, the Law Courts on the Lityeiny Prospect were set on fire, then police stations throughout the city were attacked and burned. The first Russian Revolution had begun.[1]

The struggle inside Russia intensified. While on his way to his ship on March 13, the captain of the Russian cruiser *Aurora*, which was undergoing repairs in Petrograd, was murdered by revolutionary sailors. That same day, at the island naval base of Kronstadt, just outside the capital, mutinying sailors murdered forty officers and sergeants, and arrested more than a hundred other officers. On the following day, March 14, as the Tsar's train approached the capital, it was stopped at Pskov by order of the revolutionaries. In Petrograd that day, the Petrograd Soviet issued its Order Number One: all weapons would be controlled by elected committees, and all off-duty saluting of officers was abolished. The British Ambassador's daughter reported a conversation that day between two soldiers: 'What we want is a Republic.' 'Yes. A Republic, but we must have a good Tsar at the head of it!'

The Tsar was still in his train on March 15, unable to reach his capital. As the principal stations on the way to the capital were occupied by revolutionary troops, he had been forced to make a detour to Pskov. That morning, from Mogilev, the Commander-in-Chief, General Alexeyev, urged all the army commanders by telegram to join him in an appeal to the Tsar to abdicate. He was supported by General Ruzsky, commanding the Northern Front, who was with the Tsar at Pskov, and who was insistent that only abdication would prevent anarchy. As the telegraphic replies came in to Alexeyev it was clear that the Army would not maintain the Tsar in power. General Brusilov was emphatic that abdication alone could save both the monarchy and Russia's ability to continue the war. Even the staunch monarchist General Sakharov, commanding the Roumanian Front, favoured abdication as the only means of persuading the soldiers to continue to fight. So too did the Viceroy of the Caucasus, the former Commander-in-Chief, Grand Duke Nicholas, the Tsar's cousin. By half past two that afternoon Alexeyev was able to send all the telegraphic replies to General Russky at Pskov.

Armed with the telegrams, General Russky went to see the Tsar. Within a few moments, the Tsar bowed to these representations. His uncle's participation in the unanimity weighed particularly strongly with him. Without further discussion he telegraphed to Alexeyev: 'In the name of the welfare, tranquillity and salvation of my warmly beloved Russia I am ready to abdicate from the throne in favour of my son. I request all to serve him truly and faithfully.'

---

[1] Because of the different Russian calendar at that time, the revolution of March 1917 is known to the Russians as the February Revolution. I have given throughout the dates as used outside Russia (and inside Russia once the calendar was changed at the end of 1917).

The war had claimed its first Allied sovereign. The 300–year-old imperial system over which he the Tsar had presided was over.[1] The former pomp and circumstance, and the surviving class and power structure of the Russian Empire were all but ended. The secret treaties which the Tsar had approved, the territories which he had acquired or expected to acquire, whether from the Turks or the Germans or the Austrians, were no longer valid.

The Duma moved to the Tauride Palace, where it formed a Provisional Government. Opposing it was the Petrograd Soviet, which remained in session, a rival authority to the new Government. In Zurich, on the afternoon of March 16, the calm of Lenin's study was disrupted when a fellow-exile rushed in waving a newspaper and declared, to Lenin's astonishment, 'Haven't you heard the news? There is Revolution in Russia!' But in Petrograd, the President of the Duma, M.V. Rodzianko, told the British Military Attaché: 'My dear Knox, you must be easy. Everything is going on all right. Russia is a big country, and can wage war and manage a revolution at the same time.'

The political restrictions of Tsardom were swept away by the Provisional Government, whose authority was thereby enhanced. Political prisoners were granted an amnesty and released from their Siberian exile. To the disappointment of many soldiers and sailors, however, the Provisional Government announced that Russia would remain in the war. Lenin at once denounced this decision, and the Provisional Government itself, creating the slogan, 'All Power to the Soviets!'

Two rival centres of power were operating in the Russian capital. At the head of the Provisional Government, Russia's new Prime Minister, Prince Lvov, urged active participation in the war. To countermand this, the Petrograd Soviet appointed political commissars to all military units. The main task of the commissars was to urge the soldiers not to fight. The revolutionary forces were strong and unleashed: on March 17 the Commander-in-Chief of the Russian Navy, Admiral Nepenin, who had just resigned, was murdered by a sailor. Anti-war fever was intense. But the Foreign Minister, Paul Miliukov, in a statement on the following day, announced to the world that Russia would remain with her Allies. 'She will fight by their side against a common enemy until the end, without cessation and without faltering.' The former Tsar, having returned to his headquarters at Mogilev on March 20, told the troops there that they should be loyal to the Provisional Government and loyal, also, to its determination to continue with the war.

That March, as Russia plunged into political turmoil, the war fronts continued to see facing armies unable to gain decisive advantage. The Germans had withdrawn from the Somme without loss to their new

[1] The first Romanov ruler of Russia, Tsar Michael, came to the throne in 1613. The first ruler of all Russia was Ivan the Great (House of Rurik) who proclaimed himself Tsar in 1480.

defensive line. In the air, a Canadian pilot, Billy Bishop, shot down the first of seventy-two German aircraft that he claimed to have shot down above the Western Front. On the Salonica Front, the Bulgarians, using gas shells for the first time, failed to break through the Allied positions. In Mesopotamia the British army advanced beyond Baghdad to capture Baquba, thirty-five miles to the north-east, while its commander, General Maude, pledged the Allies to promote Arab freedom. Just inside the border of Palestine, the British attacked the Turkish positions at Gaza, but although outnumbering the Turks by more than two to one, they were unable to break into the city. During the battle, German reconnaissance aircraft had been of crucial help to the Turkish defenders.

At sea, 296 French sailors were drowned on March 19 when the *U-64* sank the battleship *Danton* off Sardinia. Two days later a United States tanker, the *Healdton*, was sunk by a German submarine while in a specially declared 'safety zone' in Dutch waters. Twenty American crewmen were killed. President Wilson called Congress to meet on April 2. Eight days before, the joint German and Austrian High Command had agreed to provide railway facilities to allow Lenin, and the group of thirty-two Bolsheviks with him in Switzerland, to return to Russia, knowing that he would be a major force for civil unrest, and for the removal of Russia from the war. On March 27 the Petrograd Soviet called on all peoples to demand an end to the war. Four days later, Lenin agreed to return to Russia by rail through Germany. He knew, or feared, that were he to travel back through the territory of the Allied powers, by rail through France, then by sea from Britain to North Russia, he might well be arrested, in an attempt to ensure that Russia stayed at war.

Russian troops were still fighting. On April 2 Russian units coming from Persia and British units advancing from Baquba linked forces at the Mesopotamian town of Kizil Rabat. But on the following day, on the Eastern Front, the Germans took 10,000 Russian prisoners. The United States was still not at war, but on April 1, near Brest, the armed American steamer *Aztec* was torpedoed and twenty-eight of her crew drowned. 'The world must be made safe for democracy,' Wilson declared on the following day. There were already 533 Harvard graduates among the many thousands of Americans serving as volunteers in the Allied armies or in hospital and ambulance work behind the lines: up to that time twenty-seven of them had been killed in action.

On April 1 the British Fourth Army captured Savy Wood, only four miles west of St Quentin, whose cathedral spire could be seen from the new front-line trenches. Among the soldiers in action that day was the poet Wilfred Owen, who led his platoon through an artillery barrage to the German trenches, only to find that the Germans had withdrawn. Severely shaken by the bombardment, he fell asleep on a railway embankment and was blown into the air by a shell, 'a near-miss', comments one of his biographers, 'that seems to have left him sheltering helplessly, close to the dismembered remains of another officer. When he got back to base, people noticed that he was trembling, confused, and stammering. It seems probable that his courage was called into question in some way by the CO, who may even have called him a coward.'[1]

Despite the Commanding Officer's scepticism, a doctor diagnosed shell-shock and Owen was sent to hospital at Etretat. From there he wrote home on a postcard showing the cliffs near the town: 'This is the kind of Paradise I am in at present. No. 1 General Hospital. The doctor, orderlies and sisters are all Americans, strangely from New York! I *may* get permission to go boating and even to bathe.' Back in Britain, Owen was sent to the Craiglockhart War Hospital for Neurasthenic Officers, of whose inmates he later wrote:

> *These are men whose minds the Dead have ravished.*
> *Memory fingers in their hair of murders,*
> *Multitudinuous murders they once witnessed.*

Woodrow Wilson seemed to wish to find a way to end those murders, but the German government belittled his initiative. The German authorities were confident that they had widespread popular support. From his home in Berlin, Albert Einstein wrote to a friend in Holland on April 3 of the extreme nationalism of the younger scientists and professors around him. 'I am convinced that we are dealing with a kind of epidemic of the mind. I cannot otherwise comprehend how men who are thoroughly decent in their personal conduct can adopt such utterly antithetical views on general affairs. It can be compared with developments at the time of the martyrs, the Crusades and the witch burnings.'

Unrestricted German submarine warfare had been in operation for two months. On April 4 the United States Senate voted in favour of war by 82 votes to 6. Two days later the House of Representatives likewise voted for war, by 373 votes to 50. That day, April 6, the United States declared war on Germany. There could be no doubt about the potential impact of America's troops on the battlefield. At least a million, in due course more than three million, were to be under training in the United States. But it would clearly be a long time, at least a year and possibly more, before the vast apparatus of recruitment, training, transportation across the Atlantic, and supply once in France, could be mastered. The American army was small, its recent military experience limited to a punitive expedition in Mexico.

The task of creating an army to serve in Europe began slowly at first. It was a full month after America's declaration of war on Germany that the former commander of the Mexican expedition, General John J. Pershing, then stationed in Texas, received a somewhat cryptic telegram from his father-in-law, a United States Senator: 'Wire me today whether and how

---

[1] Dominic Hibberd, *Wilfred Owen, The Last Year*, Constable, London 1992, page 10.

much you speak, read and write French.' Before he could even reply that he spoke French 'quite fluently', Pershing had been offered the command of the American forces that would eventually be sent to France.

That April, the omens for Germany and Austria were not good. Slowly, the United States would become an active belligerent. Russia, despite the continued arrest and frequent murder of officers by their own men, was still at war. The Allied powers now outnumbered the Central Powers in manpower and resources. Germany and Austria had one geographic asset, however, that could not be taken away from them, the advantage of 'internal lines' of communication. Railway, road and river networks linked their armies, their factories and their capitals in a compact continental mass. The link between New York and London, and between Britain and France and their essential overseas supplies of raw materials and food, could be, and was, hampered by submarine attack. The links between Berlin, Vienna, Budapest and Belgrade could not be effectively disrupted.

The Allied sense of moral indignation was stimulated on April 8, when the British steamer *Torrington* was sunk off Sicily by a German submarine, the *U-55*. Not only did the *U-55* destroy one of the lifeboats, killing fourteen people in it, it also deliberately submerged while twenty of the steamship's passengers were still clinging to the submarine's hull: all of them were drowned.

That day, in a move designed to destroy one of the pillars of the Alliance, Lenin and thirty-two Bolshevik colleagues began their journey from Zurich, travelling by special train through Germany and Sweden, and then by boat across the Gulf of Bothnia to Russia. The Kaiser, told of this stratagem, approved of it. His Austrian counterpart, the young Emperor Charles, warned him, however, that a successful Bolshevik revolution in Russia could be dangerous for all monarchies, five of which had already been 'dethroned in this war'.[1]

Lenin reached Petrograd on April 16, thanks to the facilities provided to him by the Germans. His first speech, at Petrograd's Finland railway station, contained an ominous sentence for Germany: 'The hour is not far when, at the summons of Karl Liebknecht, the German people will turn their weapons against the capitalist exploiters.'

On the Western Front, a new Allied offensive was imminent. On April 5, during a sortie over German lines, Leefe Robinson, who had shot down the airship over England the previous September, winning the Victoria Cross, was himself shot down and taken prisoner. He spent the rest of the war in captivity, his several attempts to escape being foiled. His award-winning exploit did not endear him to his captors. 'The Boche harried and badgered and bullied him in every way possible,' a fellow-prisoner later

[1] The sovereigns were those of Belgium, Serbia, Roumania, Montenegro and Albania: they had each been dethroned as a result of the successful military actions of the Central Powers.

recalled. Those who had attempted to escape were particularly ill-treated, and Robinson, referred to with derision by one camp commandant as 'the English Richthofen', was frequently punished and humiliated.

British soldiers awaited the new offensive on the Western Front, but revealed nothing in their correspondence. In a letter to a friend on April 8, the British poet and painter Isaac Rosenberg wrote: 'We've been in no danger – that is, from shell-fire – for a good long while, though so very close to most terrible fighting. But as far as houses or sign of ordinary human living is concerned, we might as well be in the Sahara Desert. I think I could give some blood-curdling touches if I wished to tell all I see, of dead buried men blown out of their graves, and more, but I will spare you all this.'

On April 9, Easter Monday, British and Canadian forces launched simultaneous offensives at Arras and at Vimy Ridge. In the preparatory air struggle, when for five days British pilots tried to clear the skies for reconnaissance work, seventy-five British aircraft were shot down and nineteen pilots were killed. The first British assaults on the morning of April 9 were successful. The Hindenburg Line was pierced and 5,600 Germans taken prisoner: almost the whole of the German front-line trench system was overrun within three-quarters of an hour, and the second line within two hours. By nightfall even part of the third German line was in British control. The Canadians were also successful in the first hours, taking 4,000 prisoners.

Part of the success on April 9 came from a new artillery device, the 'rolling', or as it was later called 'creeping', barrage, whereby the targets of the artillery would move steadily and systematically forward, while the infantry followed close behind it, talking advantage of the effect of the artillery in stunning the defenders and disrupting the defences. The creeping barrage at Arras was devised, and executed, by Brigade Major Alan Brooke.[1]

The German third line, however, so much better fortified than any previous line, held fast against the renewed assaults hurled against it, even when parts of it were taken. As the day wore on, the British tanks, which were intended to go ahead of the infantrymen, fell behind them, beset by mechanical faults and trapped by the mud. Horse-drawn guns had difficulty crossing the captured German trenches: an unexpected and awkward obstacle for those artillerymen who had never had to take their guns beyond the front line before. Nor did the word 'success' mean that the suffering of the victors was less than that of the vanquished, in either this attack or any other. Among the Canadians killed on April 9 was Private Earl Hembroff, who, the previous October, had been serving on the Somme with the Canadian Field Ambulance. On that occasion he had written in

[1] From 1941 to 1945, Brooke was Chief of the Imperial General Staff, Britain's most senior army officer.

his dairy: 'Not many rats and Fritz too busy to put over gas.' Also killed at Arras on that first day of the battle was the British poet Edward Thomas, who so loved the English countryside:

> This ploughman dead in battle slept out of doors
> Many a frozen night, and merrily
> Answered staid drinkers, good bedmen, and all bores:
> 'At Mrs Greenland's Hawthorn Bush,' said he,
> 'I slept.' None knew which bush. Above the town,
> Beyond 'The Drover', a hundred spot the down
> In Wiltshire. And where now at last he sleeps
> More sound in France – that, too, he secret keeps.

Another British soldier killed on April 9 was R.E. Vernede, a 41-year-old Londoner. After being wounded on the Somme in 1916, he had refused a desk job at the War Office in order to return to the front. He was killed by machine-gun fire while leading his platoon in an attack on Havrincourt Wood. In his poem 'A Listening Post' he had expressed his confidence in the rightness of the Allied cause:

> And yonder rifleman and I
>   Wait here behind the misty trees
> To shoot the first man that goes by
>   Our rifles ready on our knees
>
> How could he know that if we fail
>   The world may lie in chains for years
> And England be a bygone tale
>   And right be wrong, and laughter tears?

On the night of April 9 the attacking forces tried to sleep in unexpected cold, with snow flurries. At least one man died from exposure. On April 10 the attack was resumed, given an added urgency for its commander, General Allenby, by the news that substantial German reinforcements were being brought up. On that second evening of the battle Allenby felt confident enough that a breakthrough was within his grasp to send a message to his commanders: 'All troops are to understand that the Third Army is now pursuing a defeated enemy and that risks must be freely taken.' Allenby's most recent biographer, Lawrence James, comments: 'Relayed to the men at the front, the message was received with incredulity.'

A sense of imminent victory persisted even on the following day, when, at Haig's insistence, cavalry were sent forward to penetrate what seemed to be a widening gap in the German lines. As men and horses trotted forward in a snow blizzard they were heard singing the Eton Boating Song, 'Jolly boating weather'. They were halted, however, Allenby later wrote, and then pushed back 'by wire and machine guns'.

On that third day of the battle, April 11, Allenby captured one of his objectives of the first day, the village of Monchy-le-Preux. But as snow blizzards became more frequent, the first German reinforcements reached the battlefield. For many of the attackers, three consecutive days in action had brought them to the limit of their endurance. Allenby was warned by a front-line officer that the men were 'suffering from cold and were tired out'. Haig now urged caution, telling Allenby that the time for 'great risks' had passed, that further infantry attacks would lead only to unnecessary loss of life, and that 'we must try and substitute shells as far as possible for men'. Allenby tried one further infantry assault, sending a Scottish battalion forward, to a point where they were accidentally hit, and hit severely, by a mistimed British creeping barrage, and then by skilfully placed German machine guns.

On April 14, in an act of widely reported heroism, ten men of the Royal Newfoundland Regiment, having lost 485 of their colleagues killed or badly wounded, held Monchy-le-Preux for five hours against a German division, until reinforcements came. At Vimy Ridge, the Canadians had gained 4,500 yards of the German line and taken 4,000 German prisoners, but at a cost of 3,598 of their own men killed and more than 7,000 wounded. That day, three British generals defied army tradition by protesting directly to Haig at the mounting casualties. Allenby argued that the troops had spent too long in the trenches and had forgotten how to fight a war of movement across country. On April 15, Haig ordered an end to the offensive. By the standards of the Western Front, Allenby could regard himself as a victor. A dent of four miles had been made along ten miles of the German front line.

In a cemetery in the suburbs of Arras, a British national memorial gives the names of 35,928 soldiers killed on that battlefield, but who had no known grave. In this cemetery there are also 2,395 individually named British graves, and a number of other graves.[1] British air losses had also been high during the Battle of Arras: 131 aircraft and 316 airmen, a third of the strength of the Royal Flying Corps in France, which called the month 'Bloody April'. Above the French lines, Captain Joseph Vuillemin began, on April 16, the first of a series of successful aerial combats that were to win him the Croix de Guerre with thirteen palms and eleven stars.[2]

On Vimy Ridge, 250 acres of shell-pocked land, given by the people of France in perpetuity to the people of Canada, are planted with Canadian trees and dominated by a massive war memorial with the names of 11,500 Canadian soldiers killed on the battlefield but never identified for burial. Throughout the battlefield, large and small cemeteries tell the story of the heavy loss of life among the attackers.[3] Sixty-seven military cemeteries

---

[1] The other individual graves are of 152 Canadians, 60 South Africans, 28 Germans, 23 New Zealanders, nine Indians, six British West Indians, one Newfoundlander, one Frenchman, one Russian and one 'unknown'.

[2] From 1938 to 1940 Vuillemin was Chief of the French Air Staff. In 1943 he became head of the Free French bomber forces then in North Africa.

[3] In the larger cemeteries, 521 British and 155 Canadian soldiers are buried at Lieven, 129 Canadians and 8 British at Givenchy-en-Gohelle, 531 Canadians and 215 British at Neuville St Vaast , 590 Canadians and 90 British at La Chaudière, 245 Canadians and 50 British at Thélus,

mark the course and destruction of this battle alone. The poet Siegfried Sassoon expressed his feelings thus:

> 'Good-morning; good-morning!' the General said
> When we met him last week on our way to the line.
> Now the soldiers he smiled at are most of 'em dead,
> And we're cursing his staff for incompetent swine.
> 'He's a cheery old card,' grunted Harry to Jack
> As they slogged up to Arras with rifle and pack
>
> But he did for them both by his plan of attack.

On April 16, the day after the Battle of Arras was brought to an end, the French launched their own attack against the German forces on the river Aisne, using twenty divisions along a 25-mile front. Planned by General Nivelle, and known as the Nivelle Offensive, the attack was a disaster, despite the first use of tanks by the French. Nivelle planned to advance a full six miles. His men were halted after six hundred yards. He had expected about 15,000 casualties: there were almost 100,000. Of the 128 tanks in action, thirty-two were knocked out on the first day. Of the two hundred aircraft planned to be in action, only 131 were available when the battle began, and these were worsted in combat with the German fighters. Every element in the planning proved disastrous on the day, even the use of black African troops to drive forward into the German lines. 'Decimated by machine gun fire,' one historian has written, 'Senegalese troops break and flee.'[1]

One of the objectives of the Nivelle Offensive was the fort of Nogent-l'Abbesse, one of the circle of forts around Reims, from which the Germans repeatedly bombarded the city. But the heights to the east of Reims were extremely well fortified, and despite the enthusiasm in Paris at news of initial successes as several heights were overrun, the German counter-attacks were successful. Two villages in the battle zone, Nauroy and Moronvillers, were totally destroyed.

As Nivelle's offensive on the Western Front was crumbling into failure, in Palestine the British launched their second attempt to capture Gaza. Again the Turks were outnumbered by two to one. This time eight tanks and the first gas shells used on the Palestine Front were intended to make victory certain. But the attack was a failure. The tanks were unsuitable for the desert conditions, three of them were captured by the Turks, and Gaza remained under their complete control. Reinforcements were called for: both Italian and French troops were brought from Europe to join the next assault.

504 British and 92 Canadians at Roclincourt, and 97 British, almost all of them Scotsmen, at St Laurent-Blangny, all of them killed on 9 April 1917.
[1] Randal Gray, *Chronicle of the First World War*, volume II, 1917–1921, Oxford 1991, page 38. All students of the First World War are indebted to Randal Gray, and to his colleague Christopher Argyle, for their outlines of the war in all its aspects.

17

War, desertion, mutiny

APRIL–JULY 1917

Far away from the battlefields, and with America's impact still to be felt, two of Germany's three partners, Austria and Bulgaria, were beginning to try to find some way of discussing peace with the Allies. Working through diplomats in Switzerland, on 12 April 1917 there was an initiative in which they tried to find out what terms would be acceptable. But the mood of the Allies was uncompromising: America's decision to enter the war seemed to open up the prospect of a decisive swing in the Allied favour. Five days later, an ominous foretaste of what was to become a storm took place on the Aisne, when seventeen French soldiers deserted their trench shortly before an attack was due to begin.

On the flank of the Aisne, General Mangin made a four-mile penetration of the German line, but when the battle was called off on April 20, Nivelle admitted that there could be no breakthrough. In the air, the Germans had also maintained ascendancy on the Western Front: on April 21, Baron Richthofen celebrated his eightieth aerial victory. On the following day, in what had so recently been an integral part of the Tsarist dominions, German troops entered Helsinki.

On April 23, on the Western Front, in an attempt to relieve the growing German pressure on the French, and lessen the potentially disastrous impact of the French mutinies, which were spreading, British troops were again in action east of Arras, at Monchy-le-Preux. Haig had been reluctant to restart an offensive he had called off eight days earlier at the request of three of his generals, but the French were insistent. Among those killed on the first day of the renewed offensive was a friend of Vera Brittain, Geoffrey. Another of her close friends, Victor, had been blinded near Arras two weeks earlier, after having been shot through the head. As often happened during the war, a letter from a soldier who had been killed reached its destination after his death. Three days before he was killed Geoffrey had written of how he hoped he would not fail at the critical moment, that he was 'a horrible coward', and that for his school's sake he so wanted to do well. Geoffrey's letter ended: 'If destiny is willing I will write later.'

Vera Brittain subsequently commented: 'Well, I thought, destiny was not willing, and I shall not see that graceful, generous handwriting on an envelope any more.' Her Geoffrey had been killed by a sniper while trying to get in touch with the battalion on his left, some hours before the start of the attack. 'Shot through the chest, he died speechless, gazing intently at his orderly. The place where he lay was carefully marked, but when the action was over his body had disappeared and was never afterwards found.' Vera Brittain's brother Edward, who had recovered from his wound on the Somme, wrote from the Western Front: 'Dear child, there is no more to say; we have lost almost all there was to lose and what have we gained? Truly as you say has patriotism worn very very threadbare.'

Haig wanted the offensive at Arras to continue. On May 1, perturbed by the heavy casualties, Allenby asked him to call it off. Some units, beset by mud and bad visibility, had advanced without proper support and 'were left isolated and were lost, as a consequence of their gallantry'. Haig, however, was convinced that more gains could be made. Two days later a night attack failed when the units, moving forward, lost contact with each other in the dark. But still the offensive was to continue, and for six days after Allenby's first protest it went on. On May 7, however, Allenby warned Haig that the reserves then being sent into the battle were 'semi-trained troops unable to use their rifles properly'.

Twice as many British troops as German were being killed in the renewed attacks that Haig now demanded. In the House of Commons on May 10, Churchill, then in opposition to the Government, pointed out that American troops would not be ready for action until 1918 and went on to ask: 'Is it not obvious that we ought not to squander the remaining armies of France and Britain in precipitate offensives before the American power begins to be felt on the battlefield?' He received no answer. There would be more offensives before the Americans arrived. Allenby's protests, too, were to no avail: within a few weeks of his warning to Haig he was sent back to London, where he learned that he was not to command again on the Western Front. He was convinced that he had been sacked.

Allenby's command was given to the victor of Vimy, General Byng. For Allenby there was a distant posting to Cairo, and command of the Egyptian Expeditionary Force. The British and Imperial troops there had twice tried to cross from the Sinai into Palestine. On both occasions they been defeated by the Turks outside Gaza. Allenby was not being sent out, however, merely to hold the line or fight a third losing battle. Lloyd George, undeterred by these past failures, gave him the instruction: 'Jerusalem by Christmas'. The capture of the Holy City would be an unexpected, exotic gift for a nation tired of the set-backs and casualties of the Western Front.

For Britain and the countries of the Empire, the number of war dead and the need to mark their graves led, on May 21, to the creation of the

Imperial War Graves Commission. It was charged by Royal Charter with the duty of marking and maintaining the graves of all members of the armed forces of the Empire who died during the war, to build cemeteries and memorials, and to keep registers and records. Around Arras itself, where battle was raging that May, more than a hundred cemeteries mark the sites and losses of the conflict. A mile and a quarter from Arras Station, a memorial to the missing lists the names of 35,928 soldiers who were killed in action in the region in 1917 and 1918, as well as all the British pilots and air crew who fell on the Western Front, but have no known grave. In the graveyard attached to the memorial are more than 2,600 named gravestones, of British, Canadian, South African, New Zealand, Indian, British West Indian and Newfoundland soldiers: also one Frenchman, one Russian and twenty-eight Germans.

On the Salonica Front, April 24 saw a twelve-hour British assault on the Bulgarian positions above Lake Doiran. After a two-day preliminary artillery bombardment, it was hoped to drive the Bulgarians out of their first line of trenches and then, bringing up artillery, to force them back out of their second line. The attack was planned for after dark. Half an hour before it was to begin, the Bulgarians, using searchlights, launched an artillery barrage of their own. Still the attack went forward. Twice the Bulgarian trenches were reached, and twice lost.

One line of advance lay up a narrow defile, the Jumeaux Ravine. Here the force of the explosion of the shells was such that men were killed by being blown against the rock surface. It was a long way from Devon and Wiltshire, from where the first British troops caught in the ravine had come, only to be killed at long distance by the heavy shells of German naval guns, always hellish when used on land. Fighting continued until dawn. While some units were forced back to their own trenches, others succeeded in taking the first line of Bulgarian trenches and holding them against four successive counter-attacks. When day came, the Bulgarians allowed British stretcher bearers to collect the wounded from the ravine. One medical orderly was even allowed to go through a gap in the Bulgarian wire to take out a man who was lying wounded only ten yards from the front-line parapet.

A French attack on the Monastir Front was meant to have taken place simultaneously, but had to be postponed because of heavy snow. When fighting was renewed at dusk on April 26 a British brigade, which had succeeded in crossing the Jumeaux Ravine, went forward too soon, and was caught by its own artillery fire. More than 5,000 of the attackers were killed or wounded during the battle.

In Petrograd, despite the existence of the warmaking Provisional Government, the Soviet was acting as a parallel source of authority, and as an anti-war focus. On the Eastern Front the anti-war movement was gaining in strength, but was not yet universally supported. Early in April the

Russian 109th division fraternised with the German troops opposite them. A loyal Russian artillery unit opened fire on the rebels, whereupon their leader, Lieutenant Khaust, arrested the two artillery officers who had given the order to fire.

On April 20 Khaust and ten other soldiers from his regiment appeared before a specially-convened Assembly of the Russian 12th Army and demanded an immediate peace, with a simultaneous laying down of arms by both sides. The Assembly, however, although made up only of soldiers, without any officers, would not support them. Its 'president', a Jewish soldier named Rom, had to intervene to prevent Khaust and his colleagues being attacked by the other men. In Petrograd, the British Military Attaché, Colonel Knox, suggested that Khaust and his fellow agitators should be arrested. He was told by the Assistant Minister of War, Colonel Yaku-bovich, that this was something the army could not and dare not do, even though it had publicly announced increased disciplinary powers. Yakubovich also told Knox that of drafts 1,000-strong sent from depots in the rear only 150 to 250 men reached the front. In the munitions factories, the technicians were being expelled. Bolshevik anti-war propa-ganda was also incessant. On April 23 the Party's newspaper, *Pravda*, asked the Russian soldiers: 'Are you willing to fight for this, that the English capitalists should rob Mesopotamia and Palestine?'

On April 24, in an unprecedented act of divisiveness, the Ukraine demanded autonomy from Russia. Strikes in the Russian factories had already reduced Russia's coal production by almost a quarter over the previous year. On April 27 Lenin, having arrived in Petrograd eleven days earlier, took the chair at the Petrograd Bolshevik Conference.

That day the sailors at Kronstadt declared their support for the Bol-sheviks and announced that they would have nothing to do with the orders put out by the Provisional Government. Two days later the Russian Commander-in-Chief, General Alexeyev, informed the Minis-ter of War that information from all sides 'indicates that the Army is systematically falling apart'. Looking at the Russian situation from Germany, General Hoffmann noted in his diary on the following day: 'We are showering newspapers and leaflets on the Russians and trying to get at them in various ways.' The Russian revolution, Hoff-mann added, 'is a godsend to us'. But at the beginning of May more than 50,000 wounded Russian soldiers demonstrated in favour of the continuation of the war, and on May 4, by a narrow margin, and to Lenin's distress, the Petrograd Soviet gave its support to the Provisional Government.

The Eastern Front would remain in place, despite a massive increase in the number of deserters, as many as two million by the beginning of May. The night life of Petrograd would also go on. 'Theatres and cabarets remained open,' the historian John Wheeler-Bennett has written. 'At the "Europe", Jimmy, the barman from the old New York Waldorf-Astoria, continued to purvey his famous concoctions. The ballet season was in full swing, with Karsavina enchanting her public, while at the opera Chaliapin had never been in better voice.'[1]

The Germans looked with alarm at the decision of the Russian Provisional Government to remain at war. 'We are giving the Russians much good advice,' Hoffmann wrote in his diary on May 12, 'telling them to behave sensibly and make peace, but they don't yet seem anxious to do so.' The Chairman of the Duma, Rodzianko, was looking for means of stimulating the war effort. That month he authorised the establishment of an all-women's battalion. It was headed by Maria Bochkareva, the daughter of a Siberian peasant and former serf who had fought against the Turks in the war of 1878, reaching the rank of sergeant. In 1914 his daughter had been refused admission into the army. After successfully petitioning the Tsar, she fought on the Eastern Front for three years, being wounded four times and decorated for acts of bravery on three separate occasions. The creation of the women's battalion made such an impact that the British suffragette Emmeline Pankhurst travelled to Petrograd to support Bochkareva's efforts, which the anti-war Bolsheviks denounced.

The ability of Russia to continue at war was everywhere being undermined. At Pernau, on the Gulf of Riga, the men of one regiment demanded of their commander that he take off his shoulder straps with their badge of rank 'as a mark of sympathy to their brothers of the Baltic Fleet' who had already declared their support for the revolution. The commander refused, and was murdered. The men of a whole Russian division, the 120th, not only crossed over into the German trenches as an act of mass desertion, but pointed out to the Germans the location of the Russian artillery battery facing them. On May 27 a battalion commander told Colonel Knox that while none of his men had deserted 'everything in the rear had gone, transport drivers, depot units etc. His men are absolutely without boots and are wasting from sickness.'

It had become clear in the Allied capitals that the United States' entry into the war would not have any influence on the battlefield for at least a year. This was a grave set-back for the Allies, especially as Germany, the country whose indiscriminate submarine warfare had forced America into the war, continued to operate at sea with relative impunity. At the beginning of May it was announced that the shipping losses of the Allied and neutral States in April was the highest of the war thus far: 373 ships, with a total weight of 873,754 tons.[2]

Among the German successes that spring was the sinking of the troopship *Arcadian* on April 15, in the Aegean, when 279 British soldiers were

---

[1] John W. Wheeler-Bennett, *Brest-Litovsk, The Forgotten Peace, March 1918*, Macmillan, London 1938, page 45.
[2] This was in fact the highest monthly shipping loss of both the First and Second World Wars. In the following month (May 1917) 285 Allied and neutral ships were sunk, with a total of 589,603 tons, and in the next month (June 1917) 286 Allied and neutral ships were sunk, totalling 674,458 tons.

drowned; the sinking of the French destroyer *Etendard* off Dunkirk ten days later, when all her crew was lost; the sinking of the British destroyer *Derwent* by a mine on May 2, when fifty-two sailors were drowned; and the sinking of the British troopship *Transylvania* in the Gulf of Genoa on May 4, when 413 soldiers were drowned, but 2,500 were saved by the Japanese destroyer *Matsu* that was escorting them.[1]

For more than three years the British Admiralty had resisted all calls for the introduction of the convoy system, unwilling to see its warships taken away from their fleets or diverted from participation, however remote, in a major naval battle. But the ever-rising scale of German submarine successes forced Lloyd George's Government to set up a system whereby all merchant ships sailing across the Atlantic Ocean would sail in groups and be given naval protection. A convoy of ten to fifty merchant ships with, possibly, a troopship attached to it, could be escorted throughout the voyage by one cruiser, six destroyers, eleven armed trawlers, and two torpedo boats each with an aerial balloon whose observers could look down from their baskets to detect underwater submarines and the tracks of torpedoes.

Only with the introduction of the convoy system on May 24, did the scale of the German submarine sinkings decline. In the first convoy, which sailed from Hampton Roads, Virginia, to Britain, the only merchant ship lost was one that fell behind the convoy. In June, sixty merchant ships sailed in convoy across the Atlantic without a single loss. Of the 1,100,000 American troops brought across the Atlantic in convoy between May 1917 and November 1918, only 637 were drowned as a result of German submarine sinking. When the American troopship *Tuscania* was torpedoed in February 1918, the convoy of which she was a part rescued 2,187 of the 2,397 troops on board.

Seven more convoy collection points were set up after May 1917. These were at Halifax, Nova Scotia, for ships coming from the Great Lakes and the St Lawrence; at Panama for ships coming from Australia and New Zealand; at Rio de Janeiro for Argentinian supplies of foodstuffs and horses, on which so much of the British war effort depended; at Murmansk for military supplies being sent to Russia; at Port Said and Gibraltar for the trans-Mediterranean, East African and Indian Ocean trade and troop transports; and at Dakar, on the Atlantic Coast of Africa, for the trade and war supplies from East and South Africa, and from the Far East.

Germany's hope of being able to starve Britain into surrender was over. But, despite the success of the convoy system, the war at sea continued to be a harsh one: on May 26 a German submarine sank a British hospital ship, the *Dover Castle*, off the coast of Algeria. Seven passengers drowned. Four years later, in June 1921, the submarine's commander, Captain

[1] Six weeks later, sixty-eight Japanese sailors drowned when their destroyer *Sakaki* was torpedoed by an Austrian submarine off Crete.

Neumann, was accused of war crimes at the Leipzig War Crimes Tribunal, before German judges. His plea that he was acting on 'higher orders' was accepted, and he was acquitted.

On the Western Front, despite the heavy casualties at Arras, the British Expeditionary Force had, in six weeks of fighting, pushed the Germans back between two and five miles, along a twenty-mile front, firing more than six million shells. Half the German divisions engaged were forced to take a period of rest and recuperation. In the first week of May, the British poet, Isaac Rosenberg, finished the first draft of a poem that described the course of a limber carrying barbed wire up to the front line on the Western Front:

> *The wheels lurched over sprawled dead*
> *But pained them not, though their bones crunched,*
> *Their shut mouths made no moan,*
> *They lie there huddled, friend and foeman,*
> *Man born of man, and born of woman,*
> *And shells go crying over them*
> *From night to night and now.*
>
> *Earth has waited for them*
> *All the time of their growth*
> *Fretting for their decay:*
> *Now she has them at last!*

For those who fought in the trenches, there were many moments of contemplation and long periods of waiting, with time to reflect on the purpose and consequences of the war. In a letter to his parents from the Western Front, a young soldier wrote on May 20: 'Nothing but immeasurable improvements will ever justify all the damnable waste and unfairness of this war – I only hope those who are left will *never, never* forget at what sacrifice those improvements have been won.' His name was Norman Chamberlain, a cousin of the future British Prime Minister. Also with time to reflect, but in the isolation of a prison cell on the Salisbury Plain, Clifford Allen, leader of the No-Conscription Fellowship, who had been in prison since the previous August, faced his third Court Martial on May 25. There was 'no substantial reason,' he told the court, 'to prevent Peace negotiations being entered upon at once'.

Quoting a recent statement by a Cabinet Minister that so far in the war 'seven million human beings have been killed in all the nations and forty-five millions wounded', Allen went on to ask: 'Will there be such a supreme difference between Peace now and Peace in say, two years' time as to justify the supreme sacrifice of, say, another seven million lives?' In years to come 'the peoples of all nations will look back with amazement when they come to realise how the Governments permitted and instigated this sacrifice to achieve so small a result.' The longer that conscientious objectors were kept in prison, Allen added, 'the more certainly you establish our hope that the spirit of Russian freedom shall not be confined within Russian national boundaries'. He was sentenced to two years' hard labour, and sent to Winchester Prison.

By mid-May the troops under Haig's command had made greater advances than at any time since the start of trench warfare two and a half years earlier. These gains included sixty-one square miles of German-held territory, more than 20,000 prisoners-of-war, and 252 heavy guns, in just over a month of fighting. The tank had become an integral part of the British infantry advance. The first German tank trial was held only that month, on May 14 at Mainz, two days before the renewed Battle of Arras ended.

On the Salonica Front, a new Allied offensive opened on the evening of May 8 with a British night attack. Like the attack two weeks earlier, it was frustrated by Bulgarian searchlights and artillery fire, so that only five hundred yards were gained on a two-mile front. On the following day, Russian, Serbian, Italian and French troops, the latter including Annamites and Senegalese, were also in action elsewhere in the line, especially north and west of Monastir. Such gains as were made were soon lost, most of the overrun trenches being exposed to Bulgarian, German and Austrian artillery fire. The Bulgarian lines could not be breached. Guarded by German heavy guns, Austrian howitzers and Bulgarian artillery, the April and May objectives, high peaks with high-sounding names, remained in Bulgarian hands. As one of the historians of the campaign, Alan Palmer, has written: 'Not a single Allied soldier had come within two miles of the Grand Couronné, the central keep of the Devil's citadel; from its ramparts the Eye would stand sentinel for another sixteen months, watching and counting and waiting.'[1]

In the plain, as summer came, the British withdrew beyond the river Struma, holding a series of bridgeheads across it that could quickly be reinforced if the Bulgarians showed signs of hostile activity. In fact, the Bulgarians welcomed the respite, and put out placards with the words: 'We know you are going back to the hills, so are we.' That summer the official British newspaper correspondent in the Balkans, G. Ward Price, commented: 'The only forces that hold the Struma valley in strength are the mosquitoes, and their effectives may be counted by thousands of millions.' Another enemy had also reached the Balkans: on May 18 the commander of the Russian forces on the Salonica Front, General Dietrichs, expressed his concern at the effect of the news from Russia on his men. 'The latest events in Russia,' he wrote, 'added to the slowness and uncertainty of postal communication and the various rumours and occasional gossip

[1] Alan Palmer, *The Gardeners of Salonika*, André Deutsch, London 1965, page 125.

reaching the trenches from the rear and spread around by good-for-nothings, can only strain the men's nerves further, worrying them and paralysing their will.'

As the Balkan impasse continued, the Italian army launched its tenth Battle of the Isonzo on the front with Austria. British artillery batteries, in action for the first time on the Italian Front, earned the Italian commander, General Cadorna's lyrical recognition: 'Amid the roar of battle was clearly heard the voice of British guns.' The battle lasted for eighteen days and although many of the hilltops captured by the Italians were lost again during the Austrian counter-attacks, it was an Italian victory, with 23,681 Austrians taken prisoner, among them more than six hundred officers.

The Italian soldiers had no illusions about a swift breakthrough. Among their many jingles was the verse:

> *Il General Cadorna*
> *Ha scritto alla Regina*
> *'Se vuoi veder Trieste,*
> *Compra una cartolina.'*[1]

Among their prisoners, the Italian soldiers took many Czechs and Slovaks, Croats, and even Italians from the Austrian province of Istria. Some then joined the Italian army to fight against their former imperial masters.

In Petrograd, the War Minister of the Provisional Government, General Guchkov, resigned on May 13, warning that there was a limit to the democratisation of the army 'beyond which disintegration is bound to begin'. On May 15 the Petrograd Soviet issued a manifesto to the 'Socialists of all Countries' demanding a 'platform of peace without annexations or indemnities'. The Provisional Government rejected all calls for peace: on the day after the publication of the socialist manifesto, the Minister of Justice, Alexander Kerensky, accepted the War Ministry portfolio. His aim was to renew the offensive abilities of the Russian army.

In the Reichstag that day the German Chancellor, Bethmann-Hollweg, offered the Russians immediate peace. The Provisional Government rejected this, but the anti-war forces were gathering. On the day of the German peace offer, a leading revolutionary, who had been interned in Canada for the past month, arrived in Petrograd: Leon Trotsky. At the same time, the Provisional Government took into its ranks six moderate members of the Petrograd Soviet, members of the Menshevik faction which Trotsky had once led, and to which Lenin and the Bolshevik members of the Soviet were implacably opposed.

War and revolution had become inextricably entwined. One of the most energetic members of the Provisional Government, Alexander Kerensky, who had just been appointed Minister of War, was determined to halt the

---

[1] *General Cadorna, Has written to the Queen, 'If you want to see Trieste, Buy a picture postcard.'*

drift to anarchy, and to peace. On May 19 he announced that no further resignations would be accepted from senior military officers, and that all deserters who did not return to their units would be punished. Three days later he replaced the vacillating General Alexeyev with the victorious Brusilov as Commander-in-Chief, and on May 25 he issued an Order for the Offensive. But on the following day it was reported that 30,000 deserters a day were reaching Kiev from the front, on their way back into Russia.

In Austria, at the end of May, when the Austrian Parliament, the Reichsrat, met for the first time since March 1914, the Polish deputies declared their support for Polish independence, while the Serb, Croat and Slovene deputies announced the formation of a 'Yugoslav Parliamentary Club'. On the following day, in an attempt to defuse nationalist discontent, the Emperor Charles promised a more nationally oriented post-war constitution.

Anti-war feeling was not only seen that spring in Russia, and in the growing number of French army desertions: on May 22 the British Cabinet had approved a scheme to 'counter-attack the pacifist movement' in Britain. Conscientious objectors were prepared to face long prison sentences rather than serve in the trenches. Poets who were in the trenches had begun to write with unprecedented bitterness. Siegfried Sassoon caught a mood of hopelessness in his description of a soldier in a working party, piling sandbags along the parapet of his trench at night, eager to get back to his tot of rum, and sleep:

> *He pushed another bag along the top,*
> *Craning his body outward; then a flare*
> *Gave one white glimpse of No Man's Land and wire;*
> *And as he dropped his head the instant split*
> *His startled life with lead, and all went out.*

The first 243 American soldiers to reach Britain did so on May 18. They were the medical staff and orderlies for a base hospital. On May 26 the first American combat troops arrived in France. By the end of that week a total of 1,308 had landed.

The arrival of the first American troops coincided with a dramatic change on the French sector of the Western Front, where the growing number of desertions turned, on May 27, to mutiny. At the Front itself, along the Chemin des Dames, as many as 30,000 soldiers had left their trenches and reserve billets and fallen to the rear. Then, in four towns behind the lines, the troops ignored their officers' orders, seized buildings, and refused to go to the Front.[1] On the following day, at Fère-en-Tardenois railway station, the mutineers tried to get to Paris, but the trains were prevented from leaving.

---

[1] The towns were Soissons, Villers-Cotterets, Fère-en-Tardenois and Coeuvres.

Two days later, at the Front, several hundred French infantrymen refused to move into the front-line trenches, where they were needed to go to the support of French Moroccan troops already in the line.

On May 28, when the French mutinies were in their second day, the commander of the American Expeditionary Force, General Pershing, and his Staff, left New York for Liverpool on board the British steamship *Baltic*. During the transatlantic voyage Pershing decided to plan for an army of at least a million men 'to reach France as early as possible'. For the French High Command, beset by its daily barrage of news from the disaffected regions, even 'as soon as possible' seemed a distant prospect.

On June 1, at Missy-aux-Bois, a French infantry regiment took over the whole town and established an anti-war 'Government'. For a week there was chaos through the French war zone, as the mutineers refused to go back into the line. The military authorities took swift action: under Pétain's guiding hand, mass arrests and Courts Martial followed, with 23,385 guilty verdicts being passed for mutinous behaviour. More than four hundred soldiers were sentenced to death, fifty of them being shot, the rest sent to penal servitude in the French colonies. For several million infantrymen, some of whom had been fighting for nearly three years, Pétain brought in immediate improvements, organising longer periods of rest, more home leave, and better food. 'I set about suppressing serious cases of indiscipline with the utmost urgency,' he explained to his army commanders on June 18. 'I will maintain this repression firmly, but without forgetting that it applies to soldiers who have been in the trenches with us for three years and who are our soldiers.' Within six weeks the mutinies were over. 'They died away with a surprising speed,' one historian has commented, 'that leaves a mystery as to which of Pétain's actions had most effect in reconciling the army to endless continuation of a dreary and dangerous war.'[1]

The scale of the mutinies made clear to the French High Command that the soldiers were unwilling to go through the torments of a renewed offensive. They would hold the line, but not go over the top. This put a considerable burden on the British forces on the Western Front, who were soon to bear the brunt of a renewed Allied effort in France and Flanders. 'The awful losses incurred by the British in the Third Battle of Ypres (Passchendaele)', writes a leading British military historian, 'were in part the result of efforts to distract German attention and strength from the weakened French sector.'[2]

From the air, a new type of warfare was introduced on the afternoon of May 25, when twenty-three German bombers set off from two airfields in Belgium for London. The machines were Gothas. There was something in

[1] Correlli Barnett, *The Swordbearers, Studies in Supreme Command in the First World War,* Eyre and Spottiswoode, London 1963, page 236.
[2] John Keegan, 'An army downs tools', *The Times Literary Supplement,* 13 May 1994.

the very name 'Gotha' that seemed to add terror. Each carried thirteen bombs. Because of cloud, only two reached England, but the five bombs dropped by one of these aeroplanes caused more casualties than in any of the Zeppelin raids before it. At a military camp at Shorncliffe, sixteen Canadian soldiers were killed. At Folkestone it was civilians who were the victims: sixteen men, thirty women and twenty-five children. When the raid was over, 95 people had been killed and 192 injured, and a new element had been introduced to warfare, that was not to find its apogee until two decades had passed. 'The ancient Jehovah is still abroad,' Albert Einstein wrote to a friend in Holland on June 3. 'Alas he slays the innocent along with the guilty, whom he strikes so fearsomely blind that they can feel no sense of guilt.'

During the next German bombing raid, on June 4, thirteen British civilians were killed.

The war on the battlefield had become one of bizarre contrast. On both the Eastern and Western Fronts the savagery of the conflict was matched by mass desertions, mutinies and fraternisation. On the Eastern Front, General Hoffmann noted in his dairy on June 1 that an armistice was to all intents and purposes 'in being at many points'. At other points there was fighting. 'It is indeed a strange war!'

Three days later, in Paris, as the mutinous French troops everywhere revealed their hatred of the war, the French Minister of War, Painlevé, estimated that there were only two reliable French divisions between the front line and Paris, seventy miles away. In an attempt to gain extra men, and also to encourage anti-Central Power sentiment, on June 4, the day of Painlevé's warning, the French Government authorised the formation of a Polish army to serve alongside the Allied forces on the Western Front. In Warsaw, Polish university students went on strike, as a manifestation of national aspirations.

In England, an anti-war meeting was held in Leeds in the first week of June. One newspaper commented on June 4: 'Leeds, as a city, did not extend a hearty welcome to the National Labour and Socialist Convention, which opened in the Coliseum this morning.' The first resolution, moved by the former (and future) leader of the Labour Party, Ramsay MacDonald, congratulated the Russian people on their revolution. There was then a call, amid cheers, for the delegates 'to fetch out Clifford Allen – and do as the Russians had done.' Bertrand Russell, who was present, championed those one thousand pacifists who, like Allen, were in prison, stating that 'by their refusal of military service, conscientious objectors had shown that it was possible for the individual to stand against the whole power of the State. That was a very great discovery, which enhanced the dignity of man.'

Among those in prison for refusing military or alternative civilian service were Stephen Hobhouse, the member of a wealthy Quaker family who had renounced his inheritance and worked for the poor in the East End of London; and Corder Catchpool, also a Quaker, who in the Second World War was to lead a campaign against the bombing of German cities.

On June 5 the registration began throughout the United States, under the Selective Draft Act, for all men between twenty-one and thirty to register for military service. This act, declared the *New York Times*, gave 'a long and sorely needed means of disciplining a certain insolent foreign element in this nation'. The reference was to America's Jews, whose pacifist elements were no greater, by proportion, than those of other Americans. Universal military service, one American rabbi insisted, was an institution deriving from the time of Moses. In support of this pro-war view there was also a verse in the Psalms which British Jews had cited two years earlier as a religious justification for going to war: 'Blessed be the Lord, my Rock, Who teacheth my hands to war and my fingers to fight.'

Within two months of the passage of the Selective Draft Act, Jews made up 6 per cent of the American armed forces, though they were only 2 per cent of the population.

On the Western Front, with the pessimistic Allenby no longer one of his commanders, Haig told his senior generals on June 5: 'The power and endurance of the German people is being strained to such a degree as to make it possible that the breaking point may be reached this year.' Two days later the British Expeditionary Force launched its second offensive in two months, against the German trenches, dug-outs and fortifications on the Messines-Wytschaete Ridge. The attack was preceded in the early hours of the morning by a phenomenal explosion, so loud that it caused panic in German-occupied Lille, fifteen miles away. This was the culminating effort of the Tunnelling Companies that had first reached France two and a half years earlier.

Nineteen mines were exploded under the German front line, with a total explosive power of five hundred tons. It had taken British, Canadian and Australian tunnellers more than six months to dig the shafts, one of which was 2,000 feet long. The deepest of the mines were placed a hundred feet below the German trenches. One of the explosions, at Spanbroekmolen, blew a crater 430 feet in diameter. Two mines failed to explode: one of them was deliberately detonated in 1955, the other remains underground somewhere to the north-east of Ploegsteert Wood, its exact position unknown, exciting periodic local nervousness, as I found on my own visits to the area in 1970 and 1971.

The effect of the explosions at Messines was devastating. Ten thousand German soldiers are thought to have been killed outright or buried alive. Thousands more were stunned and dazed, and 7,354 taken prisoner. A British artillery bombardment of 2,266 guns added to the impact. Among the British officers whose men moved forward in the immediate aftermath of the mine explosions was the twenty-year-old Anthony Eden. 'As the barrage opened,' he later wrote, 'simultaneously the noise of the guns deadened all sound from the mine, except that we could hear, even above this crescendo, the screams of the imprisoned Germans in the crater. We could do nothing for them, for we had at all costs to keep up with our barrage.' Moving forward immediately behind the British artillery barrage, Eden and his men captured a German machine gun and its crew intact. 'Presumably they were too shaken by the mine explosion to do their job in time.'

From Eden's company, only one British soldier was killed that morning: he must have gone ahead of the other men, seeking to knock out a German position. Eden recalled coming across him: 'The man had just fallen and lay spread-eagled on the ground, mortally wounded and already unconscious. I knew the rifleman for one of our most trusted soldiers and, for some reason I cannot explain, I was overwhelmed for the moment with most bitter sadness. Perhaps it was the helpless position in which his body lay, the sudden and pathetic waste of a young life, a boy determined to do his duty. Quite possibly he had been hit by a fragment of our own barrage, but that altered nothing. He had done what he set out to do and by his firm will he had helped to save many lives, for which he had paid with his own.' Eden added, sixty years after the event: 'The momentary flash of that scene is still fresh in my mind.'

The mine explosions under the Messines Ridge created throughout southern England what Vera Brittain recalled as 'a strange early morning shock like an earthquake'. On the following night her blinded soldier-friend Victor died in hospital. Her brother Edward, home on leave, was already a changed person, 'unfamiliar, frightening Edward, who never smiled nor spoke except about trivial things, who seemed to have nothing to say to me and indeed hardly appeared to notice my return'.

Within four days of the underground explosions, the Germans abandoned Wytschaete and Messines, and withdrew to a new line further east. The withdrawal was skilfully and deliberately conducted on the orders of Prince Rupprecht of Bavaria. During the withdrawal, on June 8, a 24-year-old German aviator had his first acknowledged victory. His entire squadron watched from the ground, and from the air, as he shot down an Allied plane after a prolonged dogfight. His name was Lieutenant Hermann Goering.[1]

Within a week the front-line stalemate was re-established. That June, T.S. Eliot sent the *Nation* magazine a letter he had received from an officer who had been at the front since before his nineteenth birthday. The officer was angered by what he saw as the lack of understanding at home of conditions at the front, the 'leprous earth, scattered with the swollen and

[1] Goering joined the Nazi Party in 1922. From 1935 until 1945 he was in charge of the German Air Force. He was sentenced to death at the Nuremberg Trials in 1946, but committed suicide before the execution could be carried out.

blackened corpses of hundreds of young men. The appalling stench of rotten carrion.' His description continued: 'Mud like porridge, trenches like shallow and sloping cracks in the porridge – porridge that stinks in the sun. Swarms of flies and bluebottles clustering on pits of offal. Wounded men lying in the shell holes among the decaying corpses: helpless under the scorching sun and bitter nights, under repeated shelling. Men with bowels dropping out, lungs shot away, with blinded, smashed faces, or limbs blown into space. Men screaming and gibbering. Wounded men hanging in agony on the barbed wire, until a friendly spout of liquid fire shrivels them up like a fly in a candle.'

'But these are only words,' the officer ended, 'and probably convey only a fraction of their meaning to the hearers. They shudder, and it is forgotten.'

The will of governments to continue to fight, despite the actual horrors of trench warfare, despite the chaos in Russia, despite mutiny in France, did not dissolve. The South African leader, General Smuts, who was a member of the British War Cabinet, was advocating the earliest possible British offensive on the Western Front; otherwise, he said, the Germans would 'have time to recover their spirits. . . . If we could not break the enemy's front we might break his heart.'

The offensive was planned for June 10, under Haig's command. Two days earlier, on June 8, Lloyd George called an emergency Cabinet meeting to discuss Smuts' argument. The Cabinet also had before it details of the scale of the French mutinies. Lloyd George proposed the immediate postponement of the British offensive. Instead, he argued, Britain should examine 'the possibility of a separate peace with Austria', which would isolate Germany, and might lead the Kaiser to end the war. He saw no point, Lloyd George told his colleagues, in Britain alone seeking to break through the German lines when 'the French were finding it difficult to go on, and their reserves physically and mentally exhausted'. Smuts, reluctant to see the offensive abandoned, asked that Haig be consulted as to the prospects of success. The three-word message came back from the Western Front: 'Haig was hopeful.' He was asked to come to London to explain his hopefulness in greater detail.

On June 8, the day of this War Cabinet discussion in London, General Pershing and his headquarters Staff reached Liverpool. In welcoming their arrival, one British newspaper told its readers that, whereas in 1776 America and Britain had been separated by the 'Prussian policy' of King George III, now Prussianism had served to reunite them. The *Graphic* turned to Shakespeare for its inspiration: 'Now is the winter of our discontent made glorious summer by this sun of (New) York.' It was well meant, even if Pershing was, like President Truman after him, from Missouri.

During Pershing's conversation with King George V on the following day, at Buckingham Palace, the King 'mentioned the great cost of the war, the large numbers of men Great Britain had already furnished the Army and Navy, and the tremendous losses they had suffered'. The King then mentioned rumours that the United States would soon have 50,000 aircraft in the air. Deeply embarrassed by this rather typical exaggeration of America's military power, Pershing told the King that 'such reports were extremely exaggerated and that we should not be sending over any planes for some time to come.' At that moment America had only fifty-five training planes, fifty-one of which were obsolete and four obsolescent.

On that second day in London, Pershing learned that the German sinkings of Allied shipping, a total of 1,500,000 tons in April and May, were so high that there would not be sufficient British shipping to bring the American Expeditionary Force to France or to keep it supplied once it had arrived. Fifteen ships had been sunk in British waters alone during the eleven days that Pershing was crossing the Atlantic: indeed, to guard against the possibility of a torpedo attack, his ship had not responded to any of the frequent distress calls it had received.

On June 9, the Russian Provisional Government rejected a German offer of an armistice. At the same time, in an attempt to curb the French army mutinies that had been widespread for almost a month, two different but not mutually exclusive policies were being pursued. On June 10 the first two mutineers sentenced to death were executed. In some units, one in every ten of the mutineers were shot. Nine days after the first execution, General Pétain began the formidable task of speaking in person to all the regiments in which there had been mutinous outbreaks. In two months he visited more than eighty divisions. It was a long and arduous task. A secret report sent by eighty-three Préféts to the Minister of the Interior in Paris that month, on the morale of their Departmental capitals, revealed that morale in fifty-four towns was 'poor' or 'indifferent' and in thirty-six towns 'contaminated'.

On the Italian Front, the increasingly frustrating battle for the mountain tops was renewed in the Trentino on June 10. But Italian deserters gave details of the assault to the Austrians, who were able to counter-attack with success. Six peaks were attacked by the Italians: only one, a 6,794-foot peak (known as Height 2101) on Mount Ortigaro, was captured. The Austrians were able to hold on to the 6,906-foot mountain peak. As the battle for the peaks continued it became more and more difficult. An Italian assault on the summit of Mount Ortigaro was eventually successful, and a thousand Austrians were taken prisoner, but even then the Austrians retained their hold on a nearby 6,729-foot peak, and on another main Italian objective, Mount Camigoletti. Then, to the dismay of the Italians, two weeks after its capture Mount Ortigaro was retaken by the Austrians, and nearly 2,000 Italians made captive. When the battle ended after three weeks of fighting, the line on the map had hardly changed, but 23,000 Italians and nearly 9,000 Austrians had been killed or wounded.

On the morning of June 13 the war came once more to the quiet world of civilians and cities when fourteen German bombers, flying at 12,000 feet, attacked London. More than a hundred bombs were dropped, killing 162 civilians, the capital's highest death toll of the war. In the City of London, Vera Brittain saw 'several derelict tradesmen's carts bloodily denuded of their drivers'. At a school in Poplar, fifteen children were killed and twenty-seven maimed for life. 'Such a "slaughter of the innocents" was a horribly familiar aspect of warfare in towns and villages on the continent,' writes the most recent historian of the East End, 'but in London there had been nothing comparable for 900 years. Grief, shock and anger once more turned xenophobic. Since the bomb had fallen in daylight, it was assumed the school was itself a target.'[1] The targets were in fact the nearby docks, warehouses and railway lines. Some parents were so alarmed that they sent their children out of London, a spontaneous precursor of the organised evacuations of the Second World War. Among those who were sent away, to Reigate, were the young Winogradsky brothers.[2]

That day, June 13, General Pershing reached France, landing at Boulogne and travelling by train to Paris. His arrival was the long-awaited, much-hailed harbinger of a new impetus to the Allied war powers. 'He has captured the fickle Paris crowd,' one observer noted, 'and could be elected King of France tomorrow if it depended on Paris.' But Pershing was warned by an American friend who had been living in France: 'There is a limit to what flesh and blood and endurance can stand.' The French 'have just about reached that limit'.

It was going to be many months, perhaps as much as a year, before American troops could take their place in the line in sufficient numbers to make any impact. At his first meeting with Pétain, on June 16, Pershing understood the Frenchman's meaning when he said, out of the blue, at a point where the conversation had flagged: 'I hope it is not too late.' But the French will to fight was not over. On June 15, between Pershing's arrival in France and his meeting with Pétain, the French aviator Captain Joseph Vuillemin had won a palm to his Croix de Guerre when he was flying a reconnaissance over No-Man's Land and was attacked by five German aircraft. He fought them off, and continued his reconnaissance. It was French Moroccan troops watching this exhibition of aerial skill from their trenches who demanded that the Captain be rewarded.

In the war against Turkey, the Royal Navy yacht *Managam* returned two Palestinian Jewish agents to Athlit on June 15, after they had been trained in the use of explosives in Cyprus. Their task was to blow up a section of the Haifa to Damascus railway, between Afula and Dera'a. Further south, the Damascus to Medina railway was being blown up by Arabs between Amman and Dera'a, this time with T.E. Lawrence's guidance and with

[1] Alan Palmer, *The East End, Four Centuries of London Life*, J. Murray, London 1989, p. 119.
[2] Later Lord Grade, President of the ATV television network from 1977 to 1982 (born 1906) and Lord Delfont, a leading theatrical impresario and President of the Entertainment Artistes' Benevolent Fund (born 1909). A third brother, Leslie, later head of the Grade Organisation, a theatrical agency, had been born a year earlier, in 1916.

340

British explosives. British aircraft were also in action against Turkish positions behind the lines. On June 23, flying both from the aircraft carrier *Empress* and from airfields near Gaza, they bombed the railway station at Tulkarm, the airfield at Ramleh, and the German military headquarters in Jerusalem, located in the Augusta Victoria church and sanatorium on the summit of the Mount of Olives. The main bomb damage was to a large roof mosaic of the Kaiser and his wife.

On the Western Front, the Portuguese Expeditionary Force was in action for the first time on June 17, in Flanders. On the following day the British were in action at Messines. Among those mortally wounded was Paul Freyberg, brother of the hero of the Ancre battle of November 1916, who died at Boulogne while on his way to hospital in England. The New Zealand poet Elsdon Best wrote of him:

> *Today the lonely winds are loose*
> *And crying goes the rain.*
> *While here we walk the field they knew*
> *The dead who died in pain.*
> *The fields that wait the slow hours long*
> *For sounds that shall not come.*
> *In other fields, in other earth*
> *The laughing hearts are dumb.*

On June 19, Sir Douglas Haig crossed from France to England to tell the War Cabinet why he wished the summer offensive to go ahead, despite Lloyd George's hesitations. Haig argued that Germany was within six months of total exhaustion. With one more push, the war could be won in 1917. He was strongly supported by General Smuts. Lloyd George gave way: the renewed offensive, the largest since the Somme a year earlier, would begin on the last day of July.

On June 28 fierce fighting broke out on the Aisne, where the British and Canadians made some small gains, and at Verdun, where the Germans overran a few French-held trenches.

Two days earlier the first large contingent of American troops had arrived in France, 14,000 men, who disembarked at St Nazaire. But this was to have no effect at all on the battlefield. The men had first to train, and to be reinforced by colleagues, the next contingent of whom did not arrive for another three months. America was in the war, but in France her effort was necessarily focused on building up port and training facilities, supply lines and store depots. Some gaps were immediately evident. Some of the artillerymen had not only arrived without their guns, but had no idea what those guns looked like or how they operated. Many of the infantrymen were recent recruits, as most regular soldiers had been kept back in America to act as leaven for the recruits still being assembled. Even Pershing was shocked by the poor quality of his men. His most recent biographer tells of an episode when, in the poor light of a hayloft in which American soldiers were billeted, Pétain mistook Pershing himself for a sergeant and asked him, 'Sergeant, are your men content?' Taken aback but in full control, Pershing replied, 'Oui, mon général, nous sommes très content', whereupon Pétain passed on, unaware of his mistake. On another occasion, a French general approached a 'dishevelled' American sentry. Instead of standing to attention, the American handed the general his rifle and sat down in a doorway to roll himself a cigarette.[1]

Pershing, an excellent organiser, established a network of training schools for his new arrivals, and initiated a vast apparatus of supply and preparation, essential to ensure American participation in the front line ten or twelve months hence. That participation was a long time away. The Americans had arrived but the question 'Where are the Americans?' was often asked. On July 4, however, when American troops marched through Paris to the grave of Lafayette, who had been buried at his request in earth brought from America, there was a pandemonium of enthusiasm, and great excitement when an American officer, Colonel Charles Stanton, declared in front of the assembled Parisians: 'Lafayette, we are here!'[2]

That summer yet another belligerent was about to enter the war. On June 12 the pro-German King of Greece, King Constantine, had abdicated in favour of his second son. On June 26 the pro-Allied Venizelos had become Prime Minister. All was now ready for Greece to commit itself to the Allies. Then, in a hoped-for upsurge of Allied fortunes, on July 1, encouraged to do so by Kerensky, General Brusilov launched his second offensive against the Austro-German forces on the Eastern Front, and on July 2 Greece declared war on the Central Powers.

Almost three years after the outbreak of war, one almost broken power was renewing the offensive, and one hitherto neutral power was entering the conflict.

---

[1] Donald Smythe, *Pershing, General of the Armies*, Indiana University Press, Bloomington 1986, page 30.
[2] This remark is often attributed, wrongly, to Pershing, who was present on that occasion and also spoke. Lafayette, one of the drafters of the Declaration of the Rights of Man during the French Revolution, had earlier fought against the British during the American War of Independence. He died in 1834.

18

Stalemate in the west, turmoil in the east

JULY–SEPTEMBER 1917

Inside the Russian Empire, without the Tsar at its head, power in the capital was still divided between the Provisional Government, eager to create a liberal democratic system, and the Soviets with their revolutionary doctrine. At the first Congress of Workers and Soldiers Soviets, held between 16 and 22 June 1917, the Bolsheviks had a hundred of the 781 delegates, and were emphatic that the war should cease. But with Kerensky as Minister of War, the Provisional Government moved forward with its plan to renew the offensive as soon as possible. A British journalist, Michael Farbman, returning from Petrograd to London, reported on June 28 'the growth in the power of the extremist socialists owing to mistrust of the war aims of the Allies' and, equally ominous for the Allies, the 'worn-out condition' of the Russian railways and rolling stock, which 'was rapidly destroying the means of communication'.

On July 1 a massive peace demonstration was held in Petrograd. That same day, General Brusilov, victor of the previous year's offensive, went on to the offensive in Eastern Galicia along a fifty-mile front. Thirty-one Russian divisions, supported by 1,328 heavy guns, launched the attack, the aim of which was to reach and capture Lemberg, fifty miles to the west. The front was defended by German and Austrian troops, more than 10,000 of whom were taken prisoner in the first forward thrust. On the second day of the battle, Czech soldiers fighting alongside the Russians, in a specifically Czech Brigade, prevailed upon many of the Czech troops facing them, part of the Austrian 19th (Czech) Division, to desert. Russian troops, too, were seen throwing down their rifles and refusing to go forward, standing 'sullenly with arms folded', John Wheeler-Bennett has written, 'while their officers, threats and prayers alike proving useless, spat at the silent men and went towards the enemy alone'.

In a separate Russian attack southward, General Kornilov took 7,000 Austrians prisoner: the complete collapse of the line was averted by the arrival of German reserve troops. But Kornilov continued to press forward, crossing the Dniester to take Halich and then Kalush, on the road to the

Carpathian passes and the Hungarian border, along which the Russians had marched so triumphantly in the opening months of the war.

The Russian advance reached Ldziany, threatening the Eastern Galician oilfields. In the defence of Ldziany the Austrian philosopher-corporal Ludwig Wittgenstein won the Silver Medal for Valour for his work as an artillery observer when, under heavy fire, he directed the guns in such a way as to cause heavy Russian losses 'in decisive moments'. The Austrians began to advance on July 23, and the oil fields were saved. But all was not well for the Central Powers: behind the German lines, Polish troops hitherto loyal to Germany, and forming several Polish legions within the German army, were refusing to swear an oath of loyalty to the Kaiser. More than 5,000 were arrested and interned during July. Also arrested was the leader of the Polish Legions, Josef Pilsudski, who supported the refusal of his men to remain loyal to Germany.

When the German Governor of Warsaw, General von Beseler, appealed to Pilsudski on July 21 to work in tandem with the Germans, Pilsudski replied: 'Your Excellency, do you imagine for one moment that you will win the nation's confidence by hanging Polish insignia on each of the fingers of the hand which is throttling Poland? The Poles know the Prussian stranglehold for what it is.' Pressed to become the leader of a German-sponsored Poland, Pilsudski retorted: 'If I were to go along with you, Germany would gain one man, whilst I would lose a nation.' Pilsudski was then imprisoned by the Germans for the rest of the war, and his soldiers, who had fought so bravely against the Russians on all the eastern war fronts, were interned in German camps.

National ambitions were proving a serous impediment to the warmaking abilities of the Central Powers. Germany's troubles with the Poles were mirrored by Turkey's troubles with the Arabs. In the southernmost extremity of the Ottoman Empire, Arab hostility to their Ottoman masters was having its effect. On July 6, T.E. Lawrence was present when 2,500 Arabs overwhelmed the three hundred Turkish soldiers defending the port of Akaba, at the head of the Red Sea. This brought the Arab forces to within 130 miles of the British front line in Sinai, where General Allenby was under instructions from London to reach Jerusalem by the end of the year, despite his predecessor's repeated failure to capture Gaza.

Crossing the Sinai desert, skilfully avoiding all Turkish patrols, Lawrence met Allenby in Cairo on July 10, securing a monthly subsidy for the Arabs of £200,000 in gold, subsequently increased to £500,000. For their successful seizure of Akaba, the Arabs were paid £16,000 in gold.[1] For Allenby, a personal tragedy intervened at the end of the month, when a telegram arrived announcing that his son Michael had been killed on the Western Front, hit in the head by a shell splinter, and dying five hours later without recovering consciousness. Allenby

---

[1] In 1917, these sums were the equivalent of £5 million ($8 million), £13 million ($20 million), and £432,000 ($648,000).

wept; his new colleagues found him a 'pitiable figure' in his distress. In a letter to his wife, trying to comfort her, Allenby wrote: 'Michael achieved, early, what every great man in the world's history had made it his life's ambition to attain – to die honoured, loved and successful, in full vigour of body and mind.' Michael Allenby had fought on the Western Front for eighteen months. He had won the Military Cross for bravery. He was not yet twenty years old when he was killed.

In Britain, on July 7, the Government agreed to establish a Women's Auxiliary Army Corps. This was the first time that women were to be put in uniform and sent to France, to serve as clerks, telephonists, waitresses, cooks, and as instructors in the use of gas masks. Tradition dictated that only men could hold commissions in the forces, so none of the women volunteers could become officers: those in charge were given the ranks of 'controller' and 'administrator'. The principle underlying the establishment of the Corps was the need to release soldiers who were doing menial jobs in Britain and France, for active service at the Front.

Women were already working in enormous numbers in munitions factories throughout Britain. Long hours, acrid fumes and low pay were among the negative features of the work, but the patriotic call for volunteers was as strong as for soldiers. 'The situation is serious. Women must help to save it' was one of the banners held aloft during a 'Women's Right to Serve' march in London, when news of the shell shortage became public in the summer of 1915. At Gretna, in Scotland, 11,000 women were employed in the national cordite factory. More than a third of them had been domestic servants before the war. 'With the object of keeping the workers within the factory area, and away from undesirable temptations elsewhere,' one superintendent recalled, 'no late ordinary evening trains were run between Gretna and Carlisle except on Saturdays, when the latest train left the neighbouring city at 9.30 p.m.'

Women played an essential part in providing the necessary munitions of war. The dangers were ever-present. Women working with the explosive TNT were jocularly referred to as 'canaries' because of the yellow discoloration of the skin which was a symptom of TNT poisoning. Sixty-one women munitions workers died of poisoning, and eighty-one in other accidents at work. In accidental explosions during the war, seventy-one women were killed, one at the factory at Gretna, sixty-nine at Silvertown in East London, when seventy-two women were also severely injured. The explosion at Silvertown, in which an accidental fire ignited fifty tons of TNT, devastated a square mile of London's East End, causing more destruction than all the First World War air raids on the capital combined. Because the factory was owned by Brunner, Mond and Company, there was an intensification of xenophobia, on the grounds of the German origins of the owners.[1]

[1] Sir Alfred Mond, later 1st Baron Melchett, a Liberal MP from 1906 to 1928 (and Minister of Health 1921–22), was the second son of Ludwig Mond, whose father Meyer Mond had been born in Ziegenhain near Cassel in 1811. Ludwig Mond had married his cousin Frida, the heiress of a Cologne Jewish banker.

345

On the Eastern Front, among the Russian units in action, was the 300-strong women's battalion formed in May under the command of Maria Bochkareva. Known as the Women's Battalion of Death, according to the popular Russian accounts at the time, the battalion captured 2,000 Austrian prisoners, but then the troops serving alongside it, imbued with Bolshevik ideas, and fearful that the women's success would provoke reprisals from the enemy, beat Bochkareva up and forced her to disband her battalion. But Florence Farmborough, into whose field hospital at Seret some of the wounded women were brought in mid-August, wrote in her diary: 'In honour of those women volunteers, it was recorded that they *did* go into the attack; they *did* go "over the top". But not all of them. Some remained in the trenches, fainting and hysterical; others ran or crawled back to the rear. Bachkarova retreated with her decimated battalion; she was wrathful, heartbroken, but she had learnt a great truth: women were unfit to be soldiers.'[1]

The German High Command placed more and more emphasis on the ability of the German submarine campaign to bring the Allies to their knees. The statistics for the monthly sinking of Allied and neutral shipping gave Ludendorff in particular a sense that the Allied ability to continue the war must be waning, as war supplies and food were sunk without respite on all the seas and oceans. But the statistics raised false hopes. On July 10, Walther Rathenau went to see Ludendorff to warn him that even the highest estimates of Allied shipping sunk were illusory, as the British were making extraordinary efforts to replace the lost vessels. Rathenau also drew Ludendorff's attention to 'the possibility of America building more tonnage than we sank'. The soldier was not to be deterred by figures or forecasts, however, telling the industrialist that he respected what he had said, 'but you will admit that I have to follow my feeling'.

Rathenau did not know at the time how right he was, for in Britain a shipping expert, Arthur Salter, was organising exactly the replacement programme Rathenau had warned of, to the extent that by the summer of 1917 almost no extra time was needed to make up each loss of tonnage. 'Feeling', however, as Ludendorff expressed it, had replaced facts and figures in the German search for victory.

Not only submarine torpedoes, but gas canisters seemed to the German High Command to hold a prospect of victory. On the Western Front, July 12 saw the first use of mustard gas, fired by the Germans at the British near Ypres. More than 50,000 shells were fired, and more than 2,000 Allied soldiers affected by the gas. Eighty-seven were killed. In the next three weeks the Germans fired a million gas shells, killing five hundred more soldiers and incapacitating several thousand, but they were unable to break through the British lines.

[1] When Florence Farmborough boarded the steamship *Sheridan* at Vladivostok in April 1918 one of the first people she saw on board was Maria Bochkareva. 'She has eluded the spy net of the Red Guards and is making good her escape to the United States.' (*Nurse at the Russian Front*, page 408)

On July 17 the British retaliated, firing 100,000 gas shells containing chloropicrin, and causing seventy-five German deaths. This retaliation led to no breakthrough. More Britons died that July in a single accidental explosion at Scapa Flow on board the battleship *Vanguard* than in all the mustard and chloropicrin gas attacks combined. In that one, sudden explosion, 804 sailors were killed. There were only three survivors.

On the Eastern Front, German troops were taking over from the Austrians in the central sector. 'Yesterday's news has quite relieved my mind,' General Hoffmann wrote in his diary on July 17. 'Litzmann has retaken Kalush, and there are now such strong German reinforcements in these parts that nothing need worry us.'[1] Two days later the Germans broke through the Russian positions at Zloczov on a twelve-mile front. 'The affair is developing according to plan,' Hoffmann wrote on July 21, but added: 'I should like a few more prisoners. The fellows ran away so frantically that we could not catch any of them. Only 6,000 to date, and only seventy guns.'

Austrian territory had been liberated by the Germans. 'The Emperor of Austria was here yesterday,' Hoffmann wrote on July 23, 'and he behaved in the sort of way that falls just short of direct discourtesy. There was of course no question of any thanks for the reconquest of a province for them.' Three days later the Kaiser came to Zloczov, driving from there to Tarnopol. His troops, not the Austrians, had won back Eastern Galicia for the Central Powers. 'He was of course in a brilliant humour,' Hoffmann noted.

Peacemaking efforts had continued that summer, with as little success as earlier in the year. In July the British arms manufacturer Sir Basil Zaharoff held a secret meeting in Switzerland with the Turkish War Minister, Enver Pasha, and offered the Turks $1,500,000 in gold if they would sign a separate peace with the Allies.[2] Enver was tempted, but refused. In Berlin, the Reichstag was recalled in order to vote more money for the prosecution of the war. It demanded that when peace came, it should be a peace without any territorial annexations by Germany. A 'Peace Resolution' brought forward in the Reichstag on July 19 was passed by 212 votes to 126, with seventeen abstentions. It urged the German Government to work for 'a peace by agreement and a permanent reconciliation'. But Dr Michaelis, who had succeeded Bethmann-Hollweg as Chancellor six days earlier, and was the nominee and mouthpiece of the General Staff, insisted that Germany would not seek peace. 'I do not consider that a body like the German Reichstag is a fit one to decide about peace and war on its own initiative during the war' were his dismissive words.

[1] When, in September 1939, the Germans conquered the Polish city of Lodz, it was renamed Litzmannstadt in General Litzmann's honour. The ghetto established there in 1940 became a scene of terrible torments and the deaths from deliberate starvation of many thousands of Jews (5,000 between January and June 1941, tens of thousands more after that).
[2] In 1994 this sum was approximately $13 million, or £9 million.

All thoughts of a negotiated peace were likewise dismissed by the Kaiser, who, on July 20, for the first time in almost two decades, met representatives of all the German political parties, except the Independent Socialists. In an uncompromising speech he told them of his plans for a 'Second Punic War' against England, in which the whole of Europe, under Germany's leadership, would destroy Britain's world domination.[1] The delegates of the moderate parties were shocked, all the more so when, in reference to Germany's recent victories on the Galician Front, he declared: 'When my guards appear, there is no room for democracy.' The Reichstag Peace Resolution was of no interest to the ruler of Germany.

An attempt by the former leader of the British Labour Party, Ramsay MacDonald, to gain support in the House of Commons for the Reichstag Peace Resolution, was defeated by 148 votes to nineteen. Bitterly, Mac-Donald wrote to President Wilson that American neutrality would have been better for peace. On July 27 a meeting was arranged of Bolshevik sympathisers in the East End of London. Calling themselves the London Soviet, their purpose was to demand an immediate end to the war. To encourage the local populace to break up the meeting, the Government arranged for the *Daily Express* to reveal where it would take place. It also distributed leaflets stating that a pro-German meeting was taking place and exhorting the citizens: 'Remember the last air-raid and turn up.' Eight thousand did, including many soldiers in uniform, who stormed the platform and broke the meeting up.

During the last week of June and the whole of July, negotiations took place on the island of Corfu between various south Slav representatives, about the possibility of creating a new country, partly within the confines Austria-Hungary, based on the assumption that Austria-Hungary would in due course disintegrate, and that Serbia would regain its independence. The Pact of Corfu, signed on July 20, envisaged a post-war union of the three main southern Slav groups, Serbs, Croats and Slovenes, who would form one country, ruled by the Serbian royal family. Local linguistic and religious minority rights would be guaranteed, and a constituent assembly elected by secret and universal suffrage.

The idea of this new nation appealed in particular to the United States, where there were many south Slav emigrant groups, and where the possible emergence of democratic, nationally cohesive systems on the ruins of an imperial structure was welcomed as an advance in human relations. The conflict during the negotiations, and after them, between Serbs who wanted domination by Belgrade, and Croats who wanted a unified South Slav State ('Yugoslavia') rather than a 'Greater Serbia' was acute, and unresolved.

---

[1] In the Second Punic War (218–201 BC), against the Phoenician (Punic) city of Carthage, the Carthaginians, who had already lost Sicily to Rome in the First Punic War (264–241 BC), were forced to surrender all their remaining overseas possessions, and become a dependent, tribute-paying ally. The Third Punic War (149–146 BC) ended in the capture and total destruction of Carthage itself.

Such futuristic planning was in contrast with the day-to-day problems that were created by the continuation of the war. Mutinies and discontent were still threatening the fighting abilities of several armies. On July 16, four days before the Corfu Pact was signed, French troops on the Salonica Front mutinied. Yet it was from this front that the liberation of Serbia had to come. The French soldiers were not revolutionaries: their demand was for the right to go home on leave. Three hundred of them were persuaded to accept new leave arrangements, but ninety were arrested.

Other fronts on both sides were troubled that month by unease among the troops. An Italian officer wrote from the Austro-Italian Front: 'Certain bad elements who have got into the units worry me a great deal.' In Germany, Ludendorff was sufficiently concerned about the dissemination of political propaganda among the German front-line troops to order a detailed examination of all letters being sent to soldiers at the front.

It was in Russia, however, that the main threat lay to the Allied ability to make war, or to plan for a peace based on conquest. On July 16 an uprising in Petrograd, encouraged by Leon Trotsky, demanded an immediate end to the war. Six thousand sailors at the Kronstadt naval base joined the revolt, which Trotsky thought would lead to revolution, but which Lenin, who had been recuperating from overwork and exhaustion, regarded as premature. Disturbances continued for three days. On July 18, Officer Cadets loyal to the Provisional Government, and to the prosecution of the war, broke into the offices of the Bolshevik newspaper, *Pravda*, and smashed them to pieces. Lenin, afraid of being arrested, even killed, went into hiding.

On the Eastern Front, the Russian military successes were coming to an abrupt end. On July 19, General Hoffmann ordered a counter-attack east of Zloczov that created a twelve-mile breach in the Russian lines. More than 6,000 Russian soldiers were taken prisoner; thousands more fled from the battlefield. As news of this defeat reached Petrograd, Prince Lvov resigned as Prime Minister and was replaced by Kerensky. That day, the last five hundred Kronstadt rebels surrendered. But at the front, the Russian advance had turned into a retreat, almost a rout. Tens of thousands of Russian soldiers simply threw down their rifles and fled from the war zone. Hundreds of officers were murdered. Two Allied armoured car units, one British and one Belgian, were serving on the Eastern Front near Buczacz: their officers pleaded with the Russian deserters to return to the front line, but in vain.

The Austro-German forces had begun to move forward towards the Russian border. On July 21, near Tarnopol, the British Royal Naval Air Service detachment of armoured cars took part in the Russian defence. The two towns of Halich and Stanislau[1] were recaptured on July 23,

---

[1] In inter-war Poland, Halicz and Stanislawow. Today they are in the Ukraine.

Tarnopol two days later, the Kaiser being present to watch the Austrian advance. On July 28 the Austrian army, faced not by an organised Russian defence but by 40,000 Russian deserters fleeing eastward, reached the Russian border at Husiatyn. General Brusilov, whom Kerensky had appointed Commander-in-Chief of the Russian armies, was replaced by General Kornilov, whose first Order of the Day condemned the treachery of 'certain units'.

One possible area of help for the Russians was a British offensive on the Western Front, to draw German troops and guns back from the east. It was Haig's belief that the British army could break through the German lines that summer without waiting for substantial American forces to arrive. General Pershing had made it clear that he did not intend to commit his troops to action until the summer of 1918, when he would have a million men under arms, ready for battle. Even that million was almost twice as many as the War Department in Washington thought they could provide. Haig met Pershing for the first time on July 20, noting in his diary: 'He has already begun to realise that the French are a broken reed.'

General Smuts, fresh from his slow but steady successes against the German forces in East Africa, argued before the War Cabinet in London that it was Britain's moral duty to launch an offensive on the Western Front that year. Churchill, who had just been brought back into the Government as Minister of Munitions, but who was not a member of the War Cabinet, urged Lloyd George to 'limit the consequences' of any renewed offensive on the Western Front. 'The armies are equal,' Churchill warned the Prime Minister. 'If anything, the Germans are stronger. They have larger reserves, and ample munitions. An endless series of fortified lines, with all kinds of flooding possibilities, and great natural difficulties of ground, constitute insuperable obstacles.'

What Churchill had in mind, he explained to the Minister of War, Lord Milner, on July 26, was that the United States would ultimately provide the manpower needed for victory, and that the next offensive should be postponed, or severely limited, until sufficient American troops had arrived in France to tilt the military balance of power against Germany. Britain's main part would be to manufacture the munitions, tanks and aircraft that these American troops would need, and provide the shipping to bring over both men and raw materials.

This was a long-term plan for 1918 and even 1919, which would avoid a repetition of the enormous loss of life on the Somme, and avoid further failures. Haig was confident, however, that he could achieve at Ypres in the autumn of 1917 what had proved impossible on the Somme a year earlier: a breakthrough that would breach the German trench lines altogether, and a sweep behind the German lines, forcing the Germans to pull back deep into Belgium, as much as twenty-five miles, before the potentially vast American army arrived in the line. More than two million men were already under Haig's command. Churchill's warning was ignored.

German mustard gas attacks had been continuous on the Western Front since July 12. The British medical services worked at full stretch to try to cope, but the mortality rate was high. Major J.W. McNee, in charge of a mobile laboratory, noted of one typical case: 'Exposed to mustard gas on the morning of 28th July, 1917. Admitted to casualty clearing station on the evening of 29th July, suffering from severe conjunctivitis and superficial burns of face, neck and scrotum. Respiratory symptoms gradually developed and death occurred about one hundred hours after exposure to gas.' In the six weeks following July 12, just over 19,000 British soldiers were incapacitated by mustard gas, many of them being blinded, and 649 dying within a week or ten days of the attack.

Among the British officers who were in action that summer was Siegfried Sassoon. Wounded in the neck, he was taken back to base hospital on one of the hundreds of hospital trains that crossed and recrossed the French countryside. There were five hundred other wounded men on board. 'My memories of that train are strange and rather terrible,' Sassoon later wrote, 'for it carried a cargo of men in whose minds the horrors they had escaped from were still vitalized and violent. Many of us still had the caked mud of the war zone on our boots and clothes, and every bandaged man was accompanied by his battle experience. Although many of them talked lightly and even facetiously about it, there was an aggregation of enormities in the atmosphere of that train. I overheard some slightly wounded officers who were excitedly remembering their adventures up at Wancourt, where they'd been bombed out of a trench in the dark. Their jargoning voices mingled with the rumble and throb of the train as it journeyed – so safely and sedately – through the environing gloom. The Front Line was behind us; but it could lay its hand on our hearts, though its bludgeoning reality diminished with every mile.'

Sassoon was sent back to London. When he reached Charing Cross station 'a woman handed me a bunch of flowers and a leaflet by the Bishop of London who earnestly advised me to lead a clean life and attend Holy Communion'. His stretcher was then 'popped into an ambulance' which took him to a military hospital. Sassoon, who had earlier won the Military Cross, was so badly wounded that he could have remained on home service. He decided, however, that rather than remain silent and accept the comforts of home service, he would resign from the army and speak out against what he now regarded as a wrongful war.

In a letter which was published in the newspapers that July, Sassoon wrote that it was his belief 'that this war, upon which I entered as a war of defence and liberation, has now become a war of aggression and conquest', and he went on to declare: 'I have seen and endured the sufferings of the troops, and I can no longer be a party to prolong these sufferings for ends which I believe to be evil and unjust. I am not protesting against the conduct of the war, but against the political errors and insincerities for which the fighting men are being sacrificed. On behalf of those who are suffering now I make this protest against the deception which is being practised on them; also I believe that I may help to destroy the callous complacence with which the majority of those at home regard the continuance of agonies which they do not share, and which they have not sufficient imagination to realise.'

On July 23, Sassoon was admitted to Craiglockhart War Hospital for Neurasthenic Officers. He was fortunate to be hospitalised rather than court-martialled. Influential voices had been raised in his support, and a Government Minister told the House of Commons that there seemed to be 'something wrong' with this 'extremely gallant officer'. Members should not seek to exploit 'a young man in such a state of mind'. While at Craiglockhart, Sassoon met a fellow-patient, Wilfred Owen, whom he encouraged to write of the war as both men had seen it. The result was one of the most powerful poems of the war, Owen's 'Dulce et decorum est': 'To die for the fatherland is a sweet thing and becoming.'[1]

> Bent double, like old beggars under sacks,
> Knock-kneed, coughing like hags, we cursed through sludge,
> Till on the haunting flares we turned our backs
> And towards our distant rest began to trudge.
> Men marched asleep. Many had lost their boots
> But limped on, blood-shod. All went lame; all blind;
> Drunk with fatigue; deaf even to the hoots
> Of gas shells dropping softly behind.
>
> Gas! GAS! Quick, boys! – An ecstasy of fumbling,
> Fitting the clumsy helmets just in time,
> But someone still was yelling out and stumbling
> And flound'ring like a man in fire or lime...
> Dim, through the misty panes and thick green light,
> As under a green sea, I saw him drowning.
>
> In all my dreams, before my helpless sight,
> He plunges at me, guttering, choking, drowning.
>
> If in some smothering dreams, you too could pace
> Behind the wagon that we flung him in,

[1] Horace, *Odes*, III, ii, 13.

And watch the white eyes writhing in his face,
His hanging face, like a devil's sick of sin;
If you could hear, at every jolt, the blood
Come gargling from the froth-corrupted lungs,
Obscene as cancer, bitter as the cud
Of vile, incurable sores on innocent tongues, –
My friend, you would not tell with such high zest
The old Lie: Dulce et decorum est
Pro patria mori.

The renewed assault in the Ypres Salient, on which Haig was so determined, began on July 31. Following a 3,000-gun barrage, nine British and six French divisions moved forward on a fifteen-mile front. Their first objective was the village of Passchendaele, four and a half miles beyond their starting point. In the first two days' battle, the advances were greater than during any previous Western Front offensive, in one sector two and a half miles were gained, elsewhere a mile and a half. Among the British dead on the first day was Lance Corporal Francis Ledwidge, the 26-year-old Irish veteran of the Gallipoli and Salonica Fronts. He was laying wooden planks on a muddy track, so that guns and munitions could be taken forward to the front line, and had paused for a mug of tea, when a shell exploded near him. He was killed at once. His pre-war poetry had rejoiced in pastoral Irish scenes and tales of the fairies:

And now I'm drinking wine in France,
The helpless child of circumstance.
Tomorrow will be loud with war,
How will I be accounted for?

It is too late now to retrieve
A fallen dream, too late to grieve
A name unmade, but not too late
To thank the gods for what is great;

A keen-edged sword, a soldier's heart,
Is greater than a poet's art.
And greater than a poet's fame
A little grave that has no name.

Ledwidge's own grave does have his name on it, in Artillery Wood Cemetery at Boesinghe. This cemetery was begun immediately after the battle in which Ledwidge was killed, and remained in the front line until March 1918: by November 1918 it held 141 graves. After the war bodies were brought to it from the battlefields, and from other nearby cemeteries. It now contains 1,243 British, thirty Canadian, ten Newfoundland, five Australian and three New Zealand graves, as well as the graves of 506 unknown soldiers: the little graves that have no name.

At heavy cost in dead and wounded, the British forces in the Ypres Salient advanced on July 31 and in the following days, pushing the Germans back almost a mile in places. It was nothing like as far as Haig had envisaged, but further than in any previous assault in the Salient. Among the British officers wounded on the third day of the battle was Captain Noel Chavasse, the medical officer who a year earlier had been awarded the Victoria Cross on the Somme for rescuing the wounded in No-Man's Land. Now, having again carried wounded soldiers back to his battalion's first aid post, a dug-out in the trenches, and gone out into No-Man's Land under heavy fire to tend to the wounded, he was taking a short rest in the dugout, when a shell entered it.

Most of the occupants of the dugout, almost all of them wounded men, were killed. Chavasse, the man who had brought them in and tended to them, was hit in the stomach. Bleeding profusely, he dragged himself up the stairs and managed to crawl to another aid post. Taken from there to a casualty clearing station, he was operated on by a specialist from Guy's Hospital, London. He died two days later. To a nurse who was with him in his final hours he dictated a message to his sister: 'Give her my love, tell her Duty called and called me to obey.'

Soon after Chavasse's death he was awarded a second Victoria Cross.[1] His brother Christopher wrote more than forty years later, to a friend: 'I still mourn my Noel every day of my life, and have done so for forty-four years.... I seem still to think things over with Noel, and to feel he might walk into the room any minute.' Also in the Ypres Salient another Chavasse brother, Aidan, was killed in action, 'missing presumed dead'. His name is one of the 54,896 inscribed on the Menin Gate, with no known grave.

Less than two weeks after the start of the July 31 offensive, the Belgian Government, on whose soil the offensive was being fought, signed an agreement at Le Havre with the British Government, whereby the land on which the British war cemeteries and graves in Belgium were located was 'conceded in perpetuity' to Britain. The agreement was signed on August 9, almost two years after a similar British agreement with the French. It was recognition of the mounting scale of British losses on Belgian soil.

*

[1] Only three men have won the Victoria Cross twice (the Victoria Cross and Bar): Lieutenant-Colonel Arthur Martin-Leake, of the Royal Army Medical Corps (first in the Boer War, then in 1914), Captain Noel Chavasse (both in the First World War), and Captain Charles Upham, New Zealand Infantry (both in the Second World War, first in Crete and then in the Western Desert). Chavasse and Upham were distantly related by marriage.

More than 5,000 German soldiers were taken prisoner during the three days of battle from July 31 to August 2. For the Kaiser and his commanders, however, the danger was not only on the Western Front. On August 2, as British troops took up their new positions in the Ypres Salient, trouble broke out aboard the German battleship *Prinzregent Luitpold* at Wilhelmshaven, when a stoker, Albin Kobis, led four hundred sailors into the town and addressed them with the call: 'Down with the war! We no longer want to fight this war!' A Marine sergeant and a few men persuaded the sailors to return to the ship.

There was no violence. Several hundred sailors with what were called 'bad political attitudes' were, however, sent to shore stations, and seventy-five were imprisoned. Kobis was sentenced to death and shot by an army firing squad at Cologne. Before his execution he wrote to his parents: 'I die with a curse on the German-militarist State.' Also shot was Max Reichpietsch, who had led a demonstration on another warship, the *Friedrich der Grosse*.[1] Another sailor, Willy Weber, who was sentenced to death but had his sentence commuted to fifteen years in prison, told the court: 'Nobody wanted a revolution, we just wanted to be treated more like human beings.'

On the very day of these disturbances in the German Fleet, a British naval pilot, Commander Edwin Dunning, was making military history, taking off from an air field at Scapa Flow and landing, for the first time, on the aircraft carrier *Furious*. Hitherto, planes could take off from but could not land on the deck, and had to be brought to the carrier by barge and winched back on board. After making a second successful landing five days later, Dunning was killed that same day, making a third attempt, when his plane slipped over the side of the carrier and into the sea.

On the Eastern Front the Russian retreat continued. Austrian troops recaptured the city of Czernowitz on August 3. On the Roumanian Front, on August 6, the Russian Fourth Army fled before a German assault. The Russians hoped, however, to find a point on the Eastern Front from where they could move westward again. At the end of July they had been successful in the central sector, in one engagement capturing almost a complete Austrian division, 12,000 men, and on August 8 they launched an attack on the Austrian forces defending Kowel. On that sector, south of the Pripet Marshes, the Austrian troops were facing much larger Russian forces, 863,000 to 480,000. Understandably, they were alarmed. For the Germans, this was a typical failure of their ally's nerve: General Hoffmann commented that the Austrian army resembled 'a mouthful of hyper-sensitive

---

[1] The naval historian David Woodward has written of how, in 1958, a meeting of West German officers, past and present, broke up in disarray because a speaker, a senior army officer, 'said that he preferred Reichpietsch and Kobis to the two Grand Admirals of Hitler's navy, Raeder and Dönitz, both convicted war criminals.' David Woodward, *The Collapse of Power*, Arthur Barker, London 1973, page 12.

teeth: every time the wind blows, there's tooth-ache'. German troops were sent, as they had been the previous year, to reinforce the Austrians.

The Russians launched a massive assault, with some regiments advancing seventeen times despite intense machine-gun and artillery fire. So horrifying was the stench of Russian corpses in No-Man's Land that the Russians asked the German commander, General Marwitz, for a truce in which they could bury the dead. Marwitz would not agree. There could be 'no better deterrent to future offensives', comments one historian, 'than this forest of rotting corpses'.[1]

The Austrians held off the Russian attack. The Kowel offensive continued, but the Austrian line was not broken. Kowel remained under the control of the Central Powers. Despite repeated efforts to do so, the new Russian commander of the central front, General Alexeyev, was unable to repeat Brusilov's breakthrough of 1916.

As a gesture of inter-Allied solidarity, on August 6 some 3,000 Russian troops reached the Scottish port of Invergordon, on their way to the Western Front. There, on August 10, the British renewed the Ypres offensive, but the advance was impeded four days later by heavy rain. On August 16 the village of Langemarck was taken, but a German counter-attack recovered much of the ground gained. The initiative lay, however, with the British, who were helped in capturing the fortified German pillboxes by the use of tanks, and also by a ferocious French diversionary attack on the German lines at Verdun, when more than 5,000 Germans were taken prisoner.

On August 18, as the British and French were making steady gains on the Western Front, the Italians launched their eleventh battle on the Isonzo. Three days later a British nurse on the Italian Front, Viscountess D'Abernon, wrote in her diary: 'The camp has been submerged beneath an ever rising tide of wounded. Seven hundred and seventy passed through yesterday.' At one point her casualty clearing station ran out of stretchers. 'The men seem extenuated with hunger and fatigue.... We get a very large number of head cases, also shattered legs and arms, but so far few "abdominals". I sometimes suspect that the medical officers at the front leave them purposely on one side. Probably they think it is no use bringing down desperate cases. Best to give a fighting chance to those who may win through. But the sadness and horror of it all.'

Italian troops were also in action in the Balkans on August 18, in a different task, that of firefighters, joining with all the Allied forces then in Salonica to try to put out a fire that raged beyond control. Nearly half the city was burned down, and 80,000 people were made homeless. The British base headquarters were destroyed, as were almost all the stocks of quinine, needed to fight the scourge of the Salonica Front, the malarial mosquito. A munitions store filled with grenades had also blown up. For

[1] Norman Stone, *The Eastern Front*, Hodder and Stoughton, London 1975, page 272.

the troops, who always hoped for a few days' leave in the city, writes the historian Alan Palmer, 'it was still possible to enjoy the natural beauty of the Gulf and to find some peace in the hills behind the town. But there were many high spirits who looked for something noisier; and Montmartre – or was it Babylon? – had gone up in smoke. For the rest of the campaign, Salonica remained a desolate place.'

Since the launching of their new attack on August 18, the Italians had captured five mountain peaks and taken more than 20,000 Austrian and some German prisoners. Among those brought into Helen D'Abernon's casualty clearing station was a tenor from the Hanover Opera House. 'His poor face was concealed by a sanguinary mass of bandages. It was only possible to give nourishment by means of an india-rubber tube passed underneath. It seemed as though gangrene had already set in, yet he wrote down an anxious enquiry as to whether we thought he would ever "be able to sing again".' On August 24 she noted: 'The stream of sick and wounded has swollen to a flood.' On the previous night 4,000 Austrian prisoners had passed through, on their way to be interned 'behind barbed and electrolised wire at Cividale. Some are very young, some looked like Montenegrins, some like flat-faced Kalmucks – all were slouching in a ragged tired way. But they seemed in good spirits and were laughing and singing in snatches.' Internment, a serious deprivation of liberty in peacetime, meant life in wartime.

An Austrian counter-attack on August 28 was repulsed by the Italians, who took another thousand prisoners. The Austrians withdrew to a new line. Italy had gained six miles of mountainous terrain. But there was a dark side also for the Italians: a growing number of desertions, estimated at more than 5,000 in July and a further 5,000 in August.

On the Western Front, the initial British promise was not maintained. On August 22 a mere 880 yards were gained on the Menin Road for more than 3,000 dead and wounded, bringing the casualty figure to more than 60,000 in three weeks. It was a terrifyingly heavy toll. For the Germans, who had once more beaten back a sustained and numerically massive attack, it was a triumph.

Among the terrors of the battlefield were those of mental breakdown, which had begun to make their appearance in the first weeks of the war, and had been intensified during the Somme and Verdun offensives in 1916. On the British sector of the Western Front special centres were set up in 1917 to deal with the increase in mental disorders, in particular hysteria. The centres were given the acronym NYDN centres, standing for the somewhat disingenuous 'Not Yet Diagnosed (Nervous)'. As diagnosis was being made, games and exercises were provided, there was a lending library, and concerts were given. The centres were established twelve to fifteen miles behind the line, so that the noise of battle would be muted. After treatment, men who had broken down under their experiences were sent back to Britain.

Other men, judged unstable but still usable, were transferred to employment and labour companies in the back areas. Those judged fit to return to active service were sent to convalescent homes and given further training before being sent back to the trenches. As many as a third of those brought to the centres were found to be only temporarily disordered. Dazed, silent, unable to understand questions, and confused, they made a rapid recovery and returned to the trenches. Others were shattered for life. In Britain, in addition to six peacetime hospitals that could deal with nervous disorders, an additional six hospitals for officers and thirteen for other ranks were set up in 1917 and 1918 to deal entirely with those whose mental balance had been disturbed by their experiences in the trenches, and who had been sent home for ever.

Was there a way out of the stalemate on the Western Front? In a conversation with one of the King's Private Secretaries on August 14, Lloyd George, who as early as January 1915 had favoured striking at Austria as a way to victory, and who still wanted to focus Britain's efforts on the Italian Front, spoke bitterly against his own military advisers. Britain had made 'an egregious mistake', he said, 'in not throwing our weight on the side of Italy in order to smash Austria, take Trieste and then shake hands and make peace with Austria'. Summoned to meet the War Cabinet in London, on September 4 Haig argued in favour of continuing the offensive on the Western Front. He was able to enlist in his support an appeal from Pétain for continued British activity to prevent a German onslaught on the French positions, still weakened by the aftermath of the mutinies. Pressure from the Italians for British troops to be sent to counter a possible Austrian offensive, and Lloyd George's support for this, was discussed, but it was turned down after Haig reiterated his confidence in breaking through the German lines.

Taking advantage of the turmoil inside Russia, during the first week of September the Germans achieved two victories at the extremities of the Eastern Front. On September 3, after a massive bombardment with more than 100,000 gas shells, German troops drove the Russians from the Baltic port of Riga. On the Roumanian front, at Marasesti, the Germans advanced five miles on an eighteen-mile front, taking 18,000 prisoners.

American troops had reached the Western Front, but in small numbers and with limited tasks. Throughout August, General Pershing, from his headquarters in Paris, had been establishing the basic structure for American participation in the war, still planned for the summer of 1918. On August 13 he set up a Line of Communications system to link the ports with the bases and the forward depots. On August 20 he created a General Purchasing Board, headed by a friend from his University of Nebraska days, Charles G. Dawes.[1] The Board's first and immediate act was to order 5,000 aircraft and 8,500 lorries from the French. These were to be delivered by June 1918. When Pershing's advisers told him that the creation of such a centralised purchasing agency was illegal, he brushed their objections aside, commenting later: 'An emergency confronted us and it was no time to discuss technicalities.'

On September 4 four Americans were killed during a German air raid on a British base hospital, the first United States army fatalities in France. On the following day two American soldiers, both engineers, were killed by German shellfire while repairing a light railway track at Gouzeacourt behind the lines. There was an American aspect to a Royal Naval success that September 5, when the German submarine *U-88* was sunk by British mines off Terschelling. In 1915 her captain, Walther Schwieger, had sunk the *Lusitania*, one of forty-nine ships to have succumbed to his torpedoes. Six weeks before his death he had been awarded the highest German decoration for bravery, the Pour le Mérite, in recognition of his skills in having sunk 190,000 tons of Allied shipping. No mention was made in the citation of the 30,000-ton *Lusitania*, by far his largest victim.

On the Western Front, on September 5, an episode took place the outcome of which only became known in 1991, as a result of a historian's patient detective work.[2] A soldier in one of the Liverpool Pals battalions, Private James Smith, was executed at Kemmel for desertion. He had joined the army in 1910 and fought at Gallipoli in 1915. Sent to the Western Front in 1916, he had been buried by a German shell when in the trenches. Later that year he was convicted twice for breaches of military discipline, forfeiting two Good Conduct badges as a punishment. In August 1917 he deserted, and was caught, tried and sentenced to death. Among those who were ordered to take part in the firing squad was Private Richard Blundell, who knew Smith well. After the executioners' volley had been fired, it was discovered that Smith was still alive. The officer in charge, who by tradition would then have shot Smith with his revolver, could not go through with it. Instead, he gave his revolver to Blundell and ordered him to fire the shot. Blundell did as he was ordered. As a reward for his action he was granted ten days' home leave. It began that same day. Seventy-two years later, as Blundell lay dying, he repeated again and again, in the hearing of his son: 'What a way to get leave, what a way to get leave.'

On September 6, General Pershing moved the headquarters of the American Expeditionary Force from Paris to Chaumont, near to what would

---

[1] Dawes was later author of the Dawes Plan linking German reparations repayments with foreign loans to help Germany's recovery (1924), Vice-President of the United States (1925–9), and American Ambassador to London (1929–32).
[2] The historian was Graham Maddocks, and his book, *Liverpool Pals*, Leo Cooper, London 1991; see pages 166–8. The fact of Smith's execution had been published in 1989 in Julian Putkowski and Julian Sykes, *Shot at Dawn*.

most probably be the American sector of operations. It was proving a hard task to have his men ready for action. That day Poincaré came to inspect the American troops. The parade ground had of necessity been hastily chosen, after dark, by the acting Chief of Staff, Captain George C. Marshall.[1] It proved in the morning light to be irregular, churned up and muddy. The President of France was not impressed, nor was Pershing, whose task was to turn these men into fighting soldiers, and whose credo was discipline and smartness. To add to Pershing's and the Allies' problems, the American Secretary of War, Newton D. Baker, insisted that no American troops should be sent to the front until they were fully trained. When Clemenceau, who wanted to see the Americans in action swiftly, was told that they were not yet ready, he replied acerbically that it was not a question of being ready – nobody – was ever fully ready, but of helping France, which was exhausted, had been bled white, and needed help. Pershing understood the almost desperate needs of his allies, writing in his diary on September 15: 'Recent British attacks beginning with the latter part of July have been very costly and British morale not as high as two months ago.'

Six days before Pershing wrote so gloomily, there had been an incident behind the lines, at Étaples, where British soldiers who had been hospitalised were being put through a tough two week retraining course in gas warfare and marching. Scuffles broke out in the town between soldiers and the military police, the disturbances spread, and the camp commandant and a dozen officers were thrown into the river. But the men returned to camp that night, and in the morning resumed their training. When further disturbances broke out on September 12, aimed at the much disliked Military Police, reinforcements were called in and a cavalry brigade alerted. But when concessions were made to the men, and the rigours of the training relaxed, calm was restored. The British 'mutiny' had been a muted one. When, however, Chinese labourers at Étaples demanded better conditions, their protest was suppressed by troops without compunction, or compassion.

At the time of the disturbances at Étaples, a brigade of Russian troops at La Courtine, two hundred miles south of Paris, were debating their imminent dispatch to the Western Front. Raising the red flag of Bolshevism, they refused to go to the trenches. On September 16 their camp was attacked by another Russian brigade of troops loyal to Kerensky and the war. In what quickly became known as 'The massacre of La Courtine', several dozen Russians were killed. On the previous day, in Petrograd, Kerensky had declared a Republic. He was determined to try to maintain the liberal gains since the March revolution, and to see Russia emerge from the war as a democracy. But power was slowly and inexorably

---

[1] Marshall served as Chief of Staff of the United States forces throughout the Second World War, and was Secretary of State from 1947 to 1949, when he originated the Marshall Plan for the post-war reconstruction of Europe.

50 The Italian Front: an Italian trench dug in the snow, 10,000 feet above sea level, on the south side of Mount Ortler.

51 The Western Front: two officers making their way from one platoon to another in the Ypres Salient, late 1916.

52 The Salonica Front: an observation and machine-gun post north of Monastir, captured from the Bulgarians by the Serbians, 20 November 1916.

53 The Salonica Front: a company of Annamites, French Colonial troops from Cochin China.

54 The Salonica Front: Bulgarian prisoners, November 1916.

55 The Salonica Front: a raft takes wounded Allied soldiers to a hospital ship.

56 The Mesopotamia Front: shells burst on the Turkish trenches. In the foreground, a British military field cemetery.

57 British troops enter Kut, 27 February 1917. Ten months earlier Kut had been the scene of a British surrender.

passing to the Petrograd Soviet, which remained in session at the Tauride Palace.

General Pershing, visiting the Russian camp at La Courtine, described it as 'the vilest and most unsanitary place I have ever seen'. A joke was circulating about the Russian soldiers on the Eastern Front that would have been comic but for the seriousness of Russia's failure for the Western Allies: 'How far did the Russians retreat today?' 'Fourteen kilometres, and they will retreat the same tomorrow.' 'How do you know?' 'That is as far as a tired German can walk.'

On the day of the Russian revolt at La Courtine, five hundred Egyptian labourers, who were employed by the Allies unloading stores at Marseilles, also rioted. They had been led to believe that their period of service in the docks would be of limited duration, and had just learned that it was intended that they should continue to work there until the end of the war, whenever that might be. On the morning of September 16 they refused to leave their camp for work. British and Indian troops were sent in, and an Indian Cavalry guard escorted them to work. That evening there was a further disturbance, and one of the labourers, Mohamed Ahmed, knocked a British officer unconscious with a stick and seized his rifle and bayonet, before being overpowered by three other Egyptians. Twelve days later he was tried for 'a disturbance of a mutinous nature', found guilty and shot.

On that same September 16, an episode took place on the Western Front that caused considerable anger. It was the third day of a limited offensive in the Ypres Salient, in front of St Julien. As Bernard Freyberg, recently promoted to Brigadier-General, wrote home: 'On September 16 one of our low-flying aeroplanes reported that three men in khaki had signalled from a shell-hole in No-Man's Land. An officer went out in broad daylight and brought these men in, who stated on oath that, the morning after the attack, they saw a party of our men, after being disarmed and made prisoner, bayoneted by the enemy. They said the men's screams were dreadful.'

The British offensive in the Ypres Salient was renewed on September 20. The first day's action was a success. 'All our objectives were captured to plan,' Freyberg noted, but he added, with reference to the bayoneting four days earlier: 'Not many prisoners were taken by our men. The incident of a few days before was too fresh in our minds.' Freyberg himself was wounded yet again, in five places including the lung and the thigh, after being hit by a shell burst. He later recalled the casualty clearing station to which he was taken, at Remy. 'The excising of bits of shell or bullets when possible was done at once. Simple cases were X-rayed under a screen, and the body marked with pencil, before taking the patients to the operating theatre where they took their place in a long queue of cases. Inside the tent eight teams of operators were working simultaneously. As soon as one patient was finished, he was taken away, still under anaesthetic, to make way for another anaethetised man who was put on the operating table. I waited in a queue for my turn for the anaesthetic, which was given to me by a woman doctor.'

The British objective was still the Passchendaele Ridge, beyond which lay what was hoped would be an easier terrain for the onward thrust. It was to take seven weeks before the ridge was secured, seven of the most terrible weeks in the history of British warfare. In one encounter, a British sergeant, W. Burman, used a sword to kill eleven Germans in their machine-gun post: he was awarded the Victoria Cross. An American cavalryman who was present during the battle wrote to his wife: 'The Germans shoot a gas which makes people vomit and when they take off the masks to spit, they shoot the deadly gas at them. It is a smart idea, is it not?' [1]

Each day of the war saw some incident that revealed how narrow was the margin between injury and death. A German infantry sergeant who had been wounded in the arm by shrapnel from an exploding shell at Verdun in 1916, and then hit in the arm again by a shell splinter in July 1917 on the Roumanian Front, was injured for a third time that same autumn, and gravely so. Leading his platoon across No-Man's Land towards a Roumanian trench, he was confronted by a Roumanian soldier who opened fire at thirty paces. The bullet went through his chest between the aorta and the heart, and then exited within a finger's breadth of his spine. Bleeding profusely, he managed to run back to the German trenches. After four months in hospital he volunteered as a pilot, was accepted, and was in aerial combat in the last weeks of the war. His name was Rudolf Hess. From 1934 until his dramatic flight to Scotland in 1941, he was Hitler's deputy, and a stalwart supporter of the Third Reich.

Another future Nazi leader was also wounded that September. Joachim Ribbentrop, later Hitler's Ambassador to Britain, and German Foreign Minister, had fought on both the Eastern and Western Fronts for three years. He was awarded the Iron Cross, First Class, and, as a result of his injuries, was invalided out, with the rank of Lieutenant.

---

[1] The cavalryman was Captain George Patton, later a leading proponent of mobile tank warfare, and one of the senior American military commanders in North Africa, Sicily and Northern Europe, 1943–5, when he was known as 'Old Blood and Guts'.

19

Battle at Passchendaele;
Revolution in Russia

SEPTEMBER–NOVEMBER 1917

The Germans were suffering even more severely than the British during the third battle of Ypres. After the first day of a British assault on Polygon Wood, on 26 September 1917, Ludendorff wrote: 'A day of heavy fighting, accompanied by every circumstance that could cause us loss. We might be able to stand the loss of ground, but the reduction of our fighting strength was again all the heavier.'

In Britain, questions had begun to be raised about the continuing attrition. Although the Germans were being pushed back a hundred yards here and a hundred yards there, the casualty lists were growing. On September 27 the Chief of the Imperial General Staff, Sir William Robertson, wrote to Haig: 'I confess I stick to it more because I see nothing better, and because my instinct prompts me to stick to it, than because of any good arguments by which I can support it.' On the following day Haig wrote in his diary, 'The enemy is tottering.' This was his usual argument for continuing.

In the first six days of October, five successive German counter-attacks were driven off and more than 4,000 of the attackers captured. By October 5 more than 20,000 Germans had been taken prisoner. But this was at a cost of an estimated 162,768 dead and wounded. Haig's two most senior generals, Plumer and Gough, urged him to end the offensive, but he would not do so. The British offensive was renewed on a six-mile front on October 9. One of those who took part in it, Hugh Quigley, wrote home a few days later, from hospital, about how 'the officers told us the usual tale, "a soft job", and I reckon it might have been easy enough if we had had a decent start. But none of us knew where to go when the barrage began, whether half-right or half-left....'

Quigley and the men with him reached their first objective, 'a ghastly breastwork littered with German corpses', after which he was knocked out for a while by a shell. 'One sight almost sickened me before I went on: thinking the position of a helmet on a dead officer's face rather curious, sunken down rather far on the nose, my platoon sergeant lifted it off, only to discover no upper half to the head. All above the nose had been blown to atoms, a mass of pulp, brain, bone and muscle.' Apart from that episode, Quigley added, 'the whole affair appeared rather good fun. You know how excited one becomes in the midst of great danger. I forgot absolutely that shells were meant to kill and not to provide elaborate lighting effects.' For a short while he looked at the barrage, 'ours and the Germans', as something provided for our entertainment – a mood of madness, if you like'. The mood of madness soon passed. One of the men in his platoon, loaded with five hundred rounds of ammunition, 'acted the brave man, ran on ahead, signalled back to us, and in general acted as if on quiet parade. The last I saw of him was two arms straining madly at the ground, blood pouring from his mouth, while legs and body sunk into a shell-hole filled with water.'

Then the Germans launched a massive artillery barrage, with mustard gas and high-explosive shells. 'Before us the country seemed a mass of crawling flame,' Quigley wrote. As they advanced, men 'grew nightmarish, as if under a cliff of fire'. British shells, falling short, burst near groups of men trying to go forward. 'But when the mud and smoke cleared away, there they were, dirty but untouched. The clay, rain-soaked, sucked in the shell and the shrapnel seemed to get smothered, making it useless.' At that moment a German shell burst among them. 'A man beside me put his hands to his ears with a cry of horror, stone-deaf, with ear-drums shattered.' Advancing further, Quigley himself was hit by German machine-gun fire. 'Four men carried me on a stretcher down the Passchendaele road, over a wilderness of foul holes littered with dead men disinterred in the barrage. One sight I remember vividly: a white-faced German prisoner tending a whiter "Cameron" who had been struck in the stomach. In spite of the fierce shelling he did not leave him.' Two men carrying a wounded Highlander were hit by the explosion of a shrapnel shell. They were both killed. The wounded Highlander survived. 'The only trouble was his being dropped into a stinking shell-hole. I came down myself once or twice, the path being so bad, but my stretcher bearers, Royal Army Medical Corps, were good stuff, afraid of nothing, and kind hearted, apologising for any jolting.'

Stretcher cases were needing up to sixteen men to carry them back across the mile of mud to the duck-board tracks and advance dressing stations.

On October 12, as the Allied troops drew close to the ridge at Passchendaele, heavy rain turned the fields into liquid mud. So high were the German casualties that Ludendorff was forced to divert, to Flanders, twelve German divisions then on their way to the Italian Front. So heavy was the rain, and so deep the mud, that on October 13 Haig cancelled the attack that was to have gone beyond Passchendaele. Commented one British general laconically: 'Mud stops operations in Flanders. Snow stops operations in Italy.' In the last five days of the battle for Passchendaele, during which Australian troops reached the outskirts of the village, 130 officers and more than 2,000 men were killed, and 8,000 injured. Many of those who died were injured men who fell into the mud and were drowned.

Among the Allies there was a greater sense of achievement after Third Ypres than after the Somme. More ground had been gained, and for fewer casualties. The dead and the wounded during Third Ypres totalled 244,897. Of these about 66,000 were killed.[1]

For the Germans, the Third Battle of Ypres had been a severe blow to their strength and morale. Their losses in dead and wounded were in the region of 400,000, almost twice the British. General von Kuhl, the Chief of Staff on the Flanders Front, later described the battles that culminated in Passchendaele as 'the greatest martyrdom of the World War' and added: 'No division could stick it out in this hell for more than fourteen days.'

The American troops were still in training, their numbers growing more slowly than Pershing would have liked, the supply programme hampered by the need for the Americans themselves to construct many of the docking facilities. On October 3, during an inspection by Pershing of the 1st Division, Major Theodore Roosevelt Jr., son of the former United States President, demonstrated an attack on an enemy trench. When Pershing exploded at the lack of competence, as he saw it, of the senior officers commenting on the demonstration, it was Captain George Marshall who intervened, to explain some of the training difficulties. All was not yet well with the army on whose shoulders a heavy burden of fighting was eventually to fall. 'I fear that we have some general officers', Pershing wrote to the Secretary for War, Newton Baker, on the following day, 'who have neither the experience, the energy, nor the aggressive spirit to prepare their units or to handle them under battle conditions as they exist today.'

At sea, the fortunes of the Allies were mixed. On October 2, in the Baltic, the Russian Fleet refused to obey the orders of the Provisional Government, enabling the Germans to make plans to land on the two large islands in the Gulf of Riga, Dagö and Oesel. As the Germans brought troop transports up for these further landings, the crew of a Russian minelayer, the *Pripyat*, refused to lay its mines. In the Atlantic and the Mediterranean, however, the institution of the convoy system was showing good results for the Allies. The merchant shipping losses for September were the lowest of the year, with only 159 British, Allied and neutral ships being sunk, though 293 British merchant seamen had perished in these sinkings, a high toll. On land, the Allied powers were passing through unfortunate days. On the Isonzo and Trentino Fronts the number of Italian deserters had risen by early October to 70,000. In Palestine the Turkish secret police had broken the Jewish spy ring working for the British, and arrested one of its leaders, Sarah Aaronsohn. For four days they tortured her, but

---

[1] The Somme figure for dead and wounded was 419,654, though the British official history notes: 'The clerk-power to investigate the exact losses was not available.'

she revealed nothing. Then, on October 5, she killed herself.

Influenced by the enthusiasm and practical schemes of Sarah Aaronsohn's brother Aaron, the British Government had begun to look with favour on the idea of replacing Turkish rule in Palestine by a Zionist entity under British rule. That summer, Lord Rothschild had given the British Government a draft formula for a Jewish National Home in Palestine, that would serve to encourage Jews in all the Allied armies to see the defeat of the Turks as an important aim. At first, the British Government moved slowly in its response. But on October 2, British Intelligence learned of a meeting in Berlin at which plans were made by the Germans and Turks to offer the Jews of Europe a German-sponsored Jewish National Home in Palestine. This stimulated the British search for a formula that would make the Allied offer to the Jews more attractive.

Throughout 1917 the future of the Czechs had exercised the policy-makers in Vienna and the nationalists in Prague. On August 4, as a hoped-for focus of anti-Hapsburg opinion, the French Government announced the formation on French soil of a Czech army. In Vienna, despite this inducement by the Entente, opposition remained strong to any real concessions to the national minorities. Czech national hopes had been raised by the accession of the Emperor Charles, one of whose first acts was to commute the death sentences on the nationalist leaders Karel Kramar and Alois Rasin to fifteen and ten years' imprisonment respectively. The new Emperor, who was thirty years old in August 1917, had moved swiftly to mark the change from his great-uncle's old order: appointing a moderate Prime Minister, Seidler; convening Parliament for the first time in more than three years; and proposing a federal system for Austria, in which the Czech lands would be autonomous. Dr Kramar was also released from prison.

Kramar was received back in Prague amid scenes of rejoicing. But the Hungarians were determined not to allow their frontiers to be altered in any way, and vetoed not only the Czech claim to Slovakia, but also the Roumanian and South Slav demands. Yet even the Hungarians were now being drawn into the web of uncertainty and chaos with which the future of the war was bedevilled. On September 19, Count Karolyi, the leader of the Hungarian Independence Party, had set out the details of a campaign designed to bring about an end to the war as soon as possible.

There was a humiliating moment for the Czechs on September 27, in Parliament, when an Austrian deputy, Karl Hermann Wolf, in reply to a Czech call for the integrity of the Bohemian lands, stated that the claims of Bohemia lay at the root of Austria's woes. Wolf went on to say that the new Prime Minister 'behaved with a goodness, a gentleness, a delicacy, a sweetness in which one can perhaps indulge in highly civilised circles, but which one cannot show towards tigers. In a menagerie one does not work with promises and caresses, but with the whip.'

There was uproar, and for twenty minutes Wolf could say no more, but when the noise subsided he continued in similar style. Commented the historian of Czech national aspirations, Elizabeth Wiskemann: 'The Czechs were hyper-sensitive enough – over their "servants' language" and their uncouthness, which amused the Viennese so much – without being likened to wild beasts.'

Civil unrest followed where parliamentary procedures had failed. During a strike in the Moravian town of Prostejov (Prossnitz), twenty-three workmen were shot dead and forty wounded when Austrian troops opened fire.

The Kaiser, eager to show Turkey that Germany was determined to continue the war despite the Wilhelmshaven naval mutiny, the rumblings of the Reichstag and the heavy losses in the Ypres Salient, travelled to Constantinople. He could at least point with confidence to the imminent collapse of the Eastern Front, where, beginning on October 6, more than a million Russian railway workers were on strike, making the movement of the troops to the front virtually impossible.

There were several other German successes that October. On the Western Front, a series of French attacks were beaten off. At Passchendaele, albeit with heavy losses, the German defences held and the wider British plan to advance deep into Belgium collapsed. In the Baltic, an amphibious operation was launched against three Russian islands, Dagö and Oesel, and the smaller Moon Island, with an armada of warships, including eleven battleships, and nineteen steamers for the 23,000 soldiers and 5,000 horses. The islands were defended by Admiral Altvater, but his task was made impossible by the revolutionary sailors under his command. As he later told General Hoffmann: 'The influence of Bolshevik propaganda on the masses is enormous. I was defending Öesel and the troops actually melted away before my eyes.' The islands were occupied and 5,000 Russian soldiers taken prisoner.

In German East Africa, the German forces continued to battle with the British, and prepared under Lettow-Vorbeck's tenacious leadership to invade Portuguese East Africa: after many brushes with his enemies over a vast geographical area, he was not to surrender until fourteen days after the armistice in Europe. In the North Sea, two German cruisers, the *Bremse* and the *Brummer*, attacked and broke up a Norway-Shetland convoy, sinking nine merchant ships in just over two hours. Two British destroyers that tried to intervene, *Mary Rose* and *Strongbow*, were both sunk, and 135 of their crew drowned. That same day, October 17, the United States transport ship *Antilles* was sunk by a German submarine, and sixty-seven of those on board were lost.

A German submarine commander, Martin Niemöller, whose submarine was then off the coast of Morocco, later recalled those heady days. 'On the 20th October, as night falls, we sink an unknown – probably British – steamer, near the coast, by means of a torpedo after a gunnery duel. On the 21st we have a stand-up fight with another British steamer which first comes towards us and then turns away. It is Sunday and the steamer is lucky to begin with, as she increases her distance and we have to cease firing. Shortly after noon the SS *Gryfevale* appears to have a hot bearing as she eases down and we are able to reopen fire. She runs ashore in the surf. After her crew have landed, we destroy her by gunfire and her remains are then not recognisable as a steamship.'[1]

These were German successes. There were German failures, too, that month, including the execution just outside Paris on October 15 of the 41-year-old Dutch-born dancer, Mata Hari, found guilty of spying for the Germans.[2] *The Times* reported: 'Mata Hari, the dancer, was shot this morning. She was arrested in Paris in February, and sentenced to death by Court-Martial last July for espionage and giving information to the enemy.... She was in the habit of meeting notorious German spy-masters outside French territory, and she was proved to have communicated important information to them, in return for which she had received several large sums of money since May 1916.' Her real name was Margueretha Gertruida Zelle, who had been a dancer in France since 1903, when she was twenty-seven.

Four days after Mata Hari's execution, later a carefully planned air raid against the industrial cities of northern England by eleven Zeppelins went badly awry. One Zeppelin dropped its bombs over London, four were blown off course by a 60-mile-an-hour gale and ended up over German-occupied France, one was shot down by French anti-aircraft fire at 19,000 feet, one crash landed, one fell intact into French hands and one disappeared without trace over the Mediterranean.

There was a moment of ill omen for the Germans on October 21, on the Lunéville sector of the Western Front, when the first American combat troops were attached to various French units. They were sent to a quiet sector of the front, deliberately chosen as such. The scheme was to send individual battalions, in rotation, to the front-line trenches. One American battalion captured the first prisoner to be taken by the Expeditionary Force, a German orderly who wandered into their sector by mistake.

On October 23, on the Aisne, the French launched a limited but sustained attack on the German positions defending the Chemin des Dames. The attack had been preceded by a six-day (and night) artillery bombardment in which one of the batteries of French 75-millimetre guns was operated by American artillerymen. The attack itself, by eight French divisions, assisted by eighty French tanks, advanced two miles across the pulverised terrain, taking 10,000 German prisoners, and depriving the Germans of

---

[1] Martin Niemöller later became Vicar of Berlin-Dahlem, and was a courageous opponent of Nazism. In 1937 he was arrested, and sent first to Sachsenhausen and then to Dachau concentration camps. He died in 1984, at the age of ninety-two.

[2] As I was writing this chapter a spy scandal in the United States led a leading British newspaper to publish a photograph of Mata Hari with the caption: 'First World War role model....' (*The Times*, 24 February 1994).

an important observation point at Laffaux. Among the places captured by
the French on that occasion was the Fort de la Malmaison, a former
fortress which had been sold before the war to a private builder, for use
as a stone quarry. Known as the Battle of the Quarries, the victory was
what one historian has called 'neat and compact and satisfying as a gift
package; indeed a gift to cheer a tired and discouraged country'.[1] The
Germans, unwilling to face a protracted battle, withdrew from the Chemin
des Dames to a lower position two miles further north.

The focus of German offensive planning was on the Italian Front, where
a substantial German force had joined with the Austrians to break through
on the Isonzo. It was the twelfth battle among the inhospitable high peaks,
but the first whose planning, scale and pattern had been determined by
the Central Powers. It began with a four-hour artillery bombardment, two
hours of which was with gas shells against which the Italians had no
adequate protection. The Italians, devastated by the gas, fell back in panic
as much as fourteen miles. That afternoon German forces entered the
town of Caporetto. For the Italians it was to be a name with shameful
connotations, though their men had no means of resisting such an overwhelming assault.

Death made no discrimination among the armies: among those killed
on the Isonzo that week was the 25-year-old Austrian lyric poet, Franz
Janowitz. Also in action at Caporetto was Lieutenant Rommel, who on
October 25 led his men to two mountain peaks, capturing 3,600 Italians
as he did so. By the end of that day the German army had taken 30,000
prisoners in all, and more than three hundred guns. On the following day
the Austro-German advance continued, with Austrian troops capturing
Mount Maggiore. Rommel, after a twelve-mile advance, reached the
5,414-foot summit of Mount Matajur. After fifty-two hours of fighting he
had taken more than 9,000 prisoners, at a cost of only six men killed.

On this third day of the Austro-German success against the Italians,
Haig launched a last British attempt to take Passchendaele. 'The enemy
charged like a wild bull against the iron wall' was Ludendorff's comment.
On October 26, the very day the final Passchendaele offensive began,
hoping to avert an Italian collapse in the south, Lloyd George ordered two
Western Front divisions to be sent to Italy without delay. It was too late
for any immediate redress of the military balance: on October 27 the Italian
army withdrew from its positions on the Isonzo. That day Mussolini, one
of Italy's most strident journalists, called for renewed patriotic zeal. For
as long as the struggle continued, he wrote, 'we must abandon the great
phrase "Liberty". There is another which in this third winter of the war
should be on the lips of the cabinet when they address the Italian people,
and it is "Discipline".' His exhortation to his readers on October 27 was:
'Face the enemy.' Italians must consider, 'Not the gravity of the hour but
the greatness of the hour.'

[1] Correlli Barnett, *The Swordbearers*, London 1964.

So distressed was one British liaison officer in Italy, Sir Samuel Hoare, at the widespread defeatism and anti-war feeling in Milan, and at the pro-German feeling he found in Rome, that he sought out Mussolini and obtained permission from British Military Intelligence to help finance his newspaper and to encourage outspoken articles against the Milanese pacifists. 'Leave it to me' was Mussolini's comment to an intermediary who brought him the British money. From his editorial chair Mussolini continued to advocate courage, resistance, defiance and sacrifice. On the Isonzo, where the Italians had withdrawn as far south as Udine, French and British troops were hurrying to sustain their ally.

Everywhere the Allied armies were engaged in tremendous struggles, each one potentially decisive for the outcome of the war. It was on October 30 that Canadian soldiers finally entered Passchendaele, but their casualties were heavy and they were driven back. 'The sights up there', a future Chief of the Imperial General Staff, Brigade-Major Alan Brooke, Royal Artillery, wrote a few weeks later, 'are beyond all description; it is a blessing to a certain extent that one becomes callous to it all and that one's mind is not able to take it all in.' At a conference addressed by Haig, Brooke recalled: 'I could hardly believe that my ears were not deceiving me! He spoke in the rosiest terms of our chances of breaking through. I had been all over the ground and to my mind such an eventuality was quite impossible. I am certain he was misinformed and had never seen the ground for himself.'

In Palestine, the Turkish Eighth Army, commanded by General Kress von Kressenstein, a veteran of Gallipoli, was preparing to throw back a third British attempt to drive the Turks from the southern border of Palestine. Twice before Gaza, guarding Palestine from the south, had been attacked in vain. The third attack, however, was to be different, and not primarily on Gaza at all. It had been preceded by a two-month deception plan aimed at convincing the Turks, through false orders 'inadvertently' captured, that the main assault would indeed be at Gaza, as before. Three weeks before the battle, a British officer, Richard Meinertzhagen, rode up to a Turkish guard post, allowed the guards to chase him, and, just as he disappeared from view, dropped a haversack smeared with horse's blood, to give the impression he had been wounded. Inside the haversack were carefully prepared details, all spurious, of the next attack on Gaza, and a letter from the Intelligence department advising the impracticability of an attack on Beersheba.

The main British offensive, the first in Palestine commanded by General Allenby, took place against Beersheba on October 31. The Turks, having been successfully deceived into thinking that no great attack on them was intended there, were confronted by an assault force of 40,000 men. The Turkish commander, General Ismet, was forced to throw in his reserves to meet the first assault.[1] As so often in battle, luck also played its part: the newly formed Turkish Seventh Army had already left Jerusalem for the Beersheba Front, but was not yet half way there.

The first of the attackers to go into action were New Zealand cavalrymen. On the battlefield a British soldier, Corporal Collins, while carrying a wounded man to safety, bayoneted fifteen Turks who tried to bar his way back to the British lines. He was awarded the Victoria Cross. In the capture of Beersheba itself, Australian cavalrymen carried out a full-scale cavalry charge, using their sharpened bayonets as swords. Aerial reconnaissance, a branch of warfare to which Allenby paid particular attention, had revealed that the Turks were protected by neither barbed-wire or anti-cavalry ditches. Believing that the Australians were the advance guard of a far larger force, the Turks fled back into the town. The Australians followed, capturing more than a thousand prisoners.

In the aftermath of Beersheba's capture, Gaza was also taken, the assault being preceded by a massive Anglo-French naval bombardment from off shore, with ten warships taking part. Even then the power of the Turco-German combination was not to be scorned: a German submarine moved in close to the shore and sank two of the Allied warships. But when the combined infantry and cavalry attack on Gaza came, it swept all before it, and the fortification system which it had taken von Kressenstein twenty-five weeks to build was overrun in the same number of minutes. When it was discovered that the minaret of the main mosque was being used as an artillery observation point orders were sent to the naval flotilla, and the minaret was fired on and demolished.

On entering Gaza the British troops, among them the specially-recruited Jewish soldiers of the 39th Battalion Royal Fusiliers, found a city in ruins. They also found, among the graves of the British soldiers who had died in the two previous assaults, the grave of James Bonar Law, son of the senior Conservative politician and future Prime Minister, Andrew Bonar Law. The city itself had been looted by the Turks before they withdrew. Near Huj, north of Gaza, the Turks tried to block the further British advance, using Austrian howitzers and gunners. But Allenby's cavalry, undeterred, charged at Austrian artillery and Turkish machine guns alike. Most of the gunners, seeing the attackers thundering up the hillside towards them, limbered up and galloped away to the north. Others, realising too late that they would be overrun, and that their chance of escape was lost, 'fired point blank', as Allenby's biographer Raymond Savage has written, 'into the mass as it surged up the slope. Horses crashed disembowelled on the guns at the impact, as unflinching gunners met their death.'

Three Austrian howitzers and nine field guns were captured. Cavalry

[1] Ismet became Ataturk's Chief of Staff against the Greeks (1919–22), acquiring the surname Inönü after the battle near the Anatolian village of that name. He was subsequently the first Prime Minister of the Turkish Republic (1923–37) and President of Turkey after Ataturk's death (1938–50). He was again Prime Minister from 1960 to 1965. He died in 1973, at the age of eighty-nine.

had fought and beaten artillery. The cavalry charge swept on, capturing the Turkish machine guns 'which were then swung round to harry the retreating Turks'. Von Kressenstein and the Turkish Eighth Army fell back almost to Jaffa. The way to Jerusalem, Allenby's goal, was open. From the fields and ditches around Gaza the bodies of the fallen victors were gathered up, and buried just to the east of the railway station, where they lie to this day: 3,000 British soldiers, an airman, a nurse and a nursing sister, a hundred Australians, twenty New Zealanders, nine British West Indians, two British officers from the Indian Army, four South Africans and two members of the Egyptian Labour Corps. The Jewish soldiers are identified by a Star of David on their tombstones. There are also 781 tombstones of men who could not be identified. A special Indian cemetery, containing forty graves, is divided into a Hindu and a Muslim section. At the military cemetery in Beersheba are 1,239 British and Dominion burials.

Over Britain, on October 31, the German Gothas carried out their first incendiary bomb raid of the war. The raid was not a success, little damage being done by the eighty-three ten-pound bombs which were dropped, many of which failed to ignite. Ten civilians being killed. London's anti-aircraft guns, arranged so that each battery could alert its neighbour to the incoming bombers, drove off some of the raiders altogether and dispersed others. Of the twenty-two raiders, five crash landed on their return.

United States troops were now ready to go into action. They did so for the first time on the evening of November 2, when an American infantry battalion took over from French troops at Barthelémont. At three o'clock the next morning one of its isolated outposts was subjected to an hour-long artillery bombardment, after which a raiding party of 213 Germans, from a Bavarian regiment, attacked. The Americans were outnumbered four to one. Three were killed: Corporal Gresham and Privates Enright and Hay. One was shot, one had his throat cut, and one had his skull smashed in. The raiding party then withdrew. It had lost two of its own men killed and one deserted to the Americans, but it took back to the German lines twelve American prisoners-of-war.

The survivors of the outpost were found with 'white, drawn faces and haunted eyes'. Pershing, on being told of the attack, wept. An inquiry decided that the American troops were not sufficiently trained and should be taken out of the line. Bitterly the local French commander, General Paul Bordeaux, cast doubt on 'the courage and ability with which the Americans had defended themselves'. After his critical comment was challenged, General Bordeaux retracted, asking that the bodies of the three dead Americans 'be left here, be left to us for ever', and he declared: 'We will inscribe on their tombs "Here lie the first soldiers of the famous United States Republic to fall on the soil of France, for justice and liberty." The passer-by will stop and uncover his head. The travellers of France, of the Allied countries of America, who will come here to visit our battlefield of Lorraine, will go out of their way to come here, to bring to their graves the tribute of their respect and of their gratefulness. Corporal Gresham, Private Enright, Private Hay, in the name of France, I thank you. God receive your souls. Farewell!'

Seventy-five years later a British guidebook directed visitors to this very battlefield in Lorraine, to the very site of this first American offensive action on the Western Front.[1]

On the Eastern Front, war was rapidly giving way to revolution. Despite the assertion on October 16, by the new Russian Minister of War, General Verkhovski, to Colonel Knox, that 'we will restore the Russian Army and make it in a fit condition to fight by the spring!', Knox noted in his diary two weeks later: 'There is evidently not the slightest hope that the Russian Army will ever fight again.' On November 2, hoping in part that Russian Jews might be influenced to urge their compatriots to go on fighting, Britain issued the Balfour Declaration, the letter from the Foreign Secretary, Lord Balfour, to Lord Rothschild, expressing Britain's support for 'a National Home for the Jewish people' in Palestine. The final discussions leading to the declaration had touched directly on how it might serve to rally patriotic feeling in Russia.

'Information from every quarter shows the very important role the Jews are now playing in the Russian political situation,' a senior Foreign Office official, Ronald Graham, had written to Balfour on October 24. 'Almost every Jew in Russia is a Zionist, and if they can be made to realise that the success of Zionist aspirations depends on the support of the Allies and the expulsion of the Turks from Palestine, we shall enlist a most powerful element in our favour.' It was arranged on November 3 that three leading Zionists, among them Vladimir Jabotinsky, would go at once to Petrograd to rally Russian Jewry to the Allied cause. 'It is a pity so much valuable time has been lost,' the Permanent Under-Secretary of State, Lord Hardinge, wrote that day, but he was not too despondent, telling Balfour: 'With skilful management of the Jews of Russia the situation may still be restored by the spring.'

It was too late to restore the disintegrating situation. Nothing, however attractive to a minority, or tempting in the long term, could counter the great swell of anti-war opinion. On November 3 it was learned in Petrograd that Russian troops on the Baltic Front had thrown down their arms and begun to fraternise with their German 'enemy'. When, on November 4, the Provisional Government ordered the 155,000-strong Petrograd garrison to go the front, the Bolshevik Military Revolutionary Committee urged them not to go. On the following day Kerensky ordered troops outside Petrograd, whom he believed to be loyal to his government, to enter the city. On November 6 they declined to do so. A 1,000-strong women's battalion loyal to the Government was jeered that day by the soldiers as it marched through the streets on its way to be inspected by Kerensky. That evening

[1] A.J. Peacock, *A Second Alternative Guide to the Western Front*, Gun Fire, York, page 13.

the Bolsheviks occupied the principal buildings in the capital: the railway stations, the bridges over the river Neva, the state bank and, most importantly, the telephone exchange.

The vast Empire stretching from the Baltic Sea to the Pacific Ocean, whose support for Serbia and whose alliance with France had been one of the catalysts of war in 1914, was in turmoil and disarray. On November 7 more than 18,000 Bolsheviks surrounded the Provisional Government ministers in the Winter Palace, defended by a mere thousand soldiers. From the naval base at Kronstadt had come more than 9,000 sailors committed to revolution. They were joined that day by nearly 4,000 more, and by nine hundred soldiers, who reached the capital on board a minelayer, two minesweepers, two steamers and five small naval vessels. That same day, two Russian destroyers arrived from Helsinki: they too announced their support for revolution.

Shortly after ten o'clock that evening, the cruiser *Aurora*, manned by Bolsheviks and anchored in the Neva, announced that it would open fire on the Winter Palace, and fired a few blank charges as an earnest of its resolve. By one o'clock in the morning of November 8, the Bolsheviks had overrun the Winter Palace, scattering its defenders. Lenin, elected that day Chairman of the Council of People's Commissars, was ruler of the Russian capital. Trotsky became Commissar for Foreign Affairs. 'It could not possibly last,' the British Ambassador's daughter Meriel later reflected. 'Petrograd itself might perhaps be forced to submit to such a rule for a short time, but that the whole of Russia should be governed by such men was not credible.'

Not credible, and yet a reality: the six-month-old Provisional Government had been swept away as assuredly as the Tsar had been swept away before it. In Moscow, Red Guards occupied the Kremlin. Kerensky fled from Petrograd in an American Embassy car, driving to Pskov, where he hoped to rally military forces loyal to his Government. 'He was forced to borrow a car,' Colonel Knox noted in his diary, 'as all the magnetos from the cars collected in the Palace Square had been stolen by the Bolsheviks during the night. He sent back a message to the American Ambassador, asking him not to recognise the new government for five days, as before that time he would return and restore order. In my opinion he will not return.'

Orders and decrees began to flow from the new source of power. The first decree on November 8 was the Decree of Peace. Lenin read it out that evening to an ecstatic crowd. But on the following day, when Trotsky asked the Foreign Ministry, of which he had just been made head, to translate it into foreign languages for immediate distribution abroad, six hundred officials, former loyal civil servants of the Tsar and the Provisional Government, resigned and walked out of the ministry building. On the following day, four million copies of the decree were sent to the front, calling for an end to all hostilities.

The war-making power of Russia, hitherto the eastern arm of the Allies, was broken.

20

The terms of war and peace

NOVEMBER–DECEMBER 1917

With Russia immobilised by revolution, the Allies struggled to maintain what momentum they could on their other fronts. On 5 November 1917, as news of the Russian Revolution was reaching the Western Allies, an inter-Allied conference at Rapallo heard from Foch that the Italian Second Army was 'absolutely broken' but that the First, Third and Fourth Armies 'remained intact'. The problem with the Second Army had been panic in the ranks. Confronted by a sustained Austrian assault, military order and discipline had collapsed.

The newly appointed Italian Prime Minister, Vittorio Orlando, appealed to the British and French for help. It was not sufficient, he told Lloyd George, 'merely to render some assistance, but essential that assistance should be adequate.' When Lloyd George said that it was 'in the obvious interests' of Britain and France that Italy should stay in the war, Orlando replied, as Lloyd George recounted, 'with quivering passion that this was what Italy intended to do at all cost, even at the expense of retirement to Sicily'. Lloyd George noted at this point: 'He is a Sicilian.'

The Italians had decided to fall back sixty miles, to the line of the river Piave, and try to hold the Austrians there. 'At the present moment the country was calm,' Orlando told his allies. 'It had resigned itself to the loss of territory and had discounted the retreat to the Piave.' Internal order could be guaranteed, 'unless', Orlando warned, 'the line of the Piave was abandoned. Hence the future of Italy 'depended on the decision which the Allies took now'.

The Italians asked for fifteen British and French divisions to be sent to Italy at once, declaring that the ratio of Austrians to Italians at the front was, battalion against battalion, 811 to 377. Foch declared that this estimate was a 'ridiculous exaggeration', as indeed it was. The fact that such an estimate had been put forward, Lloyd George later reflected, 'was only a further proof of the panic' that had seized the Italian General Staff. Britain and France agreed to send eight divisions between them, but no more.

This decision gave the Austrians an initial and unexpected success. On November 8, Austrian troops, hurrying down from the mountain peaks of the Julian Alps and the Dolomites, occupied Vittorio Veneto, only thirty-seven miles from Venice. From Caporetto, where the Italians had stood ten days earlier, back to the line of the Piave, involved a sixty-mile retreat of Eastern Front proportions. During the course of it, at the village of Longarone on the upper Piave, by a skilful fording of the river Lieutenant Rommel took part in the capture of 8,000 Italian troops and twenty guns. As he drew near to the village, Rommel saw a German lieutenant who had been captured by the Italians a short time earlier, riding towards him on a mule followed by several dozen Italians waving white handkerchiefs. The lieutenant had with him a letter from the Italian garrison commander in Longarone, surrendering the garrison and the village.[1]

Five days later the Central Powers had another success on the Italian Front when, on November 15, a Hungarian division crossed the Piave at its delta, capturing Cava Zuccherina, sixteen miles from Venice. The Italian military spirit had not collapsed, however, and on the night of November 15, when four battalions of German troops crossed the Piave near Ponte di Piave, the Italians drove them back, taking six hundred prisoners.

On the coast of the Eastern Mediterranean, having captured more than 4,000 Turks and fifty-nine guns at Gaza and Beersheba, Allenby was advancing rapidly towards his goal, Jerusalem. Far from their respective homes, Germans, Austrians and Turks fought Britons, Australians and New Zealanders. During the battle for Tel el Khuweilfeh on November 6, a 24-year-old Captain in the Royal Army Medical Corps, John Russell, was posthumously awarded the Victoria Cross after he 'repeatedly went out to attend the wounded under murderous fire from snipers and machine guns, and, in many cases where no other means were at hand, carried them in himself although almost exhausted'.

In a bombing attack on November 8 on the German airfield at El-Tine, in the coastal plain, eleven German aircraft were destroyed on the ground and hundreds of Turkish troops, alarmed by the aerial warfare, fled from the front line. On November 9 an intercepted Turkish wireless message revealed a serious shortage of railway engines and trucks. As Turkish forces who had been driven from Beersheba retreated into the Judaean hills, British aircraft bombed and machine-gunned their columns.

On November 11 the British War Cabinet, unused to receiving daily telegrams reporting such rapid advances, warned Allenby not to take risks with such extended lines of communication. In case he thought the politicians were being too timorous, he was reminded of the fate of the British troops who had advanced so rapidly towards Baghdad in 1915,

[1] In November 1963 I passed through Longarone: the village had been all but obliterated a month earlier when the Vaiont Dam built above it collapsed. The dam was the third highest concrete structure in the world. In Longarone and the five villages below it, 1,809 people were drowned, including 430 schoolchildren.

and had been driven back to Kut, besieged and forced to surrender. But neither the impetus of the advance nor the lure of Jerusalem could be impeded. On November 15, Australian and New Zealand troops occupied the towns of Ramleh and Lydda. This latter was the former crusader town of St Georges de Lydde, home of St George of dragon-slaying fame whom British crusaders had brought back as their patron saint six hundred years earlier. New Zealand cavalrymen entered Jaffa on November 16. Their next objective was Jerusalem.

On the Western Front, the battle at Passchendaele had come to an end on November 10 with a final Canadian advance of five hundred yards, in the face of a massive German artillery bombardment of more than five hundred guns, and continual air attacks. Since the start of the offensive on the last day of July, Haig's forces had gained four and a half miles of ground. The cost to the attackers was 62,000 dead. A further 164,000 had been wounded. The Germans lost 83,000 killed and as many as a quarter of a million wounded. A further 26,000 Germans had been taken prisoner. 'We have won great victories,' Lloyd George told the Supreme War Council in Paris on November 12. 'When I look at the appalling casualty lists I sometimes wish it had not been necessary to win so many.'

A deep reluctance to be in the casualty lists could be seen that month in the statistics following the Canadian call-up. So unpopular was the prospect of military service in Europe, that of the 331,934 able-bodied men who came within the scope of the act, 21,568 reported for military service and 310,376 applied for exemptions.[1] It was an indication of the growing grasp of the reality of war.

On November 11 Russian forces loyal to the former Provisional Government in Petrograd, having formed themselves into a substantial army, came within shelling range of the capital. It was a Sunday. Inside Petrograd it was widely believed, by those for whom the prospect of Bolshevik rule was a nightmare and an aberration, that the moment of deliverance had come. Groups opposed to the Bolsheviks set up a Committee of Public Safety, and called on the officer cadets to take offensive action inside the city. One of the Tsarist generals being held captive in the Astoria Hotel arrested the military guard put there by the Bolsheviks. Officer Cadets seized several buildings. But in the afternoon the Bolsheviks were back in control, the Astoria being captured and the Cadets driven out of their strongholds by shell and machine-gun fire. Many of the Cadets were brutally murdered after they sought to surrender.

With Russia's warmaking ability ended, and Italy pressed back to the Piave, the burden on France and Britain to sustain the Allied cause was a

[1] The call-up was on 13 October 1917. The figures of the exemptions were announced on November 10. Most of the exemptions were granted. By 1 January 1918 the figures were: 404,395 soldiers called up and 380,510 appealed for exemption.

heavy one. On November 16, France acquired a new, 76-year-old leader, Georges Clemenceau, who despite his age was determined to drive his country to victory. As Prime Minister and also War Minister, he quickly dominated France's warmaking efforts, driving his subordinates forward as he drove himself. It was not a moment too soon. A telegram had reached the Germans from Petrograd, addressed 'to all' and signed by Trotsky, announcing that the new Soviet Government wished to make peace. On November 17 the Austrian Foreign Minister, Count Czernin, wrote to a friend: 'Peace at the earliest moment is necessary for our own salvation and we cannot obtain peace until the Germans get to Paris – and they cannot get to Paris unless their Eastern Front is free.'

That moment might well have been imminent: on November 19 the Bolsheviks asked for an immediate armistice on all fronts. Defiantly, Clemenceau told the French Chamber of Deputies on the following day that his policy was 'War, nothing but war.' Listening to him as he spoke these words of defiance was the British Minister of Munitions, Winston Churchill, who was to echo those very sentiments twenty-two years later when Britain had lost its main ally, France, and London seemed as much in danger as Paris had been with Russia's withdrawal from the war in 1917.

On the day after Clemenceau uttered his stern words of defiance, equally stern words were spoken in utmost secrecy by Lloyd George to Woodrow Wilson's emissary, Colonel House. It had become clear that Pershing's hope of having a million armed Americans in Europe by the summer of 1918 was nowhere near realisation. The most recent calculation of the maximum possible had reduced that number to 525,000 by May. Nor would the United States have sufficient shipping tonnage available to supply and feed them all, possibly not until 1919. Incompetence was also proving a problem: some American supply ships were reaching France with less than 50 per cent of their available cargo space taken up. For the British, the prospect of the scaling down and postponement of the American contribution was a blow. 'It is better that I should put the facts quite frankly to you,' Lloyd George told Colonel House on November 20, 'because there is a danger that you might think you can work up your army at leisure, and that it does not matter whether your troops are there in 1918 or 1919. But I want you to understand that it might make the most vital difference.'

On the day of Lloyd George's protest, the British launched another offensive on the Western Front, their third in 1917. Its objective was the city of Cambrai and beyond. A quarter of a million British soldiers took part, facing a quarter of a million Germans, along a mere six-mile front. General Sir Julian Byng was in command of the British forces. Three hundred aircraft engaged in reconnaissance and spotting duties. But the dominant feature of the battle was that, for the first time in the history of warfare, the main thrust of the attack was carried out by tanks: 324 took part in the opening attack. Their appearance in such numbers was initially effective. They were able to crush the German barbed wire and within hours had made a break in the German line throughout the six-mile front of attack.

'The triple belts of wire were crossed as if they had been beds of nettles,' Captain D.G. Browne recalled, 'and 350 pathways were sheared through them for the infantry. The defenders of the front trench, scrambling out of dug-outs and shelters to meet the crash and flame of the barrage, saw the leading tanks almost upon them.' The appearance of these metallic creatures, wrote Browne, was 'grotesque and terrifying'.

The initial success was dampened and then stopped by ill-luck, by a design fault whereby the tank tracks broke down after a very short time in action, and by German tenacity. At Flesquières, less than half way between the starting point and Cambrai, British air observers had failed to report the German artillery batteries, which halted the tank advance in one sector, knocking out thirty-nine tanks. Seven of these were halted by a single German artilleryman, Unteroffizier Kruger, who worked his gun alone until he was shot. He was the only German soldier in the First World War to be mentioned in British military dispatches.

Canadian cavalrymen of the Fort Garry Horse (the Garrys), advancing north of Masnières, came closer to Cambrai that day than any other Allied troops. During their advance they captured a complete German engineers Staff. Then, coming upon a German artillery battery which was firing at some advancing tanks, the Canadian horsemen drew their sabres and charged. They then descended, literally, as they came to a sunken road, on a German machine-gun battery. In that short charge fifty Germans were killed. But in the sunken road the Canadians were pinned down by other German machine gunners. They thereupon dismounted, stampeded their horses towards the German lines, and managed to fight their way back to Masnières, using their sabres to break through. For his leadership during the charge, Lieutenant H. Strachan was awarded the Victoria Cross.

The first day of the Battle of Cambrai marked a decisive success for the tank and the strategy of using it to create a decisive breach in the enemy front line. The German defences had been broken, five miles gained, and more than 4,000 German soldiers taken prisoner. The British newspapers declared in triumph: THE GREATEST BRITISH VICTORY OF THE WAR and A SURPRISE FOR THE GERMANS.

The sense of achievement on that first day was real, but the set-backs at Flequières and Masnières were ill omens. On the second day of the battle a fresh German division arrived from the Russian Front. It was rushed forward from the railway station at Cambrai to strengthen the line at a point where it might have given in altogether that day, between Rumilly and Crèvecour, on the St Quentin Canal. This made the next phase of the British plan, a cavalry breakthrough, impossible. When Byng learned that this new German division was in the line, he realised that the cavalry would not be able to gallop forward east of Cambrai: that 'galloping through', the image and reality of war before 1914, would not come to pass in 1917.

News of the initial breakthrough at Cambrai, offering as it did some hope that the stalemate of trench warfare might yet be broken to the Allied advantage, was made public on November 23, and led to an unprecedented reaction. In Britain, church bells were rung throughout the island to celebrate the victory.[1] In the United States, a New York club notice board displayed the effort of Edward I. Kidder:

> *Cheer Boys Cheer*
> *We sing,*
> *Of Byng,*
> *The Britisher who won his charge,*
> *Without artillery or barrage,*
> *With no attempt at camouflage,*
> *With steady ranks, with sturdy 'tanks'*
>   *He's gained the world's undying thanks.*
> *His prowess flashes o'er the main*
> *While Hohenzollern writhes with pain.*
> *Onward in your victorious swing,*
> *We drink to you, brave warrior Byng!*

Even as the elation was at its height in London and New York, that 'victorious swing' was coming to an end. On November 23, the day on which the church bells rang out in Britain, and on which it was announced that the total number of German prisoners taken at Cambrai now exceeded 7,000, the British advance was checked in a violent battle at Bourlon Wood. Sixty-two tanks were in action there, but tank losses continued to mount, losing the element of strength as well as of surprise.

The future of the battle turned upon the fate of Bourlon Wood. Haig was insistent that the wood be taken, to enable the wider plan of attack to be renewed. At his suggestion, cavalrymen, whose intended task was to exploit the tank victory by galloping forward on horseback, were dismounted and called upon to fight as infantrymen. They should be used, Haig told Byng, 'in any numbers'. When the decision to attack was passed on to General Fielding, one of the corps commanders, he replied: 'We shall do our best, Sir, but you ask a lot of us.'

That 'lot' proved impossible to fulfil. The hoped-for mastery of the high ground above Bourlon eluded the attackers. The Germans, in a counter-attack, recovered a hundred of their captured guns. In a separate struggle for the village of Moevres, three Irish battalions succeeded, by dusk on November 23, in driving the Germans out of three-quarters of the village.

---

[1] For the first time in three years and three months of war. In the Second World War the church bells (originally intended only to be rung in the event of an invasion of Britain) were rung in November 1942 after the Battle of Alamein, three years and two months after the war had begun.

One of their companies then came under intense German machine-gun fire from a strongpoint to the south-west of Bourlon Wood. Their predicament was seen by a Royal Flying Corps pilot, who dived low to attack the strongpoint. The Germans fired at him: he was shot down and killed. The soldiers did not forget his bravery. A few weeks later a note appeared in the 'In Memoriam' column of *The Times*: 'To an Unknown Airman, shot down on November 23rd, 1917, whilst attacking a German strongpoint south-west of Bourlon Wood, in an effort to help out a company of Royal Irish Fusiliers when other help had failed.' The dead pilot was in fact an American volunteer, Lieutenant A. Griggs. He had been flying with No. 68 (Australian) Squadron.

Also in action in the air above the battlefield was Baron Richthofen's squadron. North of the village of Fontaine, Richthofen himself shot down yet another British pilot victim, Lieutenant J.A.V. Boddy, who was wounded in the head and crash landed. Boddy was later rescued by a fellow-pilot who, by chance, crash landed nearby.

In the last week of November, the first snow fell. The war of tank movement was replaced by that of hand-to-hand fighting. When, on November 27, the British made an attempt to take Fontaine, tanks were sent into the narrow streets for which they were quite unprepared. 'There was horrible slaughter in Fontaine,' Major-General J.F.C. Fuller, a senior tank officer, later wrote, 'and I, who had spent three weeks before the battle in thinking out its probabilities, had never tackled the subject of village fighting. I could have kicked myself again and again for this lack of foresight, but it never occurred to me that our infantry commanders would thrust tanks into such places.'

A German officer saw the battle from the other side. 'Armoured vehicles have entered the village,' he wrote in his report. 'It is found that they are able to conquer ground but not hold it. In the narrow streets and alleyways they have no free field for their fire, and their movements are hemmed in on all sides. The terror they have spread amongst us disappears. We get to know their weak spots. A ferocious passion for hunting them down is growing.' The Germans had discovered that individual hand grenades thrown on the top of the tanks or at their sides were ineffective. 'We tie several grenades together', the officer wrote, 'and make them explode beneath the tanks'. The new weapon had found a new adversary.

German machine gunners swept Fontaine from the north, their British counterparts from the south. The British war correspondent Philip Gibbs, wrote in the *Daily Telegraph*: 'No human being could stay alive there for a second after showing himself in the village.' Those British tanks that reached the far side of the village, and from there glimpsed the town of Cambrai itself, were called back. The British troops who had entered the village withdrew. Of the 1,500 Guardsmen who had fought in the streets, fewer than five hundred returned to their lines. Among the dead that day was Norman Chamberlain, whose cousin Neville, a future Prime Minister, later described in a privately published memoir how Norman, having led his men to their objective, came under heavy machine-gun fire. 'The ground was open, there was no cover, and orders were given to retire some fifty yards to a trench ... whether the retiring orders never reached him or whether he was unable to get back, neither he nor his men were ever seen again.'

That day, November 27, the British were forced to break off the action. Cambrai would remain in the unreachable distance. British cavalry would not be able to sweep forward behind the line of trenches and barbed wire. The area that had been gained did, however, give the British one advantage, the ability to overlook a considerable area of German-held land to the north, a benefit for future artillery attacks and possible future offensives. The Germans were determined not to let even this benefit be retained. On November 27, the day that Haig ordered an end to the Battle of Cambrai, Prince Rupprecht of Bavaria issued an order to the commanders of the German Second Army: 'Attack on November 30.'

In preparation for this attack, on November 28 the German guns fired 16,000 shells, including gas shells, on the British positions in Bourlon Wood. The attack began, as ordered, on November 30. Many British companies fought until every man was killed or wounded. In the southern sector of the battlefield, however, the Germans quickly broke through the forward British positions. Masnières was abandoned, after which the Germans blew up its bridge to prevent any Allied tanks recrossing the St Quentin Canal. Advancing almost three miles, the Germans captured more than 6,000 British soldiers and 158 guns. The German combination of gas shells, and the use of at least thirty low-flying aircraft in close air support, was as effective for them as tanks had earlier been for the British. In the air, however, the British eventually gained the advantage, eleven German and seven British planes being lost in aerial combat. Elsewhere, though falling back, the British regrouped and held the line.

At one point Captain A.M.C. M'Ready-Diarmid, of the Middlesex Regiment, not only led an attack that forced the Germans back five hundred yards, but by bomb-throwing skills remarkable by the standards of those perilous times, killed or wounded more than eighty Germans, before he was killed. In another sector a British officer tried to persuade sixty men, whom he found in flight, to turn and face the advancing Germans, by whom they were massively outnumbered. 'It's not British to run away like this,' he told them. 'Let's make a stand.' The soldiers, whose ammunition was virtually exhausted, ignored his call and continued to retreat. Later that day a German was found in the British trenches, dressed in a British officer's uniform. He was executed as a spy. He was also thought to have been the man who had tried to send the troops forward to inevitable death or capture.

Elsewhere on the battlefield, as a British position was being overrun, a hastily put together reserve was thrown into the battle, made up of headquarters officers, runners, cooks, orderlies and signallers. 'The men all fought it out,' one former Staff officer has written, 'and when on December 2 the ground was recovered their bodies lay littered indistinguishably with a heap of dead assailants.'[1]

The Battle of Cambrai, the first day of which had caused such a thrill for the Allies, had, within two weeks, failed utterly to be the turning point that had been hoped for. 'Byng captured a hundred guns and was promoted,' General Gough wrote with some bitterness nearly forty years later. 'Bells were rung in England and there was general rejoicing. But this battle was not, or could not be followed up. Byng found that his head was thrust into a narrow salient, where Bourlon Wood became a name of ill-omen to many British soldiers.'

The cavalry had not been able to sweep forward behind the German lines. The costly stalemate of trench warfare had been restored. On December 2 Haig instructed Byng to choose a secure winter line and withdraw to it without delay. The withdrawal began on the night of December 4. Using the experience he had gained at Gallipoli two years earlier, Byng was able to ensure that it was carried out without loss. But the Allied casualties at Cambrai had been considerable: 44,000 British and Canadian dead and wounded. The German casualties were 53,000.

Many of the British wounded, sent towards England, could get no further than the hospitals on the French coast. Vera Brittain was then at No. 24 General Hospital at Étaples. On December 5 she wrote to her mother: 'I wish those people who write so glibly about this being a holy War, and the orators who talk so much about going on no matter how long the War lasts and what it may mean, could see a case – to say nothing of 10 cases – of mustard gas in its early stages – could see the poor things burnt and blistered all over with great mustard-coloured suppurating blisters, with blind eyes – sometimes temporarily, sometimes permanently – all sticky and stuck together, and always fighting for breath, with voices a mere whisper, saying that their throats are closing and they know they will choke. The only thing one can say is that such severe cases don't last long; either they die soon or else improve, usually the former.'

On the Italian Front, the Austrian forces west of the Piave were battling on the slopes of Monte Grappa, almost at the edge of the plain beyond which lay Vicenza, Padua and the river Po. On November 22 they took the summit of the 3,176-foot Mount Tomba, but were driven off. Further west, in the mountains around Asiago, as sickness knocked out 7,000 of the attacking troops, no further Austrian advance was possible, and the Emperor Charles ordered an end to the attack. His own people were weary of war. On November 25, in a mass demonstration in Budapest, as many as 100,000 Hungarian workers marched in favour of immediate peace, and of the Bolshevik revolution.

[1] George A.B. Dewar, *Sir Douglas Haig's Command*, Constable, London 1922, volume I, page 412.

The soldiers at the front were precluded from such subversion by discipline and circumstance. In an Austrian attack on Mount Pertica on November 26, the summit changed hands seven times. Three weeks later the Austrians reached the 5,315-foot peak of Mount Asolone, from which they had a striking, tantalising view of the distant plains below, but their armies were to get no closer to the Italian heartland. Lieutenant Rommel, who had fought with his mountain battalion throughout the advance, was awarded the Pour le Mérite.

On the Salonica Front, the British were using 4,000 Turkish prisoners-of-war, brought in groups from Cyprus, to build a fifty-mile light railway. Military stores and camps on the front were protected from German air attack by balloons filled with explosives. One of these balloons was responsible for the death of a leading German fighter pilot, Lieutenant Eschwege, the 'Eagle of the Aegean', who had previously shot down twenty Allied aircraft in combat.

The Bolshevik call on November 19 for an armistice on all fronts had gone unanswered. Trotsky, in charge of foreign policy, pressed Britain and France to open negotiations and threatened, if negotiations did not begin, to make a separate armistice with the Central Powers. On November 21 the French Ambassador in Petrograd, Maurice Paléologue, was sent an official note informing him that the Bolshevik Government had ordered an immediate ceasefire on all fronts, and intended to begin negotiations with the Germans, with the aim of making a separate peace.

Still the Allies made no response. On November 27 the British Ambassador in Petrograd warned London: 'Every day that we keep Russia in the war against her will does but embitter her people against us.' That day, three Russian emissaries, blindfolded, crossed into the German lines near Dvinsk, with authority from Petrograd to make preliminary arrangements for an armistice. That same day, as a gesture of defiance, Trotsky published to the world the secret treaties Russia had signed with the Allied Powers between 1914 and 1917, including those giving France a free hand in the west to acquire German territory, giving Italy large tracts of Austria and Turkey, giving Roumania lands she coveted, and giving Russia herself Constantinople and the Straits.

'The Government of workmen and peasants abolishes secret diplomacy, with its intrigues, secret cyphers and lies,' Trotsky declared that day from Petrograd. 'We desire a speedy peace, so that peoples may honourably live and work together. In revealing before the whole world the work of the governing classes as it is expressed in the secret documents of diplomacy, we turn to the workers with that appeal which will always form the basis of our foreign policy: "Proletarians of all countries, unite!" '

It was not only the Bolsheviks who were seeking a way to end the conflict. On November 29 the *Daily Telegraph* published a letter from Lord Lansdowne, a former British Foreign Secretary, in which he wrote: 'We are not going to lose this War, but its prolongation will spell ruin to the civilised world, and an infinite addition to the load of human suffering which already weighs upon it.' If negotiations were begun at once, they could bring the war to an end by means of 'a lasting and honourable peace' in the New Year. The popular press denounced any attempt to sit and talk with the Germans, but Lansdowne was surprised, he wrote to his daughter, 'at the number of letters written to me by officers at the front to say that *they* welcome the letter'.

On the day that Lansdowne's letter was published, Count Hertling, the new German Chancellor, gave his public support to the Bolshevik appeal for an armistice. The Kaiser went so far as to suggest to his new Foreign Minister, Richard von Kuhlmann, that Germany should seek an alliance with Russia. The Austrians also welcomed the Bolshevik proposals to end the fighting. For the Allies it was a spectre of doom.

The Central Powers were elated. In Italy, the Austrians were within striking distance of Venice. On the Eastern Front, the Germans were transferring forty-two divisions, more than half a million men, to the west.

On December 1 the Bolsheviks seized the Russian Military Headquarters at Mogilev, where the last of Russia's wartime Commanders-in-Chief, the 44-year-old General Dukhonin, was dragged from his special train by Bolshevik sailors, who had earlier stripped him of his epaulettes. He was beaten, fell to the ground, and continued to be beaten until a sailor killed him with two bullets. The bystanders cheered. The Czechoslovak leader, Dr Thomas Masaryk, who was in the area organising some 92,000 Czech prisoners-of-war into military formations, later recalled that Dukhonin's body was 'barbarously profaned' at the railway station. Dukhonin had approved the idea of allowing the Czechs to form an army to fight alongside Russia against the Central Powers. Now the Russians themselves had laid down their arms. The Czechs would have to make their way out of Russia as best they could, and set off eastward on a 5,000-mile journey along the Trans-Siberian railway to Vladivostok, the only Russian port from which they could sail back to Europe.

On the day of Dukhonin's murder, a Bolshevik Armistice Commission left Petrograd for the Eastern Front. On the following day, as a formal ceasefire was declared throughout the battle zone, the Commission crossed into the German lines at Dvinsk, and was taken on by train to the former Russian fortress of Brest-Litovsk. There they were met by a phalanx of negotiators: Germans, Austrians, Bulgarians and Turks. A whole swathe of war zones, from the Baltic Sea to the Caucasus Mountains, was about to be ended.

The armistice negotiations at Brest-Litovsk continued for five days. The two senior Bolshevik negotiators were both Russian Jews, Adolf Joffe and Leo Kamenev, Trotsky's brother-in-law. Another of the delegates, the symbol of the equality of sexes which was part of the wider Communist philosophy, was Anastasia Bitsenko, who had only recently been released, as part of the general amnesty of Tsarist prisoners, from a seventeen-year sentence in Siberia for the murder of a former Minister of War. For the sake of revolutionary propriety, a worker, a peasant and a soldier had also been included in the delegation: the peasant had only been found at the last moment, during the railway journey, at a wayside station. These symbols of the revolution were given no part in the negotiations. The Russian naval representative, the former Tsarist commander in the Baltic, Admiral Altvater, warned General Hoffmann of the dangers of Bolshevik propaganda at the Front. His own defence of Oesel Island two months earlier had been undermined by such propaganda. 'It was the same with the army,' Altvater said, 'and, I warn you, the same thing will happen in your army.' Hoffmann did not appreciate the truth of these words. 'I only laughed at the unfortunate Admiral,' he later wrote.

On December 6, while the Bolsheviks, Germans, Austrians, Bulgarians and Turks were still discussing how to bring their military confrontations to an end, the Roumanian Government, its armies beaten back by German and Austrian forces to their eastern borders, obtained a ceasefire. Nine days later, on December 15, the negotiators at Brest-Litovsk announced the end to all fighting on the Eastern Front. Russia was no longer a belligerent.

From the Baltic to the Black Sea the guns fell silent. The Central Powers were freed from the two-front war that had been their nightmare and their burden since 1914. All that remained was to negotiate a peace treaty with the Bolsheviks that would restrict their territorial control as much as possible: Lenin put Trotsky in charge of these negotiations, which opened at Brest-Litovsk on December 22, a day on which the Kaiser was visiting his troops on the Western Front, where soon, it was hoped, the benefits of an eastern peace agreement would be seen.

The Germans were not the only beneficiaries of the collapse of Russia. On November 28, Estonia had declared her independence, and Finland did so on December 6. But war was far from over for the Bolsheviks, who on December 9 declared war on the Cossacks in southern Russia, an independent-spirited people who had refused to accept the new revolutionary authority. By the end of the month the Bolsheviks were also confronted by anti-Bolshevik Russian forces led by two former Tsarist officers, General Kornilov in the Kuban and General Alexeyev at Novocherkask. In the Ukraine, the Rada, or Parliament, rejected Lenin's appeal for the transit of 'Red' Bolshevik troops to combat the 'White' forces. Fighting between the Bolshevik and Ukrainian forces broke out on December 24. Three days later, Latvia declared its independence from Russia. On December 31 the 'Reds' occupied the eastern Ukrainian city of Kharkov. The Russian civil war had begun.

These events took place far from the Western Front, but affected it directly. On December 6, while the Bolshevik and German negotiators at Brest-Litovsk were still negotiating the final terms of a ceasefire, the British Minister of National Service, Sir Auckland Geddes, warned the War Cabinet in London that as soon as the ceasefire was agreed the

Germans would be able to transfer 900,000 men to the Western Front, giving them a superiority of eleven fighting divisions.

When the Germans transferred their artillery from east to west, they would move from their existing equality with the Anglo-French forces to a preponderance of 2,000, with a 4,000 preponderance in field guns and howitzers. Everything would then depend upon the United States: her twelve divisions, if they came into the line in 1918, would tilt the balance once more in the Allies' favour, though only slightly. She would also create a slight superiority in rifle strength. But Geddes was emphatic that more than a million new soldiers would have to come from Britain if the necessary superiority for any successful offensive was to be achieved. Men would have to come from the munitions factories and shipyards as well as from the new conscripts. Skilled munition workers who could fight would have to be replaced by women, or men unfit for military service. The nation would have to be remobilised. At the same time, in order to make the workers' sacrifices seem more fair, the tax already being levied on those who made excess profits in business or industry as a result of the war would be raised from the 40 per cent of the original tax in 1915 to 80 per cent.

At sea, the convoy system had begun to serve the Allied powers well. November's shipping losses were the lowest of the year, with 126 ships being sunk, fifty-six of them British.[1] From the United States, four American battleships joined the British Grand Fleet that December. A massive 'shipbuilding crusade' was under way in the United States, to provide the merchant shipping needed for the war in 1918. There was a disaster for the Allies on December 6, many thousands of miles from the war zones: in the Canadian harbour of Halifax a French merchant ship, the *Mont Blanc*, loaded with munitions for Europe, collided with a Belgian vessel and blew up. More than 1,600 people were killed and 9,000 injured: one in five of the city's population. In France, six days later, 543 soldiers were killed when a railway train came off the tracks near Modane: the highest death toll of any civilian railway disaster then or since.

On the morning of Sunday, December 9, in a valley just north of Jerusalem, two British soldiers, Private Church and Private Andrewes, were up early in search of eggs, hoping to find some abandoned farm, or peasants willing to hand them over. They were part of the force that had fought its way up from the Mediterranean and was now encamped three miles from the city, intent in the next few days on capturing it from the Turks. As the two soldiers foraged, they saw coming towards them a motley group, some in civilian clothes, some in Turkish uniforms, carrying aloft a large white flag. It was the Jerusalem dignitaries, including the Mayor, priests, rabbis and imams, bearing the keys of the city. They were looking for someone to whom they could surrender. The Turkish army, with its German and

---

[1] The number of British seamen lost had risen, to 376 for the month of November.

Austrian officers, had gone, slipping northward to Nablus, and eastward to Jericho and the river Jordan.

The British could enter the Holy City without fighting. More than seven hundred years had passed since Richard the Lion Heart had reached almost the exact spot reached by Church and Andrewes, but the king had been unable to go further. The two soldiers took the dignitaries to a sergeant, who eventually found a general to whom they could formally hand over their keys. On December 11, following precise instructions laid down three weeks earlier in London, Allenby entered Jerusalem on foot, to avoid emulating the Kaiser's triumphal entry on horseback in 1898. Allenby did as London told him: to show humiliation before the Holy Places, no Allied flags were flown over the city, and to avoid offending Muslim tradition, Indian Muslim troops were sent to guard the Dome of the Rock. Allenby's proclamation of goodwill, also prepared for him by the War Cabinet in London, was read out in English, French, Arabic, Hebrew, Russian and Greek. Allenby was elated by his victory, which redeemed his three years of set-back and stagnation on the Western Front. While in Jerusalem he acquired a fighting spider whose jaws could sever a scorpion's tail: he named it 'Hindenburg'.

The capture of Jerusalem caught the imagination of the Allied world. In Rome the church bells rang out, as did the bells of London's Roman Catholic Cathedral. Jews world-wide sensed a new dawn for their national aspirations. The Arabs were excited too: the name Allenby bore a close calligraphic resemblance to the Arabic word for prophet, Al Neby.

In the aftermath of the British set-back at Cambrai, some British newspapers contrasted it with the success in capturing Jerusalem. *The Times* called Cambrai 'one of the most ghastly stories in English history'. Worse seemed in prospect. Following the ceasefire on the Eastern Front, German troops were moving continuously from Russia to the Western Front. The Italian army was defending the valley of the Po with British and French help, and Venice was vulnerable to any further Austrian success. Beset by these difficulties, the British leaders responded positively to talk of a separate peace with Austria, and even with Turkey.

With Lloyd George's approval, General Smuts went to Switzerland where, on December 18, in a Geneva suburb, he held three meetings with the former Austrian Ambassador to London, Count Mensdorff. Smuts proposed that, in return for agreeing to make a separate peace with the Entente, the Austro-Hungarian Empire would be left intact, as a counterweight to Germany in central Europe. Mensdorff replied that Austria could not discuss a separate peace. Philip Kerr, a member of Lloyd George's secretariat, who had been present at the Geneva talks, then went on to Berne to meet a Turkish negotiator, Dr Humbert Parodi. But Turkey, too, was not willing to consider a separate peace. The German magnet was still strong, strengthened by the prospect of an Allied defeat.

The British diplomat Sir Horace Rumbold, who was with Smuts and

Kerr in Geneva and Berne, noted: 'Our conversations with the Turks have, of course, been prejudiced by the conference at Brest-Litovsk. In the last week we have ascertained from a number of Government Turks at Geneva that the conference in question has filled the Turks with extravagant hopes for the future of their empire. Not only do they hope to recover Mesopotamia, Palestine, etc., with the help of the Germans, but they also expect to get portions of the Caucasus and to enter into an alliance with such a state as Georgia. In fact they seem really to believe in the possibilities of the Turanian movement.' Enver Pasha in particular had hopes of spreading Turkish rule to the Turkic-speaking regions of Russian Central Asia.[1]

With the prospect of Brest-Litovsk enhancing the German warmaking powers, the Turkish negotiators in Switzerland backed off. Publicly no hint was given that diplomatic discussions were taking place; indeed, on December 14, Lloyd George declared in a speech in London that there was 'no halfway house between victory and defeat'. Two months later, an inter-Allied conference in France repudiated the weapon of diplomacy as a means to peace. A diplomatic note on December 15 from Trotsky, announcing that, as the Allied Governments would not agree to entering peace negotiations, the Bolsheviks would negotiate instead with the socialist parties of all countries, was treated with contempt.

The war would go on, that was the message of the politicians and the patriots. 'I cannot help being constantly very depressed over the immeasurably sad things which burden our lives,' Albert Einstein wrote to a friend in Holland on December 18. 'It no longer even helps, as it used to, to escape into one's work in physics.' Even Lloyd George, despite his public assertion of the need for victory, was privately uneasy at the method of warfare that was being pursued. At lunch with the newspaper editor C.P. Scott on December 19 he said that, whereas military victory was 'a necessity', perhaps 'to defeat the impending great German attack in France or Italy, or wherever else it might take place, would in itself constitute military victory'. The Prime Minister also spoke of 'stopping the useless waste of life in attacks on the West and dealing only heavy counter-strokes, while standing on the defensive'.

Knowledge that the offensives of 1916 and 1917 would not be repeated caused Churchill to write to a soldier friend on December 29: 'Thank God our offensives are at an end. Let them traipse across the crater fields. Let them rejoice in the occasional capture of placeless names and sterile ridges.'

Since the signing of the armistice at Brest-Litovsk, the Germans and Austrians, as well as the Turks and Bulgars, had been anxious to conclude a peace with Russia to satisfy their many demands. For their part, the Bolsheviks were desperate to secure their western border and to consolidate

---

[1] After the defeat of Turkey, Enver Pasha led a forlorn army in Central Asia, trying to rally Turanian feeling. In 1922 he was killed in Turkestan during a skirmish with the Bolsheviks, who established their own rule throughout the region (which formed a part of the Soviet Union until the collapse of Soviet communism in 1991).

the revolution inside it. Those who were to negotiate peace arrived at Brest-Litovsk on December 20. 'Since Russia has entered into separate negotiations,' Lloyd George told the House of Commons that day, 'she must of course alone be responsible for the terms in respect of her own territories.'

That evening at Brest-Litovsk, a banquet was given by the German Commander-in-Chief in the East, Field Marshal Prince Leopold of Bavaria, for all the delegates, among them the Austrian Foreign Minister, Count Czernin. One of the first historians of the negotiations, John Wheeler-Bennett, has written: 'The picture was rich in contrasts. At the head of the table sat the bearded, stalwart figure of the Prince of Bavaria, having on his right Joffe, a Jew recently released from a Siberian prison. Next to him was Count Czernin, a grand seigneur and diplomat of the old school, a Knight of the Golden Fleece, trained in the traditions of Kaunitz and Metternich, to whom Joffe, with his soft eyes and kindly tone, confided: "I hope we may be able to raise the revolution in your country too".' That evening Czernin commented laconically in his diary: 'We shall hardly need any assistance from the good Joffe, I fancy, in bringing revolution among ourselves. The people will manage that, if the Entente persists in refusing to come to terms.'

The formal negotiations began on December 22. 'I may regard it as an auspicious circumstance', the chief German delegate, Baron Richard von Kuhlmann, told the delegates, 'that our negotiations should begin in sight of that festival which for many centuries has promised peace on earth and good will towards men.' For Germany, Bolshevik Russia's weakness offered a chance to acquire, through the legal niceties of a negotiated treaty, the territorial gains, and much more, that she had been unable to acquire by more than three years of war.

On the Italian Front, the Austrians were determined to defeat the Italians before the winter snows, already a month late, made fighting in the mountains impossible. In a final exhortation General Conrad told his troops that they would celebrate Christmas Mass in Venice. The attack began on December 23, heralded by a massive artillery bombardment using gas shells. In the ensuing two-mile advance, two heights, including the 4,183-foot Col del Rosso, were captured and 9,000 Italians taken prisoner. But an Italian counter-attack on the following day recaptured the peaks. That night, the first heavy snow fall cheated the Austrians of their goal, and it was the Italians who celebrated Mass that night, thanking God for their deliverance. On the previous day, during a visit to the Western Front, the Kaiser had told his troops that the events of 1917 were proof that God was on the side of the Germans.

It was under British military occupation that Mass was celebrated that Christmas in Jerusalem and Bethlehem. On Christmas Day there was desultory Turkish artillery fire from the north and east, but it did not seem to signify. Then, late on the evening of December 26, the Germans and

Turks attacked. Fresh Turkish troops, who had not been involved in the demoralising retreats from Beersheba and Gaza, pushed through the British outposts on the Nablus road. For eight and a half hours, all through that night and into the following day, a series of Turkish attacks was beaten off. In an attack from the east, along the Jericho road, the Turks again advanced towards the city. At one point, seven hundred Turks surrounded a fifty-strong company of British troops, but although without artillery support, they found shelter in the ruins of an ancient monastery and held out until relief came on the morning of December 28.

Having beaten back the Turkish attempt to recapture Jerusalem, Allenby ordered his men to advance on December 28, to make the perimeters of the city secure. Armoured cars and aircraft were used to support the advance. A thousand Turkish corpses were counted on the battlefield when the advance was halted ten miles north of the city. Among the 750 prisoners taken were a number of German officers, captured by Irish troops. These Germans expressed their surprise to find that they had been fighting white troops. To encourage them to think that the fighting would be easy, they had been told that their enemy would be 'Indians and the scum of Egypt'.

For those on the high seas, death came without warning over the Christmas season. On December 23, in the Irish Sea, a German submarine sank the armed British steamer *Stephen Furness* and 101 men were drowned, while in the North Sea, off the coast of Holland, 252 sailors were lost when three British destroyers, *Tornado*, *Torrent* and *Surprise*, ran into a German minefield. A week later, on December 30, while the British destroyer *Attack* was rescuing survivors of the torpedoed troopship *Aragon*, she herself struck a mine and sank: 610 sailors and soldiers were drowned. On the following day another 198 British sailors were killed when their ship, the *Osmanieh*, struck a mine and sank: a naval death toll of more than a thousand in one week. A further 520 British merchant seamen had lost their lives in December.

As 1917 came to an end there was no prospect of peace in Europe. Even the ceasefire in the east had proved to be but a prelude to immediate civil war, with its own horrors and excesses. Nor were the Bolsheviks happy with the severe terms on which, in the peace negotiations at Brest-Litovsk, the Germans were insisting. Behind the lines, those nations whose food imports were being stopped by a naval blockade had begun to suffer greatly. In Constantinople, as many as 10,000 of the city's inhabitants had died of privation in 1917. In Austria, hunger led to strikes and food riots in Vienna and Budapest that forced the government to recall seven army divisions from the front, and to do so permanently at the beginning of 1918, to prevent violence in the streets. In Germany more than a quarter of a million civilians had died in 1917 as a result of hunger, directly attributed to the British blockade. Not only the troops on the battlefield, the sailors at sea, the airmen and the growing numbers of men in the prisoner camps, but also the once prosperous cities of Europe were suffering the torments of prolonged war.

On December 30 the Germans launched an artillery barrage against the British on the Western Front. Among those wounded was a member of the Royal Naval Division, Lieutenant-Commander Patrick Shaw-Stewart, who had fought at Gallipoli, where he was saved from a bullet 'plumb on the right heart' by a small steel mirror that he kept in the pocket of his uniform. After being hit by shrapnel on December 30, and having his ear lobe cut off, he refused to go back to battalion headquarters to have the wound dressed. Shortly afterwards a shell burst on the parapet, killing him instantly.

Knowledge of the cruel nature of the war could not be entirely confined to the war zones. On December 27 the British war correspondent and novelist Philip Gibbs, who had just returned from the Western Front, told a gathering of politicians and journalists in London what he could of the conditions of trench warfare. One of his audience, C.P. Scott, noted in his diary: 'The thing is horrible and beyond human nature to bear.' Yet it was going to continue, and to be borne, into yet another year.

58 Arab forces advance towards the port of Akaba, 6 July 1917.

59 Chinese labourers unloading 100-lb sacks of oats, Boulogne, 12 August 1917.

60 The Ypres Salient: Pack mules pass a destroyed artillery limber near St Jean, 31 July 1917.

61 Stretcher bearers carry a wounded man back to the rear, Boesinghe, August 1917.

62 A German prisoner-of-war, captured by Scottish and South African troops near Potijze, September 1917.

63 A stretcher bearer attends to a badly wounded sergeant in a trench near Polygon Wood, 26 September 1917.

64 The battlefield of Third Ypres, September 1917.

65 A stretcher-carrying party of the 2nd Canadian Division bring in a wounded man from the battlefield, Passchendaele, 6 October 1917.

21

The Central Powers on the verge of triumph

JANUARY–MARCH 1918

Even the dangers posed to the Allies by Russia's withdrawal from the war did not alter the cautious policy of the United States. On the first day of 1918, General Pershing successfully opposed an urgent request from Lloyd George that America send over as many surplus troops as possible, and incorporate them immediately on their arrival into British and French units.

Lloyd George argued that the Germans were planning 'a knock-out blow to the Allies' before a fully trained American army was ready to take its place in the line that summer. Pershing disagreed. 'Do not think emergency now exists that would warrant our putting companies or battalions into British or French divisions,' he telegraphed to the Secretary for War in Washington, 'and would not do so except in grave crisis.' Pershing did accept a request from Pétain, however, that four black regiments that were already in France should serve as integral parts of French divisions. They did so for the rest of the war.

As 1918 opened, the Western, Italian, Salonica and Turkish Fronts were each the scene not of any large-scale offensive, but of spasmodic fighting characterised by repeated raids and counter-raids. On the former Eastern Front, negotiations for a Russo-German peace treaty paused for a twelve-day break over the New Year. Behind every front line, political movements were stirring with a new enthusiasm, looking to negotiation, war-weariness and the unexpected evolution of events to satisfy their ambitious plans for statehood. The main precondition, however, for many of these hopes was the disintegration of Austria-Hungary, which could not be taken for granted.

On January 5, in an address to the British Trade Unions, Lloyd George stated that the dissolution of Austria-Hungary was not an Allied war aim. Though he could not say so, he still hoped to detach the Hapsburgs from Germany. Within the Hapsburg borders national aspirations were growing. On January 6, in Prague, a specially summoned convention, meeting in the immediate pre-war Municipal House, whose architects had sought to epitomise Czech national aspirations, called for the independence of the Czech lands of Bohemia and Moravia. Two weeks later the German-speaking peoples living in the Sudetenland region of Bohemia called for a province of their own.

The omens for national self-determination, if not for independence, appeared favourable to those who sought an Allied victory. On January 8 President Wilson, in an address to the United States Congress, set out a peace programme for Europe based upon fourteen separate points, essentially democratic and liberal in outlook. In future, diplomacy and treaty-making would always proceed 'frankly and in the public view'. Freedom of navigation would be assured on the sea. Economic barriers would be removed and 'an equality of trade conditions' established among all nations. Naval armaments would be reduced. In questions of colonial sovereignty, 'the interests of the populations concerned must have equal weight with the equitable claims of the government whose title is to be determined'. Germany must evacuate all Russian territory. Belgium must be 'evacuated and restored'. All French territory must be freed and 'the wrong done to France by Prussia in 1871' over Alsace-Lorraine be 'righted'. The frontiers of Italy must be 'along clearly recognisable lines of national-ity', thus giving Italy the Austrian province of South Tyrol. The peoples of Austria-Hungary should be given 'the freest opportunity of autonomous development'. Roumania, Serbia and Montenegro should be restored, and Serbia given access to the sea. The Turkish portions of the Ottoman Empire should be 'assured a secure sovereignty', but the other nationalities inside Turkey assured of their 'autonomous development'. A Polish State should be erected, 'united, independent, autonomous ... with free unrestricted access to the sea'. Finally, a 'general association' of nations must be formed to guarantee political independence and territorial integrity 'to great and small States alike'.

These Fourteen Points were intended as a counter to the growing appeal of Bolshevism among the soldiers of the Central Powers, and to be more attractive than a Bolshevik-inspired peace. They did not, however, satisfy to the full the hopes for statehood that had been aroused. The peoples of Austria-Hungary would be given not independence, but, in Wilson's phrase, 'the freest opportunity of autonomous development'. Many Czechs and Slovaks noted this with disappointment. Nor did Wilson give any recognition or encouragement to the aspirations of the South Slavs for a single State of their own. Austria would have to evacuate Serbia and Montenegro, but he made no mention of the other two South Slav national-ities, the Croats or Slovenes. Two days after Wilson issued his Fourteen Points, a delegation of Finns reached London, hoping to obtain British support for Finland's independence. The earlier reliance upon German patronage was set aside.

The race for national patronage was affecting both sides, as the Allies and their adversaries looked for new recruits to the conflict, or sought to isolate old enemies. On the day of the arrival of the Finnish Mission in London, the Central Powers and the Bolsheviks both recognised the independence of the Ukraine. Latvia declared its independence from Russia on January 12. On the following day, in their revolutionary Decree No. 13, Lenin and Stalin announced their support for Armenian self-determination. At Brest-Litovsk, the peace negotiations had resumed after their New Year break. This time the Bolshevik delegation was led by Trotsky, who hoped, if only by threats of world revolution, to limit German and Austrian demands for substantial territorial gains at Russia's expense. The Turks also sent a delegation to Brest-Litovsk, intent on recovering the lands in eastern Anatolia that had been lost to Russia in 1878.

The desire to continue the war, and the hope of ending it, were in conflict in every nation. But for the Allied powers, the moral imperative of victory was still being publicly asserted, and widely held. In a speech at Edinburgh on January 10, Balfour declared that he horrors of war were 'nothing' compared to a 'German peace'. With almost two million men under arms, the British Government was making plans to bring in at least 420,000 more.

Three days after Balfour's speech, the pacifist philosopher Bertrand Russell commented in a private letter: 'The world is damnable. Lenin and Trotsky are the only bright spot.' Russell's pacifism had only a few echoes in Britain. On January 14, having been wounded on the Western Front and invalided home, a British infantry officer, Max Plowman, took the rare step of resigning his commission, writing to his regimental adjutant that his hatred of war 'has gradually deepened into the fixed conviction that organised warfare of any kind is always organised murder'. Plowman added: 'So wholly do I believe in the doctrine of Incarnation (that God indeed lives in every human body) that I believe that killing men is always killing God.'

Hunger and privation at home were as much an influence for war weariness as the killing. On January 22 a secret British report, based on a careful reading of British intercepted correspondence, revealed 'a decided increase in letters for an immediate peace'. In Berlin, six days later, more than 400,000 workers went on strike, demanding peace. Within forty-eight hours these strikes had spread to six other cities. The German authorities reacted swiftly and firmly, declaring martial law in Berlin and Hamburg, and drafting many of the striking workers into the army. But the hunger that the British naval blockade had exacerbated could not be assuaged by martial law or compulsory service. Civilians were being forced to eat dogs and cats, the latter known as 'roof rabbits'. Bread was made from a mixture of potato peelings and sawdust.

From Vienna came yet more tentative talk of a possible negotiated peace. 'More foreign speeches reported today, moderate but very evasive,' the pacifist Clifford Allen wrote in his diary on January 28 (he had been released from prison because of ill-health), and he commented: 'Austria quite mild. Why can't they all make speeches round peace table instead of from platforms thousands of miles apart and at intervals of weeks or months?' The 'foreign speeches' were those of the Austrian Foreign Minister, Count Czernin, and the new German Chancellor, Count Hertling, suggesting 'an exchange of ideas' through Washington (Czernin) and discussion on 'a limitation of armaments (Hertling). Commented *The Times*: 'Neither discloses the least readiness to meet any of the demands which the Allies with one accord declare to be indispensable.'

On January 28, at a military hospital at Wimereux, on the Channel coast, the Canadian medical officer, Lieutenant-Colonel John McCrae, died. Nearly three years had passed since, in the Ypres Salient, he wrote the lines:

> *We are the Dead. Short days ago*
> *We lived, felt dawn, saw sunset glow ...*

In a naval action off the Dardanelles, 127 British sailors had been killed on January 20 when their monitor, the *Raglan*, was sunk by a German warship. That same day, in the North Sea, two German destroyers were sunk by British mines, and a German submarine sank the armed British steamer *Louvain*, killing 224 of those on board. On January 26, three German submarines were sunk, two in the English Channel and one in the St George's Channel. Five days later, in an accidental night collision in the North Sea, two British submarines hit each other and sank, with the loss of 103 submariners. On January 29, three German 'Giant' bombers flew over Britain on a raid that injured twenty civilians. The 'Giants' were followed the next night by thirty-one 'Gothas' flying over Paris, dropping 267 bombs and killing or injuring 259 Parisians.

Submarine and aerial warfare combined to create hostility even among those whose instincts were for some form of compromise peace. 'Isn't the German mentality a depressing thing,' the former British Foreign Secretary, Edward Grey, who favoured offering Germany 'economic equality' after the war, wrote to a friend on January 27. 'When one is not in office and out of London it is so uncomfortable to hate anybody and one longs more than ever for peace, but I do not see how there is to be peace with the people who still run Germany.'

In the east, Lenin's forces had entered the Ukraine and declared the triumph of Bolshevism there. The Central Powers announced their support for an independent Ukraine. On January 28, Russian Bolsheviks and Ukrainian nationalists fought against each other at Lutsk, where three years earlier German and Russian forces had battled for supremacy. On January 29, Lenin's troops entered both Kiev and Odessa. Two days later, with Ukraine falling rapidly under Bolshevik rule, Lenin established the Union of Soviet Socialist Republics, the USSR, also known as the Soviet Union. This was followed within two weeks by the creation first of the Red Navy and then of the Red Army.

Discontent was growing in more and more armies and navies. On February 1, Greek troops in the town of Lamia, who were about to be sent to the Salonica Front, mutinied. Two of their leaders were executed. On the day of the Lamia mutiny, Austro-Hungarian sailors on board ship in the Gulf of Cattaro (Kotor) also mutinied. Led by two Czech socialists, the 6,000 sailors raised the red flag and announced their adherence to Bolshevism. But they played the 'Marseillaise', not the 'Internationale', and their demands were closer to President Wilson's Fourteen Points than to Lenin's decrees: national autonomy (as already being demanded by the Slav groups in the Vienna Parliament, not independence), immediate peace, no annexation of territory, demobilisation, and better living conditions. The mutineers appealed for support to the Austrian troops in the Cattaro garrison, and to the crews of German submarines alongside them in the bay, but this attempt to widen the mutiny was rebuffed. On learning of what had happened, the Austrian naval authorities despatched three battleships from the Istrian port of Pola: eight hundred of the mutineers were taken off their ships, forty were brought to trial, and four were executed.

In France, bread shortages led to a protest, on February 5, by 3,000 people in Roanne, on the Loire, followed by looting.

On January 18, a full American division, the 1st, entered the front line, in the Ansauville sector of the St Mihiel Salient. It had been sent there to gain experience of holding the line, and took no offensive action. As soon as the Germans discovered that Americans were opposite them, they tried to demoralise them, launching a raid on an American listening post, killing two soldiers, wounding two and capturing one. Then they ambushed an American patrol in No-Man's Land, killing four, wounding two and capturing two. 'This thing of letting the Boche do it all is getting on the nerves,' one American officer noted in his diary on January 30.

American troops were arriving every week in France, where, under Pershing's vigilant eye, considerable port and base facilities were being developed for them and their stores. The American contribution to the war, though not yet marked by the participation of armies, was becoming a frequent element in war reporting. On February 5, Lieutenant Thompson was the first American pilot serving with the United States Forces in France to defeat a German aeroplane in combat. That same day off the coast of Ireland, the first American troops were killed while on their way to Europe, when the British troopship *Tuscania* was sunk by a German submarine: 166 American servicemen and forty-four British crew members were drowned.

Vocal and visible anti-war feeling in Britain was still confined to a few thousand conscientious objectors. On February 6 there was outrage among them when a former shoemaker, Henry Firth, died at the work centre for conscientious objectors at Princetown on Dartmoor. Having been in prison for nine months, he had become so ill that he had accepted alternative service at the Princetown stone quarries on Dartmoor. Admitted to hospital after collapsing at work, his request for eggs was refused on the grounds that they were wanted for the soldiers in France. Eventually the authorities relented, and three fresh eggs were granted him: they arrived the day after his death. Three days after Firth's death, Bertrand Russell was sentenced to six months in prison for advocating in public that the British Government accept a German offer to open peace negotiations.

'War is a disciplinary action by God to educate mankind,' the Kaiser told the citizens of Bad Homburg on February 10. Three days later he told a War Council convened at Homburg that there was a world-wide conspiracy against Germany, the participants in which included the Bolsheviks supported by President Wilson, 'international Jewry' and the Grand Orient Lodge of Freemasons. He made no mention of the fact that as many as 10,000 Jews, and many thousands of Freemasons, had already been killed fighting in the ranks of the German army. Nor did he seem to remember the details he had been given only two months earlier of German financial backing for the Bolsheviks, including a secret German subsidy for the Bolshevik newspaper, *Pravda*.

A week after the Kaiser's speech, on February 17, there was a dramatic development on the former Eastern Front, when the long-drawn-out peace negotiations between the Bolsheviks and the Germans at Brest-Litovsk broke down. Germany's terms were too hard for the Bolsheviks to accept. The Germans at once prepared to resume the war in the east. 'Tomorrow we are going to start hostilities against the Bolsheviks,' General Hoffmann wrote in his diary that night. 'No other way out is possible, otherwise these brutes will wipe up the Ukrainians, the Finns, and the Balts, and then quickly get together a new revolutionary army and turn the whole of Europe into a pig-sty.'

The war resumed, with fifty-two German divisions crossing the November ceasefire line, occupying Dvinsk in the north and Lutsk in the south, and moving eastward along the Russian main-line railways. Lenin realised that the Bolsheviks must give in to whatever was asked of them. 'It's not a question of Dvinsk,' he told Trotsky, 'but of revolution. Delay is impossible. We must sign at once. This beast springs quickly.' On January 19, Hoffmann received a telegram, signed by Lenin and Trotsky, accepting the conditions of peace that had been offered at Brest-Litovsk. But Hoffmann was in no hurry now to accept it. He was even vexed that the renewal of hostilities was to be cut short. He therefore replied that acceptance had to be confirmed in writing, and sent by a courier through the German lines. Meanwhile, the German advance continued. On February 20, German troops entered Minsk, taking more than 9,000 Russian soldiers prisoner. 'The Russian army is more rotten than I had supposed,' Hoffmann wrote in his diary that day. 'There is no fight left in them. Yesterday one lieutenant with six men took six hundred Cossacks prisoner.'

The war continued for a whole week, the Germans using the Russian roads and railways as if they were on a civilian excursion: in 124 hours they advanced 150 miles. 'It is the most comical war I have ever known,' Hoffmann wrote in his diary on February 22. 'We put a handful of infantrymen with machine guns and one gun on to a train and push them off to the next station; they take it, make prisoners of the Bolsheviks, pick up a few more troops and go on. This proceeding has, at any rate, the charm of novelty.'

Lenin and Trotsky knew that peace had to be made on Germany's terms. But their written request, which reached Berlin on February 21, was rejected by the Germans, who sent a note back, on February 23, demanding even harsher terms. The Germans knew that the territorial integrity of Russia was disintegrating even faster than could have been anticipated. In the Tsarist province of Finland, where Red and White Russian forces had been in conflict, the Finnish national leader General Mannerheim demanded the evacuation of all Russian troops from Finland without delay: Red and White alike. The Bolsheviks agreed to this on February 23. Then, on the following day, after a stormy session of Lenin's ruling council, during which the revolution's leader went so far as to threaten resignation, he obtained a 116 to 85 vote in favour of the new German terms. The vote in the Central Committee was even closer, seven in favour and six against. On the issue of accepting whatever Germany demanded, Lenin and Trotsky were joined by a new figure on the international scene, Joseph Stalin.

As Lenin and his colleagues prepared formally to leave the war, and to abandon vast areas of western and southern Russia, United States troops were in offensive action on the Western Front for the first time. On February 13, at the Butte de Mesnil in Champagne, American artillery batteries took part in a six-hour rolling barrage before a French attack that broke through the German lines and captured more than 150 German prisoners. Ten days later, at Chevregny, south of German-held Laon, two American officers and twenty-four of their men volunteered to take part with French troops in a raid on German trenches. The raid lasted half an hour, and twenty-five Germans were taken prisoner. *The Times* commented that although 'the actual occasion was not of much importance – February 23 is one of the dates that will always be remembered in the history of the war'.

While the Americans were fighting at Chevregny, Churchill, as Minister of Munitions, was visiting the Ypres Salient, passing through the battlefields of 1915, 1916 and 1917. 'Nearly 800,000 of our British race have shed their blood or lost their lives here during 3½ years of unceasing conflict,' he wrote to his wife on February 23. 'Many of our friends and my contemporaries all perished here. Death seems as commonplace and as little alarming as the undertaker. Quite a natural ordinary event, which may happen to anyone at any moment, as it happened to all these scores of thousands who lie together in this vast cemetery, ennobled and rendered forever glorious by their brave memory.' Among Churchill's friends who had fought in the Salient and had been killed, was an American volunteer, Henry Butters, who came from San

Francisco. 'I just lied to 'em and said I was British born,' he had told Churchill, when asked about how an American citizen could be serving as a second lieutenant in the Royal Artillery.

American participation on the battlefield was now a fact, forty-two-and-a-half months after the war had begun. On February 26, three days after that first raid, the Chief of Staff of the American 42nd Division, the Rainbow Division, was observing a French raid on the German trenches near Réchicourt. Carried away with the enthusiasm of the moment, he joined in the raid, helped to capture several German soldiers, and was awarded the Croix de Guerre: the first such award to a member of the American Expeditionary Force. His name was Colonel Douglas MacArthur.[1] A year earlier, when American troops were being recruited, there had been concern in political circles in Washington that individual American States might be aggrieved if other States were to be the source of particular divisional recruiting. It was then suggested to the Secretary for War, Newton Baker, that one complete division could be drawn from the surplus units of many different States, thus avoiding the danger of jealousies and friction. According to Baker's recollection, 'Major MacArthur, who was standing alongside, said, "Fine, that will stretch over the whole country like a rainbow." The Division thus got its name.'

Much was expected of the American forces. The British, French and even American newspapers wrote enthusiastically of how America would soon darken the skies with its aircraft. This forced Pershing to protest to Washington at the exaggeration, pointing out that, after almost a year of war between America and Germany, there was not yet a single American-manufactured aeroplane in service on the Western Front.

In the East, German troops continued their rapid advance, occupying Borisov, Gomel and Zhitomir. Along the Baltic, their forces reached Dorpat on February 24, then moved swiftly towards Reval, where on the following day the Bolsheviks scuttled eleven submarines to avoid their capture by the Germans, who entered the Estonian port a few hours later.

The continuing German successes in the east led to a renewal of patriotic zeal inside Germany. To an academic correspondent who rebuked him for his dislike of the war, Einstein wrote on February 24: 'Your ostentatious Teutonic muscle-flexing runs rather against my grain. I prefer to string along with my compatriot Jesus Christ, whose doctrines you and your kind consider to be obsolete. Suffering is indeed more acceptable to me than resort to violence.'[2]

[1] MacArthur was later Commander-in-Chief of all American and Filipino troops in the Far East (1941) and Commander-in-Chief, Allied Forces, South-East Pacific (1942–5). On 2 September 1945 he accepted the surrender of Japan, of which he then became Allied Commander (1945–51). From 1950 to 1951 he commanded the United Nations forces in Korea.
[2] 'My compatriot Jesus Christ'. In September 1917 Romain Rolland had written in his diary: 'It is noteworthy that Einstein is Jewish, which explains the internationalism of his position and the caustic character of his criticism.'

On February 25 German troops reached the outskirts of Narva, on the Baltic. In doing so, they clashed briefly with a Bolshevik detachment of just over a thousand men. On February 26 the Finnish Battalion, which had fought alongside the Germans on the Eastern Front for a year and a half, arrived back in Finland, at the town of Vasa, pledged to uphold Finland's independence (declared the previous December) and to drive the Bolsheviks from the rest of the country, including its capital, Helsinki. On the following day, German forces reached Mogilev, the former Tsarist military headquarters, and on that same day, February 27, a German aeroplane dropped its bombs on the Fontanka Embankment in Petrograd.

Lenin having agreed to resume peace negotiations at Brest-Litovsk, the Soviet delegation returned there, reaching the town on February 28. The Germans refused, however, to agree that their arrival must lead to an immediate end to hostilities. The fighting would stop, Hoffmann insisted, only when the treaty was signed. The negotiations began again on March 1. There was nothing left for the Bolsheviks to do but to accept the terms offered them. These included a Turkish demand for the annexation of Ardahan and Kars, which Russia had annexed from Turkey in 1878. On March 2, as the delegates discussed the detailed terms of the peace treaty, the German army entered Kiev, the capital of the Ukraine, which the Bolsheviks had taken only a month earlier. On the Baltic, German forces occupied Narva, the most easterly Estonian city, only eighty-five miles from Petrograd. Plans were made in the Russian capital to evacuate the Government to Moscow, and Lenin gave emergency orders 'to intensify the preparations for blowing up of railways, bridges, and roads; to gather arms and arm detachments; to transport arms into the interior of the country'.

The Germans looked set to enter Petrograd. In their rapid and virtually unopposed advance since the Brest-Litovsk negotiations had first broken down, less than two weeks earlier, they had captured 63,000 Russian prisoners, 2,600 artillery pieces and 5,000 machine guns. The weapons would be of great value on the Western Front. Throughout March 2 the German forces continued their eastward advance. Lenin and Trotsky had no choice but to instruct their delegates to sign. The German High Command was relieved: it was eager to turn Germany's military might against the Western Front.

At five in the afternoon of March 3, the Russo-German peace treaty was signed at Brest-Litovsk. The Bolsheviks accepted the harsh reality of the battlefield, giving up all claims to the Baltic provinces, Poland, White Russia (later known as Byelorussia, now Belarus), Finland, Bessarabia, the Ukraine and the Caucasus. This constituted a third of her pre-war population, a third of her arable land, and nine-tenths of her coalfields: almost all the territory, in fact, that had been added to the Tsarist dominions since the reign of Peter the Great more than two hundred years earlier. Once more, as after the fall of Bucharest at the end of 1916, the Kaiser celebrated with champagne.

Under the Treaty of Brest-Litovsk, all Russian naval bases in the Baltic except Kronstadt were taken away. The Russian Black Sea Fleet warships in Odessa and Nikolayev were to be disarmed and detained. The Bolsheviks also agreed to the immediate return of 630,000 Austrian prisoners-of-war. They permitted the Armenian areas conquered by Russia in 1916 to be transferred to Turkey.[1] Armenian soldiers fought against this distant decision, but were quickly crushed by Turkish forces moving eastward. On February 24 the Armenians had already been driven out of Trebizond, on the Black Sea. On March 12 they were driven from the city of Erzerum, on the Anatolian plateau.

The Roumanians signed a treaty with the Central Powers, at Buftea, on March 5, ceding the southern Dobrudja to Bulgaria, but being offered a former Russian province, Bessarabia, if she could extract it from Bolshevik rule. A Bolshevik Congress, meeting in Petrograd on the following day, accepted the Brest-Litovsk Treaty, and at the same time adopted the name Communist for their Party. Fearing the possibility of a renewed German threat along the Baltic, on March 12 they moved the capital from Petrograd to Moscow.

Although the situation looked bleak for the Allies on the Western Front, two items of news, one from the Eastern Mediterranean and one from the war in the air, brought a boost to Allied morale. On February 21, Allenby's forces drove the Turks from Jericho and reached the northern end of the Dead Sea, the lowest point on Earth, 1,290 feet below sea level. On the Western Front, British bomber pilots made raids on four nights in February on German barracks and airfields, including a successful attack on a main aircraft hangar near Metz.

In Britain, Lloyd George and Churchill were looking ahead with new strategies to bring victory over Germany in 1919. On March 5, in the hope of being able to secure a victory over Germany a year hence, Churchill assured Lloyd George that he would produce 4,000 tanks by April 1919, a thirteen-month programme. Victory on the Western Front could only come, he told the Prime Minister, when Britain and France had 'stronger and better armies' than Germany. 'That is the foundation on which everything rests, and there is no reason why we should not have it in 1919'.

By 1919 the American army would also be a decisive factor on the Western Front. Conscious of this, German propaganda tried repeatedly to undermine French confidence in the American soldiers and to cast doubt on the contribution they would make. On March 5 the German wireless news gave an account of the interrogation of some American troops who

---

[1] This was at the insistence of the Turkish delegation at Brest-Litovsk, led by Talaat Pasha, one of the leaders of the pre-war Young Turk movement. After the war he fled to Germany where, in 1921, he was assassinated in Berlin by an Armenian.

had recently been captured. 'They are strong young fellows but do not seem to have much desire to fight. To them it is an enterprise undertaken by New York financiers. They hate but respect the English. With the French they are on good terms. They have not the slightest idea of military operations and seem stupid and fatalistic in comparison with the war-accustomed Frenchman. They were glad to escape further fighting.' A further broadcast three weeks later stated that French officers 'do not conceal their disillusionment' over the value of the American troops, who were 'entirely incapable of carrying out independent operations'.

In the first week of March 1918, the Central Powers took four bombing initiatives. On March 4, Austrian aircraft bombed Venice, Padua, Mestre and Treviso, but lost a third of the planes taking part. Three days later, three German Giant bombers attacked London, a single bomb killing twelve people in a residential building in Maida Vale and damaging four hundred houses. On March 8, Gotha bombers dropped more than ninety bombs on Paris. Without panic, but with much fear, 200,000 Parisians left the capital by rail for the countryside. On the following day a German airship dropped its bombs on the Italian naval base and steel plant at Naples. Three days later German forces occupied Odessa. For the first time in history, one power's control of Europe stretched from the North Sea to the Black Sea, something even Napoleon had not achieved.

Within two weeks of occupying Odessa, German troops entered the Black Sea port of Nikolayev, seizing one Russian battleship, three cruisers, four destroyers and three submarines, as well as gaining control of the naval dockyard. The German triumph in the east was unprecedented, and complete. On March 8 the Kaiser refused the throne of the Duchy of Kurland, along the Baltic Sea: the region became, instead, a German protectorate. In the Middle Ages it had been the domain of the Teutonic Knights. Any criticism of German nationalism was not tolerated. There was indignation in Germany in mid-March, when a long memorandum written by the former German Ambassador to London, Prince Lichnowsky, justifying Britain's pre-war diplomacy, and criticising Germany's handling of the crisis, was published in the newspapers. Lichnowsky was asked to leave the diplomatic service.

The British continued to try to detach Austria-Hungary from Germany. On March 9, General Smuts returned to Switzerland with Lloyd George's confidant Philip Kerr, to talk to an Austrian emissary, Count Alexander Skrynski.[1] Despite the fact that Skrynski was a Pole, he rejected the conditions for peace that Smuts laid down, that 'justice must be done to all peoples' inside the Hapsburg dominions, by means of autonomy for the Poles, Czechs, Croats and other minorities. The talks continued for

[1] Count Skrynski, who had entered the Austro-Hungarian diplomatic service in 1906, was three times Foreign Minister of inter-war Poland, and Poland's Prime Minister from November 1925 to March 1926.

five days, but then the Austrians broke them off. Kerr's view, as he explained to Rumbold, was that the Austrian Foreign Minister, Count Czernin, 'may have realised that once he had started negotiations public opinion would never allow him to draw back if the Entente terms were reasonable and that once he started negotiations it was rather the case of a separate peace or the break up of Austria-Hungary.'

Those Austrians interested in negotiating with the Allies had also to consider the possibility of a German victory on the battlefield, of which they would be the beneficiaries. Behind the lines, anti-war feeling and fears were spreading. On March 16, in Vienna, an Austrian police report told of 'great and rather widespread resentment against Germany' inside Austria itself. But on March 19 a former Austrian Foreign Minister, Baron Burian, wrote in his diary: 'No one will now listen to the word "peace". Everything is based on the forthcoming offensive, as if everyone were entrusting himself without a tremor to the decision of fate.'

On March 9, the Germans began, with a series of artillery bombardments, the preliminary phase of what was to be their largest, and most essential gamble of the war: a massive offensive against the British and French forces on the Western Front. Hitherto the main military initiatives on the Western Front had been taken by the Allied powers: on the Somme, at Ypres (Passchendaele) and at Cambrai. Each of these offensives had broken themselves against superior German fortifications and defence lines. Now it was the Germans who were going to try to break through the line of the trenches. They had one overriding concern, that their victory should be secured before the mass of American troops, unbattered by battle, reached the war zone.

In the preliminary feints, a series of bombardments throughout the Western Front, among the targets of the German artillery was an infantry post in the Parroy Forest. Hit on March 7, it happened to be held by men of the American 42nd 'Rainbow' Division. Nineteen Americans were killed in the single dugout. At their funeral service a poem was read out, written by the poet Joyce Kilmer, then serving as a corporal in the Division:

> ... death came flying through the air
> And stopped his flight at the dugout stair,
>> Touched his prey –
>> And left them there –
>> Clay to clay.
> He hid their bodies stealthily
> In the soil of the land they sought to free,
>> And fled away.

Between Ypres and St Quentin the German preliminary bombardment of March 9 started with a gas attack in which half a million mustard gas and phosgene shells were fired, a thousand tons of gas in all. That day, during a German gas attack in the Salient du Feys, Colonel Douglas

MacArthur supervised the capture by a company of American troops of a German machine-gun strongpoint. He was awarded the Distinguished Service Cross. On March 11, during a further German gas barrage, MacArthur was among those gassed. His injury was classified as 'slight' and he recovered within the week. For having been injured in battle he received the Purple Heart.

The use of gas on the battlefronts led to many individual cases of panic, fear, malingering and desertion. In the German army this led to the establishment of a rule, in operation throughout the German medical services from the end of 1917, that 'alleged' cases 'of gas poisoning and malingerers who show no definite symptoms are retained for twenty-four hours to forty-eight hours for observation in medical inspection rooms of units ... with a view to returning them to their units if possible'. They were not to be admitted to local field hospitals or gas clearing stations.

On March 19, in a pre-emptive strike near St Quentin, the British fired eighty-five tons of phosgene gas, killing 250 Germans. Then, on March 21, the Germans launched their great offensive. Were it to succeed, Germany could win the war in the west on the battlefield, as she had already won it in the east, at the conference table.

22

Germany's last great onslaught

MARCH–APRIL 1918

In the early hours of 21 March 1918, Ludendorff launched the offensive that was intended to bring victory to Germany's forces on the Western Front. His objective was to drive the British from the Somme and the French from the Aisne, and to threaten Paris as it had been threatened in 1914. The omens for Germany were good. Following the signature of the Treaty of Brest-Litovsk on March 3, Russia was out of the war. The pre-war nightmare and wartime reality of a conflict on two fronts was over. The German railway system, perfected during the previous two years, was enabling the German divisions hitherto tied to the Eastern Front to be moved rapidly and efficiently westward, together with many hundreds of heavy guns and machine guns captured during the German thrust deep into Russia in the last days before the Brest-Litovsk Treaty was signed.

At the tactical level, Ludendorff had succeeded in giving the impression that the main thrust of his attack would come much further south. His drive against the British Fifth Army was unexpected, and unprepared for by Haig and his headquarters staff, who concentrated on building up their reserves behind the more northerly Third Army, protecting the Channel ports. At the same time, on the eve of the battle, the French Third Army was moved a hundred miles to the east of the British Fifth, to guard against the non-existent German sweep through the southern sector of the front. The Fifth Army's position was thus weaker than it might have been, and much more exposed. In terms of manpower, it was much under strength: its divisions, devised to be 12,000 strong, had in no instance many more than 6,000 men. After three and a half years of war, the manpower shortage was still a factor in the British army's ability to make war. From the manpower as well as from the human aspect, the losses of the Somme and Passchendaele had been crippling.

The artillery bombardment with which the battle started on March 21 lasted for five hours. At ten past five in the morning, a mile behind the front line, General Gough recalled: 'I awoke in my room at Nesle to the sound of a bombardment so steady and sustained that it gave me an

immediate impression of some crushing, smashing power.' More than
6,000 German heavy guns were in action, the intensity of their bombardment augmented by more than 3,000 mortars. Gas shells were
employed to weaken the ability of the British artillery to counter the
German barrage: in the coming two weeks as many as two million gas
shells were rained down upon the British lines.

In the air, 326 German fighter aircraft faced 261 British fighters, sixteen
of which were shot down on the first day, for fourteen German losses. The
shelling began at 4.40 in the morning. Two and a half hours later the first
wave of German infantrymen had left their trenches and were attacking
the British line. In the first day, the Germans made advances of up to four
and a half miles, taking 21,000 British soldiers prisoner. Winston Churchill,
who was visiting one of the front-line headquarters when the artillery
barrage began, was only just able to leave the battleground before the
Germans overran it.

The weight of the German assault was too great for the Fifth Army to
stand against. In the battle for Manchester Hill, a British regiment fought
to the last man and the last round. When its commander, Lieutenant-
Colonel Elstob, from the fire step of his forward trench, refused a German
offer to surrender, he was shot dead. When the news of his defiance became
known, he was posthumously awarded the Victoria Cross. Whole villages
were destroyed as the British forces defended their positions to the last: in
one of them, Maissemy, a German war cemetery contains the graves of
23,292 men. Just over a mile away, the village of Le Verguier was likewise
destroyed.

On the second day of battle, March 22, the Germans made further
advances. In a counter-attack by twenty-five British tanks, sixteen were
destroyed. Another thirty British planes were lost that day, compared with
only eleven German planes. At Beaumetz-les-Cambrai two British divisions
held out all day, but were then driven back: the local cemetery records 257
British burials. At Revilon Farm a division fought for two days after being
surrounded, bombarded from the air, and under intense artillery and
mortar fire, before being overrun. At Roupy a British battalion was fired
on by its own artillery, beat off seven successive German attacks, and then
withdrew, against orders. At Hermies Hill cemetery, near the village of
Bertincourt, nearly a thousand British soldiers are buried. The intensity of
the fighting is shown in a German report of one section of the Fifth Army
front, which concluded: 'The 7th Corps covered the retreat of the main
body even to the extent of being destroyed itself.'

On March 23, three German guns, specially manufactured by Krupp,
began to bombard Paris from a gun site at Crépy-en-Laonnoise, seventy-
four miles away. The first shell, fired at 7.16 a.m., landed in the French
capital four minutes later. More than twenty shells were fired, killing 256
Parisians. That day the British forces retreated to the Somme. The Kaiser,
returning to Berlin, declared 'the battle won, the English utterly defeated'.

The Allies had every cause to be alarmed by the speed and scale of the

German advance. Five French divisions hurried to assist the British at the southern end of their line, but they, together with the British, were pushed back. Among the British soldiers killed in action that day was a former schoolmaster, T.P. Cameron Wilson, whose poem 'Magpies in Picardy' began with the verse:

> *The magpies in Picardy*
> *Are more than I can tell.*
> *They flicker down the dusty roads*
> *And cast a magic spell*
> *On the men who march through Picardy*
> *Through Picardy to hell.*

The vast American armies on which the Allies counted to turn the tide of battle on the Western Front were still not yet ready to enter the line. On March 23, Lloyd George telegraphed to the British Ambassador in Washington, Lord Reading, asking him to explain to President Wilson that in the existing state of Britain's manpower resources 'we cannot keep our divisions supplied with drafts for more than a short time at the present rate of loss' and would therefore be 'helpless to assist our Allies if, as is very probable, the enemy turns against them later'.

Lloyd George told Reading: 'You should appeal to President to drop all questions of interpretation of past agreements and send over infantry as fast as possible without transport or other encumbrances. This situation is undoubtedly critical and if America delays now she may be too late.' As soon as this telegram was decoded in Washington, Reading called for his car and drove to the White House. Wilson received him at once, acknowledged the gravity of the situation, and asked what he could do. Reading replied that he should send a direct order to General Pershing, telling him that American troops already in France should be brigaded with British and French troops, without waiting until they were numerically large enough to form brigades of their own.

'The President was silent for a moment,' Reading's son has written. 'Then he replied that under the constitution he had power to decide without discussion with any of his Cabinet, and that he had determined to give the necessary orders. There was no more to be said.' The Ambassador's son commented: 'In those few moments and by that almost curt conversation the scales had been finally weighted against the enemy.' Wilson accompanied Reading to the door. Then, as he said goodbye, he placed his hand on his shoulders and said: 'Mr Ambassador, I'll do my damnedest!'

On March 24 the Germans crossed the Somme. As they threatened to drive a wedge between the British and French armies, they created a crisis in the Allied High Command. Haig urged Pétain to send more French troops to his assistance. Pétain refused, fearing that the Germans were about to launch a separate attack on French positions in Champagne. As the acrimonious debate continued, the battle raged. Among the British soldiers killed that day was Lieutenant R.B. Marriott-Watson, who had written, in his short poem 'Kismet':

> *Opal fires in the Western sky*
> *(For that which is written must ever be),*
> *And a bullet comes droning, whining by,*
> *To the heart of a sentry close to me.*
>
> *For some go early, and some go late*
> *(A dying scream on the evening air)*
> *And who is there that believes in fate*
> *As a soul goes out in the sunset flare?*

On March 25 the Germans broke through between the British and French armies, capturing Bapaume and Noyon. As many as 45,000 British and French soldiers had now been taken prisoner. As the British line east of Amiens was threatened with being overrun, a special force of 3,000 men was formed to hold the line. It included five hundred United States railway engineers, thrown into the struggle at its most dangerous moment. In London, the War Cabinet discussed the possibility of the British forces retreating to the Channel ports. 'It is quite evident that the Boche means to get to Amiens,' General Rawlinson wrote in his diary on March 26, 'and if he does he will cut the British Army off from the ports of Rouen and Havre, as well as separating us from the French Army. We can manage without Boulogne and Calais at a pinch....'

Rawlinson was not without hope. 'We shall have some ding-dong fighting,' he wrote, 'but, with our backs to the wall, we shall, I know, give a good account of ourselves. The Boche reserves are not unlimited.' The resistance of the Fifth Army, even in retreat and against enormous odds, was a pointer to the German army's difficulties. On March 26, on the road to Péronne, General Gough met a wounded British general whose division had been reduced, Gough wrote, 'to a small and very weary brigade'. The General told him: 'Well, we have won the war!' What he meant was this: that the Germans, who had begun the attack with a numerical superiority of four to one, were becoming disheartened by the resistance they faced, in particular by the British soldier's willingness, when all seemed lost, to counter-attack. As one British officer, a captain, went forward with twenty men, he sang a hymn to sustain his battered nerves. When he and his men approached the Germans in front of them, hands went up and the Germans surrendered. As another officer, Brigadier-General Jackson, led his decimated brigade against the German soldiers facing him, he blew a hunting horn. The German soldiers withdrew.

That day, March 26, after an emergency conference of generals and politicians at Doullens, Marshal Foch was given overall charge of the Allied forces. His first act was to order the French army then holding the line at St Mihiel to move towards Amiens. When Pétain expressed his doubts as to the possibility of holding the line in front of the town, suggesting instead a new line twenty miles further back, Foch cut this pessimism short with the words: 'We must fight in front of Amiens. We must stop where we are now. As we have not been able to stop the Germans on the Somme, we must not retire a single centimetre!'

Not only did the Germans, at Soissons, drive the French back across the Aisne, they also forced them back towards the Marne, east of Château-Thierry. It seemed to be 1914 over again. On March 27 the French were driven from Montdidier, only fifty miles from Paris. On that very day, however, near Noyon, French forces halted the German advance, while on the Somme the British took eight hundred German prisoners. There was still a ten-mile gap between the British and French armies, but Foch was doing his utmost to close it, declaring in his inimitable style: 'Lose not another metre of ground!'

As the Fifth Army held its new line, its commander, General Gough, was removed from his command. He was dismissed abruptly on March 28, seven days after the German assault had begun, and left the front on the following day. Within two weeks Lloyd George made much, in the House of Commons, of Gough's failure and that of his army. The public were satisfied at the thought of an incompetent general and poor troops being the cause of so deep a retreat. The nature of the German onslaught, and the ferocity of the British response, and the lack of manpower at the front, were overlooked. Ten years later, reflecting on those two crucial weeks, Lord Birkenhead wrote of Gough in his book *The Turning Points of History*: 'Yet with such temerity and courage did he continue to oppose and muffle the enemy's advance that, after the first terrible fortnight was passed, the front still stood and Ludendorff's last throw had patently failed. Amiens was saved; so was Paris; so were the Channel ports; so was France; so was England.'

On March 30 a successful counter-attack by British, Australian and Canadian troops, in which most of Moreuil Wood was recaptured, signified the turn of the tide for the Allies. The Germans were only eleven miles east of Amiens, but the city eluded them. They had advanced in places as much as forty miles, over-running all the Allied gains during the Battle of the Somme, taking 90,000 prisoners and 1,300 guns. But the impetus of their attack was broken, and their own losses were high. Among the German pilots killed was Ludendorff's youngest stepson, shot down over the battle-field. As the battle continued, each side committed all its energies. On a mission to the front, to report back at first hand whether the Allied line could hold, Churchill was impressed by Foch's determination and Clemenceau's courage. Clemenceau's spirit and energy were 'indomitable', he telegraphed to Lloyd George.

It was clear to all observers that a German victory on the Western Front would be the end for the Allies. 'The last man may count' was Lloyd George's comment on March 31 to the British Dominions, many of whose troops were at the centre of the action. In France, doctors and nurses were ensuring that 60,000 wounded men were returning to the battlefield each month to rejoin the fight. From Britain, more than 100,000 infantry replacements reached France in two weeks, many of them eighteen and nineteen year olds who had not seen action before. From the United States, following Lord Reading's urging, 120,000 American troops a month would eventually be reaching France. Among the ships converted for the task of transporting them was the ocean liner *Aquitania*, which brought a total of 90,000 troops to France in six transatlantic voyages. But the additional troops on the Western Front were not all on the Allied side. During April the Germans transferred eight divisions from the east to the west.

April 1, Easter Monday, marked the twelfth consecutive day of fighting. British troops again moved forward, recapturing Rifle Wood and taking a hundred Germans prisoner. Among the British dead that day was the poet and painter Isaac Rosenberg. He was twenty-eight years old, and had fought on the Western Front since the summer of 1916. In one of his poems from the trenches he had written:

> *Heaped stones and a charred signboard shows*
> *With grass between and dead folk under,*
> *And some bird sings, while the spirit takes wing.*
> *And this is Life in France.*

The perceived importance to all armies of maintaining the steady flow of letters to and from the trenches, and the nature of trench war, was such that on April 2, the day after Rosenberg's death, a letter he had written three days earlier had found its way to the Army post office, which date-stamped it and sent it on its way to London. 'We are now in the trenches again,' he had written to a friend, 'and though I feel very sleepy, I just have a chance to answer your letter so I will while I may. It's really my being lucky enough to bag an inch of candle that incites me to this pitch of punctual epistolary. I must measure my letter by the light.'

On April 2, as a result of Lloyd George's appeal to President Wilson, and a second appeal from Clemenceau made after Churchill enlisted the French leader's help, General Pershing finally agreed that American troops could join the British and French armies in small formations, well before they were numerous enough to form armies of their own. This decision was a boost to Allied morale, even if it meant that the bulk of the American troops already in Europe, who would be arriving at the rate of 120,000 a month, would not yet be in action. This put the Allies at a disadvantage: that day Churchill, who was still in France, sent a telegram to Lloyd George reporting on the attitude of the French politicians and generals whom he had consulted. 'It is considered certain here', he told Lloyd George, 'that the Germans will pursue this struggle to a final decision all through the summer and their resources are at present larger than ours.'

On April 4 the Germans launched a renewed attack at Villers-Bre-tonneux, starting with an artillery bombardment unleashed by more than 1,200 guns and sending fifteen divisions against seven Allied divisions. At first there was panic among the troops facing this renewed onslaught. Then British and Australian troops drove back the attackers, while five French divisions in the Castel-Cantigny sector also advanced. On the following day, April 5, Ludendorff called off the Somme offensive. He had decided 'to abandon the attack on Amiens for good,' noting in his memoirs that 'The enemy resistance was beyond our powers.' Prince Rupprecht of Bavaria later wrote: 'The final result of the day is the unpleasant fact that our offensive has come to a complete stop and its continuation without careful preparations promises no success.'

Despite the set-back on the Somme, the power of the Germans to fight elsewhere was considerable. Three days after the Somme offensive had been called off, as part of a long-devised plan, the Germans prepared for a new offensive along the British front further north, intending to fire 40,000 gas shells against Armentières, on the river Lys. The German objective was to cross the Lys, overrun the southern sector of the Ypres Salient, and drive to the coast between Calais and Dunkirk.

Having returned from London, Churchill reflected on the inevitability of a renewed German military initiative, as a direct result of the ending of the war on the Eastern Front. In a secret note to the War Cabinet on April 7, he proposed a method whereby Russia could be persuaded to return to the war. A distinguished Allied representative, perhaps the former United States President Theodore Roosevelt, who was then in Paris, should be sent to Russia to work with the Bolsheviks on a scheme to reopen the Eastern Front. By offering the Bolsheviks a formula such as 'safeguarding the permanent fruits of the Revolution', the Allies would then work out a plan whereby Russia could rid herself of the 'cruel and increasing pressure' of Germany, and rejoin the battle. The civil war and the German inroads into Russia could be used by the Allies to their advantage. 'Let us never forget', Churchill explained, 'that Lenin and Trotsky are fighting with ropes round their necks. They will leave office for the grave. Show them any real chance of consolidating their power, of getting some kind of protection against the vengeance of a counter-revolution, and they would be non-human not to embrace it.'

Churchill wanted Britain, France and the United States to offer to help the Bolsheviks with aid and support. 'Self-preservation will force them to tread a path which is also ours if they can be helped to gain it.' The effort 'must be made to re-build some kind of anti-German power in the East. However hopeless the task may seem it should be persevered in, and every agency – American, Japanese, Roumanian, Bolshevik – should be simultaneously invoked.'

No such effort was made to reopen the Eastern Front. On the Western Front on April 9, after a bombardment lasting four-and-a-half hours, the Battle of the Lys began. Fourteen German divisions attacked on a ten-mile front. As on the Somme three weeks earlier, the British were driven back. So too was a Portuguese division, against which the Germans sent four divisions, taking 6,000 Portuguese prisoners and creating a gap three-and-a-half miles wide in the British line. So fierce was the initial German artillery bombardment that one Portuguese battalion refused to go forward into its trenches. Further havoc was caused when 2,000 tons of mustard gas, phosgene and diphenylchlorarsine was discharged against the British forces, incapacitating 8,000 men, of whom many were blinded, and killing thirty.

The British situation was so grave that on April 9 conscription was extended to Ireland, a measure hitherto avoided because it was so bitterly opposed by the Irish nationalists. The poet W.B. Yeats wrote to Lord Haldane in protest: 'I read in the newspaper yesterday that over 300,000 Americans have landed in France in a month, and it seems to me a strangely wanton thing that England, for the sake of 50,000 Irish soldiers, is prepared to hollow another trench between the countries and fill it with blood.' It was the opinion of Yeats's friend Lady Gregory, he informed Haldane, that if conscription were imposed on Ireland 'women and children will stand in front of their men and receive the bullets, rather than let them be taken to the front'.

Irish independence was not on the Allied agenda: but in the second week of April, in Rome, the Allies sponsored a Congress of Oppressed Peoples, designed to encourage the subject masses and minorities inside Germany and Austria-Hungary to assert their rights to become 'completely independent national States' when the war was over. Even the Italian Government, so hard pressed by the struggles on the Isonzo and in the Trentino, accepted the right of the South Slavs to independence, despite earlier hopes of considerable Italian territorial expansion along the Dalmatian coast. Representatives of the Czechoslovak, South Slav and Polish National Committees sat side by side in Rome, together with the Allied publicists and professors who supported them, and many Italian journalists publicising their cause, among them Benito Mussolini.

In Canada, the anti-war feeling that had led so many men to resist enlistment at the end of 1917, re-emerged that spring. Under the Conscription Act, 320 men had been ordered to report towards the end of March to recruiting centres in Quebec, but at least a hundred failed to do so. By April 1 almost all these 'deserters' had been arrested, whereupon anti-conscription rioters ransacked and burned the building containing the military service registration office. They then fired on troops who had been sent to disperse them. 'The mob used rifles, revolvers and bricks,' *The Times* reported. 'The military found it necessary to use a machine gun before the mob was overcome.' Four civilians were killed. To calm the situation, the Canadian Government ordered a suspension in the arrest of army deserters.

*

On the Western Front, the situation was worsening for the Allied forces. On April 10 the British were driven from Messines, which had been gained at such cost nine months earlier. Almost all the officers in charge of the British gas companies were themselves incapacitated by German gas shells. 'Inferno continues,' one of them, Donald Grantham, wrote in his diary that day. 'Hun is nearing Béthune. Everyone clearing out. Everything in a muddle. Everyone flying. Refugees on road terrible. Have left behind in cellar pounds worth of kit.'

For six days the Allies struggled to defend successive lines behind the river Lys. On April 11, Haig issued a famous Special Order of the Day, in the course of which he declared: 'There is no course open to us but to fight it out. Every position must be held to the last man: there must be no retirement. With our backs to the wall and believing in the justice of our cause, each one of us must fight to the end.' Commented Vera Brittain, whose hospital wards, crowded with badly wounded men, were now much nearer the front, 'There was a braver spirit in the hospital that afternoon, and though we only referred briefly and brusquely to Haig's message, each one of us had made up her minds that, though enemy airmen blew up our huts and the Germans advanced upon us from Abbeville, so long as wounded men remained in Étaples, there would be no "retirement".'

A few days after Haig's order, Vera Brittain was leaving her sleeping quarters to return to the ward when she had to wait to let a large contingent of soldiers pass by along the main road. 'They were swinging rapidly towards Camiers,' she later recalled, 'and though the sight of soldiers marching was now too familiar to arouse curiosity, an unusual quality of bold vigour in their stride caused me to stare at them with puzzled interest. They looked larger than ordinary men; their tall, straight figures were in vivid contrast to the under-sized armies of pale recruits to which we were grown accustomed. At first I thought their spruce, clean uniforms were those of officers, yet obviously they could not be officers, for there were too many of them; they seemed, as it were, Tommies in heaven. Had yet another regiment been conjured out of our depleted Dominions? I wondered, watching them move with such rhythm, such dignity, such serene consciousness of self-respect. But I knew the colonial troops so well, and these were different; they were assured where the Australians were aggressive, self-possessed where the New Zealanders were turbulent.' Then she heard an excited cry from a group of nurses behind her, 'Look! Look! Here are the Americans!'

Among those escorting the American troops across the Atlantic was the explorer Sir Ernest Shackleton. That April, after reaching Liverpool from New York in a convoy, he wrote to a friend: 'We were twelve ships in all, and carried 25,000 United States troops. When we got to the danger zone we were met by seven destroyers; and it was a good job, because the next day we were attacked by two submarines, but before they could discharge a torpedo one of our destroyers dropped a depth charge and blew up one of the Huns; the other cleared off. We had 3,000 troops on our ship.'

Before these American troops could enter the line, the Allied forces were driven back even further: British, Australian, South African, New Zealand, French and Belgian troops. On April 12 a British division that had been brought back from Italy was thrown into the battle. That same day, in the air, 170 British planes engaged the Germans in combat above Merville, losing ten planes and shooting down five. The onslaught could not be halted. Yet the Germans, too, were feeling the effects of the daily attrition. 'We are all utterly exhausted and burned out,' Prince Rupprecht of Bavaria wrote on April 15. 'Everywhere I hear complaints of the accommodation of man and horse in the totally ravaged country, and the heavy loss from bombs, particularly in horses which could not be hidden from sight.'

On April 15 the British evacuated the Passchendaele Ridge, won at such terrible cost a mere five months earlier. From Haig and Foch came an appeal for American troops to join the battle immediately. General Pershing, having promised the French and British three weeks earlier that he would send what troops he could to the front, addressed the nine hundred officers of the 1st Division that day: 'You are going to meet a savage enemy, flushed with victory. Meet them like Americans. When you hit, hit hard and don't stop hitting. You don't know the meaning of the word defeat.'

The need for American participation was evident everywhere and every day. On April 16 more than a thousand New Zealand troops were taken prisoner. Four days later, south of Ypres, the Germans launched another massive gas bombardment, firing nine million rounds of mustard gas, phosgene and diphenylchlorarsine: a total of 2,000 tons of poison gas. More than 8,000 British soldiers were gassed, and forty-three killed.

The battle in the air was continuous, but not always to the German advantage. On April 7, the Zeppelin *L-59*, which had just dropped 14,000 pounds of bombs on the Italian naval base at Naples, and on a nearby steel plant, accidentally caught fire and exploded over the Adriatic. None of its crew of twenty-two survived. On April 20, Germany's best-known fighter ace, Baron Manfred von Richthofen, the 'Red Baron', shot down his eightieth Allied plane north-east of Villers-Bretonneux, behind German lines. The pilot, a 19-year-old Rhodesian, Second Lieutenant D.G. Lewis, was made a prisoner-of-war. But on the following day, above the Somme, Richthofen was shot down by a Canadian airman, Captain Roy Brown. He managed to land his plane alongside the Bray-Corbie road, but when nearby Australian troops reached it, he was dead. A hero had died, and a legend was born.[1]

---

[1] The fame of the Red Baron entered into language as well as history. When, on 11 January 1994 *The Times* reported a Government proposal to cut back, for financial reasons, a Royal Air Force meteorological research aircraft known as Snoopy, it gave the report the headline: 'RAF's Snoopy may have met his Red Baron.'

23

'The battle, the battle, nothing else counts' (Foch)

APRIL–JUNE 1918

A few of the long-awaited, much-needed American troops were in action on 20 April 1918, in the St Mihiel Salient. That day, two companies, 655 officers and men in all, who had been stationed in the village of Seicheprey for the past month, were caught in an attack by 2,800 German troops. Almost half of the Germans were specially trained 'shock' troops. The Americans, outnumbered by more than four to one, fell back with heavy losses. Entering Seicheprey, the Germans destroyed such fortifications as they could find and then withdrew to their original front line. Eighty-one Americans had been killed, more than two hundred incapacitated by gas, 187 wounded, and 187 were either missing or taken prisoner.

Pershing was angered by what he regarded, even in the circumstances of being outnumbered, as bad American generalship. He was only prevented from removing certain senior officers, including one who had refused to mount a counter-attack, by the decision of the French corps commander, General Passaga, to award the Croix de Guerre to those very officers, and to many others: a boost for American morale. Lloyd George was scathing. 'This kind of result', he wrote, 'is bound to occur on an enormous scale if a largely amateur United States Army is built up without the guidance of more experienced General Officers': that is, without the guidance of British and French officers. This view was also expressed at British General Headquarters, which was supervising the training of seven American divisions. 'The American Commanders and Staffs are almost wholly untrained' was the comment there, while Haig wrote in his diary that it would be 'criminal' to count on American help that spring or even summer.

Anti-American feeling was widespread in high British and French military circles, where the Americans were portrayed as amateurs, interlopers and latecomers. Winston Churchill, whose mother was American-born, understood that the real problem on the Western Front was the German superiority. In a conversation in London on April 23, he told General

Pershing that the Germans had 'plenty of artillery and ammunition, notwithstanding recent losses'.

As the struggle on the Western Front continued, the Royal Navy devised a plan to prevent German submarines from using the shelter of the canal at Zeebrugge as a base for their attacks on Allied shipping in the North Sea. Despite the growing British success in hunting submarines, they continued to be built almost as swiftly as they were being destroyed. Plans had been made to bring considerable numbers of American troops, and their supplies, across the Atlantic that summer. It had become necessary, Foch later wrote, to close 'one of the lairs from which the enemy submarines threatened the vital communications of the Allies'.

Six miles inland from Zeebrugge, and linked to it by canal, were concrete submarine shelters so thick as to be impervious to Allied air attack. As well as shelters, the base at Bruges contained the floating docks, workshops and stores indispensable to maintain, repair and arm the German submarine fleet. On an average day, eighteen submarines would be at Bruges, as well as twenty-five destroyers or torpedo boats, for the canal was wide enough and deep enough to allow the passage even of a light cruiser.

On April 23, St George's Day, three old British cruisers were sent across the North Sea, with a large naval force in support, to be sunk as blockships at the entrance to the submarine refuge. The man who planned the operation, Vice-Admiral Roger Keyes, had been the naval officer who, two-and-a-half years earlier, had been so keen to renew the naval attack at the Dardanelles. As the force set out, Keyes sent a signal for all ships: 'St George for England,' to which his deputy, Captain Carpenter, replied: 'May we give the Dragon's tail a damned good twist.' It was a daring and risky enterprise: eight Victoria Crosses were awarded for it.

The fortified Mole guarding Zeebrugge harbour was stormed, many of its facilities were destroyed, and the railway viaduct leading to it was broken. Carpenter later commented: 'We heard afterwards that a German cyclist corps was hurriedly sent to reinforce the Mole garrison, and, not knowing that the viaduct had been destroyed, they were precipitated into the sea and thus infringed the Gadarene copyright.'

The blockships were put in place just inside the entrance to the canal, but within three weeks the Germans had dredged a channel around them, and German submarines were once again able to renew their depredations in the North Sea and beyond. The British losses in the raid had been two hundred killed and four hundred wounded. In an attempt to create dissension among the Allies, the Germans made propaganda in the United States with criticism that American ships had not been asked to participate in the action.

An American Battle Squadron, commanded by a senior American naval officer, Rear-Admiral Hugh Rodman, had for some time been an integral part of the British North Sea Fleet, but its officers and men had not been called upon. Captain Carpenter later explained: 'If we had transferred a few score American officers and men to Chatham, where there were no American ships, for special training with our own, curiosity would have been aroused at once, comment would have followed and, in a very short while, the secret might have been public property'. Admiral Rodman, however, who had earlier served in the Panama Canal Zone, 'let us have the benefit of his experiences with regard to questions of salvage'.

The British public responded with enthusiasm to the story of Zeebrugge. Less was said of the simultaneous attack that day on the canal entrance at Ostend, which also led to the submarine base at Bruges. That raid, also made in force, failed to block the entrance at all. Not only the awards, but also public recognition went more readily to success.

On the Western Front, the German advance continued. On April 24, assisted by thirteen tanks, German troops took Villers-Bretonneux. That day saw the first battle between tank and tank, when a British heavy tank knocked out its first adversary and the others turned and fled. Seven British tanks then pushed forward into the German infantry positions 'and did great execution', General Rawlinson noted in his diary. 'They claim four hundred killed at least.'

The impetus of the German thrust had almost completely waned. On April 25 a British-Australian night attack recaptured Villers-Bretonneux, taking six hundred Germans prisoner. That same day, ninety-six German aircraft dropped seven hundred bombs on French positions around Mount Kemmel, and fired 60,000 machine-gun rounds, before driving the French off the hill. On the following day, however, French troops forced the Germans back from both Voormezeele and Locre. At Langemarck, on April 28, it was the Belgians who drove off a German attack.

On April 29 the Germans attacked again, using thirteen divisions along a ten-mile front. Once more they drove the British and French back, but only a small distance. They were to get no further forward. That night Ludendorff called the offensive to a halt. More than 30,000 German and 20,000 Allied soldiers had been killed within three weeks. The German drive to the coast, like the drive to Paris in 1914, had been halted.

The Battle of the Lys was a turning point not only in German military fortunes, but in German battlefield morale. Many soldiers were depressed and exhausted, seeing no further prospect of breaching the Allied line. It was nearly four years since the Archduke Franz Ferdinand had been assassinated in Sarajevo: who could now remember the causes and sequences, twists and turns, charges and counter-charges, which had led to such a widespread and all-consuming war? Yet the repercussions of Gavrilo Princip's act were being acted out in blood without any end in sight. On April 28, in a prison hospital in the Austrian fortress town of Theresienstadt, Princip died of tuberculosis, aged twenty-two. The medical help of a military surgeon, Dr Jan Levit, failed to save him.[1]

Also at Theresienstadt were 5,000 Russian and 500 Italian prisoners-of-war. Some of the Russians were from the Muslim regions of the Russian Empire: for them the Austrians had built a mosque. Those who died while in captivity are buried just outside the fortress walls, a Russian monument honouring them.[2] Forty miles from Theresienstadt, in Prague, Czech national feeling remained an ever-present threat to the unity and war-making zeal of Austria-Hungary. On April 13, in the Smetana Hall, a focal point of patriotic activity, delegates gathered from every Czech town to pledge to build a State of their own.

On what had been the Eastern Front, the Germans had continued to advance in the areas where the Bolsheviks had withdrawn or were weak. On April 5 they occupied the eastern Ukrainian city of Kharkov. Eight days later they entered the Finnish capital, Helsinki, formerly the capital of the Russian province of Finland. In Petrograd, now a city at peace, albeit under Bolshevik rule, and stripped of its Finnish and Baltic hinterlands, Prokofiev's Classical Symphony, written by the composer in the enthusiasm of social renewal, was given its first performance on April 21. Three days later the Germans entered Simferopol, the capital of the Crimea. On April 29 a senior German army officer, General Groener, established military rule throughout the Ukraine, whose 1918 harvest would be gathered for the German war effort.[3] Two days later the Germans occupied the Black Sea port and arsenal of Sebastopol.

At sea in April 1918, more than a hundred merchant ships had been sunk by German submarines and 488 lives had been lost. Troop transports were also a continual target: in May, in the Mediterranean, ninety-nine lives were lost on the *Leasowe Castle* and forty-four on the *Missir*, both of them torpedoed by German submarines off Egypt. On May 14, however, another troopship, the 46,359-ton ocean liner *Olympic*, rammed and sank the German submarine *U-103*.

To arm the Americans once they reached France, the British Ministry of Munitions, under Churchill, was making prodigious efforts to increase British munitions production, as well as manufacturing tanks and aircraft for the new ally. Early in May, Churchill was able to offer the Americans

[1] Twenty-five years later, 140,000 German, Austrian and Czech Jews were incarcerated in Theresienstadt by the Nazis. Some 33,000 died there of malnutrition and disease, and 88,000 were deported to Auschwitz and other death camps where they were murdered. Among those incarcerated at Theresienstadt in 1942 and deported to Auschwitz in 1944, where he was killed, was Dr Levit (who between the wars had been a Professor of Military Surgery). He was a second-generation Christian, but under Nazi definition of race that could not save him.
[2] A plaque was put up by the post-1945 Yugoslav Government at the entrance to the cell in which Princip was imprisoned, and where his chains, to this day, are shown to the visitor.
[3] Groener was later Army Minister, and then Interior Minister, under Weimar. It was he who, in 1919, persuaded the new Weimar Republic to retain the army in a form that would enable it, in due course, to expand.

225 heavy guns for the summer and another fifty for November, the latter for the campaign of 1919, in which the Allies hoped that the American troops, more than three million of whom were expected to be in Europe by the summer of 1919, would turn the balance against the Central Powers. The next year's campaign had begun to exercise the planners more and more. On May 24 a British tank officer, Lieutenant-Colonel Fuller, prepared a 'Plan 1919' which envisaged nearly 5,000 Allied tanks effecting a major breakthrough on the Western Front in 1919. The British Cabinet, anxious to maintain a sense of duty on the home front into the early months of 1919, decided on May 28 not to allow horse-racing during the winter season. The first National Hunt race of that season was scheduled for 1 January 1919.

The planning for 1919 took place under the shadow of a possible renewed German offensive in the summer of 1918. In an attempt to strengthen the immediate number of Allied troops in the line, a meeting of the Supreme War Council of Allied leaders, presided over by Clemenceau, met at Abbeville, near the Channel coast, on May 1. First Clemenceau, then Lloyd George and finally Foch sought Pershing's permission to reconsider his earlier change of mind, and, as President Wilson had wished, to bring the existing American troops into the line at once. Foch went so far as to say that, unless this was done, and American infantrymen and machine-gun units sent forward immediately, all would be lost. Pershing was adamant, telling the conference with some acerbity: 'I do not suppose that the American army is to be entirely at the disposal of the French and British commands,' and he added: 'We must look forward to the time when we have our own army.'

Lloyd George, while agreeing to a separate American army in principle, told Pershing: 'At the present time, however, we are engaged in what is perhaps the decisive battle of the war. If we lose this battle, we shall need tonnage to take home what there is left of the British and American armies.' This threat had no effect on Pershing, of whom Foch asked angrily: 'You are willing to risk our being driven back to the Loire?' Undaunted by the rhetoric, Pershing replied: 'Yes, I am willing to take the risk. Moreover, the time may come when the American army will have to stand the brunt of this war, and it is not wise to fritter away our resources in this manner.' Foch replied that the war might be over before the American army was ready to enter the battle. The meeting ended with a final altercation:

Lloyd George: 'Can't you see that the war will be lost unless we get this support?'

Pershing: 'Gentlemen, I have thought this programme over very deliberately and will not be coerced.'

The Abbeville meeting resumed on May 2, when Lloyd George, after pointing out that since March 21 the British casualties had been 280,000 and the French more than 340,000 men, told Pershing: 'If the United States does not come to our aid then perhaps the enemy's calculations will be correct. If France and Great Britain should have to yield, their defeat would be honourable, for they would have fought to their last man, while the United States would have to stop without having put into the line more men than little Belgium.'

Pershing told the conference that America had declared war 'independently' of the other Allies and must face it 'with a powerful army'. He also wished to emphasise 'that the morale of the soldiers depends upon their fighting under our own flag'. He then proposed a compromise, which Clemenceau and Lloyd George had no option but to accept. The 130,000 American infantrymen and machine gunners being transported across the Atlantic that May, in British ships, and a further 150,000 in June, could join the Allied line, but he would make no provision for July. American shipping resources would continue to be used exclusively to create an American army, for service in the field as such when it was ready. By the end of May there would be 650,000 American troops in Europe. As a result of Pershing's compromise, two-thirds of them would not be joining the line until they could do so as an American army. Foch was depressed, Clemenceau angry and Lloyd George bitterly disappointed, writing to the British Ambassador in Washington: 'It is maddening to think that though the men are there, the issue may be endangered because of the short-sightedness of one General and the failure of his Government to order him to carry out their undertakings.'

As the Anglo-American quarrel continued, so did the daily death toll on the battlefields and behind the lines. On May 5, a British soldier, Gunner Francis Barber, of the 32nd Siege Battery, Royal Garrison Artillery, died in a German military hospital at Condé of wounds received in action. He is one of ninety British soldiers buried at the nearby French cemetery who died in that hospital while they were in German captivity. He was thirty-seven years old. His son Stephen, born in 1914, was killed in action in Normandy in 1944.

In the east the Germans were following up their victories. On May 7 the Roumanians signed the Peace of Bucharest with the Central Powers, who gained military control of the mouth of the Danube. Bulgaria, as its reward for attacking Roumania as Germany and Austria's ally, received the coastal lands that it had lost to Roumania in the Balkan War of 1913. On May 12, at the Belgian resort town of Spa, the Kaiser and the Emperor Charles signed an agreement for the joint German-Austrian economic exploitation of the Ukraine. Two days later the Kaiser declared that Lithuania was free from the old shackles of Russian rule, and allied to Germany.

That month, national aspirations began to emerge in the Austrian army. On May 12 there was a mutiny in the heart of Austria, at the Styrian town of Judenburg, when an infantry platoon captured the barracks and munition stores, looted the food stores, and destroyed the telephone and telegraph lines. The platoon was largely Slovene. Their cry was: 'Let us go home comrades, this is not only for us but also for our friends on the fronts. The war must be ended now, whoever is a Slovene, join us. We are going home; they should give us more to eat and end the war; up with the Bolsheviks, long live bread, down with the war.'

The mutiny was quickly suppressed, and six Slovenes were executed. But the mutinies spread, and within a few weeks both a Ruthenian battalion, and a Serbian unit in the Austrian army, had mutinied, though both revolts were quickly crushed. On May 17, in Prague, a provocatively named Conference of the Suppressed Nations of Austria-Hungary was held in Prague. A fourth mutiny, by Czech troops, broke out in Rumburg four days later. They refused to go to the front unless they were paid the money due to them when they were prisoners-of-war in Russia. They occupied the town, received some support from the local Czech citizens, and threatened to march on Prague. A few took the train to Prague, declaring that they would 'put an end to the war' once they arrived, but they were intercepted before the train reached Prague, and disarmed. At the subsequent Court Martial, ten Czechs were sentenced to death and 560 imprisoned. The mutiny was over, but the local Governor warned Vienna, in no uncertain terms: 'Had the rebels succeeded in advancing southward and had they found support – and this was by no means impossible – among the civilians in these regions, we might by now have faced a regular revolution in several parts of Bohemia.'

Both in Vienna and Berlin, the authorities had to keep alert to any danger of revolution, and were responsive to any calls for help against Bolshevism. In southern Russia, the new leader of the Don Cossacks, General Krasnov, appealed to the Germans on May 16 for financial and military help against the Red Army. This was given readily, and included fifteen million roubles and 12,000 rifles. German influence extended across a thousand miles of southern Russia. That day, in Finland, the Finnish national leader, General Mannerheim, entered Helsinki at the head of 16,000 men. More than a century of Tsarist rule, six months of Bolshevik control, and most recently German military occupation, were over.

On the former Caucasus Front, Germany's ally Turkey was driving the Armenians out of what was left of their homeland, occupying the former Russian city of Kars (which had been Turkish until 1878) and pressing eastward into the Armenian heartland, occupying Alexandropol on May 15 and defeating more than 6,000 Armenians three days later. For another ten days the Armenians fought tenaciously, at one point pushing the Turks back thirty miles, but on May 26, at the Battle of Karakilise, the Turks were victorious, and 5,000 Armenians made their escape over the mountain passes. On May 28, Armenia declared her independence. It was a short-lived culmination of long-held aspirations: within two weeks, hundreds of Armenians were being massacred by Tatars south of the Georgian capital of Tiflis. The Turks, advancing three months later into the former Russian

Caucasus, and in due course reaching the Caspian Sea, murdered more than 400,000 Armenian civilians, townsmen, villagers, women and children.

In Berlin, Albert Einstein, who since his call for a post-war united Europe in 1914 had published his General Theory of Relativity, was worried that he was failing to take any part in the protests against war to which his fellow signatory of 1914, Georg Nicolai, had continued to devote himself. 'You are in no way to be "reproached" because you sit in Berlin and work,' Nicolai wrote to him on May 18. 'If anyone has a right, as a latter-day Archimedes, to cry out to the mercenaries of war, "Noli tangere circulos meos"[1] it is *surely you*!' Nicolai added that he was 'much more firmly convinced than I was at the time we wrote the Manifesto to Europeans that the impending cultural collapse can only be avoided if the idea of Europe, pure and simple, prevails.'

Five weeks later, denounced and hounded for his pacifism, Nicolai escaped by aeroplane from Germany to Denmark. In German-occupied Belgium, it was three years since the first printing and circulation of an illegal patriotic newspaper *Libre Belgique*. Its network had been wide, its operations vexing for the Germans. At the end of January 1918 most of the paper's distributors, sixty-one in all, had been arrested, the Kaiser sending a telegram of congratulations to the Military Governor, General von Falkenhausen, whom the paper had described as 'a bird of prey sent to live on the palpitating flesh of Belgium'. The Kaiser himself was 'His Satanic Majesty' in the paper's parlance.

On May 15 the sixty-one were brought to trial in Brussels. They were sentenced to imprisonment, some for ten and twelve years. After a short interval, the paper appeared once more, the next issue, number 143, being produced almost single-handed by Abbé van den Hout, who, on a treadle press, printed 7,000 copies, and then arranged for the paper to be reprinted in Antwerp. Copies of *Libre Belgique* were even smuggled into internment camps in Germany. At one of these, Soltau, readings were given from it to four or five hundred internees, among them a Belgian student, Paul van Zeeland, who had been elected spokesman for the other prisoners.[2]

On the Western Front, and above Britain and Germany, there was much activity in the air during May. The lock gates at Zeebrugge were among the British targets, as were railway junctions inside Germany itself. On May 18, in retaliation for German air raids on British cities, thirty-three British aircraft bombed Cologne, doing much damage to buildings in the

[1] Archimedes, a citizen of Syracuse, had been drawing geometric circles in the sand outside Carthage, as part of a geometry lesson, when a Roman soldier, a member of the conquering army, came across him and ordered him to stop. He refused, telling the soldier, 'Do not touch my circles', and was killed, despite an earlier order by the Roman general that his life should be spared. The phrase has come to mean 'Do not interfere with my work.'
[2] Van Zeeland was Prime Minister of Belgium from 1935 to 1937. He spent the Second World War in England. As Belgian Minister of Foreign Affairs from 1949 to 1954, he was a central figure in the moves towards European union.

city and killing 110 civilians. On the following night, twenty-eight German Gotha bombers struck at London, and forty-eight civilians were killed. Six of the bombers were shot down in flames by British pilots and three more crashed when they reached their home aerodromes. These large two-engined aircraft reached London across Kent. 'The air-raid warning was by changing the gas pressure,' a ten-year-old British schoolboy, Desmond Flower, later recalled. 'When the lights went up and down twice all window curtains had to be drawn.'

On their way to London, from whatever direction they came, the German bombers had to fly through skilfully designed anti-aircraft barrages, arranged in the form of an enormous oblong box across the countryside. The young Flower remembered how, as soon as the raid began, the anti-aircraft guns 'barked continually at the giants lumbering overhead; shell fragments pattered down like rain, but that would never prevent father from parading around outside to see what was going on, however much we implored him to come in. One night I stayed awake for a long time listening to a bomber groaning round and round trying to find a way out of the box barrage in which it was caught; it did not succeed – when it was shot down the droning stopped and I went back to sleep.'

German air raids on French munitions dumps for four successive days from May 19 led to the destruction of more than 12,000 tons of Allied ammunition. In a German air raid on the railway bridge at Étaples that month, some of the bombs missed the bridge and hit a British hospital, killing several wounded soldiers and the nurses that were looking after them. Nine members of the Women's Auxiliary Army Corps were also killed: their work in France included giving instruction in the use of gas masks, clerical work, and cooking in army camps.

On both sides the scale of the bombing raids was small, yet they were a new and visible arm of warfare, constantly improving in effectiveness. In the third week of May, British Handley Page bombers, known as 'Bloody Paralysers', attacked a German chemical works at Oppau, gas works at Mannheim and railway workshops and engines at Karthaus. On May 22, nine German Gotha bombers approached Paris. An intense anti-aircraft barrage drove eight of them away, but one got through, dropping several bombs and killing one person. *The Times* reported: 'An exciting struggle between the raider trying to get away and the guns concentrating to bring it down lasted fully half an hour.'

There were three further bombing raids on Paris in June, and considerable action in the air above the battle zones. On June 2, a day on which the Germans claimed to have shot down thirty-eight Allied aircraft for the loss of seventeen of their own, a German pilot, Hermann Goering, received the Pour le Mérite. On the following day the British instituted a new decoration for bravery in aerial combat, the Distinguished Flying Cross. A month earlier, on May 9, Hitler had been awarded a German regimental diploma for outstanding bravery.

*

The Germans were in control of two of pre-war Russia's most prosperous regions, the Ukraine and the Baltic. They had helped the Finns drive the Bolsheviks out of Finland, where German troops remained as a guarantee of independence. On May 27 an independent Georgian Republic was set up under German protection. But Germany was not to be the only military bastion against the Bolsheviks. On May 23 the British War Cabinet had taken a decision to dispatch a 560-strong military mission to the port of Archangel, and a further six hundred men to Murmansk, to guard the British military stores there, that had earlier been sent through the Arctic as Britain's military contribution to the Russian army.[1] The British also offered to train the hundreds of thousands of anti-Bolshevik Russians to defend themselves against any future Bolshevik assault. Three days later, in Siberia, 60,000 Czech troops, who had made their way through Siberia to the Far East of Russia after the Treaty of Brest-Litovsk had liberated all Austrian prisoners-of-war, turned actively against the Bolsheviks.

These Czechs, who for almost four years had been an integral part of the armies of the Central Powers, now declared themselves for the Allies, and formed a Czech Legion, determined, from afar, to see the Central Powers destroyed and Czechoslovakia become an independent State. They even tried to find a way to return to Europe to fight with the Allies. But their immediate battle, as of the last week of May 1918, was against the Bolsheviks. On May 27 they seized the Siberian town of Chelyabinsk, four days later Petropavlosk and Tomsk.

The German High Command had not given up hope of breaking the Allied line on the Western Front. On May 27 Ludendorff tried again, hoping to repeat the initial successes of two months earlier, and even to reach Paris. Four thousand guns opened fire in the very early hours of that morning, on a 24-mile front. The Third Battle of the Aisne had begun. On the French sector of the Chemin des Dames, the attacking forces drove through the lines to a depth of twelve miles, annihilating four French divisions.

Between Soissons and Reims the Germans broke through four more French and four British divisions, to reach the Aisne in less than six hours. At the village of La Ville-aux-Bois-les-Pontaverts, a British battalion and a field battery refused to withdraw despite the overwhelming fire power hurled against them. 'The guns continued to fire and resistance did not cease until every man was killed or captured,' a French memorial records at the site of the gun battery's resistance. For this action, the whole British battery was awarded the Croix de Guerre. Of the 540 graves in the Commonwealth War Graves Commission cemetery at Ville-aux-Bois, 413 are the graves of unknown soldiers.

By the end of May 28 a forty-mile-wide, fifteen-mile-deep wedge had been driven through the Allied lines. Among the British soldiers killed that

[1] It was a contribution for which Britain had submitted a bill, £757 million in all, but on coming to power Lenin and the Bolsheviks had repudiated all Tsarist and Provisional Government debts.

day was Major Bertram Cartland, who had been on the Western Front since 1914, 'which in itself', writes his daughter, 'was a miracle of survival'.[1] That day the Kaiser visited 'The California Position', a look-out post near Croanne from which, in 1814, Napoleon had witnessed one of his last victories over the allies ranged against him. Despite the ferocity of the German attack in 1918, however, the Allies were not everywhere beaten back, and at Cantigny, on the Somme, in the first sustained American offensive of the war, nearly 4,000 Americans, a full Brigade, were in action that day. The French provided the air cover, as well as 368 heavy guns and trench mortars, and flamethrower teams to assist the advance through the village. The American infantrymen were preceded by twelve French heavy tanks. Each American soldier carried with him 220 rounds of ammunition, three sandbags, two hand grenades, one rifle grenade, two water canteens, and iron rations, as well as two cakes of chocolate, and a lemon and chewing gum as thirst quenchers.

A two-hour artillery barrage preceded the attack, and Cantigny was quickly overrun. The flamethrowers were particularly effective. One American, Clarence R. Huebner, recalled how he saw a German soldier run out of a dug-out 'just as I had seen rabbits in Kansas come out of burning straw stacks'. The German ran about fifteen yards and then fell over, dead.[2]

The Americans took about a hundred German prisoners that day, but, one historian has written, 'Some they did not take. These were the last-ditch machine gunners, who fired until their ammunition was exhausted and then tried to surrender. For some American soldiers 'it was simply too much to see a buddy machine-gunned and then hear his killer yell "*Kamerad*" to escape retaliation. They killed the *Kamerad* with mixed feelings of grief and hate.'[3]

Cantigny village was under American control. 'No inch was to be given up' was Pershing's instruction. Seven German counter-attacks followed in the space of seventy-two hours. During the continuing battle two hundred American soldiers were killed and a further two hundred incapacitated by the German gas attacks. Under the strain of the continual shelling, and the fatigue of three days in action, men became, in the words of their commander, Colonel Hanson E. Ely, 'half crazy, temporarily insane'. One American lieutenant began shooting wildly at his fellow-soldiers until he was killed by a German shell. After three days of battle and bombardment,

[1] Two of Major Cartland's sons (one of them a Member of Parliament) were killed in action on the Western Front in 1940, within a day of each other, during the retreat to Dunkirk. His daughter, Barbara Cartland, became a prolific novelist.
[2] Huebner rose through the ranks to become a Major-General, commanding the 1st United States Infantry Division in Sicily, Normandy and northern Europe. 'I remember him not fondly,' my American proof-reader commented at this point in the typescript.
[3] Donald Smythe, *Pershing, General of the Armies*, Indiana University Press, Bloomington 1986, page 127. German soldiers would call out *Kamerad* when they wanted to surrender. It meant, simply, comrade, though many British and American soldiers thought it was the German for 'I surrender'.

the Americans were exhausted. When relief finally came, Colonel Ely recalled, 'They could only stagger back, hollow-eyed with sunken cheeks, and if one stopped for a moment he would fall asleep.'

The Americans held Cantigny. The impact of its capture was threefold: it deprived the Germans of an important observation point, it gave Pershing a further argument for an independent United States command, and it provided, according to one American military historian, 'the first cold foreboding to the German that this was not, as he had hoped, a rabble of amateurs approaching'.[1]

Despite the American success at Cantigny, the onward German thrust continued. On May 29 German troops entered Soissons. By the end of that third day of the onslaught, more than 50,000 French soldiers had been taken prisoner, as well as 650 artillery pieces and 2,000 machine guns. On May 30 the Germans reached the river Marne near Château-Thierry. That night Pershing dined with Foch and his senior staff officers. He later recalled: 'It would be difficult to imagine a more depressed group of officers. They sat through the meal scarcely speaking a word as they contemplated what was probably the most serious situation of the war.'

On June 1, German troops were forty miles from Paris, ten miles nearer the capital than they had been in April. On June 2 they overran one of the forts defending Reims, the Fort de la Pompelle, but a French counter-attack regained the fort, capturing two hundred German soldiers and four tanks. That day the Supreme War Council met at Versailles. Once again, as in 1914, the French Government was preparing to leave Paris and move south. Tens of thousands of civilians were fleeing from the capital as they had done in 1914, and were to do again in 1940.

Once more the French appealed to Pershing, asking for an immediate transfer of American troops to the French sector of the disintegrating front, and their temporary amalgamation with French units. Pershing, as determined as ever not to give up the prospect of an independent American army, or to see that prospect recede, resisted all arguments. Foch, distraught, repeated again and again: 'The battle, the battle, nothing else counts.' When, during the discussions at Versailles, the French asked for 250,000 American troops to join the line in June and a further 250,000 in July, Pershing stunned them by replying that apart from the three divisions ready to embark, there were only 263,852 more trained men in the United States. This was far fewer than the Allies had imagined possible, but it was the true figure, in all its precision. The great American contribution to Allied manpower would not be ready until the end of the year, possibly not even until 1919. 'Then we can expect practically nothing from the United States after the present schedules are completed,' Clemenceau remarked. 'That is a great disappointment.' Those 'present schedules'

[1] General Hunter Liggett, *AEF: Ten Years Ago In France*, New York 1928.

envisaged between 120,000 and 150,000 American troops a month, and no more.

To the suggestion that additional American troops should be sent over to Europe untrained, Pershing insisted that they complete their training while still in the United States. 'Men learned quicker in France' was Foch's reply. When Lloyd George suggested that the Americans should be trained in Britain, by the British, Pershing answered that he would not 'surrender my prerogatives' in this matter.

The British and French leaders lost patience with the American Commander-in-Chief. As Pershing was suggesting that the French mobilise the next class of French youth, Lloyd George interrupted with the words: 'Why, General Pershing, you surely would not put those mere boys into the trenches?' Exasperated, Pershing replied: 'Mr Prime Minister, you have suggested we put American boys not as well trained as the French boys you refer to into the trenches. I cannot see the distinction.'

Pershing got his way. American troops would be trained in the United States. The terms of the earlier agreement at Abbeville would be adhered to, though he agreed to a slight increase in numbers. Pershing would put into the line, as and where the French needed them, 170,000 troops in June and 140,000 in July, but not a man more. The remaining troops that were scheduled to arrive, 190,000, would become part of Pershing's own supply and support system for the future American army.

The demands of the battle activated the agreement at once, as American troops were sent to the Marne east of Château-Thierry, where they blew up a bridge to prevent the Germans crossing to the south. They were also sent, through Meaux, to the closest point of the German advance towards Paris. On their way they encountered thousands of refugees, mostly villagers and farmers, fleeing from the advancing German army, and innumerable groups of three or four French soldiers also hurrying away from the battle zone.

As the American troops drew closer to the front they found whole villages that had been looted by the retreating French troops. Where wine cellars had been looted, drunkenness added to indiscipline. A French peasant who tried to protect his property had been tied to a chair and beaten. Closer still to the front the Americans met wounded French troops falling back, the 'walking wounded', their heads bandaged, their arms in slings. 'The Boche are coming,' the French warned wearily, to which the Americans replied, as encouragement, 'We're here.' 'Ah, oui' was the French response, 'but the Boche, he is *still* coming.' When the American troops reached the front, astride the Paris-Metz road a French general instructed them to hold the line 'at all hazard'. French units were still falling back, some of the soldiers calling out to the Americans as they passed them, on June 1, that the war was over: 'La guerre finie.'

The Americans held the line. They were helped by the Germans' own exhaustion at the end of a six-day struggle, and by the great distance created by the German advance, which created formidable difficulties of supply. Not only did the Americans hold the line, however, but they also made small advances, creating an immediate boost to French military and civilian morale. One Frenchman who understood, and shared, this reaction was Jean de Pierrefeu, an officer on Pétain's Staff. 'We all had the impression', he later wrote, 'that we were about to see a wonderful transfusion of blood. Life was coming in floods to reanimate the dying body of France.'

On the British Front, General Freyberg was among those in action on June 3, when he suffered his ninth serious injury. 'I was wounded by a big shell during a minor operation,' he wrote to a friend. 'I was very shaken for a bit; it threw me several yards and wounded me in the leg and head. I had the bits out at the casualty clearing station. It was rather an ordeal.' The man in the bed next to him 'had two legs and an arm off'.

To help staunch the German advance, 10,000 French and 10,000 British troops were brought from the Salonica Front. There, Bulgarian deserters warned the Allies of an imminent offensive, but the offensive had to be cancelled because of a mutiny among the Bulgarian forces. Matters were far from well, that summer, for the Central Powers: in Hungary on May 20, in their barracks at Pécs, 2,000 Hungarian troops had refused to go to the front, occupied the camp weapons stores, and were helped in their mutiny by local coal miners. Three loyal regiments had to be ordered to suppress the mutiny.

War-ravaged, revolution-harassed Russia was becoming a new battle zone. On June 3, two German battalions landed at Poti, for service in support of the authorities in the Crimea. On the following day 150 Royal Marines landed at the northern Russian port of Pechenga, to protect Allied stores and support the local anti-Bolsheviks. That same day a member of one of the German royal houses, the Duke of Württemberg, accepted the throne of Lithuania. But another German prince, Crown Prince Rupprecht of Bavaria, was pressing the German Chancellor, Count Hertling, to open peace talks with Britain, France and Italy while Germany and Austria still held the military ascendancy in the west. His request was rebuffed, the Chancellor replying that the collapse of France at least was still likely.

The political and military wars were marching side by side. On June 3, Britain, France and Italy announced their full support for Polish, Czech and Yugoslav statehood. On the following day, encouraged to do so by the British, Dr Chaim Weizmann, the Zionist leader, met the Emir Feisal, the leader of the Arab Revolt, near the port of Akaba, and worked out with him what seemed to be a satisfactory Arab support for a Jewish National Home in Palestine. A senior British general noted after the meeting that both T.E. Lawrence, who helped set the meeting up, and Weizmann, 'see the lines of Arab & Zionist policy converging in the not distant future'. In the following week a renewed Arab offensive cut off the Turkish garrison in Ma'an. In Allenby's army on the coastal plain north of Jaffa, waiting to advance north of Jerusalem, 5,000 Palestinian Jews, many of them Russian-born, were under arms.

'I would welcome any good understanding with the Jews,' Feisal wrote to Mark Sykes a month after the Akaba meeting, and he added: 'I admit that some ignorant Arabs despise the Jews, but ignorants everywhere are the same, and on the whole such incidents compare favourably with what the Jews suffer in more advanced lands.' At that very moment, in towns and villages throughout the Ukraine, several thousand Jews were being murdered by anti-Bolshevik Whites, whose historic anti-Semitism, combining with a new hatred of the noted Jewish presence among the Bolshevik leadership, renewed the violent pogroms of a decade and a half earlier.

On June 3, German forces crossed the Marne at Jaulgonne, using eight enormous ladders, telescoped like firemen's ladders and thrown across the river. Each ladder was only wide enough for two men to crawl forward side by side. Once across, another fourteen ladders were laid down, and a small bridgehead was established with six machine guns. Again it was as though August 1914 had come again, with Château-Thierry, only six miles to the west, vulnerable to capture from both sides of the river. But at Château-Thierry, two United States divisions had already been in the line for two days, and it was American troops who attacked the German bridgehead. A hundred Germans were taken prisoner. The rest were forced to return in boats or swim back.

Also on June 3, on the other side of Château-Thierry, five miles to the west of the town, American tenacity emerged during a German attack at Belleau Wood. As the American Marine Brigade was ordered into action, Sergeant Dan Daly called out: 'Come on, you sons-o'-bitches. Do you want to live for ever?' At the end of the day 1,087 Marines had been killed. When the question arose of an American withdrawal, an American officer is said to have declared with indignation 'Retreat hell! We just got here.'

In the French Chamber of Deputies, Clemenceau reflected this spirit when he declared on June 4: 'I shall fight before Paris, I shall fight in Paris, I shall fight behind Paris.' He also spoke of 'the ultimate success that is within our grasp, that we are on the very eve of grasping if only we have enough tenacity'. Not every observer shared this confidence. On the day of Clemenceau's speech, the Secretary to the British War Cabinet, Sir Maurice Hankey, a former Royal Marine, wrote in his diary: 'I do not like the outlook. The Germans are fighting better than the Allies, and I cannot exclude the possibility of disaster.'

24

The Allied counter-attack

JUNE–AUGUST 1918

On 3 June 1918, a French codebreaker, Georges Panvin, decrypted a top-secret German radio signal which gave details of a German attack on the French sector of the Western Front scheduled to begin on June 7. The signal also revealed that the attack was to take place between Montdidier and Compiègne. This precious intelligence enabled the French to make diligent preparations. German troops were once more only forty-five miles from Paris. On June 6, the day before the new German assault, British troops advanced in their sector south-west of Reims, driving the Germans from the village of Bligny. Above the warring armies a thousand British and French aircraft were in continuous, fierce conflict. That night six British bombers attacked German railway yards at Metz and Thionville.

At midnight on June 7 the Germans prepared to launch the attack for which the French, thanks to their signals intelligence, had been alerted. As a result of having been forewarned, the French launched a massive artillery bombardment ten minutes in advance of the German one. When the German bombardment came, however, it was even more intense, with three-quarters of a million rounds of mustard gas, phosgene and diphenyl-chlorarsine being fired: 15,000 tons of gas shells. Nearly 4,000 French soldiers were incapacitated by gas and thirty-two were killed.

At 4.30 on the morning of June 8, the German infantrymen attacked, advancing more than five miles and taking 8,000 prisoners. On June 9 they advanced a further two miles, forcing the French to evacuate several strongpoints. Pershing, who was with Clemenceau that day, was asked his opinion of the outcome of the battle. 'Well, Mr President,' he replied, 'it may not look encouraging just now but we are certain to win in the end.' Clemenceau, visibly moved, took Pershing's hand. 'Do you really think that?' he asked. 'I am glad to hear you say it.' Even the indomitable Tiger of France could have his moments of doubt.

On June 10 the Germans advanced south of Lassigny, forcing the French back as far as Antheuil-Portes, a mere five miles from Compiègne, and forty-five miles from Paris. Churchill, who was in the French capital on munitions business, wrote to his wife that afternoon: 'The very critical and deadly battle on the Montdidier-Noyon front has raged all day, & the latest accounts (5.30 p.m.) are apparently satisfactory. There is no surprise here, but a blunt trial of strength – the line held strongly with troops & good reserves at hand.' Churchill added, rather ominously: 'If the French cannot hold them back on this sector, it is not easy to see what the next step on our part should be.'

Churchill was in Paris planning to co-ordinate the munitions needs of the British, French, Italians and Americans for the autumn of 1918 and the spring of 1919. The campaign of 1919 was also on Ludendorff's mind that month, as he gave orders for a great increase in aircraft production, three hundred planes a month, between July 1918 and April 1919. That day, on the Noyon-Montdidier front, six hundred French and two hundred British aircraft participated in the battle. Thirty-eight Allied and five German aircraft were shot down.

On June 11 the Allies launched a counter-attack with four French and two American divisions. Air support was again an integral part of the battle, as were 163 tanks. More than a thousand German soldiers were taken prisoner. The infantrymen were no longer acting alone, though a bombing error by the Royal Air Force that day wounded eight French soldiers and killed seventy-five horses. About forty Allied aircraft were shot down by the Germans, for the loss of nineteen German planes.

West of Soissons, five German divisions attacked on June 12, but made only small gains, the French forces again having an advantage, with nearly two hundred tanks. That day, after only four days of battle, Ludendorff halted his offensive. The Allies, however, continued to press forward. On June 14 the French used mustard gas on an extensive scale for the first time.

Even film was being used as a factor in warmaking. On June 14 President Wilson himself was driven to complain about an American film version of Ambassador Gerard's book *My Four Years in Germany*, which contained gruesome scenes of German atrocities against Belgian prisoners-of-war that had been filmed in New Jersey. But zeal for war was an indispensable part of recruiting: an inflammatory anti-war speech two days later by the socialist leader Eugene Debs led to his arrest, and a ten-year prison sentence. Socialists elsewhere were also in angry mood: on June 17 there were riots in Vienna after the bread ration had been reduced, and in Budapest there were violent scenes in support of higher wages.

In the east, the Germans continued to extend their control over large areas of the former Tsarist Empire. On June 12 they occupied the Georgian capital of Tiflis. Austrian troops, supporting Germany's virtual annexation of the Ukraine, had taken 10,000 Russian Bolsheviks prisoner in southern Russia. But it was on the Italian Front that the great trial of strength came, when on June 15 the Austrians launched a massive offensive, with fifty-five divisions attacking from the Asiago Plateau and Monte Grappa, a further fifty-one divisions attacking across the Piave.

Ludwig Wittgenstein was among the Austrian troops in action that day. During a fierce artillery and machine-gun duel, he went out on patrol to report on the situation. When two of his patrol were wounded he helped bring them back. Shortly afterwards, while he was at his gun emplacement, a shell buried the officer and three crew members. Wittgenstein took charge of the gun, for which he was recommended for Austria's highest award, the Gold Medal for Valour. 'His exceptionally courageous behaviour,' read the citation, 'calmness, sang-froid, and heroism won the total admiration of the troops. By his conduct he gave a splendid example of loyal and soldierly fulfilment of duty.' The troops facing Wittgenstein's battery were British.

On June 16 the *Observer* reported that the Italian defenders along the Piave had met the attackers 'in their first onslaught and immediately retook the few small positions that had been lost in the first moments of the fighting'. Reading this report in London, with a practised eye, Vera Brittain, whose brother Edward was then serving on the Italian Front, reflected ominously that 'the loss of a "few small positions", however quickly recaptured, meant – as it always did in despatches – that the defenders were taken by surprise and the enemy offensive had temporarily succeeded'. Six days were to pass before she received the short, standard telegram she dreaded: 'Regret to inform you Captain E.H. Brittain M.C. killed in action Italy June 15th'. Shortly after leading his men in recapturing a trench, he had been shot in the head by an Austrian sniper. 'It seemed indeed the last irony', his sister wrote, 'that he should have been killed by the countrymen of Fritz Kreisler, the violinist whom of all others he had most greatly admired.' Vera Brittain had lost her fiancé, two of her best friends, and her brother.

The day of Edward Brittain's death was the day on which the *Nation* published a poem by Wilfred Owen, who had been invalided out of the trenches on the Western Front, but was later to return to them:

> Move him into the sun, –
> Gently its touch awoke him once,
> At home, whispering of fields unsown.
> Always it woke him, even in France,
> Until this morning and this snow.
> If anything might rouse him now
> The kind old sun will know.
>
> Think how it wakes the seeds, –
> Woke, once, the clays of a cold star.
> Are limbs, so dear-achieved, are sides,
> Full-nerved, -still warm, -too hard to stir?
> Was it for this the clay grew tall?
> – O what made fatuous sunbeams toil
> To break earth's sleep at all?

433

The Austrian offensive of June 15 failed to achieve a breakthrough. On the Piave Front, the preliminary artillery bombardment was short of shells. It also suffered because the Germans had failed to provide the phosgene gas shells Austria had hoped to use. On the Asiago sector, good Intelligence enabled the Italians to open an artillery barrage of their own four hours before the start of the Austrian barrage. In the opening phase of the battle, the British and French troops holding part of the Italian line were pushed back. But a successful Allied counter-attack led to the capture of 1,500 Austrian troops. In the Monte Grappa sector, the Austrian advance was stopped after 3,300 yards, then driven back by an Italian counter-attack.

The Emperor Charles, waiting in his train at Meran in the hope of hurrying forward to witness victory, was distraught. At noon he telephoned one of the most successful of the Hapsburg commanders, Field Marshal Svetozar Boroevic, to be told: 'The Army of Tyrol is defeated, the troops have lost all that they have gained and have been driven back to the line of departure.' Boroevic, whose family had fought for the Hapsburg Emperors for many years, was a Serb.

Among the Allied advantages on the Italian Front was superiority in the air. More than six hundred Allied aircraft, Italian and British, caused havoc to the Austrian forces that had crossed the Piave on the first and second days of the battle. On June 16 the British and Italian forces continued their counter-attacks, the British taking 728 Austrian prisoners, and the Italians releasing two hundred of their own men who had been taken prisoner on the first day of the battle. On June 20 the Italians shot down fourteen Austrian aircraft over the Piave. Then, five days after launching their offensive, the Austrians began to withdraw, their retreat made more hazardous by attacks from the air by as many as fifty British aircraft.

By June 24 the last Austrian troops had withdrawn north of the Piave. In the Asiago and Monte Grappa sectors they had failed to break southward into the plain. That day, the German Foreign Minister, Richard von Kühlmann, told the Reichstag that the deputies should not expect 'any definite end to the war from a military decision alone'. The Kaiser, angered by such 'defeatism', dismissed Kühlmann from his post. He was replaced by a senior naval officer, Admiral Paul von Hintze.

On June 17, as American troops still battled on the Western Front with the Germans inside Belleau Wood, Marshal Foch asked General Pershing to transfer five American divisions to reinforce twenty French divisions: one American regiment for each French division. Foch told Pershing that people were asking 'Where are the Americans, and what are they doing?' The French troops were exhausted by the renewed German attacks and needed encouragement. Pershing still refused to disperse his force in this way, telling Foch that the American troops could do 'twice as much' under their own leaders.

Pershing recognised the strain under which the French and British had fought for nearly four years, and the draining effect of their own many previous offensives, as well as of the German offensive that March. He also knew that the three million Allied troops on the Western Front were facing three and a half million Germans. 'The Allies are done for,' he wrote bluntly to Colonel House on June 19, 'and the only thing that will hold them (especially France) in the war will be the assurance that we have enough force to assume the initiative.' America's task, in Pershing's view, was to win the war in 1919. If she could not win it then, the Allies would probably make peace. To ensure an American victory in 1919 he wanted the 800,000-strong American army to be increased to three million, and in a telegram to the War Department in Washington on June 19 he asked for sixty-six American divisions, more than two and a half million men, to be in France by 1 May 1919. This, he wrote, was 'the least that should be thought of'.

The issue of the American troops remained critical. On June 21 the Canadian Prime Minister, Robert Borden, who had crossed the Atlantic earlier that month in a convoy of thirteen ships, bringing more than 30,000 American troops to Britain, wrote to a colleague in Ottawa: 'The military situation in France is very serious and the issue of the War may depend upon the speed with which the American armies can be organised, trained and equipped.' Borden had just agreed to an American request that Canadian officers with their long battle experience should train a portion of the American troops. 'The problem,' he explained, 'is to hold the line on the Western Front until the Americans are ready to strike with substantial force.' The American troops he had seen 'are splendid men and very keen to be in the fight'. The next two months, he warned, 'will be a period of great anxiety during which we must expect a fierce attack'.

Those American troops who were already in action were giving a remarkable account of themselves, new as they were to fighting. On June 26, at Belleau Wood, the Marines who had refused to withdraw three weeks earlier finally gained the wood. More than half of the 10,000 men of the American Marine Brigade had been killed or wounded in the action. In the war cemetery at the edge of the wood are the graves of 2,288 American soldiers and the names of a further 1,060 who have no known grave. In another cemetery a few hundred yards away are 8,624 German graves.

The Germans were impressed by their new adversary. 'The moral effect of our fire-arms did not materially check the advance of the infantry,' a German Intelligence officer had written in the midst of the battle, adding: 'The nerves of the Americans are still unshaken.' After the battle Pershing visited the wounded. Men who had been gassed stood to attention beside their beds with bandages on their eyes: some would never see again. Pershing's biographer recounts a story reported in the *Cleveland Plain Dealer* of how, in a surgical ward, Pershing 'came to the bed of a soldier named Jimmie, who had been operated on the day before and who remarked apologetically through parched lips: "I cannot salute you, sir." Pershing noticed the dent in the sheets where the right arm would normally be. "No," he replied, running his hand lightly through the boy's tousled hair, "it's I that should salute you." '[1]

There were now 800,000 American troops in France, but not one of them was serving in an American army corps, a blow to Pershing's dream and intention. The troops in action were all under French or British corps commanders. Only administration and supply were in American hands. The call for American troops to enter the line had spread beyond France. On June 27 an American infantry regiment landed at the Italian port of Genoa: it would be sent forward into the line by the end of September. Meanwhile, in an advance two days later on the Asiago Front, the Italians regained three mountain peaks and captured more than 2,000 Austrian soldiers. That month the first American was killed on the Italian Front, an American Red Cross ambulance driver, Lieutenant Edward M. McKey.

Black American troops were also arriving in France, including the all-Black 369th Infantry Division. Its members were sent to work as stevedores in the docks, causing them great offence. They then demanded to be sent to the Front, but when it was pointed out that American law apparently forbade them to be stationed alongside white soldiers, they were sent to fight alongside French units. One of their white officers, Hamilton Fish, won the Silver Star.[2]

Many Black American women also volunteered to serve in France as nurses. Only five or six were accepted: neither official policy nor public prejudice was willing to see them tending wounded white soldiers in France. As many as 25,000 white American women volunteers did cross the Atlantic, mostly to work as nurses, some as signallers, typists and interpreters. They received no pay or pension.

On June 27 the British hospital ship *Llandovery Castle*, sailing from Canada, was torpedoed by a German submarine 116 miles off Fastnet Rock. Of the 283 passengers who died, some were fired on while in the water. Only twenty passengers, the occupants of one lifeboat, were saved. Of the ninety-seven nurses and hospital personnel on board, only six survived. Among the dead were all fourteen Canadian nursing sisters on board.

That June, 453 merchant seamen had been drowned when their ships were torpedoed. In the air, 505 Allied aircraft and 153 German had been shot down that month: June 27 saw the first successful parachute jump in

---

[1] Donald Smythe, *Pershing, General of the Armies*, Indiana University Press, Bloomington 1986, page 141. The newspaper article was headed: 'War Nurse Tells of Maimed Doughboy and "Black Jack".'
[2] Hamilton Fish later played a leading part in founding the American Legion, and in establishing the United States Tomb of the Unknown Soldier. Between the wars he was a champion of minority groups. He detested Communism and, on the eve of war in 1939, insisted that Hitler could be trusted. In 1941 he strongly opposed American intervention in the Second World War. He died in 1991, at the age of 102.

action, when a German pilot, Lieutenant Steinbrecher, was shot down by
the British over the Somme, and parachuted to safety.

On the Western Front, the French were seeking to reverse the German
victories of the previous months. The 'state of tension', commented *The
Times*, 'is comparable to that which preceded the former great German
attacks, as that of March 21 and May 27'. On June 30, south of Ambleny,
the French attacked with a new type of $5\frac{1}{2}$-ton tank, adopting the earlier
German tactic of advancing rapidly to their objective on one flank before
turning back to capture the troops in the centre. Only then did they search
for German soldiers hiding in caves, taking a thousand prisoners.

Behind the lines, a new spectre had begun to haunt soldiers and civilians
alike. Starting in June, in both India and Britain, influenza began its
epidemic, and then pandemic course. Reaching the Western Front, it was
to wreak its havoc there. More American soldiers were to die of influenza
in France than by the bullets of the enemy.[1]

A million American troops and military personnel were in France by the
beginning of July 1918. Their supplies were entering French ports at a rate
of 20,000 tons a day. On July 1, showing great bravery, and tenacity,
American troops attacked the village of Vaux, three miles west of Château-
Thierry. Aerial and ground photographs, and information provided by a
local stonemason, helped them take the village with the minimum of loss.

On July 4, American Independence Day, as the culmination of a nation-
wide shipbuilding 'crusade' to build transport ships for the needs of the
Western Front, ninety-five ships were launched in American shipyards,
seventeen of them in San Francisco. That day, President Wilson declared
in a speech at Mount Vernon that the Allies had four main aims: the
'destruction of arbitrary power', national self-determination, national
morality to be like individual morality, and the establishment of a peace
organisation to prevent war.

American troops were in action the Somme on July 4, alongside the
Australians, when more than a mile of ground was gained, the village of
Hamel was captured, and 1,472 German soldiers were taken prisoner. It
was during this attack that the first airborne supply to troops in battle
took place, when British aircraft dropped 100,000 rounds of ammunition
to the Australian machine gunners.

That evening, near Autrêches, the French launched two successive
attacks, gaining 1,300 yards along a three-mile front. 'In one of the quarry
caves common in the district,' *The Times* reported two days later, 'the
French captured the whole of a battalion staff, together with the entire
personnel of the telegraph, telephone, and ambulance sections, down to
the regimental cook.'

On the Italian Front, continued Italian successes along the Piave delta

---

[1] The total number of United States soldiers who were killed in action in 1917 and 1918 was
48,909; those dying of influenza exceeded 62,000.

during the first days of July resulted in 3,000 Austrians being taken prisoner. The second American to be hit on the Italian Front was an eighteen-year-old American Red Cross ambulance driver, Ernest Hemingway. He was wounded by an Austrian mortar shell on the night of July 8, while handing out chocolate to Italian soldiers in a dug-out. He was awarded the Italian Silver Medal of Military Valour. 'This is a peach of a hospital here,' he wrote two weeks later from Milan, 'and there are about eighteen American nurses to take care of four patients. Everything is fine and I am very comfortable and one of the best surgeons in Milan is looking after my wounds.' Fragments of shell had entered his right foot and his knee: several dozen other smaller fragments had struck his thighs, his scalp and his hand.

Hemingway's letter also dwelt on the souvenirs he had acquired: 'I was all through the big battle and have Austrian carbines and ammunition, German and Austrian medals, officers' automatic pistols, Boche helmets, about a dozen Bayonets, star shell pistols and knives and almost everything you can think of. The only limit to the amount of souvenirs I could have is what I could carry for there were so many dead Austrians and prisoners the ground was almost black with them. It was a great victory and showed the world what wonderful fighters the Italians are.' The Italian who was standing between Hemingway and the point of impact of the shell had his legs blown off and died soon afterwards. According to the American official history, before taking care of himself Hemingway 'rendered generous assistance to the Italian soldiers more seriously wounded by the same explosion and did not allow himself to be carried elsewhere until after they had been evacuated'.[1]

Later that month, in New York, Collier's magazine published a photograph, taken four months earlier, of a wounded American, lying on a stretcher in a trench on the Western Front, his head being bandaged by a medic. Although the photograph showed neither blood nor gore, nor any savage wound or ugliness, it nevertheless shocked Americans, who were more used to photographs such as one that showed wounded men propped up comfortably on their hospital beds, one of their number strumming a banjo, watched by smiling fellow soldiers and attentive nurses.

In the Far East, the troops of the Czech Legion, still working their way back to Europe, had reached the Russian Pacific port of Vladivostok, where they overthrew the local Bolshevik administration on June 29. On the following day, in Pittsburgh, with the approval of the United States, Thomas Masaryk signed an agreement on behalf of his fellow-Czechs whereby the Slovaks would be given an autonomous administration, their own law courts, and Slovak would be recognised as their official language and language of education, in a future Czechoslovak State. Two weeks

[1] Hemingway later wrote his own account of the episode in his novel A Farewell to Arms.

later, in the Gregor Hall in Prague, immediately opposite the main Austrian Customs Office, the National Council of Czechoslovakia was established.

With Czech troops in control of Vladivostok, on July 6 the Allies declared the port to be an Allied Protectorate. Woodrow Wilson went so far that day as to suggest the dispatch of 12,000 Japanese troops to 'rescue' the Czechs and enable them to proceed to the European war zones. Japan accepted his suggestion.[1] On the following day, a thousand miles west of Vladivostok, Czech troops defeated the Red Army units near Chita and occupied the Siberian city of Irkutsk. Just as Germany was the dominant power in southern Russia and the Caucasus, the Allies were becoming masters of the Russian Far East and of Siberia. On July 10 the British Government announced that a British regiment would be sailing from Hong Kong to Vladivostok.

Allied anti-Bolshevik sentiment was hardened six days later, when the deposed Tsar, his son and most of his family were murdered at Eka-terinburg.

On July 11 the Germans made their final plans for a renewed assault on the Western Front. Because of the spread of the influenza epidemic among the German troops, the German High Command considered postponing it, but decided to go ahead as planned. 'People have only one more hope, the German Front,' the German Ambassador in Vienna reported to Berlin on July 11, and he added: 'Even a hope in a separate peace does not exist any more.' Austria, which in 1914 had looked to Germany with such confidence to help it ward off the Russians while Serbia was being crushed, had now become Germany's captive ally.

On the Western Front, a new method of gas warfare was being used in the Allied armies. It was a railway train whose wagons were loaded with gas cylinders that could be brought up by narrow gauge railway to the war zone, and the wagons then taken off the rails and pushed manually to within a quarter of a mile of the front. On July 12 more than 5,000 gas cylinders were discharged simultaneously by this method. Donald Grantham was in charge of the attack. Martin Fox, a corporal who had been with the gas companies since their inception, has described it: 'As Zero approached, conditions became eminently suitable. Thus at 1.40 a.m. Grantham "pooped" the whole train successfully. Everybody stood well back as the detonators showered in the explosion. Immediately there ensued a terrific hissing noise as a huge release of gas commenced. The dense, grey cloud made an awe-inspiring sight as it rolled steadily forward, widening as it went. We watched it as it poured over our

---

[1] In an accidental explosion that month, on July 12, the 21,900-ton Japanese battleship *Kawachi* was blown up in Tokuyama Bay. Seven hundred of those on board were killed. Two days later, on July 14 (Bastille Day), 442 French sailors and troops were drowned in the Mediterranean, off Cyrenaica, when a German submarine torpedoed the troop transport *Djemnah*.

own Front Lines and continued across No-Man's Land. Such a threatening cloud as this we had never before witnessed. Over the enemy Lines the gas belt spread wider and wider, engulfing them from sight.'

Captain Grantham was pleased with the results of the multiple attack, noting in his diary: 'I fired train by switch near engine. Magnificent cloud.' Reports of several hundred German casualties confirmed the sense of achievement. But there were hazards for the men who carried out these new methods. On the return journey, noted Corporal Fox, the train set off before everyone was on board. 'I raced toward the front, but it was of no avail. Some of the guards scrambled onto the trucks as the train gathered speed. It rattled homewards across the plain at a frightening rate, with the men clinging on for dear life; they were enveloped in the gas which still issued from the dripping cylinders. Their respirators saved them, though it was a ghastly ride.'

An anonymous member of the gas companies penned an epitaph for their work:

> Science of the ages, the highest arts of man,
> Degraded and prostituted, that Might should take the van,
> Whilst Empire, Justice, Freedom slumbered.
> Then chemist, student, artisan answered Duty's call;
> Our arms, our arts, our poison fumes
> Gained Liberty for all.

American gas companies worked closely with their British opposite numbers. Although neither Pershing nor his Chief of Staff were supporters of gas, there were 3,400 American soldiers operating gas cylinders at the Front by the summer of 1918. But cooperation in the field was often parallel by disputes at the highest level of command. National pride could overshadow even the harsh necessities of the battlefield. On July 14, at a conference at Danny, in Sussex, presided over by Lloyd George, Haig asked for, and was given, the support of the politician in refusing a French request that four British divisions be sent to form part of the French reserve near Vitry-le-François.

Even on English soil, the conflict on the Western Front was not entirely remote. During an afternoon break in the discussion at Danny, those present went for a walk on the South Downs. 'We could hear with great distinctness,' wrote one of the participants, Robert Borden, 'the booming of the guns in France; and it was said that the sound was conveyed through the chalk and water. Thus to be in touch with the terrible realities of the conflict had a very solemn and depressing effect.'

The renewed German attack on the Western Front was launched at midnight on July 14. Its timing had been revealed by a number of German prisoners-of-war, most of them from Alsace. As a result of this Intelligence, French and American artillery were able to bombard the crowded German front-line trenches and jumping-off points for half an hour before the Germans' own bombardment began.[1] Even so the intensity of the German barrage was once again formidable. More than 17,500 rounds of gas shells, totalling thirty-five tons of explosives, were unleashed on the sectors of the front held near Château-Thierry by the American 42nd Division (Rainbow) Division.

When the Germans advanced they found that the French had set up a line of spurious trenches against them, giving the appearance of real obstacles, but in fact lightly manned. The German bombardment had largely expended itself in vain. This ruse had been devised by Pétain. The Germans rapidly overran the false defences, killing the few token defenders who had not already been killed in the bombardment, suicide troops in all but name. The 'real' trenches further back were fully manned, and almost untouched by the shellfire. As the Germans approached the defended lines, they came under heavy French and American fire. 'When they met the dikes of our real line,' one American officer recalled, 'they were exhausted, uncoordinated, and scattered, incapable of going on without being reorganised and reinforced.' That officer was the Chief of Staff of the Rainbow Division, Douglas MacArthur. Later he wrote that, after the battle, he was haunted by 'the vision of those writhing bodies hanging from the barbed wire'.

Despite the ruse that proved fatal to the German plan, as well as to so many German lives, more than a thousand American soldiers were incapacitated by gas in the early hours of July 15. Many were blinded, but only six were killed. Another American killed that day was a pilot, Quentin Roosevelt, a son of the former President Teddy Roosevelt. His plane was shot down near the village of Chamery, five miles east of Fère-en-Tardenois. To this day a plaque marks the spot were he was killed. It was said that, being short-sighted, he mistakenly (and not for the first time) tacked on to the German squadron rather than his own at the end of an aerial engagement. 'Only those are fit to live who do not fear to die,' the former President wrote about his dead son, 'and none are fit to die who have shrunk from the joy of life and the duty of life.' These words were later carved in stone on the Theodore Roosevelt monument in Washington, on an island in the Potomac.

Other monuments give testimony to the fighting of that week. At the village of Marfaux a memorial records the missing New Zealand dead, while at Chambrecy an ancient Roman column stands guard over the cemetery in which those Italian soldiers who fought alongside the French for the defence of Reims fell in action, with their general at their head. The commanders recognised the bravery of their men. 'The German has clearly broken his sword on our lines,' General Gouraud telegraphed to the French XXI Corps, which included the American

[1] As a result of similar prior information provided by British Signals Intelligence (Ultra) in 1943, the Russians were able to bombard the German positions around Kursk several hours before the opening of the third major German offensive of the Second World War.

Rainbow Division. 'Whatever he may do in the future, he shall not pass.'

The day before the July battle began, the Richthofen Squadron, its founder and his successor both having been killed, gained a new chief, Hermann Goering. After shooting down an Allied plane on July 16, his twenty-second victory of the war, he gave himself ten days' leave. That day, in the early hours of the morning, the German bombardment was switched against the French and American forces in the Champagne, where half a million gas shells were fired: 9,000 tons of mustard gas, phosgene and diphenylchlorarsine. The Kaiser was present that morning at the German First Army observation point at Ménil Lepinois, fourteen miles north-east of Reims, to watch the bombardment.

For two days it looked as if the Germans might make the finally decisive breakthrough. In one sector of the front, however, French gunners suc-ceeded in knocking out all twenty of the attacking German tanks. In another sector, 3,600 American troops, outnumbered three to one, fought and held their ground in hand-to-hand combat. In the air, 225 French bombers dropped more than forty tons of bombs on the bridges which the Germans had thrown across the Marne. Twenty-five of the bombers were lost, but the attack continued.

East of Château-Thierry the American 3rd Division blew up every pontoon bridge the Germans threw across the Marne in its sector, gaining for itself the title 'The Rock of the Marne'. As the Germans continued to pour down to the river, American infantrymen and machine gunners were waiting for them, and mowed them down. A German officer later wrote: 'Never have I seen so many dead men, never such frightful battle scenes.' The commander of the 3rd Division, General Joseph T. Dickman, had similar memories of the carnage. By noon on July 16, he later wrote, 'there were no Germans in the foreground of the Third Division except the dead'. The Americans also suffered, despite their success. The horrific nature of the battleground affected victor and vanquished alike, the wounded on both sides being vulnerable and afraid. 'Some of them cursed and raved and had to be tied to their litters,' one American medical officer wrote. 'Some shook violently ... some trembled and slunk away in apparent abject fear of every incoming shell, while others simply stood speechless, oblivious to all surroundings.'

As well as the Americans, Italian troops had been brought to the Western Front to help halt the German attacks. On July 17, when the Germans reached Nanteuil-Pourcy, it was Italian troops who drove them off. At German headquarters the mood was very different from the confidence of March. 'Fairly depressed mood,' noted Colonel Mertz von Quirnheim, of the operations section, and he added: 'Difficult question – what is to happen from now on?' The answer came from the Allied side on the following day, July 18, when Foch launched the Allied counter-attack. It began with a 2,000-gun artillery bombardment along a 27-mile front. More than two hundred tanks took part in the offensive. The German line gave way, being driven in to a depth of four-and-a-half miles. Twenty thousand German prisoners and four hundred heavy guns were captured. Jaulgonne, where the Germans had crossed the Marne six weeks earlier, was retaken by the Americans, who immediately began, with the French, the northward march to Fère-en-Tardenois.

The American area of operations on July 18, entrusted to the 1st and 2nd Divisions, was just to the south of Soissons. It started with a rolling barrage which an American eye-witness, the aviator Eddie Rickenbacker, watched from his plane. The barrage, he later recalled, 'seemed to be tearing up the earth in huge handfuls' as it moved steadily nearer to the German trenches. 'To know that human beings were lying there without means of escape – waiting there while the pitiless hailstorm of shrapnel drew slowly closer to their hiding places – seemed such a diabolical method of torture that I wondered why men in the trenches did not go utterly mad with terror.'

Rickenbacker watched while a shell 'fell directly into the trench in front of me, tearing it open and gutting it completely for a space of thirty feet. The next instant a Boche soldier sprang out of the trench alongside this point and flinging down his rifle proceeded to run for all he was worth back to a safer zone in the rear trenches. Hardly had he gone ten yards when a high-explosive shell lit in front of him. Before I saw the burst of the shell I saw him stop with his arms flung over his head. Next instant he was simply swept away in dust and disappeared, as the explosion took effect. Not a vestige of him remained when the dust had settled and the smoke had cleared away.'

As the German aviator flew on, the American soldiers left their trenches and advanced through the pulverised German lines. The Germans fought with every resource of personal bravery and technical skill to halt the onward march of their new-found enemy. Pershing's biographer cites the diary of Marvin H. Taylor, who recorded reaching a German machine-gun post where 'he encountered a dead German machine gunner seated at his weapon, his hand still on the trigger. He was slumped over, a bullet hole in his forehead and a bayonet thrust in his throat. The gun had an excellent field of fire, and many Americans had died approaching it. Taylor was a humane man, but he laughed aloud at seeing the corpse; it seemed a fit retribution for what the gunner had done to others.'[1]

By nightfall on July 18 the German threat to Paris was over. By the end of the fourth day of the French offensive an estimated 30,000 German soldiers had been killed. Among the French forces taking part was a Foreign Legion regiment, one in four of whose volunteers were killed or wounded that day. One of the Legion's heroes, Sergeant-Major Max Emmanuel Mader, a former German soldier who had fought with the Legion against the Germans since 1914, and had won the Légion d'Honneur in 1917, was in action that week. His right arm and shoulder were

---

[1] Donald Smythe, *Pershing, General of the Armies*, page 156.

blown away by a German shell. As the last rites were being administered to him in the base hospital, and his imminent death was being mourned by his devoted colleagues, he regained consciousness. Surviving a series of operations, he lived to an old age.

Advancing in Flanders on July 19, the British recaptured Meteren, taking three hundred Germans prisoner. On the Soissons Front, the French and American advance continued, with 3,000 more Germans and 150 more guns being taken. The salient the Germans had created with such high hopes in June had been made untenable. On July 21 they abandoned Château-Thierry. 'Never have such demands been made on our men's strength of character, morale and physical endurance,' a German lieutenant, Herbert Sulzbach, wrote in his diary on July 21. 'Brought in over long distances by continuous forced marches, in hot weather and without rest, and after the failure of their own offensive on which they embarked with great expectations, thrown into a defensive battle of a gigantic scale; they do their duty, they fight, they keep going. A dreadful day is drawing to its close; it really got on one's nerves, all this uninterrupted raging and roaring, and one is still alive!'

On July 22 the Germans fell back more than five miles, and were being driven back even further on the 23rd, the day on which British tanks and infantry, advancing two miles on the Somme Front, captured nearly 2,000 German prisoners. The Germans had not been pushed back like this before. On July 15 they had still expected to be receiving Allied peace proposals within two months, with Paris at their mercy. 'That was on the 15th,' the German Chancellor, Georg von Hertling, later wrote. 'On the 18th even the most optimistic among us knew that all was lost. The history of the world was played out in three days.'

On July 22 the Kaiser visited Hindenburg's advanced headquarters at Avesnes, where he was given an account of the failure of the offensive, and of the dramatically successful Allied counter-attack. That evening his companions found him in a deep depression. 'I am a defeated War Lord to whom you must show consideration,' he told them. That night he had a dream that he recounted in the morning to those around him: his royal relatives in England and Russia, as well as every German minister and every general who had been appointed since he had come to the throne in 1888, had appeared before him, holding him up to scorn. Only a single person in his dream, his cousin Queen Maud of Norway, youngest sister of King George V, had shown him any goodwill.

In order to bring the American contribution on the Western Front to the knowledge of the British public, the British Minister of Information, the Canadian-born Lord Beaverbrook, asked the American painter, John Singer Sargent, to go to France and paint a canvas on the theme of British and American troops working together.[1] The 62-year-old Sargent travelled

---

[1] Sargent was in fact born in Florence, to American parents. In January 1915 he had sent back to Germany one of his hitherto prized awards, the Prussian order, Pour le Mérite.

behind the lines, slept in a dug-out, visited the ruins of Ypres and Arras, and at Péronne saw hundreds of German prisoners locked in a cage, ankle-deep in mud. On July 24 he went on what he called 'a joy ride in a tank up and down slopes, over trenches and looping the loop generally'. A row of already obsolete tanks 'made me think of the ships before Troy'. When he came across some American troops they asked him to camouflage his large painter's umbrella. But he found nothing to inspire the painting that was required of him. 'We go on our warpath in several motors,' he wrote in his notebook, and added: 'It is very hard to see anything significant in warfare.'

The significant events were taking place where no Allied painter could go. On July 25 the Royal Air Force dropped almost three hundred tons of bombs behind the German lines in the Amiens sector of the front. On July 26, German troops began their retreat from the scenes of their former victories, pursued on the ground by Allied tanks and cavalry, and continually harassed from the air by Allied pilots. One of those pilots, Major Edward Mannock, was the most highly decorated and successful British pilot of the war, with seventy-two 'kills' to his credit. Taking up a young New Zealander, Lieutenant Donald Inglis, to show him the ropes, Mannock shot down his seventy-third German plane, then broke one of his own rules and flew over the scene of his triumph to inspect the wreckage. As he flew low to see what he had achieved, German soldiers opened fire from their trenches and the plane was brought down, exploding when it hit the ground. Both Mannock and Inglis were killed. For his bravery in action over more than a year, Mannock was awarded the Victoria Cross.[1]

On July 28, American troops entered Fère-en-Tardenois, one of the main towns taken by the Germans in their sweep forward four months earlier. A cemetery was later built near the town, covering more than thirty-six acres, in which are the gravestones of 6,000 American troops, as well as a memorial listing the names of a further 241 who have no known grave.

Advancing eastward from Fère-en-Tardenois, the Americans attacked two German-held villages, Seringes and Sergy. Their enemy was the much-feared Prussian Guard, who counter-attacked repeatedly. Finally the Americans decided on a ruse, withdrawing from Seringes as if they were pulling back altogether. Then, an American newspaper correspondent reported, 'In their ardour the Prussians walked in unwarily.' The Americans, who had withdrawn to three sides of the village, quickly surrounded it. 'The Guards fought desperately to get out – so desperately that not one was taken prisoner. The streets were filled with dead and dying. No hands went up. All fought like tigers. The ruthless Prussians had met the remorseless men from young America. When night fell, after the bloodiest day the

---

[1] The Victoria Cross is almost always won for a specific act of bravery. In the Second World War another aviator, Leonard Cheshire, won his Victoria Cross, like Mannock, for a series of actions over a period of time. In Cheshire's case the award was for his leadership.

Americans had yet known, the Yanks had maintained all their positions.'

The Americans had also taken the village of Sergy, after the Prussian Guard had twice re-entered it and driven them out. 'A great day in American history indeed', the newspaper correspondent concluded. As the Germans retreated, they were still capable of inflicting heavy casualties, and striking back at their pursuers. On the last day of July, in the Neuilly sector, sixty-eight French soldiers were killed and more than 3,000 incapacitated by gas when German artillery fired 340,000 rounds of mustard gas. That day, in London, the Dominion Prime Ministers were discussing the war at a meeting with Lloyd George and other senior ministers. Two of those present, Lord Milner and General Smuts, believed that there would not be enough men under arms in 1919 to support a victorious Allied campaign, and suggested that victory would not come until 1920.

On the other side, when questioned by Count Hertling as to whether the German army could ever take the offensive, Ludendorff replied: 'Five times thus far during the war I had to withdraw my troops, and was still able, in the end, to beat the enemy. Why shouldn't I succeed a sixth time?'

During July 31, a German deserter, found by the French, revealed that his division and several others were pulling back that day. In the early hours of August 2, near Sergy, after the American Rainbow Division had heard across No-Man's Land the rumbling of vehicles on the move, the Chief of Staff of the Division, Colonel Douglas MacArthur, went into the zone between the armies to be confronted only by what he recalled as 'the moans and cries of wounded men', apparently left behind when their comrades-in-arms had withdrawn.

MacArthur estimated that he passed at least 2,000 German corpses. Stopping from time to time to examine the dead and wounded, he identified the insignias of six different German divisions. During his reconnaissance he suddenly saw, in the light of a flare, a German machine gun pointing directly at him. When the crew did not fire, he crawled up to the gun. 'They were dead, all dead – the lieutenant with shrapnel through his heart, the sergeant with his belly blown into his back, the corporal with his spine where his head should have been.' The German front line had been abandoned. For his exploit, MacArthur was awarded his fourth Silver Star. Later that day he led his men in a successful attack on the new German line.[1]

In eight days the Rainbow Division had lost 566 men killed and more than 2,000 wounded. Among the dead was the poet Joyce Kilmer. On

---

[1] As well as MacArthur, other Americans taking part in this counter-offensive included William J. Donovan (who in the Second World War was head of the Office of Strategic Services, the OSS), and another of Theodore Roosevelt's sons, Theodore Roosevelt Jr (who in 1944, in Normandy, was to be the only general to land with the first wave of American troops on D-Day). Also present in the American sector was the French-born Pierre Teilhard de Chardin, later a distinguished Jesuit anthropologist and philosopher, who was serving as a stretcher-bearer, and who won the Légion d'Honneur for his courage at the front.

August 3 the Division went into reserve. Father Francis P. Duffy, its chaplain, who had stayed with the troops throughout the battle, later recalled: 'Back came our decimated battalions along the way they had already travelled. They marched in wearied silence until they came to the slopes around Meurcy Farm. Then from end to end of the line came the sound of dry, suppressed sobs. They were marching among the bodies of their unburied dead.'

Further north, the Germans were fighting hard to retain the town of Soissons. But on August 4 the French, after a fierce struggle, drove them from it, taking 35,000 prisoners and capturing seven hundred guns. This French success was on a scale similar to that, two years earlier, of the German victories on the Eastern Front. Now it was the Germans who had to fall back to new defensive positions. Among the German soldiers who had fought throughout the retreat was Corporal Hitler. On August 4 he was awarded the Iron Cross, First Class, for 'personal bravery and general merit'. This was an unusual decoration for a corporal. Hitler wore it for the rest of his life. The regimental adjutant who recommended him for it, Captain Hugo Guttman, was a Jew.[1]

On the day that Hitler was awarded the accolade of which he was to be most proud, one of his future adversaries, Franklin D. Roosevelt, then United States Assistant Secretary for the Navy, was making his first and only visit to the Western Front. Having come from Washington to Europe to discuss various problems of naval strategy and supply in London, Paris and Rome, he was making a much-desired visit to the scene of action. It was at the village of Mareuil-en-Dôle that what he later called his 'sensitive naval nose' told him he had reached the war zone. The smell was that of dead horses: soon he was passing their carcasses. 'The cleaning-up outfit had not yet sprinkled them with lime,' one of his biographers has written. 'The Boche had held the village the night before, and their corpses were piled up, awaiting burial.'[2] An American artillery battery was shelling the German front line, about four miles distant. Roosevelt fired one of the guns, which was aimed at a railway junction at Bazoches, eight miles to the north. A spotter plane reported that the shell had hit its target. 'I will never know how many, if any, Huns I killed,' was Roosevelt's later comment.

While he was in the war zone, Roosevelt saw an American regiment coming out of the line. He referred to this eighteen years later when, in 1936, he declared in a public speech: 'I have seen war. I have seen war on land and sea. I have seen blood running from the wounded. I have seen men coughing out their gassed lungs. I have seen the dead in the mud. I have seen cities destroyed. I have seen two hundred limping, exhausted men come out of line – the survivors of a regiment of one thousand that

[1] It would seem that Guttman emigrated to Canada after Hitler came to power.
[2] Ted Morgan, *FDR, A Biography*, Simon and Schuster, New York 1985, page 197.

went forward forty-eight hours before. I have seen children starving. I have seen the agony of mothers and wives. I hate war.' Shortly after the war, Roosevelt wrote to a fellow-alumnus who was preparing a World War One tablet for their school: 'I believe that my name should go in the first division of those who were "in service", especially as I saw service on the other side and was missed by torpedoes and shells.'

Leaving the war zone, Roosevelt dined that night at French army headquarters at Château-Thierry. On the following day he went to Nancy to inspect the American Marine Brigade, then made a pilgrimage to the battlefield of Verdun. He visited a battlefield cemetery and the ruins of the village of Fleury. On the way to Fort Douaumont his party was shelled: the German front line was little more than a mile away. During his travels he noted groups of Italian deserters who had been caught, and sent as punishment to work on the roads of France. Then he went on to Rome, before returning to the United States.[1]

In August 5, the sixteenth German Zeppelin was destroyed by a British airman, Captain Robert Leckie, who shot it down in flames over the North Sea, off Cromer.[2] It was the latest type, with seven engines. All twenty-two crew members were killed, including one of the most successful Zeppelin commanders, Peter Strasser, winner of the Pour le Mérite, and holder of the official title of Leader of Airships. A year earlier he had written: 'If the English should succeed in convincing us that the airship attacks had little value, and thereby cause us to give them up, they would be rid of a severe problem, and would be laughing at us in triumph behind our backs.'

Strasser's was the last Zeppelin to be brought down. The defences of Britain's East Coast were so effectively developed, with Warning Control Centres, Home Defence Squadrons, Searchlight Stations in place in an unbroken swathe from Edinburgh to Hove, as to make any Zeppelin raid a virtual suicide mission. Strasser's often-expressed contempt for those defences had not saved him.

On the Western Front, although they were almost exhausted by their sustained efforts during the previous four and a half months, the German troops had not given up the fight. In a counter-attack on August 6, at Morlancourt on the Somme, they regained a considerable amount of ground and took 250 British prisoners. But at the German High Command at Spa there was a sense of failure, a loss of morale and a loss of nerve. On August 7, Colonel Mertz von Quirnheim noted Ludendorff's 'completely inert mood' and he added: 'This spectacle is scarcely impressive. Woe unto us if the Allies should notice our slowdown. We have lost the war if we cannot pull ourselves together.'

---

[1] In 1921 Roosevelt was stricken by polio. From 1929 to 1933 he was Governor of New York State, and from 1933 to his death in 1945, President of the United States.
[2] In 1944, Leckie, then an Air Marshal, served as Chief of the Air Staff of the Royal Canadian Air Force.

Among the American troops in action that week was the 77th Division, the first National Army division to be in action, its troops all coming from New York. This made it as heterogeneous as a division could be, including as it did, in the words of *The Times*, 'a great number of Jews, German and otherwise, Italians, Irish-Americans, Greeks, Poles, Scandinavians, and almost every known people on earth.'

In Russia, Czech troops reached the Volga on July 24, capturing Simbirsk, Lenin's birthplace and the centre of a fertile grain region. Czech troops were now holding a 3,000-mile line from the river Volga to the Pacific. On July 25 they entered Ekaterinburg, where the Tsar had been murdered eleven days earlier. On the following day, French troops joined the British at Murmansk. The Germans were masters of the Russian shores of the Black Sea and the Caspian. The Bolsheviks were struggling to retain power in the centre.

On August 5, a thousand French colonial troops landed at Vladivostok. On the following day, four thousand miles further west, the Czech Legion captured the Volga city of Kazan. That month the struggle for power in Moscow reached a climax when Social Revolutionaries, who wanted the war with Germany renewed, wounded Lenin and murdered two of his closest colleagues. The Bolshevik response was to carry out reprisals on a massive scale. Stalin, sent to the Volga city of Tsaritsyn, conducted a ferocious red terror. 'Systematic mass terror against the bourgeoisie and its agents' was how Stalin himself described it in a telegram to Moscow. Later, in his honour, the city was to bear the name of Stalingrad, but the terror was not forgotten.

In the United States, the shipbuilding 'crusade', which in two years had doubled the number of ships sailing under the American flag, was gaining an extraordinary momentum, aimed at ensuring that, by mid-1919, there would be sufficient naval tonnage for all the Allied shipping needs. On August 5, the first ship was launched at a new shipyard, Hog Island, where marshland had been transformed into fifty, as opposed to the normal five, ship construction bays. The workers at Hog Island had their own bank, post office and weekly newspaper.

At sixteen separate shipyards, from Seattle on the Pacific to Newport News on the Atlantic, ships were being built according to emergency procedures. At Newark, where twenty-eight construction bays were erected in what had been a salt meadow, 150 identical prefabricated ships were built, each of 8,000 tons. At Camden, New Jersey, a 5,000-ton ship was built in twenty-seven days and then fitted out in a further ten. At Harriman, where a special township was built with thirty streets, sixty identical ships of 9,000 tons were built in two years, with twelve ships capable of being built simultaneously at any one time. The slogan of the shipyard workers engaged in this prodigious effort was that of Charles M.

Schwab, the Director-General of America's Emergency Fleet Corporation: 'Shoot ships at Germany and save America.'

On August 7 French, British and Dominion troops prepared for a new assault on the Western Front which was to begin on the following day. Among those who was to be in action was a Newfoundlander, Lieutenant Hedley Goodyear, whose brother Raymond had been killed on the Somme in 1916 and whose brother Stanley had been killed near Ypres in 1917. 'This is the evening before the attack and my thoughts are with you all at home,' Hedley Goodyear wrote to his mother. 'But my backward glance is wistful only because of memories, and because of the sorrow which would further darken your lives should anything befall me in tomorrow's fray.' The attack was to be the the first of what Foch called his 'liberating attacks' against the new German line, aimed at driving its defenders back along a fifteen-mile front. Goodyear understood the importance of the attack, telling his mother: 'A blow will be struck tomorrow which will definitely mark the turn of the tide.... I shall strike a blow for freedom, along with thousands of others who count personal safety as nothing when freedom is at stake.'

As Goodyear had written, the battle was a turning point. He and his fellow-Canadians advanced six miles, taking twelve villages, 5,000 prisoners and 161 guns. In the attack on Gentelles, Goodyear found himself 'early in the fight' the last unwounded officer in his company. 'I had eight machine guns and over a hundred of the best troops in the world at my command. I ordered every gun to open up.... It took us ten minutes to gain superiority of fire.... I thought the moment opportune to charge so I gave the word and the boys went in with bayonets.... I had no mercy – until they quit fighting, then I did not have the heart to shoot them.'

Australian troops were also successful that day, taking seven villages, nearly 8,000 prisoners and 173 guns. Having reached the railway junction at Bazoches, on the river Vesle, American engineers, working under heavy machine-gun fire, prepared a bridge made of tree trunks bound together, on which the American troops were able to cross the five-foot-deep river that had been filled with barbed wire. 'We have reached the limits of our capacity,' the Kaiser told Ludendorff that day. 'The war must be ended.' In the Kaiser's view, however, it had to end at a time when Germany was making progress on the battlefield, so that she could obtain at least a minimum of her 'war aims'.

On August 9, Ludendorff told an army colleague: 'We cannot win this war any more, but we must not lose it.' That day, in a daring 625-mile flight, the Italian aviator Gabriele d'Annunzio spent half an hour circling above Vienna, dropping 200,000 leaflets on the Austrian capital, calling upon its citizens to throw off their 'Prussian servitude'. Also on August 9, the British Government recognised the Czechoslovak National Council 'as the present trustee of the future Czecho-Slovak government'. Britain was the first Allied power to take this step, thus further encouraging the ferment behind the lines in the Hapsburg heartland.[1]

By August 10, the third day of the Allied offensive on the Western Front, 24,000 Germans had been taken prisoner. In the air, British pilots and observers, members of a newly created Army Co-operation Squadron, flew over the rear areas and reported back on the state of the German defences and the movement of German reinforcements. One of these aircraft, piloted by Captain Frederick West, with Lieutenant Alec Haslam as his observer, was attacked by seven German aircraft. West was hit in the leg by three explosive bullets. Almost severed, the leg fell on to the controls. West lifted it off and then, despite continuing German machine-gun fire, got the plane back to base. His report to his commanding officer on the following day was concise: 'Sir, was brought down after uneven flight yesterday at 11.45 a.m. My leg was blown off but managed to do a good landing. One Hun followed me down to twenty-five feet. Haslam wounded in ankle. I lost my left leg. Was operated. Luck to everybody.'

West was awarded the Victoria Cross. Sixty years later he explained: 'I was very young and strong and healthy and had a bit of luck. They amputated my left leg in a chapel in the field. They thought I'd go under.'[2]

That day, August 10, when seven fresh German divisions arrived to take their place in the line, a group of drunken German soldiers shouted at them: 'What do you war-prolongers want?' How long the war would still last, no one could know: it was on August 10 that Churchill told Lloyd George that the Tank Corps, for which he was building the tanks, would need 100,000 men by June 1919. On the following day, Hindenburg and Ludendorff told the new Chief of the Naval Staff, Admiral Scheer, that only German submarines could win the war. 'There is no more hope for the offensive,' Ludendorff told a member of his Staff on August 12. 'The generals have lost their foothold,' and on August 14, at a meeting of the German Crown Council at Spa, he recommended immediate peace negotiations. So too did the King-Emperor Charles, whose senior military adviser warned the Kaiser that Austria-Hungary 'could only continue the war until December'.

Ludendorff's pessimism at Spa was echoed on the following day by one of his most senior army commanders, Crown Prince Rupprecht of Bavaria, who wrote from Flanders to Prince Max of Baden on August 15: 'Our military situation has deteriorated so rapidly that I no longer believe we

[1] United States recognition of the Czechoslovak National Council did not follow until September. Although the Council was based in Paris, French recognition of Czechoslovakia was delayed until October.
[2] West was talking to William Newton Dunn, a Conservative Member of the European Parliament, and the biographer of Air Chief Marshal Sir Trafford Leigh-Mallory, the head of the Army Co-operation Squadron in 1918. West, who was later British Air Attaché to Finland, wrote to me in 1963 about the determination of the Finns before the Second World War to defend themselves against Russia. 'The Finns were ready to fight and die behind every tree.' West had won his Victoria Cross a year after Finland obtained her independence from Russia.

can hold out over the winter; it is even possible that a catastrophe will come earlier.' His greatest worry was the Allies' greatest asset: 'The Americans are multiplying in a way we never dreamed of,' he wrote. 'At the present time there are already thirty-one American divisions in France.'

The German High Command feared defeat even before the end of the year. In London, however, pessimism at the outcome of the battle in 1918 or even 1919 led Lloyd George to prepare a memorandum for the Dominion Prime Ministers, on August 16, setting out his case for delaying the decisive Western Front offensive until 1920. He was only prevented from putting forward this argument to the Dominions, as he had done before, on the last day of July, by colleagues who feared that such an attitude would lead to a relaxation in the vigorous prosecution of the war in the spring of 1919.

The Allied plans for 1919 were gaining momentum. On August 14 and again on the following day, a newly created Inter-Allied Munitions Council met in Paris. The senior American official present was Edward Stettinius, the chief purchasing agent in the United States for the Allied Governments, who was representing the War Department. He agreed that the American army would accept for 1919 a mixture of British and French weapons, and said he would increase the number of troop convoys crossing the Atlantic to Europe in order to make full use of the larger Anglo-French munitions production. A tank factory had already been built in France, at Châteauroux, to manufacture the tanks that the Americans, as well as the British and French, would need in 1919.

Other plans were also in full spate that summer. 'Maeterlinck says the God of bees is the future', wrote Churchill, who represented Britain on the Inter-Allied Munitions Council. 'At the Ministry of Munitions we were the bees of Hell, and we stored our hives with the pure essence of slaughter. It astonishes me to read in these after years the diabolical schemes for killing men on a vast scale by machinery or chemistry to which we passionately devoted ourselves.' In 1918 the Germans possessed 'far the larger supplies of the irritant mustard gas, but our outputs were broadening daily. Although the accidentally burned and blistered at the factories exceeded 100% of the staff every three months, volunteers were never lacking.'

On August 16, eight days after the French went there, American troops landed at Vladivostok. On the following day a British force, having come northward from Persia, entered the city of Baku on the Caspian Sea, a British challenge to both the Germans and the Bolsheviks in the Caucasus. 'If the Entente set up a Tsar in Russia,' General Hoffmann wrote in his diary on August 22, 'then Russia will be closed to us.' Five days later, in a remarkable twist of fate, Germany persuaded Bolshevik Russia to sign a supplementary peace treaty, in which the Bolsheviks promised to fight against the Allies in northern Russia. In what they perceived as their national interest, Lenin and the Kaiser were making common cause, as Stalin and Hitler were to do twenty-one years later, to the day. Under the treaty of 25 August 1918, Germany would have full control of all Red Navy vessels and facilities on the Black Sea.

If Baku were again to be in Bolshevik hands, Russia would have to send Germany one-third of all her oil production. In return, Germany would prevent Finland from attacking Russia. At the beginning of September, the anti-Bolshevik government of the Ukraine signed an economic agreement with Germany.

The withdrawal of Russia from the war, which offered Germany her last chance to maintain her war effort, also served as an inspiration for those everywhere in Europe who hoped that the proletariat of all the warring nations would, at some point, throw down their arms in protest. But in England, pacifists like Clifford Allen, many of whom had been imprisoned for their refusal to serve, recognised the limits of the intellectual appeal to peace. That August, Allen was in Edinburgh where, late one night, he took a tram home. 'Top of tram state of slight drunkenness,' he wrote in his diary, 'and great hilarity and much hatred of Germans. What a public we pacifists have got to face. The war spirit is becoming rapidly identical with that of a spectator of a football match, and infinite hatred.'

Unknown to the British pacifists, not fully understood by the British, French and German Governments, the war was almost over. Such was the habit of warmaking, however, and such was the impact of that 'infinite hatred' over four years, that London, Paris and even Berlin continued to think in terms of renewed offensives, retrenchment, and the war of 1919.

25

The turn of the tide

AUGUST–SEPTEMBER 1918

Considerable Allied advances were made throughout the Western Front in the second week of August, when the Germans were driven from the village of Antheuil-Portes, just north of Compiègne, at the southernmost limit of their June offensive. On 17 August 1918 they faced a French attack on Lassigny, which had likewise been overrun in June. Six times the French attacked Lassigny and were driven off with heavy casualties. But on August 20 they were in the outskirts of the town. That day Foch felt confident enough to write to Clemenceau that he could secure victory in 1919.

Throughout the Western Front, German morale was low. On August 20, a British Second Lieutenant, Alfred Duff Cooper, in action for the first time, reached a railway cutting ahead of his men. 'Looking down I saw one man running away up the other side of the cutting', he wrote in his diary. 'I had a shot at him with my revolver. Presently I saw two men moving cautiously below me. I called to them in what German I could at the moment remember to surrender and throw up their hands. They did so immediately. They obviously did not realise that I was alone. They came up the cutting with their hands up, followed, to my surprise, by others. There were eighteen or nineteen in all. If they had rushed me then they would have been perfectly safe, for I can never hit a haystack with a revolver and my own men were eighty yards away. However they came back with me like lambs, I crawling most of the way to avoid fire from the other side of the railway. Two of them who were Red Cross men proceeded to bind up my wounded.'[1]

A main French objective, Lassigny, was recaptured on August 21. When the offensive was renewed on the Somme that day, Haig expressed his

---

[1] Duff Cooper was then eighteen years old. In 1938, when First Lord of the Admiralty in Neville Chamberlain's Cabinet, he resigned in protest against the Munich Agreement. In the first years of Churchill's wartime administration he was Minister of Information. In 1944, after serving as British Representative to the French Committee of National Liberation, he became British Ambassador to France.

454

confidence that victory could come before the end of 1918. That day,
British forces advanced more than two miles and took 2,000 Germans
prisoner. Yet for every victorious headline there was a sombre subtext.
Four days before the offensive was renewed, the Newfoundland officer
Hedley Goodyear, who had led his men in the attack on August 8, wrote
to his mother: 'Don't worry about me. I'm Hun-proof.' He was killed by
a sniper between Lihons and Chaulnes. His photograph, in uniform, stood
on his fiancée's mantelpiece for the next fifty years.

On August 22, Duff Cooper was again in action. 'When we were
eventually formed up for the attack', he wrote in his diary, 'I had only ten
men, and the climax was reached when I discovered that my Platoon
Sergeant, who had been excellent all the day before, was so drunk as to
be useless. He started the attack with us but we never saw him again until
the next day. The attack itself was beautiful and thrilling – one of the most
memorable moments of my life. The barrage came down at 4 a.m. A
creeping barrage – we advanced behind it. We kept direction by means of
a star, and a huge full moon shone on our right. I felt wild with excitement
and glory and knew no fear. When we reached our objective, the enemy
trench, I could hardly believe it; so quickly had the time passed it seemed
like one moment. We found a lot of German dead there. The living
surrendered.'

Although the German forces outnumbered the Allies on the Somme Front
by forty-two divisions to thirty-two, in the Allied armies there was a sense
of purpose, even exhilaration. One by one the scenes of the most desperate
fighting on the Somme in 1916 were overrun. Thiepval Ridge was captured
on August 24. When, in Berlin, General Wrisberg told the Reichstag Budget
Committee that day that the German High Command was confident of
victory, he was met with 'distainful, mocking laughter'. 'The Germans
would give a great deal to be able to make peace,' Sir Horace Rumbold
reported from Berne to London that day, 'but they are not yet in a frame
of mind to accept our conditions.'

Each day, the Germans continued to be pushed back. On August 25,
Mametz Wood was captured. It had been the scene of ferocious fighting
and heavy casualties in 1916. On August 26 the Germans withdrew ten
miles along a 55-mile front. Only Ludendorff's fear of the complete collapse
of his armies led him to reject an appeal by his senior army commanders
to fall back further. On August 27, British troops overran Delville Wood,
yet another scene of slaughter and defeat in 1916. Two days later the
Germans began the evacuation of Flanders, giving up all the towns and
villages, hills and rivers, that they had conquered four months earlier.
Ludendorff had decided upon a purely defensive strategy, to hold the
Hindenburg Line at all costs.

Nervously, after a meeting of the British War Cabinet in London, Sir
Henry Wilson, then Chief of the Imperial General Staff, sent Haig a
telegram, warning him that 'the War Cabinet would become anxious if we

received heavy punishment in attacking the Hindenburg Line without success'. Caution had become the watchword of the hour on both sides of the line. No one wanted a return to the four years of intermittent but intensive slaughter that had just ended. On August 30 the Austrian Chancellor, Count Burian, informed the authorities in Berlin that Austria intended to open its own negotiations for peace. Mostly from the Italian Front, but also from the Balkans, and from barracks all over the Empire, by the beginning of September there were an estimated 400,000 Austrian army deserters.

The Germans were to be given no respite on the Western Front. As August ended, ferocious Allied assaults were made against them. On August 30 General Mangin, who four years earlier had won a rearguard action with two battalions in the retreat to the Marne, threw a French division against the German forces east of Soissons, driving the Germans back across the river Aisne. That day the Americans captured Juvigny, five miles north of Soissons. On August 31, Australian forces captured Péronne, forcing the Germans to abandon their fortified position on Mont St Quentin. Eight Victoria Crosses were won that day by the attacking force. Two days later, on September 2, Canadian troops attacked the Hindenburg Line at the Drocourt-Quéant switch. In a four-hour battle they broke through the last and strongest German defence line. Seven men won the Victoria Cross in the attack.

Near Arras, on September 2, a 21-year-old lieutenant in the Wiltshire Regiment, Alec de Candole, expressed in verse his hopes for a not-too-distant future:

> When the last long trek is over,
>   And the last long trench filled in,
> I'll take a boat to Dover,
>   Away from all the din;
> I'll take a trip to Mendip,
>   I'll see the Wiltshire downs,
> And all my soul I'll then dip
>   In peace no trouble drowns.
> Away from noise of battle,
>   Away from bombs and shells,
> I'll lie where browse the cattle,
>   Or pluck the purple bells;
> I'll lie among the heather;
>   And watch the distant plain,
> Through all the summer weather,
>   Nor go to fight again.

Two days after writing these lines, Lieutenant de Candole was killed in a bombing raid on German-held trenches.

*

66 Hindenburg, the Kaiser and Ludendorff study a map.

67 The Isonzo Front after Caporetto: Italian dead in a trench near Cividale. This photograph was taken when the Germans overran the position on 26 October 1917.

68 The Western Front, 1917: lifting the entrance to a First Aid Station that had been hit by a shell.

69 The Western Front, 1917: wounded men at an Advanced Dressing Station.

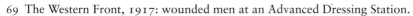

70 Peace in the East: the Russian delegation (Joffe, Karakhan and Trotsky, in dark coats) arrives at Brest-Litovsk on 7 January 1918, after the New Year break in the negotiations.

71 War in the West: the German offensive of 21 March 1918. A German artillery piece crossing a destroyed British trench. German cavalrymen watch. In the foreground, a dead British defender.

72 German and British wounded waiting to be evacuated near Bapaume, 22 March 1918.

73 Soldiers blinded by German gas reach an Advanced Dressing Station near Béthune, April 1918. Each man has his hand on the shoulder of the man in front of him.

74 Temporarily vanquished: three British prisoners-of-war, watched by their German captors, near Amiens, May 1918.

75 Would-be victors: Joffre, Poincaré, King George V, Foch and Haig at Beauquesne, August 1918.

76 The Meuse–Argonne battlefield photographed from the air. American soldiers move forward along
their trenches, surrounded by shellholes.

77 British soldiers advance through a wood during the battle in Tardenois, July 1918.

78 Dead German soldiers in a sunken road that was strongly held by German machine gunners, near
Drury, during the Battle of the Drocourt-Quéant Line, September 1918.

79 The Western Front: American soldiers at the war's end, the eleventh hour of the eleventh day of the eleventh month.

80 An American sailor, an American Red Cross nurse and two French soldiers (on either side of them) celebrate the signing of the Armistice, Vincennes, 11 November 1918.

On September 3, Foch gave the order for continual attacks along the whole length of the Western Front. By contrast, that same day, Ludendorff issued a secret order to stop defeatist talk by German soldiers on leave. 'Public feeling in Berlin is not good,' General Hoffmann noted in his diary. Three days later, on September 6, the German forces completed their evacuation of the Lys Salient. On September 8 Ludendorff ordered the St Mihiel Salient to be evacuated. He did so just as the French and Americans were preparing to launch a massive attack on the salient.

By the time of Ludendorff's order to withdraw, the Allies had assembled more than 3,000 guns and 40,000 tons of ammunition for the attack. To provide for those who would inevitably be wounded, sixty-five evacuation trains had been assembled in railway sidings, and 21,000 beds made available in hospitals. To take the troops, guns and ammunition forward, fifteen miles of road had been reconstructed using 100,000 tons of crushed stone, and 45 miles of standard-gauge and 250 miles of light-gauge railways were built.

Even as the St Mihiel offensive was in its final days of preparation, Foch and Haig were setting their own strategic sights on a more ambitious plan, a breakthrough on the Ypres and Somme Fronts. This meant that the three hundred heavy tanks Pershing believed Haig would transfer to him for the St Mihiel offensive could not be spared, while the French produced only 267 of the 500 light tanks Pershing requested from them. The successes of the previous month had encouraged Haig and Foch to think beyond a limited conquest of trench lines, or the straightening out of a salient. During August, Britain and France, and the Americans, had captured 150,000 German soldiers, 2,000 guns and 13,000 machine guns. The British and French hoped, by an offensive to be launched at the end of September, to achieve even more. Crossing to London, Haig asked the War Office on September 10 for mounted men, and all forms of munitions designed to increase mobility, for a new type of war, a war of movement, which he anticipated in the 'near future'.

In Germany on September 10, rousing himself from weariness and depression, the Kaiser spoke to the munitions workers at Krupp's, in Essen. He intended his speech to rouse their enthusiasm for the war, but when he said that anyone spreading false rumours or circulating anti-war leaflets ought to be hanged, the workers were silent.

On September 11 the Americans began their final preparations to drive out the Germans out of the St Mihiel Salient. A few days earlier German artillerymen had withdrawn some of their heavy guns from the woods above the town. The German High Command had been deceived by a deliberate American trick into believing that the main attack would come elsewhere, against Mulhouse. A copy of part of the operational orders for the attack on Mulhouse had been thrown into a wastepaper basket at Belfort and, as intended, had been found by a German agent and interpreted 'correctly', much to the Americans' advantage.

457

The battle was nevertheless to be a fierce one. 'American tanks do not surrender so long as one tank is able to go forward,' Lieutenant-Colonel George S. Patton, Jr, informed his men on September 11. 'Its presence will save the lives of hundreds of infantry and kill many Germans.'[1] When the battle began on September 12, more than 200,000 American troops, supported by 48,000 French, moved forward in pouring rain along a twelve-mile front. The lack of British and French tanks proved no obstacle to success. During the advance, the American gunners fired 100,000 rounds of phosgene gas shells, incapacitating 9,000 Germans, and killing fifty. In the air, the largest ever number of aircraft were in combat, with 1,483 American, French, Italian, Belgian, Portuguese and Brazilian planes, all under American command, in action above the battlefield.

The Germans had no way of matching these numbers, or the freshness and zeal of the Americans, many of whom were in action for the first time. 'Get forward there,' Colonel William 'Wild Bill' Donovan of the Rainbow Division exhorted his men, 'what the hell do you think this is, a wake?' Within forty-eight hours the Americans had captured 13,000 prisoners and two hundred guns. Prisoners could be captured in unusual ways. At Bouillonville, an American soldier, Sergeant Harry J. Adams, saw a German run into a deep dugout. He had only two bullets left in his pistol. Firing both of them into the dugout entrance, he called on the man to surrender. Out the German came, followed by another and, to the amazement of Adams, who now had no more bullets, by more and more men, until all three hundred occupants of the dugout had surrendered to him. Armed only with his empty pistol, he marched them back to the American lines. When the column was first seen approaching, it was thought to be a German counter-attack.

The German High Command was astounded by the swift initial American success. An officer who visited Ludendorff on September 12 found him 'so overcome by the events of the day as to be unable to carry on a clear and comprehensive discussion'. The Americans had not won their victory without considerable loss. In the American military cemetery at Thiaucourt, in which the dead of the St Mihiel battle were gathered after the war, are 4,153 graves, with a further 284 names on the wall of the missing.

At midday on September 13, French troops entered St Mihiel. When Pétain went to Pershing's headquarters a few hours later, the two men went into the town together. Pétain explained to the inhabitants that, although it was French troops who had liberated the town, they had done so as part of the American First Army, whose soldiers had made liberation

[1] As a tank commander in the Second World War, Patton won high battle honours in Tunisia and Sicily. In 1944 he commanded the United States Third Army, which advanced from Brittany, around Paris, along the Marne, through the region he had fought in 1918, across the Rhine, through northern Bavaria and into Czechoslovakia. From May to October 1945 he was Military Governor of Bavaria. He died after his 1938 Cadillac limousine collided with a military lorry in December 1945.

458

possible by their victories on the flanks. Among those liberated was an Irish girl, Aline Henry, who had been trapped there for four years, having gone to learn French in the town in June 1914. To the shock of the inhabitants, the Germans had taken away with them all the local males between the ages of sixteen and forty-five, causing consternation. But after marching them ten miles to the east, they had let them return. On entering Thiaucourt that evening the Americans captured Professor Otto Schmeernkase, described in a French communiqué as 'the German gas specialist and the exploiter of chlorine gas as a form of civilised torture'.

Entering the town of Essey that same day, the Americans were surprised to find, as MacArthur, then a brigade commander, recalled, 'a German officer's horse saddled and equipped standing in a barn, a battery of guns complete in every detail, and the entire instrumentation and music of a regimental band'. The Americans found it difficult to persuade the inhabitants of the town to come out of their hiding places: they did not know that United States soldiers were in the war.

Going forward that night through the German lines, accompanied by his adjutant, MacArthur was able to see, through binoculars, the city of Metz. It did not seem well defended. He at once proposed to his superiors a surprise attack, the continuation of the St Mihiel offensive to this further objective, and prize. 'Here was an unparalleled opportunity to break the Hindenburg Line at its pivotal point', he later wrote. MacArthur was supported in this view, and in the desire to continue the advance into Metz, by the Operations Officer of the First Army, Colonel George C. Marshall. But Foch, Pétain and Haig were already making their plans for a co-ordinated Allied offensive elsewhere in two weeks' time. They did not want a 'premature' offensive or distraction from what was to be a major battle.

The straightening of the St Mihiel Salient, and the liberation of St Mihiel itself, were successes enough. The salient had been in German hands for four years. It had earlier resisted two French attacks on it. As a victory, it was seen without blemish. 'It is as swift and neat an operation as any in the war,' wrote the *Manchester Guardian*, 'and perhaps the most heartening of all its features is the proof it gives that the precision, skill, and imagination of American leadership is not inferior to the spirit of their troops.' The American soldiers had at last obtained the recognition they deserved. To his last days, however, MacArthur believed that the victory at St Mihiel ought to have been followed up at once, and Metz taken. 'Had we seized this opportunity,' he later wrote, 'we would have saved thousands of American lives lost in the dim recesses of the Argonne Forest.'

MacArthur's keenness was in contrast to the many problems that even the victory at St Mihiel revealed. On the day that he was advocating a further advance, his divisional Chief of Staff was warning that the men were not being adequately fed or clothed. Logistical problems forced Colonel Patton's tanks to wait thirty-two hours for petrol supplies to cover the nine miles. On September 15, when Clemenceau travelled to the St Mihiel salient, he was

angered by the chaos and traffic jams on the roads. 'They wanted an American army,' he later wrote, with scorn. 'They had it. Anyone who saw, as I
saw, the hopeless congestion at Thiaucourt will bear witness that they may
congratulate themselves on not having had it sooner.' Most ominous of all
for the next offensive, a mere two weeks away, a German intelligence report
concluded: 'The Americans have not yet had sufficient experience, and are
accordingly not to be feared in a great offensive. Up to this time our men had
too high an opinion of the Americans.' St Mihiel had been a victory, but
the 'great offensive' was yet to come.

On the French and British sectors, and against the Hindenburg Line,
small attacks were launched during the St Mihiel offensive, and a series of
German counter-attacks were repulsed. But the German forces were not
pulling back. Rumours of Allied successes could also prove to be false:
the village of Pagny-sur-Moselle, the southernmost point of the fortified
German defences, which was reported to have been overrun by the Americans during the St Mihiel offensive, remained under German control until
the end of the war. Near the village war memorial is a plaque to a fifteenyear-old boy executed by the Germans 'without reason' two months after
the outbreak of war. The memorial itself depicts a soldier and his dog.

That August and September, Russia had become a focus of concern once
more for the Allies. On August 31 the British Naval Attaché in Petrograd,
Captain Cromie, had been murdered by the Bolsheviks inside the Embassy
building. On September 2 the Bolsheviks announced the institution of Red
Terror. In Petrograd alone, 512 opponents of the regime were executed.
On September 11, 4,500 American troops landed at Archangel. That day,
near Murmansk, British troops, after a successful action against the Red
Army, advanced twenty-five miles along the river Dvina.

On September 14 the Allies launched their offensive on the Salonica Front,
signalled by a six-hour artillery bombardment of the Bulgarian positions.
At German headquarters in Skopje, sixty miles to the north, the sound of
the guns could just be heard, a distant murmur above the quiet of the
morning. As had so often happened on the Western Front, however, the
artillery fire, while destroying the enemy wire, left his machine-gun nests
and artillery points relatively unharmed. A Serbian assault up the steep
Vetrenik mountain was successful, the final assault, by bayonet, being
carried out alongside French and Senegalese troops.

That day the Austrians asked the Allied powers, the United States and
the neutrals to agree to 'a confidential and non-committal exchange of
views' on neutral soil, with a view to seeing if peace might be possible.
The United States rejected this invitation at once, Britain and France soon
after. Even the German Government was annoyed by it. The war would
go on, wearing down the life-energies of millions. As an example of this
war weariness, the pacifist Clifford Allen, who saw the Assistant Secretary
to the British Labour Party, Jim Middleton, on September 14, wrote in his

diary: 'Jim is clearly broken by the sorrow of the war. He is almost haunted by the sight of train-loads of soldiers with their kit and helmets leaving Victoria and Waterloo and thundering past his home at Wimbledon. He has lost all his mirth and humour.'

As the fighting continued in Macedonia throughout September 15, a new feature in battle was a Yugoslav Division, an earnest of the determination of the South Slavs – Slovenes, Croats, Serbs, Bosnians, Montenegrins and Macedonians – to unite territorially when the Austrians had been driven out of Laibach, Agram, Belgrade, Sarajevo, Cetinje and Skopje. On crossing the former Graeco-Serbian frontier on September 15, the soldiers of this division momentarily broke off the assault to embrace each other, and also to embrace the French troops fighting with them. They were ordered back into action: the battle was far from over.

That day 36,000 Serbs, French and Italians were in action against 12,000 Bulgars and Germans. So tenacious were the Bulgarian machine gunners, however, that the French used flamethrowers, for the first time on the Salonica Front, to dislodge them, driving the defenders from three mountain peaks. On the following day, September 16, the commander of the Bulgarian Second Army, General Lukov, expressed positive interest in the Austrian peace feelers. Tsar Ferdinand, his King and Commander-in-Chief, replied: 'Go out and get killed in your present lines.'

Two Bulgarian regiments mutinied on September 16. They had no intention of fighting any longer. The German commander, General von Scholtz, one of the heroes of Tannenberg, ordered his fellow-German, General von Reuter, who was in command of the reserves, to go with his staff officers to the battlefield and, pistol in hand, to stop the Bulgarian rout. When it was clear that most of the Bulgarians would fight no longer, von Scholtz ordered a limited retreat. An appeal to Hindenburg for reinforcements was passed on to the Austrian Chief of Staff, General Arz von Straussenburg, but he had no men to spare for that distant, almost forgotten theatre of war. The only force available, which would take at least two weeks to arrive, was a German brigade then in the Crimea, which was ordered to go by sea to the Bulgarian port of Varna, then overland through Bulgaria and on into Macedonia.

On September 18, British and Greek troops attacked at Lake Doiran. There were set-backs, however: the men of one British battalion, the South Wales Borderers, having reached the summit of the Grand Couronné, were forced to retreat as a result of intense Bulgarian machine-gun fire, and ran into a British gas cloud. Their commanding officer, Lieutenant-Colonel Burges, who had been wounded three times and taken prisoner, was awarded the Victoria Cross. In an attack on Pip Ridge by three British battalions, the Bulgarian machine-gun fire was again so intense that only one in three of the attackers returned to the ravine from which they had started. At one point, Bulgarian artillery shells started a large grass fire which, fanned by the wind, forced the Greek Crete Division down from the mountainside.

After two days' fighting the town of Doiran was in Allied hands, as was the Petit Couronné, but the Grand Couronné was still held by the Bulgarians. Then, on September 20, the Bulgarian army was ordered to retreat. The British, French and Greeks, advancing to the positions they had attacked in vain four days earlier, found them deserted. Pip Ridge, the Grand Couronné and Devil's Eye, which for two years had glowered over the Allied lines, mocking all attempts to take them, were harmless and worthless. The dead of the previous days' unsuccessful battle lay, unburied, where they had fallen.

Two days later Serbian troops were fourteen miles north of the starting line. French Moroccan troops, the Spahis, rode forward on their stallions. The town of Prilep was entered on September 21, having been evacuated by the Germans and Bulgarians. The Serb inhabitants carried their first liberators on their shoulders to what had, a few hours earlier, and for the past three years, been German headquarters.

The Bulgarian defeats in Macedonia led to unrest in the Bulgarian capital, Sofia, and a mutiny among the garrison there. On September 23 there was unrest in three more Bulgarian towns, where Soviets were established by revolutionary students. Loyal Bulgarian officer cadets were sent to disperse the mutineers in Sofia (just as officer cadets had been called upon to sustain the old regime in Petrograd), assisted in their task by the German division that had just reached Bulgaria from the Crimea, too late to affect the course of the battle in Macedonia.

On September 25 British forces entered Bulgaria. Two days later a Bulgarian republic was declared in the small manufacturing town of Radomir, with the peasant leader, Alexander Stamboliisky, being declared President. Despite the support of 15,000 soldiers, however, he was unable to seize power in the capital: after three days of fighting at Vladaya, ten miles south of Sofia, the Republican forces were defeated and Stamboliisky (who in 1919 became Prime Minister under King Boris) fled into hiding.

While this abortive revolution was in progress, the Macedonian capital, Skopje, which Bulgaria had so coveted for itself, fell to the French. The Spahis, commanded by General Jouinot-Gambetta, had covered the last fifty-seven miles to it in six days. Jouinot-Gambetta was the nephew of Léon Gambetta, who in 1870 had left the besieged Paris in a balloon, to organise the resistance of provincial France against the German invaders. Now it was the Germans who were in retreat, all hope of holding the Balkans shattered, the southern approaches of the heartland of the Central Powers virtually open to an Allied advance. Chance seemed to favour the victors: a newly despatched Austrian division, the 9th, was only fifty miles from Skopje by rail when Jouinot-Gambetta and his Spahis entered the city unopposed.

On September 16, President Wilson rejected the Austrian request for peace talks. Clemenceau rejected it on the following day. A separate German peace offer to Belgium, on the basis of no claims to be made by Belgium for restitution or indemnity, was rejected by the Belgians on September 19. On the Western Front, the Allies had continued to advance. In the seven days up to September 24, the British Expeditionary Force took 30,000 prisoners, more than in any previous week of the war. Speaking to four hundred submarine officers on September 25, the Kaiser railed against treason. It was only two weeks since one of his submarines had, in pursuance of his policy of unrestricted submarine warfare, torpedoed the Union Castle liner *Galway Castle* without warning in the English Channel: 154 lives were lost.

In Palestine, on September 17, an Indian sergeant deserted from Allenby's army and crossed into the Turkish lines north of Jerusalem. There would, he said, be a major offensive in two days' time. The Turkish commanders, among them Mustafa Kemal, believed him, but Liman von Sanders did not, and no special preparations were made. At midnight on September 19 the British artillery bombardment began. Then, at dawn on the 20th, Allenby resumed the northward offensive that had ended a year earlier with the capture of Jerusalem. Within a few hours hours his infantrymen had broken the Turkish defence lines and his cavalrymen were advancing rapidly northward through the coastal plain.

Air power proved an important part of Allenby's new advance. For two hours that morning the Royal Air Force and Royal Australian Air Force bombed the German and Turkish telephone exchanges and telegraph offices at Afula, Nablus and Tulkarm, breaking all contact between General Liman von Sanders and his commanders. The main German airfield, at Jenin, was also put out of action. For seven days, as Allenby's cavalry advanced, the bombing of roads, railways and troop concentrations disrupted all the Turkish and German defensive plans.

On September 20 Allenby's troops entered the Jezreel Valley, and in two days' fighting took 7,000 prisoners. The Turks were demoralised and eager to give up the fight. At Afula, on the Haifa-Damascus railway, a Indian cavalry regiment charged the Turkish position, killing fifty and taking 500 prisoners for the loss of one man wounded and twelve horses killed. Near Megiddo, the biblical Armageddon, where the Turks were ordered to make a stand, the only shots fired were from nine German riflemen. Far from home, these soldiers were silenced by two machine guns. The British cavalrymen then rode on to Nazareth, where, in the early hours of September 21, the garrison of 3,000 was taken captive. The advancing army had covered forty miles in a single day.

Von Sanders fled Nazareth in his pyjamas. The Turks, lacking the will or means to resist, fled northward and eastward. That day two columns of Turkish troops were retreating, one from Tulkarm and the other from Nablus, through the hills and defiles of Samaria. Both columns were attacked by British and Australian aircraft. One Australian history records, of the Turks who were trying to reach Nablus from Tulkarm, in a column some two miles long: 'Pilot after pilot, flying in perfect order, dropped his bombs, and then, assisted by the observers, raked the unfortunate Turks with machine guns. Their ammunition exhausted, the airmen sped back to their aerodrome for more, and returned again to the slaughter. Some pilots made four trips on that day.'[1]

Further east, an even more intense air raid was mounted that day on the Turks trying to reach the river Jordan from Nablus. It was the most devastating aerial attack of the war. More than fifty aircraft bombed and machine-gunned the Turks and their supply column as they fled down the narrow defile of the Wadi Fara. More than nine tons of bombs were dropped, and 56,000 machine-gun rounds fired, as the Turks struggled to reach the river. The bombers first struck at the vehicles at the head of the column, so that the rest had to come to a halt. Then they methodically destroyed the long line of stationary vehicles and the panic-stricken men who were machine-gunned from the air as they tried to escape down the steep wall of the wadi, or to climb to its top.[2]

On the following day, September 22, a second aerial attack was made on the Turks descending to the Jordan down the Wadi Fara, when a further four tons of bombs were dropped and 30,000 machine-gun rounds fired from the air. 'At one part of the road,' the Royal Air Force historian, H.A. Jones, has written, 'lorries, abandoned in motion, had crashed forward into guns which had been carried with their teams into other transport wagons, and the accumulation had gone tearing on, shedding lorries and guns over the precipice on its way, until at last it had been brought to a standstill by its own weight. Along the length of the defile lay the torn bodies of men and animals.' Some of the pilots who bombed the retreating Turks became so nauseated by what they saw from the air that they asked to be spared any further sorties.

The Turks had been overwhelmed by British air power and by the speed of the Allied cavalry. How many prisoners had been taken, Allenby asked the commander of the Desert Mounted Corps on September 22. On being told that 15,000 had been captured, he laughed and told the commander: 'No bloody good to me! I want 30,000 from you before you've done'. His wish was granted. On September 23, five hundred of his horsemen captured the port of Haifa and, galloping northward, entered the crusader city of Acre. That day, in the Wadi Fara, a third bombing attack was made on the Turkish troops trying to reach the river Jordan. More than six tons of bombs were dropped and 33,000 machine-gun rounds fired. Among the vehicles smashed up in the three-day bombing attack were fifty lorries, ninety guns, and 840 four-wheeled horse-drawn vehicles. Hundreds of Turkish soldiers had been killed. Death from the air had assumed a new dimension.

---

[1] H.S. Gullett and Chas Barrett, *Australia in Palestine*, Angus and Robertson, Sydney 1919, page 36.
[2] That same day, on the Salonica Front, more than seven hundred Bulgarian troops were killed when they too were attacked by the Royal Air Force, as they tried to make their escape back into Bulgaria through the Kosturino defile.

On September 25, Australian and New Zealand cavalrymen crossed the river Jordan and entered Amman, on the Berlin-Baghdad railway. In all, 2,750 cavalrymen took part in the attack. They captured 2,563 Turkish prisoners, bringing the Egyptian Expeditionary Force's total number of prisoners, in a single week, to 45,000. Angrily, a captured German officer told his interrogators: 'We tried to cover the Turks' retreat but we expected them to do something, if only to keep their heads. At last we decided they were not worth fighting for.'

Half an hour before midnight on September 25, less than two weeks after the start, and only ten days after the finish of the St Mihiel offensive, thirty-seven French and American divisions launched a new and even more ambitious offensive. It was against the Argonne Forest and along the river Meuse. As part of the preliminary bombardment that night, the American Expeditionary Force fired eight hundred mustard gas and phosgene shells, incapacitating more than 10,000 German troops and killing 278. Almost 4,000 guns were in action, 'none of them', one American historian has commented, 'made in America'.[1]

Among the American battery commanders was Captain Harry S. Truman. 'I fired 3,000 rounds of 75 ammunition from 4 a.m. to 8 a.m.,' he later recalled. 'I slept in the edge of a wood to the right of my battery position on Friday night. If I hadn't awakened and got up at 4 a.m. I would not be here, because the Germans fired a barrage on my sleeping place!'

The six-hour bombardment continued throughout the night. Then, at 5.30 on the morning of September 26, more than seven hundred tanks advanced, followed closely by the infantry, driving the Germans back three miles. The artillery that had been so effective during the night moved forward behind the advance. 'As we marched on a road under an embankment', Truman recalled eighty years later, 'a French 155-millimetre battery fired over my head and I still have trouble hearing what goes on when there is a noise.'

By the morning of September 27, more than 23,000 German prisoners had been taken. That day, near Cambrai, the British Expeditionary Force attacked the Hindenburg Line. More than a thousand aircraft supported the attack, with seven hundred tons of bombs being dropped, and 26,000 machine-gun rounds fired from the air. By nightfall the attacking forces had taken 10,000 prisoners and two hundred guns. Even by the standards of the Western Front, the scale of the German losses was astounding: 33,000 prisoners in one day. But the fighting in the Argonne Forest showed that the German army would not give up, and the Americans suffered considerably from the tenacious defence that was offered them. As the American soldiers put it, 'Every goddam German there who didn't have a

[1] Donald Smythe, *Pershing: General of the Armies*, Indiana University Press, Bloomington 1986, page 195.

machine gun had a cannon.' One American division, thrown into a panic by a German counter-attack, fell back in disorder.

By former Western Front standards the Americans were successful. Montfaucon, which Pétain had believed could hold out until the winter, was taken on September 27, and advances were made of up to six miles. But the plan had been far more ambitious, making the set-back all the more galling.

On September 28 the British launched Haig's massive offensive against the Germans in the Ypres Salient: the Fourth Battle of Ypres. Five hundred aircraft took part. Among the New Zealand troops in action that day, at Gheluvelt, was the nine-times-wounded General Freyberg, who wrote to a friend: 'I commanded my Brigade from a horse (an ugly white German one) and advanced under a barrage on it until it was killed.' The advance on the ground was rapid, with Wytschaete falling during the day, and 4,000 Germans surrendering. Belgian troops were also in action on September 28, recapturing Passchendaele, scene of such terrible slaughter a year earlier, with little loss.

That evening Ludendorff pressed upon Hindenburg that Germany must seek an immediate armistice. What neither of them knew was that Lloyd George and his Secretary of State for War, Lord Milner, still not convinced that the speed of the British advance meant that Germany could be beaten, were insisting that Haig reduce British commitments to the offensive in order to preserve his manpower for the battles of 1919. In Britain, the focus on those battles was intensifying. 'I shall never forget going through a large workshop in the North of England late in September 1918,' a munitions expert, George Dewar, later wrote, 'and witnessing the making and testing by German rifle-fire of the plates of our new type of tank, Mark VIII; thence passing on to another workshop in the same district and witnessing the production and the testing of the engine to drive this super-tank. Mark VIII was destined never to go into action; but had the war continued, Great Britain would have assembled and despatched to the Front large numbers of that great type by the early spring of 1919.'

On the Salonica Front, more than 10,000 Bulgarian and German soldiers had been taken prisoner in the third week of September. On September 28 Bulgaria, with British and Greek troops already on her soil, began armistice talks with the French and British in Salonica. She was the first of the Central Powers to succeed in calling off the fight. At Spa, Ludendorff was insistent in his discussions with Hindenburg that Germany too must ask for an armistice with the Allies. On the following morning, September 29, the two German military leaders, the once feared combination that at different times had so nearly defeated all its enemies, went to the Kaiser and told him that the war could not go on.

Ludendorff and Hindenburg explained to the Kaiser that the problem was not only the German soldiers' will and ability to fight, but also President Wilson's deep reluctance to negotiate in any way with the Kaiser himself or his military chiefs. Grasping not only the nettle of military defeat, but also that of political democratisation, the Kaiser signed a proclamation establishing a Parliamentary regime. In the space of a single day, Germany's militarism and autocracy were all but over.

The battles continued, however, nowhere more fiercely than on the Meuse-Argonne Front. On September 29, the fourth day of the battle, the American forces were brought to a halt, partly by the unflagging German defence, partly by the incredible chaos that had developed in their lines of supply and communication. 'His soldiers were dying bravely,' a French visitor to Pershing's headquarters noted, 'but they were not advancing, or very little, and their losses were heavy. All that great body of men which the American army represented was literally struck with paralysis.'

Paul Maze, while visiting an American battalion headquarters that day on a reconnaissance task, saw a group of American soldiers who appeared to be falling back. He went forward on his motor-bike to investigate. 'They were indeed retiring,' he later wrote, 'but simply because they were not in touch with anybody; they had no news, and most of their officers had been killed in the advance. I made some of them stay where they were and place their machine-guns facing the battle, then ordered the rest to go forward and rejoin their comrades, which they immediately did. They were not in any sort of panic, but had merely sauntered back for want of instructions.'

Paul Maze returned to the battalion headquarters to tell them there about these men. 'To my amazement I found the place shattered as if by an earthquake. Three corpses lay there partly covered by a sack. They were the sentry, who had been standing at the door of the dug-out, and two of the officers with whom I had spoken before I left. Down below the Colonel sat alone, mopping his brow. "Say, Captain, this certainly is war," he commented as I entered.'

Among the artillery batteries in action on September 29 was Harry Truman's. 'Fired on three batteries', he later recalled, 'destroyed one and put the other two out of business. The regimental colonel threatened me with a court martial for firing out of the Thirty-fifth Division sector! But I saved some men in the Twenty-eighth Division on our left and they were grateful in 1948!'[1]

The congestion of essential supply vehicles behind the American lines that day was such that when Clemenceau drove towards Montfaucon, on his way to the French Fourth Army, his path was completely blocked by American trucks, some of whose drivers told him they had been held up by the traffic jam for two nights. Whatever inconvenience American

[1] In 1948 Truman was elected President of the United States, the position to which he had succeeded (as Vice-President) on the death of Roosevelt in 1945.

transport confusion might have on Clemenceau, however, America's contribution had made its mark on the German High Command. On September 30, Ludendorff told General Hermann von Kuhl: 'We cannot fight against the whole world.'

Hostilities on the Bulgarian Front ended at noon on September 30. With Bulgaria in turmoil, Macedonia liberated, and any chance of German reinforcements ended, the Bulgarian delegates then at Salonica, including General Lukov who had wanted to seek an armistice two weeks earlier, had no other course but to accept the terms they were offered: the evacuation of all Greek and Serbian territory, the surrender of all arms and weapons of war, the evacuation of all German and Austrian troops, Allied occupation of strategic points inside Bulgaria and use of the Bulgarian railroads to advance northward, and the almost total demobilisation of the Bulgarian army.

The Bulgarian collapse was a blow to Germany and Austria, both of which were suddenly cut off from all land links with their ally Turkey. The way was also opened for an Allied advance up the Danube. In London and Paris there was great excitement at the thought of Germany becoming vulnerable through the defeat of her allies. 'The first of the props had fallen,' commented the British Cabinet Secretary, Sir Maurice Hankey.

On the Western Front the battle had continued with ever-increasing ferocity. On September 29, British troops successfully crossed the St Quentin Canal, using boats, ladders, and 3,000 lifebelts taken from the cross-Channel ferries. More than 5,000 German soldiers were taken prisoner, and a hundred guns captured. On the following day, on the Ypres Front, the British were within two miles of Menin, the town whose capture had eluded them for four years. In the British and French sectors, a further 18,000 German prisoners-of-war and two hundred guns were captured. Only the Americans had been forced to a halt, in the Argonne, but they too were planning to renew the assault within a week.

Among those wounded on September 30 was Paul Maze. He had gone forward on foot to report on the whereabouts of the front line, at a point where it was being fought for by the Australians. From a shell-hole, he saw, two hundred yards away, the tops of German steel helmets: it was a front-line German trench. Raising his field glasses to have a closer look, he was shot in the wrist. As he made his way back to safety and to hospital, travelling slowly that evening to the coast in a hospital train, he could hear in the distance 'the guns making a thundering row'. It reminded him of the comment of the mother of a French friend of his, who had succeeded in reaching her son in a village immediately behind the line, during a battle. 'She had sent word and was waiting for him, a tall black figure in the middle of the road; as she spied him coming towards her down the shattered street she called out: "My dear child, why all this noise? What is it all about?" '

*

From Palestine, on September 27, Allenby's cavalrymen had ridden across the Golan Heights into Syria. Damascus lay only sixty miles away. That day, further east, at the village of Tafas, Turkish and German forces murdered several hundred Arab women and children in an act of cruel defiance for the successful harassment by the forces of the Arab revolt. On the following day, September 28, at Dera'a, where thousands of Bedouin had joined the Arab forces, wounded Turkish soldiers and prisoners were murdered as a reprisal, arousing violent anti-Arab feeling among the Indian cavalrymen who entered the town while the massacre was taking place. 'Arabs murdered in cold blood every Turk they came across' was the brief note in the 4th Cavalry Division's summary of events.

On the following day 1,500 Turks blocked Allenby's path at Sasa, holding up his advance for two days. But by late afternoon on September 30, Allenby was on his way to Damascus. That night, the Turkish authorities abandoned the city which the Ottomans had ruled for so many centuries. On October 1, Allenby's cavalrymen, having ridden more than four hundred miles in twelve days, were approaching their prize. As troops of the 3rd Light Horse Brigade, from Western Australia, reached the outskirts of the city, there was a burst of Turkish rifle-fire. No one was hit, and the officer in command, Major Olden, decided to continue. Ordering his men to draw their swords, Olden galloped forward with them towards the main Turkish barracks, where several thousand Turks were quartered. 'For the moment the enemy decision was in the balance,' one Australian history recorded. 'But the sight of the great Australian horses coming at a gallop (the Turks and natives never ceased to marvel at the size of our horses), the flashing swords, and the ring of shoes upon the metal, turned the scale.'[1] An Australian officer later recalled, 'The shooting by the Turks gave way, in a second, to the clapping of hands by the citizens.' Suddenly more shots rang out, but these were Arab riflemen, expressing their joy that so many centuries of Turkish rule were at an end. A few hours later 'Lawrence of Arabia' arrived, his Rolls-Royce escorted by Indian cavalrymen.

For twenty-four hours there was much looting by Arab and Druze. Then Allenby, leaving his headquarters at Tiberias on the Sea of Galilee, drove along 120 miles of poor roads across the river Jordan and up the Golan Heights to Damascus, installed the Emir Feisal as head of the local administration, and returned that same evening to Tiberias. It was left to the politicians to inform Feisal that, under the terms of the secret agreement negotiated by Mark Sykes and François Georges Picot in 1916, Syria, as well as the Lebanon and northern Mesopotamia, including oil-rich Mosul, was to be within the French sphere of control.

On October 1, as the British Expeditionary Force prepared to break

[1] H.S. Gullett and Chas Barrett, *Australia in Palestine*, Angus and Robertson, Sydney 1919, page 47.

through the final obstacles on the Hindenburg Line, and the Americans got ready to launch a new attack in the Argonne, Ludendorff begged the Kaiser to issue a German peace offer at once. That night German forces evacuated Lens and Armentières. North of Cambrai, Canadian troops had taken more than 7,000 German prisoners and two hundred guns in the previous five days. The German army, Ludendorff told his Staff, was 'heavily infected with the poison of Spartacist-Socialist ideas'. Ludendorff was exaggerating, but while the soldiers at the front were continuing to fight, those who were in Germany on leave, or about to be sent back to the front, were certainly prey to political agitation of the most extreme sort. The leaders of the Spartacists, Karl Liebknecht and Rosa Luxemburg, were demanding an immediate peace and the end of the monarchy. Not for them the panacea, if such it was, of a democratic or parliamentary monarchy, British style: their aim was a socialist republic.

So excited was Lenin by what appeared to be the imminent collapse of Germany, through both defeat on the battlefield and insurrection in the cities, that he wrote that week to his fellow-revolutionaries Sverdlov and Trotsky to tell them that international revolution was imminent. To assist the proletariat of all countries to throw off their shackles, he wanted the Bolsheviks to create a three-million-strong army. Near to Petrograd, however, at Pskov, an anti-Bolshevik army was being created by former Tsarist officers and released Russian prisoners-of-war, under German protection. That week, in the Black Sea, some two hundred German sailors took over the Russian battleship *Volya*, as well as four Russian destroyers and two torpedo boats. Germany's machinations in the east had outlived her triumphs in the west.

The first four days of October saw the Allied armies advancing on all sectors of the Western Front. A thirty-mile sector of the Hindenburg Line was completely overrun. But with these Allied success came news of grave difficulties on the American sector of the front, where on October 4 the renewed offensive was met by devastating German machine-gun defences, 'one damn machine gun after another' in the American soldier's parlance. That day an American force of just over five hundred men, who were holding a precarious position in a ravine about half a mile ahead of the front line, were surrounded by a much larger force of Germans. For two days they were continually attacked and shelled. On the second day, after their food ran out, they were accidentally hit by an American artillery barrage. They released their last carrier pigeon with an appeal for Americans to stop shelling Americans. The Germans then used flamethrowers against the men in the ravine, but some of the Americans clambered out and killed them. The American High Command assumed that all was over and posted the men as 'lost'. That night the Germans withdrew. The 'lost battalion', as it became known, had not been defeated. Of the 554 defenders, 360 had been killed. On the following afternoon the survivors came down from their hillside into the American lines.

*

At sea, the submarine war, on which so many German hopes had rested, continued without pause, and with more tragedies. A Spanish steamship, the *Francoli*, had been sunk off Cartagena on October 2, and 292 passengers drowned. Two days later a further 292 passengers had been drowned when the Japanese liner *Hiramo Maru* was torpedoed off the coast of Ireland. An accidental collision in the English Channel that same week led to the sinking of an armed merchant cruiser, the *Otranto*: of the thousand American troops on board, 431 were drowned.

The first German revolution took place on October 2. It was not in the streets, as Ludendorff had feared, but in the council chamber, where Prince Max of Baden, the Kaiser's second cousin, became Chancellor. Prince Max agreed to take office only after the Kaiser accepted two conditions: that henceforth Parliament alone would have the right to declare war and make peace, and that any remaining control that the Kaiser might have over the army and navy cease at once. That day, at a Crown Council in Berlin, Hindenburg reiterated Ludendorff's advice of the previous day (Ludendorff having stayed at Spa) for an immediate truce. 'The army cannot wait forty-eight hours,' Hindenburg told the Kaiser. Prince Max disagreed. He did not want to enter negotiations with the Allies with the position already surrendered. 'I hoped I could fight down pessimism and revive confidence,' he later wrote, 'for I myself was still firmly convinced that in spite of the diminution of our forces we could prevent our enemy from treading the soil of the Fatherland for many months.'

Hindenburg replied that the situation demanded an immediate armistice. If the situation was so desperate, Prince Max replied acerbically, it was for the army to raise the white flag in the field. No decision was made, for Hindenburg, like Kitchener before him on the British side, lacked the ability to argue his case, and could merely reiterate it. A message from Ludendorff was needed to articulate what had to be done, and why. This message was sent to Berlin later that day, as the result of a telephone call from Hindenburg. It stated that the collapse of the Salonica Front, 'whereby a weakening of our reserves in the west is necessitated', and the impossibility of making good the 'very heavy losses' in the battles of the previous few days, made an immediate armistice imperative 'to spare the German people and its allies further useless sacrifices'. Ludendorff's letter, to which Hindenburg appended his signature, ended with the reality of the battlefield spelt out clearly: 'Every day lost costs thousands of brave soldiers' lives.' It was a sentence that could have been written on almost any of the past 1,500 days.

Prince Max had not given up hope of delaying the appeal to the Allies. On October 3 he warned Hindenburg that too swift an armistice could mean the immediate loss both of Alsace-Lorraine and of the predominantly Polish districts of East Prussia. Such German territorial losses were implicit

471

in President Wilson's Fourteen Points. Hindenburg again telephoned Ludendorff, only to report back to the Chancellor that, whereas the loss of Alsace-Lorraine was acceptable to the High Command, the loss of any territory in the east was unacceptable. One historian has commented: 'It became more and more evident that the Chancellor had read the Fourteen Points while the Supreme Command had not.'[1]

Prince Max now chose his own way forward. During October 3 he brought two Socialist deputies into his government, one of whom, Philip Scheidemann, told him, with much wisdom, 'Better an end to terror than terror without end.' To avert terror, an armistice was essential. On October 4, having informed the Reichstag of the need for peace, and having obtained Austrian support for what he now realised could not be delayed, Prince Max telegraphed to Washington requesting an armistice.

That day, at a Franco-American conference in France, held at the small town of Trois Fontaines, plans were being drawn up for shipping American troops and munitions across the Atlantic for the campaign to defeat Germany by the end of 1919, or in early 1920. The two senior participants at the conference were Marshal Foch and the American Secretary of War, Newton Baker. They agreed to an accelerated shipping programme throughout the winter of 1918, so that by the following summer the American Army would have adequate supplies for a major offensive in 1919.

During the month of September, a total of 297 artillery units had been manufactured in the United States. The subsequent targets that were now fixed, and were in due course reached, were just over a thousand between October and December 1918, and a further thousand between January and April 1919. Every other branch of ordnance and supplies was given similar accelerated and increased production targets for the coming six months, and beyond. An expanded network of telephone and telegraph lines was even then being constructed by the American army throughout France, determined to improve and accelerate communication with the front line and, by drawing on the lessons of the Argonne set-backs, to ensure a successful campaign in 1919.

The Franco-American agreement reached at Trois Fontaines on October 4 held out hope of a considerable military advance during the early months of 1919. As Pershing's troops struggled to regain the initiative on the Meuse, their commander was calculating how many divisions he would need in France by 1 July 1919, for the decisive battle. The number of men involved, most of whom would be transported across the Atlantic in British ships, was 3,360,000: two million more than he had already. They were on their way.

[1] John Wheeler-Bennett, *Hindenburg, The Wooden Titan*, Macmillan, London 1936, page 168.

26

The collapse of the Central Powers

OCTOBER–NOVEMBER 1918

In France, the painter John Singer Sargent had been travelling behind the lines since July looking for inspiration for the painting he had been asked to do for the British Ministry of Information. On 4 October 1918 he wrote to a friend: 'For a long time I did not see any means of treating the subject given to me, of "British and American Troops Working Together". They do this in the abstract but not in any particular space within the limits of a picture.' He could still not find a subject, though the three months he had been allotted for the painting were coming to an end.' I have wasted lots of time going to the front line trenches,' he wrote to another friend six days later. 'There is nothing to paint there – it is ugly, and meagre and cramped, and one only sees one or two men.' He had gone to the Somme, still searching, when inspiration came. 'In this Somme country I have seen what I wanted, roads crammed with troops on the march,' he wrote. 'It is the finest spectacle that war affords, as far as I can make out.'

In fact, it was not troops on the march whom Sargent decided to paint. With him on the Somme was another artist, Henry Tonks, who had been asked by the Ministry to do a painting on a medical theme. In search of this, he and Sargent went to a dressing station near Le Bac-de-Sud, on the Doullens Road. 'There,' writes Sargent's biographer, 'under a perfect autumnal sky, they saw soldiers blinded by mustard gas waiting for treatment. Sargent had at last found *his* picture, though it had nothing whatever to do with the terms of his assignment. Tonks said he did not mind; far from it.'[1]

Sargent took notes, returned to his studio in London, and began work on his painting. Entitled *Gassed*, it shows two groups of blinded and blindfolded soldiers, ten in the centre of the picture and nine in the distance,

[1] Stanley Olson, *John Singer Sargent*, Macmillan, London 1986, page 261. Tonks painted two paintings on this occasion, 'An Underground Casualty Clearing Station, Arras' and 'An Advanced Dressing Station in France' (which includes a file of men blinded by mustard gas, possibly one of the files in the Sargent painting). Both these paintings by Tonks are at the Imperial War Museum, as is Sargent's.

all standing in line, each group led by an orderly. Each blindfolded man has his hand on the shoulder of the soldier in front. Some are still holding their rifles. More than twenty men are lying in a field in the foreground, their eyes also bandaged. Others are lying in the field behind. There are no doctors or nurses to be seen. In the far distance, on the horizon, dwarfed by the men who have been gassed, a football match is in progress. The painting, of considerable power, was voted 'Picture of the Year' at the Royal Academy Exhibition in 1919.

On what had been the Salonica Front, now deep inside Serbia, in the first week of October, Austrian troops were still fighting despite Bulgaria's defection. Ludendorff, however, recognised the danger presented to the Central Powers as Serbian and French forces pushed the front steadily northward, through Serbian Macedonia, towards the Danube and Belgrade. Yet in both Berlin and Vienna the instinct to brazen it out remained. On October 4 a German and Austrian 'Peace Note' was sent to President Wilson, asking him to agree to an armistice. It was made clear by both the Germans and Austrians that this was not a surrender, not even an offer of armistice terms, but an attempt to end the war without any preconditions that might be harmful to Germany or Austria. This was what Prince Max wished.

As Wilson studied the note, the war went on. On October 5, more than 3,000 Austrians were taken prisoner on the Salonica Front. Inside Germany the continuation of the fighting led to an increase in public discontent. On October 6, at Gotha, a conference of German Spartacists, whose leader, Karl Liebknecht, was in prison, demanded an end to the monarchy and the setting up of Soviets in Germany.

With the disintegration of Empires the struggle of subject peoples intensified. On October 7, in German-occupied Warsaw, a Regency Council, hitherto under German control, invoked President Wilson's principles of self-determination and declared a 'free and independent' Polish State. Its authority was challenged, however, by two other Polish groups, the oddly-named Polish Liquidation Committee in Cracow, and the left-wing Provisional People's Government of the Polish Republic, in Lublin.[1] The Germans, unwilling to see the total collapse of their Polish conquests, kept Pilsudski in prison in East Prussia. The Ukrainians, determined not to lose East Galicia to a reconstituted Poland, established a Ukrainian National Council in Lvov, and fighting began between Poles and Ukrainians throughout the region.

Germany, in turmoil, had not yet succumbed to anarchy or decided to

[1] It was in Lublin, in June 1944, that the Soviet Union established the Communist-dominated Polish Committee for National Liberation (known as the 'Lublin Poles') which the Western Allies rejected as the future Government of Poland, but which by the end of the war they were forced to accept.

surrender. On October 7, as a Polish State was declared in Warsaw, a call for a final military effort on the battlefield was published in the *Vossische Zeitung*. Written by the industrialist Walther Rathenau, its aim was to give Germany the strongest possible position from which to negotiate a peace of equality rather than of defeat. 'All men capable of bearing arms must be combed out of the offices, the guard rooms and depots, in East and West, at the bases and at home,' Rathenau wrote. 'What use have we today for Armies of Occupation and Russian Expeditions? Yet at this moment we have hardly half of the total available troops on the Western Front. Our front is worn out; restore it, and we shall be offered different terms. It is peace we want, not war – but not a peace of surrender.'

Struck by this line of reasoning, Prince Max asked Hindenburg and Ludendorff whether 'adequate reinforcement' would in fact be afforded by such a combing out of troops as Rathenau proposed. Ludendorff was sceptical: from a practical viewpoint 'it would cause more disturbance than we could stand', he replied on October 8. But Rathenau did not give up, writing to the newly-appointed Minister of War, General Scheüch, that if Germany evacuated the areas demanded by President Wilson, including the whole of Belgium and Alsace-Lorraine, this would 'make an end of our capacity for defence and thus put ourselves at the enemy's mercy'.

The argument for a German position of strength on the Western Front was becoming academic. On October 8, Wilson rejected the German Peace Note. A first condition of an armistice, he reiterated, was the evacuation of all occupied territories. The war would not end until there were no German troops on Belgian or French soil, and no Austrian or German troops in Serbia. That day, near Châtel-Chéhéry in the Argonne, an American soldier who had earlier been a conscientious objector on religious grounds, Corporal Alvin C. York, was in action. His patrol having been surrounded and outnumbered ten to one, York, single-handed, killed as many as twenty-eight German soldiers and captured 132 others, bringing back thirty-five machine guns. Asked by a divisional general how many Germans he thought he had killed, York replied: 'General, I would hate to think I missed any of them shots; they were all at pretty close range – fifty or sixty yards.' Commenting on his fellow-soldiers' shooting abilities he remarked: 'They missed everything but the sky.' He, however, was a mountaineer. 'It weren't no trouble nohow for me to hit them big army targets,' he explained. 'They were so much bigger than turkey's heads.'

Also on October 8, the day of Corporal York's exploit, the British launched an offensive on a twenty-mile front between St Quentin and Cambrai, the Second Battle of Cambrai. A smokescreen for the attack was created by the Royal Air Force, dropping phosphorus bombs. In one day, three British armies, with eighty-two tanks in support, advanced three miles and took 10,000 prisoners and 150 guns. An American division also advanced towards Cambrai, capturing 1,500 prisoners and 30 guns.

Within twenty-four hours of the start of the new offensive, the Hindenburg Line was finally overrun in its entirety. On October 9, Canadian troops entered Cambrai. The Duke of Wellington had taken the city's surrender 103 years earlier, after the defeat of Napoleon. In 1870 the Germans had captured it: they had held it again since August 1914. Now it was a free French city once more. A British cavalry division, in an unprecedented eight-mile advance, reached the outskirts of Le Câteau, taking five hundred prisoners on its gallop forward.

Battlefields from which the British had been driven in 1914 and 1915, and again earlier in 1918, were entered and crossed almost without pause. An artilleryman, Colonel Alan Brooke, visited Lens on October 9. 'Such ruin and desolation,' he wrote. 'I climbed on to a heap of stones which represents the place where the Church once stood, and I looked down on the wreckage. One could spend days there just looking down picturing to oneself the tragedies that have occurred in every corner of this place. If the stones could talk and could repeat what they have witnessed, and the thoughts they had read on dying men's faces, I wonder if there would ever be any wars.'[1]

On the following day a British officer, the poet Wilfred Owen, who had returned to the trenches after his time in hospital in Britain, wrote to a friend from the front line: 'The boy by my side, shot through the head, lay on top of me, soaking my shoulder, for half an hour.' Yet, Owen added, he was 'full of confidence' when, 'after having taken a few machine guns (with the help of one seraphic lance-corporal), I held a most glorious brief peace talk in a pill-box'. He had shot one German with his revolver at thirty yards. The rest had surrendered 'with a smile'. Owen had earlier been invalided home with shattered nerves after serving for six months in the trenches in 1917, but he had wanted to go back, explaining to his mother: 'I came out in order to help these boys; directly, by leading them as well as an officer can; indirectly, by watching their sufferings that I may speak of them as well as a pleader can.' But trench warfare took its toll again, as he later wrote home: 'My senses are charred; I don't take the cigarette out of my mouth when I write Deceased over their letters.'

Among those killed in action earlier that week was the 21-year-old Charles Read. His brother Herbert, a writer and poet who had fought on the Somme, tried to express his feelings, of both pain and pride:

> *I curse the fate that sent us*
> *a tortured species down the torrent of life*
> *soul-exposed to the insensate shores*
> *and the dark fall of death.*

> ** * **

> *All the world is wet with tears*
> *and droops its languid life*

---

[1] Twenty-two years later, Brooke, then commanding an army, was at the same spot, amid the swift German sweep forward to Dunkirk. Rereading his comment of 1918, he wrote: 'Stones had remained silent. We were starting the Second World War.'

in sympathy.
But death is beautiful with pride: the trees
are golden lances whose brave sway
assails the sadness of the day.

At sea, the relentless war went on, with a German submarine sinking the Kingstown-Holyhead ferry *Leinster* on October 10, drowning 176 passengers and crew, including several Americans.

On October 10 it was made known that 20,000 American troops had died in France in the previous two months, not in battle, but of influenza and pneumonia. Even as the armies prepared for what the Allies believed would be the final struggle, death stalked their ranks from within. But the exhilaration of imminent victory was hard to quell. On Allenby's front, Damascus had fallen nine days earlier, and an Indian division had entered Beirut on October 8.

Dramatic events were taking pace in Serbia, after three years of Austrian occupation. The Austrian 9th Division, made up mostly of Bohemians and Moravians, was showing its fellow-Slav sympathies for the Serbs, and was no longer an effective fighting force. On October 10, Serb forces entered Nis, having advanced 170 miles in twenty-five days. The city had been defended by German troops. Near Prizren, a German army corps was reported lost in the mountains, as it tried to make its way to the Albanian coast.

Every nation in the Allied line was moving forward. On October 10 the American First Army under Pershing finally succeeded in driving the Germans out of the Argonne Forest. Yet the battle did not fare as well for the Americans as they had hoped, and there was no breakthrough. Ammunition, food and other essential provisions were still being held up by the congestion on the roads. In addition, the shortage of horses had become acute. Pershing calculated that he was short of at least 100,000 horses, but when he asked Foch if France could provide 25,000, he was told to get them from the United States. This proved impossible: there was not enough shipping space. 'The animal situation will soon become desperate,' Pershing's senior supply officer reported.

Pétain's reaction to the American supply difficulties was to suggest that Pershing's First Army be dissolved, that the American effort should be limited to corps and divisions, and that those divisions which could not be adequately supplied should be distributed 'among the French armies'. Already, of the thirty American divisions fit for combat, ten were serving with the French and British forces under French and British commanders, and only twenty under Pershing. But Pershing and his First Army fought on. They were not going to dissolve themselves, or accept that they were beaten by the problems of supply.

On October 11, German forces began a systematic withdrawal from the

Western Front. But they had not given up fighting, and on October 12 Hindenburg sought to stiffen their resistance by his announcement that the granting of favourable armistice terms to Germany would depend upon a successful military resistance at the front. That day, the German Government accepted President Wilson's condition for negotiations, the complete withdrawal of their troops from France and Belgium. Hearing this news in Constantinople, the German-born Zionist Arthur Ruppin noted in his diary how he 'went for a long walk and continuously repeated to myself the one word: Peace! How much this means!'

Ruppin's excitement, like that of millions of others, was premature. Before Wilson received the German acceptance of his terms, the British and French opened a new offensive inside Belgium, between Dixmude and Courtrai. In support, American bomber aircraft attacked German lines of communication deep within Belgium. In five days the new offensive had advanced eighteen miles, taking 12,000 prisoners and 550 guns.

German troops continued to fight for the French cities under their control, unwilling to withdraw without a struggle from regions they had ruled for more than four years. But on October 13, French forces under General Debeney and General Mangin drove them out of the city of Laon, liberating 6,500 French civilians, and, in triumph, advanced further northward. The liberation of Laon was a turning point: a city that had so often been within sound of the guns during earlier battles, but had faced the humiliation of occupation for more than 1,500 days.

At a meeting at a private house at Danny, in Sussex, on October 13, Lloyd George told his senior military and naval advisers, and several senior Cabinet Ministers, of his fears that if the Germans gained 'a respite' as a result of an armistice, 'they might obtain time to re-organise and recover'. As the minutes of the meeting report, he then 'raised for consideration the question as to whether the actual military defeat of Germany and the giving to the German people of a real taste of war was not more important, from the point of view of the peace of the world, than a surrender at the present time when the German armies were still on foreign territory'.

In Berne, Sir Horace Rumbold, who had served in the Berlin Embassy in 1914, was also worried that the Germans would make peace too soon. 'It will be a thousand pities', he wrote to the Foreign Office on October 14, 'if we are called off before we hammer him completely on the Western Front. We ought to get him into his beastly country, for that is the only way of bringing home to him or to his population what war means.' That morning, among the German wounded in the Ypres Salient was Corporal Hitler, temporarily blinded by a British gas shell near the village of Wervik. He was evacuated to a military hospital at Pasewalk in Pomerania.

That same day, the American First Army, with the Argonne Forest behind it, renewed its offensive on the Meuse. At first the battle did not go well. 'Hope for better results tomorrow,' Pershing wrote in his diary that evening, and added: 'There is no particular reason for this hope except that if we keep on pounding, the Germans will be obliged to give way.'

But the Germans continued to shell the American positions with high-explosive and gas shells, and fought for every yard of ground. When, on October 15, Pershing visited the troops of the 3rd Division, then resting at Montfaucon, he found them 'disorganised, and apparently disheartened'.[1]

With more than a million men under his command, and a front of eighty-three miles, Pershing divided his army, creating a Second Army. But its problems were still acute. The shortage of horses was immobilising the artillery. As many as 100,000 men were thought to have become 'stragglers', wandering about behind the lines, away from units which depended on them to make up the necessary strength for attack. Some men hid in dug-outs: the commander of the 3rd Division authorised the throwing of bombs into dug-outs if his men refused to come out.

Deaths from influenza continued to mount. On October 15 it was announced that 1,500 Berliners had died of the disease. Four days later, on the Western Front, the Canadian air ace, Captain Quigley, who had shot down thirty-four German planes, died of influenza. Not only Europe, but Africa and Asia were affected. In Bombay, more than a thousand Indians died. In the United States, the death toll was climbing. In Vienna, the 28-year-old Expressionist painter Egon Schiele was among those who succumbed to the epidemic. In London that month, 2,225 people died of 'Spanish 'flu', as it was known, within a week: more than all the deaths from four years of German Zeppelin and aircraft raids.

On October 14, in Paris, the Allies recognised the Czechoslovak National Council, a group of determined exiles headed by Thomas Masaryk, as the Provisional Government of a future Czechoslovakia. Two days later, in a desperate attempt to preserve the unity of the Hapsburg Empire, the Emperor Charles offered complete federal freedom to all six principal nationalities of Austria: Czechs, Slovaks, Poles, Croats, Slovenes, Serbs and Roumanians. This belated offer, the historian Elizabeth Wiskemann has written, 'was spoken by nothing but a voice from the grave'. Even while they were seeking a means of placating the Allies, the Austrians could not bring themselves to detach the predominantly Roumanian areas of Transylvania from Hungary to Roumania.

Four days after the Emperor's offer, the decisive blow to the survival of Austria-Hungary was struck when President Wilson insisted that 'autonomy' for subject peoples was no longer an adequate fulfilment of their national rights. Wilson now claimed that the United States had incurred obligations towards the Czechoslovak and South Slav peoples that went beyond autonomy, or a federal agglomeration, within the Empire.

As territorial offers and counter-offers touched on age-long national hopes, the fighting on the Western Front continued. On October 16,

---

[1] Donald Smythe, *Pershing: General of the Armies*, Indiana University Press, Bloomington 1986, page 214.

as the Americans were moving forward again on the Meuse, a brigade commanded by Douglas MacArthur struggled to take the Côte de Châtillon. Taking the hill, the brigade repelled repeated German attempts to take it back. In a batallion led by Major Ross, a corporal, Joseph E. Pruett, single-handed, attacked a German machine-gun post, then, outdoing Alvin York, captured sixty-eight German soldiers. MacArthur later recalled the ferocity of the struggle. 'Officers fell and sergeants leaped to the command,' he wrote. 'Companies dwindled to platoons and corporals took over. At the end, Major Ross had only 300 men and six officers left out of 1,450 men and twenty-five officers.' But the hill was held. 'Clouded prospects wherever one looks,' a German company commander wrote that day. 'Really has everything been in vain? Such a piteous finish.'

On October 17, advancing south of Le Câteau on a ten-mile front, American troops took 5,000 prisoners and sixty guns. That same day, British forces occupied the city of Lille without a single shot being fired. The German navy evacuated Ostend and Zeebrugge. But at the very moment when all seemed lost for the Central Powers, some German leaders appeared to part with reality. Grand-Admiral Tirpitz wrote that day to Prince Max urging 'resolute reinforcement' of the Western Front with every available man, and the 'relentless prosecution' of the submarine campaign: 'Every German must understand that if we do not fight on, we fall to the level of wage-slaves to our enemies.' Summoned by the Kaiser to discuss what reply to give to President Wilson, Ludendorff declared that the German army could, and should, fight on. An Allied breakthrough was, he said, 'unlikely'. In another month winter would bring the battle to a halt. A skilful withdrawal to a new line, based on Antwerp and the river Meuse, would give the German Army the ability to plan for an offensive against the Allied line in the spring of 1919.

Prince Max was not convinced, but Ludendorff had no doubts. In Germany's spring 1919 offensive, he said, Belgium must again become a battlefield 'so that 1914 will be child's play compared to it'. The German War Minister, General Heinrich Scheüch, said that he could probably provide up to 600,000 reinforcements for the battle of 1919, but he went on to warn that if Germany's supply of oil from Roumania was cut off, the German army could only fight for another six weeks. This was the first note of realism in the current discussions. A second such note came on the following day, October 18, from Prince Rupprecht of Bavaria, who in a letter to Prince Max described the wretched condition of his troops, short of artillery support, ammunition, fuel, horses and officers, and concluded: 'We must obtain peace before the enemy breaks into Germany.'

On October 18, Haig, who had earlier been confident of victory in 1918, told a War Cabinet committee that Germany would be able to hold its new lines on the Western Front well into 1919. But Germany's warmaking powers were almost over. That day, under the terms of the September 30 armistice, the last German troops left Bulgaria. On the following day

1,200 German advisers and military specialists began to depart from Mesopotamia, together with their aircraft, guns and transport. In Austrian-occupied central Serbia, some German units remained in action, counter-attacking the Serb forces at Paracin, but most of the German forces that had been on the Salonica Front were still making their way across the mountains to the Adriatic.

That day, in a measure that ended Germany's long-held hopes of bringing Britain to her knees by naval warfare, Admiral Scheer ordered all German submarines to return to their German bases. The last torpedo was fired by a German submarine on October 21, when a small British merchant ship, the *Saint Barcham*, was sunk in the Irish Sea, and eight crewmen drowned. They were the last of 318 British merchant seamen to be killed that month.

The whole of the Belgian coast was now in Allied hands. But still the German Government resisted the inevitable. On October 22, Prince Max insisted that Germany would not accept 'a peace of violence'. Reparations had become a new feature of the armistice discussions: the Belgian Government made it known that week that it would demand almost £400 million from Germany, in compensation for damage done.[1] In an attempt to lessen the mounting discontent, and republicanism, in Germany, the Kaiser agreed to a general amnesty of political prisoners. Liebknecht, an implacable opponent of the monarchy, was among those released. More than 20,000 people went to the station in Berlin to welcome him back. Lenin, watching these events from Moscow, declared in triumph: 'Three months ago people used to laugh when we said there might be a revolution in Germany.'

On October 23 there was a mutiny in the Austrian army in Italy, when Croat troops behind the lines seized the port of Fiume. The mutiny was suppressed. Far more damaging to the fabric of the Empire than any Croat mutiny, on October 25 the Hungarian nationalist leader, Count Michael Karolyi, set up a Hungarian National Council in Budapest, the prelude to the complete separation of Austria and Hungary.

Throughout October, from his distant vantage point in the United States, President Wilson remained at the centre of the armistice discussions. In their most recent note, sent to Washington on October 20 but not received there until the 22nd, the German Government agreed to renounce submarine warfare. Sending this note back across the Atlantic to Clemenceau and Lloyd George on October 23, Wilson suggested that the Allies prepare their armistice terms.

Wilson's position was one of considerable strength. The American army's possible future role on the battlefield was alarming the Germans considerably. On October 24 the left-wing *Arbeiter Zeitung* drew its readers' attention to the fact that 10,000 'fresh, well-fed, well-equipped' American troops were reaching Europe every day, 300,000 every month, and it went on to ask: 'Do the people wish to continue war under such circumstances,

[1] The 1994 equivalent would be in excess of £10,000 million ($15,000 million).

to sacrifice the lives of many hundred thousand men, thereby destroying the remainder of the nation's manhood and imperilling their future?' A year earlier, even three months earlier, such a question would have been tantamount to treason. Now it was seen as common sense.

Meeting at Senlis on October 25, the four senior Allied commanders, Foch, Haig, Pétain and Pershing, discussed what their armistice demands would be. The main concern of the generals was to make it impossible for Germany to renew the fighting at some future date after the armistice, perhaps in the early spring. To prevent this, they insisted on the surrender to the Allies of all German artillery and all railway stock. But there was no unanimity of thought about whether the Germans were, in fact, ready to surrender on such terms. Haig still thought that, although the Germans had been severely hurt in the recent battles, they had not been beaten, and would be able, on falling back, to create a new and effective front line. The Allied armies, however, were in Haig's view 'pretty well exhausted'. He then spoke of the American army in terms that upset Pershing. It was 'not yet organised, not yet formed, and had suffered a great deal on account of its ignorance of modern warfare'. In the next battle it 'cannot be counted upon for much'.

Ignoring this criticism, Pershing pointed out that, as the American lines of supply extended 3,000 miles across the Atlantic, the armistice terms ought to include the surrender of all German submarines. This was agreed. Foch, challenging Haig's view that the Germans were not yet beaten, pointed out that since July 15 more than 250,000 German soldiers had been made prisoners-of-war, and 4,000 guns captured. The German army was retreating along the whole front. It was not only an army that had been 'beaten every day for three months', it was also 'an army that is, physically and morally, thoroughly beaten'.

The German High Command was of the same opinion, and yet, at Spa, Hindenburg and Ludendorff, distressed by Wilson's insistence that German must put forward its armistice terms, were on the verge of a final act of defiance. Turning their back on Wilson's demand, they prepared a circular letter, which they dispatched by telegram, to all Army Group commanders, describing the armistice conditions as unworthy of Germany and unacceptable to the army, and ordering a 'fight to the finish'. Wilson's demand was 'nothing for us soldiers but a challenge to continue our resistance with all our strength'. No Allied sacrifice would achieve 'the rupture of the German Front'. Following a protest from one army commander the telegram was withdrawn, but not before a military wireless operator, who happened to be a member of the Independent Socialist Party, had transmitted its text from Kovno, where he received it, to the Reichstag members of his party.

Yet another Allied offensive opened on October 24, on the Italian Front. It began with a 1,400-gun bombardment of the Austrian positions around Monte Grappa. Fifty-one Italian divisions took part in the renewed attack, together with British, French, Czechoslovak and American units. The Austrian defence was tenacious, however: their seventy-three divisions were not yet ready to give up.

On the Piave, British troops took part in a fierce struggle for the island of Papadopoli. They were veterans of the Western Front, a fact that gave them a particular perspective. 'On this occasion,' one of their chaplains has written, 'the novelty of the enterprise helped considerably to relieve the tension. There was something hideous and inhuman about a trench attack in France. The mud, the duckboards, the dead horses one passed on the way up, the sickening bark and roar of the guns, all combined to produce a sort of uncanny effect which one could only tolerate by suppressing all brooding on the situation. On this occasion, however, the situation was quite different. For months the firebrands in the battalion had been spoiling for a fight. The guns were all silent, the avenues of trees were all decked in the glories of their autumn foliage. Above all, the element of adventure which was involved in the passage of the river, and the fact that we were fighting against an enemy whom we had come rather to despise, combined to free men from the load of oppression which even the stoutest heart had felt a year ago on the Passchendaele Ridge.'

Crosse added: 'The men were out to finish the war, to give the Austrians a knock-out blow for all the crimes they had committed since the fateful murder at Sarajevo, and everyone felt that, though the expedition was a gamble, the stakes were well worth the risk.'[1] Papadopoli Island was captured, but heavy rain and flooding made any further advance impossible. In the mountains that day, the Italians re-captured Mount Asolone, which the Austrians had captured a year earlier, then lost it.

In Germany, on October 25, the newspapers published the cancelled Spa 'fight to the finish' telegram. Outraged, Prince Max went to see the Kaiser to demand that either Ludendorff resign, or the Government itself would resign. Travelling to Berlin, Ludendorff saw the Kaiser, and demanded that Wilson's latest note be rejected. If the people at home would support the army in the field, he said, 'the war can be maintained for some months'.

Ludendorff was supported by Hindenburg and, more importantly, by the Chief of the Naval Staff, Admiral Scheer. The new Minister of War, General Scheüch, also supported him. But the Kaiser had been angered that Ludendorff had telegraphed direct to the troops, and at one point shouted at him, with anger and sarcasm: 'Excellency, I must remind you that you are in the presence of Your Emperor.'

Realising that there was now no way that the war could be continued, or that he would be allowed to continue it, Ludendorff resigned. The warmaking nation had lost its War Lord. Hindenburg, the figurehead, remained, the Kaiser having refused his offer of resignation. But the Kaiser himself, the Supreme War Lord, had also become a figurehead, as Prince

[1] The Rev. E.C. Crosse, *The Defeat of Austria as seen by the 7th Division*, pages 25–6.

Max's Government continued to seek terms acceptable to the Allies. Ludendorff's successor as First Quartermaster-General, General Groener, was a realist who recognised that Germany had lost her ability to continue the war.

On the Turkish Front, the Arab forces under Sherif Hussein had reached the outskirts of the city of Aleppo, the northernmost Arab city in Syria. Allenby's army was also near, his cavalrymen eager to crown their ride through Syria with the capture of the city. Defending Aleppo was Mustafa Kemal. On October 25, as the Arabs inside the city rose in revolt, determined to welcome their liberators as free men, Kemal urged his troops to fight street by street. The commander of the Arab forces opposing him in this struggle was a former Turkish army officer, Nuri es-Said.[1]

By nightfall Kemal realised that nothing more could be done to retain this last southern bastion of the Ottoman Empire, and he ordered his troops to pull out. He was aware that any further Arab or Allied advance would lead into the Turkish heartland. Just five miles north of Aleppo he turned, not only to face the advancing enemy but, in effect, to delineate the future southern frontier of Turkey. At Haritan, where he turned to fight, 3,000 Turkish and German troops under his command halted the advance guard of Allenby's army, forcing two Indian cavalry units, the Jodhpur and Mysore Lancers, to withdraw.

On the Italian Front, the Austrians were still defending their mountain positions yard by yard. But a first sign of disintegration came on October 26, when three Hungarian divisions asked to be sent back to Hungary. Their request was granted, and within twenty-four hours they were gone. Turkey, the third arm of the Central Powers, was also in disarray. Allenby's cavalry entered the northern Syrian city of Aleppo on October 26. The Turks retreated towards Anatolia. On the Mesopotamian Front, a thousand British cavalrymen had advanced eighty-three miles in two days.

On October 26, three Turkish negotiators reached the island of Mudros, in the Aegean, to begin armistice talks. With them was General Townshend, who had been held in captivity near Constantinople since the fall of Kut two and a half years earlier, and whom the Turks asked to help them in securing an armistice. The talks were held on board the battleship *Agamemnon*, which three and a half years earlier had been among the British warships bombarding the Dardanelles. As on the Western Front, so in the Aegean, the opening of talks was not paralleled by any halt to the fighting.

Forty-eight hours after the arrival of the Turkish negotiators at Mudros, British troops reached the Bulgarian port of Dedeagatch, ten miles from

[1] Like Kemal, Nuri was a graduate of the Constantinople Staff College. In 1922 he became the Defence Minister in the Government of Iraq, and after 1930 he was several times Prime Minister of Iraq. Pro-British and anti-Communist, he was executed after the *coup d'état* in 1968.

the Turkish border, with the declared intention of invading Turkey-in-Europe. Other British troops were approaching Adrianople, a former Turkish city that had been ceded to Bulgaria in 1913.

Fighting and talking were continuing in tandem on all fronts. On the Italian Front a ferocious struggle was under way. One Austrian counter-attack captured six hundred Italians. On October 27, Italian and British troops managed to cross the Piave. It was the turning point of the battle, with more than 7,000 Austrians being taken prisoner. Mutiny was in the air, as parts of two Austrian divisions refused to counter-attack. The Emperor realised that he could not expect anything but withdrawal, retreat and flight. 'My people are neither capable nor willing to continue the war,' he telegraphed to the Kaiser that day, and he added: 'I have made the unalterable decision to ask for a separate peace and an immediate armistice.'

It was not only the Austrians who were unwilling to continue the war that day. Aboard the German High Seas Fleet, an order to go to sea for a final, desperate attack on the British Fleet electrified the Admiralty when it was decoded in London, but the order was resisted by the German sailors. Admiral Scheer did his utmost to convince the men to fight. 'An honourable battle by the fleet – even if it should be a fight to the death – will sow the seed of a new German fleet of the future,' he said. 'There can be no future for a fleet fettered by a dishonourable peace.'

The sailors were not to be persuaded. 'We do not put to sea, for us the war is over,' they chanted. Five times the order to leave port was given and five times it was ignored. Stokers on board those ships that were at sea extinguished the fires in the boilers. A thousand mutineers were arrested, immobilising the fleet. 'Our men have rebelled,' the Fleet's commander, Admiral von Hipper, wrote in his diary, 'I could not have carried out the operation even if weather conditions had permitted it.' Angry that the Imperial Navy had failed to challenge the British that day, the former Chief of the Navy Staff, Admiral Tirpitz, wrote in retrospect: 'The German people do not understand the sea. In the hour of its destiny it did not use its fleet.... Whether our grandsons will be able to take up the task again lies hidden in the darkness of the future.'

On the Western Front, an American artillery battery was moving from one front-line zone to another on October 27 when, as its commander, Captain Harry Truman, later recalled, 'the French edition of the *New York Herald* was distributed along the line. Headlines in black letters informed us that the armistice was on. Just then a German 150 shell burst to the right of the road and another to the left.' A sergeant remarked: 'Captain, those goddam Germans haven't seen this paper.'

On October 28 Austria asked the Allies for an armistice. The initiators of the confident opening of hostilities against Serbia in 1914 were at the end of their military and political tether. During the day, the Italians took 3,000 Austrian prisoners on the Piave. In the evening the Austrian army was ordered to retreat. At the Adriatic port of Pola, four young Austrian naval officers went on board a German submarine, asking for passage to Germany. 'What for?' they were asked. 'We should like to fight for Germany to the end!' they replied.

In Prague the Austrian request for an armistice led to a final upsurge in Czech national activity. Meeting in the Gregor Hall, the National Council of Czechoslovakia, which had been formed there three months earlier, assumed the powers of a government, gave orders by telephone to the Austrian officials in the Hradcany Castle to transfer power to it, took over control of the streets, and proclaimed the independence of the Czech State. That evening the Austrian troops in the Castle laid down their arms and the civil servants their pens. Without borders, without international recognition, without the approval of Vienna, with little more than a capital city under its control, a Czech national entity had come into being.

On October 29, as the Austrian troops retreated from the Piave to the Tagliamento, more than six hundred Italian, French and British aircraft struck at the long, slow retreating columns of men, stores and guns. It was a savage bombardment, against which the Austrians had no protection. Several thousand bombs were dropped, and more than 50,000 rounds were fired at the retreating army by the Royal Air Force alone. A nineteen-year-old British officer, Bernard Garside, later recalled reaching the scene of the air attack. 'All along the road were broken vehicles and all the litter out of them, dead horses sometimes with limbs off or bellies ripped open, corpses of men on the road and in the fields where they had run to escape the machine guns and bombs from the planes, all the litter from men's pockets for some reason. I don't want to go into what I saw too much, but it was terrible.' It was a repetition of the attack on the Turkish forces in retreat to the river Jordan a month earlier.

The Austrian armistice was not to come into effect until November 4. Meanwhile the retreat continued, and with it the Allied bombing.

On the Western Front, General Pershing was still worried about the German ability to start the war up again in the spring. His opinion, given on October 30, was that the Allied advance should continue until the German army surrendered. 'An armistice', he warned, 'would revivify the low spirits of the German army and enable it to reorganise and resist later on.' But Pershing's plea for unconditional surrender was dismissed by Lloyd George and Clemenceau, who were now confident of imposing strong, virtually crippling terms on Germany, even if its army did not lay down its arms on the field of battle. Foch, too, did not fear a German military revival of the sort of which Pershing feared. 'I am not waging war for the sake of waging war,' Foch told Colonel House, Wilson's emissary. 'If I obtain through the armistice the conditions that we wish to impose upon Germany, I am satisfied. Once this object is attained, nobody has the right to shed one drop more of blood.'

The armistice talks with Germany would go on. So too would the fighting.

On October 30, Tirpitz wrote to Prince Max: 'The enemy, who can well estimate our strength, will not treat us any more mercifully if we disarm prematurely, but all the more roughly and brutally, since to the sensation of victory will be added a feeling of contempt for us.' Tirpitz was confident that if Germany decided to reject the Allied terms 'the sudden need to resume the fight will have the greatest psychological effect', to Germany's advantage. If Germany rejected the proferred peace terms, he believed, there would be 'terrible disappointment' among the 'war-weary masses of the enemy peoples', which would be matched by 'the increasing strength of the heroic resistance on our front'. Prince Max rejected this call for continued confrontation and a prolongation of the war.

On the Western Front, the fighting continued. Among the British troops in action in the last days of October was the poet Wilfred Owen, advancing with his battalion through French villages from which the Germans had just pulled back. Owen was resentful that the Allied leaders had turned down the earlier tentative German requests for negotiations. 'The civilians here are a wretched, dirty, crawling community, afraid of *us*, some of them, and no wonder, after the shelling we gave them three weeks ago,' he wrote on October 29 to his fellow-poet Siegfried Sassoon. 'Did I tell you that five healthy girls died of fright in one night at the last village? The people in England and France who thwarted a peaceable retirement of the enemy from these areas are therefore now sacrificing aged French peasants and charming French children to our guns. Shells made by women in Birmingham are at this very moment burying little children who live not very far from here.' It was rumoured that Austria had surrendered. 'The new soldiers cheer when they hear these rumours, but the old ones bite their pipes, and go on cleaning their rifles, unbelieving.'

The war would go on, even as the German and Austrian armies were in retreat, and areas that had been under German control for four years were being liberated. On October 30, Colonel Alan Brooke visited the military cemetery at Douai, maintained by the German army since the end of 1914, 'looking at all the graves, French, English, Russian, Italian and German all equally well cared for'. In the middle of the cemetery, the Germans had put up a large stone monument. 'On the three corner stones are three medallions with the French, English and German crests, each face turned towards the respective country.' At each frontal face at the top was written 'Pro Patria' and at the bottom on each side, etched in stone:

A LA MEMOIRE DES BRAVES CAMARADES
DEN GEFALLEN KAMERADEN ZUR EHRE
IN MEMORY OF BRAVE COMRADES

On the Italian Front, the fighting continued. On October 30 more than 33,000 Austrian soldiers were taken prisoner. On the Western Front, a German division refused orders to go into battle. In Vienna, the Austro-Hungarian Government continued to seek an armistice with the Allies.

The Hapsburg Empire was collapsing. The Czech National Council in Prague having declared the independence of Czechoslovakia on October 28, on the following day, the Slovak National Council, meeting at Turciansky Svaty Martin associated itself with the previously non-existent entity, while at the same time insisting on the right of 'free self-determination' for the Slovak region.[1]

Also on October 29, in Agram, the Croatian Parliament declared that Croatia and Dalmatia were henceforth part of a 'national sovereign State of the Slovenes, Croats and Serbs', a state that, like Czechoslovakia, was a new feature on the map of Europe. In the Slovene city of Laibach and in the Bosnian capital of Sarajevo, similar declarations linked these regions with the emerging South Slav State of Yugoslavia. In tune with the times, the German name Agram was changed to the Slav name Zagreb, and Laibach to Ljubljana.

On October 30 the Austrian port of Fiume, which two days earlier had been declared (from Agram) to be part of the South Slav State, declared its own independence, demanding union with Italy. In Budapest, the Hungarians grasped the hour of their own separate existence, as the King-Emperor invited Count Karolyi to form a government. Karolyi did so; then, with Charles's agreement, he ended the links that had joined Austria and Hungary together since 1867, and demonstrated Hungary's new-found independence by opening armistice negotiations of his own with the French forces in Serbia. During October 30, with 'Austria-Hungary' a thing of the past, Charles gave the Austrian Fleet to the South Slavs and the Danube Flotilla to Hungary. In Vienna, workers and students demonstrated against the monarchy itself. That evening the Austrian armistice delegation arrived in Italy, at the Villa Giusti near Padua.

On the battleship *Agamemnon*, off the island of Mudros, the Turkish and British negotiators, headed by the commander of British naval forces in the Eastern Mediterranean, Admiral Wemyss, were working out the last details of the Turkish armistice, which was to come into effect at noon on the following day. General Townshend participated in this final defeat for Turkey.

The signing of the armistice ended the war in Mesopotamia, which had brought his former army to the gates of Mosul. During the four years of the British campaign in Mesopotamia, the deaths in action and from disease amounted to 1,340 officers and 29,769 men. The war in Palestine and Syria had also ended, with British troops already north of Aleppo, at the very edge of the Turkish heartland of Anatolia.

Under the terms of the armistice of Mudros, Turkey had to open the Dardanelles and Bosphorus to allied warships, accept the military occupation of the Dardanelles and Bosphorus forts, agree to the demobilisation

---

[1] Slovakia was twice to achieve its own sovereign status in the twentieth century: from 1939 to 1945 as a satrap of Nazi Germany, and on 1 January 1993, when it separated from the post-1945 Czechoslovak State in the aftermath of the fall of Communism.

of the Turkish army, release all prisoners-of-war, and evacuate its vast Arab provinces, all but a fragment of which were already under Allied control. A few months later *The Times* commented: 'The weakness of the armistice lay in that it did not bring home to the Turks in Anatolia the completeness of the defeat they had sustained and that no adequate provision was made for the security of the Armenians.'

October 30, the day of Turkey's capitulation, saw another dramatic development, the departure of the Kaiser from Berlin to Spa. From the distance of that Belgian resort town he let the politicians discuss his possible abdication in favour of his young son, with Germany to be ruled by a Council of Regency. A majority of the political parties in the Reichstag favoured such a course. They were agreed that the Kaiser would have to sacrifice himself so that his dynasty might survive. But when the Prussian Minister of the Interior, Dr Drews, went to Spa to put this point to the Kaiser himself, he was indignant. 'How comes it that you, a Prussian official, could reconcile such a mission with the oath you have taken to your king?' he asked.

With Hindenburg's full support, the Kaiser declined to abdicate. General Groener, who was also present during the Kaiser's interview with Dr Drews, and had been noisily emphatic (loudly so, as Drews was hard of hearing) that his sovereign should not abdicate, had another proposal to make. The Kaiser he said, after Drews had gone, 'should go to the front, not to review troops or to confer decorations, but to look for death. He should go to some trench that was under the full blast of war. If he were killed it would be the finest death possible. If he were wounded the feelings of the German people would completely change towards him.' Hindenburg thought this a bad idea. The Kaiser's views are not recorded.

On the Western Front, the Allied offensive continued with swift advances everywhere. On October 31 the British reached the river Scheldt. Elsewhere, preparations were being made for a final offensive. 'It is a great life,' the poet Wilfred Owen wrote home that day from his dug-out near the village of Ors, on the Sambre Canal, the next objective for him and his men. 'I am more oblivious than alas! yourself, dear mother, of the ghastly glimmering of the guns outside, and the hollow crashing of the shells. There is no danger down here, or if any, it will be well over before you read these lines. I hope you are as warm as I am....'

On October 31, in the Adriatic port of Pola, the South Slavs took over the Austro-Hungarian warships that the Emperor had handed to them. Then, to their horror, they saw an Italian torpedo-boat, which had refused to accept that these warships were no longer part of an enemy fleet, torpedo the battleship *Viribus Unitis* while it was at anchor. Several hundred sailors were drowned. That same day, Serbian troops reached the heights above their capital, Belgrade, having marched all the way from the Salonica Front in less than six weeks, liberating their towns and villages. From their vantage point above Belgrade they could see an armada of

489

boats taking the Austrian troops across the Danube to the Hungarian shore. On the following day they opened fire on the Hungarian monitors patrolling the Danube. More than four years earlier, the First World War had begun by the Austrians shelling Serb positions on these very heights.

A new American offensive was planned for November 1, on the Meuse. The preparations were intense, but the men were listless. Douglas MacArthur described how they 'drearily kept themselves in readiness for their next call to front-line duty', and, within sight of the Côte de Châtillon which they had captured with such heavy losses two weeks earlier, could not get 'those nightmarish days' out of their minds. Those training them tried to create a new zeal with slogans and exhortations. 'The best way to take machine guns is to go and take 'em! Press forward.' 'There is no excuse for failure.' 'No man is ever so tired that he cannot take one step forward.'

In the week before the American attack, three batteries of 14-inch naval guns, the standard armament for a battleship, were mounted on railway wagons and, from a distance of twenty-five miles, fired their 1,400-pound shells into the German defences. Two days before the attack began, American artillerymen, using mustard gas for the first time in action, fired 36,000 rounds of gas shells, forty-one tons, at the four German divisions facing them. Of the twelve German artillery batteries in the nearest sector to the Americans, nine were destroyed. Then, after an intense two-hour artillery barrage in the early hours of November 1, the Americans advanced. Low-flying American planes machine-gunned the German defences that had survived the bombardments. High-flying American bombers struck at German lines of communication, stores and troop concentrations behind the lines.

'For the first time the enemy lines were completely broken through,' Pershing commented. The Germans fled. An American private, Rush Young, recalled: 'The roads and fields were strewn with dead Germans, horses, masses of artillery, transport, ammunition limbers, helmets, guns and bayonets.' By the end of the day it was clear that the Germans would not be able to regroup or counter-attack. That same day, November 1, just north of the Aisne, near the villages of Banogne and Recouvrance, French troops advanced into what had been the first of the three lines set up behind the Hindenburg Line.

In Berlin, political activity was intensifying, with the demand for an end to the monarchy being voiced with particular force by the Spartacists. The Kaiser's comment about the demand, at Spa on November 1, to an emissary from Prince Max, was: 'I wouldn't dream of abandoning the throne because of a few hundred Jews and a thousand workers', and he added bitterly: 'Tell that to your masters in Berlin.' Prince Max was untroubled by the Kaiser's point of view. He had already informed the United States that the German Government was awaiting the armistice terms.

Like the Ottoman Empire whose armistice came into effect on October 31, the Hapsburg Dominions had also disintegrated. On November 1 the city of Sarajevo, where the heir to the Hapsburgs had been assassinated four years and five months earlier, declared itself a part of the 'national and sovereign State' of the South Slavs. That same day the people of Ruthenia declared their independence.[1] Revolution was breaking out in Vienna and Budapest. The former Hungarian Prime Minister, Count Tisza, had been murdered in Budapest by Red Guards on October 31. On November 2, German reinforcements transferred from the Eastern Front to the Western Front mutinied rather than go into action. In Vienna, a Hungarian infantry regiment stationed at the Imperial Palace of Schönbrunn deserted its post and returned to Hungary. That same day, in recognition of the collapse of the Central Powers and all that they stood for, the Lithuanian State Council rescinded the election of the Duke of Württemberg as King.

The Allied Supreme War Council, still suspicious of the German will to conclude an armistice, discussed that day, and then approved, plans for an invasion of Bavaria in the spring of 1919. This was to be conducted mainly by the Italians, with some French and British support. The warmaking powers of the Allies were at their height: that October nearly 5,000 machine guns had been produced in Britain, with a further 5,000 being manufactured for the month of November.

The Austrian armistice was signed on November 3, and was to come into effect the following day. In Vienna, Red revolution continued. 'The time is near when the first day of the world revolution will be celebrated everywhere,' Lenin declared on November 3 in Moscow, at a mass rally in support of the Austrian revolutionaries. In Kiel 3,000 German sailors and workers raised the red banner. The Governor of Kiel, Admiral Souchon, the man whose guns had opened fire on the Russian Black Sea ports in 1914, bringing Turkey into the war, ordered Officer Cadets loyal to the Government to suppress the revolt. Eight of the mutineers were killed, but the revolt went on.

On November 3, on the Italian Front, the Italians entered the city of Trent. Among the 300,000 Austrian soldiers taken prisoner in the Trentino was Ludwig Wittgenstein. That day, the Allies agreed to a formal German request for an armistice on the Western Front, but the fighting there continued. On the Italian Front, all fighting ended at three in the afternoon of November 4. Having crossed the river Tagliamento just before the armistice was to come into effect, a chaplain in the British 7th Division commented: 'On the right the sounds of firing were heard. This we believe to have come from the tiny American contingent, which at the eleventh hour had fulfilled their ambition of getting into the front line and were not going to be done out of their battle by any unsoldierly passivity on the part of the enemy.' That night, a British

---

[1] In 1919 Ruthenia was incorporated into Czechoslovakia; in 1939 it was annexed by Hungary; in 1944 it was annexed by the Soviet Union; in 1991 it became the most westerly part of the independent Ukraine. It has not yet achieved its own independence (as of May 1994).

artillery officer, Hugh Dalton, later recalled 'the sky was lit up with bonfires and the firing of coloured rockets.... One could hear bells ringing in the distance, back towards Treviso, and singing and cheering everywhere. It was an hour of perfection, and of accomplishment....'[1]

That day, on the Western Front, British troops attacked along a thirty-mile front between Valenciennes and Guise. The New Zealand Division led the attack on the ancient walled town of Le Quesnoy, less than five miles from the Belgian border. The Germans defended the town in force, driving off the New Zealanders, who then decided to surround the town, leave it besieged, and attack German artillery positions further east. There too, however, at the villages of Jolimetz and Herbignies, German resistance was strong. The New Zealanders then dropped leaflets on Le Quesnoy calling on the German soldiers in the town to surrender, but they refused to do so. The New Zealanders then tried a direct assault, using at one point a thirty-foot ladder up which they clambered in single file. Entering the town at last, they captured 2,500 prisoners and a hundred guns.

In the British assault on the Sambre Canal on November 4, an attempt by engineers to throw a temporary bridge over the canal was prevented by heavy German artillery and machine-gun fire. Almost all the engineers were wounded, and the canal was unbridged. The poet Wilfred Owen was seen encouraging his men to try to get across on rafts. 'Well done!' and 'You are doing well, my boy,' an officer in his company recalled him saying. The rafts proved unsuccessful, however, so planks and duckboards were put together. At the water's edge, helping his men in this task, Owen was hit and killed. Earlier he had written:

> *Voices of boys were by the river-side*
> *Sleep mothered them; and left the twilight sad.*
> *The shadow of the morrow weighed on men.*

At the place where Owen was killed, near the village of Ors, the canal remained unbridged. His battalion eventually crossed on an existing bridge a few miles lower down. On his tombstone in the village of Ors are inscribed the words of one of his poems:

> *Shall life renew*
> *These bodies?*
> *Of a truth*
> *All death will he annul.*

In the original poem, the second sentence also ended with a question mark.

By the end of November 4, the British forces on the Western Front had

---

[1] Dalton, then an artillery lieutenant, was later a leading Labour politician, a member of Churchill's Second World War Cabinet, and Chancellor of the Exchequer in the post-1945 Labour Government.

advanced five miles, capturing 10,000 prisoners and two hundred guns. Among those killed, and buried in the same cemetery as Owen, were two of the four men awarded the Victoria Cross that day, Lieutenant-Colonel James Marshall and Second-Lieutenant James Kirk. On Marshall's headstone are the words: 'Splendid in death when thou fallest courageous leading the onslaught.' Kirk's headstone is inscribed with the words of Jesus: 'Father forgive them for they know not what they do.'

Among the soldiers wounded on November 4 was Carroll Carstairs, one of the Americans who had volunteered to fight with the British army while America was still neutral. A Yale graduate, he had enlisted in December 1914. During the November attack he was hit in the hip by a machine-gun bullet and lay in a shallow trench. 'Gunther ran out to me. As I looked round he fell and I saw the rip at the back of his jacket where the bullet had gone out. He died almost at once. A private soldier shot through both arms fell at the same time, and together we lay until the battle had gone ahead and the stretcher bearers turned up. I was in too much pain to be picked up, and dragged myself on to the stretcher.'

Carstairs was then carried, as he later wrote, 'for a mile or two over broken country by two medical corps men and two German prisoners. It seemed we would never reach the end of our journey. Every step was a jolt and every jolt intense pain. We reached a field which looked like a battlefield, so many wounded lay about – British and Germans. I heard someone say, "That house is mined" which explained our being put down in a field. It was now late in the afternoon. I was so cold that my fingers stuck out stiff and numb and I couldn't move them. I had milk chocolate in my pocket and gave it away. It was dusk when a horse ambulance picked me up. The bridges blown up, horse ambulances were being used to ford the stream.'

On reaching the Casual Clearing Station, Carstairs 'was put down in a courtyard, while a Padre said, "Anyone want any tea? If you've been shot in the stomach, don't drink it as it will kill you." I drank five cups of tea and felt revived.'

Behind the lines, the German naval mutiny was spreading. On November 4, at Kiel, thousands more sailors, many factory workers and 20,000 garrison troops joined the 3,000 mutineers of the previous day. Several thousand sailors travelled from Kiel to Berlin, to raise the flag of mutiny there. On November 5 the sailors in Lübeck and Travemünde declared their adherence to the revolution. On the following day the sailors in Hamburg, Bremen, Cuxhaven and Wilhelmshaven did likewise. From his military headquarters at Spa, the Kaiser considered sending combat troops to retake Kiel, but was dissuaded from doing so by those around him.

On November 4 the Allied commanders met to plan their next attacks. The French were to launch an assault into Lorraine in ten days' time, on November 14. The Americans agreed to provide six divisions for this task, provided that they constituted a separate American army. Meanwhile, inside Germany and Austria the calls for revolution were growing. 'Germany has caught fire and Austria is burning out of control' was Lenin's comment on November 6. That day, in Berlin, the German socialist leader Friedrich Ebert proposed that the Kaiser, who was still at Spa, should abdicate 'today, or at the latest, by tomorrow'.

The American army, continuing its successful November 1 offensive on the Meuse, reached the bank of the river opposite Sedan on November 6: in the rapidity and confusion of the advance, Douglas MacArthur, commanding an infantry brigade, was taken prisoner by his own side. Thinking he was a German officer, vigilant American sentries brought him in at pistol point. The mistake was quickly discovered, once MacArthur had taken off his unusual floppy hat and long scarf. It was a day of growing confusion, conflicting orders, units marching one into another, and a rapidly growing, chronic shortage of supplies. In one division horses were in such short supply that men had to be harnessed to wagons to pull them towards the front. But chaos in the rear areas, combined with warnings that the medical personnel were at 'the breaking point', could not mask the scale of the victory. That same day Canadian troops entered Belgium, taking 1,750 German prisoners on the soil that Germany had occupied for just over four years.

Returning to Spa on November 6 after four days at the Front, General Groener warned the Kaiser in person, and the Chancellor by telegram, that an armistice must be signed at the latest by Saturday the 9th. 'Even Monday will be too late,' Groener warned. His survey of the situation, based on his personal experiences of the past few days, was a grim one: the fleet was in mutiny, revolution was imminent, and the Government's authority had fallen so low that troops would refuse to fire on revolutionaries.

On the following morning, November 7, the German armistice delegates gathered at Spa. The Centre Party leader, Matthias Erzberger, a member of Prince Max's Government, had with great reluctance agreed to lead the delegation, thereby (as we now know) signing his own death warrant. So uncertain was it that Erzberger would actually have the courage to cross into the French lines that a virtually unknown officer, General von Gündell, had been told to be ready to take his place. That morning Foch received a wireless message from the German Supreme Command, giving the names of the envoys, and asking that, 'in the interest of humanity' their arrival in France 'might cause a provisional suspension of hostilities'. Foch ignored this request. At midday the delegation left Spa for the front, crossing on to French-controlled territory. There, they were told that the negotiations would take place in the Forest of Compiègne.

On the battlefield the soldiers were still fighting, as they had done every day for more than four years. But news of the arrival of the German delegates on French soil stimulated a sudden rumour behind the lines that the war was over. That afternoon, in Brest harbour, French sailors threw their caps in the air to exuberant cries of 'Fini la guerre!' and guns fired in celebration. An American journalist in the port, Roy Howard, who was about to sail for America, telegraphed to the United Press office in New York that the armistice had been signed at eleven that morning and that hostilities had ceased at two in the afternoon. He added for good measure that American troops had 'taken Sedan' that morning.

Because of the five-hour time difference, Howard's telegram arrived in New York in time to be taken up by that day's afternoon editions:

PEACE

FIGHTNIG ENDS

was the bold headline of the *San Diego Sun* that day, the compositor having misspelt 'fighting' in his enthusiasm. In hundreds of towns throughout the United States celebrations began. In New York, Enrico Caruso appeared at the window of his hotel and sang 'The Star-Spangled Banner' to an ecstatic crowd. In Chicago an opera rehearsal was halted when a Belgian tenor burst on to the stage and cried, amid tears of joy, 'Stop! Stop! Peace has been declared', whereupon the orchestra played first 'The Star-Spangled Banner' and then the national anthems of all the Allied belligerents.

During the afternoon and evening of November 7, the news of the signing of armistice was reported in Cuba, the Argentine and Australia, leading to widespread celebrations and rejoicing. When the news reached Washington, excited crowds converged on the White House, calling for the President. His wife urged him to show himself on the portico and greet the crowds. Knowing that the news must be false, he declined to do so. Meanwhile, a telegram reached Howard from the United Press office in Paris: 'Armistice report untrue. War Ministry issues absolute denial and declares enemy plenipotentiaries to be still on way through lines. Cannot meet Foch until evening.'

On the Western Front, the advance of the Allied armies continued throughout the day, but so did German resistance. When patrols of the American 42nd Division entered the villages of Torcy and Wadelincourt, just across the river Meuse from Sedan, they were forced back by intense German artillery and machine-gun fire.

In Berlin the majority Socialist deputies in the Reichstag were demanding the Kaiser's resignation. When that was refused, they resigned *en bloc* from the Reichstag and called for a general strike throughout Germany. In Munich, Kurt Eisner, a Prussian Jew and follower of Lenin, who in his professional life was the theatre critic of the *Münchener Post*, declared the establishment of a Bavarian Soviet Republic. In Cologne, revolutionary sailors seized the city, raising the Red flag as it had earlier been raised at Kiel.

The Kaiser was in despair at the collapse of his country, and of the imperial system which had been created by his grandfather and Bismarck a half century earlier. When Prince Max begged him over the telephone to abdicate, he shouted his refusal down the line. Late on the evening of November 8, Admiral von Hintze reached Spa, to tell him that his beloved navy would no longer obey his orders. The Kaiser, who for four years had been the symbol of the warmaking zeal of the Central Powers, was broken, his proud imperial world in ruins.

27

The final armistice

9–11 NOVEMBER 1918

On the morning of 9 November 1918, the German armistice negotiators reached the Forest of Compiègne. The German military delegate, Major-General von Winterfeldt, was the son of the man who had made out the terms of France's surrender in 1870: there was some speculation among the French as to why he should have been chosen. But when General Weygand led the Germans into Foch's railway carriage, it was clear that they brought with them nothing but the aura of defeat. 'When I saw them in front of me,' Foch later wrote, 'aligned along the other side of the table, I said to myself: "There's the German Empire!" '

At Spa, the ruler of that Empire was wrestling with his future. 'My dear Admiral, the navy has left me in the lurch very nicely' was his caustic comment when he saw Admiral von Hintze again that morning. The Kaiser recognised at last that he had lost the support of his navy, whose carefully built-up might was to have been the instrument of Britain's downfall. But what, he asked, of the army, which he had commanded since 1887, and which was in the midst of defeat? Might it not still be used to restore order in Germany itself, and thus maintain the monarchy? He would, he said, lead his army not into battle, on what was left of the Western Front, but to Kiel, Munich and Berlin, to suppress mutiny and revolution. Eleven German cities were flying the Red flag, including five major ports. With Hindenburg at his side, he would restore order to the Reich.

General Groener was asked for his opinion. He spoke without pre-varication. No military operation inside Germany could succeed. Rev-olutionaries were in command of the main railway centres. Many soldiers had joined the revolution. Twenty miles away, Aix-la-Chapelle (Aachen), the nearest German city, was under rebel control. So too was the German-occupied Belgian town of Verviers, less than ten miles away. If called upon to fight, the army would not do so. There were no reserves.

The Kaiser did not seem to understand the enormity of his situation. At first he contemplated an immediate military expedition against the German rebels at Verviers and Aix-la-Chapelle. Then he suggested that he would remain quietly at Spa while the armistice was negotiated, after which, still Kaiser, he would return to Berlin at the head of his army. Groener put paid to this fantasy with the words: 'The army will march home in peace and order under its leaders and commanding generals, but not under the command of Your Majesty, for it no longer stands behind Your Majesty.' The Kaiser protested, and then asked that all his senior generals put that statement in writing. They refused to do so. 'Have they not taken the military oath to me?' the Kaiser asked, to which Groener replied: 'Today oaths of loyalty have no substance.'[1]

At that moment in the discussion, a telegram was brought in from the Commandant of Berlin. It read: 'All troops deserted. Completely out of hand.' It was eleven in the morning of November 9. Other telegrams followed throughout the early afternoon, each one disastrous for the Kaiser's authority and future. Prince Max, in Berlin, in an attempt to preserve the monarchy, announced the Kaiser's abdication and the establishment of a Regency. Then Prince Max himself resigned, handing the Chancellorship to the Socialist leader, Friedrich Ebert. Another telegram revealed that the Spartacists had seized the Imperial Palace, and that Karl Liebknecht had, from the imperial steps, proclaimed the establishment of a German Soviet Republic. In response, the Socialist leader Scheidemann, from the steps of the Reichstag, had proclaimed a Socialist Republic. The road back to Germany was blocked by revolutionaries. Even at Spa the soldiers were setting up a Bolshevik council.

At Spa, another visitor was announced. It was Admiral Scheer, who, in an attempt to stiffen the royal resolve, told the Kaiser that if he resigned the Imperial Navy would be without a leader. 'I no longer have a navy' was William's bitter comment. 'Deep disappointment sounded in these words,' Scheer later recalled. It was five o'clock in the afternoon. The Kaiser had made up his mind. He would leave for Holland, and for exile, in the morning.

In the Forest of Compiègne the armistice negotiations continued throughout the day. When Erzberger tried to explain the extent of the revolutionary danger in Germany, and the threat of Bolshevism invading central Europe and threatening the west, he used that danger as part of his plea for lenient terms. Foch replied: 'You are suffering from a loser's malady. I am not afraid of it. Western Europe will find the means of defending itself against the danger.' Once more Erzberger repeated the German Government's request that there should be a ceasefire on the Western Front for as long as the talks were taking place, and while the German delegates sought to obtain improved terms. 'No,' replied Foch. 'I represent here the Allied Governments, who have settled their conditions. Hostilities cannot cease before the signing of the Armistice.'

[1] 'Der Fahneneid ist jetzt nur eine Idee.'

The fighting therefore went on, but Germany could no longer influence the outcome of the negotiations by its actions on the battlefield. In the hundred days since the Allied offensive had opened at the beginning of August, Germany's power had been broken not by dissent or revolution behind the lines, or by political intrigue, as later nationalist and Nazi politicians were to claim, but by the military superiority of the Allied armies. In those hundred days the British army, with its Dominion forces, had captured 186,000 German prisoners and 2,800 guns. The French had captured 120,000 prisoners and 1,700 guns, the Americans 43,000 prisoners and 1,400 guns, and the Belgians 14,000 prisoners and 500 guns. The combined total, 363,000 prisoners and 6,400 guns, constituted a quarter of the German army in the field, and one half of all its guns. The warmaking power of Germany, even to defend its borders, was within a few days of collapse.

At sea the final acts of the naval war were taking place. Off Gibraltar, British ships sank the German submarine *U-34*, which had been responsible since 1915 for the destruction of 121 Allied merchant ships. Off Cape Trafalgar, a German submarine, the *UB-50*, sank the British battleship *Britannia*, forty of whose sailors were killed.[1]

On the battlefield, the Americans made small advances in Lorraine on November 9. Even then, as the Germans retreated, they left small light machine-gun units behind to hold the Americans up on every ridge. Casualties on the battlefield were few. But behind the lines, thousands of people died that day of influenza, among them the French poet Guillaume Apollinaire.

That day, recovering at his Hyde Park home from a severe bout of pneumonia contracted while in France, Franklin Roosevelt contemplated resigning as Under Secretary for the Navy and enlisting as an ordinary seaman. His visit to Europe, and his inspection of American warships and naval installations in the North Sea and along the Atlantic Coast of France, had given him a taste for action. He was not convinced that the Germans would agree to the Allied armistice terms. 'The consensus of opinion seems to be that the Boche is in a bad way and will take anything', he wrote to a former Harvard room mate on November 9, 'but I personally am not so dead sure as some others. If the terms are turned down and the war continues, I think I shall get into the Navy without question.'

On November 10 the Canadians entered Mons, where, four years earlier, the 'Old Contemptibles' of the British Expeditionary Force had first entered the line, and been driven back. Elsewhere that day, American troops were

---

[1] The commander of *UB-50*, Captain Kukat, was famous for having accepted two young camels as a gift from Senussi tribesmen in Libya in 1916, and taking them in the mine room of his submarine across the Mediterranean to the Austrian port of Pola, where they became prize exhibits at the local zoo.

in action both in the crossing of the river Meuse, and against German troops still fighting near the Briey basin. In this latter engagement a Black American division took part, suffering heavy casualties. At sea that day, a British minesweeper, HMS *Ascot*, was torpedoed off North-East England by a German submarine, and fifty-three crewmen drowned.

As these final deaths marked the self-perpetuating futility of war, the Kaiser left his headquarters at Spa for exile in Holland. His journey there did not take him back to German soil. Warned that German army units at Liège might be mutinous, he left the train that was to taking him to Holland and proceeded by car through back roads and rural by-ways.

On the night of November 10 news reached Compiègne from Berlin that the German Government had accepted the armistice terms. Germany would evacuate immediately Belgium, France, Luxembourg and Alsace-Lorraine. All inhabitants of these areas who had been deported, imprisoned or held hostage would be repatriated. The German army would surrender 5,000 heavy guns and artillery pieces, 25,000 machine guns, 3,000 trench mortars and 1,700 aeroplanes. German troops would evacuate, and the Allies occupy, all western Germany up to the left bank of the Rhine, and would in addition hold three bridgeheads across the Rhine: at Mainz, Coblenz and Cologne. The Allies would be given 5,000 German railway engines and 150,000 railway wagons, as well as 5,000 lorries 'to be delivered in good condition within thirty-six days'. All German troops in the east, including those in Russia, were to withdraw behind Germany's 1914 frontiers. All Black Sea ports were to be evacuated. All captured merchant ships were to be returned. All submarines were to be handed over, together with six battle-cruisers, ten battleships, eight light cruisers and fifty destroyers. Germany would also be required to make 'reparation for damage done' in Belgium and northern France.

The German delegates at Compiègne worked on the last details of these terms through the night, then signed them at ten past five in the morning of 11 November 1918. 'A nation of seventy millions suffers but does not die,' Matthias Erzberger, the chief German delegate declared, in a statement claiming that the terms would lead to famine and anarchy in Germany. It was the fourth and final armistice of the war. Foch immediately sent a message by telegram and telephone to all the Allied commanders: 'Hostilities will cease on the entire front November 11th at 11.00 a.m. French time.' When that moment came (the eleventh hour of the eleventh day of the eleventh month) all fighting on the Western Front would cease. The Kaiser, whom many had come to regard as the principal initiator of the war, was already in Holland, on neutral soil.

Throughout the morning of November 11 fighting continued. At American First and Second Army headquarters news of the signing arrived at 6.30 in the morning. The commanders ordered the fighting to go on until eleven. 'The men who died or were maimed in those last few hours suffered needlessly,' one American historian has written, 'and their mishandling provoked a Congressional investigation after the war.'[1] East of Verdun, near the village of Herméville, Harry Truman's battery was in action that morning. 'I fired the battery on orders until 10.45,' he later recalled, 'when I fired my last shot.' He was using a new type of shell, with a range of 11,000 metres. The extreme range of the normal 75-millimetre guns was 880 metres. The warmaking powers of the Allies, even in their final hour, were still being perfected and refined.

One British objective that morning, for a brigade that had advanced in five weeks from the Lys to the Scheldt almost to the Dendre, was to seize a bridge over the Dendre at Lessines, before the Germans could blow it up. The order to do so was received at 9.30 that morning and had to be completed by eleven o'clock. It was carried out by the much-wounded General Freyberg. As he led his men forward, he was fired on by a German outpost, one bullet piercing his saddle. The bridge was reached, and made safe, and three German officers and a hundred men were taken prisoner. For this action Freyberg was awarded a bar to his Distinguished Service Order and, in due course, a street was named after him in Lessines. It was almost the eleventh hour.

At the village of Ville-sur-Haine, just east of Mons, a Canadian soldier, Private George Price, was awaiting, as were millions of his fellow-soldiers, the ending of the war. It was two minutes to eleven. At that moment a German sniper bullet rang out and Price was killed: one of the very last casualties on the Western Front, and one of 60,661 Canadian war dead.

'Officers had their watches in their hands, and the troops waited with the same grave composure with which they had fought,' John Buchan has written. 'At two minutes to eleven, opposite the South African brigade, at the eastern-most point reached by the British armies, a German machine-gunner, after firing off a belt without pause, was seen to stand up beside his weapon, take off his helmet, bow, and then walk slowly to the rear.'

A few moments later the watch-hands reached eleven. Buchan, whose brother had been killed in action two years earlier, has written: 'There came a second of expectant silence, and then a curious rippling sound, which observers far behind the front likened to the noise of a light wind. It was the sound of men cheering from the Vosges to the sea.'[2] In Eddie Rickenbacker's American air squadron one airman cried out, as he danced in joy, 'I've lived through the war!' Another shouted in Rickenbacker's ear, 'We won't be shot at any more!'

'It's all over, an armistice has been signed,' a company sergeant in the British 8th Division announced to his men (their commanding officer had been wounded in the head the night before). 'What's an armistice mate?' asked one of the men. 'Time to bury the dead,' replied another.

The war was over. Marching into Mons, Lieutenant J.W. Muirhead saw

[1] Donald Smythe, *Pershing, General of the Armies*, page 232.
[2] John Buchan, *The King's Grace*, Hodder and Stoughton, London 1935, page 203.

the corpses of three British soldiers 'each wearing the medal ribbon of the 1914 Mons Star. They had been killed by machine gun fire that morning. As we got into Mons there were bodies of many of the enemy lying in the streets, also killed that day.... Boys were kicking them in the gutter.... The bells in the belfry were playing "Tipperary".'

On board the *Mauritania*, then twelve hours out from New York, 4,000 American troops were on their way to join the battle. When the purser announced that an armistice was imminent some of the troops expressed disappointment that they were too late to take part. In London, guns were fired to mark the moment when the gunfire ceased. Hundreds of thousands rushed into the streets. Vera Brittain, still too saddened by the death of her brother and her fiancé to rejoice, was called to join the celebrations by a fellow-nurse at Millbank Hospital. 'Mechanically, I followed her into the road. As I stood there, stupidly rigid, long after the triumphant explosions from Westminster had turned into a distant crescendo of shouting, I saw a taxicab turn swiftly in from the Embankment towards the hospital. The next moment there was a cry for doctors and nurses from passers-by, for in rounding the corner the taxi had knocked down a small elderly woman who in listening, like myself, to the wild noise of a world released from nightmare, had failed to observe its approach. As I hurried to her side I realised that she was all but dead and already past speech.'

Among those in London when the armistice came was Colonel Alan Brooke. 'The wild evening jarred on my feelings,' he later wrote. 'I felt untold relief at the end being there at last, but was swamped with floods of memories of those years of struggle. I was filled with gloom that evening, and retired to sleep early.' His brother Victor had been killed in action on the Western Front more than four years earlier, in the very first month of the war.

In Rochester, as the bells of the cathedral rang out to celebrate the war's end, Lucy Storrs was at her home giving thanks that each of her four sons had come safely through the fighting. The telephone rang. It was a friend to tell her that Francis, her second son, had died of his wounds the previous evening. In North Wales, Robert Graves had just learned of the death of two of his friends. Two months earlier, his brother-in-law had been killed. The news of the armistice, he later wrote, 'sent me out walking alone along the dykes above the marshes of Rhuddlan (an ancient battlefield, the Flodden of Wales), cursing and sobbing and thinking of the dead'.

In Shrewsbury, near the Welsh border, Wilfred Owen's parents were listening to the cathedral bells ringing out in celebration of the Armistice when a telegram arrived, announcing their son's death.

For many hours, sorrowful memories were caught up in an exuberant, drunken celebration. Streets were filled with crowds singing, dancing and rejoicing. In London, a vast mass of people filled Trafalgar Square, while others thronged the Mall. As the news of the armistice spread to every town and village throughout Europe, the celebrations spread with it. An eleven-year-old English boy, Desmond Flower, recalled how 'we paraded round the garden in our night clothes blowing anything that would blow and banging anything bangable, such as a tea-tray'.

Victory brought a visible explosion of joy to all the Allied capitals. 'Who shall mock or grudge these overpowering entrancements?' Churchill asked a decade later. 'Every Allied nation shared them. Every victorious capital or city in the five continents reproduced in its own fashion the scenes and sounds of London. These hours were brief, their memory fleeting; they passed as suddenly as they had begun. Too much blood had been spilt. Too much life-essence had been consumed. The gaps in every home were too wide and empty. The shock of an awakening and the sense of disillusion followed swiftly upon the poor rejoicings with which hundreds of millions saluted the achievement of their hearts' desire. There still remained the satisfactions of safety assured, of peace restored, of honour preserved, of the comforts of fruitful industry, of the homecoming of the soldiers; but these were in the background; and with them all there mingled the ache for those who would never come home.' At 10 Downing Street that evening, Lloyd George told his dinner guests that he was all for hanging the Kaiser. Churchill, who was present, opposed this.

In France, Pershing was angry that his advice had not been taken, and that the war had not continued until the Germans had thrown down their arms in the field. 'I suppose our campaigns are ended,' he remarked, 'but what an enormous difference a few more days would have made.... What I dread is that Germany doesn't know that she was licked. Had they given us another week, we'd have *taught* them.' The Germans, their troops still under arms, their trenches manned, their machine guns in place, their soldiers everywhere still on French and Belgian soil, felt betrayed by those who had signed the armistice, handing victory to the Allies at the negotiating table. That day General von Einem, commander of the German Third Army, told his troops: 'Firing has ceased. Undefeated ... you are terminating the war in enemy country.'

The soldiers of the victorious armies celebrated with what was to hand. 'Along in the evening', Harry Truman recalled, 'all the men in the French battery became intoxicated as a result of a load of wine which came up on the ammunition narrow gauge. Every single one of them had to march by my bed and salute and yell, "Vive President Wilson, Vive le capitaine d'artillerie américaine!" No sleep all night. The infantry fired Very pistols, sent up all the flares they could lay their hands on, fired rifles, pistols, whatever else would make noise, all night long.'

In the United States, in the town of Cedar Rapids, so many thousands of miles from France, a high school student, William L. Shirer, who was already in his school officers training unit, watched in disappointment as the armistice celebrations got under way. 'A young doctor who had married a cousin of ours', he later wrote, 'and then gone off to France had just returned, his lungs burned out by poison gas, slowly dying. Nevertheless, I found it hard to swallow the fact that I would never fight in the war to make, as President Wilson said, and I believed, the world safe for democracy.'[1]

The war was over. In a poem written to mark the signing of the armistice, Thomas Hardy wrote:

> *There had been years of Passion – scorching, cold,*
> *And much Despair, and Anger heaving high,*
> *Care whitely watching, Sorrows manifold,*
> *Among the young, among the weak and old,*
> *And the pensive Spirit of Pity whispered, 'Why?'*
>
> *Men had not paused to answer. Foes distraught*
> *Pierced the thinned peoples in a brute-like blindness,*
> *Philosophies that sages long had taught,*
> *And Selflessness, were as an unknown thought,*
> *And 'Hell!' and 'Shell!' were yapped at Lovingkindness.*
>
> * * *
>
> *Calm fell. From heaven distilled a clemency;*
> *There was peace on earth, and silence in the sky;*
> *Some could, some could not, shake off misery:*
> *The Sinister Spirit sneered: 'It had to be!'*
> *And again the Spirit of Pity whispered, 'Why?'*

---

[1] Shirer was later, as a journalist, to be an eye-witness to the triumph of Nazism in Germany, and subsequently to write a history of it, *The Rise and Fall of the Third Reich*. He died in 1993, at the age of eighty-nine.

28

Peacemaking and remembrance

On Armistice Day, 11 November 1918, Austria was without an Empire and Germany was without an Emperor. 'Militarism and bureaucracy have been thoroughly abolished here,' Albert Einstein wrote that day from Berlin on a postcard to his mother, adding: 'The present leadership seems thoroughly equal to its task.' But the tasks for the defeated nations were enormous: combating the forces of revolution on the left and militarism on the right, reviving war-ravaged economies, maintaining national morale in the face of the stigma of defeat, the growing burden of 'war guilt', a desire to recover the territories and self-assurances that had been ripped away at the last moment, and a search for scapegoats.

For the victorious powers, too, the burdens of the peace were great, including the promised provision of a better life for the soldiers, sailors and airmen returning from the battlefields. For victor and vanquished alike, the pain and bereavement of the war could never be entirely, and for many millions never at all, assuaged by medical or social amelioration. 'I don't know if I am glad or sorry to be alive,' General Freyberg wrote to a friend in Britain on November 18, as he and his men marched through Belgium towards the German frontier. 'I only know that it wasn't my fault that I am alive.'

In two remote regions, fighting had gone on after the armistice. On November 21, in central Albania, the Austrian commander, General Pflanzer-Balltin, unaware that the war was over and that the Hapsburg monarchy had fallen, took the imperial salute at a march past of Austrian occupation troops. Two days later, in East Africa, the 150 German troops and 3,000 Africans still marching under General von Lettow-Vorbeck, who had been unbeaten after four years of fighting and moving across vast areas, surrendered to the British at the Northern Rhodesian town of Abercorn.

A hundred German troops, and 3,000 Africans fighting with them, had been killed, or died of disease, during the four years of their East African saga, in which they had been forced to cover many hundreds of miles of remote and inhospitable terrain. In the British forces, 3,000 Indian soldiers had also died, as had 20,000 African labourers, porters and bearers, killed by disease during those four years, while assisting the respective armies.

On the morning of December 1 the first British troops crossed into Germany. It was a date, wrote Field Marshal Haig in his final dispatch, 'for ever memorable as witnessing the consummation of the hopes and efforts of four-and-a-half years of heroic fighting'. Ironically it was also the day on which, as Haig noted, the supply situation became 'critical': the men had moved forward so quickly that they had gone further than their food trains could reach them. And so the victors had to halt for three days, before being able to continue their triumphal march.

When the American troops crossed into Germany on December 1 they were amazed by the contrast between the ruined villages and farms of the battle zones in northern France and the 'carefully cultivated fields and prosperous villages' of Germany. The troops themselves were tired and wet: they had marched for two weeks, mostly in the rain, to towns on the Rhine which had known nothing of war and whose inhabitants resented the arrival of a conqueror who, it was being increasingly believed, had not defeated them in battle, but had secured an armistice as a result of their own leaders' failures to avert revolution and republicanism.

In Vienna, the capital city of a vast Empire that had disintegrated, hunger rapidly became acute. In an attempt to persuade the Allies to help, the municipal authorities sent the former Austro-Hungarian Ambassador in London, Count Mensdorff, a cousin of King George V, to Berne, to see Sir Horace Rumbold. 'If someone had said to me five years ago or less', Rumbold wrote to the King's Private Secretary, Lord Stamfordham, 'that Count Mensdorff would come one day to my room and implore me to get food sent to Vienna, I would have said that person was a proper inmate for a lunatic asylum.' Like millions of other parents, the King's Private Secretary had lost a son in the conflict: his only son, John Bigge, had been killed in action on the Western Front in 1915.

Several new States emerged quickly on the wreckage and fragmentation of the four defeated empires. On 1 December 1918, three weeks after the Armistice, and the day on which Allied troops crossed into Germany, the 'Kingdom of the Serbs, Croats, and Slovenes' was proclaimed in Belgrade. The borders of the new State included many minorities, among them half a million Hungarians and half a million Germans, the inheritors of Austria's defeat. There were also many tens of thousands of Roumanians, Albanians, Bulgarians and Italians within the borders of the new State. In theory, under the Wilsonian plan and the minorities legislation of the new League of Nations, each of these new minorities would be better protected than the pre-war minorities of empire had been.

The new South Slav State survived, and to a certain extent flourished, throughout the inter-war years. Its Regent, Alexander, who had commanded the Serbian armies in their epic retreat in 1915 and throughout their time at Salonica, became King on his father's death in 1921. His efforts to create a common Yugoslav patriotism, symbolised in 1929 by the change of the name to Yugoslavia, were ended in 1934 when he was assassinated in Marseilles by extreme right-wing Croat nationalists, at the start of an official visit to France. The unity of Yugoslavia was maintained under his son Peter for another seven years, until, in 1941, the German army overran Serbia as Austria had done in 1915, and Croatia declared its independence.[1]

On 4 December 1918, British troops, having marched from the Franco-Belgian border, at last reached Cologne, establishing a Zone of Occupation. Nine days later, on Friday the 13th, they crossed to the east bank of the Rhine over the Hohenzollern Bridge. The last of the Hohenzollern kings had been in exile in Holland for more than a month.

From the first days of peace, the stigma of defeat and the severity of economic hardship, stimulated the forces of revolution and fanaticism in Germany, Austria and Hungary. 'Never, indeed, in the history of the world', the German-born Zionist Arthur Ruppin wrote in his diary on December 7, 'has a people been confronted with such terrible armistice terms and admitted its complete defeat, although no enemy has yet set foot on its soil and, on the contrary, its armies are still deep within the territories of its enemies. The simple man in the street cannot understand what has happened so suddenly and feels completely lost.'

On December 13, President Wilson arrived in Europe. His had been the conditions that had led to the prolongation of the war in its last weeks, and to the armistice terms that Germany was already denouncing. His had been the troops, more than a million, on whose arrival at the front in the summer of 1918 so much had seemed to depend. His were the troops, as many as three million, which in 1919 or 1920 were to have secured the victory. Now his vision of a new Europe was to be tested at the conference table and enshrined, or tarnished, in peace treaties. To the chagrin of the American troops who waited to greet him, he did not visit the battlefields on which they had fought, suffered and in the end prevailed. He declined to review them at Montfaucon, the scene of one of their hardest battles, and when he did review them, at Langres, he found an excuse not to stay for the planned celebratory dinner afterwards. His battlefield was to be the Paris Peace Conference; his adversaries the former Allies, France and Britain, Clemenceau and Lloyd George.

Allied prisoners-of-war were returning to their homes, many of them angry

---

[1] United again, under Communist rule, in 1945, Yugoslavia broke up into its component parts in 1991, when Croatia again declared its independence, followed by Slovenia, Bosnia and Macedonia.

at what they considered harsh or negligent treatment in captivity. Among those who reached Britain on December 14 was Leefe Robinson, who had won the Victoria Cross in 1916 shooting down a German airship over Britain, but had himself been shot down over German lines in France a year later. His friends were shocked to find him bent almost double: he needed a walking stick to get about. Within days of returning home he contracted influenza. He died seventeen days after returning to England, one of 150,000 Britons, soldiers and civilians, who fell victim to an epidemic that left none of the recently warring countries unscathed.

Adolf Hitler, recovering from the British gas attack that had temporarily blinded him, returned to his regiment in Munich on December 18. His bitterness at Germany's defeat spilled over into venom against alleged enemies of Germany. The new rulers of Bavaria were socialists and Jews, led by Kurt Eisner. 'I thought I could no longer recognise the city,' Hitler wrote seven years later in his book *Mein Kampf* (My Struggle). It was those whom he called the 'Hebrew corrupters of the people' against whom he vented his anger: 12,000 to 15,000 of them ought to be held 'under poison gas', together with all politicians and journalists who participated in the Bavarian socialist regime: 'jabberers', 'vermin', 'perjuring criminals of the revolution' who deserved nothing but annihilation. 'All the implements of military power should have been ruthlessly used for the extermination of that pestilence.'

Three days after the unknown Hitler reached Munich, Dr Thomas Masaryk, who had spent the war years travelling throughout the Allied lands as an advocate of an independent Czechoslovakia, reached Prague. That night he slept in the Hradcany Castle, which was to be the centre of Czech government and the symbol of Czech independence until March 1939, when Hitler slept there to celebrate his bloodless conquest.

In Berlin, on 6 January 1919, 10,000 German Marxists and revolutionaries gathered in anticipation of revolution. During a day of fevered discussion, one of their most forceful leaders, Rosa Luxemburg, urged her Spartacist followers not to attempt to seize power before they had sufficient popular support, but she was unable to restrain them. As fighting broke out, she and Karl Liebknecht were captured by right-wing paramilitary forces and killed. Rosa Luxemburg's body, thrown into a canal, was not recovered for five months. She became a Communist heroine and, with the fall of Communism eighty years after her death, a non-person in the lands that had once exalted her.[1]

The Peace Conference opened in Paris on 18 January 1919. For Germans the date was an insult: the anniversary of the day on which, in 1870, the German Empire had been proclaimed with all the fanfare of national

---

[1] I was in Lvov in October 1991 on the day on which the street names of this then Ukrainian city were changed, and watched as the plaques on 'Rosa Luxemburg Street' came down, to be replaced by 'Cathedral Street'.

rebirth and satisfaction. In an attempt to make the German delegates more amenable to pressure, France insisted on maintaining the blockade of Germany. 'There seems to be no limit to French vindictiveness and commercial jealousy' was the comment of the British journalist C.P. Scott, reflecting the growth of a new Anglo-French animosity.

One area of conflict among the Allies concerned Germany's former colonial territories, all of which had been conquered, and none of which were to be returned. It was decided to set up a system of League of Nations Mandates, and to give these Mandates to the victorious powers. Under the terms of the mandates, certain conditions were imposed: in the African and Pacific mandates there was a strict injunction to combat the slave trade. Turkish territory was also distributed under the Mandate system, France acquiring Syria and Lebanon, Britain acquiring Mesopotamia (Iraq) and Palestine, in the western half of which Britain was already committed to introduce a Jewish National Home. South Africa was rewarded for its contribution to the Allied war effort by being given the mandate for German South-West Africa. Cameroon and Togoland were each divided between Britain and France. In the Pacific, where the German colonies had been seized on the outbreak of war in 1914, Japan acquired the mandate for the Marianas, Caroline and Marshall Islands, New Zealand the mandate for German Samoa and Australia that for German New Guinea. The phosphate-rich island of Nauru, which Australia, New Zealand and even Britain wanted, became, perforce, a mandate of the 'British Empire'.

Several of the victors were disappointed. Belgium was denied any part of German East Africa, which she had occupied and would have liked, but received instead the landlocked African territory of Rwanda-Urundi. Portugal also hoped to gain German East Africa but, because this was one of Britain's desiderata, had to make do with the 'Kionga Triangle' in northern Mozambique. Italy asked for a free hand to trade in Abyssinia, but this had not been German territory, and her request was denied. Italy was also denied most of her claims in North and East Africa, as these could only have been given at the expense of France and Britain. The most satisfied power was Britain, the result of the distribution of Germany's colonies and Turkey's empire being, in the words of the British Foreign Secretary, A.J. Balfour, a 'map of the world with more red on it'.

Among those who were disappointed by the outcome of the Peace Conference was Nguyen Ai Quoc, a 25-year-old Vietnamese who, on the outbreak of war in 1914 had been a kitchen hand in the Carlton Hotel, London. While the Conference was in session at Versailles, he asked to see President Wilson. He wanted to submit a paper to Wilson asking for 'the right of self-determination' for the Vietnamese, equality of the law for both Vietnamese and French, freedom to organise and assemble, and the abolition of forced labour: a veritable Vietnamese Fourteen Points. 'The French called it a bomb,' a fellow Vietnamese later recalled. 'We called it a thunderbolt. We were overjoyed. How could any of us refrain from admiring the man who stood up so courageously to make claims on our behalf?'

Nguyen's request to submit his proposals was refused. Forty years later, under the name Ho Chi Minh, he emerged as a national leader, determined to drive France out of Vietnam. Fifty years after his disappointment in Paris he was to engage the full military might of the United States.[1]

On January 25 the Peace Conference set up a Commission on the Reparation of Damage. The Commission was to examine what each of the defeated States 'ought to pay' to the victors by way of reparation for damage done during the war. The French, British and Italian representatives each believed that they could claim the whole cost of the war. The Belgian delegate was worried that under such an approach Belgium would come off badly: her war costs had been relatively small, but her towns and countryside had suffered the rigours of four years of occupation. Britain, given the four-year German submarine campaign against her, wanted shipping losses to be included, as well as losses from German air raids. As the discussion about reparations continued, one note of moderation emerged: the damages were not to be assessed for two years. This, Lloyd George later explained, would give time 'for passions to cool down. It also reduced the bases of valuation by giving time for a reduction of the inflated prices of the War to something in the direction of normal'.

The Germans gained no comfort from this ameliorating attitude with regard to the actual sums to be paid in reparations, or from the decision that the payment would not have to be completed until 1 May 1961, although £1,000 million would have to be paid by 1 May 1921. For them, the very concept of reparations was galling, with its clear implication not only that ill-luck on the battlefield would be penalised financially, but also, as the Allied preamble to the reparations clauses made clear, that Germany was being made to pay because of responsibility for the war itself. The Allied formula, which the Germans reduced to the two words 'war guilt', read: 'Germany accepts the responsibility of Germany and her allies for causing all the loss and damage to which the Allied and Associated Governments and their nationals have been subjected as a consequence of the war imposed upon them by the aggression of Germany and her allies.'

'... the war imposed upon them by the aggression of Germany': seldom can ten words have led to such disturbing, and in due course violent repercussions, culminating in a renewal of war, so that the Great War of 1914–18 had to be renamed the First World War, and its successor become the Second. The link between the two world wars, separated by only twenty years, was this 'war guilt' clause as perceived by Germany, aggravated by

[1] Among London's more unusual wall plaques is one affixed to the building now occupying the site of the Carlton Hotel (at the bottom of the Haymarket) recalling Ho Chi Minh's work there. In Ho Chi Minh's time the hotel was a favourite dining haunt for David Lloyd George and Winston Churchill. It was destroyed by a German bomb in the Second World War.

her extremist politicians, and set up as a target to be shot down in flames and fury by Hitler, the former corporal who was to see his mission as revenge on the Allied and Associated Powers (three of which, Italy, Roumania and Japan, were to become his allies in the Second World War).

In his opening speech at Versailles the senior German delegate, Count Brockdorff-Rantzau, declared: 'We are required to admit that we alone are war guilty; such an admission on my lips would be a lie.' The Allied press denounced this German 'insult', the *Daily Mail* telling its readers: 'After this no one will treat the Huns as civilised or repentant.' Brockdorff-Rantzau had gone on to point out that the Allied blockade of Germany was still in force. 'The hundreds of thousands of non-combatants who have perished since November 11 by reason of the blockade', he said, 'were killed with cold deliberation, after our adversaries had conquered and victory been assured them. Think of that when you speak of guilt and punishment.'

The blockade of Germany remained in force, and would do so, the Allies insisted, until the treaty was signed. If the treaty were not signed, *The Times* pointed out, the occupation of the whole of Germany could be added to the blockade as a threat and a weapon. Norman Angell, who in 1909 had warned that war would cripple victors and vanquished alike, denounced the continuing blockade as a weapon 'against the children, the weak, the sick, the old, the women, the mothers, the decrepit', as wicked as the sinking of the *Lusitania* had been.

Inside Germany the forces of the right sought to reassert themselves. On February 21, Kurt Eisner was shot in the back and killed while on his way to the Munich Parliament: his assassin was a 22-year-old German aristocrat, Count Anton Arco-Valley. The violence that followed included the murder of fifty released Russian prisoners-of-war near Puchheim, the murder of twenty-one Catholics arrested in their club in the city and shot in prison, the murder of three of the leaders of the Soviet experiment, and the murder as a reprisal of eight imprisoned rightists. As the forces of the right reasserted themselves, Hitler found employment in Munich, working for the army in persuading returning German prisoners-of-war at Lechfeld camp to turn their backs on defeatism and the Left. He took as his theme the corrupting influence of a 'Jewish Marxist world conspiracy', stimulating a new source of national ferment that had not been present among the forces for disruption in 1914.

The Allied armies of occupation remained on the Rhine. But millions of soldiers were slowly being demobilised and sent home. Some would never recover from the mental anguish of their war experiences. Some would remain trapped in a mental world bounded on all sides by their wartime service. Some would build new lives for themselves in which the war would become increasingly distant and remote. Some would find the forgetfulness of others a source of anguish.

Even as the wounded recovered, some only slowly, in the hospitals, there were incidents that caused distress. On February 23, from his military hospital bed in Rouen, the American volunteer Carroll Carstairs wrote to his father about the night superintendent nurse who berated him and his fellow officers for wanting, when their wounds were causing them agony, to 'disturb' the surgeon. 'The officers all hate her,' Carstairs wrote. 'One evening when she arrived they let out cat-calls and boo'ed. She said "I thought you were officers and gentlemen, but I see I'm in a stable." Everyone laughed. It was strange to watch them, these trapped, these swathed and prostrate marionettes, arms and legs at acute angles outstretched in splints hoisted with ropes that run through pulleys fastened to the ceiling, on the ends of which sandbags dangle. It was grotesque to watch them in this inquisition of weird and painful, of cruel and impossible positions, their beds shaking with their hysterical laughter.'

For returning American soldiers there was the shock, on reaching home, of finding how little their exploits and achievements were known there. When the converted German liner *Leviathan* docked in New York on 25 April 1919, General MacArthur, who had commanded the Rainbow Division in the last weeks of the war, was surprised to be met at the gangplank not by a mass of dignitaries full of praise and ceremonial, but by a young boy who asked him who the men were. 'We are the famous 42nd,' he replied. The boy then asked him if they had been in France. 'Amid a silence that hurt,' MacArthur later wrote, 'with no one, not even children, to see us, we marched off the dock, to be scattered to the four winds – a sad, gloomy end of the Rainbow.'

Siegfried Sassoon expressed in words the anger he felt at even the soldiers forgetting. In a poem entitled 'Aftermath, March 1919', he wrote:

Have you forgotten yet?
Look down, and swear by the slain of the War that you'll never forget.

Do you remember the dark months you held the sector at Mametz –
The nights you watched and wired and dug and piled sandbags on
*   parapets?*
Do you remember the rats; and the stench
Of corpses rotting in front of the front-line trench –
And dawn coming, dirty-white, and chill with a hopeless rain?
Do you ever stop and ask, 'Is it all going to happen again?'

Do you remember that hour of din before the attack –
And the anger, the blind compassion that seized and shook you then
As you peered at the doomed and haggard faces of your men?
Do you remember the stretcher-cases lurching back
With dying eyes and lolling heads – those ashen-grey
Masks of the lads who once were keen and kind and gay?

Have you forgotten yet? ...
Look up, and swear by the green of the spring that you'll never forget.

At the Paris Peace Conference, Lloyd George was beginning to have doubts as to the wisdom of the severity of the terms under discussion, a severity on which the French, and Clemenceau in particular, were insistent. On March 25 he went for the day to Fontainebleau, to work out in his own mind how Germany ought to be treated. In a memorandum which he wrote at the end of the day he declared that his concern was to create a peace for all time, not for a mere thirty years. A short peace might be possible for punitive measures against Germany. But unless the Germans were placated, they would go Bolshevik, and Russian Bolshevism would then have the advantage 'of the organizing gift of the most successful organizers of national resources in the world'.

Once the initial shock of war had passed, Lloyd George warned, 'the maintenance of peace will depend upon there being no causes of exasperation constantly stirring up either the spirit of patriotism, of justice, or of fair play, to achieve redress.... Our peace ought to be dictated by men who act in the spirit of judges sitting in a cause which does not personally engage their emotion or interests, and not in a spirit of a savage vendetta, which is not satisfied without mutilation and the infliction of pain and humiliation.'

Lloyd George went on to criticise those clauses which were even then being drafted, and which might prove 'a constant source of irritation'. He suggested that the sooner reparations disappeared the better. He deprecated putting Germans under alien rule, fearing that by doing so 'we shall strew Europe with Alsace-Lorraines'. He emphasised that the Germans were 'proud, intelligent, with great traditions', but that those people under whose rule they would be placed by the Treaty were 'races whom they regard as their inferiors, and some of whom, undoubtedly for the time being, merit that designation'.

At the centre of the Fontainebleau memorandum was Lloyd George's warning of the danger that lay ahead if the treaty as planned was finalised. 'I am strongly averse to transferring more Germans from German rule to the rule of some other nation than can possibly be helped,' he wrote. I cannot conceive any greater cause of future war than that the German people, who have certainly proved themselves one of the most vigorous and powerful nations in the world, should be surrounded by a number of small states, many of them consisting of people who have never previously set up a stable government for themselves, but each of them containing large masses of Germans clamouring for reunion with their native land ... a new war in Eastern Europe.'

The British Prime Minister's arguments fell on stony ground: when the Fontainebleau memorandum was discussed on March 26, Clemenceau remarked icily: 'If the British are so anxious to appease Germany they should look ... overseas ... and make colonial, naval, or commercial concessions'. Lloyd George was particularly angered by Clemenceau's remark that the British were 'a maritime people who have not known invasion'. Angrily he countered: 'What France really cares for is that the Danzig Germans should be handed over to the Poles.'

These acrimonious exchanges were symptomatic of a growing rift between Britain and France. For Clemenceau, the treaty seemed the best chance France would have of designing effective protection against a Germany that was already almost twice as populous as France, and who must be shown by deliberate, harsh action that it would not pay to think of revenge. Lloyd George regarded this as a recipe for future conflict. Back in Paris from Fontainebleau, he opposed, but in vain, the transfer to Poland of all predominantly German areas. His protest failed to undermine French determination for the maximum reduction of German territory.

Even while the debate about how to treat Germany continued, a sequence of commemorations continued to remind victor and vanquished alike of the divisions, pain and hatreds of the four-year struggle. On 7 May 1919, the day on which the German delegates at Versailles received the draft Treaty of Peace, the body of Edith Cavell was brought back to England on board the destroyer *Rowena*. Eight days later a memorial service in Westminster Abbey was attended by a great multitude. In the streets, crowds, including large numbers of schoolchildren, watched her coffin go by, carried on a gun-carriage.

'During the passing of Nurse Cavell through London,' wrote *The Times*, 'a wonderful stillness rested over streets which at the midday hour are usually clamorous with sound.' In her honour, Canada named Mount Cavell in the Rockies and the United States named the Cavell Glacier in Colorado. In London, her statue was erected just to the north of Trafalgar Square; for several months after it was unveiled men would stand near it to make sure that passers-by removed their hats.

On May 29 the German peace delegation at Versailles submitted a memorandum to the conference protesting at the proposed terms. While willing to disarm 'in advance of all other peoples', they wanted the victors to agree to abolish conscription and reduce their armaments 'in the same proportion'. They were willing to renounce German sovereign rights in Alsace-Lorraine, but wanted a plebiscite to be held there. In agreeing to pay reparations up to a certain limit, they specifically repudiated the notion of war guilt and demanded a neutral inquiry into the responsibility for the war. These submissions were rejected. The denial of war guilt struck a raw nerve with the British. 'I could not accept the German point of view,' Lloyd George later wrote, 'without giving away the whole of our case for entering into the War.' Reviewing the considerations 'which impelled us to throw in our lot with Belgium, Serbia, France and Russia', he had 'not one wavering doubt as to the culpability of the Central Powers'.

The Allied answer to the German delegates was unequivocal: 'Throughout the war, as before the war, the German people and their representatives supported the war, voted the credits, subscribed to the war loans, obeyed every order, however savage, of their government. They shared the responsibility for the policy of their government, for at any moment, had they willed it, they could have reversed it. Had that policy succeeded they would have acclaimed it with the same enthusiasm with which they welcomed the outbreak of war. They cannot now pretend, having changed their rulers after the war was lost, that it is justice that they should escape the consequences of their deeds.'

For the Allies the wounds of war were too close, and the victory too close, to allow any other response. On 30 May 1919 the first of the American war cemeteries on the Western Front was dedicated, that at Suresnes, with 1,551 graves and 974 names on the wall of the missing, those soldiers with no known grave. It seemed self-evident that Germany was culpable. But the Germans were not prepared to accept that their 'deeds' called for 'justice'. Returning in June to his home in Hanover, Hindenburg set to work to write his memoirs, blaming Germany's collapse not on the army, but on the disruptions and revolutions on the home front. This was the 'stab-in-the-back' legend that was to be exploited by many German politicians in the next decade, not least by Hitler, who was to be the last Chancellor in Hindenburg's own Presidency, which ran from 1925 until his death in 1934.

As the Paris Peace Conference continued its intense daily deliberations that June, the atmosphere of anti-Germanism seemed to intensify, as if the Allied diplomats and negotiators were a jury about to condemn and a judge about to pass sentence. One of the British participants, the historian H.A.L. Fisher, wrote in a private letter to a friend on June 11: 'The moral atmosphere in Paris isn't encouraging. All the small States out for more territory and France is not unnaturally in fear of a revived and vengeful Germany. My own view is that passion still runs too high to get a really enduring settlement now, but that if a Treaty *tel quel* is signed there will be an appeasement and by degrees readjustments and modifications can be introduced which will give Europe a prospect of stability.'

The prospects of stability through appeasement were still far off, both in Europe and on what had once been the Eastern Front. On June 17, outside the Russian naval base at Kronstadt, three British coastal torpedo boats, led by Captain Gordon Steele, Lieutenant Dayrell-Reed and Lieutenant Agar, penetrated the naval defences. Dayrell-Reed was killed on entering the harbour. Steele and Agar continued, torpedoing a Bolshevik cruiser. They were both awarded the Victoria Cross.

The intervention against Russia was multinational: British, French, Italian, Czech, Roumanian, Serb, Japanese, Latvian, Baltic German, Finnish and American forces all taking part, as well as anti-Bolshevik Russians and Russian Cossacks. Britain provided the Russian anti-Bolshevik forces with more than half a million rifles and five hundred million rounds of ammunition. British soldiers, including a detachment of men who were expert in releasing gas, were sent to North Russia, among them Donald Grantham, who took advantage of his new posting to study the local geology.

In one of their last decisions before they left Paris, the Allies decided not to continue with this new, distant and increasingly costly conflict. Before the Americans withdrew from Archangel and Vladivostok, 174 had been killed in action or died of their wounds. On 18 November 1919, in one of the last acts of bravery of the First World War, an American officer, Major Sidney Graves, rescued a number of Russian civilians caught in the crossfire of rival factions. He was awarded the Distinguished Service Cross.

The fate and future of the Germans who were to come under Czechoslovak and Polish rule, whose vocal champion Hitler was to become in the summers of 1938 and 1939, were in evidence twenty years before they formed part of the public and much-publicised prelude to the Second World War. On 15 June 1919, representatives of the German-speaking Sudeten regions of Bohemia, Moravia and Silesia, parts of Austria which were to be integrated intro Czechoslovakia, submitted a memorandum to the Paris Peace Conference protesting at their sovereign rights being handed over to the Czechs. 'The subject nation can never tolerate such domination,' they declared. Six days later, with reference to the Germans who had come under Polish rule, on 21 June 1919 the *Vossische Zeitung* wrote: 'The flight from West Prussia and other parts of the Eastern marches, which are about to be transferred from Prussia to Poland, to the Western and Central German provinces, is increasing to such an extent, that the Germans remaining there are very depressed.' The towns on what was to be Germany's new eastern frontier had become 'dangerously crowded' with refugees. 'In Pila (Schneidemühl), whole families had to be herded in stables and other buildings quite unsuitable for human habitation.'

Neither the three and a half million Germans of the Sudetenland, nor the hundreds of thousands in what was to become the Polish Corridor, had any hope of reversing the pattern of decisions that were even then about to be finalised. At the Paris Peace Conference, the Germans continued to seek modifications of the treaty, but the Allies would not allow it to be subject to negotiation. Then, on June 21, anticipating that the German Fleet, which had been interned at Scapa Flow since the armistice, would have to be handed over to the Allies under the treaty, its commander, Rear-Admiral von Reuter, gave orders for the ships to be scuttled.

The first ship to go down was the battleship *Friedrich der Grosse*, sixteen minutes after midday. Two years earlier she had been the focus of the first German High Seas Fleet mutiny. By five o'clock in the afternoon, seventy-four German warships, sixteen of them the largest of their time, had gone to the bottom of the sea. By a curious irony, the scene was witnessed by a party of Scottish schoolchildren on board the tug *Flying Kestrel*: they were on an excursion, and were thrilled to witness what they assumed was some gigantic naval display laid on for them. In an unsuccessful attempt to force some of the German crews to return to their ships and stop them sinking, fire was opened from a few of the small British craft nearby, and eight

German sailors were killed. The last of the German warships, the *Hindenburg*, went to the bottom at five o'clock that afternoon. Four ships were towed ashore by the British before they could be sunk. By scuttling the ships, Admiral Scheer wrote, 'the stain of surrender has been wiped from the escutcheon of the German Fleet'.

On June 22, at Versailles, the German delegates agreed to sign all the clauses in the peace treaty with the exception of those relating to 'war guilt'. As the Allied leaders prepared to give their response to this final act of defiance, news reached them of the scuttling of the Fleet at Scapa Flow. They at once decided not only to reject any alterations in the treaty, but to give the Germans only twenty-four hours in which to sign it. When the German delegates asked to be given forty-eight hours, Lloyd George told his colleagues that 'after carefully considering the matter he felt the sinking of the German ships in the Orkneys weighed principally with him against granting the German request'. The sinking of these ships was 'a breach of faith'. The German request was refused.

There was one further obstacle to signing. The German Government, unwilling to face the odium of having authorised the signature, resigned. The President of the newly created German Republic, Friedrich Ebert, refused to accept its resignation. He then asked Hindenburg and Groener (Ludendorff's successor as Chief of Staff) if Germany would be able to defend herself in the event of a renewed Allied attack. Hindenburg walked out of the room to avoid pronouncing the unpronounceable, that Germany was defenceless. General Groener remained in the room and told the truth: in the east the German position was 'reasonable', in the west it was 'hopeless'.

With four hours left before the Allied deadline, the German Government agreed to sign the Versailles Treaty. In doing so it made a final protest: 'The Government of the German Republic has seen with consternation from the last communication of the Allied and Associated Governments, that the latter are resolved to wrest from Germany by sheer force even the acceptance of those conditions of peace which, though devoid of material significance, pursue the object of taking away its honour from the German people. The honour of the German people will remain untouched by any act of violence. The German people, after all the frightful suffering of the last few years, lacks all means of defending its honour by external action. Yielding to overwhelming force, but without on that account abandoning its view in regard to the unheard of injustice of the conditions of peace, the Government of the German Republic therefore declares that it is ready to accept and sign the conditions of peace imposed by the Allied and Associated Governments.' When this uncompromising yet 'yielding' message reached the Allied negotiators at Versailles they ordered guns to be fired in celebration. On the following day, in Berlin, Ludendorff finished writing his war memoirs, which he dedicated 'To the heroes who fell believing in Germany's greatness.'

On 28 June 1919, the Treaty of Versailles was signed between Germany and the 'Principal Allied and Associated Powers': the representatives of twenty-seven victorious powers appended their signatures to the 200-page document.[1] Under the treaty, Germany was punished both territorially and financially. Her territory was reduced in both the east and west, her army, navy and air force were disbanded, and her responsibility for the war was expressed in the financial liability imposed on her to make reparations, especially to France and Belgium. Articles 42 to 44 forbade Germany from fortifying the Rhineland or having any armed forces there. Article 80 forbade German union with Austria 'except with the consent of the Council of the League of Nations'. Articles 100 to 106 transferred the port of Danzig from German sovereignty and made it a Free City under the protection of the newly created League of Nations. Articles 119 and 120, in five lines, deprived Germany of all her colonial possessions. Article 170 forbade Germany from importing any arms, ammunition or war materials. Article 191 forbade her from building or buying submarines. Article 198 forbade her from having any military or naval air forces.

Germany was to be denied the ability to make war. Under Article 231 of the Treaty, she was forced to accept, with her allies, 'responsibility' for the loss and damage caused as a result of the war 'imposed upon' the victors 'by the aggression of Germany and her allies'. This was the war guilt clause, which served as a preamble to the reparations demands, and to which the German negotiators had particularly objected. While some Allied negotiators, including the British economist J.M. Keynes, thought the reparations clauses were too harsh, others praised them, led by Rudyard Kipling:

> *These were our Children who died for our Lands.*
> *They were dear in our sight.*
> *We have only the Memory left of their Home,*
> *Treasured sayings and Laughter.*
> *The Price of our Loss shall be paid to our Hands,*
> *Not another's hereafter.*
> *That is our Right.*

Every week that followed the signing of the Treaty of Versailles had some ceremony that reminded the victors of their grievance, and made impossible any talk of Treaty modification, or of acceptance of its unfairness, as a few people, including the economist J.M. Keynes, were already arguing. Ten days after the signing of the Treaty there was a spur to anti-German feeling when a memorial service was held in London for Captain Fryatt, the steamer captain shot by the Germans in Brussels in 1916 for having dared to ram a German submarine. Fryatt was then reburied in Dovercourt.

*

[1] The 'Principal Allied Powers' were the United States, the British Empire, France, Italy and Japan. The 'Associated Powers' were headed by Belgium, Portugal and Roumania. The rest, each of whom had declared war on Germany, were Bolivia, Brazil, China, Cuba, Ecuador, Greece, Guatemala, Haiti, the Hedjaz, Honduras, Liberia, Nicaragua, Panama, Peru, Poland, the Serb-Croat-Slovene State (Yugoslavia), Siam, Czechoslovakia and Uruguay.

On July 14, two weeks and two days after the signature of the Treaty, when the power of Germany to harm its neighbours seemed ended for all time, a Victory Parade in Paris linked the day of the fall of the hated fortress of the Bastille with the fall of the German Empire. The day began with a march of a thousand French veterans: the blind, the lame and the mutilated. Then soldiers, bands, commanders, troops from every Allied nation, followed in procession under the Arc de Triomphe and down the Champs Élysées to the Place de la Concorde. There the Strasbourg statue was unveiled for the first time since 1871, before the marchers moved on to the Place de la République, the site of the French Revolution's triumph in 1789.

The procession was headed by two men on horseback, Foch and Joffre, the two Field Marshals who had been at the helm, or near it, since August 1914. Eleven Allied units, each about 1,500 strong, marched in their alphabetical order, as at the Olympic Games. In this triumphant instance Americans marched first, led by General Pershing on horseback, then Belgians, British, Czechs, Greeks, Italians, Japanese, Portuguese, Roumanians, Serbs and Poles, followed at the end by the French, on whose soil so much of the fighting had taken place, and whose losses were the highest of all those present. There was no place for Bolshevik Russia, which had turned its back on the war at a critical time, making it even more critical. Nor was there a place for China, which had declared war on Germany in 1917, and whose labourers were even then working to clear the battlefields of barbed wire and unexploded shells. As for those nations which had been defeated, they could read full accounts of the triumph in their newspapers on the following day: the Austrians, the Bulgarians, the Germans and the Turks.

Among those in Paris watching the celebrations was Winifred Holtby, who had witnessed, as a schoolgirl, the German bombardment of Scarborough in December 1914. Later she had served in France as a nurse. Her biographer, Vera Brittain, has written of how 'calling, during the day, on the plump French Madame who did her laundry, Winifred found the gay, voluble little woman sobbing beneath a cherry tree in her cottage garden for the son who would never return to gather the ripe fruit from the laden boughs. Did this sudden recall to reality bring back to her mind the old drunken woman who had told her at Rudston on August 3rd, 1914, that war was "bloody hell"? At any rate, she returned to Yorkshire to find that for some – amongst whom she did not yet include herself – the War's tragedies, far from being over, had hardly begun.'

On 1 September 1919 the last American combat division left France, sailing from Brest. In the previous months, 300,000 American soldiers had crossed the Atlantic from east to west each month, back to the United States. Each returning soldier received his discharge papers, a uniform, a pair of shoes, a coat and a $60 bonus. More than three and a half million men went through this process. Remaining in France was a small group of men who were to work on the military cemeteries, supervising the gathering of bodies, their identification, burial, and memorial. An American occupation force of 16,000 men was also sent to Germany, as part of the Allied presence on the Rhine, based at Coblenz.

Prisoners-of-war were beginning to be released. In their camps, tens of thousands had died in the influenza pandemic. Of the 300,000 Austrian troops taken prisoner at the beginning of November 1918, as many as 30,000 had died in captivity by the autumn of 1919. Among those who eventually made their way home was the philosopher Wittgenstein, who arrived back in Vienna on August 25. There he was united with his brother Paul, who had lost his right arm on the Eastern Front. A concert pianist, he was learning to play with his left hand only, and rebuilt his career as a teacher.

In Britain, those Conscientious Objectors who had been in prison were also being released, but only slowly. In March 1919 there were still 1,200 in prison and 3,400 doing alternative labour service in special camps in Britain. As a collective punishment for their views, they were deprived of the vote for five years after the war, both in parliamentary and local government elections.

On September 10, Austria signed the Treaty of St Germain with the Allied and Associated Powers. To Italy she ceded the South Tyrol, Istria, part of Dalmatia and her Adriatic islands. The Bukovina was ceded to Roumania. The former South Slav provinces of Slovenia, Croatia, much of Dalmatia, Bosnia and Herzegovina became part of Yugoslavia, putting Sarajevo, the scene of Gavrilo Princip's assassination of Franz Ferdinand, under Slav rule. Hungarian independence was recognised, as was the independence of Poland and Czechoslovakia. Poland was given the former Austrian provinces of Western and Eastern Galicia, including the cities of Krakau (Cracow) and Lemberg.[1] Czechoslovakia was given the former Austrian provinces of Bohemia and Moravia, including the German-speaking Sudetenland. The Austrian army was to be limited to 30,000 men, she was to have no air force, and she was forbidden to unite with Germany.

On November 27, Bulgaria signed her peace treaty at Neuilly. Thrace, her only outlet on the Aegean Sea, was ceded to the Allies, who later transferred it to Greece. The South Dobrudja, a small strip of land along the Black Sea shore, was transferred back to Roumania. Yugoslavia acquired the small enclaves of Strumica and Tsaribrod. Bulgaria was to have no aircraft, no submarines, and an army limited to 20,000 volunteers. Reparations for damage done was to be paid at more than two million gold francs every six months, for thirty-seven years: until 1957. In addition, Yugoslavia was to receive 50,000 tons of coal a year for five years.

In Hungary, the turmoil of nine months of Communist rule and terror under the leadership of Bela Kun postponed the peacemaking. But on

---

[1] In their Polish form, Kraków and Lwów.

4 June 1920 the last main territorial bloc of what had once been the Central Powers accepted the terms of defeat, agreeing to a series of decisions that had already been carried out on the ground. By the Treaty of Trianon, Czechoslovakia acquired the former Hungarian regions of Slovakia and Ruthenia. Transylvania was transferred to Roumania, creating a grievance that has lasted for three-quarters of a century. The Banat region was transferred to Yugoslavia. The Hungarian army was not to exceed 35,000 men. Hungary no longer had access to the sea, though her former maritime activities in the Adriatic were evident in the rank of her Regent, Admiral Horthy, who in the last year of the war had been Commander-in-Chief of the Austro-Hungarian Navy.

All over Europe, and in every country that had sent men to fight in Europe, the memorials to those who had been killed in the war were being designed and put in place. Every town and village from which men had gone to war erected a memorial to its dead, with their names carved in stone. Charlotte Mew wrote, in September 1919, after one such memorial had been unveiled in Britain:

> *For this will stand in our Market-place*
> *Who'll sell, who'll buy*
> *(Will you or I*
> *Lie each to each with the better grace)?*
> *While looking into every busy whore's and huckster's face*
> *As they drive their bargains, is the Face*
> *Of God: and some young, piteous, murdered face.*

On 9 November 1919 a bronze plaque was affixed to one of the pillars of the Town Hall of the Belgian village of Saint Ghislain, in memory of one of the first British casualties of the Battle of Mons, an artillery officer, Major C. Holland, killed in action on 23 August 1914. Collective monuments recorded the deaths of regiments, special units, even animals. Some monuments linked the First World War dead with those of past wars: at Newark, New Jersey, an American memorial contains forty-two sculpted figures representing American soldiers from each era of the nation's history, starting with the Revolutionary War against Britain. On Tower Hill, opposite the Tower of London, a monument records the deaths in the First World War of 12,000 merchant seamen and fishermen 'who have no grave but the sea'. The monument to the British Machine Gun Corps at Hyde Park Corner carries the inscription:

> *Saul hath slain his thousands*
> *But David his tens of thousands*

On 19 November 1919 the United States Senate rejected the Treaty of Versailles. This was a blow to those who had hoped the Americans would not only help to maintain the treaty, but make an important contribution to the political and economic recovery of Europe. 'The whole Treaty had been constructed', one of its British participants later wrote, 'on the assumption that the United States would be not merely a contracting but an actively executant party. France had been persuaded to abandon her claim to a buffer state between herself and Germany in return for a guarantee of armed support from the United States. The whole Reparation settlement was dependent for its execution on the presence on the Reparation Commission of a representative of the main creditor of Europe. The whole Treaty had been deliberately, and ingenuously, framed by Mr Wilson himself to render American co-operation essential.'[1]

Ten years later Clemenceau would write rhetorically to the Americans, his indignation still at fever heat: 'Your intervention in the War, which you came out of lightly, since it cost you but 56,000 human lives instead of our 1,364,000 *killed,* had appeared to you, nevertheless, as an excessive display of solidarity. And either by organizing a League of Nations, which was to furnish the solution to all the problems of international security by magic, or by simply withdrawing from the European schemes, you found yourselves freed from all difficulties by means of a "separate peace". But all this is not so simple as it might appear. The nations of the world, although separated by natural or artificial frontiers, have but one planet at their disposal, a planet all the elements of which are in a state of solidarity, and, far from man being the exception to the rule, he finds, even in his innermost activities, that he is the supreme witness to universal solidarity. Behind your barriers of sea, of ice, and of sun you may be able perhaps for a time to isolate yourself from your planetary fellow-citizens, although I find you in the Philippines, where you do not belong geographically. . . .' Clemenceau added, as a parting shot: 'It was not enthusiasm that flung you into our firing lines; it was the alarming persistence of German aggressions.'

The Treaty of Versailles came into force on 10 January 1920, a mere three weeks after the Senate had rejected it. Henceforth Europe would be left to its own devices to work out how the various clauses were to be implemented, and to take action, or not to take action, if they were broken. With the coming into force of the treaty came the establishment of the League of Nations. It was already in some ways a flawed organisation, with Russia not a part of it and Germany not yet included, and with China aggrieved because the Japanese, despite Allied protests, had annexed the Chinese province of Shantung, previously held by Germany. But the League enshrined the hopes of millions who looked to it to resolve international disputes without the need to go to war. These hopes were encapsulated in the twenty-six articles of the League Covenant, which provided for collective consultation, and then collective action, in the event of unprovoked aggression.

Article 16, intended to act as a deterrent to aggression, stated that an act of war against one member of the League would be deemed an act of

---

[1] Harold Nicolson, *Peacemaking*, Constable, London 1933, page 207.

war against all, and that the military, naval and air forces of the members could be combined 'to protect the covenants of the League'. Article 23 was designed to curb the arms trade, secure the 'just treatment' of native peoples, combat the drug and white slave trades, and provide for the international prevention and control of disease.

The League Covenant represented the highest aspirations of the victors to build a new world, and to guard it. But the turmoil created by four years of war could not so easily be laid to rest. Every aspect of the League's work was the object of debate and dispute. Even in the new national States, which had been born of the aspirations of pre-war minorities, there were new post-war minorities whose rights were continually being eroded, and for whom the League offered the hope rather than the reality of support. The German-speaking minorities in Poland and Czechoslovakia, the Hungarian minority in Roumania and Czechoslovakia, the Ukrainian minority in Poland, all had grievances of the sort that, before 1914, had fuelled the drive to war. The old imperial systems had gone, but some of the problems which they had failed to solved were still a source of concern, and at times of anguish.

Four Empires had fallen in 1918, and with them their rulers. Following the signature of the Treaty of Versailles, the Allies issued a list of 'war criminals' to be surrendered to the Allies, at the head of which was the Kaiser, then in exile in Holland. The Dutch Government resisted all requests to extradite him, just as he himself, as Hitler's forces drove through Holland in May 1940, declined Churchill's offer of asylum in Britain, content to live under German occupation, and to die in exile.

Turkey became a Republic, headed by her war hero, Mustafa Kemal. Austria and Hungary turned their backs on the Hapsburgs, turning their palaces and castles into museums. The Tsar had already been murdered by the Bolsheviks, who, with the growing strength of the Red Army, reasserted Russian authority over most of the former Imperial domains, including much of the Ukraine, the Caucasus and Central Asia. The civil wars by which this was done were savage, with terrible reprisals being carried out.

The violence inside Germany that had been so strong in 1919 did not abate. The defeated nation became a prey to those who sought some militaristic solution to its problems: the seizure of power, or at least the disruption of existing power, by those who did not accept the conditions or even the reality of defeat. On 15 March 1920, during a struggle between the armed forces of right and left in Dresden, a bullet damaged a painting by Rubens in the Zwinger art gallery. In an open letter to the city's inhabitants, Oskar Kokoschka implored the citizens to do their fighting 'in some other place, such as the firing ranges on the heath, where human civilisation is not put at risk', and he added: 'Pictures cannot run away from places where human protection fails them, and the Entente might make the argument that we do not appreciate pictures the excuse for raiding our gallery.'

The Weimar Republic survived several attempts to destroy it by violence. Right-wing fringe attempts to seize power were defeated: Kapp in Berlin in March 1920, Hitler in Munich in 1923. Standing somewhat self-consciously among Hitler's unknown supporters on the day of his attempted coup was one well-known war hero, General Ludendorff, who marched bravely with the leaders as they tried to force their way past a police cordon into the main square. Sixteen of Hitler's followers and three policemen were killed. 'The Munich Putsch definitely eliminates Hitler and his National Socialist followers,' commented the *New York Times*. Weimar had reasserted its authority, as it was to continue to do for most of the succeeding decade. Under the leadership of Weimar, Germany limited the scale of reparations payments and, at Locarno in 1925, entered the European security system. But in 1933 Hitler and his Nazi Party swept away the stability that might have led to Germany's eventual return to normal life without a new war.

'. . . to the memory of that great company'

Throughout Europe, wherever armies had clashed, or towns and villages had been bereaved, monuments continued to be put up, some small, some large, a few, as at Vimy or on the Somme, immense. Many of these monuments were often idealised beyond visual recognition of the conflict. In Budapest, to this day, a Hungarian cavalryman, shot on the battlefield, stands in his stirrups, his hand over his heart, as Jesus, descending from the Cross, beckons the way to heaven, leading the dead man from the dark clouds of war to the bright light of eternity. The cavalryman's sword and helmet lie on the ground at his horse's feet. The inscription reads: 'From Christ's faith, from the blood of heroes, arises the homeland.'

War memorials in Russia suffered the fate of so much in that land of continuing turmoil and destruction. In Moscow, a Brotherhood Cemetery was established soon after the outbreak of the war, and a church built in memory of the dead. In Soviet times both the church and the cemetery were destroyed. Today only one gravestone is left.

Books also served as memorials. In February 1920, the British war correspondent Philip Gibbs published *Realities of War*, in which he wrote of the need to avert 'another massacre of youth like that five years' sacrifice of boys of which I was a witness'. Franz Werfel's novel *The Forty Days* described the Armenian torment, centred around the struggle to hold out against the Turks on Musa Dagh (Moses's Mountain), within sight of the Mediterranean: 'These women's howls had died into a low, almost soundless, windy sigh. It went with the corpse-washing, the enshrouding, like old comfort.'

Werfel's book was a cry of pain. Philip Gibbs's book was a stark portrayal of the cruelties and barbarities of war. In it he also wrote, of the moral aspect of the war: 'The evil in Germany (enslaving German boyhood) had to be killed. There was no other way, except by helping the Germans to kill it before it mastered them.' In France, there was a similar widespread sense of the necessity of the war, exacerbated by the bitterness felt against the Germans for 'war crimes' committed against

French civilians and for the devastation caused by the war on French soil.

This bitterness was continually revived by ceremonies and memorials. On 18 March 1920 the French Minister of War, André Lefèvre, unveiled a memorial to one of the destroyed villages of the war, Ornes, north east of Verdun. Its buildings had been reduced to ruins, the Minister declared, but its name had become a part of history. But neither monuments nor 'history' could express the inner torments that the war had created for those who survived the fighting. A Canadian historian, Desmond Morton, noting that 60,661 Canadians were killed in action, had written: 'Many more returned from the war mutilated in mind or body.'

During a debate in the House of Commons on 8 July 1920, Churchill recalled an aspect of the fighting on the Western Front that was often overlooked. 'Over and over again,' he said, 'we have seen British officers and soldiers storm entrenchments under the heaviest fire, with half their number shot down before they entered the position of the enemy, the certainty of a long, bloody day before them, a tremendous bombardment crashing all around – we have seen them in these circumstances taking out their maps and watches, and adjusting their calculations with the most minute detail, and we have seen them show, not merely mercy, but kindness, to prisoners, observing restraint in the treatment of them, punishing those who deserved to be punished by the hard laws of war, and sparing those who might claim to be admitted to the clemency of the conqueror. We have seen them exerting themselves to show pity and to help, even at their own peril, the wounded. They have done it thousands of times.'

In the summer of 1920, the Red Army forces under General Tukhachevsky, which had defeated the anti-Bolshevik forces of General Denikin in southern Russia in March, turned against Poland. The Poles, ambitious for territory in the east, had advanced as far as Kiev. As Tukhachevsky drove them westward, almost to Warsaw, Poland appealed to Britain and France for help. Among the French military advisers sent to Poland, to help the Poles resist the Bolshevik onslaught, was Colonel de Gaulle, who had taught Tukhachevsky French when they were both prisoners-of-war of the Germans in 1917.

The danger of Communism spreading through Poland to Germany was acute. Sympathy for Poland, one of the most recently re-created States, was widespread. But there were very few people who desired to return to a European war. On July 28 Churchill wrote in the *Evening Standard*, of the British people: 'They are thoroughly tired of war. They have learnt during five bitter years too much of its iron slavery, its squalor, its mocking disappointments, its ever dwelling sense of loss.'

A week later, on August 4, the sixth anniversary of the outbreak of the First World War, Lloyd George delivered an ultimatum to Russia's emissaries in London: the advance on Warsaw must end, or Britain would come forward as the champion of the Poles, just as in 1914 she had championed Belgium. Lloyd George's willingness to go to war was made otiose within forty-eight hours, when 150,000 Polish troops halted Tukhachevsky's advance at Radzymin, only fifteen miles from Warsaw. For the new Poland, this was the Miracle of the Vistula. By August 15, Pilsudski had driven the 200,000 Russian soldiers back to the river Bug, defeating them at Brest-Litovsk, and taking 70,000 of them prisoner. On October 12, the Bolsheviks agreed to an armistice. Once again, they had been defeated by a western neighbour. With that defeat, the violent clash of armies east of the Vistula, which had been almost continuous since August 1914, was at an end.[1]

As a result of the subsequent, substantial Polish advance, a Russo-Polish frontier was established in 1921, by the Treaty of Riga, which incorporated into Poland's eastern regions considerable areas of Lithuania, White Russia and the western Ukraine. Unique among the post-war States of Europe, Poland, with territory gained from Germany in the west, from Austria in the south, and from Russia in the east, was territorially satisfied, though Russia remained, under its Bolshevik leaders, ambitious for the return of those territories lost to Germany at Brest-Litovsk that had not been regained.

Some warmaking went on. In Afghanistan, Britain crushed a revolt and reasserted its influence over the Emir. In Anatolia the military struggle between Turks and Greeks culminated in the defeat of the Greeks and their mass exodus from the mainland. In Morocco, France continued to seek to subjugate the Moroccan tribes in the Sahara desert: the death of forty-one Legionnaires at Djihani, eleven years after the end of the war in Europe, created shock and anger in France.

One short-lived post-war success, in terms of justice and the righting of a wrong, was the establishment of an independent Armenia. This was one of the main decisions of the Treaty of Sèvres, signed on 10 August 1920. The much-mutilated people were to be sovereign throughout the eastern region of the Ottoman Empire which had done so much to harm them. Although the Turks still remained in control of the city of Erzerum, the Armenian leader, Boghos Nubar Pasha, assured the Allied leaders that he would soon drive them out. In addition, across the former Ottoman-Tsarist border, in the areas that had been conquered by Russia in 1878, a new Armenia had been set up, with Kars as its capital, which would be united to the area carved from Ottoman Turkey at Sèvres. Armenia would rise again and re-establish its ancient glories.

Under the Treaty of Sèvres, the United States would be Armenia's defender, the treaty stating specifically that the frontiers of the new State would be 'settled by the arbitration of President Wilson'. This paper triumph was short-lived, despite being inscribed in a formal treaty. In

---

[1] But not the human suffering: famine in the Ukraine was followed by Stalin's purges, and by the murder and deportation to Siberia of millions of Russians.

September 1920, after the United States had turned its back on direct involvement in the problems of Europe and Asia Minor, Turkish forces marched into the new Armenia, conquering them within six weeks. Simultaneously, from the east, Bolshevik forces moved into the former Tsarist areas. Independent Armenia ceased to exist, less than a year after it had achieved international recognition. In March 1921 the Treaty of Moscow, negotiated by the Soviets and the Kemalists, established a new Turkish-Soviet border, on both sides of which the Armenian people were once more under alien rule.

Other beneficiaries of the Treaty of Sèvres were likewise disappointed in their national aspirations in Anatolia. The Kurds, afforded local autonomy, with the right to secede in one year from Turkey, found no one in the international world willing to champion them further. Greece, given the Smyrna region of western Anatolia, was driven from it in a series of bloody battles, with Mustafa Kemal, the victor of Gallipoli, finally establishing his right to be called Atatürk, the Father of the Turks. The Treaty of Sèvres had become a dead letter, and, only two years after the Great War had ended, the Allied powers began once more their negotiations with Turkey for a peace treaty.

Outside Anatolia, the Treaty of Sèvres formed the basis of the territorial settlement eventually established in the former Ottoman lands. The Hedjaz became independent. Syria, to the distress of the Arabs who had hoped for sovereignty there, became a French mandate. Palestine and Mesopotamia became British mandates. In Palestine the terms of the mandate embodied the Balfour Declaration of November 1917, establishing a Jewish National Home and inviting Jews to immigrate to it. Within two decades the number of Jews had grown from the 50,000 living there in Turkish times to 500,000. The Arabs of Palestine also multiplied through immigration, while resentful of the British promise to the Jews, and rising in revolt against the British in 1936. In the eastern, or Trans-Jordanian part of the Palestine mandate, Jews were excluded, and the Emir Abdullah was given substantial authority.

On 14 October 1993 a London newspaper, the *Independent*, published an obituary of Lieutenant-Colonel Henry Williams, who had just died at the age of ninety-six. Williams had fought at Neuve Chapelle, on the Somme and at Ypres, and been wounded and gassed. After the armistice, as a member of the War Graves Commission, he was put in charge, on what had been the Western Front, of 5,000 men whose task was to exhume, where possible identify, and then to rebury the bodies they found. His volunteers came from Britain, France, Belgium, Poland and Latvia.

Williams, and the head of the Commission, Sir Fabian Ware, had the idea of taking one of the unidentifiable soldiers from the Western Front and reburying him in England, where his grave could become a focal point of prayer and contemplation for the hundreds of thousands of parents, widows and children whose loved ones had no known grave. At first the

War Office was sceptical. But Ware and Williams persevered. In the autumn of 1920 Williams was asked to select five unknown soldiers from the main British battlefields in France and Flanders. One soldier was then chosen from the five, to become the Unknown Soldier. The coffin was made of a British oak tree from the Royal Palace at Hampton Court, and the magnificent lead sarcophagus was escorted through northern France by French cavalrymen. The soldier was then brought to Britain on a French destroyer, the *Verdun*, thereby associating the wartime losses of the two Allies.

On 11 November 1920, two years to the day, and to the hour, since the war ended, the funeral and burial of the Unknown Soldier took place in London. A Guard of Valour formed entirely of holders of the Victoria Cross was mounted outside Westminster Abbey. On the way to its burying place, the coffin halted at the Cenotaph – the Greek word for empty tomb – which was unveiled by the King, who then continued on foot behind the gun-carriage to the Abbey. The Unknown Soldier was the focus that day of the yearning of many of those who would never know where their son's or husband's or father's body had been buried, or ground into the earth. The King's Private Secretary, Sir Alan Lascelles, wrote in his diary: 'Pipers marched before him, Admirals of the Fleet and Field Marshals of England on his right hand and on his left, and all London stood bare-headed as he went; while on the coffin lay the steel helmet which each one of us wore, and the long crusader's sword selected for him alone from the King's armoury.'

Henry Williams remained in France and Flanders for seven years, searching for bodies and reburying them. The land on which they were buried was given by the French and Belgian Governments to the Imperial War Graves Commission 'in perpetuity'. Earlier, when a Belgian official asked Williams who was going to compensate the landowners for the land thus taken away from them, he burst out: 'Look, we've *paid* for the land! You've got our chaps that have died to keep it yours.'

The body that had been chosen to lie in the Abbey in perpetuity had no name. 'Of all symbols', Lascelles wrote, 'he is the most nameless, the most symbolic; yet few that Man has ever devised can have given such a clear cut image of reality; for every one of us who has his own dead could not fail to see that they too went with him; that, after two years of waiting, we could at last lay a wreath to the memory of that great company.' It was the same day, and the same hour, on which the French Unknown Soldier was brought to the Arc de Triomphe with equal ceremonial.

In Britain, the Cenotaph became the national focal point of the annual Armistice Day parade. An estimated 400,000 people went past it in the three days after it was unveiled. In Paris the Arc de Triomphe, a monument commemorating Napoleon's victories of more than a century earlier, became the scene of France's annual Armistice Day ceremony. When the Germans entered Paris in June 1940 they marched through it on their way down the Champs-Élysées. In November 1944 Churchill and de Gaulle celebrated the first Armistice Day in liberated Paris under the once more triumphal arch.

Each warring power eventually unveiled a memorial to its Unknown Soldier. The Polish memorial contains the body of a soldier killed in the Russo-Polish War of 1920. The German memorial at Tannenberg in East Prussia, unveiled in 1927, contained the tombs of twenty unknown soldiers from the Eastern Front. In 1931 an Unknown Soldier's tomb was unveiled in Berlin, placed in a neo-classical guard house built for the Palace Guard two hundred years earlier. In 1933 the Nazis attached a large cross at the back of the hall, 'to emphasise', one historian has written, 'the sacredness of the nation which they claimed to have saved'.[1]

In the aftermath of the war, acts of violence reflected some of the bitterness which war, and defeat, created. On 26 August 1921, while walking in a wood near Baden, Mathias Erzberger, who had negotiated the Armistice with Foch in 1918, was assassinated by two nationalist fanatics. On 24 June 1922 Walther Rathenau, accused by extremists of having been in league with the Entente to defeat Germany (he who had supported the deportation of 700,000 Belgian labourers to work in Germany in 1916) was assassinated by nationalist anti-Semites in Berlin.

Outside Russia, Communist efforts to overthrow the post-war governments failed everywhere. The Communist regimes that were established in Munich and Budapest were both destroyed, more bloodily in Budapest than in Munich. In Italy and Spain, right-wing regimes came to power, led by Mussolini in Italy and Primo de Rivera in Spain, committed to the prevention of Communism in all its guises.

The process of peacemaking took longer than the war itself. The war lasted four years and three months. It was not until July 1923, four years and eight months after the end of the war, that the western borders of Turkey were finally established. Having torn up the Treaty of Sèvres in September 1920, occupied Armenia, re-established Turkish power over Anatolian Kurdistan, and driven the Greeks from the Smyrna province on the Aegean, Mustafa Kemal agreed to sign the Treaty of Lausanne, and abided by it. By this treaty, Turkey would remain sovereign across a thousand miles of Anatolia, from the eastern shores of the Aegean to the western slopes of Mount Ararat. The Allied plan, embodied in the Treaty of Sèvres, for non-Turkish control of European Turkey, Constantinople, and the Zone of the Straits, was abandoned. Gallipoli, where the Turks had first shown that they could not be attacked with ease or impunity, was to remain under Turkish sovereignty.

The one concession made to Allied sensibilities was that the military cemeteries on the Gallipoli Peninsula would be accorded a special status, open in perpetuity to those who wished to make the pilgrimage there.

[1] George L. Mosse, *Fallen Soldiers*, Oxford University Press, Oxford 1990, page 97.

Visitors came quickly: one grave at Anzac, that of Private George Grim-wade, Australian Army Medical Corps, has next to it a stone brought from his home in Australia 'and placed here in ever loving remembrance by his parents, April 1922'. Parents could decide what extra inscription to put on the regular headstones. On that of Trooper E.W. Lowndes, of the 3rd Australian Light Horse, are added the words: 'Well done Ted.' At the southern tip of Cape Helles, on the clifftop overlooking two of the landing beaches that were most bitterly fought over in April 1915, a tall obelisk, the Helles Memorial to The Missing, lists the names of 20,763 men who died on the peninsula but have no known graves.

An era of peace was ushered in after 1918 amid many hopes, and the protective hand of the League of Nations. Not armies, navies and air forces, but disarmament was the method chosen to keep that peace. Inside each multinational State, minority rights would be upheld by the Minority Treaties of the League and the minority guarantees of modern con-stitutions. Modernity itself was to be based upon talking, compromise, adjustment, arbitration, common sense, economic interdependence, and a desire to settle disputes at the conference table. A cynic might feel that all these elements had existed in Europe before 1914.

In the post-war world, treaties would form a legal framework of inde-pendence and the sanctity of the new frontiers (but, some people asked, had not Belgium's frontier been guaranteed by treaty before 1914?). In August 1920, with the signing of a treaty between Czechoslovakia and Yugoslavia, the first step was taken among the new States of central Europe to create a Little Entente of mutual recognition and protection: within a year Roumania had joined them. The Locarno Agreements of 1925 brought guarantees, with British and Italian support, to the thrice-fought-over Franco-German frontier. The inviolability of the Belgian frontier was also guaranteed by Locarno. At the same time, the two new States of Poland and Czechoslovakia signed military alliances with France, giving their frontiers impressive support. The nations that felt aggrieved, especially Germany and Hungary, would be able to seek redress of their grievances through the good auspices of the League. Plebiscites, the demo-cratic application of one man, one vote, had already adjusted the Franco-German and Polish-Czech frontiers in the immediate post-war period. Land-grabbing, whether the Italian seizure of Fiume from Yugoslavia in 1919, the Polish seizure of Vilna from Lithuania in 1920, or the Lithuanian seizure of Memel from German East Prussia in 1923, were frowned upon: they were precedents that were to be avoided in the new era, though it was during the new era that they took place.

Pacifism also flourished in the post-war era, focusing its efforts on a call for universal disarmament. As Germany, Austria, Hungary and Turkey had effectively been disarmed by the treaties, the pacifist pressure was on the victor powers, especially France, to cut back their armaments to a minimal level. In 1925, the year in which the Locarno Agreements appeared to offer a legal and diplomatic framework in which to avoid a future Franco-German war, with all that entailed in terms of repercussions, an Anti-Conscription Manifesto was launched, signed among others by Albert Einstein and Mahatma Gandhi. 'It is debasing human dignity,' they wrote, 'to force men to give up their life, or to inflict death against their will, or without conviction as to the justice of their action. The State which thinks itself entitled to force its citizens to go to war will never pay proper regard to the value and happiness of their lives in peace. Moreover, by conscription the militarist spirit of aggressiveness is implanted in the whole male population at the most impressionable age. By training for war men come to consider war as unavoidable and even desirable.'

Treaties, civilised behaviour, trade, disarmament: did these pointers to permanent peace have any echoes with the idyllic aspects of the pre-1914 years, or were they the manifestation of a new pragmatism born of more than four years of suffering and destruction? On 15 November 1920, at the first meeting of the League of Nations Assembly, a proposal not to increase armaments for two years had been opposed by six countries who were not even willing to try so short a moratorium: they were France, Poland, Roumania, Brazil, Chile and Uruguay. France became the most heavily armed State in Europe, with Germany disarmed under the Treaty of Versailles: a cause of German grievance as well as of inequality. On 4 August 1928, the fourteenth anniversary of Britain's declaration of war on Germany, Sir Horace Rumbold, who had been in Berlin in 1914, was again in the German capital, this time to present his credentials as Ambassador to the German President, Hindenburg. That afternoon he walked in the streets around the Embassy. 'There was hardly a soul about. Two under-sized soldiers whom I met in the course of my walk represented the Reichswehr, which was then limited to 100,000 men. The great German military machine had been scrapped for the time being, but, as it subsequently turned out, only for the time being.'

'The time being' was over eleven years later, when a new national leader in Germany, the former corporal who had been temporarily blinded by gas on the Western Front in 1918, decided that he could reverse the verdict of defeat by rearmament, national mobilisation, terror, tyranny, diplomacy and war. Ten years after the end of the war he was already a political figure to be reckoned with in Germany, speaking in strident tones of the need for revenge, for rearmament, for the return of lost territory, and for the elimination from German life of the scapegoat he had chosen for his and their own country's defeat, the Jews of Germany. Had a few thousand of Germany's Jews been gassed in 1918, Hitler wrote in *Mein Kampf* in 1925, Germany could have averted defeat. Not for him the proved patriotism of the hundreds of thousands of Jews who served in the German army, or the memory of the 12,000 German Jewish soldiers who had been killed in action between 1914 and 1918.

The post-war period lasted two decades, twenty precarious years of peace from the Great War to the second European War. During those two decades the literature of the war reflected all its emotions, from patriotic enthusiasm and national self-assertiveness to individual suffering and disillusionment. Histories, novels, films, plays and poems, music, paintings and cartoons, even postage stamps, kept the four years of war before the eyes of the millions who had served in it, and the millions more who had watched it from their homes, in newspapers and on newsreels, and heard of it through the letters and home leaves of the participants. Almost every general sought to describe and justify his conduct. Thousands of participants gave their accounts of the various episodes of the war. Ten thousand forgotten moments of glory were resurrected, as in 1923, when General Mangin described in *Des Hommes et des Faits* (Men and Facts) his recapture of the village of Onhaye in August 1914, at a time when the French front was almost everywhere falling back. It had been one of the heroic actions of the early weeks of the war.

War museums were opened everywhere, and in the Soviet Union, anti-war museums. Relics of the war became part of many monuments. In England, in 1924, a Tank Museum was established at Bovingdon at which the very first tank, known variously to the troops as 'Big Willie', 'His Majesty's Landship Centipede' and 'Mother' was on display. It is no longer there: in 1940, when the call went out for scrap metal to feed the munitions factories, 'Big Willie' was sent to the scrap heap, to become a part of the shells and shrapnel of a new war.

Even before the battlefields could be cleared of the detritus of war, they became the focus of a thriving travel industry. In the immediate aftermath of the war, most of those who visited them were in search of the graves of their relatives, or the scene of their loved ones' final battle. Vera Brittain, seeking the grave of her fiancé, visited the Western Front in 1921. Hiring a car in Amiens, she 'plunged through a series of shell-racked roads between the grotesque trunks of skeleton trees, with their stripped, shattered branches still pointing to heaven in grim protest against man's ruthless cruelty to nature as well as man.'

Almost every year during the inter-war years travellers were joined by dignitaries and veterans at a series of ceremonies, mostly at the opening or unveiling of monuments. On 16 July 1922, at Jonchéry-sur-Vesle, President Millerand unveiled a monument to Corporal André Peugeot, the first French soldier to be killed in the war. The monument, which was destroyed by the German occupation forces a month after the capitulation of France in 1940, was rebuilt in 1959, forty-five years after Peugeot's death.

On 24 July 1927, King Albert of the Belgians was present at the opening of the Menin Gate, the massive Memorial to the Missing that replaced the twin lions that had marked the exit from Ypres during the war years.[1] The

---

[1] Those lions now reside in Canberra, Australia.

ceremony ended that day with the sounding of 'The Last Post' by buglers of the Somerset Light Infantry, and a lament played by pipers of the Scots Guards. The idea that 'The Last Post' should be sounded every evening was that of the superintendent of the Ypres police, P. Vandenbraambussche. It was, and still is, done by buglers of the Ypres fire brigade. The money for this was raised in Britain 'to ensure the sounding of The Last Post each evening for all time'.

No year went by without another impressive ceremony taking place, and another imposing monument being unveiled. On 4 November 1928 both Foch and Weygand were present at La Ferté-sous-Jouarre for the unveiling of a memorial to the 3,888 British soldiers who were killed during the retreat from the Marne but who had no known graves: Unknown Soldiers to whose gravestone relatives and friends could make no pilgrimage. Now their names were inscribed on a wall of white stone.

There was a glimpse of the way in which the opening of memorials had become routine when, in July 1931, General Sir Hubert Gough, who had commanded the British Fifth Army in 1914, met King Albert of the Belgians in London. 'I suppose, sir, you are very busy?' Gough asked. 'Oh yes, I am very busy doing the only job left in my profession,' the King replied. 'What is that, sir?' asked the General. 'Unveiling war memorials!' answered the King.

The inter-war guide books to France, to Belgium, to northern Italy, to Yugoslavia, to Poland, to the Ukraine, to Turkey and to Palestine incorporated the remnants and memorials of the war as an integral part of their presentation. Findlay Muirhead's best-selling guide to north-eastern France drew attention, in 1930, while describing a journey from St Pol, to a nearby hill which 'commands a splendid view of the Lens-Arras battle-field'. At Arras, in the Place de la Gare, could be found the Head Office of the Imperial War Graves Commission in France and Belgium. In the Grande-Place about a third of the houses had been destroyed by German artillery fire but 'are being rebuilt in the former style'. In the suburbs of Lens the miners' pre-war brick houses had 'offered little resistance to shell-fire' but the mines themselves, 'devastated in 1914–18 by artillery fire and by the German policy of systematic flooding' were again in working order. Muirhead also noted, of the city of Reims: 'Shattered by the bombardments of 1914–18 it holds the place of honour among the martyred towns of France.'

Honour was a word much turned to, and sometimes rejected, in the inter-war years. 'The causes of war are always falsely represented, its honour dishonest and its glory meretricious,' Vera Brittain wrote in her memoirs *Testament of Youth* in 1933, 'but the challenge to spiritual endurance, the intense vitalising consciousness of common peril for a common end, remain to allure those boys and girls who have just reached the age when love and friendship and adventure call more persistently than at any later time.' While that 'vitalising consciousness' lasted, she reflected, 'no emotion known to man seems to have quite the compelling power of this enlarged vitality'. Civilisation could not be rescued from the 'threatening forces of destruction', she feared, unless it was possible 'to impart to the rational processes of constructive thought and experiment that element of sanctified loveliness which, like superb sunshine breaking through the dark clouds, from time to time glorifies war'.

Vera Brittain had lost her fiancé, her only brother and two close friends in the war. For two years as a nurse she had looked after desperately wounded soldiers brought straight from the battlefield. On reading this passage after the Second World War, a former soldier, Hugh Boustead, a veteran of the Somme, commented: 'I have seen too much of what men do to one another – the torturing and mutilating of the Whites by the Red Army in Russia, savagery in Africa and Arabia, above all the butchery on the Western Front. This is evident to anyone who thinks about war; what is less obvious is "the compelling power of this enlarged vitality". That constitutes indeed the real problem of any League or United Nations.'

The 'butchery on the Western Front' was depicted for a wide public in and beyond Europe, in Erich Maria Remarque's novel *All Quiet on the Western Front*, an unalloyed portrayal of the life and death of a group of German soldiers. The writing was direct, the tone bitter: 'Bertinck has a chest wound. After a while a fragment smashes away his chin, and the same fragment has sufficient force to tear open Leer's hip. Leer groans as he supports himself on his arm, he bleeds quickly, no one can help him. Like an emptying tube, after a couple of minutes he collapses. What use is it to him now that he was such a good mathematician at school.'

Remarque's book was first published in Germany in January 1929 and in Britain two months later. Its title derived from the death of the narrator, killed in October 1918 'on a day that was so quiet and still on the whole front, that the army report confined itself to the single sentence: "All quiet on the Western Front".' In 1930 Universal Studios in Hollywood turned the book into a film.[1] When it was first screened, the magazine *Variety* wrote: 'The League of Nations could make no better investment than to buy up the master-print, reproduce it in every language, to be shown to every nation until the word war is taken out of the dictionaries.'

That the First World War would lead to a universally agreed system of international co-operation was one of the hopes of those who studied its origins and its course. On 15 June 1929 the German historian Emil Ludwig, biographer of the Kaiser, wrote in the introduction to his book on the origins of the war: 'This book demonstrates the peaceable intentions of the masses of all nations in July 1914. May it contribute to strengthen

---

[1] *All Quiet on the Western Front* was one of the first talking films, and, as the film historian Barry Norman has written, the first great anti-war film: directed by Lewis Milestone, 'it makes no concession to public demand for a happy ending; nor should it, for ultimately war has no happy ending. . . . The final shot, of a soldier reaching out to touch a butterfly only a second before he is mortally wounded by an enemy bullet, still provides one of the most vivid and unforgettable moments in all cinema.' The film won two Oscars, for best film and best director. Its star, Lew Ayres, became a Conscientious Objector in the Second World War.

the idea of a Court of Arbitration, which is no Utopia, but a growing reality – not a permanently insoluble problem, but the inevitable outcome of recent experience.' Ludwig believed there was no way forward except by such a Court and concept of arbitration: 'There is only this alternative: either to do it now, or to wait for another war.'

Arbitration and negotiation did begin to make a mark on the post-war divide, but only slowly and, as it turned out, too late. On 8 July 1932 agreement was reached at Lausanne, in Switzerland, whereby Germany was virtually freed from her Reparations payments. The German liability, which had stood at $25,000 million, was reduced to $2,000 million, with the strong indication that even this remaining sum would not have to be paid in full, and certainly not before the original treaty date of 1961, then three decades away. But there was an ominous comment from the British Ambassador in Berlin, Sir Horace Rumbold. 'It must be borne in mind', he wrote to the Foreign Office in London, 'that it is a German characteristic never to admit that any arrangement is entirely satisfactory from the German point of view'. Hitler and his Nazi Party certainly had no intention of admitting that the Lausanne agreement had helped Germany. Renunciation of the Treaty of Versailles was a main platform of his next election campaign, and a much-publicised aim once he became Chancellor six months later.

In August 1932 the French President, Albert Lebrun, inaugurated a memorial at Verdun: the Ossuary of Douaumont. Marked by a high tower, it had taken ten years to build. In it were placed the remains of 130,000 soldiers, French and German, whose bones were found on the battlefield. These bones could (and can) be viewed through special windows set at ground level. In the cemetery in front of the Ossuary are the graves of 15,000 French soldiers, each of whom had been identified. A monumental gateway nearby leads to the spot where, in 1919, a line of protruding rifles and bayonets revealed the existence underground of the bodies of French soldiers who had been killed when their trench was blown in on top of them. This too, the 'Trench of Bayonets', became a memorial, covered in a concrete canopy held up by concrete columns.

'The Marne and Verdun will ever remain among the greatest feats of war,' commented Clemenceau in his book *Grandeur and Misery of Victory*, first published in 1930. 'Yet mutual butchery cannot be the chief preoccupation of life. The glory of civilisation is that it enables us – occasionally – to live an almost normal life. The Armistice is the interval between the fall and rise of the curtain.' When Clemenceau wrote these words twelve years had passed since that armistice. Nine more were left before the curtain was to rise again.

The Armistice was a recurring memory of great power for the former victors, galling to those whom they had defeated. On 11 November 1932, in a glade in the Forest of Compiègne, a ceremony was held to celebrate the signature of the Armistice there fourteen years earlier. The railway coach used by Foch for the armistice negotiations was brought to the glade, and a monument unveiled, showing the German eagle being cut down by a sword, with an inscription describing how, that on that very spot, the boastings of the German Empire had been brought low. The railway carriage was kept in a special shed, to protect it from the elements. Less than eight years later, in June 1940, it was brought out of its shed, and used by Hitler to sign his armistice with France. For that ceremony, the monument of German's humiliation was hastily covered by a large swastika flag. The carriage was then taken to Berlin as a captured trophy. It disappeared in April 1945 on a railway line fifty miles south of Berlin, between Elsterwerda and Grossenhain, where it is thought to have been destroyed in a British bombing raid. The carriage now at Compiègne is a similar one, with most of the original relics of 1918 duly reinstated in it.

With Hitler's coming to power in Germany in 1933, fears of a new war, and preparations for war, went side by side. German rearmament, illegal under the Treaty of Versailles, was begun in earnest. Aspects of the First World War were looked at in a new light. German 'guilt', whether for invading Belgium, or for her conduct during the war, was denied. On 7 May 1935, the twentieth anniversary of the sinking of the *Lusitania*, the Nazi Party newspaper *Völkischer Beobachter* interviewed Karl Scherb, the officer who had first sighted the ocean liner. He defended the sinking as retaliation for the British 'hunger blockade'. He also said that the submarine's only orders were to 'do as much damage as possible to suspected British troop transports'. Captain Schwieger had not been guilty of wilful murder. 'He merely did his onerous duty.'

Captain Schwieger could not join the debate: he had disappeared at sea while in command of *U-88* in the autumn of 1917. Had he lived he might well have been brought to trial by the Allies, adding another cause for anger in inter-war Germany.

The controversies of the war, fought for four years in government departments and at army headquarters, were refought for the next forty years in books and magazines. The passage of time brought an increase in bitterness. In 1936, in the final volume of his war memoirs, Lloyd George wrote of the British military commanders: 'Some of the assaults on impossible positions ordered by our generals would never have been decreed if they had seen beforehand with their own eyes the hopeless slaughter to which their orders doomed their men.' Two years later, in the foreword to the abridged edition, he wrote of how, as Prime Minister, 'I saw how the incredible heroism of the common man was being squandered to repair the incompetence of the trained inexperts (for they were actually trained not to be expert in mastering the actualities of modern warfare) ... in the narrow, selfish and unimaginative strategy and in the ghastly butchery of vain and insane offensives.'

*

On 30 May 1937 five solemn ceremonies took place in France: the dedication of five American war cemeteries, followed in August by the dedication of an American war cemetery in Britain.[1] These ceremonies called
forth strong emotions of confidence in the cause as well as personal
sadness. Even as the last of the ceremonies was taking place, the cause was
being renewed. On 22 July 1938, as war again threatened Europe, and
Hitler demanded the Sudetenland from Czechoslovakia, the Imperial War
Graves Commission completed its task of cemetery building for the First
World War. That day, King George VI unveiled the Australian National
Memorial at Villers-Bretonneux in Northern France. Almost a year later,
at Easter 1939, members of the Old Comrades Association of the British
Machine Gun Corps gathered in the French town of Albert, to unveil a
plaque on the Town Hall to the 13,791 members of their corps who had
been killed in action. It was just over a quarter of a century since the Battle
of the Somme in which they had suffered their heaviest casualties. It was
less than a half a year before war would break out again, bringing German
troops once more to Albert, this time not for five months as in 1918 but
for nearly five years. A few miles away from Albert, one of the four model
tanks of the British Tank Corps Memorial bears bullet marks from the
opening battles of the Second World War.

The politicians and commanders who led their nations in the Second
World War had all been involved in some way in the First. Hitler and
Mussolini had both served in the trenches. In the British Cabinet on the
outbreak of war in September 1939, seven out of its twenty-two members
had won the Military Cross on the Western Front during the First World
War. One Minister, Earl De La Warr, as a seventeen-year-old conscientious
objector, had opted to serve in the merchant navy.[2] Only one had been too
young to serve. Almost all had lost brothers or relatives in battle. Neville
Chamberlain's nephew Norman, to whom he was close, had been killed
in action in 1917.

The Great War battlegrounds of the Eastern, Western and Serbian Fronts
were overrun by Germany in 1939, 1940 and 1941. The regions where
the most savage fighting had taken place in 1914–1918 became part of
Nazi-occupied lands. New cruelties were perpetrated, which for the civilians under occupation completely overshadowed the cruelties of the
earlier war. The sturdy brick buildings of one Austro-Hungarian garrison
and cavalry barracks in East Upper Silesia, from which in 1914 the imperial
soldiers set out to fight on the Eastern Front against Russia, became in the

---

[1] The cemeteries in France are Aisne-Marne (at Belleau), Flanders Fields (Waregem), Meuse-
Argonne (Romagne), Oise-Aisne (Fère-en-Tardenois), Somme (Bony) and St Mihiel (Thiaucourt).
The cemetery in Britain is at Brookwood, where 468 American servicemen who died in Britain
are buried: most of them were seriously wounded men who had been brought back to Britain,
where they died of their wounds, some of them in 1919 and 1920.
[2] One of Earl De La Warr's two sons, Thomas Sackville, was posted missing, presumed killed,
on air operations in 1943, aged twenty.

Second World War the focal point of the concentration camp of Auschwitz, where as many as a million people were put to death: at least 800,000 Jews, many thousands of Russian prisoners-of-war, Polish political prisoners, and captives of a dozen other nations. Another Austro-Hungarian barracks, the eighteenth-century garrison town of Theresienstadt, where Gavrilo Princip had been held as a prisoner, and where he died in the First World War, became between 1941 and 1944 the place of incarceration and death for more than 33,000 Jews. A further 88,000 were deported from there to be murdered in the east.

As German troops swept across the Somme in May 1940, they were watched by a former a British soldier, Ben Leech, who had fought there in 1916. Between the wars he was one of the of gardeners tending the war cemeteries: his was a cemetery near the village of Serre. After the fall of France, the local German commander gave him permission to continue his work. He did so, and also joined the local French resistance, helping twenty-seven Allied airmen to escape after they had been shot down over the First World War battlefield. He hid the airmen in the cemetery tool shed, within a few yards of German soldiers who from time to time came to look at the First World War graves.

Having conquered Belgium and northern France for the second time in twenty-five years, the Germans were confronted by the many thousands of memorials to the previous conflict. One in particular gave offence: the memorial to those French soldiers who were the victims of the first German gas attack in April 1915. The monument, at Steenstraat, in Belgium, showed three soldiers. One was standing against the Cross in almost exactly the position normally taken by Jesus, but was clutching his neck. The other two were in agony at the base of the Cross, writhing from the effects of the gas. The inscription described 'first victims of asphyxiating gas'. The German occupation authorities gave orders for the Belgians to cover both the inscription and the figures with cement, but the cement soon cracked, exposing them again. On 8 May 1941, just over twenty-six years after the gas attack itself, the Germans forced Belgian workers to lay explosives, and the monument was blown off its pedestal.

Immediately after the end of the Second World War, Herbert Sulzbach, then a British Army interpreter, was addressing a group of German prisoners-of-war. In the First World War he had served in the German Army, winning the Iron Cross, First Class. Being Jewish, he left Germany after the rise of Hitler, and in 1939 enlisted in the British Army. In 1945 he was a staff sergeant at Comrie, in Scotland, where 4,000 Germans were being held prisoner-of-war. Just before Armistice Day 1945 he read them John McCrae's poem 'In Flanders Fields'. He then told them how they should celebrate Armistice Day itself: 'If you agree with my proposal, parade on November 11 on your parade ground and salute the dead of all nations – your comrades, your former enemies, all murdered fighters for freedom who laid down their lives in German concentration camps – and make the following vow: "Never again shall such murder take place! It is the last time that we will allow ourselves to be deceived and betrayed. It is not true that we Germans are a superior race; we have no right to believe that we are better than others. We are all equal before God, whatever our race or religion. Endless misery has come to us, and we have realized where arrogance leads.... In this minute of silence, at 11 a.m. on this November 11, 1945, we swear to return to Germany as good Europeans, and to take part as long as we live in the reconciliation of all people and the maintenance of peace...!"'

Almost every year, long after the Second World war had ended, there was some ceremony to bring back thoughts, if not memories, of the increasingly distant First World War. In 1966 the graves of the German crewmen shot down over Britain when their Zeppelins were bombing London and the East Coast were brought from three graveyards to their final resting place in Cannock Chase, Staffordshire. A plaque was set up with the inscription in German and English: 'Side by side with their comrades, the crews of four Zeppelins shot down over England during the First World War, here found their eternal resting place. The fallen were brought here from their original burial places at Potters Bar, Great Burstead and Theberton. The members of each crew are buried in caskets in one grave.' On 11 November 1968, fifty years after the Armistice, a plaque was affixed to the wall of a house in Ville-sur-Haine, just outside Mons, where the last Canadian soldier to be killed in action had been shot by a sniper two minutes before the guns fell silent. In July 1994, several more plaques and memorials were unveiled on the Somme.

On 22 September 1984 Verdun was the site of the public reconciliation of France and Germany. 'In a gesture of reconciliation', reported *The Times* under a photograph of the scene, 'President Mitterrand and Chancellor Helmut Kohl hold hands as the French and West German national anthems are played at Verdun, a scene of one of the most bitter battles of the First World War. Before visiting the graves of French soldiers, M. Mitterrand and Herr Kohl paid tribute to the German dead at Consenvoye, one of the many German cemeteries in the area.' President Kohl's father had fought at Verdun in 1916. President Mitterrand had been taken prisoner by the Germans nearby, in 1940.

The destructiveness of the First World War, in terms of the number of soldiers killed, exceeded that of all other wars known to history. The following list gives the number of those who were killed in action, or who died of wounds received in action. The figures are inevitably approximate, nor do they encompass all the victims of the war. In the case of Serbia, more civilians died (82,000) than the soldiers listed here. In the United States army, more soldiers died of influenza (62,000) than were killed in battle. The number of Armenians massacred between 1914 and 1919 was more than one million. The number of German civilians dying as a result of the Allied blockade has been estimated at more than three quarters of a million.

The number of war dead of the principal belligerents was, according to the minimum estimates:

Germany:	1,800,000
Russia:	1,700,000
France:	1,384,000
Austria-Hungary:	1,290,000
Britain:	743,000
Italy:	615,000
Roumania:	335,000
Turkey:	325,000
Bulgaria:	90,000
Canada:	60,000
Australia:	59,000
India:	49,000
United States:	48,000
Serbia:	45,000
Belgium:	44,000
New Zealand:	16,000
South Africa:	8,000
Portugal:	7,000
Greece:	5,000
Montenegro:	3,000

The Central Powers, the losers in the war, lost 3,500,000 soldiers on the battlefield. The Allied Powers, the victors, lost 5,100,000 men. On average, this was more than 5,600 soldiers killed on each day of the war. The fact that 20,000 British soldiers were killed on the first day of the Battle of the Somme is often recalled with horror. On average, a similar number of soldiers were killed in every four-day period of the First World War.

From the last moments of the war itself, its human suffering was embedded in the fabric of the societies upon which its perpetuation had depended. The wounded men of all nations were to be a legacy of war which ended only with their deaths, or with the deaths of those who had lived with them and guarded their broken bodies or minds, or both. Ten days before the armistice, the pacifist Clifford Allen wrote in his diary of a young girl and a discharged soldier living in a cottage near him in Surrey. 'He has lost both legs and propels himself about cheerfully in a mechanical chair. The other evening he was sitting talking to his bride when the kettle started to boil over. He forgot he had no legs and jumped up to seize the kettle only to fall into space on his sore stumps.'

The post-war human suffering of the former combatants took many forms. Hundreds of thousands of sons and daughters in the former warring countries watched while their fathers, with physical wounds that would not heal, suffered, wasted away and died. At the beginning of 1922 as many as 50,000 former British soldiers were receiving government pensions for the continuing effects of shell-shock. Multiply that figure proportionately through all the armies, and one reaches more than a quarter of a million men mentally damaged by the war.

Some who had suffered the severest physical wounds recovered to lead an active life for many years. A Welsh officer, Lieutenant Tudor Williams, had been blown up by a shell and buried alive in September 1916, during the Battle of the Somme. His own men had dug him out. A piece of shrapnel had penetrated his right lung and ended up in the lining around his heart. Despite bouts of ill-health as a result of his injury, he was a Grammar School headmaster from 1929 until his death in 1955. When he went into hospital a year before his death, the radiologist who examined him was fascinated by the piece of shrapnel moving in and out with each heart beat. Williams was one of four brothers, each of whom served and survived.

The last of those who fought in the First World War are now appearing in the obituary lists. Each of their stories reflects different aspects of the distant war. On 2 February 1991 the *Independent* published an obituary of Colonel Monty Westropp, who had been severely wounded in the head at Delville Wood, during the Battle of the Somme, returned to the trenches in time for the Battle of Arras, where he was shot through the leg during the attack on Fresnoy and spent seven hours crawling through the mud of No-Man's Land, dodging several German patrols, before reaching the British trenches. He died a month before his ninety-fifth birthday.

On 24 August 1992, George Jones, Australia's last surviving First World War air ace died. He had fought as a private at Gallipoli, then served as a pilot on the Western Front, flying 113 missions and shooting down seven German aircraft, including two in a single action. Despite being badly wounded in the back, he returned to duty in October 1918, shooting down two more planes before the Armistice. In 1942 he became Chief of the Australian Air Staff, ending his service career as an Air Marshal. He was ninety-five when he died.

These were among the dozens of obituaries that I set aside as they were published. Even as I was writing this chapter, the roll call was continuing, like a muffled drum. On 31 January 1994 the *Daily Telegraph* obituaries included Thomas Glasse, aged ninety-five, who had served from 1914 to 1917 with the Middlesex Regiment, and Albert Frank Barclay Bridges, aged ninety-eight, who had seen action in the Battle of Jutland in 1916. On 19 February 1994 *The Times* published an obituary of the 96-year-old E.H.T. Robinson, a former assistant night editor of the paper, who in 1918, during the Arab Revolt, had been blown up by a Turkish shell and left for dead in the desert. In the same paper, on 26 May 1994, was the obituary of Colonel Terence Conner, who had fought against the Turks in Mesopotamia, at the battle of Dujaila in 1916, and in the recapture of Kut a year later, when he had been wounded. Almost thirty years later, during the Second World War, he distinguished himself in Burma, leading a battalion of the same regiment (the 26th Punjabis) with which he had fought in Mesopotamia, in the struggle in March 1945 to wrest Meiktila airfield from the Japanese. He was ninety-nine years old when he died.

The phraseology of the First World War continues to be a feature of conversation eight decades after the outbreak of the First World War: being subjected to a 'barrage' of complaints, being 'bombarded' with forms, joining the 'rank-and-file', finding oneself in the 'firing-line', and going 'over the top' are among the images and terminology of a war that are with us still. As with the American Civil War which preceded it by half a century, the images and echoes of the First World War will continue to impinge on public consciousness for generations far removed from its harsh realities.

The eightieth anniversary of the outbreak of the First World War coincided with the fiftieth anniversary of one of the main turning points of the Second World War, the Normandy Landings of 1944. During a visit to Normandy during the final week of work on this book, I chanced upon a Second World War headstone in a British military cemetery a few miles inland from the beaches. It commemorated the thirty-year-old Sergeant A. Barber, Royal Artillery, who had been killed on 2 August 1944, almost thirty years to the day after the outbreak of the First World War. He had been four years old when his father died in France in 1918. The inscription on his grave reads:

> *Dear son of Ann Barber*
> *His father killed in action*
> *1918 is buried at Condé*
> *remembered*

This remembrance of the dead, linking the two world wars of this century, brought home to me the links between the individuals who fought, and those who remained to guard their memories. All wars end up being reduced to statistics, strategies, debates about their origins and results. These debates about war are important, but not more important than the human story of those who fought in them.

Bibliography

The vast number of books published about the First World War defies the reading ability of any one individual. In her concise study of Britain and the origins of the First World War, first published in 1977, Zara Steiner listed 335 books for British policy alone. For each of the belligerents a similar list could be compiled. Immediately after 1918 several hundred volumes of diplomatic documents were published by the various former warring powers, likewise restricted to the origins of the war. Other volumes have supplemented these official ones with yet more material, sometimes suppressed by the official writers, sometimes overlooked by them or unknown to them.

Tens of thousands of volumes cover the campaigns, battles, war policies, strategies and individual actions of the combatants, on land, at sea, in the air and behind the lines. A 32-page article by Martin van Crefeld on the railway problems facing the Germans on the Western Front in the first two months of the war lists fifty-eight specialist works. Alan Palmer's 243-page study of the Salonica Front contains 140 books in its bibliography. The 399-page biography of General Pershing by Donald Smythe, with its detailed references to the American army in France in 1917 and 1918, lists more than five hundred relevant publications. Each of Lyn Macdonald's six eye-witness books, including the one on the front-line casualties and those who worked to save them, contains several hundred interviews and contemporary testimonies. To attempt a single-volume history of the war is, from the bibliographic point of view, to attempt not only Everest, but Pelion and Ossa.[1]

In this bibliography I have listed only those books whose factual and documentary material has been of significance during the preparation of this book. It represents, as any such bibliography must, a personal, often random choice. For every page that I myself have written here, I must have

[1] The Pelion range of mountains is in eastern Thessaly. According to Greek fable, the Titans hoisted up Mount Ossa on to the top of Pelion, in order to scale the heavens and dethrone Zeus – 'a strenuous enterprise,' comments *The Nutall Encyclopaedia*, 'which did not succeed'.

studied, and benefited from, several hundred, perhaps several thousand pages written by others. I am grateful to their authors for the knowledge and stimulation they have provided, for their own memories of the war, and for the archival material which, in the course of their own researches, they have gathered together.

Christopher Andrew, *Her Majesty's Secret Service, The Making of the British Intelligence Community*, Viking, New York 1986.

C.F. Andrews (editor), *Mahatma Gandhi: His Own Story*, Allen and Unwin, London 1930.

Norman Angell, *The Great Illusion*, Heinemann, London 1909.

Norman Angell, *Human Nature and the Peace Problem*, W. Collins, London 1925.

H.C. Armstrong, *Grey Wolf, Mustafa Kemal, An Intimate Study of a Dictator*, Penguin, London 1937.

Bernard Ash, *The Lost Dictator, A Biography of Field Marshal Sir Henry Wilson*, Cassell, London 1968.

Brigadier-General C.F. Aspinall-Oglander, *Military Operations Gallipoli*, two volumes, William Heinemann, London 1932.

Robert B. Asprey, *The German High Command at War, Hindenburg and Ludendorff and the First World War*, William Morrow, New York 1991.

Major-General Sir George Aston, *The Biography of the Late Marshal Foch*, Hutchinson, London 1929.

C.R. Attlee, *As It Happened*, William Heinemann, London 1954.

Stéphanie Audoin-Rouzeau, *National Sentiment and Trench Journalism in France during the First World War*, Berg, Oxford 1992.

Anthony Babington, *For the Sake of Example, Capital Courts-Martial 1914–1920*, Leo Cooper, London 1983.

Karl Baedeker, *Paris, Handbook for Travellers*, T. Fisher Unwin, London 1900.

Karl Baedeker, *Berlin and its Environs, Handbook for Travellers*, T. Fisher Unwin, London 1912.

Carlos Baker, *Ernest Hemingway Selected Letters 1917–1961*, Scribners, New York 1981.

Thomas A. Bailey and Paul B. Ryan, *The Lusitania Disaster, An Episode in Modern Warfare and Diplomacy*, Collier Macmillan, London 1975.

Bruce Bairnsfather, *Bullets & Billets*, Grant Richards, London 1916.

A.J. Barker, *The Neglected War, Mesopotamia 1914–1918*, Faber and Faber, London 1967.

B.S. Barnes, *This Righteous War*, Richard Netherwood, Huddersfield 1990.

Correlli Barnett, *The Swordbearers: Supreme Command in the First World War*, Eyre and Spottiswood, London 1964.

Alexander Barrie, *War Underground*, Frederick Muller, London 1962.

Alex Bein (editor), *Arthur Ruppin: Memoirs, Diaries, Letters*, Weidenfeld and Nicolson, London 1971.

V.R. Berghahn, *Germany and the Approach of War in 1914*, Macmillan, London 1973.

Count Bernstorff, *The Memoirs of Count Bernstorff*, William Heinemann, London 1936.

Lieutenant-Colonel J.H. Boraston (editor), *Sir Douglas Haig's Despatches (December 1915–April 1919)*, J.M. Dent, London 1919.

Vahdah Jeanne Bordeux, *Benito Mussolini, The Man*, Hutchinson, London 1927.

Henry Borden (editor), *Robert Laird Borden: His Memoirs*, two volumes, Macmillan, Toronto 1938.

Tancred Borenius, *Field-Marshal Mannerheim*, Hutchinson, London 1940.

Alan Borg, *War Memorials from Antiquity to the Present*, Leo Cooper, London 1991.

Hugh Boustead, *The Wind of Morning*, Chatto and Windus, London 1971.

Vera Brittain, *Testament of Youth, An Autobiographical Study of the Years 1900–1925*, Victor Gollancz, London 1933.

Vera Brittain, *Testament of Friendship, The Story of Winifred Holtby*, Macmillan, London 1940.

Captain D.G. Browne, *The Tank in Action*, William Blackwood, London 1920.

Julius Bryant, *The Iveagh Bequest, Kenwood*, English Historic House Museums Trust, London 1990.

John Buchan, *The King's Grace, 1910–1935*, Hodder and Stoughton, London 1935.

Meriel Buchanan, Petrograd, *The City of Trouble, 1914–1918*, W. Collins, London 1918.

James Callaghan, *Time and Chance*, Collins, London 1987.

Captain A.F.B. Carpenter, VC, *The Blocking of Zeebrugge*, Herbert Jenkins, London 1923.

Carroll Carstairs, *A Generation Missing*, William Heinemann, London 1930.

F.L. Carsten, *War Against War, British and German Radical Movements in the First World War*, University of California Press, Berkeley and Los Angeles 1982.

Martin Ceadel, *Pacifism in Britain, 1914–1945, The Defining of a Faith*, Clarendon Press, Oxford 1980.

Neville Chamberlain, *Norman Chamberlain: A Memoir*, John Murray, London 1923.

William Henry Chamberlin, *The Russian Revolution 1917–1921*, two volumes, Macmillan, New York 1935.

Peter Charlton, *Australians on the Somme, Pozières 1916*, Leo Cooper, London 1986.

Winston S. Churchill, *The World Crisis*, five volumes, Thornton Butterworth, London 1923–31.

Alan Clark, *The Donkeys*, Hutchinson, London 1961.

Ann Clayton, *Chavasse, Double VC*, Leo Cooper, London 1992.

Georges Clemenceau, *Grandeur and Misery of Victory*, George G. Harrap, London 1930.

Mark Cocker, *Richard Meinertzhagen, Soldier, Scientist and Spy*, Secker and Warburg, London 1989.

F. Seymour Cocks, *The Secret Treaties and Understandings, Text of the Available Documents*, Union of Democratic Control, London 1918.

Colonel Codeville, *Armistice 1918, The Signing of the Armistice in the Forest Glade of Compiègne*, Friends of the Armistice of Compiègne, no date.

Edward M. Coffman, *The War To End All Wars, The American Military Experience in World War 1*, Oxford University Press, New York 1968.

Israel Cohen, *The Ruhleben Prison Camp, a record of nineteen months' internment*, Methuen, London 1917.

John Gardner Coolidge, *A War Diary in Paris, 1914–1917*, The Riverside Press, Cambridge Massachusetts 1931.

Rose E.B. Coombs, *Before Endeavours Fade, A Guide to the Battlefields of the First World War*, Battle of Britain Prints International, London 1986.

Bryan Cooper, *The Ironclads of Cambrai*, Souvenir Press, London 1967.

Gordon A. Craig, *The Politics of the Prussian Army 1640–1945*, Clarendon Press, Oxford 1955.

Martin van Crefeld, *Supplying War, Logistics from Wallenstein to Patton*, Cambridge University Press, Cambridge 1977.

Rev. E.C. Crosse, *The Defeat of Austria as seen by the 7th Division*, H.F.W. Deane, London 1919.

Betty Cunliffe-Owen, *Thro' Gates of Memory, From the Bosphorus to Baghdad*, Hutchinson, London 1924.

Viscountess D'Abernon, *Red Cross and Berlin Embassy 1915–1926*, John Murray, London 1946.

Hugh Dalton, *With British Guns in Italy, A Tribute to Italian Achievement*, Methuen, London 1919.

Norman Davies, *God's Playground, A History of Poland*, two volumes, Clarendon Press, Oxford 1981.

C. Day Lewis (editor), *The Collected Poems of Wilfred Owen*, Chatto and Windus, London 1963.

F.W. Deakin and G.R. Storry, *The case of Richard Sorge*, Chatto and Windus, London 1966.

I. Deutscher, *Stalin, A Political Biography*, Oxford University Press, London 1949.

George A.B. Dewar, *The Great Munition Feat 1914–1918*, Constable, London 1921.

George A.B. Dewar, assisted Lieut.-Col. J.H. Boraston, C.B., *Sir Douglas Haig's Command, December 19, 1915, To November 11,1918*, two volumes, Constable, London 1922.

Bill Newton Dunn, Big Wing, *The biography of Air Chief Marshal Sir Trafford Leigh-Mallory, KCB, DSO and Bar*, Airlife Publishing, Shewsbury 1992.

Anthony Eden, Earl of Avon, *Another World, 1897–1917*, Allen Lane, London 1976.

Brigadier-General J.E. Edmonds, *Military Operations, France and Belgium*, eleven volumes, with map cases, Macmillan, London 1926–47.

Howard Elcock, *Portrait of a Decision, The Council of Four and the Treaty of Versailles*, Eyre Methuen, London 1972.

Vivian Elliot (editor), *Dear Mr Shaw, Selections from Bernard Shaw's Postbag*, Bloomsbury, London 1987.

Anita Engel, *The Nili Spies*, Hogarth Press, London 1959.

Cyril Falls, *Was Germany Defeated in 1918?*, Oxford University Press, London 1940.

Florence Farmborough, *Nurses at the Russian Front, A Diary 1914–18*, Constable, London 1974.

Anthony Farrar-Hockley, *Death of an Army*, Arthur Barker, London 1967.

Charles Fenn, *Ho Chi Minh, a biographical introduction*, Studio Vista, London 1973.

Robert H. Ferrell (editor), *The Autobiography of Harry S. Truman*, Colorado Associated University Press, Boulder 1980.

Joachim C. Fest, *Hitler*, Weidenfeld and Nicolson, London 1974.

Leslie Field, *Bendor, The Golden Duke of Westminster*, Weidenfeld and Nicolson, London 1983.

Hamilton Fish, *Memoir of an American Patriot*, Regnery Gateway, Washington DC 1991.

Louis Fisher, *The Life of Lenin*, Weidenfeld and Nicolson, London 1965.

Desmond Flower, *Fellows in Foolscap, Memoirs of a Publisher*, Robert Hale, London 1991.

Norman Franks and H.H. Hauprich (editors), *The Red Air Fighter by Manfred von Richthofen*, Greenhill Books, London 1990.

Sir Frank Fox, *The Royal Inniskilling Fusiliers in the World War, A Record of the War as seen by The Royal Inniskilling Regiment of Fusiliers, thirteen Battalions of which served*, Constable, London 1928.

Franz Joseph, Prince of Hohenzollern, *Emden, My experiences in SMS Emden*, Herbert Jenkins, London 1928.

David Fraser, *Alanbrooke*, Collins, London 1982.

David Fraser, *Knight's Cross, A Life of Field Marshal Erwin Rommel*, HarperCollins, London 1993.

Paul Fussell, *The Great War and Modern Memory*, Oxford University Press, London 1975.

Paul Fussell (editor), *The Bloody Game, An Anthology of Modern War*, Scribners, London 1991.

Brian Gardner (editor), *Up the Line to Death, The War Poets 1914–1918*, Methuen, London 1964.

Hans W. Gatzke, *Germany's Drive to the West (Drang nach Westen), A Study of Germany's Western War Aims during the First World War*, The Johns Hopkins Press, Baltimore 1950.

Imanuel Geiss (editor), *July 1914, The Outbreak of the First World War: Selected Documents*, B.T. Batsford, London 1967.

Tony Geraghty, *March or Die, France and the Foreign Legion*, Grafton, London 1986.

James W. Gerard, *My Four Years in Germany*, Hodder and Stoughton, London 1917.

James W. Gerard, *Face to Face with Kaiserism*, Hodder and Stoughton, London 1918.

Philip Gibbs, *Realities of War*, William Heinemann, London 1920.

Hugh Gibson, *A Journal from our Legation in Belgium*, Doubleday, Page, New York 1918.

Mary Gibson, *Warneford, VC*, The Fleet Air Arm Museum, Yeovilton 1979.

John Giles, *Flanders Then and Now, The Ypres Salient and Passchendaele*, Picardy Publishing, London 1979.

Captain Stair Gillon (editor), *The Story of the 29th Division*, Nelson, London 1925.

General Sir Hubert Gough, *Soldiering On*, Arthur Barker, London 1954.

Robert M. Grant, *U-Boat Intelligence 1914–1918*, Putnam, London 1969.

Robert Graves, *Goodbye to All That*, Cassell, London 1929.

Randal Gray and Christopher Argyle (editors), *Chronicle of the First World War*, volume I, 1914–1916, Facts on File, Oxford 1990.

Randal Gray and Christopher Argyle (editors), *Chronicle of the First World War*, volume II, 1917–1921, Facts on File, Oxford 1991.

Lavinia Greacen, *Chink, A Biography* (of Major-General Eric Dorman-Smith), Macmillan, London 1989.

Viscount Grey of Fallodon, *Twenty-Five Years, 1892–1916*, two volumes, Hodder and Stoughton, London 1926.

H.S. Gullett and Chas Barrett (editors), *Australia in Palestine*, Angus and Robertson, Sydney 1919.

Leslie Halliwell, *Halliwell's Film Guide*, 7th edition, Grafton Books, London 1989.

Michael Hammerson (editor), *No Easy Hope or Lies, The World War I Letters of Lt Arthur Preston White*, The London Stamp Exchange, London 1991.

Harry Hanak, *Great Britain and Austria-Hungary during the First World War*, Oxford University Press, London 1962.

Lord Hardinge of Penshurst, *Old Diplomacy*, John Murray, London 1947.

John Hargrave, *The Suvla Bay Landing*, Macdonald, London 1964.

Ian Hay, *Carrying On – After The First Hundred Thousand*, William Blackwood, London 1917.

A.P. Herbert, *The Secret Battle* (with an introduction by Winston Churchill), Methuen, London 1928.

Dominic Hibberd, *Wilfred Owen, The Last Year 1917–1918*, Constable, London 1992.

A.A. Hoehling, *Edith Cavell*, Cassell, London 1958.

Major-General Max Hoffmann, *War Diaries and other papers*, two volumes, Martin Secker, London 1929.

Peter Hopkirk, *On Secret Service East of Constantinople, The Plot to Bring Down the British Empire*, John Murray, London 1994.

Alistair Horne, *The Price of Glory, Verdun 1916*, Macmillan, London 1962.

Alistair Horne, *Macmillan, 1894–1956*, volume I of the Official Biography, Macmillan, London 1988.

Charles F. Horne (editor-in-chief), *Source Records of the Great War*, seven volumes, The American Legion, Indianapolis 1931.

James J. Hudson, *In Clouds of Glory,*

American Airmen Who Flew With the British During the Great War, University of Arkansas Press, Fayetteville 1990.

Sidney C. Hurst, *The Silent Cities, an Illustrated Guide to the War Cemeteries and Memorials to the 'Missing' in France and Flanders, 1914–1918*, Methuen, London 1929.

Ulug Igdemir (and others), *Atatürk*, Ankara University Press, Ankara 1963.

Major-General Sir Edmund Ironside, *Tannenberg*, William Blackwood, London 1925.

Vladimir Jabotinsky, *Turkey and the War*, T. Fisher Unwin, London 1917.

Robert Jackson, *The Prisoners, 1914–18*, Routledge, London 1989.

D. Clayton James, *The Years of MacArthur*, volume I, 1880–1941, Leo Cooper, London 1970.

Lawrence James, *Imperial Warrior, The Life and Times of Field-Marshal Viscount Allenby, 1861–1936*, Weidenfeld and Nicolson, London 1993.

Roy Jenkins, *Mr Attlee, An Interim Biography*, William Heinemann, London 1948.

Nigel H. Jones, *The War Walk, A Journey along the Western Front*, Robert Hale, London 1983.

Geoffrey Jukes, *Carpathian disaster, death of an army*, Pan/Ballantine, London 1973.

Hans Kannengiesser Pasha, *The Campaign in Gallipoli*, Hutchinson, London 1931.

Robert Kee, *The Green Flag*, volume II, *The Bold Fenian Men*, Weidenfeld and Nicolson, London 1972.

Count Harry Kessler, *Walther Rathenau, His Life and Work*, Gerald Howe, London 1929.

J. Davidson Ketchum, *Ruhleben, a prison camp society*, Oxford University Press, London 1965.

Professor T.M. Kettle, *The Ways of War* (with a memoir by his wife Mary S. Kettle), Constable, London 1917.

Rudyard Kipling, *The Irish Guards in the Great War*, two volumes, Macmillan, London 1923.

Sir Ivone Kirkpatrick, *Mussolini, Study of a Demagogue*, Odhams, London 1964.

Alexander von Kluck, *The March on Paris and the Battle of the Marne 1914*, Edward Arnold, London 1920.

Major-General Sir Alfred Knox, *With the Russian Army 1914–1917, being chiefly extracts from the diary of a Military Attaché*, two volumes, Hutchinson, London 1921.

Olda Kokoschka and Alfred Marnau (editors), *Oskar Kokoschka Letters 1905–1976*, Thames and Hudson, London 1992.

Oskar Kokoschka, *My Life*, Thames and Hudson, London 1974.

John Laffin, *Battlefield Archaeology*, Ian Allan, London 1987.

John Laffin, *Brassey's Battles, 3,500 Years of Conflict, Campaigns and Wars from A-Z*, Brassey's Defence Publishers, London 1986.

John Laffin, *World War I in Post-cards*, Alan Sutton, Gloucester 1988.

Lieutenant-Colonel Francis Lean (founder), *The Royal Navy List, Special War Supplement*, Witherby, London 1917.

Prince Lichnowsky, *Heading for the Abyss, Reminiscences*, Constable, London 1928.

Liddell Hart, *Foch, The Man of Orleans*, Eyre and Spottiswoode, London 1931.

Peter H. Liddle, *The Soldier's War 1914–1918*, Blandford Press, London 1988.

Peter H. Liddle, *The 1916 Battle of the Somme, A Reappraisal*, Leo Cooper, London 1992.

War Memoirs of David Lloyd George, six volumes, Odhams, London 1933–6 (two-volume edition, 1938).

David Lloyd George, *The Truth About the Peace Treaties*, two volumes, Victor Gollancz, London 1938.

Wm Roger Louis, *Great Britain and Germany's Lost Colonies 1914–1919*, Clarendon Press, Oxford 1967.

General Ludendorff, *My War Memories 1914–1918*, two volumes, Hutchinson, London 1929.

Emil Ludwig, *July 1914*, G.P. Putnam, London 1929.

Kenneth S. Lynn, *Hemingway*, Simon and Schuster, London 1987.

C.A. Macartney, *The Habsburg Empire, 1790–1918*, Weidenfeld and Nicolson, London 1968.

Lyn Macdonald, *The Roses of No Man's Land*, Michael Joseph, London 1980.

Lyn Macdonald, *1915, The Death of Innocence*, Headline, London 1993.

David Macfarlane, *The Danger Tree, Memory, War, and the Search for a Family's Past*, Macfarlane Walter and Ross, Toronto 1992.

Brian McGuinness, *Wittgenstein, A Life, Young Ludwig, 1889–1921*, Duckworth, London 1988.

Robert Machray, *The Polish-German Problem*, George Allen and Unwin, London 1941.

Louise Mack (Mrs Creed), *A Woman's Experiences in the Great War*, T. Fisher Unwin, London 1915.

Major-General Sir W.G. MacPherson (editor, with others), *Medical Services, Diseases of the War*, volume II, *Including the Medical Aspects of Aviation and Gas Warfare, and Gas Poisoning in Tanks and Mines*, His Majesty's Stationery Office, London 1923.

Graham Maddocks, *Liverpool Pals, A History of the 17th, 18th, 19th and 20th (Service) Battalions The King's (Liverpool Regiment) 1914–1919*, Leo Cooper, London 1991.

Arthur Marwick, *Women at War 1914–1918*, Fontana, London 1977.

Dr Thomas Garrigue Masaryk, *The Making of a State, Memories and Observations*, George Allen and Unwin, London 1927.

Werner Maser, *Hitler's Letters and Notes*, Heinemann, London 1974.

Major-General Sir Frederick Maurice, *The Life of General Lord Rawlinson of Trent From His Journals and Letters*, Cassell, London 1928.

Paul Maze, *A Frenchman in Khaki*, William Heinemann, London 1934.

Lt-Colonel J.W.B. Merewether and the Rt Hon. Sir Frederick Smith, *The Indian Corps in France*, John Murray, London 1917.

Michelin Illustrated Guides to the Battlefields (1914–1918), *The Marne Battlefields (1914)*, Michelin, Paris 1917.

Martin Middlebrook, *The First Day on the Somme, 1 July 1916*, Allen Lane, London 1971.

Hugh Robert Mill, *The Life of Sir Ernest Shackleton*, William Heinemann, London 1923.

Oscar E. Millard, *Uncensored: The True Story of the Clandestine Newspaper 'La Libre Belgique' Published in Brussels During the German Occupation*, Robert Hale, London 1937.

Captain Philippe Millet, *Comrades in Arms*, Hodder and Stoughton, London 1916.

Ministry of Information, *Chronology of the War*, three volumes, Constable, London 1918–20.

Field-Marshal Viscount Montgomery of Alamein, *A History of Warfare*, Collins, London 1968.

Geoffrey Moorhouse, *Hell's Foundations, A Social History of the Town of Bury in the Aftermath of the Gallipoli Campaign*, Hodder and Stoughton, London 1992.

J.H. Morgan, *German Atrocities, An Official Investigation*, T. Fisher Unwin, London 1916.

Ted Morgan, *FDR, A Biography*, Simon and Schuster, New York 1985.

Captain Joseph Morris, *The German Air Raids on Great Britain 1914–18*, Sampson Low, Marston, London, no date.

Edwin W. Morse, *The Vanguard of American Volunteers in the Fighting Lines and in Humanitarian Service, August 1914–April 1917*, Charles Scribner's Sons, New York 1919.

Desmond Morton, *Silent Battle, Canadian Prisoners of War in Germany 1914–1919*, Lester Publishing, Toronto 1992.

George L. Mosse, *Fallen Soldiers, Reshaping the Memory of the World Wars*, Oxford University Press, Oxford 1990.

Captain E.O. Mousley, *The Secrets of a Kuttite, an authentic story of Kut, Adventures in Captivity and Stamboul Intrigue*, John Lane, London 1921.

Findlay Muirhead and Marcel Monmarché (editors), *North-Eastern France*, The Blue Guides, second edition, Macmillan, London 1930.

Claud Mullins, *The Leipzig Trials*, H.F. & G. Witherby, London 1921.

Otto Nathan and Heinz Norden (editors), *Einstein on Peace*, Shocken Books, New York 1968.

Lord Newton, *Lord Lansdowne, A Biography*, Macmillan, London 1929.

Harold Nicolson, *Peacemaking 1919*, Constable, London 1933.

Martin Niemoller, *From U-Boat to Pulpit*, William Hodge, London 1937.

Barry Norman, *100 Best Films of the Century*, Chapmans, London 1992.

Viscount Norwich, *Old Men Forget, the Autobiography of Duff Cooper*, Rupert Hart-Davis, London 1953.

Stanley Olson, *John Singer Sargent, His Portrait*, Macmillan, London 1986.

Peter Padfield, *Himmler, Reichsführer-SS*, Macmillan, London 1990.

Peter Padfield, *Hess, Flight for the Führer*, Weidenfeld and Nicolson, London 1991.

Alan Palmer, *The Gardeners of Salonika*, Andre Deutsch, London 1965.

Alan Palmer, *The Lands Between, A History of East-Central Europe since the Congress of Vienna*, Weidenfeld and Nicolson, London 1970.

Alan Palmer, *The Kaiser, Warlord of the Second Reich*, Weidenfeld and Nicolson, London 1978.

Alan Palmer, *Who's Who in Modern History, 1860–1960*, Weidenfeld and Nicolson, London 1980.

Alan Palmer, *The East End, Four Centuries of London Life*, John Murray, London 1989.

Ian Parsons (editor), *The Collected Works of Isaac Rosenberg*, Chatto and Windus, London 1984.

A.J. Peacock, *A Second Alternative Guide to the Western Front (From Nieuport to Pfetterhouse)*, Gun Fire, York, no date.

John J. Pershing, *My Experiences in the World War*, two volumes, Frederick A. Stokes, New York 1931.

E. Alexander Powell, *Fighting in Flanders*, William Heinemann, London 1914.

Anne Powell (editor), *A Deep Cry, A Literary Pilgrimage to the Battlefields and Cemeteries of First World War British Soldier-Poets Killed in Northern France and Flanders*, Palladour Books, Aberporth 1993.

Julian Putkowski and Julian Sykes, *Shot at Dawn*, Wharncliffe, Barnsley 1989.

Hugh Quigley, *Passchendaele and the Somme, A Diary of 1917*, Methuen, London 1928.

Sir Walter Raleigh and H.A. Jones, *The War in the Air, Being the Story of the Part Played in the Great War by the Royal Air Force*, six volumes, Oxford University Press, Oxford 1922–7.

Oliver Ransford, *Livingstone's Lake, the Drama of Lake Nyasa*, John Murray, London 1966.

A. Rawlinson, *The Defence of London*

1915–18, Andrew Melrose, London 1923.

Herbert Read, *Collected Poems*, Faber and Faber, London 1966.

Marquess of Reading, *Rufus Isaacs, First Marquess of Reading*, Hutchinson, two volumes, London 1945.

John Reed, *The War in Eastern Europe*, Charles Scribner's Sons, New York 1916.

Sir Stanley Reed, *The India I Knew 1897–1947*, Odhams Press, London 1952.

Jehuda Reinharz, *Chaim Weizmann, The Making of a Statesman*, Oxford University Press, Oxford 1993.

Erich Maria Remarque, *All Quiet on the Western Front*, G.P. Putnam's, London 1929.

Rush Rhees (editor), *Ludwig Wittgenstein, Personal Recollections*, Basil Blackwell, Oxford 1981.

Robert Rhodes James, *Gallipoli*, B.T. Batsford, London 1965.

K.A. Rice (editor), *Garside's Wars, Memoirs of Bernard Garside*, Hampton School, Hampton Middlesex 1993.

Donald Richter, *Chemical Soldiers, British Gas Warfare in World War One*, University Press of Kansas, Lawrence Kansas 1992.

Raymond Laurence Rimell, *Zeppelin! A Battle for Air Supremacy in World War I*, Conway Maritime Press, London 1984.

Keith Robbins, *Sir Edward Grey, A Biography of Lord Grey of Fallodon*, Cassell, London 1971.

George H. Roeder, Jr, *The Censored War, American Visual Experience During World War Two*, Yale University Press, New Haven 1993.

Theodore Roosevelt, *America and the World War*, John Murray, London 1915.

E. Rubin, *140 Jewish Marshals, Generals & Admirals*, De Vero Books, London 1952.

Sir Horace Rumbold, *The War Crisis in Berlin, July-August 1914*, Constable, London 1940.

Ward Rutherford, *The Russian Army in World War 1*, Gordon Cremonesi, London 1975.

Siegfried Sassoon, *Memoirs of an Infantry Officer*, Faber and Faber, London 1930.

Raymond Savage, *Allenby of Armageddon, A Record of the Career and Campaigns of Field-Marshal Viscount Allenby*, Hodder and Stoughton, London 1925.

Admiral Scheer, *Germany's High Sea Fleet in the World War*, Cassell, London 1920.

J.D. Scott, *Vickers, A History*, Weidenfeld and Nicolson, London 1962.

Hugh Seton-Watson, *Eastern Europe Between the Wars, 1918–1941*, Cambridge University Press, Cambridge 1946.

R.W. Seton-Watson and others, *The War and Democracy*, Macmillan, London 1914.

Sir Ernest Shackleton, *South, The Story of Shackleton's Last Expedition, 1914–1917*, William Heinemann, London 1919

Dorothy and Carl J. Schneider, *Into the Breach: American women overseas in World War I*, Viking, New York 1991.

Harold Shukman, *Lenin and the Russian Revolution*, B.T. Batsford, London 1966.

Harold Shukman (editor), *The Blackwell Encyclopedia of the Russian Revolution*, Basil Blackwell, Oxford 1988.

Peter Simkins, *Kitchener's army, The raising of the New Armies, 1914–16*, Manchester University Press, Manchester 1988.

General Sir Horace Smith-Dorrien, *Memories of Forty-Eight Years' Service*, John Murray, London 1925.

Donald Smythe, *Pershing, General of the Armies*, Indiana University Press, Bloomington 1986.

Dudley Sommer, *Haldane of Cloan, His Life and Times*, George Allen and Unwin, London 1960.

Major-General Sir Edward Spears, *Liaison 1914, A Narrative of the Great Retreat*, Eyre and Spottiswoode, London 1930 (reprinted 1968).

Major-General Sir Edward Spears, *The Picnic Basket*, Secker and Warburg, London 1967.

Gertrude Stein, *Wars I Have Seen*, Batsford, London 1945.

Leonard Stein, *The Balfour Declaration*, Vallentine Mitchell, London 1961.

Zara S. Steiner, *Britain and the Origins of the First World War*, Macmillan, London 1977.

G.R. Stevens, *A City Goes to War*, Edmonton Regiment Associates, Brampton, Ontario, 1964.

Norman Stone, *The Eastern Front, 1914–1917*, Hodder and Stoughton, London 1975.

Norman Stone, *Europe Transformed, 1878–1919*, Fontana, London 1983.

Ronald Storrs, *Orientations*, Nicholson and Watson, London 1937.

Herbert Sulzbach, *With the German Guns, Four Years on the Western Front 1914–1918*, Leo Cooper, London 1973.

Michael Summerskill, *China on the Western Front, Britain's Chinese Work Force in the First World War*, Michael Summerskill, London 1982.

Eliezer Tauber, *The Arab Movements in World War I*, Frank Cass, London 1993.

A. J. P. Taylor, *War By Time-Table, How the First World War began*, Macdonald, London 1969.

John Terraine, *The Smoke and the Fire, Myths & Anti-Myths of War, 1861–1945*, Leo Cooper, London 1980.

The Times History of the War, twenty volumes, The Times, London 1914–19.

Lowell Thomas, *Raiders of the Deep*, William Heinemann, London 1929.

Grand-Admiral Von Tirpitz, *My Memoirs*, two volumes, Hurst and Blackett, London 1920.

John Toland, *Adolf Hitler*, Doubleday, Garden City, New York 1976.

Ulrich Trumpener, *Germany and the Ottoman Empire 1914–1918*, Princeton University Press, Princeton New Jersey 1968.

Barbara W. Tuchman, *August 1914*, Constable, London 1962.

John Turner, *British Politics and the Great War, Coalition and Conflict, 1915–1918*, Yale University Press, London 1992.

Nigel Viney, *Images of War, British Art and Artists of World War 1*, David and Charles, Newton Abbot 1991.

G. Ward Price, *The Story of the Salonica Army*, Hodder and Stoughton, London 1917.

L.F. Waring, *Serbia*, Williams and Norgate, London 1917.

Stanley Washburn, *Field Notes from the Russian Front*, Andrew Melrose, London 1915.

V.A. Weeks, *London County Council Record of Service*, P.S. King, London 1922.

Stanley Weintraub, *A Stillness Heard Around the World, The End of the Great War: November 1918*, Allen and Unwin, London 1985.

Franz Werfel, *The Forty Days*, Hutchinson International Authors, London 1945.

John W. Wheeler-Bennett, *Hindenburg, The Wooden Titan*, Macmillan, London 1936.

John W. Wheeler-Bennett, *Brest-Litovsk, The Forgotten Peace, March 1918*, Macmillan, London 1938.

Brand Whitlock, *Belgium under the German Occupation, a Personal Narrative*, two volumes, William Heinemann, London 1919.

Evelyn Wilcock, *Pacifism and the Jews*, Hawthorn Press, Stroud, Gloucestershire 1994.

Charles Williams, *The Last Great Frenchman, A Life of General de Gaulle*, Little, Brown, London 1993.

Jeffery Williams, *Byng of Vimy,*

General and Governor General, Leo Cooper, London 1983.

Samuel R. Williamson, Jr, *Austria-Hungary and the Origins of the First World War*, Macmillan, London 1991.

H.W. Wilson, *The War Guilt*, Samson Low, London 1928.

Trevor Wilson (editor), *The Political Diaries of C.P. Scott, 1911–1928*, Collins, London 1970.

Elizabeth Wiskemann, *Czechs and Germans*, Oxford University Press, London 1938.

David Woodward, *The Collapse of Power, Mutiny in the High Seas Fleet*, Arthur Barker, London 1973.

Sir Llewellyn Woodward, *Great Britain and the War of 1914–1918*, Methuen, London 1967.

Z.A.B. Zeman, *The Break-Up of the Habsburg Empire 1914–1918*, Oxford University Press, London 1961.

Z.A.B. Zeman and W.B. Scharlau, *The Merchant of Revolution, The Life of Alexander Israel Helphand (Parvus) 1867–1924*, Oxford University Press, London 1965.

Marshal of the Soviet Union G. Zhukov, *Reminiscences and Reflections*, volume I, Moscow 1985.

Alfred Zimmern, *The League of Nations and the Rule of Law 1918–1935*, Macmillan, London 1936.

I have also drawn on documentary material from several of my own published works:

Britain and Germany Between the Wars, Longmans, London 1964.

Plough My Own Furrow: the Story of Lord Allen of Hurtwood, Longmans, London 1965.

The Roots of Appeasement, Weidenfeld and Nicolson, London 1966.

First World War Atlas, Weidenfeld and Nicolson, London 1970 (which includes an itemised bibliography).

Winston S. Churchill, *The Challenge of War, 1914–1916*, William Heinemann, London 1971.

Sir Horace Rumbold, Portrait of a Diplomat, William Heinemann, London 1973.

Winston S. Churchill, *World in Torment, 1917–1922*, William Heinemann, London 1975.

Churchill, A Life, William Heinemann, London 1991.

Maps

1 Europe in 1914

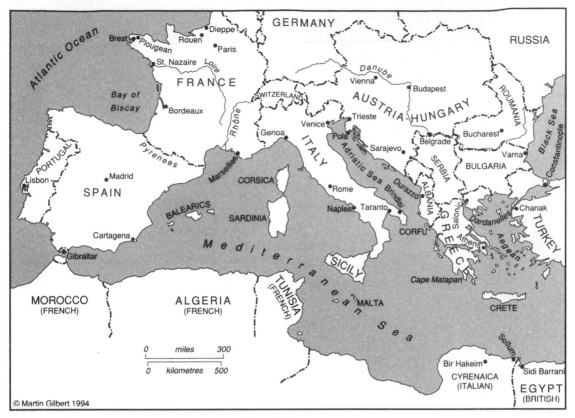

2 The Mediterranean

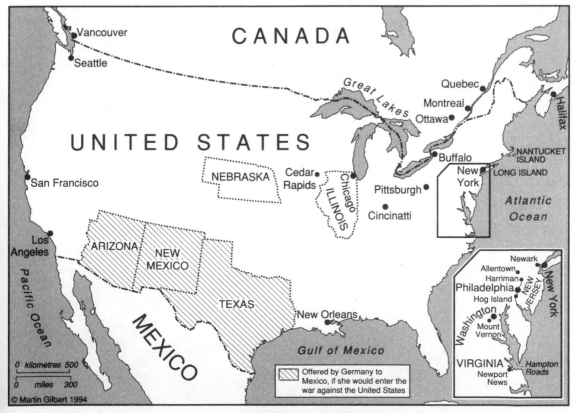

3 The United States and Canada

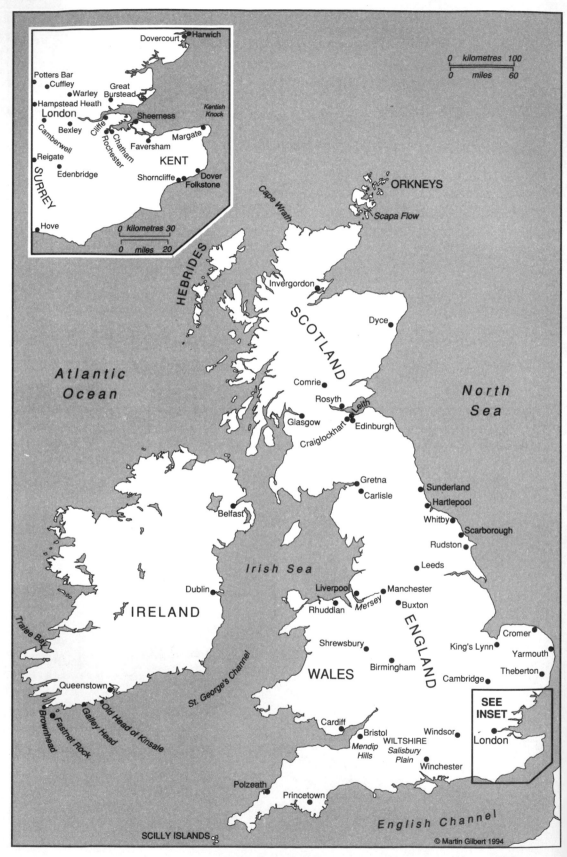

Inset map (top left):

Dovercourt • Harwich
Potters Bar
Cuffley
Warley
Great Bursted
Hampstead Heath
London
Sheerness
Kentish Knock
Bexley
Cliffe
Chatham
Rochester
Camberwell
Margate
Faversham
Reigate
KENT
Edenbridge
SURREY
Shorncliffe
Dover
Folkstone
Hove

0 kilometres 30
0 miles 20

Main map:

0 kilometres 100
0 miles 60

ORKNEYS
Scapa Flow
Cape Wrath
HEBRIDES
SCOTLAND
Invergordon
Dyce
Atlantic Ocean
Comrie
North Sea
Rosyth
Leith
Glasgow
Craiglockhart
Edinburgh
Gretna
Carlisle
Sunderland
Hartlepool
Whitby
Scarborough
Belfast
Rudston
Irish Sea
Leeds
Dublin
Liverpool
Manchester
IRELAND
Rhuddlan
Mersey
Buxton
Tralee Bay
Shrewsbury
ENGLAND
Cromer
King's Lynn
Yarmouth
WALES
Birmingham
Theberton
Cambridge
Queenstown
Old Head of Kinsale
St. George's Channel
Brownhead
Fastnet Rock
Galley Head
SEE INSET
London
Cardiff
Windsor
Bristol
WILTSHIRE
Mendip Hills
Salisbury Plain
Winchester
Polzeath
Princetown
English Channel
SCILLY ISLANDS
© Martin Gilbert 1994

4 Great Britain

North Sea

Kiel Canal

Baltic Sea

Kiel

Travemünde

Lübeck

Cuxhaven

Pasewalk

Hamburg

Wilhelmshaven

Parnewinkel

River Elbe

Rastede

Soltau

Bremen

HOLLAND

Sachsenhausen

Döberitz

Gardelegen

Ruhleben

Berlin

Potsdam

Hanover

Burg

Zossen

Karthaus

Wittenberg

GERMANY

Esterwerda

Grossenhain

Essen

Halle

Torgau

Düsseldorf

Leipzig

Cologne

Dresden

Aix-la-Chapelle (Aachen)

Ziegenhain

Gotha

SAXONY

Limburg

Bad Homburg

River Rhine

Frankfurt-on-Main

Mainz

River Main

Trier

Würzburg

Oppau

Mannheim

Ludwigshafen

LORRAINE

BAVARIA

Metz

Karlsruhe

Landshut

Strasbourg

Dachau

FRANCE

ALSACE

Lechfeld

Puchheim

Munich

Lake Konstanz

Friedrichshafen

Konstanz

SWITZERLAND

AUSTRIA

0 miles 50

0 kilometres 75

© Martin Gilbert 1994

5 Germany

GERMANY

RUSSIAN POLAND

RUSSIAN EMPIRE

SILESIA

Rumburg

Sudeten Mountains
• Theresienstadt

Cracow

Carlsbad
Konopisht • Prague

Olmütz •
• Prossnitz

Neumarkt

WESTERN
GALICIA

Lemberg

Brody

Czernowitz

EASTERN GALICIA

BOHEMIA

MORAVIA

• Brünn

• Turciansky Svaty
Martin

RUTHENIA

BUKOVINA

River Danube

SLOVAKIA

• Bratislava

Vienna •

Budapest •

River Theiss

AUSTRIA

Judenburg •

HUNGARY

Kolozsvar •

TYROL

TRENTINO

SLOVENIA
Laibach
Trieste •
ISTRIA
Fiume
Pola •

Agram •

CROATIA

Pecs •

BACKA

BANAT

TRANSYLVANIA

ITALY

DALMATIA

BOSNIA
Sarajevo •

SERBIA

ROUMANIA

River Danube

Adriatic Sea

HERZEGOVINA

MONTENEGRO

BULGARIA

Cattaro
Cetinje

ALBANIA

GREECE

The borders of
Austria-Hungary
in 1914

The Hungarian
Kingdom
1867-1918

0   miles   100

0   kilometres   150

© Martin Gilbert 1994

6 Austria-Hungary

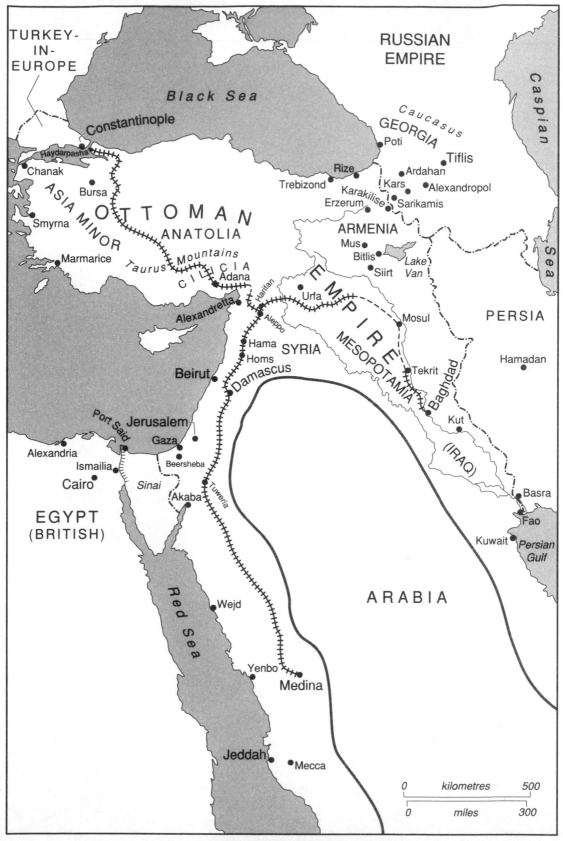

TURKEY-
IN-
EUROPE

RUSSIAN
EMPIRE

Black Sea

Caspian

Constantinople

Caucasus

GEORGIA

Poti

Haydarpasha

Tiflis

Chanak

Rize

Ardahan

Bursa

Trebizond

Karakilise

Kars

Alexandropol

Smyrna

O T T O M A N

Erzerum

Sarikamis

ASIA MINOR

ANATOLIA

ARMENIA

PERSIA

Marmarice

Taurus Mountains

Mus

C I L I C I A

Bitlis

Lake Van

Adana

Siirt

Harran

Alexandretta

Urfa

E M P I R E

Mosul

Hamadan

Aleppo

Hama

SYRIA

MESOPOTAMIA

Tekrit

Homs

Beirut

Damascus

Baghdad

Port Said

Jerusalem

Kut

Alexandria

Gaza

(IRAQ)

Ismailia

Beersheba

Cairo

Sinai

Basra

EGYPT
(BRITISH)

Akaba

Tuweria

Fao

Kuwait

Persian Gulf

Red Sea

Wejd

A R A B I A

Yenbo

Medina

Jeddah

Mecca

0	kilometres	500
0	miles	300

7 The Ottoman Empire

AUSTRIA - HUNGARY

ROUMANIA

Bucharest

DOBRUDJA

Danube

Constanta

SOUTH
DOBRUDJA

Mangalia

SILISTRIA

River Danube

Varna

Belgrade

S
E
R
B
I
A

Nis

Tsaribrod

BULGARIA

Burgas

Black
Sea

Sofia

Radomir

River Maritsa

River Vardar

Skopje

Adrianople

Bosphorus

River Struma

Constantinople

Prinkipo

A
L
B
A
N
I
A

Monastir

Drama

THRACE

Ferrijik

Sea of
Marmara

Kavalla

Dedeagatch

Bursa

Gallipoli Peninsula

Bulair

T
U
R
K
E
Y

Salonica

Cape Helles

Chanak

LEMNOS

Mudros

Troy

G
R
E
E
C
E

Aegean

ANATOLIA

CORFU

Lamia

SKYROS

VIDO
ISLAND

Sea

Smyrna

Ionian
Sea

Athens

Patras

Piraeus

C
Y
C
L
A
D
E
S

SYRA

KOS

Cape Matapan

CERIGO

RHODES

| 0 | miles | 100 |
| 0 | kilometres | 150 |

CRETE

© Martin Gilbert 1994

8 Bulgaria, the Black Sea and the Aegean

THE ALLIED
INTERVENTION
IN NORTH RUSSIA

White
Sea

Archangel

NORWAY

SWEDEN

Gulf of Bothnia

BRITAIN

North
Sea

DENMARK

London

Jutland ×

Petrograd

Baltic Sea

Riga

BELGIUM

HOLLAND

THE
WESTERN
FRONT

Verdun

Berlin

GERMANY

Tannenberg

FRANCE

SWITZ.

Lodz

THE
EASTERN
FRONT

RUSSIAN
EMPIRE

THE
ITALIAN
FRONT

Caporetto

AUSTRIA - HUNGARY

Przemysl

Lemberg

ITALY

Rome

Adriatic Sea

THE
SERBIAN
FRONT

Belgrade

SERBIA

THE ROUMANIAN
FRONT

BULGARIA

THE
SALONICA
FRONT

Salonica

Black Sea

THE
GALLIPOLI
FRONT

Aegean

Constantinople

OTTOMAN EMPIRE

Caspian Sea

Mediterranean Sea

Trebizond

Sarikamis

THE
CAUCASUS
FRONT

Baku

CYRENAICA

THE PERSIAN
FRONT

Bir Hakeim

THE SENUSSI
FRONT

THE
PALESTINE
FRONT
Gaza

Damascus

Jerusalem

Cairo

EGYPT

Suez

Akaba

Baghdad

Kut

Hamadan

THE ARAB
FRONT

Red Sea

THE
MESOPOTAMIAN
FRONT

Basra

Persian
Gulf

0   kilometres   500

0   miles   300

© Martin Gilbert 1994

9 The War Fronts

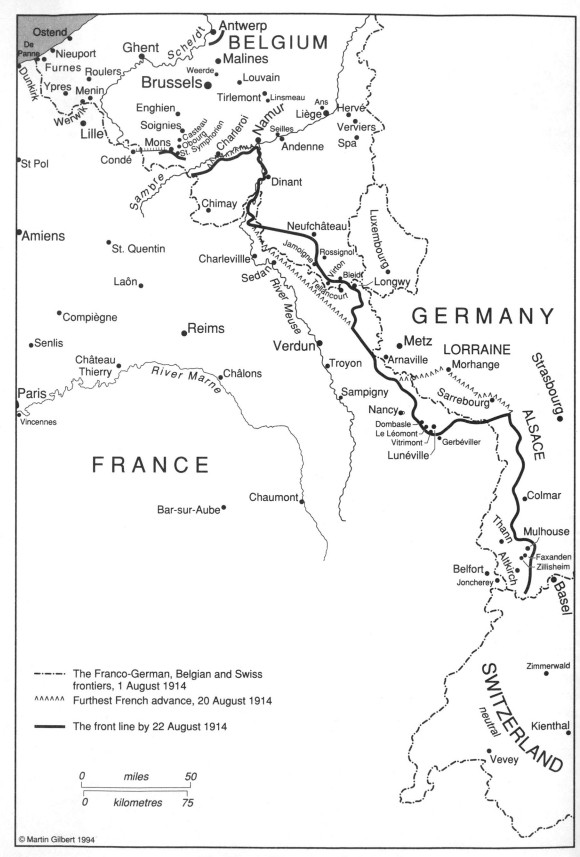

Ostend
De Panne
Nieuport
Furnes
Dunkirk
Ypres
Menin
Werwik
Lille
St Pol

Ghent
Enghien
Soignies
Mons
Condé

Antwerp
BELGIUM
Malines
Weerde
Louvain
Brussels
Tirlemont
Linsmeau
Casteau
Obourg
St. Symphorien
Charleroi
Namur
Seilles
Andenne

Ans
Liège
Hervé
Verviers
Spa

Luxembourg

Sambre
Dinant
Chimay
Neufchâteau
Charleville
Jamoigne
Rossignol
Sedan
Virton
Bleid
Longwy
Tellancourt
River Meuse

Amiens
St. Quentin
Laôn
Compiègne
Senlis
Reims
Verdun
GERMANY

Château Thierry
River Marne
Châlons
Troyon
Metz
LORRAINE
Arnaville
Morhange
Strasbourg

Paris
Vincennes

Sampigny
Nancy
Sarrebourg
ALSACE
Dombasle
Le Léomont
Vitrimont
Gerbéviller
Lunéville

FRANCE

Chaumont
Bar-sur-Aube

Colmar
Thann
Mulhouse
Faxanden
Zillisheim
Altkirch
Belfort
Joncherey
Basel

Zimmerwald

SWITZERLAND
neutral

Kienthal

Vevey

—·—·— The Franco-German, Belgian and Swiss
frontiers, 1 August 1914

ΛΛΛΛΛΛ Furthest French advance, 20 August 1914

——— The front line by 22 August 1914

0   miles   50

0   kilometres   75

© Martin Gilbert 1994

10 The Western Front, 1–22 August 1914

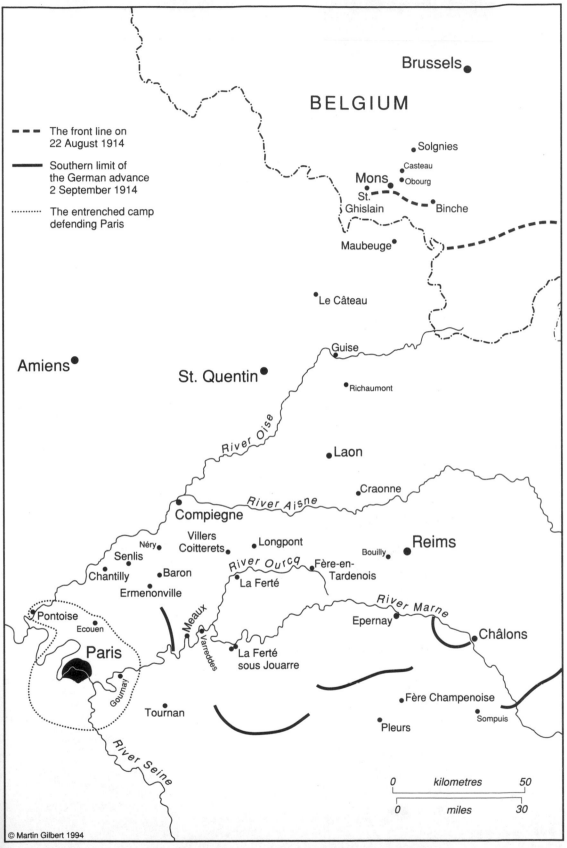

Brussels

BELGIUM

- - - The front line on
22 August 1914

—— Southern limit of
the German advance
2 September 1914

.... The entrenched camp
defending Paris

Solgnies

Casteau

Mons   Obourg

St.
Ghislain   Binche

Maubeuge

Le Câteau

Guise

Amiens

St. Quentin   Richaumont

River Oise

Laon

Craonne

River Aisne

Compiegne

Villers
Coitterets   Longpont   Reims

Néry   Bouilly

Senlis   River Ourcq   Fère-en-
Tardenois

Chantilly   Baron   La Ferté

Ermenonville   River Marne

Pontoise   Meaux   Epernay   Châlons

Ecouen   Varreddes

Paris   La Ferté
sous Jouarre

Gournay   Fère Champenoise

Tournan   Sompuis

Pleurs

River Seine

0   kilometres   50

0   miles   30

© Martin Gilbert 1994

11 The Western Front, 1914, from Mons to the Marne

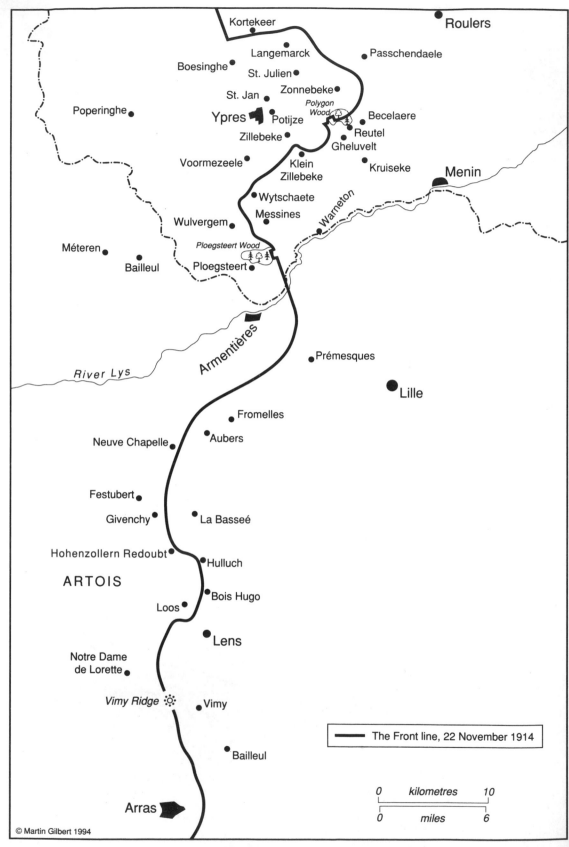

Kortekeer

Roulers

Langemarck

Passchendaele

Boesinghe

St. Julien

Zonnebeke

St. Jan

Polygon Wood

Becelaere

Poperinghe

Ypres

Potijze

Reutel

Zillebeke

Gheluvelt

Voormezeele

Klein Zillebeke

Kruiseke

Menin

Wytschaete

Messines

Warneton

Méteren

Wulvergem

Ploegsteert Wood

Bailleul

Ploegsteert

Armentières

River Lys

Prémesques

Lille

Fromelles

Neuve Chapelle

Aubers

Festubert

Givenchy

La Basseé

Hohenzollern Redoubt

Hulluch

ARTOIS

Bois Hugo

Loos

Lens

Notre Dame de Lorette

Vimy Ridge

Vimy

────	The Front line, 22 November 1914

Bailleul

Arras

0   kilometres   10

0   miles   6

© Martin Gilbert 1994

12 The Western Front, 1914–15

LETTLAND
LITHUANIA

Baltic Sea

Dvinsk

Lake Naroch

Memel

Kovno

Vilna

Chertoviche

Königsberg

Stalluponen

Gumbinnen

Minsk

Danzig

EAST
PRUSSIA

Rastenburg

Masurian Lakes

Lyck

Grodno

RUSSIAN EMPIRE

Frogenau

Tannenberg

Bialystok

Thorn

River Vistula

Przasnysz

River Bug

Novo
Georgievsk

Warsaw

Brest-Litovsk

River Bzura

Bolimow

River Vistula

POLAND

*Pripet
Marshes*

Kalish

Lodz

Wlodawa

Kowel

Piotrkow

Kholm

Krasnostaw

Lutsk

Rovno

Krasnik

Czestochowa

Kielce

River San

VOLHYNIA

Bedzin

Molodych

Brody

E A S T E R N   G A L I C I A

SILESIA

Tarnow

Cracow

WESTERN GALICIA

Przemysl

Lemberg

Zlochov

Tarnopol

Limanowa

Gorlice

Sanok

River Dniester

Buczacz

Barish

Husiatyn

Neumarkt

Dukla Pass

Smolnik

Stryj

Halich

Kalush

Bartfeld

Lupkow Pass

Uszok
Pass

Stanislau

Okna

Rokitna

AUSTRIA - HUNGARY

Carpathian Mountains

Delatyn

Kolomea

Czernowitz

Jablonitsa Pass

Seret

FRONT LINES ON:
—————— 1 May 1915
· · · · · · · 13 July 1915
– – – – – 15 August 1915
∧ ∧ ∧ ∧ 20 September 1915

0   miles   100

0   kilometres   150

Budapest

© Martin Gilbert 1994

13 The Eastern Front, 1914–16

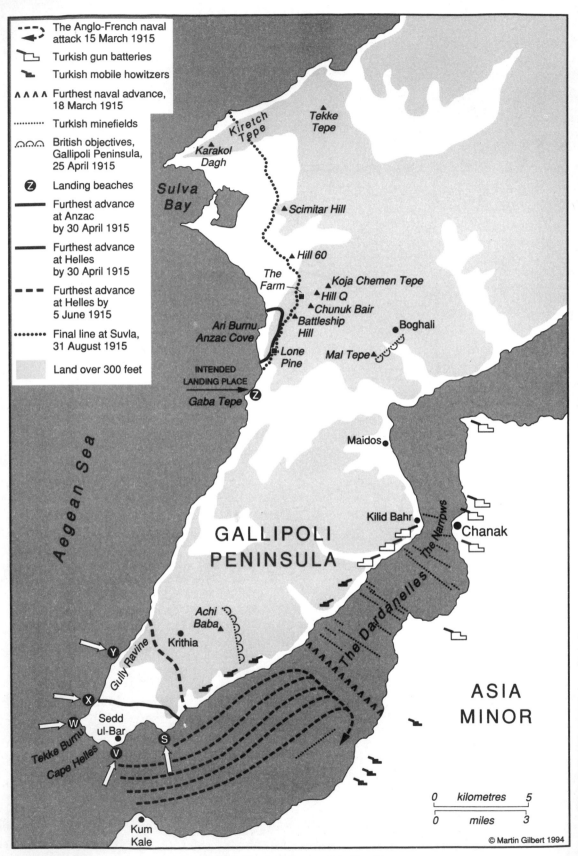

Legend

- - - - → The Anglo-French naval attack 15 March 1915
- Turkish gun batteries
- Turkish mobile howitzers
- ∧ ∧ ∧ ∧ Furthest naval advance, 18 March 1915
- .... Turkish minefields
- ◠◠◠ British objectives, Gallipoli Peninsula, 25 April 1915
- **Ⓩ** Landing beaches
- ——— Furthest advance at Anzac by 30 April 1915
- ——— Furthest advance at Helles by 30 April 1915
- – – – Furthest advance at Helles by 5 June 1915
- •••••••• Final line at Suvla, 31 August 1915
- Land over 300 feet

Kiretch Tepe

▲ *Tekke Tepe*

▲ *Karakol Dagh*

Sulva Bay

▲ *Scimitar Hill*

▲ *Hill 60*

The Farm

▲ *Koja Chemen Tepe*

▲ *Hill Q*
▲ *Chunuk Bair*

Ari Burnu
Anzac Cove

Battleship Hill

● *Boghali*

Lone Pine

▲ *Mal Tepe*

INTENDED LANDING PLACE →

Ⓩ

Gaba Tepe

Aegean Sea

● *Maidos*

GALLIPOLI PENINSULA

● *Kilid Bahr*

The Narrows

● *Chanak*

The Dardanelles

ASIA MINOR

▲ *Achi Baba*

● *Krithia*

Gully Ravine

Ⓨ

Ⓧ

Ⓦ

Sedd ul-Bar

Ⓢ

Tekke Burnu

Ⓥ

Cape Helles

● *Kum Kale*

0 ___ kilometres ___ 5

0 ___ miles ___ 3

© Martin Gilbert 1994

14 The Dardanelles and Gallipoli

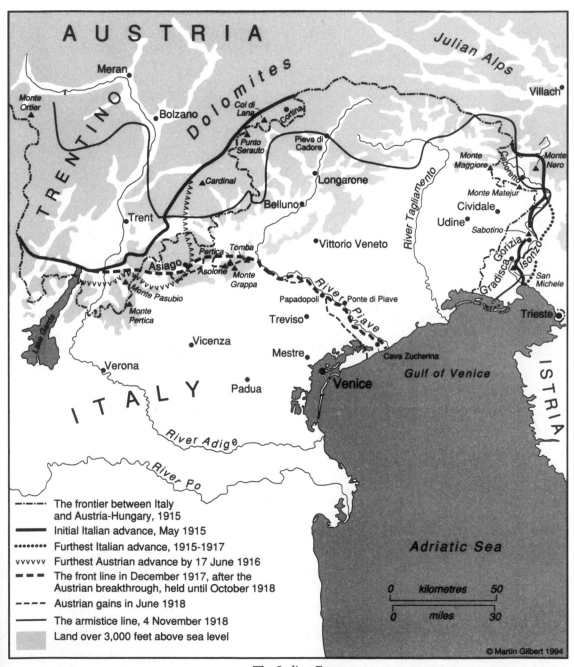

AUSTRIA

Julian Alps

Meran•

*Monte
Ortler* ▲

TRENTINO

Bolzano•

Dolomites

Col di
Lana ▲ •Cortina

Villach•

Pieve di
Cadore

Monte
Maggiore• ▲Caporetto ▲ *Monte
Nero*

Punto
Serauto ▲

Longarone•

River Tagliamento

Monte Matejur

▲Cardinal

Belluno•

Cividale•

Trent•

Udine•

Sabotino

Vittorio Veneto•

Pertica Tomba

Asiago• Asolone

▲

Monte
Grappa

Gorizia

Isonzo

Monte Pasubio ▲

Gradisca

San
Michele

Monte
Pertica ▲

River Piave

Papadopoli •Ponte di Piave

Treviso•

Lake Garda

.Vicenza

Mestre•

Cava Zucherina

Gulf of Venice

Trieste•

Verona•

Padua•

Venice

ISTRIA

ITALY

River Adige

River Po

Adriatic Sea

—·—·— The frontier between Italy
and Austria-Hungary, 1915

——— Initial Italian advance, May 1915

•••••••• Furthest Italian advance, 1915-1917

vvvvvv Furthest Austrian advance by 17 June 1916

– – – The front line in December 1917, after the
Austrian breakthrough, held until October 1918

- - - - Austrian gains in June 1918

——— The armistice line, 4 November 1918

░░ Land over 3,000 feet above sea level

0	kilometres	50
0	miles	30

© Martin Gilbert 1994

15 The Italian Front

| Serbian defence line, 7 October 1915 |
| Serbian front line by 1 November 1915 |
| Final Serbian defence line, 23 November 1915 |
| Serbian retreat to the sea |

AUSTRIA - HUNGARY

River Danube

HUNGARY

ROUMANIA

Sabac

Lesnica

River Jadar

Belgrade

River Danube

BOSNIA

Sarajevo

River Drina

Kragujevac

SERBIA

Paracin

Knjazevac

Nis

River Morava

Novi Pazar

Tsaribrod

HERZGOVINA

MONTENEGRO

Kosovo

Pristina

Sofia

Radomir

BULGARIA

Cattaro

Cetinje
Mount Lovcen

River Drin

Prizren

Skopje

San Giovanni
di Medua

Adriatic
Sea

ALBANIA

River Vardar

Strumica

Durazzo

Prilep

MACEDONIA

Monastir

ITALY

Valona

GREECE

Salonica

Aegean
Sea

| 0 | miles | 50 |
| 0 | kilometres | 75 |

© Martin Gilbert 1994

16 Serbia

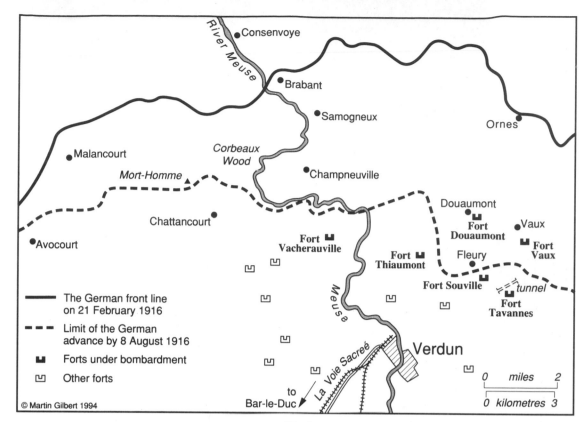

The German front line
on 21 February 1916

Limit of the German
advance by 8 August 1916

Forts under bombardment

Other forts

© Martin Gilbert 1994

0   miles   2

0   kilometres   3

River Meuse

Consenvoye

Brabant

Samogneux

Ornes

Malancourt

Corbeaux
Wood

Champneuville

Mort-Homme

Douaumont

Fort
Douaumont

Vaux

Fort
Vaux

Chattancourt

Fort
Vacherauville

Fleury

Avocourt

Fort
Thiaumont

Fort Souville

tunnel

Fort
Tavannes

Meuse

Verdun

to
Bar-le-Duc

La Voie Sacreé

17 Verdun

SERBIA

Tsaribrod

The Salonica front,
September 1916

Sofia

The Salonica front,
November 1916 to
14 September 1918

Vladaya

Radomir

The Salonica front,
29 September 1918

Prizren

ALBANIA

Skopje

River Vardar

River Struma

BULGARIA

Veles

Prilep

Negotin

Strumitsa

Kosturino

Strumitsa Station

Doiran

Fort Rupel

Vetrenik

Drama

Monastir

Kajmackalan

Kavalla

Florina

GREECE

Salonica

Aegean
Sea

0   miles   50

0   kilometres   75

© Martin Gilbert 1994

Gulf of
Salonica

18 The Salonica Front

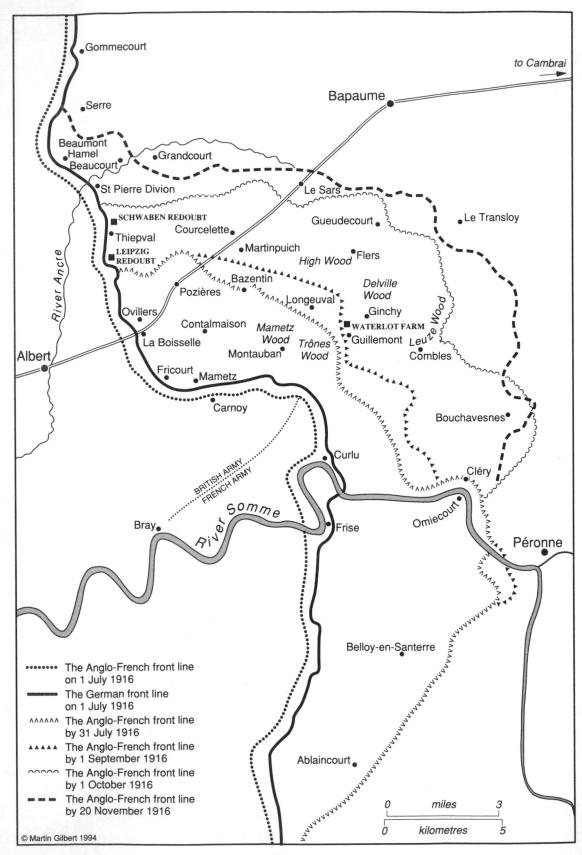

Gommecourt

to Cambrai →

Bapaume

Serre

Beaumont
Hamel
Beaucourt

Grandcourt

St Pierre Divion

Le Sars

Le Transloy

River Ancre

SCHWABEN REDOUBT

Courcelette

Gueudecourt

Thiepval

LEIPZIG
REDOUBT

Martinpuich

Flers

High Wood

Pozières

Bazentin

*Delville
Wood*

Ovillers

Longueval

Ginchy

Leuze Wood

Contalmaison

WATERLOT FARM

La Boiselle

*Mametz
Wood*

*Trônes
Wood*

Guillemont

Combles

Montauban

Albert

Fricourt

Mametz

Bouchavesnes

Carnoy

BRITISH ARMY
FRENCH ARMY

Curlu

Cléry

River Somme

Omiecourt

Péronne

Bray

Frise

Belloy-en-Santerre

Ablaincourt

```
••••••••  The Anglo-French front line
          on 1 July 1916
_____  The German front line
          on 1 July 1916
^^^^^^    The Anglo-French front line
          by 31 July 1916
▲▲▲▲▲     The Anglo-French front line
          by 1 September 1916
∩∩∩∩∩     The Anglo-French front line
          by 1 October 1916
- - - -   The Anglo-French front line
          by 20 November 1916
```

© Martin Gilbert 1994

0 — miles — 3

0 — kilometres — 5

19 The Somme

RUTHENIA

River Theiss

EASTERN
GALICIA

RUSSIA

River Pruth

Czernowitz

• Siget

BUKOVINA

▲▲▲▲▲ Initial Roumanian
advance, 27 August
to 18 September 1916

━━━ Austro-Hungarian
counter-attack by
26 November 1916

⇢ Lines of Austro-Hungarian
advance, 26 November 1916
to 7 January 1917

MOLDAVIA

Jassy •

• Kolozsvar

AUSTRIA - HUNGARY

Bacau •

TRANSYLVANIA

Hermannstadt •

Kronstadt •

• Marasesti

*Rotenturm
Pass*

Petrosani •

*Torzburg
Pass*

Rucar •

• Focsani

Mount Lescului ▲

Ploesti •

Pitesti •

Buftea •

Iron Gates

• Turnu
Severin

ROUMANIA

Bucharest •

• Craiova

WALLACHIA

• Tutracaia

River Danube

Zimnicea •

0   miles   50

0   kilometres   80

SERBIA

BULGARIA

© Martin Gilbert 1994

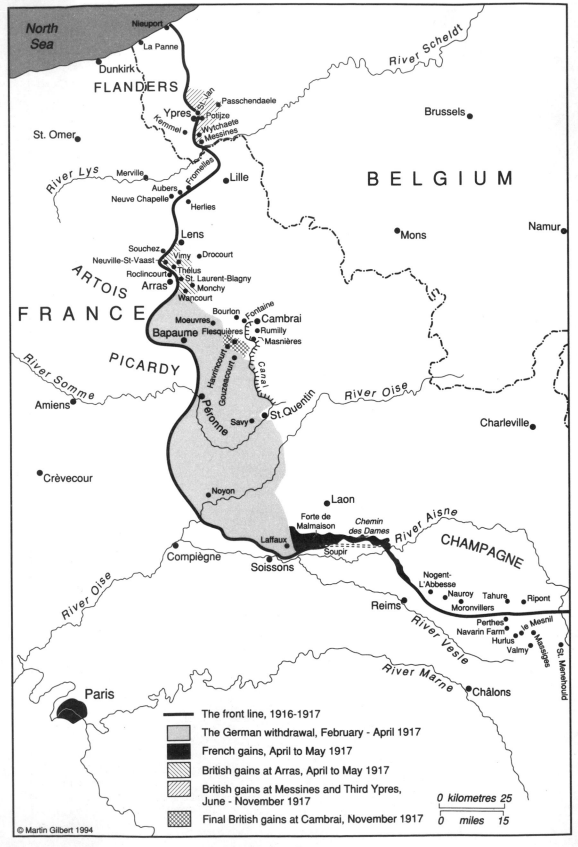

North Sea

Nieuport
La Panne
Dunkirk
FLANDERS
St. Omer

River Scheldt

St. Jan
Ypres · Passchendaele
Potijze
Kemmel · Wytschaete
Messines

Brussels

River Lys
Merville
Aubers
Neuve Chapelle
Fromelles
Herlies
Lille

BELGIUM

Lens
Souchez
Neuville-St-Vaast
Roclincourt · Thélus
St. Laurent-Blagny
Arras · Monchy
Wancourt

ARTOIS

FRANCE

Vimy · Drocourt

Mons

Namur

Bourlon · Fontaine
Moeuvres · Cambrai
Bapaume · Flesquières · Rumilly
Masnières
Havrincourt
Péronne · Gouzeaucourt
Savy · St. Quentin

Canal

PICARDY

River Somme
Amiens

River Oise

Charleville

Crèvecour

Noyon
Laon
Forte de
Malmaison
Laffaux · Chemin
des Dames
Compiègne · Soupir
Soissons

River Aisne

CHAMPAGNE

River Oise

Nogent-
L'Abbesse
Nauroy · Tahure · Ripont
Moronvillers
Reims · Perthes · le Mesnil
Navarin Farm
Hurlus · Massiges
Valmy · St. Menehould

River Vesle

River Marne
Châlons

Paris

The front line, 1916-1917
The German withdrawal, February - April 1917
French gains, April to May 1917
British gains at Arras, April to May 1917
British gains at Messines and Third Ypres,
June - November 1917
Final British gains at Cambrai, November 1917

0 kilometres 25
0 miles 15

© Martin Gilbert 1994

21 The Western Front, 1916–17

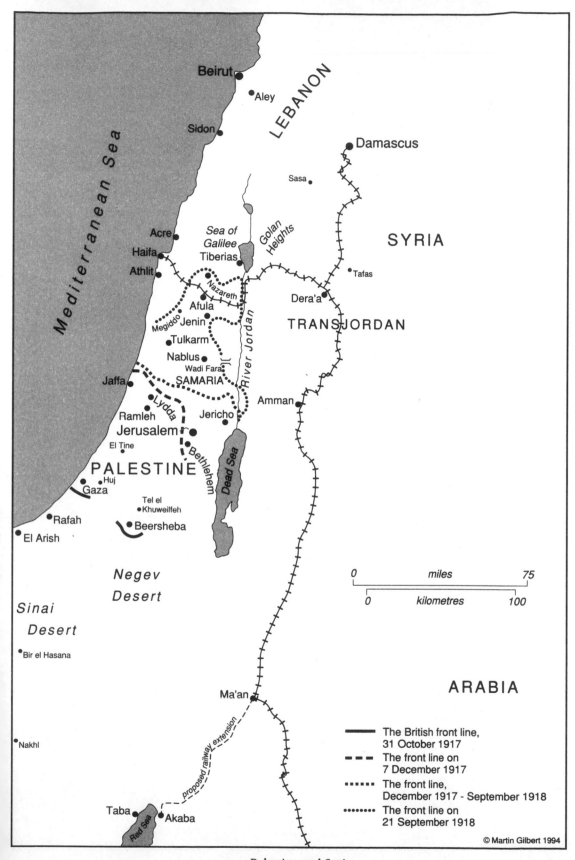

Beirut
Aley
LEBANON
Sidon
Damascus
Mediterranean Sea
Sasa
SYRIA
Acre
Sea of Galilee
Golan Heights
Haifa
Tiberias
Athlit
Tafas
Nazareth
Dera'a
Afula
Megiddo Jenin
TRANSJORDAN
Tulkarm
River Jordan
Nablus
Wadi Fara
Jaffa
SAMARIA
Lydda
Amman
Ramleh
Jericho
Jerusalem
El Tine
Bethlehem
Dead Sea
PALESTINE
Huj
Gaza
Tel el Khuweilfeh
Rafah
Beersheba
El Arish
Negev Desert
Sinai Desert
Bir el Hasana
miles
0   75
0   100
kilometres
ARABIA
Ma'an
Nakhl
Proposed railway extension

	The British front line, 31 October 1917
	The front line on 7 December 1917
	The front line, December 1917 - September 1918
	The front line on 21 September 1918

Taba
Akaba
Red Sea

© Martin Gilbert 1994

22 Palestine and Syria

Hamadan •

Tekrit •

Khanikin •

Kizil Rabat •

Paitak Pass

Kermanshah •

Bakuba •

P E R S I A

Baghdad •

Ctesiphon •

River Tigris

River Euphrates

M E S O P O T A M I A   (I R A Q)

Hanna
Dujaila •
Wadi •
Sheikh
Sa'ad •
Kut

Amara •

Nasiriyeh •

Kurna •

Shatt al Arab

0 *kilometres* 75
0 *miles* 50

Shaiba • **Basra** • Abadan •

Fao •

K U W A I T

Kuwait •

Persian Gulf

—— Further British (Ctesiphon)
and Russian (Hamadan) advance,
November 1915

✳ Kut, beseiged from
December 1915 to April 1916

--- Main British forces
awaiting the advance to
Baghdad, 1916 - 1917

© Martin Gilbert 1994

23 Mesopotamia

White Sea

Archangel

Gulf of Bothina

Vasa

FINLAND

Baltic Sea

Kotlas

Helsinki

Kronstadt

Reval

Narva

Petrograd

Pernau

Dorpat

Pskov

Riga

Dvinsk

Nizhni-Novgorod

Kazan

Kovno

Tver

Moscow

Vilna

Smolensk

Borisov

Tula

Minsk

Mogilev

Orel

Samara

River Volga

WHITE RUSSIA

Gomel

Brest-Litovsk

Kursk

AUSTRIA-HUNGARY

Zhitomir

Kiev

Kharkov

BESSARABIA

UKRAINE

Tsaritsyn

Odessa

Nikolayev

Novocherkassk

Rostov-on-Don

Astrakhan

ROUMANIA

Sea of Azov

KUBAN

Caspian Sea

Simferopol

Sebastopol

Feodosiya

Novorossisk

Black Sea

C a u c a s u s

GEORGIA

Constantinople

Poti

Tiflis

Ardahan

Kars

Alexandropol

Baku

Trebizond

OTTOMAN EMPIRE

PERSIA

0	kilometres	500
0	miles	300

- - - - The armistice line, December 1917

^^^^^^ Limit of German occupation, under the Treaty of Brest-Litovsk, March 1918

© Martin Gilbert 1994

24 The Eastern Front, 1917–18

25 The Western Front, 1918

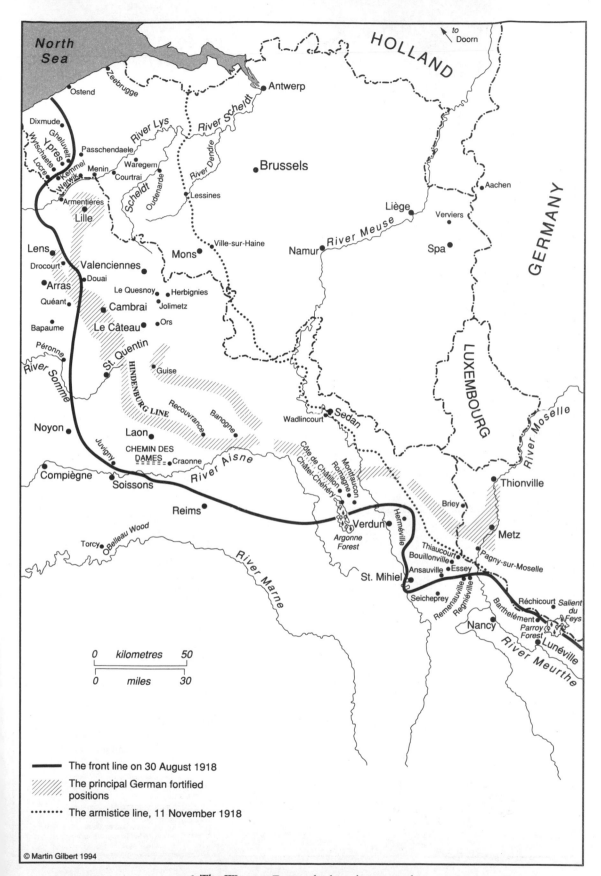

North
Sea

HOLLAND

to
Doorn

Ostend
Zeebrugge
River Lys
River Scheldt
Antwerp

Dixmude
Gheluvelt
Ypres
Wytschaete
Locre
Passchendaele
Kemmel
Menin
Werwik
Waregern
Courtrai
River Dendre
Brussels
Aachen

Armentières
Scheldt
Oudenarde
Lessines

Lille
Ville-sur-Haine
Liège
Verviers

Lens
Mons
Namur
River Meuse
Spa

Drocourt
Valenciennes
Douai

Arras
Le Quesnoy
Herbignies

Quéant
Cambrai
Jolimetz

Bapaume
Le Câteau
Ors

Péronne
St. Quentin

River Somme
HINDENBURG LINE
Guise

Recouvrance
Banogne
Wadlincourt
Sedan

LUXEMBOURG

Noyon
Laon
CHEMIN DES
DAMES
Craonne
River Aisne

Côte de Châtillon
Châtel-Chéhéry
Montfaucon
Romagne

River Moselle

Compiègne
Juvigny
Soissons
Thionville

Reims
Briey

Hernéville
Verdun
Metz

Torcy
Belleau Wood
Argonne
Forest
Thiaucourt
Bouillonville
Pagny-sur-Moselle

River Marne
St. Mihiel
Ansauville
Essey

Seicheprey
Réchicourt
Salient
du
Feys

Remenauville
Regniéville
Barthelément
Parroy
Forest

Nancy
Lunéville

River Meurthe

GERMANY

0   kilometres   50

0   miles   30

—— The front line on 30 August 1918

///// The principal German fortified
positions

······ The armistice line, 11 November 1918

© Martin Gilbert 1994

26 The Western Front, the last three months

27 Siberia

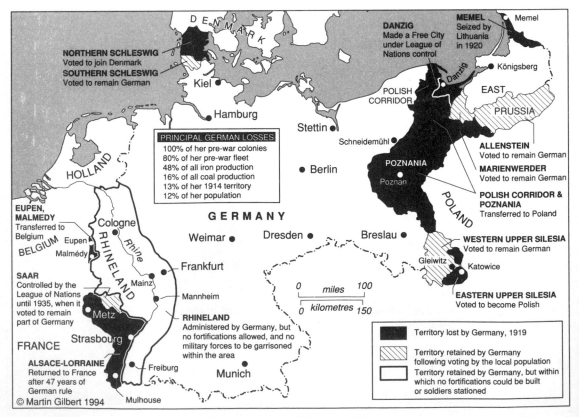

28 German territorial losses in Europe

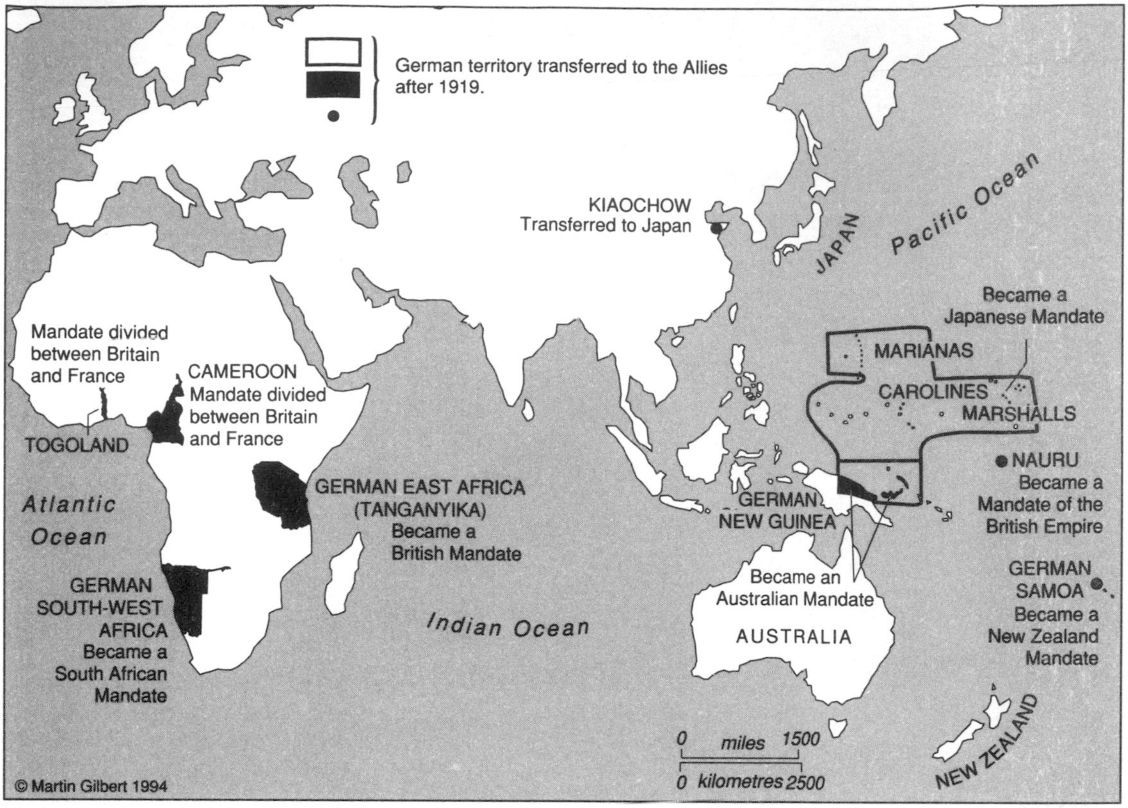
German territory transferred to the Allies after 1919.
KIAOCHOW
Transferred to Japan
JAPAN
Pacific Ocean
Became a Japanese Mandate
MARIANAS
CAROLINES
MARSHALLS
NAURU
Became a Mandate of the British Empire
GERMAN NEW GUINEA
Became an Australian Mandate
AUSTRALIA
GERMAN SAMOA
Became a New Zealand Mandate
NEW ZEALAND
Mandate divided between Britain and France
TOGOLAND
CAMEROON
Mandate divided between Britain and France
GERMAN EAST AFRICA (TANGANYIKA)
Became a British Mandate
Atlantic Ocean
GERMAN SOUTH-WEST AFRICA
Became a South African Mandate
Indian Ocean
0 miles 1500
0 kilometres 2500
© Martin Gilbert 1994

29 German losses overseas

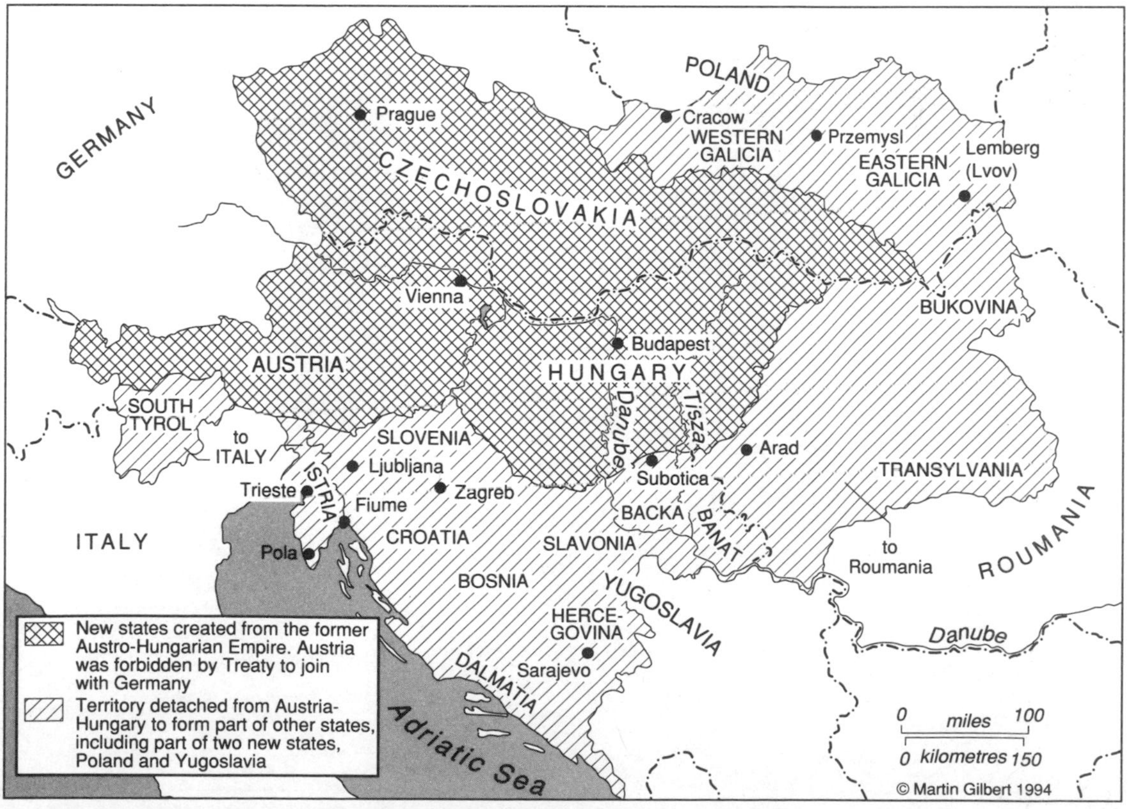
GERMANY
POLAND
Prague
Cracow
WESTERN GALICIA
Przemysl
EASTERN GALICIA
Lemberg (Lvov)
CZECHOSLOVAKIA
Vienna
BUKOVINA
Budapest
AUSTRIA
HUNGARY
Danube
Tisza
SOUTH TYROL
to ITALY
SLOVENIA
Ljubljana
Arad
ISTRIA
Subotica
TRANSYLVANIA
Trieste
Zagreb
Fiume
BACKA
BANAT
CROATIA
ITALY
Pola
SLAVONIA
to Roumania
ROUMANIA
BOSNIA
YUGOSLAVIA
HERCE-GOVINA
Danube
Sarajevo
DALMATIA
Adriatic Sea
New states created from the former Austro-Hungarian Empire. Austria was forbidden by Treaty to join with Germany
Territory detached from Austria-Hungary to form part of other states, including part of two new states, Poland and Yugoslavia
0 miles 100
0 kilometres 150
© Martin Gilbert 1994

30 The fragmentation of Austria-Hungary

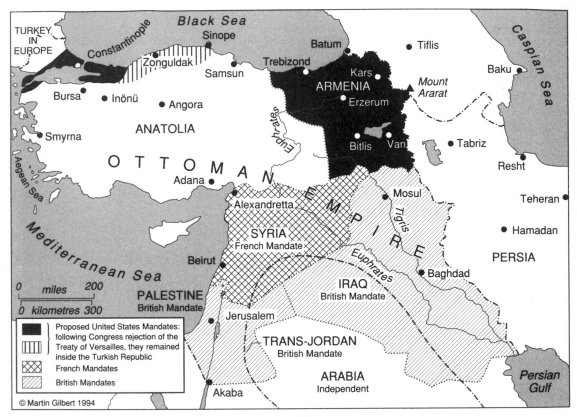

TURKEY
IN
EUROPE

Constantinople

Black Sea

Sinope

Batum

Tiflis

Zonguldak

Trebizond

Kars

Baku

Caspian Sea

Samsun

Bursa

Inönü

Angora

ARMENIA

Mount Ararat

Erzerum

Smyrna

ANATOLIA

Euphrates

Bitlis

Van

Tabriz

O T T O M A N   E M P I R E

Resht

Aegean Sea

Adana

Mosul

Teheran

Alexandretta

Tigris

Hamadan

Mediterranean Sea

SYRIA
French Mandate

Euphrates

Beirut

Baghdad

PERSIA

0   miles   200

0   kilometres   300

PALESTINE
British Mandate

IRAQ
British Mandate

Jerusalem

TRANS-JORDAN
British Mandate

Persian Gulf

ARABIA
Independent

Akaba

Proposed United States Mandates:
following Congress rejection of the
Treaty of Versailles, they remained
inside the Turkish Republic

French Mandates

British Mandates

© Martin Gilbert 1994

31 The disintegration of the Ottoman Empire

Index

compiled by the author

INDEX

INDEX